μ

WITH

EVANSTON PUBLIC LIBRARY

P9-CRE-781

305.4209 Feminis

The feminist memoir
project : voices from
c1998. JAN - 1999

DEC 04 1998

The
Feminist
Memoir
Project

SHORT TERM
LOAN

The
Feminist
Memoir
Project

Voices from
Women's
Liberation

Three Rivers Press · NEW YORK

EVANSTON PUBLIC LIBRARY.
1703 ORRINGTON AVENUE
EVANSTON, ILLINOIS 60201

Credits for the essays can be found on the facing page.

Copyright © 1998 by Rachel DuPlessis and Ann Snitow

All rights reserved. No part of this book may be reproduced or transmitted in any form or by any means, electronic or mechanical, including photocopying, recording, or by any information storage and retrieval system, without permission in writing from the publisher.

Published by Three Rivers Press, a division of Crown Publishers, Inc., 201 East 50th Street, New York, New York 10022. Member of the Crown Publishing Group.

Random House, Inc. New York, Toronto, London, Sydney, Auckland
www.randomhouse.com

THREE RIVERS PRESS and colophon are trademarks of Crown Publishers, Inc.

Printed in the United States of America

Design by Lynne Amft

Library of Congress Cataloging-in-Publication Data
The feminist memoir project: voices from women's liberation / edited by
    Rachel Blau DuPlessis and Ann Snitow.—1st ed.
        1. Feminism—United States—History—20th century.
    2. Women's rights—United States—History—20th century.
    I. DuPlessis, Rachel Blau, 1941–   .   II. Snitow, Ann, 1943–   .
    HQ1426.L59   1998
    305.42'0973—dc21   98-5660

ISBN 0-609-80384-0

10 9 8 7 6 5 4 3 2 1

First Edition

The following are the copyright notices for the essays contained in this book:

An Activist Love Story, copyright © 1996 by Paula Allen and Eve Ensler; *Catching the Fire*, copyright © 1996 by Rosalyn Fraad Baxandall; *In the Wilderness of One's Inner Self: Living Feminism*, copyright © 1996 by Lourdes Beneria; *Home Before Sundown*, copyright © 1996 by Anselma Dell'Olio; *A Year of Living Dangerously: 1968*, copyright © 1996 by Dana Densmore; *Outlaw Woman: Chapters from a Feminist Memoir-in-Progress*, copyright © 1996 by Roxanne Dunbar; *Coming of Age: Civil Rights and Feminism*, copyright © 1996 by Barbara W. Emerson; *Ambivalence About Feminism*, copyright © 1996 by Barbara Epstein; *On the Origins of the Women's Liberation Movement, from a Strictly Personal Perspective*, copyright © 1996 by Jo Freeman; *What Feminism Means to Me*, copyright © 1996 by Vivian Gornick; *Sisters in Struggle: A Belated Response*, copyright © 1996 by Beverly Guy-Sheftall; *Two Letters from the Women's Liberation Movement*, copyright © 1996 by Carol Hanisch; *Our Gang of Four: Friendship and Women's Liberation*, copyright © 1996 by Amy Kesselman, Heather Booth, Vivian Rothstein, and Naomi Weisstein; *"Ain't I a Feminist?": Re-forming the Circle*, copyright © 1996 by Shirley Geok-lin Lim; *We Called Ourselves Sisters*, copyright © 1996 by Priscilla Long; *History Makes Us: We Make History*, copyright © 1996 by Elizabeth Martinez; *"How many lives are here. . . ."*, copyright © 1996 by Kate Millett; *A Fem Feminist's History*, copyright © 1996 by Joan Nestle; *Sisterhood in Black and White*, copyright © 1996 by Barbara Omolade; *The Buried Yes*, copyright © 1994 by Minne Bruce Pratt; *Skirting*, copyright © 1996 by Yvonne Rainer; *Notes from the Aftermath*, copyright © 1996 by AnnJanette Rosga and Meg Satterthwaite; *A Marriage Disagreement, Or Marriage by Other Means*, copyright © 1996 by Alix Kates Shulman; *"Feisty Characters" and "Other People's Causes": Memories of White Racism and U.S. Feminism*, copyright © 1996 by Barbara Smith; *The Art of Getting to Equal*, copyright © 1996 by Nancy Spero; *On Becoming a Feminist/Lawyer*, copyright © 1996 by Nadine Taub; *"For the People Hear us Singing, 'Bread and Roses! Bread and Roses!' "*, copyright © 1996 by Meredith Tax; *To Hell and Back: On the Road with Black Feminism in the 1960s & 1970s*, copyright © 1996 by Michele Wallace; *Days of Celebration and Resistance: The Chicago Women's Liberation Rock Band, 1970–1973*, copyright © 1996 by Naomi Weisstein; *My Memoir Problem*, copyright © 1996 by Ellen Willis; *Primary and Secondary Contradictions in Seattle, 1967–1969*, copyright © 1996 by Barbara Winslow; *Clenched Fist, Open Heart*, copyright © 1996 by Alice J. Wolfson.

To Women

"pessimism of the intellect;
optimism of the will"

TABLE OF CONTENTS

ACKNOWLEDGMENTS

A book such as this incurs many debts, more than we can possibly remember—ironic perhaps for a book of memoirs. But, like all memoirists, we shall do the best we can. We should like first to pay tribute to the memory of Diane Cleaver, who as our literary agent, had confidence in the underlying vision of this book, her last project. We still mourn her sudden death in April 1995. Heide Lange, of Sanford J. Greenburger, then continued, and we thank her very much for seeing the book to its home at Crown. Then, for her patience, her persistence, and clear sense, we thank our editor Betty A. Prashker of Crown Publishers, Inc., for being a committed and serious part of this vision. Thanks also to our copy editor, Sonia Jaffe Robbins.

To our contributors we offer our deepest thanks. We engaged with them in many rounds of conversation, debate, and edits, over quite a number of years. They have our admiration and gratitude for their good will, patience, and feminist faith. We thank them for their willingness to search memory, to reveal themselves, to open controversy, and to abide with us in this long and taxing process. We thank them too for all they are, all they have accomplished in the women's movement, and all they gave to both of us in comradeship.

We owe thanks to the many people with whom we discussed this book from one angle or another, even if we did not or could not take all the advice that was offered. A few of these should be specially mentioned. We are greatly in the debt of Jo Freeman, whose historical and record-keeping work has been a basis for constructing an understanding of the women's movement. We would also like to thank Alice Echols and Sara Evans, whose work in women's history has already taught us so much about ourselves. We received specific help from Ros Baxandall, Virginia Blaisdell, Aviva Goode, Linda Gordon, Beverly Guy-Sheftall, Amber Hollibaugh, Judith Levine, Claire Moses, Barbara Omolade, Amy Schlegel, Barbara Seaman, Barbara Smith, Alan Snitow, Meredith Tax, Michele Wallace, Sue Wells, and Barbara Winslow. Ann would like to acknowledge the secretarial assistance of Bob Schaffer and Belinda Blum. We would also like to acknowledge many people who, finally, for one reason or another, didn't write for us, but with whom we had serious, useful, pertinent conversations. Of course we couldn't address, or find, or know all those who truly belong in such a record as this. So we see this book as just one volume of an urgent project, a project to be taken up by many others.

We editors received a great and abiding pleasure talking to each other throughout, and we feel very grateful to each other for this time of reflection and hard work that we have had together. Each of us would like to pay tribute to the patience and clarities of the other.

To our families, who lived with this and other projects from the busy, busy twain over the past five or six or seven years, we give our dear thanks and love. This means Robert S. DuPlessis and Daniel Goode, with special thanks to Koré Simone DuPlessis, feminist without portfolio, who can have the phone back now.

The
Feminist
Memoir
Project

A FEMINIST
MEMOIR PROJECT

Rachel Blau DuPlessis and Ann Snitow

The memoirs and responses you are about to read were written by people transformed by the contemporary United States women's movement. Focusing on second-wave feminism beginning about 1965, this book explores how it felt to live through and contribute to massive social change. In the context of a general upsurge of political energy, feminism created a movement of breadth and staying power, hope and influence. Changes were swift and startling. There was a readiness difficult now to fathom. Feminism entered every corner of life, and is there now; the women's movement, with its bracing defiance, shifted social life everywhere.

We two editors, old friends, looked at our lives and saw that feminism had been decisive. For us, there was a before the women's movement and an after. But when the histories of the sixties began to appear with the women's movement relegated to the footnotes and the margins, we realized how urgently we wanted to read women's own accounts of their diverse historical participation and agency. So we began this memoir project.

We asked our authors to focus on the initial burst of excitement and engagement that marked their entry into the women's movement. We asked what motivated them to political action. We also asked them to take a long view of feminism's effects and problems. Because feminism has kept moving in our lives, changing its meanings, we wanted both to create a record and to speculate about that record. Memories and reflections occur in several layers here. Thirty people wrote memoirs. Then six more read all these essays, speculated about them, and added still more memories, still more layers to interpret. We've arranged the memoirs in a loosely chronological order, to give a sense of the tempo of that dynamic time. The responses are set in a special section that begins an ongoing and diverse process of interpretation. The book seeks thereby to avoid closure. We sought to put responsive and critical readings inside this book because to us feminism is not a closed episode, an innocent, buoyant, and sealed moment of youth. On the contrary, with all necessary second thoughts and with our reevaluations of the short-term possibilities, for us feminism is alive—and is worth a lifetime of engagement.

It's hard now to evoke the sea of misogyny in which more than one generation of women struggled before the women's movement. Perhaps just saying it that way will help. This level of misogyny often made women turn against themselves, creating the bile of self-hatred and the nausea of self-doubt. How much did feminism change things? One general claim feels solid: gross and unapologetic prejudice against women is no longer an unremarked-upon given of everyday life. In the long years before second-wave feminism, women and girls were unquestioningly belittled. Daily insulted without remark. Definitely tracked away from achievement. If middle-class, told to leave jobs when married. If working-class, forced into unacknowledged doubled work days. Often fired when pregnant. Aggressively ignored or ignorantly aggressed upon. Assumed as helpers, and when unhelpful, called bitches or witches. Humiliation seemed fitting and pride made one faintly ridiculous. The prevailing assumption of the inferiority of women was the starting point from which one planned one's moves and shaped one's life—whether acquiescent or angry. The very difficulty of describing this prefeminist atmosphere today is a measure of how dramatically things have changed. These facts seemed to many at that time to cross class and race, although the situation of "woman" took different forms in a variety of social sites.

The early days of the second wave of American feminism (from about 1966 through the 1970s) felt to some like Day One, but of course, as even its name makes obvious, it wasn't. This new wave had a long past, rising out of the richness and diversity of U.S. civil society: in women's movements of the nineteenth and early twentieth centuries (including women's suffrage); in the more recent Black Civil Rights and anti–Vietnam War struggles. These last had been influenced in their turn by a wide range of left and liberal groups active since the thirties, including the once broad-based communist and socialist movements with an official stand against "male chauvinism." The eventual explosion had also been prepared by civil defense movements concerned with Cold War politics, like SANE and Women's Strike for Peace, by labor movements and union groups, like the UAW Women's Department. There were also Black women's organizations such as a Mt. Vernon/New

Rochelle group, which wrote "A Historical and Critical Essay for Black Women" after a number of years of political work beginning in the early 1960s. In their recent research, Rosalyn Baxandall and Linda Gordon identify some of these unrecognized precursors to the women's movement that diversify its origins.

In the essays in this volume, you can get glimpses of these origins, and glimpses, too, of how unknown they were to the initiators of this wave. Education had supplied no information about nineteenth- and early twentieth-century feminist struggle and thought. There was a blank where there should have been a recognition of continuities and a confrontation with past limitations. Following a well-established U.S. system of values, women's liberation set out to invent itself from scratch.

There's no way to name a single spark for a fire that became so general so quickly, but in the late fifties and early sixties there were a variety of feminist beginnings. Many experiences formerly endured as woman's fate were transformed by incipient feminism into hooks, drawing one into the swiftly forming, collectively created new state of mind. For some it was the contraceptive pill, first introduced in 1960, which brought new possibilities. The Pill, as health activists like Barbara Seaman and contributor Alice Wolfson found, threatened women's health, and, in Deirdre English's phrase, sometimes "freed men first." But for a mass of women, it created a decisive break between sexual pleasure and pregnancy. For still others the jolt into feminism was the terror involved in seeking a (then-illegal) abortion, or knowing someone in that complex panic. Perhaps it was the discovery that sterilization, especially for women of color or poor women, was the price exacted by official hospital boards for allowing a legal termination of pregnancy.

For some it was the analysis of middle-class white women's discontent—and their underutilization as a social resource—proposed by Betty Friedan's best-selling 1963 book *The Feminine Mystique*. The National Organization for Women (NOW) that Friedan helped found in 1966 was an attempt to institutionalize the drive for women's civil rights in the aftermath of the 1961 Presidential Commission on the Status of Women. Sometimes incipient feminism was helped along by the disgruntled observation that there were virtually no women in authority anywhere—in schools, in courts, at work. In the stunning new ethos, women who had been traumatized by rape or other kinds of gender violence grasped that this trauma was compounded by their treatment by those in authority—doctors, police officers, judges. In short, for many women, the contradictions with which they had been living were suddenly both plain and intolerable.

As contributor after contributor to this collection makes clear, and as Sara Evans demonstrated in *Personal Politics,* published in 1979, the first book to give the new movement a history, the formative and galvanizing source for the women's movement was the Civil Rights movement: its strategies, analyses, and high sense of political vocation. In its attention to racial oppression, the Civil Rights movement had already made the case that justice in the United States would require fundamental social change. The women who initiated the early phases of women's liberation were indebted to this analysis. Contributor Roxanne Dunbar remembers thinking, on the analogy of civil rights, "The freedom of women would require a social revolution."

The dynamism of the sixties catalyzed all this rich political material, mobilizing mass movements. Many people sought to understand the motors of change. The Civil Rights movement said moral, spiritual, and militant resistance to unjust power would bring justice. The intellectual tradition of Marxism suggested that economic contradictions generated the opportunity for new social forms. The free-flowing atmosphere of youth culture said that commitment to personal liberation would transform society. The rage, fear, and political frustration inspired by the Vietnam War's brutalities and irrationalities, the erosion of democratic values in the conduct of that war and elsewhere in political life—these suggested the time had come to confront the deep structures of society. Rising desires clashing with many unmet claims for social justice created intense political hopes and passions. A wide range of boiling, expanding movements sought a United States renewal.

The women who became feminist activists shared with their generation this social, spiritual, and emotional yearning for a better world for all. A few early Civil Rights leaders and organizers had an analysis of gender along with race, a linkage lost later—some say because of bitter internal conflicts among male leaders; others say because of the narrowing of goals that came in defensive response to violent backlash. There were contradictions between the radical ethos in such groups as SDS (Students for a Democratic Society) and SNCC (Student Nonviolent Coordinating Committee) and their proud, unthinking male chauvinism. Women in these groups began to see how the movements to which they had given their passion and energy were exploiting them. They began to wonder if "liberation" could apply to the women. Influential analyses of the place of women in these movements included Mary King and Casey Hayden's 1965 position paper on women in SNCC and Shulamith Firestone and Jo Freeman's critique of SDS in 1967.

So it was that many who became feminists began by questioning the radical questioners. In the summer of 1967, for example, SDS women addressed SDS men with a militant yet generous statement about "male chauvinism," which ended, "Freedom now! We love you!" It was published in *New Left Notes* next to a condescending cartoon of a cutsey doll-woman holding a picket sign: "Our Rights . . . Now!" At the same time, contributor Barbara Omolade remembers endorsing Black nationalism with all her heart, while knowing how that movement positioned her differently from her brothers. By bringing the apparently ridiculous, irrelevant, or shocking issue of gender, sexuality, and women to the forefront of their analyses, women radicals became outsiders to the rebels as well as to the establishment.

The second phase, following fast, often simultaneously in many places, was the declaration of a feminist consciousness. Women passionately connected with the prevailing apocalyptic atmosphere, the sense of a real ending of an oppressive time. They hoped thrillingly, wildly, even absurdly, and worked for social change with the rare urgency that comes from believing in the immediate possibility of a fundamentally different world. Their questions were scandalous and compelling, examining traditions—from culture and society to home and intimacy. Why do they call us "girls"? Why is housework "women's work"? Why are women paid less than men? How does "this ad exploit women"? Where were "the great women artists"? What were the origins of the so-common hatred of women? These were burning questions that needed answers. Each woman seemed like a presenting symptom for which feminism was the cure.

Indeed, the joy of feminism, for those who felt it, often had spiritual proportions. Like a conversion experience—"the scales dropped from my eyes; I saw all things new." One's inabilities and blockages, resentments, hidden griefs, all the paraphernalia and picturesque qualities of "girlhood" and "womanhood" suddenly were ripped open, suddenly fell apart. And "all things"—from the most mundane and habitual to the most enormous—seemed changed. The repetition of this moment of conversion suggests that there was shared meaning and experience, and, at the same time, that a myth came to structure the moment of origin. Those who felt outside this mythic oneness saw it increasingly as a myth that excluded them.

"Sisterhood" was the first explanatory model—the proposition of sheer solidarity among women. Out of this moment of separation from men came the opportunity to see one's gender in isolation from other social identities. This isolation was a startling and suggestive proposition, and the moment that gender seemed separable as a theme for specific analysis was bold and radical. Also, inevitably, very brief, since female solidarity was also a fantasy, a metaphor, a fiction. As feminism exploded into a mass movement, all kinds of protagonists with their multiple identities, allegiances, and needs complicated the assumption that there was one universal identity for all women. There sometimes were and continue to be moments of narcissism in the self-proclamations of identity politics, but new identities making new claims for justice were then above all mighty and liberatory forces, carrying new political hopes and knowledge.

The critique of gender-as-monocause and sisterhood-as-monocure came immediately from many locations: from third-world feminisms and communities of color both inside and outside the U.S.; and from postmodern philosophers skeptical of any system of meaning that claims to explain all. In addition, the strategic meaning of "sisterhood" was contested: did the solidarity of women mean that men were outside this ideal and needed to change, as Redstockings argued, or was this a sisterhood of oppression where women had to take the initiative to throw off their shared victimization, as Cell 16 said? But all feminist feeling, whether based in "sisterhood" or based in critique, was accompanied by modes of analysis and generalizing that were vital intellectually and socially. For if, as de Beauvoir said, one is not born, but becomes a woman, so too, the understanding of oppression is not an essential inheritance: it is a creation of ongoing political analysis.

The Civil Rights movement had taught women the power of struggling on their own behalf, but in this switch of analytic loyalty to gender, to their own oppression, white activists often left race to the side. Jo Freeman points out that many white women grieved over their expulsion from Civil Rights groups in the Black Power phase of the late sixties, though they carried that radical vision with them into the women's movement. But, as Barbara Omolade says, when white women emerged from other movements to organize around their interests, they also unified unselfconsciously around their whiteness.

So was the women's movement white? Yes and no. Black women were already organized on their own behalf in the Civil Rights movement, and many became feminist activists—often inside the Black community. If feminist activism is currently minimized in accounts of the sixties, in their commentaries Barbara Smith and Beverly Guy-Sheftall point out that African-American participation in feminism is even more unacknowledged. The National Black Feminist Organization was founded in 1973, and the Combahee River Collective was meeting from 1974. As Barbara Emerson points out, politically active Black women often recognized and analyzed the applicability of feminism's insights to their situation, whether they identified with white women's particular feminist demands or not. In *Black Macho and the Myth of the Superwoman,* Michele Wallace claimed feminism as her own, and as deeply relevant to the sexual politics of Black activists and Black communities, though she was sometimes named a race traitor for her analysis. The white-black issue oversimplifies the politics of location, for a feminist analysis was formulated in many ethnic groups, as contributor Betita Martinez shows. All were looking for their own precise point of oppression around which to organize.

In this proliferation of political intensities, old conditions became visible and new analyses and desires became thinkable. An extraordinary push to popularize these new ideas followed, led by serious feminist journalists, above all by Gloria Steinem. *Ms.* began in 1972 as an investment by *New York* magazine seeking a market-share in a newly emergent social group of professional women. Marketing and militancy coexisted in a fascinating bond at this moment of high capital flow and high consumption, but on balance the allegiance of *Ms.* to the social movement made it a vital feminist magazine of mass outreach. Jane O'Reilly's article in *Ms.* invented the word "click" to mark a change of consciousness. This dry little word implies by its very crispness that somehow the insights about women's secondary status were already deeply known, and needed only that "click"—a key opening a lock, a button pushed—to be activated.

Fissioning out of this mix, women became angry. Incidents of sexism that would once have been accepted without remark were received with rancor and studied with suspicion. Men asked for coffee and were answered with formerly unthinkable rejections. "Coffee" became the symbol of the thousand ways women had coddled and catered to men. At a union meeting, the professional organizer joshed that the real settlements get made in the men's room. He waited for the usual conspiratorial laugh, and was surprised to be met instead by hostile silence. For reasons that probably can never be fully tracked, in the early days of this wave of feminism, many women's conventional compliance, their habits of supporting men's projects and egos, simply evaporated—or went underground—to return later, though perhaps in significantly altered forms.

From the energy of this rage came witty and provocative demonstrations. Contributor Carol Hanisch instigated the movement's first national action, the Miss America Pageant Protest in Atlantic City in 1968, against the use of conventionally sexualized women as cultural icons. To protest the lack of full disclosure about side effects of the birth-control pill, Washington D.C. Women's Liberation organized a mothers and babies sit-in at the office of Robert Finch, Secretary of Health, Education and Welfare. Feminists in New York demonstrated against segregated want ads in the *New York Times* in 1967, eliminating them by 1968. These gross trappings of the sex-gender system must already have been undermined for these want ads, divided neatly into Male and Female, to topple at one push. A few immediate changes, coupled with some early attention to feminism in the media, made it seem as if the gender system of inequality and prejudice was ready to crash and burn.

Some of these early actions might seem, in hindsight, lively but naive. The comic demonstrations mounted by some feminists against heavily marketed bridal fairs didn't appeal to women for whom marriage was a place of privacy and nurturance in a hostile world. The bravura of certain actions alienated some people because they encoded thoughtless assumptions about race and class. This list of inadequacies could continue, of course, but merely to patronize these early actions is to lose sight of the real power of this utopian moment, when many things seemed possible that today seem once again far off.

By 1970, these private wrongs and political actions had coalesced into a public demonstration of female power. The first March for Women's Equality, August 26, 1970, down Fifth Avenue in New York was an announcement that this movement was in full force. This march and strike commemorated the fiftieth anniversary of women's right to vote and seemed symbolic of neglected agendas—and of the woman-power present and ready to move for social change.

From the start, the feminist movement was polyphonic. There was no central group, no central leader, no single political analysis, and no single moment of access. As the feminist theater activist Anselma Dell'Olio was leaving for Italy in 1974, burned out and sure the movement was finished, in Atlanta, Georgia, Minnie Bruce Pratt was feeling the first stirrings of new desires and new politics that were to become feminism for her. And later, immigrant Shirley Geok-lin Lim was evaluating why the feminism that was exciting in the sixties didn't include her, as she negotiated her "belated entry into the feminist project." The recollections in this book show only some of the range: local habitations of feminism with their own atmospheres; individual times of entry to the movement; and many quite different political agendas. Obviously, more such accounts are urgently needed in an on-going feminist memoir project.

The authors here were part of women's movements in Boston; Seattle; New York; Chicago; Washington, D.C.; San Francisco; New Mexico; Georgia; and elsewhere. Though cities seem germinal in these particular essays, in fact, feminist groups, on a staggered timetable, started everywhere. Not only did feminism exist in many places, it also took many political and cultural forms: Heather Booth began "Jane" in Chicago, an abortion referral service at the time of illegality. Nancy Spero was one of the founders of A.I.R., a gallery for art by women. Barbara Omolade helped to create the first state-funded shelter for battered women. Florence Howe began The Feminist Press. Ann Calderwood began the journal *Feminist Studies*. Naomi Weisstein started a women's rock band.

In one breath, feminism named sexist abuses and opposed them. Activists located and then fought: Sex-role stereotyping. Sexual harassment. Domestic violence. The wage gap. Marital rape and date rape. Street hassling. Homophobia. The battering of women. The objectification of women. Childhood sexual abuse. The double day that women work, first on the job, and then at home. The feminization of poverty. Workplace discrimination.

Feminists established means of redress in hundreds of situations in which women had once been passive or resigned. They started women's shelters; they changed how the police interview rape survivors. They deeply reformed birthing and other health practices. They demanded control of their bodies in all kinds of different situations—in sex, in reproduction, on the street, and at work. They put preschool child care on the national agenda. They criticized images everywhere—for example, the depiction of passive girls in children's books. They were interested both in making divorce no-fault and marriage rather better—though then they worried about whether men benefited more than women from these reforms. They fought for the participation of girls and women in sports. They struggled for expansion of female opportunities in the workforce. They proposed equal pay for jobs of comparable worth—though then they worried about what it would take for all women actually to acquire the skills to benefit from this kind of demand. They reinterpreted a lesbian past, and future. They recovered the biographies, issues, and works of under-appreciated women once active in history and culture. They worked for family leave for birth and adoption. And these are only a few of women's struggles during this period. Different classes of women benefited materially and immediately in different ways. But the proliferation of both questions and demands was broad, and the motivation was both newly shameless self-interest and outrage at social injustice. In the intense 1970s, the freshness of these feminist formulations and the mobilized social moment raised hope. Then, the scale of the tasks galvanized political energies instead of daunting people, as they can do now, in the 1990s.

In the rush of first rebellion, feminism created organic intellectuals. Astonishingly enough to themselves, women were suddenly speaking in public; acting in flamboyant, polemical skits; gathering and analyzing statistics; criticizing everyday institutions; drawing up planks for programs; composing analytical and personal essays; publishing and distributing documents; writing punchy and engaging leaflets; sketching political cartoons; organizing speak-outs; and making unconditional demands. Contributor Barbara Winslow remembers taking center stage to defend feminism, when only a minute before her sole political identity had been as the wife of an outspoken New Left leader. In February 1969, after a New York hearing about abortion laws where the experts were fourteen men and one nun, women set up a counter-hearing. Twelve gave evidence about their (illegal) abortions, claiming that as women they were the true experts on unwanted pregnancies. (This formulation, "unwanted" pregnancies, was a radical break with female compliance at the time and has, in the 1990s, once again become taboo.) And at every moment, more feminists were created: Gloria Steinem remembers these hearings "as a light coming on in a dark room. Indeed, it was the beginning of my realization that the position of females was political, not 'natural,' and that it could be—must be—changed." (She is writing in 1996, introducing *In the Company of Women,* an anthology of interview-memoirs with women active in Minnesota; edited by Bonnie Watkins and Nina Rothchild.)

Women thought on their feet, trying to keep up with things that were happening in a hurry. They also dug in and began inventing institutions, disciplines, strategies. Some began studying the past for models and female heroes, unearthing whole histories of feminism before this one. The movement was nicknamed a "wave" for good reasons. It poured over everything. People gained what footholds they could in the flood.

One starting point of the early feminist analyses—often appearing first as best-selling, grass-roots pamphlets—was the deconstruction of everyday life. Feminists initiated public scrutiny of the smallest and most unregistered bits of female experience. A pamphlet with the provocative title of "The Myth of the Vaginal Orgasm," by Anne Koedt, inaugurated the whole debate about sexuality. Another by Naomi Weisstein raised questions about how psychologists were conventionally constructing "woman." Meredith Tax's "Woman and Her Mind: The Story of Everyday Life" was an underground classic, selling 150,000 copies. Tax announced the deep revulsion many women feel at street harassment and linked that feeling to a sweeping analysis of patriarchal institutions. Similarly Barbara Smith's "Toward a Black Feminist Criticism" began a key confrontation by naming white feminist limits and failures, and denouncing the invisibility of Black lesbians in both Black liberation and women's liberation politics. This often-reprinted essay appeared first in *Conditions* ("a feminist magazine of writing by women with an emphasis on writing by lesbians"), then as a pamphlet from Out and Out Books, one of a growing number of women's independent publishing ventures central to this time.

These working papers initiated loud conversations, new arguments and genres, schools of thought, and whole fields for analysis and research. In fact, women's studies began here, with the scrutiny of gender institutions and practices, in such bold anthologies as *Notes from the*

First, Second, and *Third Year; No More Fun & Games;* and several mass-market paperbacks, such as *Sisterhood Is Powerful* (edited by Robin Morgan) and *Woman in Sexist Society* (edited by Vivian Gornick and Barbara Moran). Pat Mainardi's famous and infamous title "The Politics of Housework" made something out of what had been called nothing. Kate Millett's 1970 title *Sexual Politics* proposed an apparently absurd and shocking combination of words. All this writing felt extraordinarily fresh. The new feminists placed the once-discounted materials of female life in the context of power and control. Now they talked of politics, not of custom, nor of individual choice, nor of private sorrow.

One of feminism's structural inventions was the voluntary small group practice called "consciousness raising" (CR) where women spoke about their histories and daily lives. They spoke personally and then generalized; they spoke privately in order to generate a changed public discourse; they confessed and told secrets in order to couple the private and public spheres. Uncountable thousands of such small groups met across the country during these early years. Through consciousness raising, women reinterpreted themselves and the institutions in which they lived. The existence of these groups gave rise to broad theoretical debates about the relationship between discourse and politics: Is making new words a political act? Does a change of discourse change social conditions? What are the strengths and weaknesses of the small group form? Is the small discussion group only a first stage of activism? Or should it be an ongoing political activity?

Men and women experienced the sense of a change among women no matter where they were. The new expectations were pervasive. Even the most committed misogynist found himself in an altered social configuration. Male unconsciousness was a lost art, giving way to defensiveness, or lip service, or rant. There was action everywhere, often in the little encounters of daily life—questions of errands and jokes. For some, feminism could be a word overheard on the street, or, as Lourdes Benéria tells us, a button worn by another person and glimpsed in a moment, or a picture on the newsstand, or a rumor that turned out, amazingly, to be true.

Beginning about 1970, for a few years, media attention spotlighted feminism. This created an atmosphere of glamour around a white, free, young, pretty, gutsy few. The mirror was held up to these vivid young for a year or so (say 1970–72); then it was smashed. The press found out that women really meant it. They kept complaining, kept analyzing. They were lesbians, women of color, poor women, angry divorced women, smoldering critical women, overworked women who weren't laughing at male defections from housework or child care or relationships. Once the message started to repeat and gain in intensity, the media decamped. Women had burst beyond the surface packaging in which the media wrapped them. But as Ros Baxandall notes, the work of organizing was sometimes aided by the media's superficial infatuation. Even hostile media got the word out. Once out, the dynamism of the ideas, and their historical ripeness, carried them in many directions.

In response to this brief, distorted star turn, and with mixed success, feminism tried to resuscitate its own name—the word "feminism" itself, to rescue it from its reputation as unfashionable (plain girls with bad clothes), shrill (that monstrous regiment), or class- and race-bound (for middle-class white ladies only). The continuing difficulty of rehabilitating the word "feminism" for radical action shows how hard this struggle was. From the first, nasty and trivializing names were applied to activists. When they said women's liberation, they got back—lib and libber. They said woman, and got back—chick or girl. These early moves to discredit feminism prefigured the later backlash, for one measure of the strength of the new feminist paradigm has always been its ability to excite outrage and reaction.

Indeed, in the years since 1980, and accelerating as we worked on this book, the word "feminist" has fallen (and been pushed) into a place beyond disrepute—a nadir, even when people responded to issues feminism raised or agreed with some feminist demands. In general, the current lack of symbolization of political action could make what these activists did evaporate, leaving little residue. We would like this book to stand against the belittling and the demonizing, not only of feminism but of many of the political struggles of the sixties.

We two editors remember feeling, in those early days, a paradox of time: Everything was happening fast, but we were also engaged in slowing down the rush of daily events, registering them, taking them in, analyzing acts and gestures in bursts of angry and joyous understanding. Then once again we moved into fast forward, as we tried to overturn, or at least outrun, the sexism we could suddenly see, the demeaning and reductive assumptions about female possibility. We editors, formerly somewhat suspicious participants in the middle-class ethos of universal opportunity, learned, in short, that both custom and ideology had produced and policed us as Female Selves.

The discovery of a shared condition had great power when it was new. In the first light of this discovery, liberal feminists and radical feminists seemed sisters; cultural feminists and socialist feminists were, briefly, almost the same. Women who didn't identify with feminism were nonetheless stirred by it. In its early form, feminism made universalist claims, far more than the particularist ones we now associate with "identity politics." But in many ways and for many women this "moment of unity" was a false promise on which feminism was usually unable to deliver. Since the beginning of the women's movement, women of color have criticized their "inclusion without influence," in Lynet Uttal's term. Women of color thereby initiated a new level and intensity of the feminist analysis of difference. They expressed rage and disgust (though not surprise) at the racism they found in the women's movement, just as women, both white and of color, had only just expressed those same emotions of outrage and irritated recognition toward men.

Feminism also made women of color acutely aware of their "double jeopardy," in Frances Beale's phrase of 1970, identifying racism and sexism as interlocking systems of oppression. From the beginning there had been calls for the end to "sexism, racism, violence and poverty," as the founding documents of the Women's National Political Caucus said in 1971. But these fine words did not register the difficulty of expecting a movement of women to address all oppressions. Feminism set out with the ideal of resisting domination in all spheres, but it was at the same time "about women," "for women," "by women"—a unity that could not hold, since some women participate in the oppression of others, and of each other. Hence early feminist idealism ran the risk of reductionism, and increasingly feminists had to confront the pitfalls of static identity politics. For identity is in historic motion, constantly requiring reconfiguration. However, the thrill of recognizing the importance of this new category of identity, "woman," and of including women's new claims as part of a more general politics of liberation carried the work of raising an inclusive feminist consciousness very far, before both outside resistance and internal contradictions—particularly about sexual orientation, race, and class—slowed the movement down.

So amid this ferment and passion, the women's movement had its internal costs, its splits, its shortcomings. Differences of race, class, and sexual orientation emerged and were only partially acknowledged as real sources of conflict. Indeed, the emphasis on shared experiences in consciousness raising—in other words, the concept of sisterhood itself—assumed the similarity of all women and initially blocked the recognition of the complexity of differences.

At the same time, difference was inevitably exploding, making itself known. Personal relations struggled to keep up with movement principles. Consciousness-raising groups developed their own versions of the speakable and the unspeakable, their own customs and rigidities, as Priscilla Long and Barbara Epstein point out. Individuals in sisterly bonds and groups working toward feminist practice could, for example, collide, split, and hate in mere weeks, motivated by conflicts among strong personalities and by disagreements about how to define feminism. There were fissures, confusions, and rancors; envy, malice, and spite: aspects of all group life at any time, but a shock at a time of such heightened idealism. People's motives were—inevitably—mixed.

The survival of movement energy amid so much unlooked for conflict came in part from the relative economic prosperity and the social mobility of those times. Thus, rather than dying as they might in other periods, political groups had the material preconditions to give rise, in a fervent mitosis, to new groups. Some wanted a separate culture for women, while others wanted gender to disappear. "Politicos" targeted the modern capitalist state, while "radical feminists" saw the ancient form—patriarchy—as the root cause of modern evils. Some wanted to separate the need for feminism from a women's movement whose public face was overwhelmingly white. People suffered the buffeting that comes from fighting out meaning and setting forth direction in a time of often dizzying political opportunity. Directly or indirectly, the essays in this book reverberate with these conflicts. People writing here remember pain as women came to disagree—fiercely—over one crux or another: the polemical rejection of males that occurred in some groups; the splits between lesbians and straight women; the debates over whether lesbianism was a revolutionary vanguard; the acknowledgment of social class and race undermining the proposition of a universal female subject; the uneven interest in children.

Thus feminism offered kinetic, but also contested criticisms of social institutions and practices. Attacking common places, feminists revalued or redefined or criticized the meaning of "work" for different classes of women, and they interrupted each other's fantasies of "love." While some women fled from oppressive homes, others felt that getting rid of male authority was less the point than building men's presence and their responsibility in women's lives and the lives of children. Lourdes Benería found feminism tone deaf to motherhood. Yet at the same time, Priscilla Long and Ros Baxandall remember child-care movements evolving from feminist energy. Feminism revolutionized what it meant to be a lesbian, as Joan Nestle writes here, and at the same time those changes catalyzed conflicts in both older lesbian and new feminist communities. Some feminists saw sexuality as a natural part of women's territory, while others, like Gayle Rubin, radically questioned feminism's assumption that, about sexual values and practices, women are automatic experts and feminism knows best. These differences of feminist interpretation about the nature of sexuality and sexual practices for women (and men) led eventually to debates about pornography, sadomasochism, and censorship.

One can argue about how much feminism has accomplished. Such speculation is usually polemic in disguise, the assertion, by this group or that, that feminism is the cup half empty or half full. In the late sixties, a wide variety of women demanded great changes in every aspect of the culture, and got only small bits of what they wanted. The women's movement won only some reforms and some adjustments in social mores—nothing like what people desired: the structural transformation of public and private life, social justice, and the end of violence and domination.

But a low estimate of what feminism did and continues to do is shortsighted. A movement shapes expectations it cannot satisfy. Some movements grind down in rage and bitterness for this very reason, but feminism, polyglot and structurally loose, has been able so far to keep growing and changing. It has constantly broadened its concept of liberation and deepened its recognition of the difficulty of achieving that liberation, the limitations of its own founding ideas. Many feminists are no longer confident that "women's experience" is a coherent, single position from which to launch a demand. The word "woman" is harder to romanticize for politics than it used to be. As Elizabeth Spellman and Denise Riley have both pointed out, women are never only women, and claims can no longer be made—as they were initially and blithely—in women's general name. At the start, the little formative groups of the women's movement met in homes, familiar domestic spaces that maintained the intimacy, sometimes the cliqueishness that Jo Freeman derides as ultimately inimical to public acts. But if some wished to create the movement as a home, and to extend home out into the world, others have been busy cutting that particular umbilical cord.

But none of these revisions has stopped women's groups from continuously emerging, working for serious change at every level from the intimate to the global. This morning's mail brings some typical letters. In California, a lesbian law group is advocating for lesbian rights in childbearing, custody, and adoption, using concepts carved out by feminist thinkers about what full female autonomy might look like. In Atlanta, a group is fighting hate crimes: racial crimes, gay bashing, and discrimination against women. And here's a mailing from the activist funding organization RESIST; they've given money to dozens of women's political action groups this year, like an economic-development training program and a women and cancer health project. There's a call from WHAM (Women's Health Action Mobilization) for helpers in their abortion clinic defense, and an update from the Center for Reproductive Law and Policy, an activist think tank of lawyers devoted to questions of reproductive freedom, another embracing feminist concept. The Center for Women's Global Leadership announces its annual training session for women leaders from around the world. Women are organized into plural and diverse women's movements, and the idea that they need to organize on their own behalf is alive like a yeast in U.S. culture—and far beyond.

These hundreds of local, national, and international groups continue to place women's oppression in the large pattern of how a post–Cold War world functions. They keep pressuring institutions; finding their way into new locations; inventing social forms; burgeoning here and there; pushing into the media, the schools, the courts, the workplace; repositioning social demands; responding to the basic changes in the gendering of things that is partly the cause and partly the result of movement work. Certainly in the United States, when explosive public events occur—nationally, such as Anita Hill's claim of sexual harassment against Supreme Court nominee, now Justice, Clarence Thomas, or locally, such as the murder of a battered woman by her estranged husband or boyfriend—feminism is there, one force making these events visible. Years of ongoing political work and consciousness-raising encounters large and small have fostered great debates about events that had no public face before feminism.

For all this, we continue to want more from feminism than it has delivered. If we insist on a family metaphor for our politics, then feminism becomes a mother who did not give enough, and whose shortcomings and slowdowns we regard with contempt. But when we criticize the family metaphor and go beyond that familiar, familial rage, feminism's strengths and weaknesses become a collective and political responsibility. "The personal is political" has been a great rallying point. But the interplay between the personal and the political requires constant rethinking. Earlier on women could bear to name themselves as victims because the end of victimization was in sight—through feminist politics. In contrast, the word "victim" today is like a heavy stone: no one expects victimhood to budge soon, so once again, few want to acknowledge a "sisterhood" of timeless pain and sorrow. And those who enshrine victim status run the risk of seeming to claim that such status is in itself a source of power.

If feminism is sometimes hard to pin down, if some groups take a turn toward what others consider conservative solutions, or if its very structurelessness is sometimes a tyranny or a weakness, nonetheless all this proliferating variety has been part of feminism's unusual staying power. Aspects of feminism have proved intrinsically interesting to many different kinds of women and men. Even the most hostile critic— inside feminism or without—confronts women's activism as a social force and must reckon with its effect in a changing gender landscape. On balance, feminism has offered an exhilarating challenge to the wasteful gender systems in which people live.

A book about remembering raises questions about why we remember. Anyone active in the feminist politics of the 1970s who teaches women's studies knows the experience of having to explain and, sometimes, to defend one's connection with that time. How can one narrate these ideas and this history to another generation? And just what is it that one has to tell? Are acts of translation and transmission necessary for feminism to avoid skipping a generation, as it seems commonly to do? One might well ask, why rake over "1968," exposing oneself, in a vigorously traditionalist and often reactionary time, to the charge of utopian fantasy—or worse.

The category "women," so fresh and surprising on that fictive but evocative Day One of the Second Wave, is familiar now, to some an oversimplification, to others a banality. The irony of this feminist success is hardly lost on activists, who are now well along on the second thoughts that typify the richness of contemporary feminist thinking. Nostalgia and sentimentality for the opening gambits of the women's movement don't cut much ice for people who have to figure out what to do now, in this historical time. But ignorance of that time thirty years ago is also an odd handicap, like running a relay race with no idea of what's being handed on to you from the runner just behind.

Recently a younger feminist theorist told one of the editors that the problem of the relationship between the feminist generations is far more of a difficulty for the old than for the young, that it is time for the old to let go of seventies politics, to practice a little strategic forgetfulness. This is a useful provocation. Certainly the history of feminist thought and action is problematic to summarize, introducing expectations of narrative coherence or models of progress, or offering insights that don't automatically or reliably fertilize the minds of another generation. Certainly, too, those who were active at the beginning of this wave need to question the stories of feminism they will tell, to see limitations, to recognize what people were capable of thinking then, and what not. As Katie King has remarked: "Origin stories about the women's movement are interested stories, all of them."

Also when we think about that time, mistakes and embittering conflicts loom large. Race- and class-bound formulations, sometimes foolish fantasies about female goodness, scarifying disagreements about sexuality—all these can make different feminists embarrassed to be wrongly lumped together as one erring "feminism." Nor have feminists acquired confidence about what actions of ours will make the changes we want, rather than reproduce, in thin disguise, the world we know. The whole process of change is much slower than sixties activists thought. The word revolution, used so constantly in 1968, has suffered a drubbing, not only from conservative backlash and a general erosion of hope, but also from a necessary and salutary rethinking of how change happens. Utopian wishes taken literally have led to disappointment, a feeling that younger people are right to resist as best they can. Older feminists must recognize, too, the need for each generation to develop a voice speaking from its own time, and appreciate each generation's difficulty in hearing the stale, or strange, or, to them, antediluvian rhetoric of its elders.

As we write in 1997, celebration of a feminist past is entirely out of style. Old rhetoric is like last decade's clothes: nothing dates worse. Feminism is not only repressed as an obstreperous act by one's parents, but it is also compressed into a narrow set of gestures. Ambivalent or hostile acts of memory can give rise to caricature as feminism ages in a culture that detests age, receding fast into what Henry Louis Gates, Jr. calls "a recent bygone era." But all this silences a vivid past, patronizes a conviction that occasionally moved mountains. We do not apologize for or belittle the urgency with which our contributors once proposed revolution. We want to project a possible future time of coalitions, when feminism will be a force, one key element in a wide range of liberationist activism and multicultural thinking. Reading these essays, we were often critical of our movement and yearned for much more analytical distance. Yet we want more from the past than a safe sense of its limitations. The task is to entertain doubts and develop new formulations without censoring memory or deprecating an earlier self.

In considering the renaissance of a U.S. women's movement, we editors keenly felt the dearth of memoirs. We couldn't find many autobiographical essays that described the experience we remembered, the feeling that, with the rise of a women's movement, we were suddenly and irrevocably living in history. We began to worry about the possible loss of that part of a historical record that comes from the layering and interaction of many texts. Legitimation comes in part from being woven into the subsequent story. This wouldn't be the first time women dropped out of the national political narrative, and the reluctance to listen to women remains a pervasive social problem. We saw the nuances and specificities of our stories, the nature of our debates, and the principles animating us thinning out in public consciousness, rendering our private memories of richness isolating or grotesque.

We hope for many histories of the women's movement. Surprisingly few have been written to date, though we are all indebted to Alice

Echols for the attentive account in *Daring to Be Bad: Radical Feminism in America, 1967–1975.* Our book is one piece of that project—a set of memoirs. Though it contains facts, it also contains rival accounts and interpretations of those facts, and we make no effort to sift evidence and make one story. (We have also, at the suggestion of our copy editor, Sonia Jaffe Robbins, not imposed one style of capitalization on these essays, allowing each writer her choice in capitalizing political terms.) Historians reading this book may notice disparities, jump-cuts, and contested material. Our interest is in establishing a document, and in the act of memory itself. We invite speculation on the problem of inter-pretation, and to that end we asked for the response pieces here. They are meant to model the task we value—the constant effort to find a pol-itics of liberation. In early CR groups, what one said was granted the fine new status of truth unmodified. We editors no longer believe in this dream of authenticity, of pure raw material, but this makes the material here more precious to us as evidence of ongoing social thinking. We find meaning in how our writers have chosen to put their pasts before us.

What is the status of a memoir? Certainly it is a historical docu-ment. Like any document, it is partial, a lens, a work not just mediated in language but constructed by language. Writing any memoir is an act of shaping, selecting, combining, eliding, repressing, and reconstruct-ing. Memoir writing raises questions of completeness, of veracity and the fictive, issues of privacy, of partiality, of mediation. To say "memoir," however, announces a goal—of describing events with their affects attached, of examining a complex of acts and feelings in social and per-sonal space, of making an honest and ethical attempt to restore a sense of history's specifics. There will always be unbridgeable space between the story of the one and of the many; highlighting one memory often casts another in shadow. The past is inside us in flickering and mysteri-ous ways that can never be fully acknowledged nor easily represented.

In making *The Feminist Memoir Project,* we have accepted the para-dox in all such undertakings: the effort to pull out single moments from the flow is falsifying, yet at the same time we have wanted to capture such moments—images that can endure, that fix feminism in history, and that contribute to feminism's ongoing life now. For amnesia about political movements is not only an innocent effect of general forgetful-ness, but is socially produced, packaged, promulgated, and perpetuated. This book stands against historical forgetting.

In this spirit of discovery and reconstruction, we have provoked people to write memoirs and some responses as documents of the second wave of feminism. We feel that women's movements have usually erred in a silent direction, have been all too willing to disappear, to blend into the background of other events, to forget to assert female political presence and creative interventions. So we are deeply grateful to our memoirists and respondees, many of whom were typically reluctant to begin, too busy with current projects and engagements, slow to write about their own achievements and institution-building. We asked each of the women here to talk about feminism in her own voice, to choose what stories to tell. We didn't ask people to write as public figures, nor to produce full historical accounts of public events. Our prospectus and questions assumed some partisanship on the part of all our writers, but we asked as well that they explore the ambiguities of personal change and their ambivalences about the feminist milieu.

It should be as clear to you as it was to us that no matter how big a book we made, we would inevitably exclude. Only many memoirs of consciousness, communities, groups, issues, and struggles could begin to get at the richness and the contradictions, could hint at the scale of what was, from the first, a mass movement. The book in your hands makes the best sense as an invitation to further dialogue and documentation. Many others must write. Every woman has her story, her still-changing stories, of her encounter with modern feminism. We hope the pieces here communicate both the sturdiness and the complex desires of women activists, but we don't think that they can represent the tens of thousands of people who were and are active. This is not the (mythical) full story. Instead these essays are symbolic moments, offering a sense of the particularities and values that are at stake when history is being made.

These stories are a political inheritance, but we intend no elegy. We seek knowledge of a collective experience, and we hope to link the passions feminism stirred in this generation to a past, a present, and a future.

Our Gang of Four: Friendship and Women's Liberation

Amy Kesselman, with Heather Booth,
Vivian Rothstein, and Naomi Weisstein[1]

About my involvement in women's liberation in the late 1960s, I often say, "Feminism saved my life." It replaced self-hatred with both anger and political analysis; it made sense of the world, reconnected me with other women, and gave shape to a host of unformed thoughts and feelings that had lurked for years in the shadows of my consciousness. All of this happened (with lightning speed) for me and for hundreds of other women's liberation activists in the three years from 1967 to 1970.

A pivotal element of this transformation was the intense friendship among the women who were re-creating feminism together. Formerly women's close friendships had been seen as secondary to the main business of life: finding a man. For those of us trying to move into male terrain, any relationships with women could be stunted by the suspicion that these female bonds would interfere with our efforts to be accepted as equals by men. I, for one, felt profoundly ambivalent about my friendships with women at the City College of New York. I did care about my women friends and felt more comfortable with them than I did with men, but at the same time, I was troubled by the way women together seemed to accept and reinforce their marginality in the male-dominated world.

Friendships in the early years of women's liberation were different. They reinforced our strengths, not our weaknesses, and provided the matrix within which many of the ideas of women's liberation developed. Thinking about this memoir immediately evoked my relationships with Heather Booth, Vivian Rothstein, and Naomi Weisstein, with whom I

---

[1] With the assistance of Virginia Blaisdell

had worked intensively in the women's liberation movement in Chicago in the late 1960s. The electric energy of the early days of women's liberation lent passion and intensity to our friendship, and our friendship in turn fostered the contributions we each made to the emerging movement in the city in which we lived.

To reflect on the role of our friendship in the development of the feminist movement in Chicago from 1967 to 1971, this essay will draw on the memories of all four of us. It combines a historical narrative with quotations from writings by and interviews with Heather, Vivian, and Naomi. They also helped to shape and revise the essay as a whole.

I. Becoming Politically Active

All of us were committed new left activists before the reemergence of feminism. The radical movements of the sixties had been the center of our lives for several years.

Heather Booth Speaks

After growing up in Bensonhurst in Brooklyn, New York, I moved with my family to Long Island when I was in high school. My family's strong loving support passed on values of caring for others and responsibility for building a better society. Even though I was the head of many high school clubs (yearbook, choir, study groups), I was looking for but never finding ways to act on those social values. After I heard Dr. King speak, I dropped out of the high school sorority and one of the cheerleading teams when it was clear that they discriminated against blacks and against girls who did not fit some standard definition of "pretty." But I was still searching for other meaningful activity.

It was a time of movements. On February 1, 1960, Negro students in Greensboro, North Carolina, sat in at a Woolworth's counter to demand the service they were being denied because of their race. I joined the support effort for the sit-ins organized by the Congress on Racial Equality (CORE) and began to identify a whole new world of meaningful concerns and actions. Within weeks after leaving home to go to college at the University of Chicago in 1963, I was active in a political campaign for A.A. Sammy Rayner against the local political machine. Within months, in the Friends of the Student Non-Violent Coordinating Committee (SNCC), I helped in organizing the South Side freedom schools set up during a school boycott to protest the unequal school conditions created by the superintendent of the public schools, Ben Willis. By the summer after my first year of college, 1964, I joined the Mississippi Freedom Summer Project to focus the eyes of the nation on the denial of voting rights to black citizens. Following that summer, I did national traveling to talk about the civil rights movement on college campuses throughout the country.

It was a time of youth movements. For the first time in U.S. history a majority of people in their late teens were going to college. These new experiences in an intellectual environment away from home were transformative.

In my first year at college, I also confronted the ways that women were treated differently from men. Women students, for example, had different rules about when they had to return to the dorm. When I stayed out past eleven p.m. (giving support to a friend who was very depressed about a broken love), I was searched for contraceptives. I was outraged that they would humiliate me, and I was also very embarrassed: "How could they think this of me?" Others felt that outrage. Over the next two years, women staged "sleep outs" until they changed the rules.

In 1965, a friend at the university from the Summer Project found out she was pregnant and became distraught. She asked for help in finding an abortionist. I located someone. She was safe and relieved. Word spread. Others asked. This is how I began what became known as "Jane," a significant abortion counseling service at a time of illegal and unsafe abortions. I don't remember really discussing it with anyone (I was much too scared) or even immediately seeing this as an activity related to women's organizing. It was simply the right thing to do in the face of a desperate situation. I left "Jane" in 1968, three years later, after my first child was born; I recruited others, who later expanded the service, even actually performing the procedure themselves. The women in "Jane" performed over 11,000 abortions until April 1973, when the first legal abortion clinics opened in Chicago.

The next year, another friend was raped at knife point, at home, in her bed. When she went to student health for a checkup, she was told this was not covered and was even given a lecture on her promiscuity. Outraged, several of us sat in at the student health office until she got the checkup and they changed their thoughtless policy. Now, I did not take this action with particular boldness or courage. In fact, I was petrified. Would someone yell at me? Would I get thrown out of school? What would happen to our friend? Would I know what to do? Would I have time to finish my homework for school tomorrow? My heart was always pounding. I almost never felt I knew enough, or was smart enough, to be confident. But we acted in spite of not knowing enough, being smart enough, or being confident enough. And the policy changed. We learned that if you act, you can change the world.

In the mid 1960s, at a very large student political meeting, I was shouted down by one male student and told to shut up. I did shut up. Then I proceeded to tap each woman at the meeting on the shoulder and suggest we leave. That was the beginning of our own organization, the Women's Radical Action Project (WRAP), which became one of the most dynamic groups on campus.

Amy Kesselman Speaks

I grew up in Jackson Heights, Queens, feeling alienated from just about everything in my life. I absorbed political consciousness from my parents, who had been Communists in the 1930s. But in the fearful atmosphere of the McCarthy era, their messages about politics were muted and confused. In high school, I helped to organize a discussion group called "Discussions Unlimited," an ironic title since we were told we couldn't discuss politics, sex, or religion. I picketed my local Woolworth's in support of the black students who were attempting to integrate lunch counters in the South. In 1961, my senior year, I was suspended from school for five days for distributing leaflets that protested civil defense drills. These drills, endemic in the fifties, perpetuated the futile belief that standing against a wall could save us if a nuclear bomb were to drop on New York City.

When I entered City College in 1962, I was much more interested in politics than course work. I read Marx instead of doing homework and became involved in the tiny but vocal student movement. I thought and read about politics all the time and took myself seriously as an activist. Indeed, I wanted desperately to be a leader in the left. In my junior year, I organized a campus committee against the war in Vietnam and was elected its president. But most of the time, when I was with my male colleagues, I felt stupid and inadequate. While I was excited about being part of a movement to end the war, my memories of college activism are filled with petty humiliations and frustrations.

My most vivid memory of political frustration is of a sit-in at the administration building, aimed at getting the administration to refuse to release male students' grades to the draft board, since boards would then draft those who didn't do well. The steering committee of the sit-in was composed of nine men, each representing a different political faction, and me, representing the Independent Committee to End the War. We started out with over three hundred participants, but as final exams approached, the ever-practical City College students began to attend to their school work. Losing numbers, we were losing strength. Thus when the administration offered a compromise, I thought we ought to consider it. The other members of the steering committee absolutely refused to discuss this with me. "What, give in now!" they proclaimed to me, as if they were talking to a hostile reporter or to an ignorant bystander rather than to a comrade in struggle. I felt discounted and hurt, and consequently felt certain that I must be wrong in my political analysis, perhaps lacking in guts or perseverance. We eventually had to leave the building without achieving any of our goals. I didn't realize until five years later, after I had become involved in women's liberation, that I had been right in my assessment and that the stubbornness of the men on the steering committee was counterproductive macho posturing. At the time of the sit-in, however, there was nobody to talk to nor did I have the vocabulary to express my feelings or ideas. I had talked with my friends about male chauvinism in a general way, but no one wanted to unite on the basis of our femaleness for fear that it would further delegitimate us in the eyes of the male leaders. When I read Juliet Mitchell's article "Women: The Longest Revolution," published in *New Left Review* in 1966, I thought "Yes, yes, yes." Yet the essay was abstract and theoretical; there was no one I could talk to about its implications for my life.

When I graduated from college, I could not imagine myself taking a job or going to graduate school within a society I considered hopelessly corrupt. Instead, I became a full-time activist, pouring my energy into the movement to end the war in Vietnam and to create a more just and generous world. I was moving slowly and with difficulty away from the Marxist orthodoxy of my college years, noticing that the active agents of social change in the 1960s were not members of the proletariat but middle-class young people. With this in mind, I moved to Chicago to work with an organizing project in a middle-class neighborhood: Citizens for Independent Political Action (CIPA), whose slogan was "If a machine shortchanges you, kick it." Chicago, with its obdurate political machine, seemed like the belly of the beast: hence the perfect place to build a revolutionary movement. My job was to work with neighborhood high school students. To the leaders of the organization this meant organizing draft resistance, but I developed other activities: organizing a coffeehouse where students could hold discussions and hear speakers and helping students to create underground newspapers.

Yet Chicago proved no more hospitable to female leadership than City College. While there were many women involved in the grassroots organizing projects in Chicago's neighborhoods, the leadership was male and just as given to posturing as the students I had worked with before.

Vivian Rothstein Speaks

As a child of German-Jewish immigrants who fled from the Nazis in the late 1930s, I had a keen sense that "they could come after us at any time." My mother's immigrant community in which everyone had lost their families and homes in Europe, and my own Jewishness, combined with my father's absence to make me feel like an outsider looking into mainstream America. When I became a scholarship student at Berkeley, a member of the first generation in my family to attend college, I was a ripe candidate for 1960s activism.

At college I took a job tutoring African-American kids from Oakland. There I learned about civil rights campaigns against discriminatory supermarket chains, restaurants, car dealerships, and hotels. My weekends were spent in ever larger demonstrations demanding improved services or jobs for the Black community. Two days after my eighteenth birthday, I was arrested, together with five hundred others, in front of the major automobile showrooms on auto row in San Francisco. The passion and the call for justice of the civil rights movement stirred my own desires to be part of something moral in American society. But no matter how active I was, there seemed to be room for me only as a body going limp in mass demonstrations.

In an effort to make more of a difference and to play a more meaningful role, I went South in the summer of 1965 as a civil rights worker. After I had spent ten days in jail together with hundreds of other summer volunteers and local Black activists for parading without a permit, I was dispatched to an outlying rural area to register voters, run a freedom school, and recruit kids to integrate the local schools in September. I took the mandate to develop community-organizing skills seriously; my goal was to return North to work in poor white and Black communities.

In order to become a full-time organizer, I dropped out of school and moved to Chicago to work in JOIN Community Union, a Students for a Democratic Society (SDS) project organizing southern white Appalachian migrants around welfare rights, tenant issues, block clubs, and neighborhood empowerment. While most of the block organizers were women and most of the neighborhood leadership that emerged from our effort was female, the political leaders of the organization were male. Through the civil rights movement and community organizing in urban ghettos, I had developed the skills needed to bring people together to address their problems, as well as the strategic sensibility and confidence to help others find their voices. But the movements of the time didn't welcome me either as a leader or as an intellect.

Still, it was hard to complain. The movement gave me opportunities that barely existed for women in the larger society—to be a social critic, to develop a vision for eradicating poverty and racism, to stand up to the power structure—be it landlords, city officials, ward committeemen, or county welfare workers. In contrast, the primary jobs for women outside the home in those days were in ghettoized female professions—as teachers, nurses, secretaries. The movement encouraged me to make history and to fight for social justice in society at large.

In 1967 I was invited to participate in a peace conference between antiwar Americans and Vietnamese from both the North and the South. I was subsequently invited to visit North Vietnam as part of a peace delegation investigating the civilian impact of American bombing of the North. The trip thrust me into the role of public speaker for the peace community. It changed my sense of my personal power forever. When a close movement ally commented that the trip to Vietnam had made me into a different person, my then husband remarked that our friend simply had never listened to me before. But although I had organizing skills and growing self-confidence, I still remained marginal to the movement leadership.

Naomi Weisstein Speaks

I grew up in the church of socialism and knew that all my life politics would be part of what I did. I also grew up with certain assumptions that we would later recognize as feminist: I knew that my life could not be devoted to husband and children, that I must have a career, and it wouldn't be such a bad thing if I didn't marry at all. I was ten in 1950, twenty in 1960. And in that harsh, repressive, and wildly woman-hating decade, I was in the closet most of the time on two accounts—my socialism and my feminism.

In my New York City junior high school, I had a girl gang. We terrorized the posh East Side neighborhood in which our school was located, walked home through the Park to the scuzzier West Side, where most of us lived, went to each others' houses, taught each other how to masturbate, and were so tight with each other that many of us didn't want to go to different high schools, because we would have to give up our friendships. When I got to the elite and highly selective Bronx High School of Science, my world collapsed. I went from a cozy and comfortable two years in an all-girls school to a heterosexual oven. All my music, my art, my writing, my acting in plays, my power, the standing and popularity that I enjoyed in the first fourteen years of my life vanished in a day, as it became clear that the only thing on which girls were judged was their ability to negotiate the world of heterosexuality. I came to Bronx Science with braces, glasses, no breasts to speak of, redheaded, and with a considerable amount of baby fat. I could see myself fast on the way to becoming a nerd nonperson in this environment. Furious and desperate, I insinuated myself into a girl group of smart dressers by the strength of my humor, sarcasm, and painfully, carefully calculated cool. They took me in, made me borrow money for clothes and contact lenses, gave me a padded bra to wear, told me not to open my mouth and smile so my braces didn't show, and helped me immeasurably to maintain some sort of standing through my four years of high school by having boyfriends. But I can still feel my resentment, rage, and despondency at this state of affairs, especially because it seemed as if my future were closing down on me. It seemed as if all my girlfriends were grooming themselves, first for boyfriends, and ultimately for husbands and families.

After Bronx Science, I went to Wellesley and flourished; I graduated Phi Beta Kappa and went to graduate school in psychology at Harvard.

The first day of graduate school, the chairman of the department had the entering graduate students to lunch and, after eating, sat back in his chair, lit his pipe, and announced, "You know, women don't belong in graduate school." The male graduate students assented, leaned back in their chairs, puffed on their training pipes, and said, "That's right. No man is going to want you. You're out of your natural roles."

At that time, Harvard's Lamont Library, which contained the assigned course readings on reserve, barred women, including those who took those courses. "Women will distract men from their work," said the librarian. "You want distraction," I shouted, "I'll show you distraction." I organized a demonstration in the library consisting of women graduate students dancing slinkily while I played the clarinet.

At Harvard, I was again facing the heterosexual juggernaut. But four years at Wellesley had toughened me up, and I was determined that this time I was going to call some of the shots. Besides, I had lost all of my baby fat, and so I figured I was in a relatively strong position. I hauled out my padded bra, shortened my skirts, and revved up to cruising speed, picking up law, medicine, and business school students and an occasional truck driver or cop. But my fellow female graduate students were not doing very well. When they weren't posing as total victims, they were accused of being castrating. There was a lot of weeping, a lot of taking it. I felt strongly that we should mount a collective struggle against the barriers to our finding satisfying, loving relationships with men. So we formed a syndicate, and we blacklisted notorious abusers, calling them to tell them they were on the blacklist. We would also call boys we wanted to go out with, and tell them that other women they had been out with had told us it was OK for us to date them. That was a very important principle; you never tread on another woman's turf.

Also, we went cruising together. Our M.O. was to go into big graduate dining rooms, walk up to a table full of boys, introduce ourselves, and say, "Mind if we sit down?" And it was kind of a successful thing for a while. But as is often the case in certain kinds of actions, we had our quisling, who told on us to the psychology department. The males were outraged. It was a violation of their sacred right to victimize and abuse us. And I got a lot of pressure from the males to stop what I was doing. The pressure was sufficient to intimidate most of my female friends into going back to the old system.

In spite of this hostile atmosphere, I finished my course work quickly. But when I wanted to do my dissertation research, they wouldn't give me the equipment that I needed, because they said that I would break it. This, I realized, was sexist. I pointed out that male graduate students used the equipment all the time, and broke it all the time, and that I didn't expect to be any different.

I was thrilled by my work on vision and the brain. We were at the dawn of the cognitive revolution, and I was hell-bent on continuing. Since I wasn't able to use the Harvard equipment, I moved to New Haven to work on my dissertation. I joined CORE in 1963, and found to my shocked dismay that I couldn't talk in meetings. This was quite something for me, because all my life I had been performing. I never had any difficulty talking in public. So here I was in CORE, and all of a sudden I was too terrified to speak. I didn't understand it at all. I didn't understand it until Chicago, until Heather and I started talking about women's position in these movements for social change.

At Yale I organized another syndicate. On one of its outings I met Jesse Lemisch, then an instructor in history and then as now a New Left activist. Against the current of the male misogyny of the time, he was surprisingly enlightened (and still is). Like a wolfhound sniffing out trails beneath the snow, he detected the cant and cruelty in attitudes toward women, and struggled against these attitudes. We got married and moved to Chicago together, where Jesse got a job teaching at the University of Chicago.

I, however, couldn't find a job. This was in '64; the universities were dripping jobs. Wherever I went, chairmen would say things like, "How can a little girl like you teach a great big class of men?" I found myself totally isolated in my position as faculty wife. People at parties treated me as an appendage to Jesse, which meant that I was completely ignored. It was a half-life again.

In the spring of 1965, Jesse and I participated in an anti-Vietnam War sit-in on State Street, and our political life began anew. We joined Chicago SNCC and Chicago SDS, both of us delighted to be back in the movement, and especially delighted to be part of a NEW Left, a Left that was open, generous, and at that time infused with a spirit of beloved community and vision.

During the sit-in at the University of Chicago administration building in 1966 I found, though, that once again I couldn't speak in public and that no woman was speaking except for Jackie Goldberg, a seasoned organizer from Berkeley. I tried. I got up on a chair and announced that we were organizing classes in the administration building, but no one would listen. I shouted for a while, and then I said, "Fuck," and got off the chair. I felt very weird.

II. FINDING EACH OTHER; FINDING OUR VOICES

"Building an American women's liberation movement," Vivian recalled,

> was a matter of survival for politically conscious and skilled women in the late 1960s. We were smart, we were dedicated, we had revolutionary ideas—but who besides ourselves gave a damn? We had hit the glass ceiling on the left and there was nowhere for us to go. We were hungry for political discussion with others who took us seriously, and we slowly began to find each other. It seems like a whole lifetime away, but it's important to remember that at the time there were no women on the Supreme Court, almost no women elected officials, no wage-earning women characters in TV sitcoms, and that abortion was illegal. Yet we saw ourselves as serious agents of social change (the Movement was, after all, our vocation), and we needed the validation of others who viewed us and themselves in the same way.

Between the years 1966 and 1967, we discovered each other and found the validation we craved. For all of us, as these anecdotes show, proto-feminist ideas had been percolating for several years. Hence we responded eagerly when other women in the radical movement began to articulate anger and frustration. Heather remembers going to a conference of the Students for a Democratic Society in 1965 because the "woman question" was on the agenda.

> The "woman" discussion, with both men and women in it, started off slowly. Then the women began trying to share their experiences. Several of the men, used to dominating the discussion, would often cut off the women, talk over them and deny their experience. I was one of the people who tried to keep the group together. After all, the civil rights movement was about people working together across differences, not dividing. Jimmy Garrett, a black SNCC organizer I had known in Mississippi, then stood up and told the women they needed to talk alone together and get their act together, so he

was leaving. I realized he was right. The group divided and several of the women met late into the night.

Naomi and Heather met at the University of Chicago sit-in in 1966. They shared their consternation about how few women were speaking and talked about their own struggles and frustrations. Heather was drawn to Naomi's "electric energy and piercingly challenging mind." "She was also so hysterically funny," Heather remembers, "that I would pee in my pants at some of her wit and antics." After the sit-in they taught a course together on women at the University of Chicago in the organizer's school that Staughton Lynd had started and repeated it the following summer. There were both men and women in the course, which questioned women's position in everything from beauty pageants to child rearing. Naomi recalls:

> I remember that Heather and I were stunned by the antiwoman reflex response to most of what we said and we'd look at each other and start laughing. When we talked about beauty contests, somebody said, well, it's important because otherwise women will let themselves go. When we talked about whether or not being a secretary was a free choice somebody said, well, women have smaller hands and so they're better for typewriters. Heather said, make the keyboard bigger, and many people looked at each other and rolled their eyes as if what Heather was saying was absolutely unthinkable. But Heather was a born organizer, and gently and genuinely made people start to think about alternatives. She was inclusive, reasoned, humorous and egalitarian. It was just stunning. Teaching this course with Heather marked the beginning for me of the amazing grace of the early women's liberation movement.

I knew almost no one when I moved to Chicago in 1967. CIPA, the organization I had come to work with, was located in a lower-middle-class neighborhood and had a core group of twenty to thirty members. Women were active in the organization, yet the leadership was predominantly male. The attitude of the CIPA leadership toward women was reflected in its theme song.

> *I was walking to the polls one day,*
> *For to cast my vote and have my say,*

I was taken by surprise by my precinct captain's lies.
All of a sudden my poor vote was stole away.

This college kid came to my door;
Said vote for Gene and end the war.
Throw away your picket sign; toe the Democratic line.
T'was the same thing that we heard in '64.

Then this CIPA chick came to my pad;
Laid it on me that the system's bad;
Tweedledum and Tweedledee; as everyone can see,
The choices that we're offered are so sad.

Women were expected to work hard but we were trivialized and discounted in myriad subtle and not so subtle ways. I felt lonely and isolated, and besides, had not figured out how to go about reaching the high school students in the neighborhood.

One day, shortly after I arrived in Chicago, I was sitting in the CIPA office waiting for young men to come to the office for draft counseling. Heather, whom I had just met through her husband, Paul, called. We talked for two hours about her experience working at a local psychiatric hospital. I felt that I had been awakened from a deep sleep: her observations were brilliant; she listened appreciatively to my ideas; together we figured things out. When I got off the phone to confront a surly CIPA leader, outraged by my "gossiping" on the phone to my girlfriend instead of working on the draft counseling project, something clicked in my consciousness. The excitement I felt while talking with Heather highlighted my dissatisfaction with my work in CIPA.

I first met Naomi after having seen *The War Game,* the movie about a hypothetical nuclear disaster. Steve, the man I was with, was friends with Jesse from the University of Chicago and the four of us went out for coffee after the movie. Naomi asked me what I thought. I always had complicated thoughts about movies in those days, but usually no one wanted to hear them. I said I thought the movie was liberal (a dirty word on the left in those days) because it presented people as powerless. Naomi was thinking along the same lines. She told me about experiments in social psychology that demonstrated people's willingness to defy authority when the possibility is presented to them. Naomi remembers:

Amy's comments astounded me because she was thinking about agency, about people shaping the world and resisting forces that seemed absolute and overwhelming. I was obsessed with agency in those days. In addition to thinking about agency in terms of the New Left, I had been trying to figure out how to begin a program of research that would explore questions of agency in the brain. I wanted to talk to Amy forever.

Throughout 1966 and '67, Heather, Naomi, and I talked about what it meant to be female in our society at every possible opportunity. Each time we talked, we generated new insights. The world seemed to be coming dramatically and miraculously into focus.

After the patronizing and hostile treatment of the women's resolutions at the National Conference for New Politics in September 1967, outraged women in Chicago organized the West Side Group, which included Heather, myself, Naomi, Sara Evans Boyte, Shulamith Firestone (who left for New York after a few months), Laya Firestone, Jo Freeman, Evie Goldstein, Sue Munaker, and Fran Rominski.[2] The autonomy of the group was a major step away from allegiance to the male-dominated left. I was cautioned by a male activist that the women's group would divide the movement. He was (as we used to say) a "heavy" in the Chicago movement, and I wanted his approval more than I'd like to admit. But when he unleashed his ample rhetorical powers on me, I remember thinking, "could he be right?" and then, after a minute or two, "he's full of shit," and finally, "I'll be damned, he's threatened!"

The discussions in the Westside Group continued the developing of feminist analysis that had begun informally in groups of two and three. This process generated a similar intense excitement. Naomi recalls,

The best part of the group was that we all took each other seriously. We had become so used to the usual heterosexual chill that it was a giddy and slightly terrifying sensation to talk and have everybody listen. All of a sudden we were no longer inaudible. I can hardly describe the joy! Unbelievable! The sound system had just been turned on. We couldn't wait to go to meetings, where we talked ecstatically about everything. We talked about the contempt and hostility we felt, not only walking down the street, but from our

---

[2] See Alice Echols, *Daring to Be Bad: Radical Feminism in America 1967–1975* (Minneapolis: University of Minnesota Press, 1967), pp. 45–50, for a description based on Jo Freeman's recollections of women's efforts to be included in the resolutions of the National Conference for New Politics.

male friends in the New Left. We talked about our inability to speak in public. We asked ourselves what we should call the thing that was squelching us. Male supremacy? Female subordination? Male chauvinism? Capitalist debris?

Vivian joined the West Side Group shortly after participating in a 1967 delegation of American peace activists that visited Vietnam. It was the Vietnamese, she recalls (not the American peace activists),

> who insisted that women be represented in the delegation. That's how I came to visit Vietnam, where I was introduced to the Vietnamese Women's Union. This was, then and now, the largest membership organization in Vietnam, running its own women's institutions including schools, clinics, museums and economic enterprises. That's where I first understood the importance of independent women's organizations.

Heather, Naomi, and I were immediately drawn to Vivian's sense of moral purpose, her intelligence, and her unshakable commitment to organizing. The four of us began to spend time together, always talking about women's condition and how to change it.

So after years of feeling judged and humiliated by the male heavies of the new left, I finally felt that I had political comrades—people with whom I could develop ideas without feeling judged or dismissed. We had no interest in mystification; our collaborative effort to understand women's position in the world and to develop strategies for changing it meant that we all needed clarity and honesty. Suddenly and jubilantly, I was released from the need for the approval of the male left establishment.

One of the most important insights that emerged in our discussions, which Naomi brilliantly developed in her influential article "Psychology Constructs the Female," was the power of people's expectations to shape individuals' behavior. Our friendship was a crucible for this idea. We had created a countervailing force to the sexism around us, and the transformative effects clarified in a graphic and immediate way the power of social context. Naomi remembers that the West Side Group talked about "whether it was true that we were less aggressive, less creative, less profound, less artistic, less 'linear' (whatever that means), less honorable, less smell-free and less funny" than men. Our confidence to steer through this "nature versus nurture" debate was immeasurably enhanced by our knowledge that each of us could see in ourselves the changes made possible by the respect and attention we lavished on each other.

These ecstatic, wildly stimulating discussions in the West Side Group happened almost despite ourselves. In fact, we believed that, once we had concluded that women's oppression existed, we should move quickly to action. Yet while we repeatedly attempted to steer our discussions in a programmatic, action-oriented direction, ideas about the politics of personal life welled up uncontrollably. In such talk, we developed, as women throughout the country were also doing, some of the central ideas of women's liberation. Although some of the time we sensed the importance of our discussions, we often felt guilty about not being "on the streets." Naomi comments:

> Much of the way we handled this conflict was to question whether we were really oppressed and how and whether capitalism had really done all of this to us or whether women's subjugation preceded capitalism. In other words we kept talking, but centering the subject around the left assuaged our guilt, and using the categories we'd inherited persuaded us that we were doing something almost as important as action. So we talked about whether Jackie Kennedy was our sister or our enemy and whether we were too middle-class, had too much "white skin privilege" and were too well educated to be complaining at all. But when a movement starts, its force quickly becomes greater and more powerful than the social constraints we bring to it; thus we couldn't really suppress our desire to talk about what we wanted to talk about. So after we had kicked around capitalist disaccumulation for a while, we zoomed back and talked about monogamy, and our egalitarian, anti-hierarchical vision of utopia and community, and where children fit into our scheme. And we talked about cosmetics. Suddenly, it was no longer an imperative of nature that we paint our faces and squeeze our breasts into little cones. Some of us decided to give up makeup and brassieres. It was a brave thing to do. I remember the feeling I had the first time I went out without my eyeliner. It was like wearing a big day-glo sandwich sign saying "HATE ME, I NO LONGER CARE WHETHER I'M PRETTY."

In the years between 1967 and 1970, women's liberation exploded in Chicago and throughout the country. For the women in Chicago, the tortuous process of moving toward an autonomous women's movement was complicated by the close ties we had to the left and by the central role that the movements of the sixties played in our lives. The process was accelerated somewhat for me by my contact with women from other parts of the country at the first national gathering of women's liberation activists in November 1968, in Lake Villa, Illinois. While this meeting has been described as polarized and divisive (as, for example, in Alice Echols's book *Daring to Be Bad),* I remember the conference as enormously stimulating. It pushed my thinking deeper about issues of personal life, and it convinced me of the importance and the viability of an autonomous women's movement.

From 1968 to 1970, the four of us organized women in a variety of contexts, reaching out to new women, forming groups, identifying issues of common concern, and helping other women play leadership roles. I helped to form a women's group in CIPA and taught a course on women's role in society at the Chicago high school where I worked. Since there were no texts, I used *The Second Sex,* as well as the many mimeographed pamphlets—from New England Free Press and other sources—that circulated among women's liberation activists. Heather started a women's group in Hyde Park. Vivian was organizing high school students in a Chicago suburb and speaking widely against the war in Vietnam. She had an audiotaped message made by a Vietnamese woman about the effects of the war on Vietnamese women. "I took this tape," she remembers, "to many gatherings of American women who were hungry for a connection to women's experiences in Vietnam. In this way I was able to serve as a bridge linking women who cared about each other even though they would never meet or know each other's names."

Naomi, who felt "the women's movement gave me my voice, or gave it back to me," had become an extremely effective speaker who gave talks about women's liberation all over the country. As a member of the women's caucus of Loyola SDS, Naomi also helped to organize a variety of activities against the war, in support of legalized abortion, and against various expressions of what they sometimes called "the Catholic patriarchy." Women's liberation activities in those days sometimes provoked outrageous backlash activities by men. At Loyola, for example, the women's caucus gave out leaflets at the senior prom, questioning, according to Naomi,

> whether marriage and babies were all women wanted to do with their excellent Loyola educations. It was very mild but the men

went berserk and formed themselves into a phalanx of human bodies past which we could not go to distribute our leaflets. Their legs were spread and their arms were folded over their chests, I think in an unconscious imitation of the Black Muslim bodyguards "The Fruit of Islam."

While we worked with lots of other women, we always looked to each other for political support and guidance, consulting each other about almost everything we did. Together we developed a vision of the independent women's movement that was both rebellious and pluralistic, that confronted the prevailing notions about femininity but was sympathetic to women's varied approaches to survival. Such a movement would support women who wanted to make changes in their lives but, in Naomi's words, would "steer a generous course away from denouncing women for the choices they made in their efforts to get through the day." It would be a movement that organized women to confront the myriad forms of sexism in their lives, won concrete victories, and challenged the power relations of gender in both private life and social institutions. We envisioned a radical transformation of society, but we believed that we had to build a movement around the specific injustices that women experienced. "We felt that people's consciousness develops through action," Vivian commented, "not through being hit over the head with a political line." For us, the feminist rallying cry "the personal is political," first articulated by women in New York Redstockings, implied not only that problems previously seen as private had political origins, but also that they should be addressed politically through collective activity. We tried to change the balance of power in a wide range of arenas, from singles bars to typing pools. We felt a strong sense of connection with other people's struggles against injustice, but we argued against those who urged us to abandon feminism in favor of the fight against racism and imperialism. We believed that people organizing on their *own* behalf was the lifeblood of movements for social change. Hence we fiercely defended the legitimacy of the independent women's movement.

We were radical, but were repulsed by the gyrations of the radical movement in 1969, which was so engorged by revolutionary rhetoric that it was becoming increasingly irrelevant to American society. According to Naomi:

We constantly tested our ideas against the American political reality of the time and resisted the temptation of the withdrawal politics that had begun to gather force in the late 1960s. We didn't have the least desire to join a seed gathering commune in the Nevada desert on the one hand or on the other to chirp sayings of Chairman Mao from the little red book.

We helped each other articulate our politics in the Chicago women's movement and began talking with other women about creating an organizational presence that would embody our vision. Vivian's contact with the Women's Union in Vietnam had convinced her of the importance of autonomous women's organizations. "In order to be politically potent," she realized,

> women must have opportunities to develop skills and leadership. This development was unlikely to happen in mixed organizations because of competition from men and the distance women had to first travel in building confidence and abilities.

In our early discussions about forming an organization, we expressed our belief that "an independent women's organization" would provide a context in which we could "develop our political priorities together instead of in relationship to men," and would enable feminists to "to use our power as a political block in the movement." Recognizing that women's groups in Chicago often had difficulty moving "from personal discussion to political action . . . ," we saw a need for an umbrella organization that would connect groups with each other, develop leadership, and generate ideas for action projects.[3]

The new organization that we helped to create, the Chicago Women's Liberation Union (CWLU), was inspired in part by the women's union Vivian had encountered in North Vietnam. "The idea of the organization's structure," according to Vivian, "was to decentralize action, to provide support for a variety of efforts, and to bring all the women's organizing together to increase its visibility and its impact."

At the founding convention, the four of us worked energetically against the arguments of women who opposed a separate women's orga-

---

[3] These quotations are from notes from an organizational planning meeting.

nization. In response Naomi and I, with several other women, wrote a women's history play called *Everywoman,* which we hoped would bring people together. We began the play with a comical riff about two witches who wanted to start the revolution. The two witches, played by Naomi and me, threw various instruments of women's oppression into the cauldron—padded bras, curlers, high heels, a typewriter, the Suzy Stain doll that cries real tears, and concluded with items representing capitalism and the nuclear family. Then, with the help of a theatrical smoke bomb, which was much smokier than we anticipated and caused the audience to cough and choke for the rest of the play, the cauldron exploded. Short excerpts from the writings of women activists from all over the world were incorporated into the narrative of the play. Women positioned in the audience yelled out, "Who are you?" "Tell us your names!" and the witches responded with a prose poem modeled on 1930s popular front rhetoric.[4]

> I am all women, I am every woman. Wherever women are suffering, I am there. Wherever women are struggling, I am there. Wherever women are fighting for their liberation, I am there.
>
> I am at the bedside of the woman giving birth, screaming in labor; I am with the woman selling her body in Vietnam so that her children may eat. I am with the woman selling her body in the streets of American cities to feed the habit she acquired from her boyfriend.
>
> I am with the woman who never sees the light outside her kitchen; I am with the woman who never sees the light outside her factory; I am with the woman whose fingers are stiff from endless typing and whose legs ache from the high heels that she must wear to please her boss; I am with the groupies following the rock bands, bands whose every song is a triumphant celebration of women's degradation. I am with the women who wanted to be scientists and architects and engineers and poets and who ended up being scientists' wives and architects' wives and engineers' wives and poets' wives.

---

[4] See, for example, Tom Joad's speech in *The Grapes of Wrath* and Alfred Hayes and Earl Robinson's "I Dreamed I Saw Joe Hill Last Night."

I am with the woman bleeding to death on the kitchen table of a quack abortionist; I am with the woman answering endless questions of the inquisitive caseworkers. And I am with the caseworkers, whose dreams of making a new social order have long been smothered in the endless bureaucracy, the endless forms, the racism of their institutions.

I am with the beauty queen painting her face and spraying her hair with poison; I am with the black prostitute straightening her hair and lightening her skin; I am with the young child for whom an apron is the only thing she has been taught to dream of; I am at the hospital where a beaten child is being treated for wounds caused by a mother driven beyond desperation, past sanity, past compassion; I am with the forty-five-year-old file clerk, raped and strangled in her one-room walk-up.

I am with all women; I am all women and our struggle grows.

I am with the Vietnamese guerrillas, fighting for the right to control their country; I am with the women in Ireland, living on the streets of Derry with their children because their houses have been burned or they have been evicted.

I am with the underground in the Latin American cities, arranging supplies for the guerrillas, hearing the secret police in every footstep. I am with the welfare mothers in New York and Hartford and Wisconsin who will not be turned away by the indifferent legislators.

I am with the airline stewardesses fighting to retain their job after they reach thirty and their market value has decreased; I am with the witches hexing Wall Street and the bridal fairs and the beauty contests; I am women struggling everywhere.[5]

At the very end, the two witches chanted in unison:

---

[5] In 1970 when Naomi read this at a conference at Yale, Rita Mae Brown commented that lesbians were invisible, so she and Naomi wrote the following line to be inserted before the airline stewardesses: "I am with the women who have loved other women as sisters, as lovers."

And where there are women too beaten down to fight, I will be there; and we will take strength together. Everywhere; for we will have a new world, a just world, a world without oppression and degradation.

"Afterwards," according to Naomi, "all of us were crying. The play had generated a shared feeling of unity, vision, and hope, and a sense that we were at a historic moment."

The CWLU, remembers Vivian (who was a primary architect of the organization's structure, and its first paid staff person), "was organized as a 'union' of locals, each engaged in its own activities such as producing the organization's newsletter, running an abortion service, a graphics collective, a liberation school." We tried to link together a wide variety of work groups: some organizing specific groups of women, some organized around a task, and some offering a service to women. Vivian, who organized the enormously successful Women's Liberation School, remembered, "We felt it was important to try to win victories, but also to build 'counter institutions,' or services to give people a vision of how things could be run in a better society and to give people a sense of some effectiveness in the bleak political environment of a city run by an entrenched political machine." The Liberation School for Women, with its motto "what we don't know, we must learn; what we do know, we should teach each other," was an early model for campus-based Women's Studies programs. It attracted hundreds of women to its courses.

Heather, who had small children at the time, worked with Day Creamer (later Piercy) and Kathy Blunt to organize the Action Committee for Decent Childcare (ACDC), a multiracial organization of parents and providers that succeeded in getting the city of Chicago to allocate a million dollars for child care, to revise its licensing codes, and to institute a citizen review of the licensing process. Naomi organized the Chicago Women's Liberation Rock Band, which toured widely, experimenting imaginatively with musical and comedic approaches to infusing feminism into popular culture (described elsewhere in this volume). I worked with high school students and the CIPA women's group. As organizers, Vivian remembers, we tried "to be in the background, to build leadership from community people, to help issues emerge, empower people to take collective action and, as an organizer, to organize oneself out of a job." We tried hard in the early years of the

Union to emphasize action instead of ideology and to involve people of various political persuasions in the emerging women's movement.

Like the women's movement all over the country in 1969 and '70, the Chicago movement grew rapidly. New projects and groups seemed to be springing up every week. For a while the four of us felt that we were finally working within an organization that reflected our politics. In fact, we all played leadership roles within the Union. However, we were deeply committed to avoiding what we called the "star system" and sometimes generated clumsy structures and systems aimed at creating an egalitarian environment. The speaker's policy of the CWLU was an example of both the best and the worst aspects of our efforts. The policy mandated that the many requests for speakers about women's liberation be met by all members on a rotating basis. Periodic training sessions strengthened people's skills and confidence and enabled us to share techniques. Since communicating ideas to others requires you to think them through yourself, the rotation policy was a wonderful method for helping people deepen their political understanding of women's liberation. But some people were better speakers than others and our sometimes rigid application of the speaker's policy prevented us from using the gifts of talented speakers like Naomi who could, in her words, speak "to 3,000 Loyola Catholics, insult their favorite priest, and get a standing ovation nevertheless." While Naomi was one of the most ardent advocates of the rotating speakers policy and was also an organizer of the training sessions, she felt that the policy sometimes generated an ethos of repressive vigilance against individual performance.

Meanwhile, feminism had affected our personal lives in a variety of ways. Vivian remembers how painful it was to become "so acutely aware of the ways in which women are mistreated that I became hypersensitive to sexism and discrimination."

> So every party I went to, my relationship with my family, my marriage, and of course every encounter with American mainstream culture, i.e., films, literature, history, music, etc., became a source of anger. It became more and more difficult to continue to exist in this society with a heightened women's consciousness. But then what alternatives were there? We all experimented with different ways to either avoid or integrate our consciousness into our daily lives, to somehow diminish the contradictions.

Naomi and Jesse reevaluated their marriage. Jesse learned to cook; they moved closer to Naomi's job at Loyola University and resolved that while they were both looking for new jobs, it would be Naomi's job that would determine their next move. Giving up cruising was one of the most important changes in Naomi's personal life.

I loved cruising because of the challenge of figuring out how you talk to strange men and what you say to them. . . . I gave it up because it was not appropriate for a revolutionary feminist to range through the environment looking for men to charm, and I also gave it up because no matter how good I was at it and no matter how enjoyable I found it, there was an element of servitude, subordination and the demeaning assumption of male superiority. After all, why flatter men? Do they deserve it?

Heather had her first child in 1968 and her second in 1969. "When I turned to my women's community for support," she remembers, "there was little room for children. . . . Some thought we should make no exceptions, accept no distractions from our work for children, child care, crying babies, exhausted mothers." She spent the next few years finding ways to juggle employment, mothering, and political activity. She remembers reading "The Politics of Housework," by Pat Mainardi, and struggling with Paul about "who washed dishes, who made the plans, and who thought about making plans."

I had become increasingly frustrated by my relationships with men, and had begun to question the limits I had placed on my friendships with women, which were often intense and exciting, while those I had with men were superficial and unsatisfying. Encouraged by writings of women like Anne Koedt ("Loving Another Woman"), I decided to abandon what had become an increasingly demoralizing effort to develop a meaningful heterosexual relationship, and, instead, allow my relationships with women to grow to include erotic passion and commitment. I was not alone. During those years countless previously heterosexual women all over the country began to have sexual relationships with other women. Every day someone else became a lesbian. The sudden visibility of lesbianism in the women's movement is usually described as the "coming out" of women who had previously suppressed their lesbian feelings, or as the adoption of lesbianism as a political choice by women's liberation activists who saw it as part of a political strategy of disengagement from the patriarchy. While these accounts certainly describe the experience of some women, they omit the experience of many of us who had neither felt erotic feelings for women in the past nor agreed with Jill Johnston's insistence that "feminism was the theory and lesbianism was the practice." The current tendency to see all sexual orientation as preordained makes it difficult to understand the ways that the women's liberation movement created an atmosphere in which people could change their sexual practices and desires, joyously, freely and in a spirit of discovery. For me the connection between lesbian possibility and feminist politics had to do with expanding options for one's personal life. I argued strenuously against those who felt that lesbianism was the only true expression of feminist politics. In my personal life, allowing myself to love women erotically opened up the possibility of a level of intimacy and commitment that I had never felt before.

The concept of personal life as political transmuted, in the early seventies, into what were, at best, exciting efforts to develop new ways of living and loving and, at worst, rigid imperatives about "correct" forms of personal life. These ideas affected us all in different ways. Vivian recalls that "creating new forms for our personal lives was more painful and difficult than we thought it would be." She and her husband, Rich, joined a commune because

> by the early 1970s, the center of political and personal excitement and intensity for me was increasingly focused on activities with other women. For a number of us who were married to politically involved men, it became more and more difficult to maintain bonds of common activity and analysis with our mates, so we organized living collectives to broaden the community with whom we shared our private lives. The commune I lived in had a political foundation, expected members to share incomes and child-care responsibilities, and made collective decisions about the work priorities of each resident.

> However, we soon found that we were expending increasing amounts of energy making our commune conform to the notions we were developing of "liberated lifestyles," even though we had all been raised with the values of fairly traditional American society.

The contradiction between how we actually felt and what we were supposed to feel about these new social forms brought our emotions into battle with our politics. Many relationships fell by the wayside in the process.

I was lonely. My closest friends in Chicago, Heather, Vivian, and Naomi, were all married. It was clear to me that if I wanted to develop romantic relationships with women, I needed to move to somewhere more supportive of lesbians. In 1970, I left Chicago to live in a San Francisco commune, to explore relationships with women, to write about my high school teaching experience, tie-dye my clothes, and figure out what I wanted to do with my life.

The political environment was also changing. The left had degenerated into a constellation of warring sects whose ideological disputes were seeping into the women's movement. According to Heather, in the early 1970s

> the women's movement was moving away from the sisterhood of the earliest years to increasing sectarian battles over the meaning of "true feminism." There was a harsher edge to the political conversations; harsher judgments were made about potential allies. A great deal of time was being taken up at meetings in inwardly focused discussions of the correct position, and less on outreach and mobilization. This reinforced my aversion to sectarian purity and my commitment to developing mass level popular activity.

A profound sense of loss permeated the letters we wrote to each other after I left Chicago. I felt that I had lost my political home, and I have never felt as personally and politically close with any group of friends since. Clearly much of the intensity of our friendships had its roots in the sense of power and urgency we all felt politically in the late sixties and early seventies. By the mid 1970s the action-oriented, visionary women's liberation movement that we tried to build had dissipated, hard to sustain in the changed political climate. The radical wing of the movement focused on building an alternative culture that was increasingly isolated from most people's daily lives, while the mainstream women's movement, led by NOW, fought important battles but rarely engaged in sustained grassroots struggles. Painfully absent was the sense of both the necessity and possibility of a radically transformed world. In 1973 Vivian wrote: "It is so hard—when we once felt we were making history and the lives of hundreds of people were dependent on our actions—to resolve ourselves to less significant and far less ambitious work. I feel that shift tremendously. Now that I don't feel I'm making history, I don't know exactly what to do with my life."[6]

As the earth shifted beneath us, we found different moorings. I floundered for a while, organizing Women's Studies conferences on the West Coast with the New University Conference. The cannibalistic debacle of the left in the late sixties shook me deeply. I began to question the wisdom of depending on the vicissitudes of a social movement for one's identity and source of satisfaction. It seemed to me that centering one's entire life on political activism was dangerous for both the individual and the social movement, since if people's whole identities depended on their political work, they would tend to hang on to projects or groups beyond their usefulness. So I decided to go to graduate school to study women's history and teach Women's Studies, hoping that I could communicate the power of feminism in the classroom while developing a professional life as an academic.

Heather, on the other hand, wanted to continue to be a political organizer; she felt that getting people to work together was to be her life's work. But after 1972 she found the atmosphere in the CWLU so acrimonious that she no longer recruited other women to it, and she began to think about creating a more broad-based movement that would have an easier time connecting to the lives of most people. After being fired from a job for union organizing, she filed a lawsuit and won a back-pay award. She used the money to found the Midwest Academy, a training school for leaders of mass organizations. Its first session trained the developing leadership of such groups as NOW, Nine to Five, and other working women's organizations.

Naomi, too, found what she described as "the sectarian mayhem" of the Chicago Women's Liberation Union intolerable and felt that she had been "driven out" of the Chicago Women's Liberation Rock Band (see her article in this volume). She felt continuously trashed for exerting leadership and being a professional scientist. "The rage against

---

[6] Vivian Rothstein to Amy Kesselman, January 1, 1973.

women who stood out in any way had reached monstrous proportions," she recalled. When she encountered similar hostility in the Women's Studies Program in Buffalo where she moved in 1974, she began to look for new ways to express her politics.

> I made the life-saving decision that my feminist activities should shift to the national arena. I decided to start writing and speaking again and to do solo performances—I had worked up some stand-up comedy. I also began to organize in professional organizations, figuring that I would be a small fish in a big pond there and hence I would not be as totally resented.

For Vivian, the last two years of work in the Chicago women's liberation movement had been extremely painful. Her position as coordinator of the CWLU made her the target of a wide range of political and personal criticism. The commune she lived in was rife with tensions. Recommitting themselves to their marriage, Vivian and her husband decided to leave communal life behind and move to Denver, Colorado. After she left Chicago, she got a job with the American Friends Service Committee doing antiwar work and had two children.

The different directions in which we moved strained our relationships. Being in our late twenties and early thirties, we were tense and uncertain about our identities and felt easily judged, hurt, or abandoned by each other. I sometimes felt that Vivian and Heather were disappearing into the nuclear family, trying to blend in with "the folks." In contrast, becoming a lesbian had made me feel more at odds with mainstream culture. Naomi felt that Vivian and I didn't understand or approve of her decision to seek a national audience for her work.

During the late 1970s, Heather built the Midwest Academy into an extremely influential organization which trained thousands of organizers. She was a founder and co-director of Citizen Action, and she played leadership roles in a variety of political and issue campaigns, including the National Mobilization for Choice and Carol Mosely Braun's Senate race. As I complete this essay in June 1996, she is director of the Campaign Training Academy of the Democratic National Committee.

Vivian moved from Colorado to North Carolina, where she became prochoice coordinator for Planned Parenthood. Today she directs a California nonprofit that runs a network of shelters and services for battered women and their children, runaway teens, and homeless adults and families. Organized on principles similar to the Chicago Women's Liberation Union, this $2.3 million agency is structured in a decentralized manner, which encourages project-based leadership and decision-making.

Naomi became a professor of psychology at SUNY-Buffalo, where she did pioneering research in cognitive visual neuroscience. In 1982 she contracted an extremely serious case of Chronic Fatigue Immune Dysfunction (CFIDS) and has been confined to her bed ever since. Nevertheless, she has remained active in her field and, with the help of her husband, Jesse Lemisch, has been able to make her still eloquent and witty voice heard from time to time on various women's issues.

I went on to graduate school to study women's history and have taught Women's Studies at SUNY-New Paltz since 1981. I'm currently writing a history of the women's liberation movement in New Haven, Connecticut.

Writing this essay in the mid-1990s has required us to reach across the distances created by the different choices we each have made in the last twenty-five years. It has been mostly joyous but sometimes painful, as we recognized the ways that we hurt each other in the past. But most important, this process has felt familiar. It is still exhilarating to talk with each other; we have rediscovered how deeply we still appreciate each other's skills and talents; and we still feel the sense of connection that we forged in those three intense years in Chicago. We all remain deeply committed to the feminist vision we developed together, even though that commitment has taken different forms in each of our lives.

Friendships like ours were not unique among women's liberation activists. These friendships were made possible by the belief that sisterhood is powerful and, at the same time, were an important source of that belief. Such friendships all over the country were central to the energy and insights of women's liberation activists in the 1960s.

Coming of Age:
Civil Rights and Feminism

Barbara W. Emerson

In 1994, I asked Barbara Emerson to contribute to this volume, a book meant to add some depth and variety to the alarmingly thin historical record gathered so far about this wave of the Women's Liberation Movement. Our prospectus cast a very wide net and asked about many things, yet when Barbara Emerson's memoir arrived, it had cast an even wider net; it had mentioned feminism hardly at all. Instead, Barbara had written an exciting story of commitment and adventure, a coming-of-age story about being a young girl at the center of the Civil Rights Movement, in which her father, Hosea Williams, was—and continues to be—a key leader.

Reading this piece, I felt the tension of the unsaid. I thought maybe she disparaged the women's movement, seeing it as a very poor relation, an often ambivalent cultural movement about intangibles, subjectivities, images, a movement that chose not to—or could not—confront state power as the Civil Rights Movement did in its heroic period.

But when we sat down to talk, a less polarized picture emerged—of individual lives played out in counterpoint to mass social movements. Barbara's particular distance from feminism places it as part of a much larger story.

Ann Snitow

In June 1963, I had just finished the tenth grade in Asbury Park, New Jersey. My mother and I agreed that the time had come for me to get to know the father that I had never shared a home with. She had done her part. She had devoted fifteen years to "raising" me as a "good little Negro girl." I had integrated all of the appropriate values, ways of behaving, and life expectations for what it meant to be Negro and female. Neither of us knew that by the time I reached the point of actualizing those meanings as an adult, the world would have changed radically, and me with it. "Good little Negro girls," prepared for adulthood as I was in the fifties, emerged in the sixties into a world where you were a "big, 'bad' Black Woman" instead. The rules for what it meant to be a person of African decent changed, and quickly thereafter, what it meant to be a woman changed.

My journey to Black Womanhood started as soon as the school year ended in 1963. I packed everything I owned and headed "down South" to join "The Movement." Now, I didn't really leave my mother's home with that purpose in mind, but that is exactly what happened. I left home to live with my father, Hosea Williams, for my last two years of high school and a better shot at college. But my father was a civil rights activist. So as soon as I arrived in Georgia, I was immediately in "The Movement."

Now, up until this point, the Civil Rights Movement had been just images on TV to me—freedom riders; lunch counter sit-ins; people marching; dogs attacking demonstrators; kids who looked to be about my age being knocked against buildings by the force of fire hoses because they were protesting segregation. Sure, having been born in the South, I had memories of segregation and what it had meant to me, but it was nothing like TV. I remembered the "colored only" waiting room at the train station; the Jim Crow car on the train where all the Black people sat when my mother and I traveled from southwest Georgia to the Jersey shore; having to bring our lunch because we weren't allowed in the dining car; I remembered the little white girl who lived across the street who asked one day, "You're a nigger, ain't you?" and my grandmother saying I was never to go over to her house again.

I arrived in Savannah, Georgia, in July 1963. But my father wasn't there to greet me. He was in the Chatham County jail for leading demonstrations against segregated public facilities. Finding my father in jail was just the beginning of a summer that was strange, exciting, frightening, and liberating. For instance, while my family had a new house in the upper-middle-class Negro neighborhood of Savannah, very near historically Black Savannah State College, we never slept in it. Too dangerous. The still-dead grass in the center of the lawn where a cross had burned was a reminder that our father was hated by other men and the whole family was not safe in that home. So my summer was spent working in the

Crusade for Voters office by day, going to mass meetings in the evenings, and moving from house to house at night to avoid being arrested. At our freedom rallies, men would turn in their knives and weapons before joining the nonviolent march through Savannah's streets to the City Hall, past the jail where my Daddy was held for thirty-nine days. The Savannah authorities thought "cutting off the head would kill the body." But, nightly, the body grew as more and more people—adults, older people, but especially young people, teenagers—hundreds of them—got strength from songs like, "Oh Freedom," "Ain't Gonna Let Nobody Turn Me Round," "We Are Soldiers in the Army." We'd listen intently to nonviolent tactics and then we'd move, as one, through the Savannah night, willing and ready to be arrested for demanding an end to the segregated parks, movies, restaurants, libraries, and other <u>public</u> facilities. In a word, demanding FREEDOM. I learned to always carry my toothbrush and my I.D. I still do. One of my hardest jobs as the oldest of five children was to keep my sister, who was eleven, from throwing herself into police "paddy wagons." She had been arrested several times and was convinced that if only she could get into the jail she would be able to see Daddy, for she, like all of us, was afraid for his life.

Our demonstrations went on through the summer, led by members of the Crusade for Voters Youth Group: fifteen- to twenty-one-year-olds who were determined to have their rights. We kept the pressure on and got some help from the Southern Christian Leadership Conference (SCLC), led by Dr. Martin Luther King, Jr., the organization formed to coordinate activities of nonviolent groups devoted to integration and full citizenship for Blacks (FREEDOM) and that was exactly what we were. I remember one night standing in our kitchen, eating the only thing in the refrigerator—some fruit—with a minister SCLC had sent from Atlanta to speak at a rally. We talked well into the night. I told him about how I had come from New Jersey only weeks ago and had demonstrated almost every night since. He told me that I had been "baptized by the fire of 'The Movement'" and I would never be the same. I knew he was right—in those weeks I had grown up, rapidly.

In August, we boarded a "freedom train" and headed for Washington. One of our group, Ben Clark, a high school senior known as "Little Hosea" for his role in leading demonstrations, came to the train hidden in the trunk of a car because he was wanted by the Savannah police. We arrived in the Nation's Capital the next morning for the now historic March on Washington—200,000 Americans of all races demanding legislation to end discrimination in education, housing, and employment: FREEDOM.

By the time school started that September, the Savannah mayor and the City Council had conceded to many of our demands and I got to see my father for the first time. He had been in jail for thirty-nine days, had grown a full beard, and had lost twenty-five pounds! But I was never so glad to see him. I entered a segregated Catholic high school (the one Clarence Thomas had attended the year before), not because we were Catholic, but because all of Savannah's public schools remained segregated, separate, and unequal. The Catholic schools were segregated too, but offered a better education. That fall, John Fitzgerald Kennedy was assassinated and the country was in shock. I remember feeling numb and scared because if "they" could get the president surely "they" could get anyone.

During the week I attended school, taking the usual college prep courses and trying to make my way through second-year French, without ever having had the first year. But it was a small school and French was the only language offered, so I took French! On weekends, it was Movement work: voter education on Saturdays; going door-to-door in the Black neighborhoods, trying to convince people to try and register to vote and of how important it was to try. Funny thing was, most of us doing the convincing were too young to vote!

Sundays meant church, then dinner, then a mass meeting at one of Savannah's Black churches. I remember one Sunday in particular when the guest speaker was Dr. King. He gave us courage and said Savannah was one of the first Southern cities to integrate because we, especially the young people, had demanded our rights. When I was introduced to him he said, "Hello, daughter, give me a hug." I did, and whenever I saw him, and he had not seen me for a while, no matter how busy he was, he'd say, "Hello, daughter, give me a hug." That's what I thought of when I saw pictures of him receiving the Nobel Peace Prize.

In 1964, Congress passed a major Civil Rights Act to prohibit discrimination in public accommodations and employment. It seemed as if the Movement was getting results. But then, three young civil rights volunteers from New York and Mississippi were murdered in Mississippi for trying to help Blacks register to vote and it was *déjà vu*. . . .

I spent the summer of 1964 in forced exile back in New Jersey. My mother, not a relentless activist, felt I needed a chance to be a teenager, but I was bored. There were large riots that summer. When I returned to Savannah in the fall, my father wasn't there to greet me, again! But this time he wasn't in jail. This time, at Dr. King's request, he had gone to Atlanta to join SCLC's executive staff. We packed only our clothes, rented a trailer for my stepmother's forest of plants, and headed to Atlanta to join Daddy. The Movement has been his, and my, full-time work since then. We simply do it in different settings.

Again, I enrolled in a Catholic high school. It was a new school and I would be in the first graduating class. But still, it was segregated because white parents were afraid for their children to travel to a school in a Black neighborhood, though Collier Heights was the most upper-middle-class Black community in Atlanta. That fall, I prepared for my SATs, took the last of my college-prep courses, and took French one-on-one with the principal because this school taught only Spanish and I put my foot down—I was not taking third-year Spanish without having had the first two years! And it was a good thing that I took the December 1964 SATs because by early 1965 my attention was on Selma. Now I had never been to Alabama, but since I sat in on strategy meetings at SCLC during the Christmas break, I knew that SCLC, and therefore I, would be going to Alabama to demonstrate because Blacks there were not permitted to register, not to mention to vote.

On Sunday, March 7, 1965—known as "Bloody Sunday"—we watched the news from Selma where 200 state troopers, some of them on horses, using tear gas, night sticks, and whips, charged into 525 Black marchers. At the head of the marchers was John Lewis and Daddy. He had organized the march and was trampled for it. Later that evening, he called and said he was OK and that he would see us soon—in Selma. I was ready to leave right then, but my stepmother insisted that I go to school for mid-semester exams first.

Two weeks later, we headed to Selma to join Daddy. It looked as if everyone else in the country who cared about FREEDOM was as anxious as I was to be in Selma. Thirty-two hundred people—Black, white, young, old, priests, nuns, rabbis—left Selma on March 21 for the first leg of a fifty-mile march to Montgomery to dramatize the denial of voting rights for Blacks who had attempted to register to vote in Selma.

I returned to Atlanta after the Selma-to-Montgomery march, made up a lot of schoolwork, and graduated salutatorian of my class. Ironically, we graduated with the seniors from the white Catholic schools who had been afraid to come to our school. The day before graduation, the Senate passed the Voting Rights Act, providing for federal examiners to oversee voter registration and elections.

During the summer of 1965, Dr. King appointed my father national director of voter registration and political action. We organized SCOPE (Summer Community Organization and Political Education Project), which brought in 1,100 Northern students who spent their summer doing voter registration and political education programs in seven Southern states, greatly increasing the numbers of Black registered voters.

My role in SCOPE was that of fiscal officer; I was responsible for seeing to it that all of the staff members received their weekly fifteen-dollar stipend. I did all of the record keeping and budget management. I still have a mark on my side from the metal petty cash box I carried everywhere for safekeeping. We operated out of the "Freedom House" in Atlanta, which had been the King family's home. It became a twenty-four-hour-a-day hub of activity. Dozens of Movement people worked, planned, slept, ate, and learned to organize there. At the end of the summer, most of us went back to our campuses knowing that we had made a difference. America had thousands of new voters who, prior to our efforts, had been denied that basic right—a right that we would surely exercise as soon as we were old enough to vote! Some stayed on and never went home.

In 1966, I participated in the Meredith March Against Fear in Mississippi. James Meredith was shot from ambush, shortly after beginning a pilgrimage for voting rights. The march covered 260 miles and was taken up by several civil rights groups. It was the march where "Black Power" was first put into words.

In December 1967, Dr. King announced plans for a massive civil disobedience campaign in Washington the next spring. The purpose was to be to pressure Congress and President Johnson to end poverty by providing jobs and a guaranteed income. Since I was already in Washington at American University, this time the Movement was coming to join me. By Easter, I had put in many hours before and after classes at the D.C. SCLC office organizing the Poor People's Campaign. One April afternoon while I was en route back to the dorm, Martin Luther King was shot, and the country and I have never been the same.

The Movement's leader died, but the legacy of the Civil Rights Movement has been spread across the national and international landscape. The demonstrations that were for me a coming of age became a model for voicing political opinion that has been adopted by groups of all types. The revival of the democratic principle of equity through inclusion spurred rights of workers, women, senior citizens, the disabled, gays and lesbians, just to name a few. The building of these movements to bring about change in people's lives has been so widely adopted in the world that we have seen students face tanks, walls tumble, iron curtains fall, and apartheid and governments topple. Until all of us are free to reach our greatest potential, none of us is free.

Interview with Barbara Emerson

After several discussions, on January 16, 1996, Barbara Emerson and Ann Snitow sat down with a tape recorder. This is their reorganized rendition of what they said to each other:

Ann Snitow: So, Barbara, we asked you to write about the Women's Liberation Movement, and you wrote a piece about coming of age in the Civil Rights Movement. How come?

Barbara Emerson: Because in becoming a woman (or a womanist) for me, the essential part was coming into adulthood immersed in the Civil Rights Movement. So it's difficult for me, if not impossible, to make a distinction between my feminism, or myself as a feminist, and myself as a civil rights activist, because the two were so intricately bound. I didn't see a distinction, but I named the Civil Rights Movement, I claimed that because that was what was essential.

AS: In our prospectus for this book, Rachel and I wrote pages about the personal, how we wanted detailed, specific impressions of how our writers first encountered the women's movement. Instead, you told a typical maturation story; it was a heroic story of being in this movement, joining this very intense community, and you constructed it without that itchy distinction we kept making between public and private memory. I wonder what you think about that now when you look back at how you decided to interpret our questions about "the personal"?

BE: I interpreted that as meaning what happened to me personally, as opposed to what happened around me. But it was necessary that I put it in the context of what was happening around me, because it was another one of those situations, and it's not the only one that I've experienced in my life, where it was difficult for me at times to tell where I stopped and the situation or the movement or the program or the job ended. You know, there's sort of this permeable boundary around me, because I have the ability to become so intensely involved in things. My autonomy and liberation and self-determination came from being part of a group, so the focus was more communal.

AS: You weren't willing—or interested?—in writing about the ways in which the Civil Rights Movement was sexist?

BE: Well, it certainly was sexist, but I think that was endemic in the times that we were in, I mean, men were sexist in the Civil Rights Movement, and women were accepting of it because that was the way that the world was. We had not had the feminist movement at that point. It didn't seem to me that it was unnatural or detrimental because that's just the way that it was. We hadn't reached that level of consciousness.

AS: In your piece, you described being a daughter, The Daughter, because your father is a famous civil rights activist, a great patriarchal figure clearly, and you also were called "daughter," so generically, by Martin Luther King, Jr., who recognized you as a daughter of the movement. Do you think there was a tension between being loyal to the Civil Rights Movement and telling the personal story of the difficulties of being a woman in that movement?

BE: But I didn't see it as being difficult, being a woman. It might have been difficult being fifteen, running with adults and being expected to contribute and carry the weight of an adult. "Daughter" was not a gender designation to me, it was an age designation, which is why I called the piece "Coming of Age in the Civil Rights Movement." In 1966–67, what was most significant to me was becoming an adult and the fact that the world had changed for me as an African-American person becoming an adult. So the gender issue was not nearly as significant to me as age and race were. And probably whatever detriment the gender issues caused, I didn't see it then. If you require me to put myself into a hierarchy of identities, I'm an African-American woman, in that order. A person of African descent, born in America, who is a woman. Now, I realize full well that lots of women see their gender, or see, feel, think their gender first and then their race. It doesn't happen to come to me that way.

AS: I was also thinking of questions of loyalty to the community, putting the beloved community first, because in some sense the intactness of a community of struggle takes precedence over other identities.

BE: I guess you could parallel it with the military or lots of other social groupings where your other identities become secondary to the communal identity.

AS: The first time you went down to join your father was the summer of 1963?

BE: Yes. I just realized that a lot of what we are talking about is a matter of timing. You know, I was fifteen to twenty during those five years that I talk about in the piece. If I had done all that at the same age as other people usually did, then I might have seen the whole thing within the setting of other movements, like the women's movement. But because I am my father's daughter, I got on board earlier, and when I got on board, the Civil Rights Movement was what was happening. The "boys" I was working with were all older, in college.

AS: You were an apprentice?

BE: No, I wasn't an apprentice to these guys. I went toe to toe with these guys. They were five to ten years older than me, and they were men, but I worked as long, I worked as hard, and I kicked as much butt as they did. And it was just because . . . probably because I happened to be a female version of my father, and that just happened to be me.

AS: Being his daughter gave you the position, the opportunity, but then you used it. You were able to use it.

BE: Yes. And I would be as forceful as I could, go as far in the situation as I could. For some reason my father felt an inordinate amount of trust in me, young as I was. We had never lived in the same household. We didn't know each other. But I just soaked up his attention like a sponge. We were at a point where we needed what each other had to bring.

AS: And he accepted you, let you play the game, even though you were a girl. In your piece you say that you were brought up to be a good little Negro girl, and then suddenly there was this bad, Black woman you're supposed to become, which was this new empowered image that came through the Civil Rights Movement, and then subsequently through the women's movement. But then, in one of our discussions, you and I confessed to each other that although we were supposed to become bad, we didn't at all, that in some way badness had nothing to do with it. . . . For our quite different reasons, badness was a luxury we couldn't afford.

BE: When I said "bad," I didn't mean bad in the sense of not good, but bad in the sense of strength and power, that kind of "bad," which is not bad. It's the slang sense of "bad." You know, you're big, you're "bad," and bad is good. It's because you're just . . . I mean, I'm trying to think of the contemporary word for it. It's not hip, it's not cool, but it's *"bad."* It's like dynamite, you know, in order to carry off what you're trying to do. So it's not bad in a negative sense of doing mischievous or evil things.

AS: Actually, in the Civil Rights Movement as you lived it, service was a very high ideal.

BE: Yes. I mean, it's an unrelenting one. [Here Barbara showed the only two rings she wears: one, which she got in Africa, meaning "unselfish devotion to service" and, also, "to thine own self be true"; the other, three bands, one red, one black, one green: African liberation colors.]

AS: The combination.

BE: In my own maturation, my own development, this adaptability and flexibility is something that I have been striving for, because even with all of the freedom I have now, I still have felt constrained to be good, and to do 150 percent.

AS: Speaking of having to be good, and the tension between serving others and serving yourself, there are a lot of pieces in this book written by white women who say: I was active in the Civil Rights Movement, or I was active in tenants' rights, or I was busy doing draft resistance, and then I realized I was doing all this to help

others. And then along came the women's movement and finally
this was for myself. For these white women, Civil Rights was
doing for others; only the women's movement was doing for
themselves. They didn't fully identify with Civil Rights.

BE: The Civil Rights Movement was doing for self, whereas the
women's movement was doing for others. It was for white
women who needed to be liberated, and I agreed that they
needed to be liberated as women. But I did not see that as my
primary oppression.

AS: You once told me that the women's movement didn't seem nearly
as political as the Civil Rights Movement to you. Can you
describe that distinction?

BE: Yes, because to me the Civil Rights Movement was political in the
sense that it had to do with basic political rights. The women's
movement, it seemed to me at that point, had to do with personal rights. For instance, the right to work. Well, everyone that I
knew who was capable of working worked. It wasn't that you as a
woman had to, or could, say, I want to be out of the house and I
want to have my own job, and I want to have my own career. All
the women that I knew who could work did work, and the ones
who didn't probably took care of children for somebody else who
could work. So white women's demand for the right to work
seemed to me to be a personal demand. I didn't see the limitations on white women at that point, because it seemed to me that
there were women already doing what I aspired to do who were
white women, so I didn't see that as a political issue.

AS: What other aspects of the women's movement seemed apolitical?

BE: It was apolitical because it had to do with personal assertiveness
and the right to work, the right to go to school. I wasn't aware of
the discrimination and harassment of women in school and in
the workplace, because I had not yet entered either one of them,
or at least I had not entered higher education, and my primary
and secondary education was mostly segregated, whether it was
in New Jersey or in Georgia, it was segregated. So I never had a
sense that whatever limitations were placed on me were placed
there because I was a girl.

When my mother had my brother, I was convinced that she
was broken-hearted, and I consoled her. I really had empathy for

my mother, that she now had a boy and surely she was disappointed, even though she was very brave and said that she was going to be OK. Because this was a boy, not a girl like me, and I was the greatest thing going, so being a girl was the greatest thing going, and all of my relatives and my mother and everyone that I knew confirmed it, because I was the first grandchild and in lots of instances the only child around. When my brother was born I was seven, so it just seemed to me that being a girl was just the number one thing to be. So it wasn't until many years later that I . . . I'm trying to remember now, when did I figure out that there was a disadvantage to being female? I can't put my finger on that. Because as I said, in early childhood, I was on this pedestal, and when I got into elementary school, I couldn't beat up the boys, but I always outsmarted them, and I was quite able to get them to do whatever I wanted. Maybe somewhere in adolescence, when boys began demanding what they wanted, and I was still determined that what I had, they weren't getting, then maybe I had some realization that girls were not all powerful. I guess I was quite a chauvinist up until the time that I was thirteen or fourteen.

AS: So racism was the earliest experience and then the movement for Civil Rights came along. You told me the other day that in a sense you had exhausted some primary passion for a new movement by completely engaging yourself in Civil Rights, that about the women's movement there was no urgency. It was something that other people needed to do because they were feeling bad about themselves as women. But that isn't how you were feeling. . . .

BE: Or bad about their situation. Yes, that's it exactly, I think that's a good way to put it because my identity did not have to do with the fact that I was a woman, and if women had issues that they needed to struggle for, then they needed to struggle for them, and that was fine. But the issues that I saw the women's movement struggling for were not a priority to me, or not then, not until later. I was looking back over my notes and, when I think about it, I conceived of my struggles as women's struggles only after 1975, just because of the way that my own personal life had developed. It was in 1975 that I got divorced, and then I had to be on my own as a single parent, as a woman, and it was liberating. I thought: I don't have to have a man to do this, if I have to, I can do this. But maybe that was when I had one of my strongest realizations of the fact that girls were not as powerful as I thought they were. It was in 1977 when I went out to buy a house on my own, and when I would go to real estate offices and they would ask me, where was my husband, and I would say, "I don't have a husband, but I have a checkbook." And I would get this from men and women. I remember even going to places where the couple who were selling the house simply did not want to deal with me because I was a single woman. That was 1977.

AS: How old was your son then?

BE: My son was five, because one of the reasons that I was buying this house was so that he could have a yard and a dog and a house and 2.5 cars or whatever, like other kids. In terms of gender-based political discrimination, that might have been one of the earlier points that I felt it. Now, personally, I certainly had experienced it in my marriage. I came to the realization that, as Ntozake says in *For Colored Girls,* "somebody almost took all my stuff." There came a point when I decided, OK, I have to keep my stuff, and you can't have it all. So that was a point of awakening as a feminist, that I'm entitled to my stuff, and if I have to be in the world by myself in order to have my stuff, then I will. That feeling was around 1975 even.

AS: So the women's movement had been out there as a sort of public force for, say, seven or eight years, and in 1975 it provided a way of thinking about your marriage, a way of thinking about what was happening to you?

BE: Right. I hadn't identified with feminism prior to that. But feminism gave me a sanction, a vision: I don't have to stay in an unhappy marriage for "the sake of the children" and for financial security. And I think personally that that is one of the services that the women's movement has done for lots of women who may not even count themselves as feminists. It's laid a groundwork for saying: I can, I have a right, I have an entitlement to be a whole, complete person in and of myself, and I have the right for that whole, complete person to function within interpersonal relationships, within the workplace, within whatever setting that I choose.

So I think that was really how my coming to consciousness of what it is to be a woman, and what it is to be a feminist, came about. Certain things were possible because this movement had started to change the way that people think. That's probably a good way of putting it: I became a feminist indirectly, and I suspect that that's the route that most women took. Probably more so women of color, but I'm not so sure about that, because I think a lot of white women who would now say that they are feminists didn't become feminists in an activist kind of way, and that's what movements are supposed to do. There's a cadre of folks that lead these things, and if they are successful, they bring about a kind of social change that allows the rest of the people, both women and men in this instance, to be able to think and perceive and interact with one another in a different kind of way than before this movement. That's how it works. Things move, things change.

AS: You described the whiteness of how feminists made their early demands for work, for career. Do you think feminism had any effect on your work expectations?

BE: The key people were teachers I had as a kid in the segregated public school system of Asbury Park, New Jersey. The academic experience that made me be able to have a doctorate today was the fourth and fifth grade, when I had my first male teacher, a Black man named Mr. Beatty, who was fresh out of college himself. He made such demands on us as fourth and fifth graders. It was his mission, that we're going to uplift ourselves, each one teach one, that kind of thing.

And when I got to the sixth grade, my teacher, Miss Stafford, who was a very large, imposing Black woman, asked me, what are you going to do when you grow up, and when I said I was going to be a secretary, she looked down at me and said, no, you're not. And until I realized that she had even greater ambitions for me, I was crushed because I thought that to be a secretary was the epitome of what a girl could do and I thought she was saying I was aspiring too high. She repeated, no, because you are going to college.

AS:　Those great teachers gave you a different notion of what was possible.

BE:　Right.

AS:　And the women's movement? The right to rebel against a marriage that wasn't satisfying. Anything about work?

BE:　A certain kind of independence, I think that's what the women's movement sanctioned.

AS:　Even though it's certainly true that Black women all around had independence, that the world was full of Black women who were working, running households, independent.

BE:　But that didn't seem to me to be necessarily by choice. It was by circumstance.

AS:　The difference was choice.

BE:　It was choice, it was having options. Because I had friends who were enlightened women, several of whom actually were more involved in the women's movement than I was, who could not believe that I had given up a man, a house, an English Tudor in the suburbs on Long Island that was newly furnished, and two cars. We had it all. This man was already working on a doctorate, and I was going to give all of that up because I could. But ten years earlier I would not have, because I would have thought that I had made it, and I had made it by standards for being a woman, and being a Black woman. You had a man, you had a house, you had a car, you had a kid, and you had a degree. What more did you want? You wanted yourself too?

AS:　It sounds like Civil Rights and the women's movement were both in the mix, raising your expectations about what was possible and the amount of freedom you could have.

BE:　Yes. Right. It was somewhere in there that I decided that I could have a man, a house, a car, a kid, and myself.

AS:　You could also give up some of those and still maintain yourself?

BE:　But I was convinced that I could have all of that. I never felt that it was career or family. I always felt that I could choose to do both. Time was the only limitation. And I think the ability to think in that frame of reference came from my coming of age when I did, because the psychological shackles of being Black were loosened by the Civil Rights Movement, and the psychological shackles of being a woman were loosened by the women's movement, and I sort of moved along these paths that were being opened up for me without realizing, until hindsight, that that's how I was able to do it, because it had become OK. And getting back to the good-bad discussion, for me it had to be OK in order for me to do it, because if it wasn't OK and ultimately good, then I couldn't have let myself want those freedoms. Do you see what I'm saying?

AS: Yes. That's really interesting. And you didn't need to break with either your mother or your father or your extended family in order to have your own life. On the contrary, they were all part of the story of aspiration. Somehow you got the idea that you could have everything.

BE: Yes. That's true, and the baggage that I continue to carry along with the belief that I can have what I want is my sense of responsibility, the unrelenting responsibility to help other people. I have to do for other people. There's gender in the mix there, you know, along with all the other factors: not only do I have to do for myself, but I have to do for other people, be the nurturer.

AS: Do you think that the radical U.S. women's movement of the seventies—in all the ways you describe encountering it—was racist?

BE: Only in the sense that I thought it was a white women's movement, not necessarily because I thought it was exclusionary of women of color, but simply because I thought the agenda was a white women's agenda. It was what white women needed.

AS: The radical feminists I knew and worked with in the seventies were all professed antiracists, and as I said, many of us were inspired by experiences in the Civil Rights Movement. So if you would have said to us back then, this women's movement you are building is a white movement, we would have been very defensive about that.

BE: What's wrong with its being a white movement, if by that we mean that it was addressing the needs of white women? Now, what would be wrong would be for white women's movements to deny that women of color have different needs, and to deny the sisterhood that's necessary for all of us to address the problems of women. It would be wrong; but to say that it was a white movement at that time in history is simply a statement of fact, and it obviously was needed by white women, so it was a white movement. Now if we remain stuck in that definition, then women's movements are going to dissipate, because they certainly won't meet the needs of women of color, and I don't think they will continue to meet the needs of white women either, because we're at another place in history now.

A Year of Living
Dangerously: 1968

Dana Densmore

In January 1968, I got a phone call from my mother, Donna Allen. "Women's liberation!" she pronounced in a tone of incantation. The resonance and ring with which she invested the words conveyed her sense that the words themselves, sacred and momentous, constituted in their utterance the missing piece of a puzzle. Each word and all it signified, connoted, and implied—for each word a great rich world of context—was electrically alive to both of us.

We knew "women," being women ourselves, and coming from a long line of independent-minded, woman-valuing women. We also knew the disrespect women met in the world, as a gender, and we had watched as many fine, intelligent women's brilliant and heroic efforts came to very little. We knew "liberation," the central value and key verbal formula in many of the progressive causes in which we had always been activists. "Liberation" represented a heady, psychologically and ideologically clean process of thought and commitment. Injustice, perceived and analyzed, was met with a self-sacrificing determination to right the wrongs. It felt "clean," wholesome, and unsullied, because the impulses were relatively unfettered by the inhibitions and the trade-offs necessary in mainstream politics which make one feel compromised and bought off. To those who spoke of "liberation," matters were simple: If it was wrong, it must be changed. What more was there to say? The clean energy that welled up when conscience was clear and committed seemed equal to any adversity.

Two rich words, each with important values to us—but we had never heard them uttered together. The implications were dizzying. Suddenly the progressive causes we had always worked for were revealed as having been other people's causes. Was it possible that we could finally be turning to the most radical cause of all?

"It has begun!" The words were galvanizing, chilling; the implications were massive, dangerous, and revolutionary; their seriousness precluded euphoria. I knew that the liberation of women was not going to be easily won, nor won through any moderate means. I knew that once I had embarked on this path, there would be no stopping short. Reality shifted, and I felt myself to be in a new world.

My mother, Donna Allen, a national antiwar activist and a founder of Women Strike for Peace, had been in New York at a meeting to plan a peace demonstration, and, from fellow activist Bernardine Dohrn, had heard rumblings of women's discontent in SDS and other organizations in the movements for social justice. Some women were asking whether it was ideologically defensible to fight for the liberation of every single class and category other than women, while accepting female subservience.

"Liberation for *us!*" my mother said in her phone call. "It has begun! Women are organizing, and we're going to turn the men's world upside down, throw the bums out, and run things as they should be run!" In her enthusiasm she skipped over the hard part, but I wasn't fooled. I knew that the disaffection of a few women was only a small start in a very big job.

A thorough-going, smirking disrespect for women permeated every aspect of society. I despair of conveying to young women of the nineties the chilling and depressing effect of this: they can't imagine how we could have been such low-self-esteem wimps to put up with it (*"I would have smacked him one!"*). I try to explain how it feels when it seems that all men, including all the men one respects, sneer and ridicule or, at their best, condescendingly take for granted the inferiority of women. And how it feels when it seems that all the *women* around one take that supposed inferiority for granted. The most self-respecting women did little better than to try to deny, each in her embattled isolation, that she was herself that contemptible thing: "I'm different!"

Hence the most exciting thing about Donna's news was that women were starting to identify themselves as women, to connect with other women, not protesting their difference from that ugly stereotype but questioning the stereotype itself, and protesting the treatment that resulted from it. Could it be that we would break free from the chilling and depressing effects of all those smirks and sneers, that we would assert our own reality over the false and demeaning one? Having heard the words, "women's liberation," I knew that for me there was no going back. And I suspected the same would be true for many other women.

At the time of the phone call, I had been very active in the draft resistance movement, counseling conscientious objectors, men who opposed the Vietnam War, and the undecided, who were confused or questioning. I helped them to understand their options and to sort through the ins and outs of the law and the procedures and practice of draft boards and the Selective Service. With others, I supported the men refusing induction through "The Resistance": a loose support group of and for men who had already refused or were about to refuse induction, and the women who were keeping a world of meaningfulness and love around the men who were setting their lives in turmoil.

Yet the weekly dinner meetings of The Resistance were exercises in self-laceration for the women. It went without saying that we cooked and cleaned up while the men bonded, strategized, and postured. They were laying their balls on the line, and we were . . . what? The girls enjoined to say yes to the boys who said no? Of course, in reality we were more than that. We would not personally be going to jail, but our lives were equally disrupted. We were preparing to go to Canada or Sweden with husbands who chose exile, preparing to postpone children or to raise those we already had without the support of husbands who chose jail. But for "the boys" we were nonentities. Though of equal intelligence and thoughtfulness, and equal commitment, we had no legitimacy as part of the struggle. Should a woman have the temerity to voice a thought in the course of one of the conversations, there was a silence in which the men looked embarrassedly away from her before picking up just where they had been.

After Donna's two magic words—"women's liberation"—I went to no more Resistance dinners. We women had been playing an inauthentic game, going through the motions of the required role, appearing to accept the attitudes that allowed the men to treat us dismissively while they used us as tools of service and psychological support. Although we certainly knew that we were not the intellectual and moral inferiors they indulged themselves in believing us to be, we did agree to a kind of moral inferiority when we said to ourselves (and very occasionally to one another) that their stand of courage and conscience mattered so much more than our human dignity that we would continue to support them as they were. Our courage in standing up to the United States government for what we believed was not matched by the courage to stand up to our male comrades for what we knew to be the truth of ourselves.

Serving others and sacrificing self in almost every aspect of our lives, women remained psychologically vulnerable to the accusation of being "selfish" if we requested for ourselves a level of respect that was only common decency. Leftist men saw this vulnerability; therefore, the word "selfish!" was used as a weapon against their women comrades and supporters.

Anything smacking of a real challenge to the phallocentrism of The Resistance was put down so brutally that such presumptions were rare. The women were not slow learners; most evidently learned from the example of others' experience and made no attempt to enter the public conversation. The unthinking brutality furthermore made it seem clear that forcing the men to change was out of the question; our only option would be to disengage from them, and in fact the men were riding so high in their macho exhilaration that even our departure seemed likely only to strengthen the male bonding. I no longer cared how they might muddle through without me; I departed and never looked back to see.

I began following up leads to women's liberation and, by the beginning of May 1968, was corresponding with Joreen [Jo Freeman], editor of a newsletter published in Chicago entitled *Voice of the Women's Liberation Movement.* I was now part of an actual movement, although I needed the right catalyst to launch me into activism. I had done the basic thinking; my consciousness was already raised. Now I needed comrades who were ready for revolution; I didn't want to sit around with housewives concerned about getting more help with child care from their husbands or with New Left women wanting to persuade their male cohorts to be more respectful. The magnitude of the problem obviously required a much more radical and activist approach. But would I find any such comrades?

Although I had left The Resistance, I did continue for a while to do draft counseling, where my knowledge was eagerly sought and appreciated by the often rather desperate clients. This counseling organization, the Boston Draft Resistance Group, sponsored a "free school" in July, during which there was a workshop, offered by a woman named Roxanne Dunbar, on Valerie Solanas's *Scum Manifesto,* characterized in the program as a document of female liberation. Roxanne had just arrived in town inspired by Valerie in a way analogous to my galvanization in January. She was also transcending the usual leftist causes: she had been on her way to Cuba when she read about Valerie's shooting of Andy Warhol.

She thought to herself, "It has begun!" and canceled her trip. This attack seemed to symbolize some break with business as usual for women.

The *Scum Manifesto* was a wild, crazy, man-hating diatribe filled with energy, nastiness, and taboo truths. It seemed to say all the things we rational, nice, good-hearted, inauthentic women never said, things we scarcely permitted ourselves to think. It repeatedly turned men's hostile stereotypes of women upside down and blatantly asserted them to be true of men: and it did so in a way that rang true. It wasn't nice, it wasn't even fair (not to the "nice men," the "men who weren't like that"), but the *Scum Manifesto* was perfectly exhilarating. It invited us to recognize that being "fair" to the "nice men" was paralyzing us and distorting our perception of reality.

The other women who came to Roxanne's workshop, women who very likely came with expectations of an earnest liberal appeal for fairness, received what may have seemed to them to be paranoid rantings. To me, anything less would have seemed an underestimation of the problem. Roxanne and I left the workshop talking about organizing a women's revolution.

We thereupon placed an ad in the underground paper for a women's group. Several women showed up, including Betsy (who later took the surname Warrior), a dedicated and stalwart comrade who hung in through all the Cell 16 wars and remains still on the front lines for women, and Betsy's friend Stella. Later Roxanne recruited Ellen, who lived downstairs from her, a poet whose toughness and courage had been earned in brutal life battles. Some other women joined us at times, but it was essentially this core that floundered through the theoretical and activist makings of a revolution, in isolation, five or so women against the patriarchy. We were a mixed group: former college professor, former prostitute, space avionics computer consultant, welfare mother. But for us differences of class and background faded to irrelevance before the magnitude of the shared caste of gender and the magnitude of the task before us.

It was a terrifying and dangerous time. We felt that we were laying our lives on the line in a way the boys of The Resistance weren't even contemplating. We saw the violence and hatred that demands of personhood and dignity for women brought out in men who until then appeared normal. These were many women's "nice men." They were the apparently dignified conservatives, the open-minded liberals, the justice-hungry leftists, the apolitical hippies. These men gave us every indication that they would choose open warfare, to the death, rather than yield any privilege, including the psychological privilege of feeling superior. We felt we were girding for an apocalypse in male-female relations. It was startling—and deeply disturbing—how frequently men responded to our direct but courteous remonstrances about sometimes small issues of behavior with the verbal and body language of physical violence.

The language of all-out physical combat and warfare would issue in response to what might seem to us equally mild propositions for social or behavioral change. Perhaps we would object that the calendar featuring nude women on the wall of the meeting room was embarrassing to us and a distraction from the seriousness of the meeting's deliberations. Or we'd opine that we'd like to see half the Supreme Court be women. Or we'd assert that there was something wrong with an ad that undertook to sell a computer by picturing it with a partially clothed woman draped over it. Or we'd recommend that the setting of the air conditioning should consider the way the women were dressed, not just the way the men were. Or we'd urge that fathers should sometimes be the ones to stay home when children were ill.

Then, astonishingly, their faces would get red, veins would stand out on their necks, chest and arm muscles would tighten and lift, and in tones of anger and agitation they would talk irrationally and in complete *non sequitur* of our having made men the "enemy," talk of our castrating them (a shocking and disturbing image of physical mutilation), talk of our wishing to "kill all the men." They pointed out by innuendo and outright threat that we could not hope to impose our views on them as long as we were vulnerable to rape, a vulnerability, they emphasized ominously, which their physical strength and our anatomy made permanent. The threats sometimes extended to graphic descriptions of injuries attendant on rape.

What on earth could be going on here? Did any stance but subservience make us enemies, in their view? Was a wish for any modified behavior that accorded us human decency equivalent to a wish for their death? Were they saying that they would die before yielding psychological or social privilege and pretensions? Was it really their view that the threat of physical violence against us was the foundation of gender relations, with their pious ideologies evaporating as soon as we criticized or

questioned? If men really believed that in facing challenges to their privileges and pretensions they were defending themselves against enemies
who wished to kill them or to cut off their body parts, what could we
expect from them? We therefore prepared ourselves for the day when it
would be women against men over the barricades. The prospect was terrifying: we had no wish for this, and certainly had no intention of initiating any such thing.

But we did mean to insist on our humanity and to urge other
women to do the same, to decline to make ourselves into the myth and
idol "woman" (which fond fantasy men were demanding we incarnate),
and to decline to play the games of subservience. We meant to do this
until the whole system of female subservience crumbled. Men gave us
reason to expect that when we became sufficiently effective, sufficiently
threatening, they would organize to come after us. Meanwhile we faced
the hatred and threats of individual men in private challenges and in our
political street actions.

In one action, we picketed the Playboy Club, at night, in an
unpopulated and desolate part of town, trying to hand leaflets to men
or to their wives and dates. Now, I had encountered danger and the
threat of violence before. I had been charged by New York City police
on horseback wielding clubs to break up a peace demonstration. I had
faced angry rednecks threatening me in a very personal way with rape,
mutilation, and lynching in a civil rights sit-in in the South. And one
night during the Cuban missile crisis, my sister Martha and I were
picketing the White House as part of an around-the-clock vigil for
peace; at 2 A.M. we found ourselves alone, two teenage girls with our
peace signs facing off against Nazi Party members who took ugly issue
with our stance. But looking back, I think I may have felt most vulnerable facing the well-dressed patrons of the Playboy Club and the
hatred aroused by our challenging the systematic objectification of
women through sex.

In another political event at a local movie house, we sponsored a
showing of *The Queens,* about a transvestite beauty pageant. The film
portrayed men making themselves into women who were so convincing
that one forgot that they were men. This evinced, we thought, better
than any arguments in a leaflet, that womanly appearance and feminine
mannerisms were purely convention. Around this time or a little later,
our first black woman member had joined the group: Marianne, a feisty

character who had been laughing raucously at our showing of *The Queens*. Somewhere else we had connected with our first out-and-militant lesbian member, Gail, a poet. In addition, Roxanne had acquired an apartment-mate, Maureen, whom she recruited into the group. She had also found Marilyn, high-strung and intellectual, who was to stay with us into Cell 16. Betsy and Stella and Ellen from the original group were still with us.

Still somewhat under the spell of Valerie Solanas, we considered what should be done in her defense. Roxanne and I went together to visit her at Mattawan, the mental institution in which she had been incarcerated after shooting Andy Warhol; later I made a visit on my own. Valerie was enraged about the publication of the *Scum Manifesto* by Maurice Gerodias: he was making money from her work, and had distorted her message on the book's cover, putting all the emphasis on it being S.C.U.M. for "Society for Cutting Up Men," something which, for Valerie, had been only a snicker-worthy side joke on the title of her intended organization. Her actual purpose was to speak to women who considered themselves "scum"—that is, the unladylike women who weren't afraid to tell the nasty truth about gender relations. We considered retaliatory action against Gerodias. Our isolation and sense of living on the edge were taking a toll.

In August 1968, there was a meeting in Maryland of women mostly from New Left movements to talk about women's liberation. Roxanne and I drove down from Boston, bearing our revolutionary ideas. These women wanted to talk about improving their treatment from their leftist male comrades and about their wish for more respect from their lovers. However, Roxanne was not one to try to meet people on their own level; on the contrary, she considered shock tactics to be the most salutary. Whether intending to shock or whether naively expecting this to be enthusiastically received, she insisted on reading aloud to them from the *Scum Manifesto*. To make matters worse, we talked about celibacy as a revolutionary tactic. The other women were horrified by us. They thought Valerie was clearly crazy (as her incarceration in a mental institution only confirmed). And they weren't a bit impressed by our political analysis on that: as Roxanne and I interpreted the ideology of patriarchy, when a man shoots someone, he is either justified or a criminal, but when a woman shoots someone, well, she must be crazy, since women don't do such things. Such a woman gets shut up in a mental institution where they can keep her drugged to mute her. And even if Valerie *were* crazy, we proposed that she was still worthy of our support as one probably driven to illness by the same pressures we were facing, and also valuable as theoretician and symbol.

More surprising than their reaction to Valerie were their stories of abusive relationships with men. Why stay? They're all that way, was the response; besides, we need sex. Why? Uncomprehending looks. They seemed to think that we were hopelessly out of touch with reality: how could one talk to people so unaware of basic psychology and physiology? These women had not missed the message of the so-called sexual revolution: to wit, that a woman who doesn't make sure she "gets plenty" (from men, of course) will "dry up inside," as one woman there anxiously characterized it. We responded to their stories of abusive male-female relationships with the suggestion—rather mild, so it seemed to us—that women aren't going to be able to respect themselves so long as they stay in such relationships. We suggested that women did not, in fact, need sex. What we needed was autonomy.

I doubt that we did more than scandalize; but Roxanne had greater faith than I in scandal as an organizing tactic. She believed people could be shocked and bullied out of complacent self-delusion; she felt it was probably the only way they would be. She was a great admirer of the tactics of the Chinese revolution. My faith was in finding a way of telling the truth so accurately, in ways so consonant with people's own experience, that the person herself had to acknowledge it: something in her soul would turn with gladness to what was its own. I was, of course, trying to do that at the conference, but in such a short bit of time, with our coming in so at odds with the women there on so many levels, I doubt that it could have succeeded.

Although we were disappointed not to find women more in tune with our own views, we came home feeling enlightened about the nature of the work to be done and energized by the clear direction. I saw that it wasn't going to be enough to say a couple of magic words; we needed to explain why we saw what we did. We decided to start a theoretical journal.

We called the journal *No More Fun & Games: a Journal of Female Liberation.* The main title was meant to show our uncompromising intentions. We were not promising men that the liberation of women was going to be to their advantage; on the contrary, we were going to end the game playing they found so appealing. The subtitle asserted our name for the movement: "female" rather than "women's" liberation. In addition it was "a" journal, not "the" journal, thus inviting others to publish other journals, each contributing the particular perspective of their group to weave a rich tapestry of female liberation theory. Roxanne had wrangled a typesetting machine from IBM—under pretenses that didn't bear looking into. We had it for the weekend only, so we worked all day and far into the night, each woman in our group typesetting her own articles. We were a strange manic crew, still "scum" as Valerie would have had us, but now, as our numbers increased, our bonds were looser. Ideologically, we were surfing on the same exhilarating wave, tolerant of differences of style and perspective, coherent in the importance of the primary goals, feeling fully committed to the cause. But we would no longer have trusted one another with our lives as the tighter group had rather rashly been prepared to do earlier in the summer.

The journal, which came out in late August 1968, contained no address at which we could be contacted; we sold it on the street for a dollar a copy (pretty much exactly what it cost to print, as I recall). The issue was also undated. Looking back as editor and publisher of some of the later of the six issues, it seems strange that it never occurred to us to date the first issue, but it accurately reflected our state of mind then. We didn't foresee an orderly future that would in turn become history and require documentation. Instead, we saw ourselves on the verge of a great upheaval. Perhaps it was like the anticipation of the end of the world for early Christians.

The journal reflected our diversity, a dizzying mix of styles reflecting our group and the each-woman-speaks-her-mind editorial philosophy. The issue featured practical what-to-do analyses of ways we were tricked into supporting our own oppression. There were views on left movement politics, essays with an academic tone, militant diatribes, Marxist-influenced analysis, poetry, drawings, and collages. The cover drawing, done by my sister Indra, was a naked woman whose massive curls of hair completely enclosed and imprisoned her. In fact, our first prospective printer had refused to take the job, claiming that the cover was pornographic, but perhaps he was really more confused and offended by it being brought to him by women. Or perhaps he'd had a peek at the contents.

I wrote quite a few pieces for this journal. Essays on sexuality and celibacy inspired by our conference in Maryland. A couple of ambitious analyses of how women's current condition came to be, how that condition was enforced, how women reacted to it, and what needed to be done; some of that analysis was noticeably influenced by Simone de Beauvoir's classic *The Second Sex,* which I had been reading. A short bit addressing the draft resisters and the irritating slogan "Girls say yes to boys who say no" left me with a sense of closure on my experience with The Resistance.

The journal was exciting. It said things that hadn't yet been said, things no one else was saying, things that needed to be said, things that had the shock of truth. Our message, as it emerged in gradually more coherent form in later journals, was to women, not men. It was women that we intended to change. We didn't flatter ourselves that we had anything we could say to men that would have any weight in balance with the privileges that the subordination of women conferred. (Oh, probably Roxanne thought some bullying of men couldn't hurt, but she only tossed her harangues out as a public service, for their own good, as it were; she didn't imagine that our liberation would come from them.)

We meant to empower women to reject enslavement on its many levels. We threatened men not with violence but with the refusal to play the games through which women built up men and misrepresented themselves, through which men manipulated women and rewarded them for inauthenticity. It was my focus in particular to expose the games, in as much telling detail as possible, so that women could see them for what they are and not be taken in.

The matter of a name for our group had been given some thought. We had toyed from the beginning with the name Women Against Society, and had even told importunate representatives of the media (who seemed unable to focus on the issues until they could get our label) that we were "tentatively" using that name. But we resisted the idea of having any name; it seemed limiting and invited pigeonholing and marginalization. We wanted to act in the name of liberation for women in the broadest and most radical sense. But we were certain and explicit about one thing regarding names, and had talked about this from our first meetings. We wanted the *movement* to be characterized as "female" liberation, not "women's" liberation, as it had begun to be called in the first stirrings by the women of the student peace and civil rights movements. To us, "woman" was a constructed and conventional role, created by men for their convenience and satisfaction. With the term "female" we went to the root of the matter, clearing away all the false accretions and making room for whatever was true in our natures to show itself. The term "feminism" had a respectable past history, but it was too close to the prescriptive term "feminine" to sit comfortably with us.

As it turned out, there was no stopping the media from its determination to name us: they began calling our group "female liberation," thus sabotaging our wish for that name to be used by the movement; to try to free it for the movement we eventually (about a year later) assigned ourselves the name Cell 16. The name was meant to convey that we were just one cell of the movement for female liberation, like a single cell of a complex organism. The hopes for the name female liberation denominating the movement received its final blow a few months after that when members of the Socialist Workers Party who had infiltrated our group incorporated the name "Female Liberation" in order to take over our office and lay claim to the journals. But these are other stories, and not the stuff of 1968.

In November there was to be another, larger conference for women in Chicago. The indefatigable Roxanne used her left movement contacts to connect with Abby Rockefeller, known to have given money in the past to progressive causes. Roxanne wanted to ask her for money to send one of us (me, as it turned out) to Chicago for the conference. Her pitch provided the magic words for Abby ("It has begun!"). Later that winter, Abby was to became part of the group, and remained among our most dedicated, most radical, and most thoughtful members, an important balance to Roxanne's compulsive energy, and remaining long after Roxanne moved on.

The conference in Chicago was huge (so it seemed at the time) and exhilarating. The general impression was one of tremendous richness. Women came from all around the country. Women from the thick of the civil rights struggle in the South. Women with particular contributions, like Anne Koedt (who seemed very much in tune with my approach), with her forthright article "The Myth of the Vaginal Orgasm." The Redstocking women from New York offered the "pro-woman line," proposing that anything women do is right and good and that it's just a matter of looking at any female action from a women's perspective to see its intelligence and value. This was refreshing, and often revealed more truth than the conventional view, which could be called the "anti-woman line": that anything women do is trivial or base. Much of the analysis of the conference, however, suggested that men were being unfair and that they should have this pointed out to them so that they would change, thus solving the problem. As I saw it, men knew perfectly well that they were being unfair to women, and chose their behavior because it was to their advantage. Thus men wouldn't voluntarily change. We had to change. And declaring everything women did to be good wasn't going to create change if it justified and honored things we were doing that locked us into the system of subservience and oppression.

At that point, the suggestion that women must change struck many as critical of women, and, by putting the burden on the "victim," seemed to multiply the unfairness of gender relations. Though this was a touchy issue for those sick of the atmosphere of societal disrespect for women, I had no problem with admitting that we had fallen for some of the tricks, taken some of the bribes. I had no fantasy that women were perfect; I considered women to be human, with the full range of human strengths, weaknesses, and potentials. But in some women's insistence on men doing the changing, I saw more of the same trained-in passivity that I thought we needed to break out of: women once again expecting men to do the work for us, to rescue us from our problem. What's wrong, one might ask, with being rescued? It seemed to me that we would never experience ourselves as powerful so long as men were handing us things—even if they would, which I knew they wouldn't. If we took control of our lives ourselves, maybe we would know better what to do with that control and those lives.

As I saw it then, and still do, the thing we want as women is full humanity, not male privileges and not female privileges. And it had always seemed to me, even before I read de Beauvoir, that full humanity is about deciding what one wants for oneself out of life, and then working to make one's choices a reality. Until we are fully self-respecting, how can we really demand respect from others? It seemed to me that many women had the whole situation backward. They believed they would respect themselves when others respected them. But no one, male or female, will be likely to truly respect anyone who does not respect herself. Hence I thought we must learn to respect ourselves by giving ourselves reasons for self-respect: by giving up passivity, by resisting the stunting and crushing of our wills and aspirations, by taking action and taking risks, by rejecting excuses about the barriers to women, substituting a determination to knock down, climb over, or slip around any obstacles. If, despite our determination, we didn't accomplish everything we'd like, it wouldn't be for lack of will and aspiration, nor for lack of courage and energy. When I thought about women attaining full "humanity" or "personhood," it was *not* a code for getting to live like men, but something rather higher—living authentically.

Of the female liberation groups, we in our Boston group seemed the most wholeheartedly ready to overturn and to sacrifice everything: the old coherence and whatever conveniences or privileges it might be offering us, all our systems of getting along in the man's world, our very lives. Of course, as it turned out over the next twenty years, it was not necessary to sacrifice our lives, and it did not come to armed revolution. We had been misled by men's vicious response to our suggestions for change. In fact, it turned out that men were a great deal more dependent on women than they let on, and, as long as we had the ability to leave them, we had a trump card. When enough women were willing to say they didn't need men, willing to walk out and make it stick, men began to change. Of course, the men tried every trick of manipulation and bullying, used economic pressure and played on our sense of responsibility to our children. And of course there was violence: then and still now, many women who leave men are murdered by them, and sometimes their children are murdered as well. But enough succeeded in leaving that men learned that certain behavior was not in their interests, and things began gradually to improve.

Didn't this come from women following the very strategy we recommended, whether or not they knew it was ours? We proposed women respecting themselves, valuing their lives, and insisting on being treated fairly if they are going to give of themselves, whether in the workplace or marriage or anywhere else. I still think our uncompromising approach was right. One has to be willing to face it all, to say that one's dignity and self-respect are more important than keeping a man or a job, more important perhaps even than life, if it comes to a need to take some risk.

Although our positions late in 1968 included some that were startling to a wide spectrum of the emerging women's movement, gradually over the years much of what we insisted on became mainstream.

I am amused today to find young women who scornfully declare that they are "not feminists," taking for granted their rights to do some things we scandalized our feminist comrades for suggesting in the early days. I spoke the other day to a young "not-a-feminist" with a shaved head and remembered the scandal, the uproar, the outrage Cell 16 created at a feminist conference in New York City in 1969. We were speaking from the stage on the subject of the political implications of our making ourselves into conventional womanly women through the cultivation (often at the expense of great time and effort) of stereotypical feminine appearance. To dramatize this, we included a bit of guerrilla theater: one of our number who had luxuriant long blonde hair had decided to cut it to a more practical chin length. To help us make the point about femininity, she had also agreed to have us cut her hair on stage. There was pandemonium in the hall, with women standing up and screaming, "Don't do it!" One woman shrieked, "Men like my breasts, too; do you want me to cut them off?" In 1994, in contrast, my young "not-a-feminist" acquaintance considered her shaved-head haircut practical and rather interesting. If it shocked anyone, or if someone chose to regard it as "unfeminine," so much the worse for them.

What were our characteristic perspectives and positions in 1968, and why were they controversial within the movement in the historical context in which they appeared?

First, we saw the female liberation movement as demanding our primary allegiance. The wave of activism that sparked the tinder of women's discontent and the groundwork laid by Betty Friedan into a real and powerful movement came from the women of the civil rights and antiwar struggles who became unable to ignore the contradictions between the assertions by their male comrades of belief in social justice and the men's insistence that women occupy an inferior social caste. Yet most of these women maintained their allegiance to the movements, seeking only greater equality within the organizations. We challenged these allegiances by insisting that the women's revolution was the first and only true revolution. Thus we withdrew our energies from other progressive movements, inviting the men to join us if they genuinely cared about social justice, but knowing that it was we who would be the visionaries and leaders of that genuine revolution. Society as it exists has too many privileges for men for them to be willing to change it in any thoroughgoing way; true social justice will cost them too much. It is women who, as we saw it, would remake society on the model of the true interdependent community. We thought it was time for women to stop giving their energies to support men in their partway justice.

Second, we insisted on rejecting every prescriptive description of how we must look, act, speak, or think if we are to be "true women." The controversy this occasionally provoked, such as that aroused by our haircutting at the first Congress to Unite Women, always astonished us. We thought it obvious that whatever women did was by definition "feminine," and "woman's nature" must necessarily be defined by the full richness and complexity of women's natures. Of course, what most women did most of the time under the current system was a distorted expression of their real strengths and aspirations. But as circumstances and our thoughts, choices, and actions changed, we would continue to see "woman's nature" unfold and display itself in its self-defined authenticity. When it has had a chance to unfold freely, we might then discover whether there is such a thing as "woman's nature" distinguishable from "human nature."

Let me emphasize that by "human nature" I don't mean "the way men are." Given the despotic dichotomy distorting human nature into such brutally stultifying and corrupting roles as "womanliness" and "manliness," we cannot see what any true expression of human nature is and we will not know it until all humans are free of such roles.

Meanwhile, we had to dig out from under the weight and influence of cultural demands that we act, look, and think in certain ways not selected by ourselves and mostly not in our own interests. These demands were enforced, should we deviate, by accusations of psychological deformity, by social ridicule and ostracism, and, worst, by having our opinions and analyses dismissed as the self-justifications of someone who has failed at what was most essential. We were lectured that our envy of men's penises was not being properly sublimated in the service of an individual penis.

This effort to dig out from under the normative dictates of men's fantasy of "woman" was a major activity of most parts of the women's movement. The media image of feminists as unattractive women who are bitter because they can't get a man has frightened off women for decades and still does. Even many who were prepared to call themselves feminists have wanted to dissociate themselves from the unattractive, presumably bitter ones. Until pioneers made a more relaxed version of womanhood acceptable, some women would not risk an overt feminist politics.

Our next characteristic and sometimes controversial position concerned sex. In flagrant disregard for the ethos of the sixties, we advocated celibacy as the appropriate alternative to abusive relationships and considerably downplayed the importance of sex. We thought that the ideology of sex as a *need* was a myth perpetrated by men for their own convenience. We took for granted and, indeed, would have insisted on our own sexual freedom. But we classed sex with other enjoyable but optional activities: fun at the beach, ice cream sundaes, amusement park rides. We might choose to do any of these occasionally, but we would consider the price that was paid. If the price was too high, any could be passed up without regret.

Beyond the matter of whether one ought to stay in an abusive relationship, we questioned how much time and energy ought to go into working out "personal" relationships even of a more promising sort, and asked whether women ought to be devoting themselves to raising children. Although we didn't condemn good sexual relationships or worthwhile family life, should these be found, it is true that, at that historical moment, we thought it best for women to stay free for making the revolution. Even good relationships take time and energy, time and energy that we needed in getting the word to women about the possibility of a better way of life, time and energy that we needed for the struggle. And isn't it obvious that a *guerrilla* must be free? Hence we wondered at women who professed to be dedicated to fighting for female liberation and who also chose to have children. We felt that children became the hostages of the system; women's need to protect children make us vulnerable to male threats and bribes. We might be willing to bring the world down on our own heads through a revolution total enough to effect true liberation for all, but we flinch in contemplating the danger to innocent little ones. Of course, in our apocalyptic thinking, we never envisaged this struggle being one that would go on for twenty, fifty, a hundred years. In this, too, we were progeny of the sixties: we were going to remake the world in the next two or three or five years. There would be plenty of time for "a personal life" later.

Finally, it was one of our most important contributions to promote martial arts training so that women could defend themselves physically from the random violence to which they are prey because of their gender, and, if necessary, from violence directed at us because of our demands for dignity and personhood. But this stance too created its share of scandal. Many of our potential comrades in the fledgling women's movement came from a political tradition of nonviolence. This was further reinforced by the nurturer's distaste for violence and the passivity our training as "women" has produced in us. Hence our proposal that women equip themselves to return violence for violence seemed to many abhorrent and exactly wrong.

Of course, the whole point of martial arts training is to stop the intended violence promptly by our own physical competence, and to discourage the pattern of violence against women by making it more dangerous for the would-be assailant. When women do not play into the scenario of the helpless and frightened victim, the whole encounter, intended as a power trip, denies our assailant satisfaction. Further, our confidence in our own physical competence lends us an air of assurance and easy alertness, a way of moving through the world in harmony with it, which is the very best deterrent to being selected as victim by a would-be attacker. But even when expressed at its most philosophically high-minded, the idea of women training themselves to fight back offended and alarmed many women.

Furthermore, one doesn't like being reminded of one's vulnerability when the "cure" involves years of hard work, as martial arts training in fact does. In later years, promoting self-defense for women and offering that training, I ran into much resentful rage from women over this. Once again, the burden of redress was falling on the woman, on the "victim," not on the male perpetrator. "Let men change!" women shouted angrily at me, as if I were to blame for the unpleasant state of affairs. "Why should I have to disrupt my life to learn to defend myself?" Well, the world is unfair; but frankly, I'd rather depend on myself than on some perpetrator who has been ordered to behave nicely to me.

When we originally began formulating the politics of self-defense, our own experience with self-defense training didn't extend past a YWCA course that some of our group had taken in the summer. But a very important chapter was about to open. In November, Jayne West, Abby's friend and housemate, had a narrow escape when some men tried to pull her into a car one afternoon on a pleasant Cambridge street just outside of Harvard Square. Abby and Jayne took action and began serious martial arts training; I followed a week later.

Within a few months of beginning our training, which we pursued in classes five and six times a week, we were presenting self-defense workshops at women's conferences. Our teacher, Mr. Kim, gave us his studio one night a week to teach a women's class. It was filled not just with our group, which was itself growing, but with women whom we had convinced by our political analysis about the importance of self-defense training.

How can a woman have any sense of dignity or privacy, Abby asked, if she has to walk around conscious that she is at the mercy of almost any pathetic creep of a man who jumps out at her? To experience one-self as powerful, one needs a certain sense of security in her person, or at least the confidence that she will acquit herself respectably if attacked, that she would resist as if she truly valued her life.

My joining Abby and Jayne at Mr. Kim's school was the beginning of the rich collaboration that became Cell 16. The distinctiveness of Cell 16 came from the weaving together of the unusually strong characters, personalities, and intelligences of the five women who were its nucleus: Abby, Jayne, Betsy, myself, and (until the fall of 1969) Roxanne—enriched by the other lively and original women who worked with us.

The groundwork for all that was to come of our part of the women's movement had been laid in 1968, a year of exhilaration, terror, and upheaval such as everyone should have in her life, but perhaps not more than once.

Outlaw Woman: Chapters from a Feminist Memoir-in-Progress

Roxanne Dunbar

I

Ever since I left my isolated, rural, and impoverished childhood in Oklahoma, I have felt like an outlaw, even in the women's movement which I helped initiate in 1968. So I choose the name "Outlaw Woman" for my memoir mindfully. Mine is not the story of a moderate feminist. I was an extremist. My childhood icons were Belle Starr, Calamity Jane, and Annie Oakley, along with Bonnie and Clyde, Billy the Kid, Pretty Boy Floyd, Jesse James, and Al Jennings, all from my part of the world. My grandfather had been an anarchist-socialist, a local western Oklahoma leader of the Industrial Workers of the World, a Wobbly. For those and other reasons, mainly my rural working-class background, my worldview was different from the emerging mainstream of the women's movement, which I perceived to be controlled by white, urban, middle-class professional women and leftist women from a similar background.

From the time I left Oklahoma at twenty, I have rarely met anyone who came from a background or worldview similar to mine—rural poverty, Southern Baptist, yet powerfully infused with agrarian populism, that is, a deep mistrust for the government, for all governments, for city people, and especially for "easterners," as we called everyone east of the Mississippi and north of the Mason-Dixon line.

As a teenager, I ran away from rural poverty and a violent alcoholic mother to the city, where I fell in love and married a rich boy, at least by my standards—his father was a construction superintendent. We migrated to San Francisco where I enrolled at San Francisco State for the purpose of learning everything I could about the world, majoring in history.

I was ashamed of my background and never talked about it. My husband's goal was to help me to "rise above" my class and social status. I drew further and further away from myself and cut ties with my family. My husband controlled my every thought and action. Then I had a baby, which freed me from his control; I was now a mother, and to him could do no wrong.

I read Simone de Beauvoir's *The Second Sex* in the summer of 1963. My daughter was nine months old. The book affected me powerfully, with its analysis of marriage and the family as the seed of female bondage. Three months after I read the book, I left my husband. The following year he fought for custody of our daughter and won. Though I had visitation rights, I paid a heavy price for my newfound freedom.

II

On the eve of 1968, I was in my fourth year as a history doctoral student at UCLA, writing my dissertation. I was privileged: an assistant instructor in the male-dominated history department, living in a financially, socially, and intellectually comfortable and secure world. But this world was increasingly intruded upon by the Vietnam War, by black activism, and by my own growing political and feminist consciousness. UCLA was no Berkeley, but there were rumblings of discontent in which I was active. Vietnam War teach-ins had begun in 1965. The nearby Watts rebellion that same year had sharpened my perception of institutionalized racism and the provocative role of the police. The election of Ronald Reagan as governor in 1966 had galvanized students and some faculty, for Reagan had gained popularity by campaigning against the University of California.

I was part of a small group of UCLA teaching assistants who formed a trade union. The same group led protests against the Vietnam War. My field of history was Latin America, so I was also learning about U.S. imperialism, about the longtime dictators Somoza, Trujillo, Duvallier, Stroesser, and Batista before them, whom the United States had installed and financed, and about the revolutions against them, about Cuba, about Che Guevara. As well, among my closest friends were exiled South Africans, so I learned about apartheid and about African national liberation movements.

Although I considered myself a radical and even a Marxist, it did not occur to me to leave the protective confines of academia until fate struck a blow that changed my life forever. In the spring of 1967, my best friend was killed in an airplane crash. Audrey Rosenthal, one of the group of radicals on campus, had gone to London with her companion, an exiled white South African and a member of the African National Congress. She was a courier for the African National Congress when she died. The summer of 1967, spent in London with exiled South African revolutionaries, transformed my consciousness. It also transformed me into an angry feminist, experiencing, as I did, the subservient role of women in even a revolutionary organization. I returned from London a self-identified "committed revolutionary," burning with the realization that a women's liberation movement would be essential, first, for me and other women to function as revolutionaries, and, second, for real social change even to take place. I returned with a new vision, compelled to make my way into the revolutionary vortex.

III

I moved to Berkeley on New Year's Day, 1968. There I was surrounded by the volatile protest and organizing around the "Free Huey" movement. The Black Panther Party had burst on the scene a year earlier with their black-bereted street patrols, and armed with legal and loaded shotguns. I seethed over the secondary role of women, and the absence of discussion of women's oppression in the movements that surrounded me. Women were to be supportive; in the black power movement, national liberation came first; for leftists, socialism had to be established before women would be free; for the antiwar movement, draft resisters and army deserters came first, all male. "Girls say yes to boys who say no" was their slogan. All left movements cautioned that women should wait.

1968 wasn't just my personal watershed, but a historic year, a magical number that I cannot fully explain, although I know that I was swept up in the tide that made that year historic. I cannot separate my personal odyssey from this tidal wave. In a sense, I think of 1968, and certainly women's liberation, as having saved my life, or my sanity. The night of the assassination of Martin Luther King, alienation from my own past and from everything about the United States and its history ravaged my mind. I felt enraged and helpless. I felt therefore that I had to learn to be a revolutionary and imagined that Cuba was the fount of such knowledge.

Two photographs of me tell part of the story of my transformation in 1968. Both are passport pictures, taken one year apart. The first was in May 1967, for my first passport to go to London, and the other, in May 1968, for the Cuban visa. From the 1967 picture, a total stranger stares at me. She could have stepped from the pages of *Vogue*. Her long, blonde hair is wavy, well-coiffed, corn-silk shiny. Her averted dark eyes are made up with care, enlarging and softening them. She smiles slyly, sexily, benignly. I marvel at this photograph still, trying to recall how I could have possibly convinced my fine, straight dark hair to be such a natural blond, managed and thick, how my hard black eyes could appear soft and evasive, my dark complexion lightened to ivory, my prominent cheekbones hidden under makeup. In contrast, the 1968 picture is more familiar, an adult version of my childhood photographs—a dark-skinned woman with short dark hair, a long forehead, high cheekbones, and unsmiling coals-of-fire eyes staring directly into the camera.

I left for Mexico and spent six weeks trying to obtain a visa for Cuba. Just when I got it in early June, two more bullets changed my decision to go. Robert Kennedy, in whom I had guarded hope if he were to become president, was assassinated. And Andy Warhol survived an assassination attempt by a woman, Valerie Solanas, who was described in the press as "a super-woman power advocate" and the author of a tract she named the *S.C.U.M. Manifesto,* the acronym standing for the "Society for Cutting Up Men." I was a fan of Warhol's art and art movement, particularly his experimental films, so I did not celebrate his victimization. Yet I was intrigued and even thrilled by the existence of a "super-woman power advocate." Exiled in Mexico and bound for Cuba, I interpreted Valerie Solanas's act as a signal that a women's liberation movement had begun in the United States.

Instead of going to Cuba, I went to Boston, intent on finding—or founding—a women's liberation movement. I chose Boston because it was there that the nineteenth-century feminist and antislavery movement was centered, and where at the same time young factory girls had started the labor movement. A part of my transformation in 1968 was a reclamation of my working-class and rural roots to go with my revolutionary fervor.

IV

June 1968, Boston. I answered an ad in *Resist,* the local draft-resistance newsletter, asking for volunteer teachers. I arrived at the cavernous warehouse-office in the Boston Back Bay district. I explained that I was a history doctoral student, and that I wanted to volunteer to teach a course on the nineteenth-century feminist movement—women's history. Kay crossed and uncrossed her bare, milky-white thighs. Brad flipped through a pile of papers. I noticed Kay fingering little red booklets that were somehow familiar.

"What are those?" I asked. Both of them sighed, apparently in relief.

"We are an authorized chapter of the Industrial Workers of the World, the IWW, Wobblies. You know about them?" Kay said and pointed to a red and black button on the side of her beret.

I was stunned. The IWW. It no longer existed. My own father had told me about its death long ago.

"My grandfather was a Wobbly. He named my father after the founders, Moyer and Haywood. I didn't know it was still around," I said.

"No shit. Yeah, it's still alive, hard as J. Edgar Hoover tried to destroy it," Brad said. I marveled at the fact that my grandfather had the same adversary, J. Edgar Hoover, in 1918, that my generation had more than half a century later.

"So the IWW's kind of symbolic now, you mean?" I asked.

"We're getting it going again. Hey, why don't you sign up to teach labor history?" Kay said.

"No, that's not my field," I said. I didn't tell them that feminist history wasn't my field either, that my idea in teaching the course was to recruit women for my own women's liberation project.

"Aren't you a Marxist?" Brad asked.

"Yes, but I don't know labor history well enough to teach it. I would teach feminist history from a Marxist perspective," I said.

"Look, we don't want no chicklib here," Brad said. Kay lit a cigarette. I dropped the subject.

"Hey, can I join the IWW?" I asked.

Their faces lightened and Kay said, "Sure thing. Just a dollar."

I gave them a dollar and took the thin, crisp booklet in my palm—a ghost from the past. I clutched the little red book as I walked through the Boston Commons and over the Charles River Bridge to Cambridge, recalling the stories my father used to tell me about my grandfather and the Wobblies.

Talk about my grandfather and the Wobblies had thinned in the early fifties as the new Red Scare escalated: a commie in the family tree became dangerous again. The rage about our poverty was covered over with pride for just being white and "real" Americans. I myself grew fiercely patriotic. I won first prize in a county speech contest for my original oration, "America Is Great Because America Is Good." I had spent the summer of 1954 baby-sitting in a home with a television, avidly watching the McCarthy-Army hearings, rooting for McCarthy, adoring the young Roy Cohn. I began to doubt my father's stories for the history I learned in school was completely different from what he'd told me. And then my father no longer even told those stories.

By 1968, my father supported George Wallace for president and claimed that his own father had been duped by communists. It seemed to me that I bore the responsibility to carry on my grandfather's radical convictions.

But I also wondered about those convictions. The Socialists and Wobblies had supported women's suffrage but had opposed feminism, including the female Socialists. That was what had defeated them, I believed, more than the Klan or the Justice Department: the twin monsters of male supremacy and white supremacy. These would have to be defeated for any permanent change in the United States. Women's liberation and black liberation would have to be central to the new revolution.

The freedom of women would require a social revolution. A social revolution would require liberated women. The two were inseparable. That was why no revolution had triumphed and created real freedom and equality, not the Leninist nor the Trotskyist nor the Third World liberation movements. Perhaps China, perhaps Vietnam, I thought but also doubted. Control of women was too much for the men to give up, even when they condemned authoritarianism and militarism in theory as did Marx and Engels, Lenin, Fanon, and the Wobblies. A special reserve of my anger was directed at Freud, also formerly one of my heroes, for having labeled women "hysterical" when they resisted their "natural" roles. Then there was Marx, who told his daughter that his favorite virtue in a man was strength and in a woman weakness, although what he hated most in a person was servility. And Che, too, who wrote in his guerrilla warfare manual: "The woman as a cook can greatly improve the diet and, furthermore, it is easier to keep her in these domestic tasks; one of the problems in guerrilla bands is that all works of a civilian character are scorned by those who perform them."

Male supremacy *was* all-pervasive. Women would have to create an autonomous movement, worldwide, and a new reality in order to even struggle for equality.

V

I did not know how to go about starting a women's liberation group, so two weeks after I arrived in Boston, I put an ad in the local counterculture newspaper, with Dana Densmore. I had met Dana at the draft-resistance office, where she did volunteer draft counseling. Dana was tiny but tough and athletic, a mountain climber. She worked as a computer scientist at MIT. Her husband was a geophysicist and very supportive of her independence. Her mother, Donna Allen, validated everything Dana and I were doing as feminists. Her own activist and intellectual example encouraged me, just knowing women could be like her. I had never even had a female instructor in eight years of university.

Meeting: 4 July 1968
ANNOUNCING:
Formation of the
FEMALE LIBERATION FRONT FOR HUMAN LIBERATION
Goals are personal-social, surely inseparable.
To question:
All phallic social structures in existence.
The historic-psychological role of females.

The ability of any human to be half a person.
To demand:
Free abortion and birth control on request.
Communal raising of children
by both sexes and by people of all ages.
The end of man's exploitation of
human, animal, and natural resources.
For females no longer or have never been able
To Breathe!
(Men are invited to contribute money, materials)

Eight women showed up for the meeting: three Irish-Catholic clerical workers, two single mothers on welfare, one filmmaker. And there were Dana and me. It was amazing how eight women from such different backgrounds could have more in common than not. At some level, we had all experienced the same pain when we discovered we were not considered equal to boys, or when we saw our mothers crushed by abuse or alcoholism, or simply losing hope or a reason to live. We didn't want to watch our daughters lose the light in their eyes or our sons acquire an aggressive glint. And we wanted freedom for ourselves.

Some of the women believed that for women to be liberated we had to validate women's experiences, to change social definitions about women's work, and to raise the status of housework, childbearing, motherhood, changing diapers by demanding that women be paid for those services. I disagreed.

"Those tasks should be validated for men's participation. The whole society must be organized to participate in them. To promote traditional female roles as positive would be to validate what already exists—slavery," I insisted. I could trace my rejection of marriage in a straight line back to reading *The Second Sex* in the summer of 1963. I came to understand that the family as an institution, not just my own family or my own marriage, was the root of women's subjugation. Women were reduced to their "natural" function and thereby dehumanized. Their sole power lay in sexuality and childbearing. Reduced to those functions women atrophied and became twisted, indeed became oppressors, particularly of their children. They lived through their sons, who become their fantasy lovers, and they formed daughters in their own twisted image.

One of the women said: "A woman begs for someone to talk with, just a moment of friendship. A man thinks a screw job is what she needs. She submits to it in hopes to talk afterwards, but afterwards he has better things to do, like smoke grass or go see another woman or sleep. And she ends up as lonely as before the encounter. There is nothing more sickening than the male assumption of the magic of his cock. It is something I have tolerated as a form of illness in men for years and for which I now have utter contempt."

I told them about my radical activities and how they led me to see that women's liberation would be necessary for a social revolution to be realized. "I was so wrong to assume that women were liberated in Cuba because of the revolution. There is no promised land."

The working-class women at the meeting suggested that we integrate Boston bars that did not allow women. One said, "I can drink any man under the table." I read aloud from Valerie Solanas's *S.C.U.M. Manifesto,* and they loved it. We discussed picketing the Playboy Club and studying karate together, forming street patrols to escort women walking alone, organizing prostitutes. And we decided to start a journal.

I suggested we read *The Second Sex* and discuss it for the next meeting. The filmmaker told us that in de Beauvoir's new book, *Force of Circumstance,* she had written that the greatest achievement of her life was her relationship with Sartre. Of course, Sartre would never say that his greatest achievement in life was his relationship with her. I was disappointed in my mentor.

I told the women about losing custody of my daughter, about being condemned by my husband and his family, and how I had lost her for going off on a trip by myself. "Men have always gone on the road or off to sea without consequences. They are heroes, from Ulysses to Kerouac. A woman who ventures forth on a quest is considered a deserter."

The second meeting was even more exciting than the first one. Two of the new women were computer programmers, another was a biophysicist, two more women on welfare, even a working prostitute, and a poet. Betsy and Marilyn, the two women on welfare, were very strong and involved in the local branch of the National Welfare Rights Organization. They brought their kids along—each had a daughter. The poet, Gail, was a lesbian activist with the Daughters of Bilitis. She had been organizing for years in Boston's gay bars, trying to bring hope and courage to other gays, counseling them about alcoholism and suicide. She believed that many homosexuals, male and female, would support female liberation.

Later on that year, when we needed money to repay me for the printing costs of our journal, we held a benefit, showing a feature-length documentary, *The Queen,* about a female impersonator beauty contest.

"The Queen"   Monday-September 30-ONLY
Benefit showing for FEMALE LIBERATION
Kenmore Sq. Theater

The Drag Queen Is Everywoman.
To please "The Man" wear a mask.
A Queen chooses the slavery of a female.
We are born slaves.
We are whores—A hot water bottle for your bed.
We are pimps—Filling your ego with hot air.
We are dolls—to be dressed in pretties for each new
occasion.
THE QUEEN IS EVERYWOMAN
$2.00 for women and homosexuals, $3.00 for others

We were surprised by our success. Both shows sold out, and we made enough money to print the second issue of the journal. The audience was diverse: male and female homosexuals, heterosexual couples, students, groups of women.

In retrospect, it's amazing to see the seeds of feminist activism, gay liberation, feminist theory articulated, as action-oriented gestures, by our group in 1968.

VI

All of us in the group felt the need to link up with other women's groups that we heard existed. Luckily, we found out about the first national women's liberation organizing meeting, which was to be held early in August at Sandy Springs, Maryland. The gathering was small and by invitation only. We had not been invited by the organizers. But Dana Densmore's mother, Donna Allen, had been invited. She arranged for Dana and me to go in her place. They didn't know what they were in for.

The twenty New Left women, from recently formed women's groups in New York, Washington, D.C., Chicago, Baltimore, and

Gainesville, Florida, had known each other for years from being involved in the Civil Rights movement, in Mississippi Summer, and in the Students for a Democratic Society. All in their mid and late twenties like Dana and me, their main concern appeared to be how to avoid becoming "man-haters." They seemed worried that they might be accused of it; to me it seemed that they already hated or distrusted men.

The main organizer was Marilyn Webb from Washington, D.C., SDS. All I knew about her was a June 1968 article in SDS's *New Left Notes*, "Women: We Have a Common Enemy," in which she called on radical women to unite with men for women's liberation. She wrote: "We have developed our own kind of femininity and enjoy being women who love men and do not see them as the enemy. We are not the cold, gray-suited women of the Twenties, nor the 'masculinized' ones of the present. Staid suits have been replaced by the colorful dress of a turned-on generation of women who are asserting themselves as females as well as intellectuals."

Dana and I came on strong. The first thing we did was to read a passage on sex from Solanas's *S.C.U.M. Manifesto*:

> Sex is not part of a relationship; on the contrary, it is a solitary experience, non-creative, a gross waste of time. The female can easily—far more easily than she may think—condition away her sex drive, leaving her completely cool and cerebral and free to pursue truly worthy relationships and activities; but the male, who seems to dig women sexually and who seeks constantly to arouse them, stimulates the highly-sexed female to frenzies of lust, throwing her into a sex bag from which few women ever escape. Sex is the refuge of the mindless. And the more mindless the woman, the more deeply embedded in the male 'culture,' in short, the nicer she is, the more sexual she is. The nicest women in our 'society' are raving sex maniacs. But, being just awfully, awfully nice they don't, of course, descend to fucking—that's uncouth—rather they make love, commune by means of their bodies and establish sensual rapport.

We hit a nerve. Those radical women were horrified and did not appreciate Valerie's humor nor the way she used words as a tactic to raise consciousness. Yet these women appeared to have more contempt and lack of hope for men than I'd ever imagined having. I suggested that women force men to raise children, and insist that they work in the day-care centers we envisaged, so that men would become civilized and sensitized by seeing life grow. They nearly all believed that men would desert or harm the children, even let them starve, or pervert them. I had never thought that of men. For all my resentment about my ex-husband, I knew he did not behave that way with our daughter. If they believed men were so inherently evil, what were they doing with men in their lives?

I told them I felt they were self-righteous, thinking that women were morally and biologically superior to men. They refused to accept that women were socialized to be caretakers and that men could be, too. Being responsible for children would make men change, I argued. But those women were not yet willing to give up their control over someone weaker than themselves, their children, and unwilling to admit that men were human, too. Dana pointed out that women could not be solely responsible for the survival of the human race while men made war and controlled everything. I said that both women and men must be liberated so we could strike at the real enemy—the state with its power elites that kept us all down.

Toward the end of the meeting the women were a little less afraid of us. They were impressive women, but they conceived of a women's movement in only two ways. I disagreed with both. They saw the potential of organizing a mass movement of women against the war and against racism on the basis of women being mothers of boys who die in war, and of being sisters across racial boundaries. On the other hand, they wanted to organize very private consciousness-raising groups of like-thinking movement women, women like themselves, to share their complaints about their oppressive private situations, to let off a little steam. In my view, they were not talking about a women-centered movement for the liberation of women.

I was troubled—as all the women at the conference were—that we were uniformly white-identified. Except for me, all were from middle-class backgrounds. Most of the women who had joined our group in Boston came from working-class backgrounds, but all were white. Yet I was also bothered that the women at the Sandy Springs meeting said that they believed black women and other minority women would reject women's liberation and accuse white radical women of racism and selfishness for talking about "our own personal problems." They felt we shouldn't even go public until we had linked up with leading black women and obtained their "approval." I suggested Flo Kennedy and Shirley Chisholm—black women who were also outspoken feminists— but they were dismissed as "NOW reformists."

In the end they decided to go ahead and organize a national conference at Thanksgiving in Chicago, and to try to persuade Kathleen Cleaver and other Black Panther women to participate. I objected to Kathleen Cleaver, insisting she was no feminist, rather an honorary male. That shocked them. It disturbed me that they wanted Kathleen Cleaver's stamp of approval. It seemed to me they were patronizing black women.

Yet the conference was an important experience for me. I left confident that most of the women there would become active in a real women's liberation movement if we could get it going. I thought of Frantz Fanon's observation that the oppressed were inherently radical, and that it was a matter of removing masks to uncover that radicalism. I believed that radical feminism lay behind the masks of the women at that conference.

VII

After the Sandy Springs conference, I went to New York to visit Kathie Sarachild of the women's group Redstockings, who had been at the conference and had been more sympathetic to Dana and me than most of the others. She put me in touch with Ti-Grace Atkinson, president of the National Organization for Women, who, to my surprise, was supporting Valerie Solanas, along with black civil rights lawyer Flo Kennedy, also an active NOW member. I met with Ti-Grace and Flo and they explained to me that Valerie was confused and unstable and not very communicative, but they arranged for me to visit her at the New York Women's House of Detention, where she was being held until her sanity hearing.

I was allowed to talk with Valerie only on a telephone and to see her through a scratched and filthy Plexiglas window. I don't think she figured out in the five minutes we shared who I was or what I was doing there. All I could make out clearly were her piercing black eyes. I had the odd feeling of looking into a mirror. They were the same as my eyes. The experience was sobering. I saw madness in Valerie's eyes. I saw my mother's eyes. I identified with her explosion, which came at the same time as my own. I felt almost as if she were in prison in my stead, and I felt deeply grateful to her. In a strange way, her act of violence had quelled my own growing personal rage, directing me away from violence and toward collective action. I realized that Valerie's act had marked her. She had gone over some line and probably would not be able to become a whole person, much less a leader in the women's liberation movement. But I felt a responsibility and commitment to defend and support her and to give voice and credence to the concerns that drove her to the extreme. If we were lucky, I thought, she might even recover and direct her energy and anger to the new movement which had come too late for her.

As Dana and I drove in silence back to Boston, I pondered the fact that Valerie had ended up in an institution for the "hopelessly and criminally insane." Neither Che nor Huey nor Fidel nor Mao nor Stokely ever had to face that fate—jail, prison, even death, but never a mental institution. Why should a woman who tried to kill a man in the name of a cause be classified as insane? Valerie disappeared after she was freed, only to turn up dead as a bag lady in San Francisco in 1988.

Ti-Grace and Flo felt as I did. I immediately liked the two women. Flo was past middle-age and very wise, an outspoken feminist who had remained single and childless all her life. Ti-Grace was warm and generous. She put me up in her flat and gave me a set of keys to stay there anytime. I stayed with her for three days of nonstop talking. Ti-Grace was a few years older than me, a tall, attractive strawberry blond, intelligent and intellectual. She came from a wealthy Louisiana oil family and despised the social role cut out for her. She had never married and opposed the institution on principle. Ti-Grace and Kathie took me to women's meetings and introduced me to dozens of feminists, some reformists, some radicals, some extremists.

VIII

Only a month after we had begun meeting, our still unnamed women's group published the first issue of our still unnamed journal, eighty pages, the first avowedly feminist journal since the nineteenth century. I typed all the articles on an IBM Composer I had gotten for a weekend on loan, pretending to be a prospective buyer, and I paid for the printing from my remaining savings. We published all material submitted by our group members, whether their own work or something from another source they thought important. We eschewed all editorial policy or any particular "line."

The most controversial stance taken in the journal, and the one which mythologized our group as having taken "vows of celibacy," involved our essays supporting celibacy. Dana argued in her essay, "On Celibacy," that "sexual liberation" had nothing to do with women's liberation. On the contrary, it was a new strategy to maintain male supremacy and to control women. "This is a call not for celibacy but for an acceptance of celibacy as an honorable alternative, one preferable to the degradation of most male-female sexual relationships."

My essay with much the same message was titled "Asexuality." I reasoned: "Considering what one must go through to attain a relationship of whole to whole in this society, or any other I know of, the most 'normal' person, the most moral, is the celibate."

In pairs and alone we sold the journal on the streets of Cambridge and Boston, as Valerie had done with her *S.C.U.M. Manifesto* in Manhattan. We engaged women in discussions of women's liberation and fended off catcalls, slurs, and even physical attacks by men. Within two weeks we collected nearly half its cost.

At the end of August, I went to New York to sell the journal and place it in bookstores. But I ended up spending most of the time glued to Flo's TV watching the police riot in Chicago at the Democratic convention. Antiwar protesters and young McCarthy supporters clogged the parks and streets of Chicago and were beaten brutally by Mayor Daley's police. The event lay outside my orbit, as I soared in the world of women's liberation, but it was to me a parallel breaking of structures.

In New York there had grown up a kind of myth about the "Boston women," as they called our group. No one could believe that we had put out an eighty-page journal. I heard outrageous stories, for instance, that we had organized prostitutes and black women into secret revolutionary cells. In fact, there was one prostitute, and one black woman who had recently joined our group, but our core group numbered only eight. We did not yet even regard ourselves as a "group," and certainly not as an organization. In fact, we stressed the importance of individuality as the source of our energy and power and feared "group thinking." I never wanted to fall into the evangelical insanity I had experienced as a child. I knew that even if the other women abandoned our feminist project, I would keep going, publish the journal, hawk it on the streets. Each of them felt the same. We strongly believed that only when each one of us felt autonomous and powerful could we multiply that power by joining together, but that our separate selves should never be submerged, not for any cause, ever. So the myths about us, while amusing, were also disturbing, particularly the myth of me as a leader. I did not feel like nor want to be a leader, whatever that meant. And to me it meant a patriarchal construct.

IX

In early September, a television station flew me to New York to be in a discussion with Betty Friedan, the author of the best-selling *Feminine Mystique* and a founder of NOW, and with Rona Jaffe, the novelist. I was reluctant to be in a public situation with two NOW feminists with whom I was certain to disagree. Ti-Grace had told me that Betty and other founders of NOW were hostile to women's liberation and that Ti-Grace and Flo were under attack for supporting Valerie Solanas. Nevertheless, they encouraged me to go on the show, and to be as unity oriented as possible, while raising radical feminist ideas.

Betty Friedan, however, had no desire for friendly gestures toward or unity with a radical feminist. She began a verbal assault on me in the dressing room when I refused to have makeup applied, and she did not stop until the show was over. I was dressed in my very best army surplus white cotton sailor trousers and a white man's shirt. She said that I, and "scruffy feminists" like me, were giving the movement a bad name. Ironically, I felt as if I were back under the thumb of my husband, who had constantly criticized my appearance.

I told Betty Friedan that I thought she feared losing her celebrity leadership position to a movement of women committed to collective action without leaders. She called me an anarchist; I agreed with her that's what I was. She was steaming when she huffed out of the studio.

The whole experience led me to question the viability of television for talking about the movement if it only pitted feminist against feminist. But a week later, I was on another airplane to New York for another television show.

X

One night near midnight, I heard noises at the door, and found my neighbor and a member of our women's group, whom I shall call Susan, crumpled on my doorstep. She was bruised and battered, her clothes torn and muddy. She begged me not to tell her husband, saying he was upstairs with the children asleep. She was a Boston Irish native, and confided to us that she had supported her "illegitimate" children by working as a "call girl" until she married her present husband, an Irish factory worker. Susan wrote poetry. She had brought some of her poems to the first meeting and all of us were stunned by her consciousness of women's oppression. We had published them in the first issue of the journal. Susan was a fragile, quiet-spoken blond woman, who could dress up and transform herself into a sexy bombshell—a "female impersonator," as we came to call the result after seeing *The Queen*.

I calmed Susan, ran a hot bubble bath, and coaxed her into it, massaging her neck and shoulders. She blurted out that she'd been raped.

"We have to report it," I said.

"No cops, no way. To them women exist only to be fucked," she shrieked and began sobbing again. "Anyway, the cops around here know I used to hustle. And I've just washed away the evidence." But I convinced her to file a report.

"I will do it for all women, to raise consciousness," Susan agreed.

The police treated Susan as a suspect rather than the victim. Tests were made, reports filed. We stayed cool and spent hours filling out forms. Susan filed for legal aid and was assigned a pro bono lawyer.

"I have to tell you something. I know the man who raped me. I know his name," Susan said at the end of the exhausting week. She said he was a "john" from the old days, an English professor who claimed to admire the poetry he had seen in our journal, and said he could get her into the Harvard poetry workshop. He had called her to go out to dinner to discuss it. But with a knife to her throat, he raped her on the banks of the Charles River.

"Now that I've told you the truth, you won't want to support me," she said.

"It would be easier if he were a stranger, but at least we have a case now that we have a name. You'll have to give the police and the lawyer his name."

Her lawyer was an idealistic young man involved with Planned Parenthood, interested in establishing a test case based on the principle of the integrity of a woman's body, whether on a date, whether raped by a husband, or even a prostitute forced to have sex against her will. None of us had even considered rape as something that could happen to prostitutes by their customers, or to wives by their husbands.

The trial day arrived. The courtroom was packed with scandal seekers. The professor-defendant had hired a well-known criminal lawyer and had lined up an array of character witnesses. I was Susan's only witness. The jury was half women.

Our strategy was for me, as an expert witness, to present a female liberation perspective about rape. Susan's lawyer put me on the stand and questioned me for an hour. I traced the history of patriarchy and woman as property.

We won, and a sweet victory it was, even though the penalty was light—six months in jail, suspended, and a $200 fine. But Susan was satisfied.

After the trial, I took the court transcript and rewrote what I had said into my first manifesto on female liberation. "Caste and Class: Female Liberation as the Basis for Social Revolution."

XI

After I had written the essay, and inspired by Susan's case, at our next women's group meeting I told my own hidden story of rape.

For my last year of high school, after my mother became nonfunctional and violent from drinking, I went to live with my sister and to work in Oklahoma City. I'd never had a boyfriend, not even dates, although I had a lot of male buddies. Then a boy who was one of a clique of seniors from Northwest High, the rich kids' school, who regularly attended the Sunday night Baptist Training Union that I never missed, asked me out. He was movie-star handsome in a kind of swarthy, rugged way, Marlon Brando as a biker in *The Wild One*. He always arrived on his stripped Harley or in the '52 Chevy convertible he'd souped up. I thought he was far beyond my reach.

Then one warm spring night he walked over and said to me: "Can I ask you something? Would you go out with me after Training Union?" For a full minute my voice was trapped in my throat. He stopped walking and stared into my eyes. "Yes," I said.

He drove a long way. He wanted to show me where he lived, way up in a new subdivision northwest of the city. He stopped in front of a big brick house but we didn't go in.

"My mom's a lush. She'll be drunk by now, and my old man will be asleep." I felt relieved that we shared the tragedy of drunken mothers, but I didn't speak of mine.

The top of the convertible was down, the air warm, the stars glittering above. It was so romantic, like something out of the movies I dreamed of experiencing.

"It's pretty up here," I said.

"You want to see a really nice spot?"

"Sure."

He drove across the Northwest Highway and off on a dirt road to a bare hilltop. There were no houses, no cars, only the city spread out below. He kissed me, a long, lovely kiss. My first real kiss. His lips were soft, his skin as smooth as a baby's. He stopped and opened the glove compartment. He took out a small, flat box and opened it. I couldn't tell what it was. A ring? Was he going to propose? I was overwhelmed. What would I say?

"Have you ever seen one?" he asked.

"What is it?" Extreme anxiety gripped me. Something was wrong. This wasn't a marriage proposal but something else.

He took the thing out and placed it in the palm of my hand. It felt like a deflated balloon. And then I knew it was a condom. I'd never seen one, but I'd heard the girls talk about them. One girl's words rang in my ears: "Look where to run when they pull a rubber out." I automatically looked out into the empty darkness around us. He unbuttoned his trousers and took out his erect penis and slipped on the condom. Time stopped. I stared. I had never seen a penis. He gripped my wrist.

"This way you won't get pregnant," he said. I jerked away and grabbed the door handle.

"No," I said. He held my arms. I knew absolutely that I did not want to go all the way with him, or anyone. I had not known how I would respond in such a situation, but now I knew.

"No, no, no," I yelled. I heard the echo of my voice, louder and louder, until he put one hand over my mouth and another around my throat.

And he penetrated me causing a sharp pain. Fats Domino's voice from the radio sang, "Ain't that a shame?"

After I finished my story, each of the women told her own story of rape and near-rape, often by close relatives.

XII

Our group turned attention to the second issue of the journal. In the first nameless issue, we had listed twenty possible titles thrown out by members of the group, deciding to discuss them and to solicit reactions from readers: The Fourth World, The Fourth Dimension, The End of History, We Shall Undermine, Listen Man, Shut Up, The Key to Liberation, You Listen Awhile, It's My Turn Now, Women Together, Women Unite, Women Strike Sex, Females Against Sex, Man Listen, Sisters Hear. But the name we finally chose was from a four-line poem of mine in the first journal: "It's all over now/No more fun and games/No more manly fame/I am mine." We chose *NO MORE FUN AND GAMES: A Journal of Female Liberation.*

Our main problem was money to produce the journal and to organize, but help soon came with a new member. As the Thanksgiving 1968 Chicago national women's conference drew near, a newly hired organizer, Helen Kritzler, showed up, saying she was in Boston to fundraise for it and wanted my help. She was going to see Abby Rockefeller, who lived in Cambridge, and wanted me to go along.

"One of *the* Rockefellers?" I asked. "I don't think I'd be the right person," I said and gestured to my oversized army surplus trousers and shirt, my combat boots. Helen said not to worry, that Abby was already active in the Civil Rights and antiwar movements, and that she gave most of her trust income to organizing projects, especially the Boston draft resistance.

Abby and I talked for three hours. What I said to her gave voice and concreteness to her own anger and thinking. She wrote a check for the Chicago conference and joined our women's group.

After a tense discussion in our group, I decided not to go to the Chicago Women's Liberation conference. We decided Dana Densmore should go, distribute our journal, and report back to us. We feared that our group might end up meaning just Roxanne Dunbar to other women, which would defeat our whole attempt to become a powerful force of equal individuals. I felt I had made many mistakes that I hoped I would not repeat, the main one being getting into the spotlight.

But I was sorry I had not gone when Dana returned from that historic first national women's conference. Two hundred women were there, from thirty cities in the United States, and even some from Canada. Dana felt that many were hung up on sex and men, but not all. She was impressed with Anne Koedt, who wrote "The Myth of the Vaginal Orgasm," which our group had discussed and distributed. Anne and Ti-Grace Atkinson had organized a workshop at the Chicago conference to discuss the paper, and the meeting went on into the night. Dana said she had proposed that celibacy be a choice for women, which was received as far more controversial than suggestions of sadomasochism, group sex, or homosexuality. "The myth of sexual liberation has so brainwashed them that they cannot distinguish between celibacy and frigidity," Dana said.

Dana was also drawn to Shulamith Firestone's argument that pregnancy was destructive and oppressive and that women should choose not to bear children or raise them. In another workshop on alternative lifestyles, all agreed that standard marriage arrangements should go, although most felt that marriage itself should not be condemned. Dana said all the workshops were riveting, but that the plenary sessions were chaotic. The feminists rejected the left while the New Left women regarded consciousness raising and women-centered movement as bourgeois and counterrevolutionary. Arguments had polarized, just as at the Sandy Springs meeting.

The women in our group concluded that the radical feminist/New Left split was a false dichotomy and that a third alternative was necessary. We argued that a women-centered, anti-imperialist movement with the goal of socialism was necessary and possible. The main lesson we took from the first national women's conference was to remain autonomous and develop our own theory and base of operations. We surmised that if we were on to something, the movement would follow. Meanwhile, our journal formed the core of our identity.

Soon the journal was no longer our only means of communicating female liberation. Abby bought us an electric A.B. Dick mimeograph machine and an IBM Selectric typewriter so we could create and print timely commentaries to distribute locally. The New England Free Press, one of the major radical printing houses and distribution centers, agreed to print and distribute some of our essays, the first being my "Female Liberation as the Basis for Social Revolution."

Abby offered the basement of her Cambridge house near Harvard Square for office space. The basement had a separate outside door, allowing Abby privacy, which had not been possible in my flat.

Each day various members of our group emerged from this underground workshop and hit the streets, selling the journal and handing out the informational flyers we produced by the thousands on our new mimeo.

"We need a name. Our group is more than just the journal. Everyone's calling us whatever they want, like 'Boston women' or 'female liberation.' If we don't name ourselves others will do it for us," Dana said at a meeting in the new office.

"What's wrong with calling ourselves female liberation?" I asked.

"But that's the name we are promoting for the whole women's movement, not just our group. The movement is the organism and we're a cell of it," Dana said, sounding like the scientist she was.

"I almost feel like a member of a cell hidden out in this windowless basement," said Jeanne, who considered herself a hard-core anarchist.

Since Abby's address was 16 Lexington we decided to call our group Cell 16. Then when people asked about the other fifteen cells, we could make them guess.

Cell 16 was considered by other women's groups to be heavy on "theory," but like Redstockings, NOW, and Radical Women in New York, we were action-driven. We had confronted the issue of rape by defending Ellen, we had protested women's fashions and advertising-ordained images by publicizing *The Queen,* and even by the way we presented ourselves in public.

Then we organized our first real street action—a picket of the Playboy Club in Boston. For that we were featured as female lunatics in the morning paper. We were protesting pornography. Our group quickly became high-profile and controversial, not just among the antiwar organizations led mainly by men, but among the other radical women organizing women's projects in the Boston area. They were secretively clustered in "consciousness-raising" groups. Our group was contemptuous of what we called their "T-groups," which we considered touchy-feely self-indulgence. We thought that we were more revolutionary and pushed for more radical women's liberation positions.

XIII

Then we took on the issue of street violence against women. Abby Rockefeller and her roommate, Jayne West, had been studying tae kwan do for a few months. On a cold, late November night after a meeting in Boston, Abby, Dana, and I, with a few other women, were walking along when suddenly a car full of men pulled up close to the curb and moved along with us, the men taunting us and yelling obscenities. I ran toward the car and jammed my fist through the open window, aiming for the driver's giddy grin. He easily evaded my swing. I stood my ground, fists on my hips, and yelled at them.

"Who the hell do you think you are, talking to us uninvited?"

Blinded by fury, years of accumulated fury at men for intruding upon my privacy in the streets, I really forgot momentarily that the other women were with me. I had no fear. Then the driver opened his door and in one seemingly well-practiced movement, reached down behind his seat and brought up a tire iron. He stood on the curb facing me, inches from me. He was tall and strong, poised with his muscular arm bracing the weapon above his head like the Arm & Hammer logo. I refused to budge. I saw his eyes move from my face to the side and then I heard a thump as he brought the tire iron down. It stopped in midair, just short of my skull. A look of shock spread over his face. Abby had stopped the blow with a tae kwan do defense called an "upperparts block." The man's smirk crumbled in terror. He jumped back into the car and screeched off, leaving the smell of burning rubber. Then he skidded to a stop halfway up the block and yelled at the top of his voice, the words echoing off the buildings: "Fucking lezzies!"

We checked the welt on the side of Abby's forearm. Her face flashed joy, and anger—at me. I felt both foolish and exhilarated. Women defending women was something new and wonderful to us. For me, being defended by a woman was one of the most satisfying moments of my life up to then.

After that, we formed a women's class at Abby's tae kwan do studio and promoted self-defense for women. Some of us went out on street patrols to escort and defend women, and to recruit them to our class and to female liberation.

XIV

December 1968. Two deep-winter New England experiences forced me to face the fact of class differences among women and began to make me wary of the direction women's liberation was taking.

Smith College, western Massachusetts. I sat on the edge of an avocado-colored, velvet-upholstered French provincial chair. I was at this all-women's college to answer questions about women's liberation from the daughters of the ruling class, many of them the future wives of presidents of the country and of corporations, of senators and governors. I was uncomfortable in the elegant residence hall. "Sisterhood," the term created by women's liberationists in New York, had its limitations.

We filed into the formal dining room. Some twenty women lived in each of the several residence houses, with a house mother in each. In preparing the formal dinners, they learned about flower arrangements, table settings, serving food and wine. They placed me at the head of the table as the guest of honor, the student president at the other end. Bowls of creamy clam chowder were served first, and we ate in silence. The main course was rare prime rib of roast. I declined a serving and asked for more clam chowder.

A woman asked: "Are you a vegetarian?" The silence was broken and all eyes focused on me.

"I don't eat dead animals, not unless I'm willing to kill and dress them myself, and I can't stomach doing that." Several women poked bloody slices of meat to the sides of their plates.

"Is it a religious matter?"

"No, I am not religious," I said.

"Do you think everyone in women's liberation should be vegetarians?"

"I don't believe in rules of behavior. I think each person should be fully aware of what's going on and of the implications of every act and word, and make decisions accordingly."

Sears. The edge of Cambridge. The day after the gig at Smith, I accompanied Betsy and her daughter to a National Welfare Rights Organization demonstration in front of a huge Sears store. It wasn't clear to me why they had chosen Sears for the demonstration—they were demanding supplemental funds from the welfare department for winter clothing for their children. There were around three hundred women, about a third black and Puerto Rican, the rest white—three-fourths of welfare recipients in the Boston area were white.

Suddenly someone yelled through a bull horn. "Let's go. Charge!" I was swept along with the crowd inside the store. Once inside, the women surged into the children's department, taking coats, rubber boots, caps, scarves, long underwear. I watched in amazement as the demonstrators yelled at the saleswomen: "Charge it to welfare!" and left with their loot.

Looting. A shoplift-in. Outlaw women.

Two worlds, the poor and the rich. There was no question that I felt at ease with the looters and an outsider with the rich women. The trick would be to organize the privileged women to join with the poor, otherwise the poor would be once again abandoned.

History Makes Us,
We Make History

Elizabeth (Betita) Martinez

It has been a terrible century, has it not? In the sense of: awesome. Not just bad, more like *extreme*. Such high hopes of profound change, such setbacks—the clock of justice leaping forward, then grinding in reverse. Revolutions rising and falling, leaders rising and falling, hopes rising and falling and rising again.

This I have come to know in the course of living through five international wars, six social movements in these United States, and seven attempts to build socialism in other countries. (Yes, I went to see those societies for myself, from Cuba to Russia to China.) Here at home I spent ten years in each of three movements: the Black civil rights struggle, the Chicano movimiento, and the Left effort to build a revolutionary party. The struggle that grips me most today is the one to uproot racism, that pox on this land where I grew up brown. Fighting it soon became linked to women's struggles; the two cannot honestly be divided—although some would have it otherwise.

From all this living and struggling, one lesson looms large: there is no separating my life from history. There is no separating anyone's life from history.

When World War II ended, humanity longed for peace and created the United Nations to help that dream come true. So my first job just out of college had to be working for the UN, for five years, researching the effects of colonialism upon Africa. Later the postwar smugness of white middle-class U.S. society sparked an alienated, mostly white middle-class generation of poets and pot, anger and angst. So I had to link up with the Beats of Lower East Side New York in the 1950s, while working in publishing and the photography world.

Then great mass movements exploded in these United States, sparked by the spirit of upheaval around the world. So I went to work, first part-time and then full-time, for the Student Nonviolent Coordinating Committee (SNCC), and from there to the movimiento in New Mexico. And when most of the mass movements declined in the early

1970s, it seemed clear to many who had been fighting for social change that we needed more committed, permanent organizations, in particular a Marxist party, and so I joined one.

Thus it went, on to the present, together with the inescapable awareness of being a woman in a world dominated by men no matter how revolutionary they might otherwise claim to be. *Chingado,* I had more wondrous and disastrous relationships than you can count—with poets, artists, revolutionaries (a few really were), junkies, and various combinations thereof. Not to mention a beautiful and amazing daughter who survived us all, Tessa, now a fine actress. Not to mention the hundreds, maybe thousands, of youth whom I have met or come to work with, and their passion for justice today.

It's been almost half a century of hating injustice, laughing at our own mistakes, loving the beauty of the planet, and cherishing so many *compas.* Out of all that have come many writings, with the early books on the Mississippi Summer Project and on revolutionary Cuba published under the name Elizabeth Sutherland because I thought it would have a more literary ring in the Eurocentric publishing world. Who would publish someone named Martinez then? Also out of that half-century came many letters, poems, and diary entries, which whisper some truths.

1958. In that Lower East Side Manhattan world of Beat poets, junkie painters, LSD experiments (in my living room, yet), where Black and White hung together better than anywhere else in society, I found my poet too. Small, with wild eyes and long spells of madness, soon lost to heroin, but for a while I loved his fire and stood guard over it. He and I went to Cuba together, three months after the January 1959 triumph of the Revolution, and that lit a flame that never went out. Until then life had seemed to leave me ill-defined. The UN had remained dominated by imperialist powers, not the road to peace and justice I sought. Cuba changed that. I began to see who I was.

September 15, 1960. An experience she called mystical: In Cuba, again, two years after the Revolution. She was on a bus tour of the island with a load of lefties from many countries—middle-aged people nostalgically singing Spanish Civil War songs and lumbering off the bus to look at some fishing cooperative or to be herded into their hotel for the night. It was about the fifth day of the tour and the bus was headed for that night's sleeping place. Nobody was singing; it was dark inside the bus except for little lights at some seats. The feeling came like a flood, a feeling of unity that she called god. She waited for it to recede, not trusting it, but time passed and the feeling lingered. If it could be defined, it was unity with the Cuban night: the hard bright stars and the softness together made the Revolution.

Her lover was with her and she told him about it, but he could hear only Church talk. It seems some things are not to be shared.

> *What can be shared? And with whom? How?*
> *Were ancient people as lonely as modern people?*
> *Are men ever as lonely as women can be?*

1964. I could no longer see my life separate from history. But where was I in this history? Whose is my struggle? Questions rampaged through my mind, way down under the surface, but on top it was one big love affair with revolution and social justice and the infinite courage of these 1960s. I had begun working full-time in the Black civil rights movement, with SNCC, and it would have been foolish to ask, "Are you willing to die for justice?" Of course I was—so were thousands of people in this nation and all around the world.

There were also hours of sheer delight in being alive and kinda crazy.

New York City, August 27, 1966. I took my daughter, Tessa, and her friend Valerie to the Beatles movie *A Hard Day's Night*. Nobody screamed, but they sat there speechless. When it was over we all got up without a word and RAN out of the theater and across Second Avenue, Valerie in front and then me and then Tessa, running running up three blocks to the car which we jumped into and I started it in a sec and drove sixty miles an hour up Fifth Avenue to Doubleday bookstore, which is open until midnight, yeah yeah yeah. And I parked the car where it says NO PARKING NO STANDING NO LIVING NO NOTHING and we all raced into the store with Tessa leading this time and zoomed up to the record counter where we collapsed with our tongues hanging out.

WHERE ARE YOUR BEATLES RECORDS SIR??? There it was, the movie sound track itself, what could you want in life now? WRAP IT PLEASE. The open-mouthed clerk held out the change but we had no time for that, had to get home to play it play it play it. So I drove up Park Avenue through 3 red lights, Valerie had to go home because her mother doesn't believe in beatles and she was late for dinnah, and now I am here with the music and beloved Tessa and 2 jumping kittens.

and there is no death tonight.

Sometimes life seems to come down to great simplicities, like: figuring out how to be useful to humanity. But that can be very complicated, even painful. How to be useful, with whom, and under what conditions? For example: in 1966 when SNCC voted to expel all white staff members it did not address the question of two Chicanas on staff, including me. I wasn't Black but I wasn't white either, what the hell was I? It was too early, perhaps, to expect an answer to that from SNCC. Then and in years to come, those questions continued to roll in and out, like a relentless tide.

The next year brought the women's movement home for me, through New York Radical Women, a small but potent group in the "consciousness-raising" tradition that included Chude Pam Allen, Kathie Amatniek Sarachild, Shulamith Firestone, Anne Koedt. It was almost entirely white but that did not bother me at first. So many moving moments, as when Shulie told of going to an Orthodox Jewish school where the boys said in morning prayers, "Thank you, lord, for not making me a woman." I still see her sad, angry eyes and dark hair when she spoke.

Then came the night that Martin Luther King was assassinated, April 4, 1968. The streets of New York and the nation, the hearts of people everywhere, were filled with rage. But at our women's meeting, nobody mentioned King's death, no one said we should talk about it before our usual business (some who might have done so were absent). Stunned and speechless, I left and walked down 14th Street on the Lower East Side toward the subway. Big glass store windows were asking me to break them with any handy object. It was a night of more anguish and anger than I could remember. It was a night to realize that if the struggle against sexism did not see itself as profoundly entwined with the fight against racism, I was gone.

Three months later I went to New Mexico and the Chicano movement; the question of Who-am-I had been demanding such a move for a long time. Nuevo Mexico, New Mexico, brought love at first sight. When I arrived on the plane after dark and saw the silhouetted mountain range called Blood of Christ, Sangre de Cristo, there was no doubt: I smelled *Home*.

I settled in impoverished northern New Mexico, 150-year-old center of resistance to the Anglo occupation, to start a newspaper of the struggle whose name in Spanish means: Cry of the North, *El Grito del Norte*. We of the newspaper often went to the village of Tierra Amarilla, Yellow Earth, where armed Mexicans had been rising up against the gringo land robbery since 1848. Just the year before, on June 5, 1967, they took over the village courthouse. Tanks with a thousand National Guardsmen were sent down the narrow dirt roads to crush a spirit of resistance that had no intentions of dying. It was nurtured then, as before, by poverty, patience, and a capacity for surprise no outsider could foresee. I learned of a whole new world in northern New Mexico.

Tierra Amarilla at Dusk

Birds make evening noises, tired and dreamy
Fields stretch toward blackening mountains
and dry cows low.
Ugly dogs bark, brown-eyed children whine
Across town, women stoke their wood stoves,
staring into quick flames,
Their old young faces unreadable.

The sun goes down in an orange universe
a young macho walks the dirt road alone
where there is nothing to do at night,
just barren streets, shabby bars, abandoned homes,
a sad brown squatness, an ancestry of failure.

Then I see it!
A big, black top hat sits on the young man's head
crazily crowning his work-shirt and muddy boots.
It says: I am special, rich in my own way,
centuries of pride course through my veins.

And the laughter of survivors rings out in the dusk—
it's those unreadable women who never give up.
My heart runs to meet my love,
this town I love, this Tierra Amarilla.

August 25, 1969. A lot of feminism—both rage and celebration—had traveled with me to New Mexico. The women's movement there was mostly university-based and white at the time, and even independent-spirited Chicanas saw it as alien. They believed that the feminism of those years required a declaration of war on all men, which made no sense in the face of the constant racism against Raza men as well as women. Yet many, especially the younger Chicanas working with *El Grito del Norte,* did recognize the inequality and how male self-respect often rested on the disrespect of females. As for myself, I looked hard at the sexism in the movimiento, and knew a Chicana feminism needed to be born.

I am Elizabeth
Angry and proud and ancient
and beautiful, but not for the reasons you think.

This is the age of newfound heritages
When black calls back to African queens and Nat Turner
When brown calls back to Cuauhtemoc and Zapata
When red calls back to so many bravehearts
But who do I call back to?
What did you men with your history books ever give me
Except a token female who never fought for her kind?
Except "our women," always "our women,"
in postures of maternity, sadness, devotion,
tears for the lost husband or son
"our women," nothing but shadows
reflections of someone else's existence
BASTA!

Sexism from Chicano movement stars sometimes compelled proclamations from me that do not read like news today but at the time were uncommon. So much so, and so threatening to men, that I did not circulate this statement when written in 1970. It became part of a pamphlet on Chicano movement problems distributed four years later.

April 1970. First, we should define sexism. Sexism is an institutionalized social reality, like racism or capitalism or colonialism. It is a system of power relations, the system that says men as a group are superior to women as a group, and therefore deserve certain privileges. That certain social roles should be assigned to men and other roles to women; that women's roles and women's work have less dignity and status than those of men, with the exception of child-bearing (for nine months, a pregnant woman has a certain status); that women are essentially objects, possessions of the man or the male-dominated society.

Women are oppressed primarily by that system and secondly by men who believe in that system. Women *as a group* cannot oppress men *as a group* because—as we said before—sexism is an institutionalized reality, and there are no institutions which give women power over men. . . . This doesn't mean there are not *some* women who oppress *some* men. The rich white woman with a Black chauffeur obviously oppresses him but women as a group cannot oppress men as a group.

There are three major reasons why the oppression of women and sexism must be dealt with in any movement organization (including Chicano groups):

1 Because as people fighting oppression, we must be concerned with all forms of oppression. It is a matter of principle and revolutionary consistency. We cannot have a double standard, we cannot be hypocrites, in the fight against oppression. . . .

2 Because the oppression of women weakens our strength as a group. We have less force and less unity. This is a matter of tactics, not principle, but it is just as important.

3 Because sexism is the cause of serious problems in many organizations. In one case, a man who ran an alternative school eventually forced it to close. He put the women down when they criticized him; he frightened into silence women who might have criticized him; he drove

out women who were hard workers. Although he did
this to a few men also, his basic strength came from getting men on his side, and thus dividing the sexes.

The super-macho is haunted by the need to prove his manhood.
We understand that gringo colonialism and racism have made the
Chicano insecure about his manhood. But it is time to snap: we
can't go on blaming the gringo for this, or defending sexism.

The super-macho is very disturbed by homosexuality. He doesn't
like it in women because that threatens his importance. Women
who do not need men for sexual satisfaction are a put-down in his
mind. Homosexuality in men bothers the super-macho even more.
It challenges his definition of himself and his manhood. The
oppression of homosexuals is wrong.

The more that we free ourselves and our culture from all these
oppressive attitudes, the stronger our movimiento will be.

New Mexico also brought a love affair that seemed uniquely happy
by virtue of our lives spent in joint political work. It ended with dramatic betrayal of the values which the collective built around *El Grito
del Norte* had aimed to observe: among others, absolute honesty in relationships, mutual accountability and respect, no sexism.

The pain faded with new work and the building of lifelong friendships, especially with women. Then another betrayal—this time political—brought more loss and loneliness. This one was a classic of the
movement years, complete with strong suspicion that it had been engi-
neered by a government agent who infiltrated our organization and
then destroyed it. With a move from New Mexico to California came
new hope for me, in a new party-building organization. Ten years later
it too would collapse.

But even as the century ebbs, a whole new life shines before me:
creating tools to empower young people—especially young Latinas—
with knowledge about themselves, about their own history, a knowledge
that they rarely find in school. With such tools they can tear down an
old world and fight for a new one. They can envision the end of inhu-
man history: the countless millennia of domination and suffering.

In these same recent years a song of balance began to hum inside my head, a woman's song. Replacing deadly dogmatisms with a dialectic of human change, I became proud, not ashamed of our long, long march toward the beauty that could be.

> *In China twenty-five years ago they told me:*
> *A communist is straight and sturdy as a pine tree,*
> *supple as the willow.*
> *I have remembered those words a long time.*
> *How splendid to be two kinds of trees at once,*
>
> *Honor the pine-willow,*
> *Seek to be like the pine-willow,*
> *raise your children to be pine-willows,*
> *small or tall.*
>
> *When pine-willows fill the forest*
> *Then human history begins.*

Ambivalence
About Feminism

Barbara Epstein

One day during the spring of 1967, walking down Telegraph Avenue in Berkeley, I met a friend who told me that she and a number of other women had just formed a women's consciousness-raising group. They were mostly women who were involved in the antiwar movement, and wives or girlfriends of male leaders of the movement. She asked if I would like to join. I asked what kinds of issues they talked about. Mostly, she said, about being treated as sex objects by men. I thought: I wish I had their problem. It did not seem possible to say this—so I said that I didn't think the group would be right for me.

I encountered the beginnings of feminism again a few months later, at a youth conference of the Communist Party (of which I was a member). Every summer for the last several years the Party had held a weeklong retreat for Party youth. By 1967 the Communist Party was attracting substantial numbers of young people; there must have been a hundred or more at this retreat, held at a summer camp in upstate New York. Toward the end of the week a group of women demanded that an afternoon be devoted to discussing the problem of sexism in the Party, first in a meeting of women only, then in a meeting of women and men. Many women complained that the men regarded them as sexual objects, as girlfriends or potential girlfriends; they were not taken seriously in political discussions. I remember thinking that in the political circles that I was part of, men tended to assign women to categories: some were seen as sexual beings, and not taken very seriously in political discussions; others were treated as comrades, listened to with respect, and mostly treated as asexual. I knew more about the second category than the first, since that was the one that I belonged to; it seemed to me that in its own way it was as much of a problem as being regarded as a sexual object. But it did not seem possible to talk about this.

I was thinking of leaving the Communist Party, after having been a member for nearly five years, and in fact in a position of leadership for a good part of that time, but not out of feminist dissatisfactions. I felt that the Party was rigid and dogmatic, unable to learn from the movements that were surging around it, and that membership in the Party reinforced my own tendency toward intellectual rigidity. Nevertheless I wanted to be part of the left, and felt ambivalent about the emergence of feminism because, while I thought the issues that were being raised were important, the way in which they were being raised felt like the beginning of a split. I did not want to have to choose between a women's movement and the left; what I wanted was a better left. When I joined the Party, at the age of eighteen, in my first year at Radcliffe (in 1962), I had assumed that I was joining for the rest of my life; now, at twenty-two, I was reconsidering, and several months later, back in Berkeley where I was a graduate student, I did indeed leave. Outside the Party I found a dynamic but chaotic left, and growing pressures toward separatism, from both women's liberation and the black power movement. I then participated in a series of left organizations, and also in a series of women's organizations. My dissertation was in women's history, and I got a job in which I taught women's history, among other subjects. I was for many years on the editorial collective of *Socialist Revolution* (later *Socialist Review*), which was committed to socialist feminism. But despite all this activism, I continued to feel ambivalent about feminism, or at least about the particular form that it had taken in the political world of which I was a part.

Over 1968 and 1969 the radical women's organizations that we called "the women's movement" (excluding the more liberal, establishment-oriented groups) proliferated at an astonishing pace. In Berkeley, women's consciousness-raising groups sprang up everywhere; when Women's Liberation (which for a while played the role of umbrella organization to grassroots feminism) held a public meeting, it was difficult to find a hall big enough for the crowd. The women's movement consisted of countless groups that were only informally related to each other. Nevertheless, ideas traveled fast, partly because in the women's movement, as in the antiwar movement, people traveled a lot, and national networks were often as strong as local ones. Alice Echols's history of this period, *Daring to Be Bad*,[1] places the New York groups at the center of the politics of radical

---

[1] Alice Echols, *Daring to Be Bad: Radical Feminism in America, 1967–1975*, Minneapolis: University of Minnesota Press, 1989.

feminism. My memory of this period, from the perspective of the Bay Area, supports her account. Local groups were formally autonomous, but ideas drifting in from what were seen as the hyper-radical groups in New York were very influential.

The women's movement was in many ways caught up in the same cultural currents that shaped the youth movement as a whole, despite the efforts of many feminists to distance themselves from what many referred to as "the male-dominated left." Feminists, like leftists, tended to assume that whatever was more radical was better, more legitimate, than what was less radical. Feminists and leftists also tended to assume that radicalism meant militant separatism. Feminists were not the first to equate radicalism with separatism: among the youth movements of the sixties, the black movement first made this connection. This definition of radicalism was accepted almost without discussion elsewhere in "the movement" partly because of the great moral authority of the black struggle, and partly because the call for separatist politics (or, more exactly, a collection of separatisms) struck a chord for many young people. This call for autonomous movements, organized around particular oppressed groups, spoke to the desire for a radical politics that would escape the deadening, imposed unity of the Old Left approach. I think that a definition of radicalism as separatism also appealed to a generation that felt radically separated from the generation before, and, increasingly, radically separated from American society as a whole. Politicizing the already existing social and cultural separation of the youth of the sixties helped turn a painful and confusing fact into an active stance, a basis for self-respect and for creating communities.

For the women's movement, the term separatism was used in a variety of ways. Sometimes it meant a vision of a separate women's society, though few pursued such visions very far, given the difficulties of reproducing such a society. More often it meant creating a movement, and a community, in which women were at the center of each other's lives—in political work, perhaps in personal life. In Berkeley, at least, establishing one's credentials as a feminist tended to require emphasizing how little men mattered to one. Women who were in relationships with men often apologized for them; one friend of mine used to refer to the fact that she was married as a vestige of an unliberated past. Some women defended their relationships by suggesting that their husbands or boyfriends were exceptions to the rule, the only nonsexist men in existence. For single women to acknowledge that they might like to be involved with men, or for women in couples to acknowledge that they might like to preserve those relationships, violated a set of unspoken rules. One might get away with continuing a relationship as long as one spoke of it with sufficient disdain; similarly, one might get away with belonging to an organization of men and women as long as one made it clear that one found it very unpleasant to work with men and did so only because it was necessary in order to achieve some political goal (such as integrating feminism into a socialist perspective). To acknowledge that one wanted to be part of a radical community that included men as well as women was at that time, in that milieu, likely utterly to discredit one as a feminist.

This pull toward separatism in the women's movement was understandable. Given the extent of male domination of the left/antiwar movement, and given the depth of male hostility to feminism, feminists emerging from this milieu had to assume a militant, uncompromising stance—and in effect police each other's behavior—in order to create space for a women's movement and win some degree of respect for it from the left/antiwar movement that they were leaving. These pressures, however, created an atmosphere in which women felt free to judge each other's behavior, and in which bad faith was rampant. In Berkeley competing feminist groups were given to accusing each other of having members who harbored connections with men. In my experience, at least, even in consciousness-raising groups there were unspoken rules: women could talk freely about their anger toward men and their commitments to women, but it was very difficult to express more positive feelings about men, or speak of ambivalence about entering a community confined to women. Feminism seemed to me to impose a set of rules about what one could say about one's feelings and experience. What I was not allowed to say was, for me, at least as important as what I could say.

I was not the only woman who was ambivalent about feminism. The women's movement was made up overwhelmingly of young, white, middle- to upper-middle-class, university-educated women. The demography of these groups was probably more or less representative of the northern student and antiwar movement, in particular SDS, which was at the center of that movement. But the women's groups were not representative of what we called "the movement" more broadly: there was also Black Power, the beginnings of La Raza and of the American Indian Movement. By 1969 women-of-color activists were pointing out that the feminist movement was overwhelmingly white; some were also arguing that while female separatism might be appropriate for white women, they were not about to desert their communities. In the late sixties and early seventies, it was difficult for women of color to make themselves heard.

The feminism defined in the late sixties and early seventies was in the most immediate sense a reaction to the extreme sexism of the New Left/antiwar movement, and on a deeper level was a response to the role of women in the middle-class nuclear family of the fifties, an attempt on the part of middle-class young women to extricate themselves from the role that their mothers had occupied. In the spirit of a generation that tended to regard its own experience as universal, the radical feminists of the late sixties believed, first, that the sexism of the antiwar movement revealed that any political project that brought men and women together would be oppressive to women, and, second, that the nuclear family was the source of women's oppression, the institution that had to be dismantled. However, neither of these assertions fitted my experience.

As an early teenager I had been part of the peace movement and the left of the late fifties/early sixties. I had no experience at all of being oppressed as a woman (or girl) in these movements. I had never lived in a nuclear family: I grew up with a severely disturbed single mother. For me the left was an important vehicle for creating community and for developing a sense of myself as a social actor rather than a passive recipient of fate. My doubts about feminism were based on an unusual history; I could not claim to represent any particular social group. But I think that many people who grew up in the fifties had childhoods in which it was not the nuclear family that was the problem: despite the ideology of the time, many of us grew up in settings that hardly fit that norm. Revolt against the nuclear family was nevertheless at the center of radical feminism.

Many women who did not like the direction that radical feminism was taking in the late sixties simply stayed away from it, or remained at its edges. But still I could not resist the women's movement. The women's movement was concerned with issues that were crucial to me (and that were ignored by the left): how to create equal relationships between men and women, and a community or society based on gender equality. Also, by the time the women's movement emerged, the left, or what we called "the movement," was at the center of my life, and one could not be part of the movement without addressing feminism. I suspect that I was not the only woman, even the only white woman, for whom feminist separatism was more a problem than an answer.

I became involved in the peace movement and the left when I was a ninth-grader in Elisabeth Irwin, a New York City high school, in 1958. My encounter with the left began with a social studies class assignment, a report on the 1958 New York gubernatorial elections. Anxious to do a good job, I interviewed not only members of the campaign staffs of the Democrats, Republicans, and Liberals, but also went to the office of the Independent Socialist Party, which, it turned out, was a coalition of various left groups. The Independent Socialists to whom I talked said that for them the election was a chance to air criticisms of capitalism. That sounded intriguing to me. They invited me to join a high school study group on Marxism, where I read Engels's *Socialism, Utopian and Scientific* and Plekhanov on the role of the individual in history. This was a whole lot more interesting than anything I was being given in high school. I transformed my report on the New York elections into a paper on socialism and communism, and spent the year reading and interviewing people in the various left groups in New York. By the end of the year I was a convinced socialist and Marxist. The school that I attended was politically progressive. Many of the students were from left-wing families; many of the teachers were radicals, including Communists and ex-Communists who remained progressive. While some teachers had no particular politics and no intention of encouraging radicalism, in general the school offered a friendly environment for developing a radical politics.

Meanwhile, I was also gradually becoming an activist. In 1959, during my sophomore year in high school, I joined Student Sane, the student wing of the Committee for a Sane Nuclear Policy. Over the next few years I was one of a small group of high school kids who built an extensive network of high school peace groups in New York City and the surrounding suburbs. The citywide air-raid drills that had been established when we were in elementary school were still in effect. We regarded these as fruitless and frightening. Khrushchev was talking about peaceful coexistence; our view was that the United States was needlessly keeping the cold war going, and that the function of the air-raid drills was largely to instill fear, to make people feel that they needed the bomb to be safe from the Soviet Union. Each year we organized protests against the annual air-raid drills. When I was in the tenth grade we encouraged kids around New York to refuse to take part in the drills. This protest was so effective that next time the air-raid drill was held after school hours. In 1960 we organized high school students to join a protest organized by pacifists outside City Hall, which would involve refusing to take cover when the air-raid sirens sounded. Hundreds of people came to this protest, including large numbers of students. The police roamed the edges of the crowd, making arrests, but the paddy wagons could not hold enough people to make a dent in the size of the crowd. That was the last air-raid drill in New York City.

During my high school years we students in Sane were actually engaged in two battles: in addition to fighting the authorities over such issues as air-raid drills, we were also conducting a battle with the adults in our own organization. In the spring of 1960, Sane organized an astonishingly successful public meeting over the issue of nuclear fallout and human health. The crowd filled Madison Square Garden; it seemed that, after years of McCarthyism, fear, and apathy, a mass peace movement was emerging. The main organizer of the event, Henry Abrams, was a leftist who was widely regarded as having some connection to the Communist Party, either a member or a sympathizer. A few days after the Madison Square Garden meeting, Senator Thomas Dodd summoned Norman Cousins, the head of Sane, and raised the issue of Communists in Sane. Cousins said that he would see that Communists were removed from leadership positions in the organization. As a result the Sane National Board issued an order: anyone in a position of leadership, down to the level of local chapters, was required to sign a statement that he or she was not a member of the Communist Party. Many members, many entire chapters, especially those in and around New York City, left the organization in protest.

The students remained in the organization but refused to sign. The battle between the insurgent students and the adult organization became the focal point of generalized generational distrust. We saw the adults as sellouts, hypocrites, people so concerned with maintaining their legitimacy that they were willing to accept the myths of the cold war. Placing ads in the *New York Times,* signed by prominent people, seemed to be their favorite form of political action; we regarded this approach with contempt, and spent our time organizing demonstrations that we hoped would be large and noisy. The adults could not conceive that any well-informed, well-intentioned person would not share their hostility to Communism. Our opposition to their anti-Communism convinced them that we were either card-carrying Communists—or something so close to it that lack of Party membership was irrelevant. In any event, we were young hotheads who were undermining their public stance of respectability.

This conflict touched feelings on both sides that ran fairly deep. The adults were caught up in hostilities on the left; we reminded them of their Communist adversaries. I suspect that we also reminded some of them of their own teenage children. We were also shaped by the recent history of the left in the United States. We thought that anti-Communism was stupid and cooperation with McCarthyism was cowardly. Many of us were sympathetic to Marxism and in favor of some sort of socialism. The adults also reminded at least some of us of our own parents. At one point Eric Holtzman, the head of Student Sane (and a graduate student), came to a meeting of representatives of high school Sane chapters. He told us that at the last board meeting (which he, as the head of Student Sane, attended) one of the adults had raised a complaint about a member of Student Sane—my friend Peter, at the time fifteen years old. While using the mimeograph machine in the Sane office, Peter had gotten into an argument with one of the adults about the issue of excluding Communists. The adult had said that Communists could not be allowed in Sane because they were required by the Communist Party to support any position taken by the Soviet Union. Peter said he didn't think that was the case. Several days later Peter returned, pulled a copy of the constitution of the Communist Party, USA, out of his pocket, and showed the adult in question a clause assuring members of their right to dissent. The adult, horrified by this, had reported at the next board meeting that members of High School Sane were running around with copies of the constitution of the Communist Party in their back pockets. Eric said that we should stop trying to argue with the adults, there was no way of getting them to see reason, we would only get ourselves in trouble. We agreed. We passed a resolution urging members of High School Sane not to talk with adults unless it was unavoidable.

The year these issues came to a head I was the chair of High School Sane; I therefore found myself at the center of the conflict, and was accused of being a Communist even though I was only 17 at the time, too young to be a member of the Party. But the atmosphere in Sane was too heated for anyone to think of such technicalities. The old leadership won the organization's elections and denounced us at Student Sane as card-carrying Communists or readers of the *National Guardian* (evidently, in their minds, only a shade less evil than Party membership). They threatened to break with us. We broke with them.

I don't think it ever occurred to me that there was anything remarkable about my leadership role in Student Sane—as a girl, that is. I was certainly aware that it was unusual for a teenager in those days to be spending her time organizing illegal demonstrations and publicly refusing to deny her (nonexistent) membership in the Communist Party, but it seemed no more unusual for a girl than for a boy, and in fact our little group of core activists included both boys and girls. One of the central activists, a girl, had parents who seemed entirely oblivious to her political activities. Another, a boy, had parents who had narrowly escaped Auschwitz; they were so fearful of repression that they forbade him to have anything to do with left politics. He used to sneak out his bedroom window to come to meetings. In my case, my father, an ex-Communist who had become quite conservative, was extremely unhappy about my left-wing views, but knew relatively little about what I was doing; he and my mother were divorced, and I lived with my mother. My mother, an ex-Communist who remained progressive, was concerned that my politics might get me into trouble, but took the view that my decisions were up to me.

The movement circles that I was part of in New York were small, but they went beyond Student Sane. Every year the Elizabeth Irwin student body took on a political project: one year it was participation in the student marches on Washington for integrated schools, another it was support for the Fair Play for Cuba Committee (a left-led, and, for the time, strikingly interracial organization, which opposed U.S. intervention in Cuba). Some students were involved in political activity outside school: civil rights, peace, or attending classes at the School for Marxist Studies. Some of us were involved in left Zionism. I spent two summers on a kibbutz, and participated in HaShomer HaTzair, the Marxist-Zionist youth organization, in New York. The circles of young radical activists that I was part of revolved around intersecting communities, which were held together by political values, comradeship, and friendship, between boys and girls as well as between members of the same sex. There were romantic relationships, but it was the sense of comradeship, the emphasis on community, that held the movement together. In retrospect it is clear that leaders in this community of young radicals were more likely to be men than women, but there were many more women (or girls) among the leaders than would be the case a few years down the road, in the New Left. It also seems to me, in retrospect, that in gaining the status of comrades, women tended, in some subtle way, to be desexualized.

The political culture that I am describing was influenced by the Old Left (it included many red diaper babies, and it built on the legacy of radicalism in the thirties), but it had more the flavor of a youth movement than the Old Left did. It was largely Jewish, and I think most extensive and most developed in New York City. It preceded the New Left, and had some impact on it, particularly in the state universities, such as UC Berkeley and the University of Wisconsin, where there were large numbers of red diaper babies and others who in one way or another had become radicals in the years of the late 1950s before the New Left itself emerged. SLATE, the UC Berkeley radical student party of the late fifties and early sixties, included many such people. Some of the women who had been part of SLATE later had ambivalent reactions to the women's movement, reactions quite similar to mine.

In 1962 I entered Radcliffe, then so thoroughly integrated with Harvard that it was a women's college in little more than name. There was a small group of liberal/left students, mostly centered around Tocsin, a peace organization; there was also a small socialist club. In the fall of 1964 we organized a campus SDS chapter, which became the center of student radicalism. Meanwhile, during my first year, I had joined the Communist Party, which had a small Harvard club (by the sixties the term "club" had been substituted for the term "cell," in an effort to sound more American and less conspiratorial). I joined the Party partly out of my experience in the peace movement as a high school student. The Communists had been the only group on the left that had been consistently supportive and helpful toward us. I also joined partly out of a romantic view of the movements of the thirties and the Party's role in those movements, and partly because, in 1962, I couldn't see anyone else who was trying to organize a movement with socialist politics.

Through my college years, then, I was simultaneously a member of the Communist Party and SDS, but I felt more committed to the Party than to SDS. In the Party, it seemed to me that on the whole other Party members, including men, treated me as an equal and listened to me with respect. In SDS, I often felt pushed aside. This may have been partly a result of subtle cultural differences. In the Party, my history as a leader of the high school peace movement in New York, the fact that I was a socialist and knew something about Marxism, earned me respect—as did, of course, the fact that I was willing to join the Communist Party, hardly a common decision for a college freshman in 1962. In SDS, which was mostly made up of liberal students who were beginning to question liberalism, my already-radical politics made me something of an oddity and my membership in the Party made me odder yet—not to say threatening. Though I was at one point on the steering committee of the Harvard/Radcliffe SDS chapter, and had many friends in SDS, I never felt entirely assimilated into the organization. I was not the only Party member who was simultaneously an active member of SDS, but I was the only woman in this position. The fact that I was a woman, and perhaps more than that, the fact that I was not assertive enough to carve out a unique space for myself, left me feeling a little marginal.

One difference between the Party and SDS, in the early sixties, was that the Party regarded "male supremacy" as something to be seriously opposed, while SDS had not yet begun to think about the issue. Of course, the Party's understanding of what would later be called sexism was very limited: it did not include any criticism of the family or of conventional male and female roles. Their antisexism referred mostly to the need for gender equality in public life as well as the need to promote women's involvement in the left. But this was better than nothing, which was what prevailed in SDS. I remember once, while I was a member of the steering committee of Harvard/Radcliffe SDS, reading in the student paper one morning that SDS had decided to hold a demonstration that day. I was quite surprised, because I had not been included in any discussion of this decision. I called a friend of mine, also a member of the Communist Party, and also on the SDS steering committee. He told me that he and the other two members of the steering committee (all men, all living in the same Harvard house) had decided late the night before to hold the demonstration. It was too late to call me, he said, and certainly too late to call me to a meeting; women were not allowed in the Harvard houses after a certain hour. I protested that the decision should have been held off until I could be consulted; he argued that what the New Left was about was spontaneity. Even after I raised this at a meeting of the SDS steering committee, no one saw anything wrong with what had happened. Since my friend was also a member of the Party, I raised it at a Party meeting. There it was agreed that this was an example of male chauvinism. It was impressed upon my friend that he, at least, as a Communist, should have protested against a decision being made without me. He apologized.

This double story suggests differences between the Party and early SDS that went beyond their respective politics of gender. My friend was right: the New Left *was* about spontaneity; the Party was not. In a context in which men had advantages over women (in this case, three men and one woman on the steering committee—and the editor of the student paper down the hall from the three men), spontaneity was likely to mean women being disregarded. The Party had a structure that was conducive to dealing with individual member's complaints; SDS did not. Not that Party clubs always dealt with issues of discrimination in as straightforward a manner as this: in the thirties, for instance, internal charges of racism were often used in a quite opportunistic manner (there were public "trials" of white party members accused of racism, the purpose of which was in fact not to determine who had done what but to publicize the party's antiracism). But the Party club at Harvard did not have enough power or influence, at this point at least, for posturing of this sort to have any purpose. The Party club was really a group of more or less like-minded friends, mostly red diaper babies or in some way products of Old Left culture, who were actually hybrids, somewhere between an Old Left and New Left mentality. The Party club was in a sense a support system for socialists who wanted to be part of the New Left, to find some way of negotiating it as socialists—perhaps even influence it a little. There was room, in this context, for concern about how individual Party members were being treated. Not that the community offered by the Party was perfect by any stretch of the imagination, nor that its antisexism was particularly reliable.

But as the sixties wore on, it made less and less sense to be a member of the Communist Party. The New Left, by this time mostly focused around opposition to the war in Vietnam, had become a mass movement among students and other young people. The Communist Party had some legitimate criticisms of the New Left/antiwar movement—

most importantly, the Party criticized the antiwar movement for becoming too radical too fast, for aiming at revolution, or at least talking about it, when it had little more than a student base that could not conceivably carry out a revolution. This, along with the Party's cultural stodginess, the hostility at least of most of the adults in the Party to the cultural changes taking place among young radicals, gained the Party a reputation as conservative and irrelevant. And in fact the Party was increasingly irrelevant: all it could do was to carp from the sidelines while the New Left and then the antiwar movement took the center of the stage, and, for better or for worse, transformed the nature of radicalism in the United States.

Young people like myself who joined the Party in the early sixties did so, I think, largely out of a kind of nostalgia, a desire to sustain a culture, a particular system of meaning, that was fading, or had already faded. Some of the young people who joined the Party in the early sixties were from Communist families; they had grown up with the belief that radicalism meant Communism, that one could not be a self-respecting person without being a Communist. I remember one man, for instance, who joined the Party, at Harvard, as his act of protest against Kennedy at the time of the Cuban missile crisis. After he joined he called his mother, in New York, and told her that he had just had his bar mitzvah (in those days, one did not say over the phone that one had joined the Communist Party). His mother understood immediately what he meant, and congratulated him. Most red diaper babies, however, were not particularly tempted to join the Party. They had been shaped by the culture of the Old Left in ways that often made it possible for them to make particular contributions to the New Left and the other movements of the sixties. But they had seen the weaknesses of the Party first hand, and, in most cases, wanted to find something better.

In a sense I joined the Party because I was not a red diaper baby, but wished I had been. For me, the left was the answer to an impossible family situation, a way of constructing community, and a sense of meaning, out of isolation and chaos. My parents had both been Communists, but my father left the Party, in the mid-forties, to begin a political trajectory to the right: by the time I was in college he was voting Republican and supporting the war in Vietnam. My mother left the Party somewhat later than my father, remained progressive in her views, but was not involved in political activity. My father was a doctor whose identity was tied up in his efforts to be an artist and an intellectual. My mother was first a teacher in, and then the director of, a day-care center for the children of working mothers. By the time I was five or six my father had become hostile to radicalism, and my mother had also left the Communist Party and was at most on the fringes of the radical community.

My parents' political differences were only the most superficial layer of the problems that I was confronted with as their child. The world of committed radicals seemed warm and alive to me in a way that contrasted sharply with my family. My parents had been married in name only. They never lived together, the marriage had been secret, and the day I was brought home from the hospital, my father demanded a divorce. The reason for this unusual state of affairs was that my father was living with another woman, whom he employed as the nurse/secretary in his office, and was engaged in a long-term affair with yet another woman, who was married, and, before and after I was born, had several children who might or might not have been his. My father told my mother that the marriage had to be a secret because his own father, an Orthodox Jew, would not have approved his marriage to a non-Jewish woman. It seems more likely that the main reason for the secrecy was his desire to protect his multiple relationships (all with non-Jewish women). The incident that provoked my father's demand for a divorce from my mother was that while my mother was in the hospital, having me, her brother happened to come to New York. He called my father's office and asked the nurse how the doctor's wife and baby were doing; this was the first time the nurse, my father's lover, had heard of either.

My father was able to maintain three relationships at once because he had a warmth, charm, and intelligence that led three women to put up with an arrangement that damaged each of them, and the children of two of them. He was also profoundly angry and selfish. His childhood had produced a deep self-hatred, and a simultaneous attraction to and rage at women; he was too absorbed in his own problems to be able to consider the impact of his actions on other people. He had been born in Russia, in a shtetl near Bialystok, at a time when the Jewish Pale of Settlement was being ravaged by pogroms. At the age of sixteen my grandmother had been forced to marry my grandfather, whom she did not like.

When he was about ten, my father told my grandfather that often, when he was out of the house, a strange man came to visit my grandmother. As a result of this information (and no doubt more as well), there was a divorce. Since my grandparents had had a Jewish marriage ceremony, not a civil service, there could have been a quiet Jewish divorce. But my grandfather insisted on a public trial, in which my father was brought to the stand to testify against his mother. Custody of my father and uncle was given to my grandfather; he arranged for his sons to live with one of the few Jewish families in town. Neither of them saw their mother again until they were adults. At the age of fifteen, my father entered Harvard, where he felt ostracized because he was a Jew and also because he was younger than most of the other students. He went on to medical school, became a doctor, and moved to New York, where he thereupon joined the Communist Party. Later, when he had become a conservative, he told me that his youthful radicalism had simply been an expression of the anger that he felt about life in general. It seemed to me that the same anger underlay his later conservatism. All his life he felt sharply that as an immigrant and a Jew, he was an outsider to American life. The three women that he became involved with were all non-Jews. When I was three, he insisted on changing my name, and my mother's, from Epstein to Easton, a name he found by searching the New York telephone book for something close to Epstein, but non-Jewish.

I grew up living with my mother. When I was a small child, my father was around a certain amount; though my parents were divorced, I can remember getting up in the morning to find my parents having breakfast together. When I was eight his visits became less frequent, more regularized, more formal; ostensibly he was coming to see me. I later learned that this was when my parents ended their relationship—which had been going on for years, and to which the marriage and the subsequent divorce had been more or less irrelevant. Hence I grew up surrounded by a confusing mixture of secrets, lies, and silences. For example, I was told that my parents had been divorced when I was little; in fact, my parents continued their relationship until I was about seven, when my father married the other woman he had been involved with, who by this time had had several children, possibly my father's, possibly her husband's. My father married her when I was eight, but I was not told about this. As a child, I was told that my father slept at his office. He came to visit two evenings a week, and took me out every Sunday afternoon. I dreaded his visits. Looking back on all this, I knew at the time, on some level, that I was not being told the truth, but I found my parents' world so frightening that I didn't want to ask questions, I simply wanted to have as little to do with them as possible. Neither of my parents was concerned with how all of this felt to me, and I had no other adult to turn to. I grew up deeply suspicious of all adults. When I was fourteen, my father told me that he had been married for six years, that he and his wife had a daughter, then four years old, and that there were five other children from his wife's previous marriage. I met the wife and children, but the cloud of mystery persisted. Why had this marriage been a secret for so long? Why did one of my siblings introduce me to friends by name, avoiding describing me as a stepsister? I later discovered that it was not entirely clear whether I was a step- or half-sister. In any event, my relationship to this family remained tenuous and uncertain.

My mother's background was very different from my father's. She had grown up in a small town in southern Illinois, in the Bible Belt, where fundamentalist Protestantism prevailed (and still does). In my mother's town, like many others in the region, a law, which remains on the books, ordered any blacks or Jews who might enter the town to leave before sundown. My mother remembered seeing a Jew being chased out of town when she was a child. Catholics, who were more likely to find themselves in such a town than either blacks or Jews, were somewhat more politely asked to leave.

My mother was the second child of the town doctor. Her father, whom she adored, was rarely home, and when he was, barely seemed to notice her; her mother, who soon had five children, was harried and often angry, especially with my mother. From a very early age my mother struck people as odd, as somehow not entirely there. She kept to herself, she did not seem to fit in with other children, she was virtually incapable of following directions or abiding by routines. This enraged my grandmother. In a later era my mother might have been recognized as a disturbed child who needed help; my grandmother simply saw her as willful and disobedient. My mother spent a great deal of time by herself, reading and thinking. She felt herself to be different from the people around her; she was open to ideas that were not accepted in her community. She decided, for instance, that she was an atheist. My grandfather firmly believed in college education, for girls as well as boys, and sent my mother to a nearby Christian college. After a year there, my mother simply left for New York. She graduated from Barnard and then got a Master's in early childhood education; she taught at a day-care center in a settlement house; eventually she became the director of the center. She also joined the Communist Party, married and then divorced my father, and raised me as a single mother.

What was amazing about my mother was that she was able to do well in her profession, and earn the respect of the people she worked with, for she was not really able to connect with people, nor for that matter was she interested in doing so. She was never quite focused; she was always losing things, forgetting things. She did not seem to know or care how she was dressed; she often did not notice that her blouse was unbuttoned or her skirt hem undone. People saw her as eccentric and distant, but hardworking, dedicated, capable. She got along with people as long as they did not try to become close to her—in which case she became frightened and suspicious. Sometimes she imagined that people were conspiring against her; as I grew older this occasionally included me. But she was respected for her integrity and egalitarianism. As a white Protestant from a culturally narrow and racist background, it was striking how easily she worked with blacks, Puerto Ricans, Catholics, Jews, and how utterly devoid she seemed to be of any sense of superiority.

The problem with my mother, for me at least, was how distracted and distant she was, how often she seemed lost in her own internal universe. At the age of three, convinced that I was going to be abandoned soon, I persuaded a neighbor child, who was in the first grade, to teach me how to read. By the time I was five I had mastered this crucial skill for negotiating the world on my own.

Probably what enabled me to survive this bleak emotional environment was that I began school at the age of three and became friends with another little girl. She also had problematic parents; in spite of this she was full of energy and optimism. Toward me she was generous and loyal. Throughout our childhoods we formed a crucial, utterly reliable support system for one another. We spent a great deal of time together, either at her house or at my house; in any conflict with our parents, we could count on each other's support. So as to avoid conflict, we divided up the world between us: Elinor was good at math, science, dance, athletics, art; I was good at social studies, language, music. We were among the best students in our class, but there was never any competition between us; our alliance was too important for us to allow it to be endangered. At a very early age I decided that I was a Jew. I think this was partly because my father was Jewish, and unreliable as his visits were, he was more emotionally available than my non-Jewish mother. It was also because Elinor was a Jew.

If my friendship with Elinor saved my childhood (and survived it—she and I remain close friends, perhaps more accurately pseudo, or chosen, sisters), it was my involvement with the left that saved my adolescence. I joined the left during what was in retrospect one of its most generous and nurturant moments. In the late fifties and early sixties the left was very small but, after the long winter of McCarthyism, beginning to grow again. The result was that anyone who became part of the left was likely to be greatly appreciated by everyone else; we were much more aware of what we had in common than what divided us, grateful to find a few fellow spirits, pleased by any signs that the movement was growing. It was a very optimistic moment. In some ways the emergence of the New Left itself, centered in SDS, was a step backward from the radical culture of the late fifties and very early sixties that had preceded it: the pre–New Left culture was more interracial, more conscious of its links to the movements that preceded it, more radical (that is, more willing to criticize capitalism and espouse socialism)—and there was more room in it for women's activism and gender equality. In other ways the New Left/early SDS was a step forward. It appealed to a new constituency: liberal, middle-class white students with no radical background. It allowed liberal students to examine the hypocrisy of mainstream, cold war liberalism, to express their outrage—and to gradually move toward radicalism.

Luckily for me, the left of the late fifties and early sixties was a warmer place than the outside world, and for the most part a place where one could say what one thought and be listened to with respect. This was the case both in the Communist Party and in SDS, in its early days. But there were limits, especially for women. My freshman year I made two friends at Radcliffe; the three of us joined Tocsin, and then SDS. One of the two had come to college already thinking of herself as a feminist and a socialist (her parents had been Communists, one of her aunts had been an organizer of working-class women, and a suffragist). She often raised the issue of feminism and criticized the way women were treated in Tocsin and SDS. But if any of us were to mention feminism in a meeting, the men were likely to look at us as if there were something wrong with us. It did not seem worth it to pursue the topic outside of our conversations with each other. This did not affect our commitment to the left; it was still a better place to be than anywhere else that we knew of.

The question of how women were treated in the movement became more pressing as the movement became larger, angrier, less attentive to internal process. In the early sixties, the New Left was small enough that it was possible to integrate new people, to construct a culture in which a kind of decency and mutual sensitivity usually prevailed. This was disrupted by the war in Vietnam. By 1966, opposition to the war was dominating political activity. Students were streaming into SDS, which was at the center of antiwar activity, and an atmosphere of impatience and anger was replacing the earlier orientation toward building something like what southern civil rights activists called "the beloved community." Demonstrations became huge and unruly. By this time I was at Berkeley, where radicalism was generally understood to mean, among other things, a skepticism toward potentially bureaucratic structures and a reluctance to become bogged down in time-consuming, democratic procedures. There was no membership organization at the center of the movement, playing the role that SDS had played at Harvard and elsewhere. Instead, each major demonstration or series of demonstrations was organized by an ad hoc committee, composed of what appeared to be self-appointed leaders. Predictably these were almost always men.

The movement began to flirt with violence in a way that would barely have been thinkable several years earlier, not only in response to the war, but around other issues as well. In 1969 there was a strike on the Berkeley campus for a Department of Ethnic Studies. The two principal organizations directing the strike were the Third World Liberation Front, a mostly black student group, and AFT 1570, the teaching assistants' union, of which I was a member. At one point a demonstration was held during which the police came onto campus, arrested a number of people (for picketing in a particular place where picketing was forbidden by the administration). A riot broke out; the police chased protesters around campus and beat a number of people. That evening I attended a meeting of the steering committee of AFT 1570, as the History Department representative; it was argued that in order to keep the strike going there should be another demonstration within the next few days, and that the police should again be induced to come on campus and provoked into violence. I argued against provoking violence. Only one person—a regular member of the steering committee, and a Communist—agreed with my criticisms. He called me later and asked me to repeat what I had said at the steering committee meeting at the next general meeting of the union. I agreed. At the next general meeting I described the discussion that had taken place at the steering committee meeting and said that I thought that provoking violence would in the long run destroy the left, that if we had to do that to keep the strike going, perhaps we should not keep the strike going. I was virtually booed off the stage. The leaders of the union stopped speaking to me, many of my friends ostracized me, and for years subsequently I heard myself described as an "objective racist" (presumably, because the Third World Liberation Front was pressing for greater militancy, and because I was raising questions about the conduct of a strike whose aim was the establishment of a Third World college).

The prevailing attitude of everything-for-the-struggle, dissenters-be-damned enhanced the power of movement leaders; in this atmosphere there could be no democratic controls. In the melee, the gap between men and women widened, and authoritarian and sexist behavior became more common. I frequently found myself being told what to do by men who felt entitled by their movement status to hand out orders. I was given a hard time in particular for not participating in illegal demonstrations that might lead to being thrown out of graduate school. Believing that my academic training was my security, I was not willing to do this. This was not the sort of argument that was likely to be listened to with sympathy in the movement—at least not from someone who was white and middle class. I also felt that the movement was my security, and that it was being destroyed, gratuitously, by people who might well lose interest in it within a few years.

Women's liberation had emerged a few years earlier and was gaining momentum; by 1969 male authoritarianism in the antiwar movement was driving large numbers of women into the women's movement. By this time the sexual revolution was in full swing, especially in movement circles; for women it often seemed to mean increased vulnerability to unaccountable men. For some women, the women's movement meant being able to participate in antiwar demonstrations with groups of women, and making decisions in that context about what felt safe and what did not. For many of us it meant a kind of collective intervention in the sexual revolution, an attempt to prevent it from being entirely male-defined, an effort to raise the issue of gender equality in the swirling chaos that seemed to surround us. It also meant suspicion of abstract principles (so often used by men to legitimize their power), a return to personal experience and perceptions as a legitimate basis for political analysis.

My response to the women's movement was a combination of relief that personal issues, especially relations between men and women, were being raised as a legitimate topic of discussion in the movement, disappointment that the way in which these issues were framed often did not speak to my experience, and a fear that all this was leading toward a split in the movement along lines of sex. The feminist analysis of the late sixties, at least within the circles that I was part of, seemed to revolve around a protest against men's reduction of women to sex objects, and the subordination of women within the nuclear family. As I said, I had rarely, if ever, had the experience of being treated as a sex object: men who wanted such relationships were not likely to be attracted to me. And I had never experienced or even witnessed firsthand anything that easily fit the category of female subordination within the nuclear family. My father had certainly had a great deal of power over my mother and me, but it could not be blamed on the nuclear family, or at least not directly. In fact my experience, with my father and in my own relationships with men, was that men exercised power not by directly ordering women around, or by paying the bills and making women economically dependent, but by assuming a stance of emotional distance, keeping one foot out the door, sometimes in a bid for greater power, sometimes just out of fear of being trapped in a relationship. For me the issue was not just that men had more social power than women, but also that they were afraid of women and/or of intimacy. This combination produced the stalemate between men and women—at least in my life. My analysis was certainly compatible with a feminist analysis; over the years a great deal of feminist writing has appeared on men's fear of women and of intimacy. But at the time, it seemed difficult to say these things. There was pressure to adopt the stance that one was tired of being ordered around by men, and was not very interested in relationships with them.

Indeed, it often seemed to me that there was as much pressure toward striking poses in the women's movement as there was in the antiwar movement—they were simply different kinds of poses. In the early seventies I was a member of the Berkeley-Oakland Women's Union, a socialist-feminist organization that served as an umbrella group for a variety of activist projects around such issues as women's health, child care, and education, and which tried to devise a broad agenda for socialist-feminist politics. At one point a group of radical feminists came to a general meeting to challenge our right to call ourselves feminists: they pointed out that we had women in our midst who also belonged to organizations that included men. (I was a case in point; I belonged to the socialist New American Movement, and was a member of the editorial collective of *Socialist Revolution.*) The implication of this charge was that women who worked with men politically were the carriers of a male-dominated, male-oriented politics; the logic of the debate seemed to require that one assert how little one was affected by men. A special meeting was arranged between the two groups for a discussion of this issue, and in fact one woman after the next from the Berkeley-Oakland Women's Union rose to say that her political activity, intellectual concerns, and life revolved around women. I remember one woman in particular, married with two sons, who protested that she cared only about women. It did not seem to me that feminism had managed to create an arena in which one could count on being able to speak honestly.

So I was disturbed by the pressures toward political (and sometimes personal) separatism generated by the women's movement, and further disturbed by the fact that there seemed to be no room for even discussing this issue. I wrote an article, published in *Socialist Revolution,* in which I argued that autonomous women's groups were an important part of the movement, but that feminists should see themselves as part of a broad movement for social change including both men and women. I heard rumors that several feminist activists, two of them socialists, at one point associated with *Socialist Revolution,* had said, after reading my article, that I had gone too far, that they would henceforth refuse to associate with me politically. I was told this, by a man on the *Socialist Revolution* collective, it seemed to me, as a kind of warning. Not that I should stop working with men myself (after all, we were both members of the same collective), but that I should stop arguing with feminist separatism, presumably lest I give socialism, or at least the journal *Socialist Revolution,* a bad name with feminists. It sometimes seemed as if the course of least resistance would have been to mouth a separatist line and then to ignore it in practice, both politically and personally.

Because the women's movement emerged out of a break with the left, and possibly also because so many men on the left remained so resistant to feminism, the women's movement tended to think of itself as very different from the left. In fact the women's movement and the New Left/antiwar movement had a great deal in common. They were based on the same cohort of the same generation (mostly white, mostly middle-class young people); they were driven by the same desire to construct a more authentic way of life than that which mainstream society offered. Their confidence that this could be done was buoyed by the prosperity on which the middle class had come to rely, which by the mid-seventies was coming to an end. Neither the New Left/antiwar movement nor the radical women's movement were able to sustain or reproduce themselves: both turned out to be political expressions of a particular moment. To some degree this was due to large social and political changes over which the movements themselves had no control. The war in Vietnam had angered so many Americans that, for a time, protest acquired a certain legitimacy. Radicalism seemed almost reasonable to people who otherwise had no sympathy for it. The recession that followed the war undermined the youth culture that had supported both the left and the women's movement, and created a mood of apprehension that was easily exploited by the right.

Feminism survived this shift in public mood better than the left, but the militant radical feminism of the late sixties and early seventies faded. Feminist consciousness continued to spread, but mass activism gradually disappeared. In the nineties a women's movement still exists but in a very different form. There are the established women's organizations, relatively cautious and often highly bureaucratic. There is the world of academic feminism, including women's studies programs and feminist scholars elsewhere in the humanities and the social sciences. And there is a large arena of diverse and decentralized organizations and projects. The established organizations pursue the traditional goals of liberal feminism in that they tend to focus on the goal of institutional equality for women. Feminists in academia and in the fragmented world of small feminist projects and groups tend to identify themselves with a broader social critique, which they trace back to the radical women's movement of the late sixties.

But the left and the radical women's movement of the late sixties and early seventies were not destroyed by external forces alone: they also participated in their own demise. By the late sixties, the movement as a whole was focused on opposition to the war in Vietnam. Between 1973 (the Paris Peace Accords) and 1975, when the war came to an end, the antiwar movement collapsed. Radical activists who had expected that once the war ended the movement would turn to issues of domestic social change found themselves without a mass movement. The collapse of the movement was reinforced by the shift to the right in the political climate of the United States in the mid-seventies, and also by recession. It became much more difficult to live on virtually nothing—the lifestyle that had prevailed in the movement. Activists went back to school, or found jobs. Radical feminism outlasted the antiwar movement by a few years, but in the context of increasing cultural conservatism, its critique of the family and its call for a feminist revolution seemed less and less relevant.

Further, both movements regarded radicalism as a goal in itself, and defined radicalism in terms of the purity of one's position, the thoroughness of one's break with the status quo. This view of radicalism produced a process inside the movement that might be described as bidding up: whatever passed for radicalism at one moment quickly became unsatisfactory, vulnerable to being displaced by a yet more radical stance. Inside the radical women's movement this "bidding up" process produced a politics that was less and less compatible with the lives of heterosexual women, many of whom were becoming more, rather than less, enmeshed in families and careers, both settings that required various kinds of compromises. These contradictions did not lead most feminists to reject feminism, but for most, the women's movement itself receded into memory. A similar process took place on the left: by the early seventies radicalism had reached its limits, unless one was prepared to go to prison or join the underground.

For me, the moral of this story is not that radicalism is to be avoided. We need a radical critique of the status quo, in relation to gender and many other issues, as much now as we did in the sixties. There is now a very wide arena in which feminist rhetoric is not only accepted but expected; women are more integrated into public life, particularly at its lower and middle levels. Most women continue to have considerably fewer resources and less power than most men, and relations between women and men, even in arenas in which feminist rhetoric is widely practiced, remain very much as they were before the women's movement emerged. We still need a radical critique, and a movement to develop it and give it force. But we can learn a few things from the mistakes of the radical feminism of the late sixties. First, the measure of a movement's politics is not the purity of its posture, but its ability to bring about motion toward a more egalitarian society. Secondly, a movement for a better society has a responsibility to promote egalitarian, mutually respectful relations within its own ranks. Women of color have been reasonably successful in establishing the importance of their experiences to any developing feminist analysis. The same point needs to be extended not only to other categories of identity (class, for instance) but beyond categories of identity, to the great variety of personal histories and orientations, or needs, produced by a society in which gender relations are in flux. Feminism in the nineties—if it is to have any political force—has the daunting task of making room for all of this diversity and at the same time providing some practical agenda for change.

Home Before Sundown

Anselma Dell'Olio

In 1966, not long out of college, I moved from Rome, Italy, to New York City. A search through the *New York Times* apartment ads brought me into contact with Ti-Grace Atkinson. A pale, willowy redhead with an aristocratic manner, she was looking for someone to share her townhouse apartment in the East 70s. She talked about being dropped from the Social Register after her divorce from a mainline Philadelphia man. Then she had coolly decided to make her mark in the world through art criticism and was majoring in aesthetics at Columbia. Ti-Grace had a silver-framed portrait of herself in her wedding dress, behind a cracked pane of glass, sitting on the mantelpiece. We talked about things I had never spoken to anyone about before, such as food bingeing and feminism. She told me she had "a correspondence with Simone de Beauvoir," who had put her in touch with Betty Friedan. She showed me an invitation to a meeting that Friedan had sent her. Did I want to go with her? Curious and impressed, I agreed to meet her in front of the address on the postcard, a few minutes before the meeting.

Still, I almost missed the founding of New York NOW, the National Organization for Women. When I arrived at the street in the West 70s, I couldn't find the building. It was a dark and windy night, and as I was peering around, wondering what to do, I bumped noses with Ti-Grace. We suddenly realized that the address was in the *East* 70s, so we zipped across the park in a cab. Ti-Grace was already a feminist, and really didn't need to hear the speeches at the meeting. I did. I was fresh off the boat from Europe, and had been culturally influenced, through voracious reading, to believe in the overwhelming and oppressive "supremacy" of the American woman. That evening I was especially struck by Flo Kennedy, a witty, irreverent black lawyer, and by Muriel Fox, a sleek PR woman. Both of them sported full makeup, tailored suits, and hats. There was a small crowd of elegant and substantial-looking men and women in the huge marble foyer of the East 70s town house, complete with a spiral staircase; yet revolution was in the air.

Friedan gave the most impressive speech, reeling off Labor Department statistics documenting the political, social, and economic discrimination against women in the United States. My mind was reeling, too. I was having trouble integrating the indisputable evidence that was being presented with what I had gleaned from books, magazines, and newspapers about the status of (American) women. Friedan's presentation of the truth gave me my first taste of how the media—wittingly and otherwise—manipulate information. One's mid-twenties is none too soon to learn not to believe everything you read. When a form for joining the new organization was passed around, Ti-Grace signed with a flourish, and handed it to me, taking it for granted I would do the same. I did, although I still had reservations. I was as ignorant as a goat on the subject.

I buckled down to study over the next year or so, attended NOW meetings, worked on committees, and, after the women's movement got going, dove into a CR group. Consciousness raising was a new idea in 1968, and those encounters packed an intellectual and an emotional punch: along with the opening of the mind went the opening of the heart. My sense of unbelonging had a focus and a name. I was in a state of quasi-hysterical delight and excitement all the time, due no doubt to the ecstasy of relief; relief from a tension I had always had, between who I was, and who and what I was supposed to be. Ever since I could remember, I had been filled with anger and rebelliousness. I overflowed with high spirits I was always trying to stifle (to please authority figures), and I wasn't happy about it. One leg was tied to a post and the other was trying to run like hell. I was endowed with a lot of good luck and not much training in how to use it. Feminism allowed me to make the leap from rumbling volcano, always threatening to explode, to rebel with a cause. It was like teaching an illiterate to read. It taught me that the weight on my shoulder was a chip, and how to get rid of it before it grew into a boulder.

I never met or heard of a member of my mother's or my father's family who could be described as "weak" or passive. My maternal grandmother, Jenny Bernstein, traveled alone at age thirteen from somewhere in Bessarabia to Detroit, where her older sisters and brothers quickly married her off to a tall, thin peddler, to get her out of the way. Jenny and Harry Grosz had four daughters in five years, and then Harry died of tuberculosis. Jenny was eighteen years old, untutored, with four baby girls to support, living in Watts, then a still-rural district of Los Angeles. So Jenny raised chickens and vegetables to sell to neighbors. She turned her home into a tavern for supplementary income, not too great a sacrifice, for she loved company, and a good time. Husband number two was a redheaded circus performer who was violent when drunk, which was most paydays. He would drive the family to town, then wander off and disappear, which is how my mother, age ten, learned to drive a Model T: out of necessity. A fifth daughter was born. At some point husband number two wandered off for good and eventually died.

Luigi, the Italian-speaking orphan whom the family adopted, worked jobs down at the produce market in Los Angeles, to help out my grandmother. There he met Gerry (Girolamo) Dell'Olio, a produce jobber who spoke no English. Gerry had only recently emigrated from Apulia, a region on the southeastern coast of Italy. His father and his father's father were Tolstoyan figures: big, tall, broad-shouldered men who worked their own land, and were much loved and revered by their families and the surrounding community. When as a child I asked my father, who had never known poverty, why he decided to leave Apulia, he answered that there were seven children in his family, and he was Wednesday. Despite his considerable talents and achievements, he would always be the low man in the patriarchal chain of command. For a man of Gerry's considerable temperament, this was unacceptable. My paternal grandmother's reaction to her son's decision to leave for the United States was to declare that she would never see him again. She kept her word by dying a few months before he was due home for the first time in twenty-five years. That told me what I needed to know about the women on my father's side.

Gerry's journey to California was a rite of initiation by which he earned his entry into the New World. He took off with a hundred dollars in his pocket and no visa for legal admission into the United States. He stopped in Paris and obtained forged papers to enter Canada, which were guaranteed to pass for the real thing. Arrested upon arrival, incarcerated for deportation, he escaped and made his way to the Bronx Italian ghetto, where he wondered why anyone would leave the coast of Italy to live with cockroaches in a tenement. His first (and only) job as a hired hand was to deliver ice by horse and wagon in Manhattan. The first delivery was to a building on Central Park West, at which the doorman ordered him to carry the long and heavy block of ice to the tenth floor, on foot. He left the horse, the wagon, and the ice, and took a train to California. By the time he met Luigi, Gerry had a Model A Ford and his first piece of land, a farm with no house on it in central California, near Fresno. He strung up a hammock between two peach trees, lay down on it, and contemplated his progress, his solitude, and his future.

Luigi invited Gerry home, where he spied my barefoot and bashful mother, hiding in the kitchen. They fell in love with no common language but that of the heart, and soon eloped to Mexico in my father's Model A. Gerry was twenty-five, Rose fifteen. My grandmother Jenny (who was just thirty), told my mother she would have black babies if she married the dark Italian. Rose's life had not been golden. There was the fun of cagily eating one's cornflakes while leaving enough milk to get a second helping of cereal; and the comfort of "Jewish tea": hot water with a splash of milk in it. But she had been responsible for selling Jenny's home-grown vegetables door-to-door at age five, and had cried in desperation when a housewife squeezed and ruined some rhubarb, and then refused to buy it. And she had witnessed Jenny's mortification by social workers. Once Jenny told the social worker she had no food in the house. When the social worker searched through the kitchen cabinets and found a lone box of oatmeal, she had berated Jenny in front of her five little girls for lying about the family's destitution. Rose dropped out of school at thirteen to contribute to the family's upkeep by working for an Orthodox Jewish family. Since Orthodox Jews are not allowed to do any work at all, even turning on lights or lighting an oven, on the Sabbath, it was a common practice to hire someone else—in this case a poor Jewish girl, to do housework on Saturdays. Rose was regularly hauled off these jobs by the truant officer, but the family's need of her earnings was too great for her not to keep working. There was more, and there was worse, so she took her chances and ran off with the swarthy stranger to an unknowable future.

Shortly after, the country fell into the Great Depression. Rose was Gerry's secretary, treasurer, housekeeper, wife, and all the family he had in America. My father made and ran liquor during Prohibition: a great risk, as he was still without papers. (Many years later, when I was eleven and taking civics in school, I helped him study for his citizenship examination.) Meanwhile, he would disappear with his truckloads of illegal whiskey for weeks at a time, leaving my mother with her three babies, and money that had to last until his eventual return.

After losses of an eldest son and her beloved sister, and many mis-carriages, Rose was able to bring me to term, and then some: I weighed fourteen pounds, ten ounces at birth. Rose often told me the story of how grueling and draining carrying and giving birth to me had been. Her arches fell, her teeth went bad: I sucked up all the nourishment. She very much wanted a boy to replace the one she had lost. When my heartbeat in the womb proved to be exceptionally strong, the doctor "all but guaranteed" I would be a boy. The doctor told my exhausted mother that she hadn't had a baby, she'd had a football player. My mother's response, always included in the retelling, was: "All that trou-ble for a girl." She was so pleased that she nursed me until I was sent off to boarding school at eighteen months of age. Photographs of Rose holding me show a strapping blond baby the size of a large three-month-old, and a tall, strung-out woman with rubber tires under her eyes. She looks like a demolished fifty year old: she was only thirty.

Soon after his arrival in California, my father had been befriended and helped by an order of Italian nuns, the Missionary Sisters of the Sacred Heart of Jesus, who ran an orphanage in Los Angeles. When I was a year and a half old, the mother superior came to the house and saw that my mother was close to a nervous breakdown. She took me from Rose's arms with the words: "Give her to us." This was not a tragedy. I was whisked from a patriarchal home, where my father was an absolute dictator, to a universe where women were in charge of everything.

The founder of the order was a farm girl from northern Italy, Frances Xavier Cabrini. She was born in 1850, and died, a U.S. citizen, in Chicago in 1917. She was canonized by Pius XII in 1946, and was the first American saint. Appropriately, she was made the patron saint of immigrants. Against formidable odds, she founded a vast archipelago of schools, orphanages, hospitals, and convents throughout the Americas and Europe. She dreamed of rescuing the helpless army of abandoned, unwanted baby girls in China, but was sent to tend to the New World immigrants instead. Every year her adventurous life was commemorated in plays at Cabrini schools all over the world. It was the life of a woman who gently but firmly wrested control of her (and her order's) destiny from the Church hierarchy, until she answered only to the Pope, who was safely tucked away in the Vatican. She accomplished her vision without ever disobeying a superior. She was essentially her own superior

for the last thirty years of her life. Her nuns (her "daughters") closely followed her instructions for the molding of the female character.

At Villa Cabrini Academy, simplicity and a joyful attitude were as
important as the Golden Rule and the Ten Commandments. Duplicity
and ulterior motives were as unacceptable as stealing. Punishment for
breaking rules was swift and just. We were treated with rough affection
and no sentimentality. The nuns were our commanding officers. There
was no difference in rank between the housekeeping nuns, who ran the
dormitories, refectories, laundry, and kitchens, and the teaching nuns.

There is a lot to be said for a good boarding school. It can be a boon
to the child, and to the mother, especially. In later years Rose would say
she lay awake at night, thinking about us, and crying. She no doubt did,
and probably felt she should. But surely her life was made easier. She
was no longer torn so many different ways, and was able to pull herself
together, emotionally and physically.

Perhaps as a result of those years, I have always been comfortable
with women; and I am always surprised by those who feel women's
company is second best. Working with women in a disciplined environment is something I really enjoy. No wonder that when I was introduced to feminism, we became fast friends. It was a homecoming. Still,
I don't want to understate the doubt and fear I felt at the beginning.
Was feminism selfish? Was this the most important cause I could
espouse? I also had a certain investment in not being a joiner. In the
end, my curiosity was stronger than my doubts. The movement aroused
enormous interest quickly, and after I had devoured the standard texts,
I was impatiently drafted by Friedan and Atkinson to help out with
speaking engagements, interviews, and other public tasks. "Battle of the
Sexes" articles had long been a newsroom cliché. We sure fit that profile,
and our rhetoric was tailor-made for the sound bite and the talk show.
In no time we were hot, hot, hot.

Our every demonstration and most meetings were well attended by
reporters and journalists. It was not unusual for the newswomen (we
insisted they be women) to bag their notebooks and join on the spot.
For many, it was the first opportunity they had gotten to cover politic
instead of being automatically assigned to soft-news events. In those
days no demonstration was too small to be covered by print or TV news.
We were regularly invited to be guests on radio and TV talk shows; in
fact, one talk-show host recruited the whole lot of us as he strolled by

our midtown demonstration on his way to lunch. You didn't have to be a media star to rouse their interest. The first time I had the responsibility for a demonstration was against Colgate-Palmolive on Park Avenue in 1967. The TV news crews showed up, and, probably because I was the tallest and the loudest, stuck microphones in my face, and so I rattled off our case against discrimination toward women assembly-line workers at the C.P. plant in Ohio. This happened over and over at demonstrations. The same evening we would see ourselves prominently featured on the news without too much distortion of our message.

Politically, I was destined for the Left. My father was antifascist when the Italian-American community was heavily pro-Mussolini. Both my parents were Roosevelt Democrats, and later supported Truman, Stevenson, and Kennedy. As a compulsive reader in a home not overflowing with great books, I moved from the funny papers to hard news when I was eight. The first articles I remember were about Joseph McCarthy and the House Un-American Activities Committee. My parents had started taking us for long stays in Italy at about the same time. When I was fourteen, and the last child home, they decided to spend half of every year in Italy. As I was in boarding school, they asked me where I would prefer to study. Unhesitatingly I chose Italy.

I graduated from high school and college in Rome. Memories of Fascism were still strong in the country. I cut my first professional teeth in the intensely committed, pro-Communist atmosphere of the Italian movie business of the sixties. In Rome I had found myself in the midst of the great flowering of Italian cinema in the sixties. Entry-level jobs in radio, television, but above all films, came my way with no great effort on my part. Just being part of the international community was enough. I apprenticed with Luchino Visconti, Michelangelo Antonioni, Francesco Rosi, Mario Monicelli, and others. I loved living in Rome and working in films, but after Kennedy was assassinated, and the Civil Rights and student movements began to emerge, I knew it was time to return to the United States.

I was interested in becoming involved with public policy and thought about working for the Democratic Party. It all came together when I joined NOW and became a feminist. Finally politics included me, and I was able to become a conscious, active, committed member of the community. Finally I knew who I was, and where I belonged. The strength I derived from feminism gave me the confidence to move back into show business, after sidetracking myself for a few years as a promotional copywriter and editor for Avon International. At Avon I butted my head against the barriers for women in management, until I was finally considered a candidate for executive training. It was such a struggle that I soon asked myself why I was fighting so hard to join a club I had no real interest in. Bored and unchallenged by corporate life, I haunted movie theaters and legitimate theaters, and hung around backstage when I knew people in the company. After seeing the original production of *Jacques Brel Is Alive and Well and Living in Paris* several times, I knew cabaret was what I wanted to do. One night when I was backstage, talking to visiting actors Anne Meara and Jerry Stiller, they told me the director of a new political cabaret, the DMZ, was looking for performers. With feminist-induced courage, I auditioned with an Italian folk song (a cappella!), which I later adapted for the New Feminist Theater, called "Bella Ciao." I was hired as an understudy to the only woman in the cast of four. (One of the men was a superb and kind-to-novices black actor named Morgan Freeman.) I went to every rehearsal, and watched the director like a hawk. And bided my time.

Are you an equality feminist, or a difference feminist? This was the watershed question then, around 1969–1970, and in many ways, it is now. In the early days of the second wave, there were uptown feminists and downtown feminists, and the split was roughly between those who wanted a more equal share of the patriarchal pie, and those who wanted a different pie altogether, in which all that is now voiceless and valueless would be expressed and take pride of place, in our now male-oriented and male-defined culture. I believed then, and believe now, that both views are necessary, and that both enrich the feminist dialogue. But I tilt toward one, for I fail to see how equality feminism necessarily harms women, or prevents the evolution of a new value-system, and I have yet to perceive any political course of action emerge from the often interesting and even engrossing discussions of difference feminism. The prowoman line in the early days of second wave feminism was a version of difference theory; hence the prowoman line was anti-action and pro-consciousness raising. At that time, however, the feeling was that CR groups were political: radically female guerrilla tactics that would spread exponentially throughout the culture, and change it from the grassroots up.

My first CR group—New York Radical Women, later New York Radical Feminists—was made up primarily of downtown women who espoused the prowoman line. I understand the attraction of women deciding what the standards are, rather than accepting the prevailing, thus patriarchal, power structure. But it is slippery terrain. For one thing, our "difference" is not so easily defined, and could be construed as the "feminine" values traditionally ascribed to women—nurturing and nonviolent caring. In any event, the prowoman line also addressed pragmatic issues: was a dead marriage better than a dead-end job? What to do about male infidelity? On that issue, after all the women in the room had had their say, I think it was Kathie Sarachild who summed up by concluding that, since (a) most men were unfaithful, and (b) most women didn't like it, then (c) men were just going to have to be forced to stop it. In retrospect, I find it odd that, on the one hand, we were busy documenting how we, as women, had been damaged by centuries of patriarchal oppression and discrimination, and on the other, we implied that the damage wasn't permanent, or even very deep, since whatever we expressed was virtuous and worth promoting and obtaining, by decree, if necessary.

The uptown women who generally espoused equality feminism were more mainstream in their politics, not necessarily tied to the ethos of the sixties and the student movement. But uptown or downtown, there was an outpouring of ideas, brains, wit, and talent, the likes of which I have never experienced again. Women's bibliographies (including books written by and about men, such as Goncharov's *Oblomov,* a classic study of passivity, albeit with a male protagonist) and histories were circulated. We all read and wrote frenetically, pressing books and essays on one another, talking, arguing, discussing until all hours of the night. It was one huge, movable, impromptu women's university. I read Eleanor Flexner's *A Century of Struggle* in one big gulp. I never knew that the first wave of feminism had spent a hundred years fighting just so women could vote, or that the roots of political feminism had sprouted within the abolitionist movement. It is a scandal that this book is not required reading in high school.

I had never participated in a demonstration in my life until I joined the movement. At an early NOW meeting, we were wrangling foolishly among ourselves, when Kate Millett stood up and declared we had better plan and execute an action to focus our energies and get us off one another's throats. Millett, a witty, professorial bohemian, was convincing, and we voted (long live Robert's Rules of Order) to strike the *New*

York Times Sunday edition until they agreed to desegregate the discriminatory *Help Wanted: Male, Help Wanted: Female* ads. On the designated Saturday (fall, 1967?), we turned up at the *Times* truck-loading entrance on 43nd Street, determined to lie down in front of the trucks to prevent delivery if we did not get an affirmative answer from management by Saturday evening. We made signs under the supervision of our graphic artists, and stapled them to sticks—something we'd seen in movies, I suppose. This caused our first incident with the police. As we walked in a circle on the sidewalk, chanting slogans, the cops, without warning, converged on us, yanking the signs out of our hands. Surprised and uncomprehending, we resisted, and the plywood sticks splintered painfully in our hands. We found out the hard way that it is illegal to have "sharp objects" at demonstrations in New York City. (Later on we learned to save cardboard dowels from rolls of tin foil or paper towels, to use instead.) It was my first demonstration, and I quaked internally at the idea of making a fool of myself, chanting and shouting in the street. The police aggression dispelled my boarding school sense of propriety, and my very Italian fear of *la brutta figura:* losing face.

Millett, Atkinson, and the rest of our group were heartened, as more and more women arrived to join the demonstration. Any trace of embarrassment vanished as reporters turned up in droves. Public relations were always a strong point of the feminist movement. We had solid PR professionals, like the soignée revolutionary Muriel Fox, to advise and guide us. No newspaper, TV, or radio station was left in the dark about our actions and purposes. Eleanor Holmes Norton, the head of the New York State Civil Rights Commission, gave us a boost when she came by to express solidarity. Norton and Representative Shirley Chisholm were the two Black women leaders of that era. Two buttoned-down and revered members of the Black Establishment, they never feared to place themselves in the forefront of constructive change. In our demonstration against the *Times,* we were spared getting our demonstration frocks covered in crankcase oil when management unexpectedly capitulated to our demands, hours ahead of schedule. We had won our first battle, and didn't even have to miss dinner.

Actually, I don't remember doing much cooking in those days. There were married women in NOW, who had proper home lives. But most of the downtown women were single, and lived alternative lifestyles. I was midtown and unmarried, though invariably in some kind of serially monogamic relationship. I don't remember setting a table, or sitting down to one already set, from 1966 to 1975. I think we considered it unspeakably bourgeois. Once Shulie Firestone and I were commenting favorably on the fiercely feminist tone of an article written by Sally Kempton (now Swami Durgananda) for *Esquire* magazine. I expressed happy surprise that such a revolutionary piece should appear in the Establishment press, and asked if she knew anything about Kempton's (feminist) credentials. "Oh, you know," said Shulie, with a wave of dismissal, "she's married and gives dinner parties." I should have reminded Shulie, who was the first to point it out to the rest of us, of the Stanton-Anthony dichotomy. There are many accommodations a woman can make to a job or a profession, but wifehood is a continuing education in withstanding institutionalized subordination (as I have since had occasion to learn firsthand). In any case, few of us were married in those days.

Staging demonstrations, making signs, printing and mailing press releases, and so on, all cost money, and it more or less came from our own pockets. Those of us who still held regular jobs collected involuntary contributions from our employers. From 1966, until I resigned in 1969, at Avon International, I raided the mail room for photocopies, stationery, stamps, and even printing privileges, with the collusion of the mail-room guys. One day I discovered why they were so sweet and cooperative about helping me produce feminist documents. I had worn a bikini to the company picnic my first year with the company, a shocking event in 1966, at a relatively conservative company like Avon. Snapshots commemorating this landmark occasion were mail-room contraband. I had made another unwittingly popular move when I convinced the prettiest and most traditionally feminine woman in the office to stop wearing a girdle, standard marching gear for working women at that time. (For years my mother would send them to me by the box, where they would lie unused, curling and yellowing in the tissue paper.) I denounced these medieval instruments of torture as barbaric and unhealthy. Garter belts (panty hose weren't yet on the market) were sexier and a lot less constricting. Hence to the men in the Avon mail room, feminism didn't look all that threatening, at least for the time being, and came with compensations. Never mind that these particular incidents sprang as much from a European education as from a feminist consciousness.

Meanwhile, Ti-Grace Atkinson was pressuring me to take on a more public role, and thought my initial reluctance was due to a lack of commitment to the movement. I insisted on being thoroughly prepared, because I was certain our adversaries were well-read, well-informed, and capable of destroying anyone less than brilliantly primed. I passed my "finals," and completed my conversion to the cause, during an appearance on *The David Susskind Show*. Kate Millett, Ros Baxandall, Jacqui Ceballos, and I were to be the guests. We met before the show to work out strategy, rehearse tough questions, and psyche each other up. It was 1968, and the show would eventually be titled *Four Angry Women*. The four of us felt the responsibility of going on the air for the first time, as a group representing a broad spectrum of the movement, on a program that was nationally syndicated. We needn't have worried. It quickly became apparent that Susskind, a macho precursor of Dick Cavett, had done no noticeable preparation. He had an excellent woman producer, who booked the show and, no doubt, wrote the questions. But the man himself just talked off the top of his head. There wasn't much in it, on this topic. Certainly nothing original, informed, or devastating, except for the shock: so *this* was how much we mattered. A man with his own show (and we know how most men feel about their work) had not felt it necessary to go to any trouble at all to talk to four very different, eloquent, highly politicized women for an hour on the air, on a show with his name on it. My parents saw the program in California. My mother said to me: "If I were younger, I'd be out there on the barricades with you." My father, I was told, said: "Who does she think she is, Fidel Castro?"

I enjoyed doing the show, and was on the lookout for material that would broaden the political reach of the cabaret. I had no financing, and no way to pay anybody. I put an advertisement in the theatrical trade papers, which said: "Actors, male and female, with singing skills, wanted for Feminist cabaret theater showcase production." Or words to that effect. The first response was from a transvestite, who thought we were looking for female impersonators, followed by gay men looking for dates. It took one hundred years to win the right for women to vote, and fewer than fifty years later, there were literate people who didn't know what the word "feminist" meant. So I signed up for an acting class at the New School, and convinced some of the students to come and work for the feminist theater. There would be no money, but it would be a showcase. During the Susskind show, I had announced that I was starting a feminist theater, and the response was overwhelming: I was deluged with material. Jacqui Ceballos, with her habitual enthusiasm, impulsively committed us to do a benefit performance for NOW in March 1969. This was early January. I quit my job at Avon. My stomach tied in knots, I locked myself into my apartment, took the phone off the hook, and started reading from the pile of manuscripts I had received. There was a lot of good material, some of it very funny, and one pearl: Myrna Lamb. She would eventually have a mainstream (or damn close to it) success as a playwright when Joseph Papp produced her musical *The Mod Donna* at the Public Theater. We started rehearsals in Jacqui's Upper East Side apartment, with her kids filling in for the actors who hadn't been cast yet. The second writer of talent who revealed herself to us was Rita Mae Brown, a saucy, penniless young southerner who came aboard as my assistant director. She was a gifted poet, and made her debut as an artist reading her poem "The New Lost Feminist" in our first show.

I was on an emotional roller-coaster ride with my boyfriend at that time, which went on for years. This, and the fact that he was an older man who lived on the Upper East Side and drove a Ferrari, made me an object of suspicion in some quarters of the movement. (My image improved when I switched to a composer/college professor.) Rita would tease me, saying I wasted my time on men. It seemed to me that her specialty was seducing straight women. There was no chance of getting away from sex in those days. Rita was one of the ringleaders who responded to Betty Friedan's warning of "a lavender menace," threatening the feminist movement by forming a guerrilla group of that name. They staged an invasion of the Second Conference to Unite Women wearing lavender T-shirts with *lavender menace* emblazoned across the front and back. It was great theater and good fun, and defused a potentially divisive issue. Feminists were always being attacked as lesbians, and some women who had worked hard to found the movement, like Friedan, were terrified we would be destroyed if the issue was allowed to surface, and incorporated as part of the feminist platform. Many straight feminists disagreed. In the end, the innovators won, and the movement was not annihilated because of it.

But it was exhausting to have women, as well as men, badgering us for sex. For a while, there was pressure to prove how liberated we were by having affairs with women. There was a lesbian-activist line, which claimed that the only true feminist was a lesbian feminist, and that consorting with men was retrograde and counterrevolutionary. If you resisted, you were labeled "repressed," "brainwashed," or "man-junkie." It may seem funny now, but it was taken pretty seriously for a while. A woman had to get out there and test her sexuality to make sure she wasn't suppressing her natural inclinations. Sometimes I wonder how we got any work done at all. Messy relationships, intra-gender or otherwise, were the order of the day, and the personal was decidedly political. My boyfriend (the older man) and I fought all the time. He seesawed between being proud of me as my public role grew, and angry at the amount of time I spent on and at movement activities.

As the date for the feminist theater debut performance drew near, we had to secure a performance space. I talked to the owners of the Martinique Theatre, on West 32nd Street, and they agreed to let us have it when it was "dark," for the price of the insurance coverage. Jacqui Ceballos surged into high gear, seeing to the nuts and bolts business of tickets, handbills, and PR. Jacqui Michot Ceballos is a belle and a gentlewoman with a seductive Louisiana drawl. A stranger to manipulation and deviousness, she walked away from a husband and a life of wealth and prestige in Colombia to become a feminist and raise four small children by herself in New York City. No matter how heated the discussion, Jacqui never raised her voice or made unkind remarks. Never mealymouthed, she was much in demand as a public speaker, and was one of the protagonists of the famous Town Hall debate on feminism together with Germaine Greer, Jill Johnston, and Norman Mailer (the referee), and most of the New York intellectual elite in the audience. With her clear-eyed, soft-spoken feminism, a revolutionary in Establishment drag, she surely reached far more women "in the interior" (as she used to refer to the country between the coasts) than those of us who snorted fire and wore jeans or miniskirts.

Jacqui's tireless work on behalf of our debut-benefit paid off, and our first performance was sold out, standing room included. Our cast was an adventurous admixture of committed feminists and apolitical actors; and it gradually dawned on the latter that they had hitched their wagons to a political star that, should it ingloriously fall, could incinerate their ambitions. I was being given ultimatums right and left, which I ignored. Opening night we threw ourselves into the Rubicon without life jackets.

It was a triumph that fulfilled exaggerated expectations. TV news cameras and the pencil press were everywhere. With our shaky professionalism, we had zeroed in on the zeitgeist: we were trendy, we were a hit, we were the toast of the town. And merciful Minerva! we were funny. The audience laughed, roared, at all the jokes. We ended the show with a rousing parody of "The Battle Hymn of the Republic," written by Ruth Herschberger, and performed by the entire cast and crew, gathered onstage to ring down the curtain as we sang:

> Our eyes have seen the future and rejoice at what's to be;
> Every woman in position to achieve equality.
> We will vote ourselves to power with our own majority.
> Yes the time for NOW is now!
> Glory, glory hallelujah, etc.
>
> There'll be men upon their knees to us and begging for their lives
> And some we'll spare, and some we won't, for justice is our knife
> There'll be judo, and karate,
> And a rifle for each wife
> For it's liberation time . . .

Just so it won't seem too perfect: I had been advised by Rita Mae just before curtain time, that my boyfriend and my best friend were together out front. (I had gotten her a job at his firm.) I was aware that a liaison was brewing, but I never expected them to turn up together on opening night. I must have called on all my resources, because somehow the show went on. After endless curtain calls, and testimonials for the TV cameras by celebrities in the audience, and after the pandemonium out front died down, and after the previously mutinous cast members crowded into my dressing room to swear their undying fealty, and the television crews, reporters, friends, and supporters had packed up and left for the opening night party, I broke down. I was far from being a blameless participant in that nasty, classic little triangle; I was overwhelmed by the show's success, and devastated by the ruthless curiosity of the new couple. So much so, that I never made it to our big celebration at the Village Gate. I sat on the curb at a bus stop on Sixth Avenue, and wept uncontrollably. I mated with misery on what should have been the happiest night of my life. This was a pattern that it took me years to break. I could own my failures, but not my successes. There is nothing untrue in the theory of women's fear of success. Blaming men was a necessary step, but it was only through working to transcend my conditioning that I was able to break the grip of this problem.

On Sunday, May 18, 1969, the *New York Times* splashed a review across the front page of the Arts & Leisure section: "Is Motherhood Powerful? Not Any More" ran the headline. We received high praise for consigning to the historical dustbin the Close-Binding Intimate Mother, a monster produced by the Feminine Mystique. In reexamining the double bind women constantly face between emotional and intellectual fulfillment: "The New Feminist Repertory Theatre, like the new feminist movement, starts with no dogma and is really working at what other radical theaters pretend to be doing: searching for a path in uncharted territory." There were many other reviews, almost all of them favorable, with even-handed critiques of performance levels. This was heady stuff, but as our box office was submerged with reservation requests, I felt it was time to professionalize.

A young woman agent put me together with a talented songwriting team: Bobby Paul and Arthur Morey. Paul was a professor of anthropolgy, as well as a trained composer, and Morey had studied political science with Hannah Arendt at the University of Chicago. Paul's music was richly melodious, and Morey's lyrics politically driven. We were a match, and, not to put too fine a point on it, I indoctrinated them. We spent long hours schmoozing all over the map and discussing feminism. We showed one another our "mud pies": in my case the material and reviews accumulated so far; in theirs the theatrical songs they had been writing together since they were undergraduates at Harvard. Once we knew we shared a sense of humor, we had no doubts. Then the two of them went off and wrote an evening's worth of songs I would be proud to have written. People often assumed that I had written the lyrics. At the most I inspired them. I did translate and adapt several Italian political folk songs. With these songs, a fistful of poems, a sketch, and a monologue or two, the New Feminist Cabaret Theater was born. We immediately obtained bookings all over New York, and at colleges across the Northeast and Middle West. We hired another woman singer/actress, and the four of us would drive or fly to our gigs. Interest was high, we were in demand, and so we developed yet another parallel career: auditioning for the music industry.

The music was always so well reviewed, and we received so many requests for records, that our agent had us start meeting with record companies. The subject was hot, and the companies were interested. In the music business of the late sixties and seventies, the suits wore counterculture camouflage; they were cool, casual guys. When we performed our feminist cabaret songs, their expressions slithered around like an arpeggio run amok: curious, appalled, seduced, provoked, defensive. They were most anxious to let me know they did not beat their wives.

We were criticized by some feminists for being a mixed group. My purpose in founding a feminist theater was to reach people of both sexes, and to move the discussion of sex roles beyond the stereotypes. I would have looked for very different material had I wanted to stimulate discussion only among women. There were other feminist theater groups who were composed exclusively of women, and performed only for all-women audiences. I saw some of them perform, and enjoyed their productions, without ever feeling moved to emulate them.

Yet in some parts of the movement, success was called a male identification and outspoken women were often called power-mad. Hence there was certainly a need to address intra-movement issues. By the early seventies, there were signs of burnout all around. Kate Millett had been viciously attacked by a group of women for having the temerity to sign her own book, *Sexual Politics,* with her name. Shulamith Firestone was so terrified of retaliation for writing (and signing, and being paid for) *The Dialectic of Sex* that she locked herself in her Alphabet City apartment.

I had been purged from my first consciousness-raising group. I had always been looked at askance by some of the more radical, left-wing feminists. In fact, with the benefit of hindsight, I can see that I was always a "foreign body" in the downtown milieu, despite forming lasting political and personal friendships there. The counterculture, fully expressed amid downtown feminists, was for me the proverbial nice place to visit. But I always lammed it back uptown emotionally and physically as soon as I could. The grungy apartments, mangy crash-pad lifestyle were not for me. Nor were counterculture men, heaven forfend. I've always preferred my machismo up front and declared, where I can see it.

After being purged, I was able to form another CR group, with Letty Cottin Pogrebin, Eleanor Perry, Ene Riisna, and others who were writers, editors, screenwriters, televison producers, and journalists. When I contrast the NOW meetings with the Redstockings or Radical Women meetings, or my first CR group with the second, I am struck by how much more revolutionary it was to hear establishment women talking feminism than it was to hear similar rhetoric from SNCC and SDS refugees in jeans and granny glasses. If for no other reason, the establishment women had a lot more to lose. Yet there was a tendency to gauge one's feminist credentials by look, address, and degree of hairiness. At a time when feminists were still being ridiculed as rejects from the marriage market, or lesbians, I wore eye makeup and miniskirts, even hot pants. (Fashion note: jeans were my uniform; but my favorite items of clothing from that era were a pair of burnt orange velvet hot pants and a tobacco suede midiskirt, worn with a ribbed poor-boy turtleneck sweater and knee-length brown leather boots. Si!) What made me a useful movement spokesperson to the country at large made me anathema to many radical women. But not to all. Robin Morgan and I were guests on a TV talk show in the late sixties, when the hostess tried to set us against one another by pointing out the difference in our styles. Robin, a charter member of Radical Feminists, and a recovering actress who had espoused the full counterculture look, replied with a line from the Black Liberation movement: "Better a natural woman in an artificial look, than an artificial woman in a natural look."

In the early 1970s when I traveled to college campuses, after my speech and the discussion period, a large group of women moved over to the dorms with me and we sat up till dawn, talking feminism and swapping experiences. We learned from one another, and we had good fun. By 1975 all this had changed. My sense that feminism had lost forward movement also came from these college audiences. The students still filled the halls, but their participatory enthusiasm was gone. The young women and men who had been so lively and stimulating just a few years earlier were now quiet and passively attentive. Gone were the probing, challenging questions, the wholehearted involvement. They seemed zoned-out on tranquilizers. The teachers and organizers confirmed my impressions. What emerged now was the students' concern for the future. Interest in ideas was limited to how it would affect landing a good, safe job. Some women students were readjusting their ambitions, hedging their bets with secretarial and other traditionally female courses.

Most depressing of all, the movement felt brain-dead. The inner tensions and fighting never led to an open debate about the implications for women of competing with one another for power in the movement and in the marketplace. Power and success were dirty words; nobody was supposed to want, enjoy, or, god forbid, seek it. Those who did achieve often felt obliged to be apologetic, and under an obligation to teach other women their skills, and/or share the credit. It made some women very angry that you could not turn every feminist into a public speaker or writer by drawing lots, by sharing skills, by decree. The attacks, the jealousy, the envy, all got shoved under a rug. This pattern was clear even earlier than the mid-seventies, and I had a bead on it from the first.

Even when the Second Congress to Unite Women was held in New York City (1970), I was running on empty. The intra-movement attacks had taken their toll. But the final straw was learning how many other feminists had been attacked even more violently, and more harmfully, than I had been. Once I realized that what was happening constituted a pattern, I wrote "Divisiveness and Self-Destruction in the Woman's Movement." When I was finished, I took it to the conference. A vocal group toward the front of the auditorium did its best to drown out my voice and prevent me from continuing, once they saw who I was and heard what I meant to discuss. They were a radical left-wing group called the Class Workshop. Luckily for me there were far more women who wanted to hear what I had to say than not, and the CW people were forced to let me read my paper. The reaction to it was tumultuous. As the CW women roared their dissent, scores of women rushed toward me to ask for copies, and to communicate similar experiences.

Every Second-Wave feminist has a theory about why the movement lost steam. Mine was that our refusal to wash our dirty linen in public, i.e., to examine and thus politicize the new experience of (nonsexual) competition between/among women, brought us to an intellectual and emotional impasse. Our inability to create a philosophical life jacket for the burgeoning numbers of movement burnout victims forced them to retreat from activism and heal themselves as best they could. Female ambition and achievement had long been demonized by the patriarchy in the name of the feminine mystique, but now once again by the hostility, aggression, and masked rage of some women. As I wrote then, if you are an achiever, you are immediately labelled a thrill-seeking opportunist, a ruthless mercenary, out to make her fame and fortune over the dead bodies of selfless sisters who have buried their abilities and sacrificed their ambitions for the greater glory of Feminism. Productivity seems to be the major crime—but if you have the additional misfortune of being outspoken and articulate, you are also accused of being power-mad, elitist, fascist, and finally the worst epithet of all: *a male identifier.*

My last major movement effort was to organize a fund-raiser for women political candidates, together with Bonnie Lobell, a political professional, and Ene Riisna, a TV producer. Margaret Stern, a member of my CR group and a wine-industry executive, got the Four Seasons restaurant to lend us their establishment, and persuaded a distributer to donate wine in abundance. Another friend knew a cheese importer who donated massive amounts of fine cheeses. Riisna and I were having lunch in her apartment, wondering who we could hit up for bread or crackers. Riisna picked up a box of Ry-Krisps sitting on the table, and called the importer cold. On the strength of what we had put together so far, he agreed to give us all the Ry-Krisps we needed! He and all the other contributors were repaid with a credit and a thank you on the program. We staffed the party for free with women who wanted to come but couldn't afford the fifty-dollar ticket. It was a huge success, and every last cent we earned went to support women running for office, under the auspices of the National Women's Political Caucus. There was literally no overhead. From the mix of movers and shakers present at that event, it was clear feminism had arrived. No longer just a fad, we were respected, accepted, and courted for our votes and political clout. It was good to end on a high note, but I was running out of gas.

As I was recovering from public and private burnout at my parents' home in California in the early spring of 1975, a small ray of hope arrived one day: a call from Gloria Steinem. She had just read for the first time "Divisiveness and Self-Destruction in the Women's Movement," and was stunned that it had been written five years before. "How did you know?" she said. "It's as if you had lived my life before I did." She asked if *Ms.* magazine could print it. Could they? Yes! Did they? Not quite. When it finally appeared, no doubt after being picked over by the collective, horizontal decision-making process at *Ms.,* it had been gentrified, circumcised, and bowdlerized until it was purged of any heat or light it may originally have had. My adamantine affection, friendship for, and loyalty toward Steinem just made my disappointment worse: I couldn't even work up a good hate. But understanding was no consolation. I was at a dead-end; my part of the Great Adventure had ended with a whimper.

During the revolution, if you can call the worm turning a revolution (as the great Flo Kennedy used to say), some feminists would dismiss me and women who looked and dressed like me with the epithet "beauty queen." Now that I found myself in Hollyweird, where principles easily bleach out in the sun, I figured I might as well play the game, since it was the only one in town. I sat for a sultry set of 8 × 10 glossies, lied about my age, and forged a résumé laden with TV dreck to replace my useless previous life's uncommercial credits. Not that it did me any good. For two endless years in Lost Angeles I acted in a play at La Mama, desk jockeyed for a movie company, and collected unemployment. I also seriously applied myself to the study of metaphysics. Finally the gods took pity. I was offered a job as dialogue writer, coach, and actress on an Italian film by Marco Ferreri, with Gérard Depardieu and Marcello Mastroianni: locations in New York, and studio work in Rome. I was going back to Italy. I was going home. The odd thing was, I was cast as the director of a feminist theater . . .

I had never expected to return to Italy for good. But I kept on getting work in films, and every time I would travel back to the States, I could feel my American ties loosening. Yet Italy was just entering the Years of Lead in 1977: terrorism, the Red Brigades, the abduction and assassination of Aldo Moro. And the Italian feminist movement was in full bloom. For me it was a time warp, and I felt like an impostor when I was invited to participate. I never really felt foreign in Italy except when I was with Italian feminists. The long, tedious philosophical arguments, the obsession with Communist politics and the Politics of Difference, the abhorrence of pragmatism were not my cup of tea. I did what I was asked to do, whatever was useful: participate in a press conference, sign a manifesto, give a speech on American feminism, march in the March 8th Feminist parade. Eventually the movement lost visibility here, too. Meantime I worked in films and journalism, and in 1987, I rather suddenly married an Italian whose mother is a feminist. Over the last year or two, beginning with the invitation to write this memoir, I have again begun to write about feminist issues. A year and a half ago an Italian editor who read a rough draft of this memoir asked me to write for a monthly political magazine, roughly equivalent to *The New Republic*. I have continued to do so, and in my work for *Liberal* and other publications, I have followed the rising of the Third Wave, which started in the United States, and is sending out ripples to the rest of the world, including Italy. I am most interested that in 1995 Pope John Paul II started seriously addressing feminists as such, and feminism as a social movement, which has brought great good to the world. The seeds we planted almost thirty years ago, inherited from the First Wave, are now beginning to germinate, and I'm enthusiastic about the diversity. It's so much better to have it out in the open. Feminism, god be praised, is not monolithic. I see our work now with a longer view: this is a lifetime's, many lifetimes' enterprise. Feminism is an unfolding, a slow blossoming, and each generation works some part of the vineyard. At times it seems to die out and disappear, as it did between the two World Wars, and in the late seventies to early nineties. Now we begin again, writing, arguing, communicating with one another, and with the rest of the world. Sometimes feminism will seem to skip a generation, as younger women appear to fail to appreciate the work that went into exposing and changing the feminine mystique.

In 1994, in my first ending to this piece, I wrote: "Once we're through dusting off these memories, maybe we can move on to making some new ones. There's a lot of work to be done: places to go, people to see, received ideas to challenge. Maybe we could get together to discuss it. My place, or yours? And make sure to call me for the next demonstration. . . ." For I used to wonder if the good times were all behind me, if feminism would ever coalesce into a movement again in my lifetime. As it happens, the invitation to participate in this book was a harbinger of the Third Wave. I am contented beyond words to be back working in our vineyard again, and roundly grateful to have made it home before sundown.

On the Origins of the Women's Liberation Movement from a Strictly Personal Perspective

Jo Freeman aka Joreen

I backed into feminism through an intellectual route. Not that I lacked the personal experience of discrimination that generated the proverbial "click" of so many of my contemporaries; I just didn't see it. As was true of others, I grew up believing that there were three sexes: men, women and me. Thus I was quite capable of carrying all of the stereotypes and biases about women that my culture fostered without making the personal connection or feeling demeaned thereby. I knew about woman's place. I just didn't know my own.

Although born in the South at the end of World War II, I was raised in Los Angeles, mostly in the San Fernando Valley, home of the Valley Girls. In the McCarthyite fifties, with its emphasis on complete conformity, this was a good place to grow up white, middle class, and culturally deprived. I was not a Valley Girl. But growing up among them I learned, and believed, all the negative stereotypes about females in our society. Boys, clothes, and popularity seemed to be all the other girls cared about. Those few of us who were interested in other things—learning, careers, politics—kept to ourselves and kept our mouths shut. Fortunately, my mother knew this was not a nourishing environment and got me out of there by engineering my last-minute graduation from high school at age 15. Two weeks after my sixteenth birthday she put me on a train to the University of California at Berkeley with a large trunk. Since the dorms and the boarding houses were full, I had to find my own accommodations. My mother didn't believe in protection.

Berkeley in the early sixties was a great place to go to school. It was my personal and intellectual liberation. I still think of it as my spiritual home. But it wasn't a place where women, or their absence, were particularly noted. During my four years in one of the largest institutions of higher education in the world—and one with a progressive reputation—I not only never had a woman professor, I never even saw one. Worse yet, I didn't notice. Even today, the student life is probably the most egalitarian experience a woman will ever have. Discrimination is more subtle, more covert, than in the outside world, so much so that unless your nose is rubbed in it, you don't see it.

When I entered college in 1961, the country was just emerging from the straightjacket of McCarthyism. The Civil Rights Movement was catching the public imagination with its dramatic defiance of the old order. A new, young, Democratic President was calling us to public service. The House Un-American Activities Committee—that political enforcer of cultural conformity—was in retreat. All things political seemed possible. Yet no one thought women were political. Nor did anyone think abortion was a public concern. We accepted the fact that it was illegal without question. If you got knocked up, it was your own damn fault. Child care was also a personal problem; the fact that it was a woman's personal problem was not something we thought about. As for gay rights, most of us didn't know what "lesbian" meant. Those that did thought it was a mental disease. If there was a "woman's issue"—and no one my age thought there was—it was whether or not a married woman should work if her husband could support her.

As a child of the sixties, I was raised on civil rights. My mother was a Southern renegade who served in the Women's Army Corps during World War II and got right on race. Her views were strengthened by teaching on the east side of Los Angeles, where she found more friends among her Negro[1] colleagues than white, largely because of their common Southern cultural heritage. The Civil Rights Movement's demonstrations and boycotts in Alabama, her home state, became dinner table conversation and her support was unequivocal. When the movement came to Berkeley in the fall of 1963, I didn't need to be recruited; I was ready. I had already had major confrontations with my Southern relatives when we visited Alabama, and with the segregationist whose locker faced mine during my last year of high school gym. As was found to be true of most sixties activists, I did not rebel against parental

---

[1] This was the proper term in those days, so I use it here.

values; I acted them out. My mother was the true rebel; I was merely her daughter.

The Civil Rights Movement became an intellectual as well as political compulsion. I read everything I could find and delved further into history to read about the abolitionists. Learning that this movement had been the incubator for the woman's rights movement, and seeing the parallels between that time and my own, led me to speculate that the next major movement would be one of women. I didn't tell anyone, because I knew everyone would laugh at me, but I did tuck it into the back of my mind as something to look for. "Women" also became a subtext for my reading about black Americans and the social and psychological consequences of racism. I looked around and applied what I learned by analogy. This in turn forced me to confront my own very real prejudices about women.

As I plunged into civil rights activism my only doubt was about committing civil disobedience. For kids of my class and generation, getting arrested was beyond the pale. It took six months of reading, discussion, and introspection to decide that civil disobedience was not only possible, but necessary if my beliefs were to be more than theoretical positions. My mother disapproved. She found out about my first arrest, on March 7, 1964, from a colleague whose daughter read the fine print in the San Francisco newspaper listing all 167 arrestees. Her scorching phone call still rings in my ears, as does her final admonition that if I ever got arrested again, I could forget about further financial support. Six weeks later I was arrested again; I've been self-supporting ever since.

I was arrested three times that year and again in Alabama and Mississippi in 1966. All told, my record was five arrests on ten counts; three convictions on four counts; twenty-eight days in six different jails in three states. As I was to learn, criminal records have many long-term consequences apart from the official penalty, particularly when one applies for jobs, school, or fellowships. Although I am now a member in good standing of the New York State Bar, my mother's anger that I was ruining my life was not irrational.

My second arrest kept me away from Mississippi summer. I spent two weeks in court and enrolled in summer school so I could graduate early and join the freedom fighters in the South. By the time sentence was pronounced in late July, I was so impatient with study and so anxious to "put my body on the line" that I wanted to go South without my degree. Jim Townsend, my poli sci honors professor, talked me out of this. Instead I sublet my apartment and hitchhiked to Atlantic City to join the vigil of the Mississippi Freedom Democratic Party at the Democratic Convention. I returned a month later with a couple of hundred dollars from selling buttons on the boardwalk and a lot more knowledge about civil rights, the Democratic Party—and men.

The Berkeley Free Speech Movement happened my senior year. I was on the executive committee from the very beginning to the very end, but I was not an insider. I was in the minority faction of hated moderates. We thought of ourselves as the loyal opposition—agreeing with the goals but not always with the tactics. The radical faction saw us as a fifth wheel, and the fact that I was the official representative from the University Young Democrats didn't help any. The few women in the leadership got there because of their relationship to important men. Ordinary women were supposed to do the scutwork and take care of the boys. The sexual revolution was just starting and complaints of unwarranted sexual pressure were hesitantly surfacing. Sleeping around was called "FSMing." Those that didn't do it were prudes. Besides being a Democrat, I was a prude. I'm not sure which was worse.

Within a week of graduation I was on my way to Atlanta to join SCOPE—the 1965 summer project of the Southern Christian Leadership Conference (SCLC), otherwise known as Dr. King's organization. Most went for the summer; I went for the duration. SCLC concentrated on voter registration to illuminate the need for the Voting Rights Act then being debated in Congress. Even after the bill passed, SCLC tended to use both staff and volunteers more as shock troops to garner publicity than as local community organizers—which was the SNCC strategy. SCLC would send mostly black teams of subsistence staff workers to the small towns of Alabama to register voters while also testing the waters for the feasibility of marches and demonstrations. For this men were preferred, though not exclusively. After the summer was over, the director of Southern Projects, Hosea Williams, tried to keep the remaining women in the office, but some of us got out. I credit my escape not only to my willfulness and intentionally poor typing skills, but to the hand-cranked mimeograph that two friends in Berkeley, Tony and Carolyn Scarr, had sent me. Until you've written out 300 mass-meeting leaflets by hand, you don't know how valuable this was to any project director—and I went with the machine.

For a year, I worked in Newberry, South Carolina; and Abbeville, Selma, Greenville, Birmingham, and Tuskegee, Alabama. Although I was not conscious of it at the time, my observations of black women in these communities contributed a great deal to my becoming a feminist by reforming my attitudes toward women. Since I lived with local families, often at risk to them, and spent most of my days knocking on doors in black neighborhoods or standing in line at the courthouse, and most of my nights going to meetings, I had a lot to observe. Black women seemed different from white women. They seemed stronger. More important, that strength was accepted, not denigrated. They occupied more social space than white women, played more roles, were a bigger presence in their communities. None fit the "clinging vine" stereotype popular then—or seemed to want to. Some of the subconscious contempt in which I had always held women because of this "feminine ideal" began to melt away. In effect, the black women I saw and worked with provided a different model of what it meant to be a woman in our society, and the black community a different attitude. This opened up a whole realm of possibilities.

In June of 1966, the South exploded again. After James Meredith was shot trying to walk from Memphis, Tennessee, to Jackson, Mississippi, the civil rights organizations took up his call to finish the walk. People from all over the country, even the world, joined the trek. Hosea sent the male staff to the March, leaving the women in Atlanta. New arrivals flooded the office; among them I found a woman with a car and filled it with other women. When we arrived in Memphis, Hosea looked at me, shook his head, and said, "When Atlanta told me a car full of women had left, I knew it was you." He assigned me to stay with the March and phone in hourly reports.

As the days wore on under the hot Mississippi sun, more and more white women began to complain, and since I was one of the few white female staff members, a lot of them complained to me. Black women may also have complained, but not to me. I heard the phrase "male chauvinism" for the first time; I didn't even know what it meant. Someone in the leadership had decided that women should only walk on the inside of a double march line. Each woman needed a male protector beside her; two women could not walk together. Men were not so restricted. No one believed this "protection" was real. Snipers would shoot from the inside where the bushes and trees were, not the outside where the Mississippi Highway Patrol kept the passing cars away. The inside line walked on the shoulder of the road where the rocks were; the outside walked on the asphalt. And none of the men who were so adamant about our need for protection ever offered us their sun hats or first place in the water line.

Nor were we protected from the men, who, when we camped for the night, became somewhat predatory. What is now called sexual harassment was then called "prove you believe in civil rights." I certainly had heard this line before. But in my year in the Southern movement it had seldom been more than a hopeful request. True, one white woman had been raped at an SCLC retreat the month before. I was not there, but she and I had talked about it. Judy (not her real name) attributed her attack to the distribution of a paper entitled "Stresses and Strains on the White Female Civil Rights Worker," written by Dr. Alvin F. Poussaint. Based on Dr. Poussaint's treatment interviews with women during Mississippi summer the year before, the paper said white women became civil rights workers either because they had a White African Queen Complex, or wanted to sleep with black men.[2] The paper had been passed out at the retreat by Rev. Andrew Young because he thought it would help movement workers understand white women. A lot of the males at this retreat weren't seasoned SCLC staffers but gang kids from Chicago, recruited by SCLC in hopes of starting a project. Judy and I thought the distribution of this paper by highly respected authority figures—a psychiatrist and a minister—was misinterpreted by the Chicago kids as legitimating sexual assault. Many of these same males had come to the Meredith Mississippi March. I thought they brought their crazy ideas about white women with them and spread them around.

Wanting to be neither "protected" nor "prey," women met nightly to discuss what to do. We made a few cautious complaints to the March

---

[2] The paper was later published as "The Stresses of the White Female Worker in the Civil Rights Movement in the South," in 123:4 *American Journal of Psychiatry,* 1966, pp. 401–5. The footnotes clarify that it was based on interviews with women who sought psychiatric help because they had problems coping with life in the Mississippi summer project, not a random sample of female movement workers. A careful reading would dissuade someone from generalizing to the entire population of white female civil rights workers, but a casual reading would not.

leadership, but we accepted their response that they really had more important things to worry about than sex among the marchers—who after all could just go home. We kept our complaints away from the press, as our first loyalty was to the Civil Rights Movement, and we saw nothing productive in publicity. As women have done for eons, we endured in silence. But we did talk to each other. Meeting with these women nightly resurrected my observation of a couple of years earlier that the next big movement would be one of women. Little did I know that similar events were happening elsewhere in the country.

After the March, SCLC set up a voter registration and demonstration project in Grenada, Mississippi, and as usual, I was the only female staffer. On August 18, 1966, just as things were heating up, the *Jackson Daily News,* which billed itself as "Mississippi's Greatest Newspaper," exposed me in an editorial headlined "Professional Agitator Hits All Major Trouble Spots." The editors didn't actually call me a Communist; they just accused me of working with Communists (Bettina Aptheker in the Free Speech Movement), participating in Communist organizations (SLATE—a Berkeley student group), and advancing Communist causes (the FSM). And there were a few errors. Among others, I was not 25, but only 20. What prompted Hosea to put me on the next bus for Atlanta was not the editorial allegations; it was the five photographs: front, side, hair up, hair down. "This thing makes you Klan-bait," he said. "We don't need more martyrs right now." For once, I didn't argue.

This ended my usefulness as a civil rights worker, but I wasn't ready to admit it. Back in Atlanta I did chores for SCLC's press department, and then jumped at the chance to do chores for Coretta Scott King. During the six weeks I worked for her, my admiration grew. She was much more than a minister's wife and mother. Her personal ambitions and concerns had been stifled by Dr. King's prominence and the need to play her part in the Civil Rights Movement, but they had not been lost; she had plans to move on to her own concerns when times were less intense. Before I left, my growing admiration led to another feminist "click." I realized that I was 21 years old, and she was the first woman I had ever met that I truly admired. What did it mean to live so long, and see so much, and only see men worthy of great esteem?

It was time to leave, but I was so emotionally attached to the movement that I found it hard to do. In October I joined SCLC's Chicago project, but it was not successful, and SCLC eventually withdrew. In

January I switched to a program run by the Urban Training Center for Christian Mission (UTC). Under the sponsorship of the United Church of Christ, I spent the next six months as photographer and coeditor of the *West Side TORCH,* a community newspaper published by the West Side Organization. I loved this job, but UTC only paid $34.50 a week, and unlike my stint with SCLC, now I had to pay my own rent.

In the meantime, news of a new feminist consciousness was percolating. I didn't know about the October 1966 organizing meeting of the National Organization for Women until I read an interview with Dr. Alice Rossi in the *Chicago Daily News.* I wrote her a letter but received no reply. Over the next year I wrote a few more letters to NOW names in the news, including Betty Friedan, but, again, no reply. In the spring of 1967, I met Barbara Likan, a German immigrant whose son was active in the antiwar movement. Barbara wanted to organize women, but had no idea how to do it. She gathered around her an eclectic group of men and women who met monthly to talk about how woman deserved more respect for her role as first educator. I wasn't impressed.

While I worked for the *TORCH,* I looked for ways to organize women. Saul Alinsky held a workshop at UTC, and afterwards I asked if I could enroll in his Industrial Areas Foundation to learn how to organize. Women don't make good organizers, he told me. We might let you in, but you'll have to pay your own tuition of $10,000 per year. In July I applied to the Institute for Policy Studies, a New Left think tank in Washington, D.C., which sponsored students who wanted to do political research and organizing. "I want to organize women," I told Art Waskow and Robb Burlage. "There's no future in that," they replied. My application was denied.

Occasionally I dropped into the national office of SDS where, in June of 1967, I learned that Heather Booth and Naomi Weisstein were teaching a course on women at a free school (i.e., non-credit, no tuition) at the University of Chicago. I made the last class, and heard Jane Adams talk about a forthcoming National Conference for a New Politics. The organizers planned to nominate an alternative Presidential ticket. We should run a workshop on women, I said. Jane liked the idea and organized two meetings of New Left women to talk about it. They didn't like it. I hitched to New York where I broached the possibility to women at the Fifth Avenue Peace Parade Committee and other antiwar organizations. They acknowledged that women had problems, but weren't ready to devote energy to solving them. We were in the middle of a horrid war; because men could be drafted, men had more problems.

Lefties from all over the country came to Chicago for the NCNP over the Labor Day weekend in 1967. I went there not knowing what to expect and found a woman's workshop on the program! Barbara Likan had had the same idea I had but took a more direct route. She convinced the conference organizers to have a woman's workshop by offering the services of her good friend, Madeline Murray O'Hare, to chair it. O'Hare was famous as the plaintiff in the Supreme Court decision to remove prayer from the public schools. A devoted atheist, she had never shown much interest in women, but, after all, she was a celebrity; that was enough to entice the men.

Black Power was at its zenith; the conference was segregated by mutual agreement. Blacks met with blacks. Whites met with whites. Sometimes they met together. The thirty to forty women who voted to keep the men out of our workshop merely followed suit. We met every day and hammered out a resolution to put before the plenary. By today's standards, it wasn't very radical—equal pay for equal work, abortion on demand—but in those days it seemed very daring. None of the New Left women I had met earlier in the summer came to the workshop. Ti-Grace Atkinson paid a visit from New York to talk about NOW, but no one paid her much attention.

Five of us went to the Resolutions Committee only to be told that they already had one from women, and there could only be one. It had come from Women's Strike for Peace, whose distinguished representatives had not attended our workshop. The Resolutions Chair told us to combine our resolutions. The fact that WSP's was about peace, not women, was not relevant. Theirs began, "We women take our stand on the side of life." I said I'd submit our original one as a minority report and walked out. On my way, I ran into Shulamith Firestone. Shulie didn't believe what I told her and went to find out for herself. She returned madder than I was.

We stayed up all night writing our own minority report. The more we talked, the more we wrote, the more radical it got. The next day we waited all day for the women's resolution to be put on the floor, passing our minority report around, recruiting support, and preparing for a floor fight. When the time came, meeting chair William Pepper ignored

us. "All in favor, all opposed, motion passed," he said. "Next resolution." As we stood there in shock, a young man pushed his way in front
of us. He was instantly recognized by the chair. Turning to face the
crowded room he said, "Ladies and gentlemen, I want to speak for the
forgotten American, the American Indian." We rushed the podium,
where the men only laughed at our outrage. When Shulie reached Pepper, he literally patted her on the head. "Cool down, little girl," he said.
"We have more important things to do here than talk about women's
problems."

Shulie didn't cool down and neither did I. I invited everyone from
the summer meetings to my apartment where Shulie and I told them
what had happened. The other women responded to our rage. We continued to meet almost weekly for seven months, usually at my place on
Chicago's West Side. But we didn't know what to do. We were all action
oriented, but we didn't have the resources to call a march, demonstration, or even a conference. So we talked. And we wrote.

Most of the women at these early meetings had some affiliation
with SDS. We learned from them that SDS women had been discussing
their role in the movement for a couple of years. Only the previous summer an SDS national conference had passed a resolution calling for
women's full participation. But the men regularly ridiculed them and
nothing happened. In the fall of 1965 two SNCC women, Casey Hayden and Mary King, had written "A Kind of Memo" on women in the
(civil rights) movement, which had circulated widely even before publication in a movement magazine in 1966.[3] But despite all this talk,
nothing had happened.

While we talked, I was looking for a job. My fellowship at the
TORCH had expired and it was time to decide what to do with my life.
I pursued journalism and photography for a few months, but was
turned down by all the major papers. At my one interview with the
Chicago Sun Times I was bluntly told that very few women were hired
because "women can't cover riots." My application to teach public
school was turned down because of my arrest record. Want ads listed
jobs separately by sex; when I called the ones under "men," whoever

---

[3] Casey, Hayden, and Mary King, "Sex and Caste: A Kind of Memo," 10 *Liberation*,
April 1966, pp. 35–36.

answered the phone was very surprised and not interested. I finally found a job under "women" as an assistant editor on a trade magazine. I soon learned that I was already bumping the ceiling for women. Men started as associate editors and went up. Women ended as associate editors, but only after years in the trenches. There was no future in this. Having heard that merit was the only thing that mattered in academia, I applied to graduate school in political science at the University of Chicago.

At the end of October 1967, Shulie moved to New York, where Staughton Lynd had told her to look up Pam Allen.[4] Together they went to meetings—anti-war, SDS, anything they could find—looking for recruits. Later that fall, they formed New York Radical Women. Among the first members were Anne Koedt, who was to write some of the most important early pamphlets,[5] and Robin Morgan, who published the first commercial compilation of movement pamphlets.[6] Others included Kathie Amatniek, Carol Hanisch, Peggy Dobbins, and Rosalyn Baxandall.

In Chicago, two or three dozen women attended meetings of what became known as the West Side group. The regulars included Heather Tobis Booth, Vivien Leburg Rothstein, Naomi Weisstein, Sue Munaker, Sara Evans Boyte, Amy Kesselman, Fran Rominsky, and Laya Firestone (Shulie's sister). These women lived in the two neighborhoods in Chicago, Rogers Park to the north and Hyde Park to the south, which had concentrations of radicals, and by the end of 1967 two more women's groups had formed in each of these.

All of us traveled. Airfare was cheap. Conferences were plentiful. People moved. Almost from the first meeting, members of the West Side group were telling their friends all over the country that something was happening. After Heather spoke to Marilyn Salzman Webb, a new group quickly formed in Washington, D.C., at the same Institute for

---

[4] Pam later wrote a major pamphlet called *Free Space: A Perspective on the Small Groups in Women's Liberation*, New York: Times Change, 1970. A short version was published in *Notes from the Third Year* and reprinted in *Radical Feminism*, ed. by Anne Koedt, Ellen Levine, and Anita Rapone, New York: Quadrangle, 1973, pp. 271–279.

[5] Three of these were reprinted in *Radical Feminism*.

[6] Robin Morgan, ed., *Sisterhood Is Powerful: An Anthology of Writings from the Women's Liberation Movement*, New York: Vintage, 1970.

Policy Studies that had told me only a few months previously that organizing women was a waste of time. After Kathie Amatniek visited
Boston, her friend Nancy Hawley invited friends to dinner and organized a group there. Similar contacts resulted in the formation of groups
of radical women in Berkeley, California; Madison, Wisconsin; and a
lot of other big cities and university towns.

I later determined that in addition to Chicago, women in Toronto,
Seattle, Detroit, and Gainesville, Florida, had started small groups independently of each other and in turn spread the word to others around
them. Chicago birthed more new groups because it was a New Left center and the Westside women were politically well connected. My
impression was that Heather Booth was personally responsible for the
formation of more early groups than any other single person, but all of
us were missionaries.

We sowed our seed on fertile ground. By 1967 the number of grad-
uates of the civil rights and student movements had multiplied. There
was a very rich Movement culture—off campus as well as on. Every
medium-sized city and university town had a critical mass of people
who identified themselves as radicals or Movement workers of some
sort. Although disagreements were many and debates often acrimonious, underlying it all was a critical perspective that held the Movement together. Rooted in a Christian theology that exalted the moral
superiority of the underclass, as propounded by the Civil Rights Movement, and influenced by the anti-capitalist attitudes of the Old Left,
this perspective was articulated through hundreds of small publications,
unending conferences, and regular demonstrations. Because there were
so many publications looking for articles, it was easy to get published,
and even easier to run off a pamphlet on a mimeo and distribute it. And
because the New Left was committed to participatory democracy, it was
easy to get space at a conference merely by asking for it. This culture created what I later called a "cooptable communications network."[7]

News that women were organizing spread through this network
like a chain reaction. The men helped as well. Every time the issue was
presented in a public forum, they laughed. They put us down for not

---

[7] "The Origins of the Women's Liberation Movement," 78:4, *American Journal of Sociology,* Jan. 1973, pp. 792–811.

being really political. When the men laughed, the women signed the mailing list. Their experience with radical men had prepared them for our message. We didn't have to create a feminist consciousness; we just had to let them know they were not alone.

On the surface, the first new feminists looked alike and had similar backgrounds. We were mostly white women in our early twenties holding down "straight" jobs to support our political work. Few were students. Virtually all were political, having worked in civil rights, campus protest, community organization, or antiwar activities. But we didn't all think alike; more importantly, we didn't have the same reference groups. Most of the New Left women were married or living with New Left men and often still involved in New Left activities. In their minds, the New Left set the standards for discourse and action that they wanted to meet. These were the people whose respect they sought. In contrast, Shulie (along with her sister Laya) had not been previously political. She was an art student rebelling from her orthodox Jewish upbringing, with no preexisting framework for her feminist thoughts. I don't know who or what her reference group was, but it wasn't the New Left. I was a leftie, but without an organizational anchor, and unlike so many of my other left colleagues, I wasn't convinced that capitalism was the root of all evil. My reference group was the Civil Rights Movement, even though I was no longer actively involved in it.

Our political backgrounds shaped our thinking; they gave us the frameworks through which we analyzed the world and the vocabulary to articulate our thoughts. Race and class were constant concerns. Even though there were no minority or working-class women in our group, there was an unspoken assumption that "their" approval was necessary for our legitimation. But there was no way to obtain their approval. Our contacts with minority women were few, despite our roots in the Civil Rights Movement and community-organizing projects. The message white women got from black activists was to stay away; our presence, our ideas, our whiteness, were oppressive. A couple of black women came to our early meetings but didn't come back. We accepted the fact that blacks wanted to keep their distance from whites and assumed this applied to other minority women as well.

Even without a black presence, the Civil Rights Movement was the mother of us all. But among my generation of political activists, leftist frameworks were also important, and the left had different priorities from the Civil Rights Movement. The latter was primarily a movement for inclusion into American society. A piece of the pie, equality for all, was its dominant theme even while it criticized that society. The leftist perspective said inclusion was desirable only once society had changed sufficiently for equality to be meaningful. And the most meaningful change was one that destroyed capitalism.

Although I did not then realize it, being a radical was part of the identity of the New Left women. They debated whether they were women radicals or radical women—a fine distinction not important to me. They denounced the Suffrage Movement for being a single issue reformist effort which had changed nothing, a view I did not share. No one called herself a feminist; it was still a pejorative term. I was even reluctant to use it for myself, although I had a more positive evaluation of my foremothers' efforts than the radical women.

The first battles of the West Side group were over who our constituency was. Who were we speaking to? Who were we organizing? Was our task to organize women for the New Left, or into an independent movement? In retrospect these very questions smack of hubris—who were we to decide for other women how they should relate to the left? But at the time they seemed of great importance. The idea that women should organize themselves purely in pursuit of their own interests, and not also for a larger cause, was alien to us all. The first paper written in the fall of 1967 was addressed "To the Women of the Left."[8]

In the soil of these different backgrounds sprouted the first major split—that between the politicos and the feminists. Since I was virtually the only feminist in the West Side group after Shulie left, I did not appreciate this difference until I saw it also in New York. Politicos emphasized context; they said capitalism was the enemy. Feminists emphasized women; they said the enemy was men (or as I preferred it, male-dominated institutions). This battle was hottest in New York, where there was a balance of power between politicos and feminists. In places like Chicago where the politicos dominated, any ideas not clothed in anti-capitalist rhetoric were simply ignored. Every time I wanted to add to the discussion, I had to be careful how I expressed myself.

---

[8] *New Left Notes,* November 13, 1967, as "Chicago Women Form Liberation Group."

My frequent trips to New York and heavy correspondence kept me from feeling isolated, but also made me realize that many of the arguments in all of the new groups were ways of staking out turf as well as articulating issues. Although I was on the feminist side in Chicago, I never saw women's situation independently of other political issues, so I was well aware that in New York I would have been a politico. How substantive is an ideological disagreement if the same views would be on different sides in different places? None of our discussions ever generated any consensus. But even while we passionately debated what women should do, an independent feminist movement was growing on its own, creating new techniques and new issues.

The most important of these was consciousness raising, though I myself never experienced this kind of classic small group. We in the West Side group did not talk about our personal lives. When the discussion occasionally drifted into the personal realm, someone would jerk us back to the more general subject at hand with the admonition that we weren't being *political*. This view I did share; I saw no value in talking about personal experiences, an attitude I later discarded only with great reluctance. The West Side group contributed many things to the emerging movement, but consciousness raising was not one of them.

One major contribution from Chicago was the first national movement newsletter. I spent long hours sitting on my couch typing the mimeograph stencils with my manual portable typewriter propped on a chair in front of me. No one knew what to call the newsletter, so I put "the voice of the women's liberation movement" in the tagline of the first issue, with a plea for suggested names. There were none, so for the next issue I elevated *VWLM* to the bannerline, sending the new movement name all over the country. Calling our movement "women's liberation" was a bold stroke, but not an original one. Thanks to various national liberation movements, the phrase was in the air. I had read enough history by then to know that women's refusal to accept their place was called the "woman problem" or "woman question." I wanted to reshape people's thinking from "the problem with women" to "the problem of women's liberation." The name did catch on, but was quickly used to denigrate the movement through such diminutives as "woman libbers," "libbies," or "libests."

I edited the first, second, and fifth of the seven *VWLM* newsletters, and, with a few gaps, maintained the mailing list and handled the correspondence. Since subscriptions didn't really cover the cost of producing and mailing the newsletter—and we gave most of them away free—we paid for the postage by selling the many pamphlets we were beginning to produce. This work put me in touch with incipient feminists around the country. I got a thrill every time some new person or group sent me something unexpected, such as the Grinnell College students' report on and photos of their "nude in" to protest against *Playboy* recruiting on campus. The newsletter got better and bigger with each erratically produced issue. Someone designed a good-looking bannerline, and Naomi Weisstein contributed her hilarious and perceptive cartoons.

The newsletter was where I first publicly used the name Joreen. Feminists in other cities were dropping their patronyms in favor of more descriptive ones like Kathie Sarachild, Laura X, and Betsy Warrior. Although it seemed daring at the time, it wasn't. Name changes were common with changes in identity. Men changed their names when they became brothers or priests, women religious when they became sisters. There were noms de guerre and noms de plume. And of course all women were expected to change their names when they married. What bigger change of identity could there be? Rather than create a new patronym, I combined Jo Freeman into Joreen.

When I left Chicago in April of 1968, the West Side group dissolved. By then I was well aware that my presence wasn't particularly appreciated—to use an understatement. What I experienced wasn't so much direct criticism or put-downs as a form of shunning, but no one would tell me why. Although the group met in my apartment, outside of the meetings no one talked to me. No one ever called me, or told me much when I called them. Articles were written without my input. And at the weekly meetings, people generally ignored what I said, except when I volunteered to do work. When I asked others about this, I was told it was just my imagination. I was given a couple of dark hints about my "male" ambitions—such as going to graduate school—and told no one responded because I didn't have anything valuable to say.

When I returned in June to start graduate school, I tried to reconnect with everyone and find out about meetings, but they were all very elusive. There weren't any meetings, I was told, despite talk of a national conference since January. I learned that a planning meeting for this conference was to be held in Sandy Springs, Maryland, when

I was asked to contribute to the airfare of the two women selected (by whom?) to attend from Chicago. When I said I wanted to go, I was told there was no money available for me; others had already been chosen.

I stuck out my thumb and went. Heather Booth gave me $5 toward my expenses. At Sandy Springs, I found the atmosphere so cold that I was unable to speak unless spoken to. I was also silent at the larger conference held at a camp outside Chicago the following fall. Over 200 women came from all over the country. They talked about everything, publicly and privately. I said not a word publicly, and very little in private. The men in the FSM and the Civil Rights Movements had not been able to shut me up. But the radical women silenced me.

By early 1969, the movement was taking off, especially in Chicago. A woman not previously involved in movement activities volunteered her Hyde Park house to be a women's center. She moved her personal possessions and those of her three kids upstairs and let any woman who needed it use the downstairs. This was one of the first such centers in the country. SDS roused undergraduates at the University of Chicago to hold a lengthy sit-in in the administration building after Marlene Dixon, a popular professor, was fired by the Sociology Department. My response to the sit-in was to burrow into the University archives to find out just how often women had been appointed to the faculty since the University was founded in 1892. There were so few in sociology that I expanded my search to six departments—the social sciences plus history—to have enough.[9]

The sit-in stimulated lots of meetings all over campus. I spoke about my research at four of them. I particularly remember a Political Science Department colloquium where I informed our illustrious department that it had hired the first woman on any social science faculty—for a one-year appointment in 1893. It had also hired the fewest.

---

[9] "Women on the Social Science Faculties Since 1892," at the University of Chicago, in *Discrimination Against Women, Hearings Before the Special Subcommittee on Education of the House Committee on Education and Labor, on Section 805 of H.R. 16098,* held in Washington, D.C., in June and July 1970, Washington, D.C.: U.S. Government Printing Office, 1971, pp. 994–1003.

She was the last woman to appear on a Political Science Department faculty roster in the history of the University.

I was energized by the sit-in, but not the way SDS organizers had in mind. During the weeks it lasted, I wrote "The BITCH Manifesto,"[10] which Marlene edited and commented on for me; "The 51% Minority Group,"[11] a compilation of economic statistics, which sold well in pamphlet form before being published in Robin Morgan's book; and two term papers, which were soon published. The one on sex-role socialization was reprinted fifteen times, mostly in sociology textbooks, before it became dated.[12] The other, on sex discrimination law and public policy, expanded to become my Master's thesis and contracted for publication in a law review.[13] I also wrote "The New Feminists" for *The Nation*—the only publication to respond positively to my many queries. It was reprinted in Japan.[14]

During the sit-in, I talked about my research to my fellow students, and in response to popular demand agreed to teach a "free course" (no credit, no pay) in the spring quarter. To get a room I needed a professor to sponsor it. All the left-leaning men and every woman faculty member I asked turned me down. Finally, Don Scott, a very junior history professor in the undergraduate college, agreed to "front" the course. The University of Chicago didn't give him tenure.

---

[10] "The BITCH Manifesto," *Notes from the Second Year,* ed. Shulamith Firestone and Anne Koedt, 1970. Reprinted in *Masculine/Feminine,* ed. Betty and Theodore Roszak, New York: Harper & Row, 1969, and in *Radical Feminism,* ed. Anne Koedt, Ellen Levine, and Anita Rapone, New York: Quadrangle, 1973, p. 50–59.

[11] "The 51% Minority Group: A Statistical Essay," in *Sisterhood Is Powerful,* ed. Robin Morgan, New York: Random House, 1970, pp. 37–46.

[12] "The Social Construction of the Second Sex," in *Roles Women Play: Readings Towards Women's Liberation,* ed. Michele Garskof, Belmont, California: Brooks/Cole, 1971, pp. 123–41, and many other places.

[13] "The Legal Basis of the Sexual Caste System," 5:2 *Valparaiso University Law Review,* Spring 1971, pp. 203–236.

[14] *The Nation,* Vol. 208, No. 8, February 24, 1969, p. 241. Translated and reprinted in *Fujinkoron,* a Japanese women's magazine, July 1969, p. 239. My query letter was turned down by *The Progressive* and *The New Republic,* and others that I don't remember. *The Nation* not only responded positively, but five years later asked me to write a sequel. I learned many years later that this magazine had regularly published stories about women's activism throughout its long history. Indeed, its chief editor, and eventual owner, for most of the postsuffrage era was Freda Kirchwey.

Out of developing departmental women's caucuses came the idea to organize a campuswide conference on women to start off the 1969 fall quarter. I took on the major burden of putting it together, though it was a group effort. Our conference was packed and filmed by NBC. Students, and some faculty, presented panel discussions. Naomi Weisstein gave an inspiring keynote address.

That fall the major press came sniffing around on the trail of a major story. Most of the reporters came from New York and didn't know anyone in Chicago; Robin Morgan told them to call me. The movement in general had an aversion to the press. They blamed it for negative coverage. They criticized anyone named in the press for being on an ego trip. As a former (minor league) reporter myself, I had no such aversion. I wanted to get our story out. I gave the press background reports on my research and on the new movement, insisting that they not quote me. Of course, as the one willing to answer questions, sometimes I did get quoted—and filmed. I knew the press didn't always write what we wanted, but thought it was up to us to give them good information that would persuade them to view us positively. And I could see that at that point any publicity was good for the movement. No matter how negative the press reports were, the women who read them knew something was happening and looked for groups to join.

Chicago had a lot of talk shows; since they weren't national, they were hungry for local newsmakers. Once my name appeared in the press, I was asked to appear on many of them. I did do a couple, but the roar of "ego trip" was so loud that I stopped. To forestall movement criticism, I once brought on three other women with me, without telling the host what I intended. He freaked when we all walked on stage and invited us to come back some other day, which never happened. Caught between my desire to get our message out and my vulnerability to personal attacks from my "sisters," I switched strategies. My academic adviser, Ted Lowi, was a hot item on the talk-show circuit because he was articulate and loved to make controversial statements. Feminism was controversial. I watched his appearances and briefed him on the best answers. A quick study, he became one of our best propagandists. No one I knew attacked him for ego tripping.

By late fall of 1969 I knew I had to leave the movement. No one in it wanted me to stay, or so it seemed. When I went to meetings some people literally moved away from me. My phone calls weren't returned. I didn't get mailings. Everything I did or said was ignored or criticized. I felt like I didn't exist. I heard that a citywide organization was being formed, but no one would tell me when or where the organizing talks were being held. This deliberate isolation was a very different experience from any I had had in previous political groups. I had been at odds with the radical faction in the Free Speech Movement, but that was a political fight; we challenged each others' strategies, not our worth as human beings. As a white female in the mostly black and male Civil Rights Movement, I wasn't "one of the boys," but I never doubted that I was one of "us" not "them." Yet among the radical women of Chicago I was a pariah. Worse, no one would tell me why; I was bewildered. I heard allusions to my being "too male" and an "elitist," but didn't know what these meant. I asked Naomi what was going on and she said I was being trashed.

As 1969 ended I "dropped out." I did this very quietly. I didn't make an announcement or write a letter or publish a manifesto. I simply stopped going to the women's center. Nothing happened. It was as though half my life disappeared. The people I had seen regularly, and talked to when possible, simply weren't there anymore. When I didn't take the initiative, contact ceased. Since all my life apart from going to class and the library had been devoted to the movement, this left a major void.

Although I left the movement, it didn't leave me. Being a feminist was too much a part of my core identity. Being trashed by feminists preyed upon my mind; wondering why was a minor obsession, a constant background noise that interfered with thoughts about everything else.

I tried to take evasive action by doing feminist work in other places, but nothing seemed to help. I was already a member of Chicago NOW, having helped Catherine Conroy and Nan Wood start that chapter in August 1968. I had kept my NOW membership a secret, to avoid condemnation for consorting with a reformist organization. Once I had left women's liberation, I could be "out" as a NOW member. I agreed to speak at NOW's national conference in the spring of 1970, and went to NOW pickets of the EEOC, the *Chicago Tribune,* and men-only bars and luncheon rooms. I liked the action, but not the meetings. I don't think that was a reflection on NOW, though the generation gap was palpable in our different ages, dress, and lifestyles. My disaffection was more a consequence of my general state of mind.

I had made a few speeches, but with the great press blitz about the movement in 1969–70, invitations poured in. If I hadn't dropped out, I would have turned most of them down to avoid sisterly disapproval. Since this no longer mattered, I accepted speaking gigs pretty much any place anyone asked me to go; it was the only outlet for my missionary zeal. This way I could stay in touch with the movement, if not in Chicago at least in the rest of the country. I thought of myself as Freeman's flying feminist freak show, with a bag of lectures on different topics; a self-defense demonstration; a suitcase full of books, buttons, and pamphlets; and whatever else anyone wanted. I also felt like a fake; I was speaking about a movement that I was no longer a part of, except to talk about it.

Before 1970, I had only spoken in Chicago, mostly to community and university groups. Male ridicule was a frequent experience, but it just steeled me. After the press legitimated feminism as a trendy topic, the range of invitations to speak expanded and the ridicule receded. I soon became a staple on the small-college lecture circuit, especially women's colleges. I think I spoke at every small Catholic women's college in the Midwest in the next few years. They gave me a new appreciation of the virtues of sex segregation. I heard those sisters say things that were much more radical than anything I had heard in the West Side group—at least when it came to women.

In front of an audience, as a featured speaker, I was fearless. I handled hecklers as though they were mere opponents in a friendly game. But as a face in the crowd I displayed an allergic reaction to women's groups—all of them. A feeling of coldness would come over me; I withdrew and became distant. In mixed-sex groups, though, I was as feisty as ever. I don't think any of my male political science colleagues ever thought I wasn't there. I also developed a locational depression. When in Chicago, I felt lousy. When I left, I recovered. Between speaking gigs and trips to New York, I traveled once or twice a month. In New York I could talk to other feminists and particularly sought out Anne Koedt, who was one of the few founts of sanity in the movement. She too had been trashed, as had many others. In June of 1970, a bunch of us congregating at her apartment compared notes and realized how pervasive the personal attacks had been. We were all suffering as a result and most were leaving as well. We dubbed ourselves the "feminist refugees." Ti-Grace Atkinson was not there, but a statement attributed to her summed up our feelings: "Sisterhood is powerful," she said. "It kills sisters."

At Anne's I met Anselma Dell'Olio, who had given a speech about trashing, though not by name, at the spring 1970 Second Congress to Unite [sic] Women. I sent the written version to the Chicago Women's Liberation Union, with a note affirming my support of her analysis, which it later printed in the CWLU newsletter. But I heard nothing from the organization or anyone who read the piece. Indeed, the only contact I ever had with CWLU was a phone call from someone claiming to represent it after I was one of four feminists profiled in an April 1970 issue of *Newsweek,* which examined the new feminism. The profile featured a real mug shot—as bad a photo as any taken by the cops while booking me for civil rights arrests—and labeled me a "raging gut feminist." The CWLU caller offered neither congratulations nor commiseration. She called to inform me that the Union had decided to censure me for appearing in the press without its permission.

Even though it was a relief to learn that I was not the only target of feminist anger, knowledge alone did not provide much succor. What made the attacks on all of us so debilitating was the pervasive ideology of sisterhood. Because all women were supposed to be sisters, isolation and censure were particularly harsh, just as rejection by family is more painful than by roommates, colleagues, or friends, let alone strangers. On some subconscious level we thought of the women's liberation movement as our true and proper home, unlike the predominantly male movements we had serviced for so many years. We assumed acceptance and expected to create a community in which the talents male movements had not allowed us to use would flourish and we would be our real selves, not what the men wanted us to be. Instead we found ostracism without explanation. When our "sisters" didn't want us, we knew we would never have a home.

Although I never told this to anyone, I came to think of the women's liberation movement as a sorority, or more accurately a lot of sororities. Each group was very selective, pledging only those who would easily fit in. New recruits were "rushed," or better yet, sponsored by an established member. If they didn't fit in, they were squeezed out through isolation, but never told why. In college those of us who didn't pledge were called "GDIs"—God Damned Independents. While the Greeks dominated student government, off-campus political groups were populated by GDIs. In the women's liberation movement, I was still a GDI; I could preach and practice feminism on my own, but could not be a "sister." This interpretation clarified for me why trashing was less common in NOW, as well as other groups that were more structured and more engaged in traditional political work. Joining NOW was more like joining an off-campus political group; you didn't have to rush, you just had to pay your dues and work.

When Anne and Shulie were putting out the third and last issue of their compilations of movement papers, *Notes from the Third Year,* they asked me to write about trashing. I declined. I didn't want to wash the movement's dirty linen in public. I did offer to write about "The Tyranny of Structurelessness," which I hoped would shed some light on the problem without being an exposé. By the time I finished the paper they had more copy than they could use, so I sent it to the journal *Second Wave.* Many others have published it since, not always with my permission.[15] Although I wrote it rapidly, motivated by my need to understand immediate events in a small population, it resonated with political activists everywhere. To this day, when I go to conferences, I run into people who've read it recently, often in other languages. It's probably the most famous article I've ever written; certainly the longest-lived. Eventually I did write about trashing.[16]

In the summer of 1970, I took advantage of a student charter flight to travel in Europe to visit emerging feminist groups. Hilda Smith was doing her dissertation research in London and introduced me to the

---

[15] "The Tyranny of Structurelessness," *The Second Wave,* Vol. 2, No. 1, 1972, p. 20; *Berkeley Journal of Sociology,* Vol. 17, 1972–73, pp. 151–165; *Radical Feminism,* ed. Anne Koedt, Ellen Levine, and Anita Rapone, New York: Quadrangle, 1973, pp. 285–299. *Women in Politics,* ed. Jane Jaquette, New York: John Wiley and Sons, 1974, pp. 202–214. Revised version published in *Ms.,* July 1973, p. 76. These are the places that asked my permission to publish or reprint it; the others did so on their own.
[16] Joreen, "Trashing: The Dark Side of Sisterhood," *Ms.,* April 1976, pp. 49–51, 92–98. Anselma Dell'Olio, "Divisiveness and Self-Destruction in the Women's Movement," was printed as a sidebar. The pervasiveness of trashing was confirmed by the overwhelming amount of mail *Ms.* received in response to the publication of these two articles, a large sample of which was printed in a later issue.

British feminists, most of whom thought the American women were too domineering. A month later I sailed to Belgium with a packet of feminist pamphlets on my back. While I only met a couple of interested women there, in Holland I hit pay dirt. Women and younger lefty men had created the "dolleminas." On the other side of the generation gap, Joke Kool-Smit, a professor of languages at the University of Amsterdam, had organized the Dutch equivalent of NOW, known as Man/Vrouw/Maatschappij. We hit it off. Sharing experiences and observations with the Dutch women illuminated some of the ways in which both custom and policy controlled women's actions that I had not been able to see up close in my own country. I left lots of American feminist pamphlets with them, which Joke later wrote were influential on their thinking.

For the next couple of weeks, I hitched in Denmark, Norway, and Sweden, where feminism was flourishing and pretty much everyone my age and younger spoke English. The Danish feminists called themselves Redstockings, after the New York group, but had their own feminist philosophy. The Swedish were very cool and distant. No one would talk to me without a formal introduction and an appointment. I didn't learn a great deal about the Swedish movement beyond the fact that they believed they didn't need one since they were so far ahead of everyone else in the "sex role" debate. In Norway, I found friends. I had written in advance to European women whose names were on the *VWLM* mailing list. Siri Nylander Maeland had learned of our movement while in the United States in 1969. Now back in Norway, she asked me to speak at the University of Oslo so local feminists could use the occasion to organize a mass movement. Of course I agreed.

That is why I was in Oslo on August 26, 1970, when American feminists were marching down Fifth Avenue in the first contemporary mass feminist demonstration. I told the Norwegians I needed to do something to commemorate the day and suggested picketing the American Embassy. "Nah," they said, "everyone does that. Hold a press conference. We need the publicity for your lecture." I had never done this before, and was quite surprised when reporters from the numerous Norwegian papers and the one TV station crowded into the room to hear an obscure American feminist. I was even more surprised to see my mug on TV and in all those papers.

My lecture a few days later, given in a slow, measured, well-articulated English I had taught myself while hitchhiking, was a success. Elisabet Helsing and her fellow feminist organizers did a marvelous job of putting it all together. Hundreds of people came; many joined. New feminist groups sprouted everywhere. They called themselves "Nyfeminstene." Elisabet and I corresponded for a while and then lost touch. I've often wondered how their movement fared, though when I read in the papers how many women are running their government, I know they did something right. I've never been back, but Norway will always hold a special place in my heart.[17]

Back in Chicago, my locational depression returned. I felt I was hanging off the edge of a cliff by my fingertips. In early November, I dropped off the cliff. The precipitant was a bad fall in my judo class, which ripped the ligaments in my left shoulder. The pain was excruciating. The clinic physician gave me Darvon for the pain. It made me high. Very high. When I started to rearrange the furniture in my apartment I knew I had to stop taking that drug. When I did, I dropped like a rock.

In December of 1970, I said to myself, "If I can't study, I might as well earn some money." The department stores were hiring extra help for the holidays; I became a dry-cleaning clerk at Marshall Field. That job was very good therapy; it gave me a place to go and things to do every day, but it ended Christmas eve.

The day after Christmas, Hilda Smith and I drove to Boston. Months before, she had organized a panel on the new feminist movement for the annual meeting of the American Historical Association, and asked Juliet Mitchell, Alice Rossi, and me to speak. Several hundred people came to our panel, and they responded as if they were at a revival meeting, a complete break from the usual professional atmosphere. But then what we had to say was new and unusual—though not very historical. Even the press were there. We were all in the news.

Shortly after I returned home, I got a letter postmarked in Boston without a return address. It was addressed to "Jo Freeman (GUT FEM-

---

[17] In 1996, Elizabet Lønnå published a history of Norwegian feminism since 1913 in which my visit is discussed. *Stolthet og Kvinnekamp: Norsk Kvinnesakforenings Historie fra 1913.* Oslo, Norway: Gyldendal Norsk Forlag, 1996, 230–234.

INIST) Doctoral Candidate, University of Chicago, Chicago, Illinois."
Inside was a six-page handwritten hate letter, which concluded: "They
ought to put your tits (if you got any) in a wringer and then kick your
ass 100 times." Some clerk at the University of Chicago, assigned the
task of looking me up in the directory and forwarding this letter, had
stamped on the envelope in bright red: "Please inform your correspon-
dents of your correct address."

Two Letters from the Women's Liberation Movement

Carol Hanisch

1. THE 1968 MISS AMERICA PROTEST: THE ORIGINS OF THE "BRA-BURNER" MONIKER

On September 7, 1968, the Women's Liberation Movement protested the Miss America Pageant in Atlantic City. It was, for its time, a daring act of defiance against everything that women were supposed to be.

Thirty years ago, no "respectable" woman would think of going to work, to church, to the store, or to most other public places without a breast harness (those cutting and often scratchy, padded, and even underwired bras), a butt binder and tummy flattener (better known as a girdle), hobbles (crippling and spine-damaging high heels), leg shapers (expensive and uncomfortable nylons held up by girdles or garter belts), correctly curled or straightened hair (achieved with smelly, toxic chemicals and/or hair curlers often slept on with great discomfort), and, of course, a mask of face powder (to cover a shiny nose), lipstick, mascara, and sometimes false eyelashes.

One could be fired from one's job for "inappropriate dress"—and that meant women wore skirts, not pants, no matter what the job or what the weather. When I was in college in the early sixties, women were required to wear skirts to class—except when the weather was below zero! Men wore the pants—both literally and figuratively. In many situations, they still do.

One evening in the summer of 1968, the women's liberation group to which I belonged—New York Radical Women—was watching a feminist art film called *Schmearguntz,* which contained flashes of the Miss America Pageant. It brought out my own strong feelings about beauty contests. The idea crept into my head that protesting the pageant in Atlantic City just might be a way to bring the fledgling Women's Liberation Movement into the public arena—to reach out to other women with our ideas and our dreams of a better life.

Like our foremothers in the nineteenth century, several of us had been politically educated in the struggle for the rights of Black people, particularly in the southern Civil Rights Movement. We were ready to apply what we had learned to a struggle for the freedom of women. We knew we would have to build a mass movement of women willing to take risks and do the work necessary to achieve progress for our sex as a whole—not just for a few tokens. We knew that to do this we would have to unite women by taking on those issues that spoke to the oppression we all experienced in our daily lives.

And here was this American icon—the Miss America Pageant—telling women what to look like, what to wear, how to wear it, how to walk, how to speak, what to say (and what not to say) to be considered attractive. In short: look beautiful (no matter the cost in time and money), smile (no matter what you're feeling), and don't rock the boat. We did some consciousness raising about the pageant in our group, and everyone came out loving the idea of a protest. As Ros Baxandall was to remark later on the David Susskind TV show, "Every day in a woman's life is a walking Miss America contest." It seemed just the boat to start rocking!

It was a clear, warm fall day when over a hundred of us, some from as far away as Florida and Detroit, came together on the Atlantic City boardwalk in front of Convention Hall. We spent the afternoon picketing and talking to women, many of whom watched us with skepticism or thoughtful silence. A few joined us. Several of the men, particularly the young ones, were quite hostile. "Go back to Russia!" "You're all a bunch of Lesbians!" "Mothers of Mao!" "Which one's your girlfriend?" "Man haters!" they'd yell, shaking their fists. Male reporters also verbally attacked us in a very unprofessional manner. They no doubt felt threatened because we had put out the word that we would talk only to female reporters. As a result, major news organizations sent women previously relegated to doing research and rewrite on their first outside assignment. One woman reporter even thanked us for getting her out of the research library.

We did some street theater: crowning a live sheep Miss America; chaining ourselves to a large red, white, and blue Miss America dummy to point up how women are enslaved by beauty standards; and throwing what we termed "instruments of female torture" into a Freedom Trash Can. It was the latter that brought about the "bra-burner" moniker. It wasn't that we hadn't intended to burn bras—we had—but along with other "instruments of female torture," including high heels, nylons, garter belts, girdles, hair curlers, false eyelashes, makeup, and *Playboy* and *Good Housekeeping* magazines. One of the members of our group— a Yippie who was a bit of a press hound—had quipped to a reporter that we were going to burn our bras, and the media had a field day. Everything else we were to burn was quickly forgotten. Atlantic City officials refused to let us have a fire on the boardwalk, anyway, so nothing in fact was even burned there, but "bra-burner" became the put-down term for feminists of my generation. The risqué implication of the term "bra-burner" made the action more than even many feminists wanted to own. Had the media called us "girdle-burners," nearly every woman in the country would have rushed to join us.

One of our members worked for a bridal magazine and was able to acquire a block of sixteen tickets so we could continue the protest inside Convention Hall. In order not to arouse suspicion, we, too, put on dresses, high heels, and makeup. Smuggling in a large banner in an over-sized handbag, we took our seats in the balcony very near the stage and discovered that not only did we have an excellent view of the proceedings, but there were several burly policemen in riot gear in the wings, probably a first for the pageant.

When the outgoing Miss America stepped to the microphone to deliver her farewell speech, it was the signal for the four of us who had volunteered to hang the banner to make our move. For an instant I couldn't get to my feet. I thought, "Do I really have to do this?" Interrupting this woman's speech on live TV seemed so rude, not to mention that we might get arrested.

But one of our number had stood up and was moving toward the balcony. We quickly dropped the banner—reading "Women's Liberation"—over the railing, tied it as securely as we could, and began shouting, "Women's Liberation," "No More Miss America," "Freedom for Women." All eyes turned toward us, but we were not a large enough group to totally disrupt the pageant. The outgoing Miss America hesitated briefly and then continued her speech. Once we had started shouting, joined by the other women protesters in the balcony, my reluctance turned into an intense feeling of exhilaration. We had broken some chains. We had dared to expose and defy this idol of femininity and replace it with the hope of feminism. Oh, happy day!

The police came bounding up the stairs, took down the banner, and hustled us out of the hall, but they didn't arrest us. We returned to the boardwalk picket line and triumphantly added our high heels to the Freedom Trash Can. The crowd, perhaps realizing by then that we were quite serious, was growing more and more hostile. The police decided it was time that we get out of town. They had to form a line to protect us as they escorted us to our buses.

When we read the morning papers, we knew our immediate goal had been accomplished: alongside the headline of a new Miss America being crowned was the news that a Women's Liberation Movement was afoot in the land and that it was going to demand a whole lot more than "equal pay for equal work." We were deluged with letters, more than our small group could possibly answer, many passionately saying, "I've been waiting all my life for something like this to come along." Taking the Women's Liberation Movement into the public consciousness gave some women the nudge they needed to form their own groups. They no longer felt so alone and isolated.

The protest also helped bring about some relief from the uncomfortable dress code. Manufacturers began to offer softer, stretchier, more comfortable underwear. Pantyhose replaced garter belts in situations where bare legs were still taboo. Pantsuits for women became widely available and allowable, and high heels became the exception rather than the rule.

Many of us in the eye of the hurricane were convinced that women's situation would change dramatically in a few years. In some ways it did. But we did not yet understand just how entrenched male supremacy is or how intertwined with the corporate powers that dictate public policy and benefit from the exploitation of women as underpaid labor in the workforce, and as unpaid housework and reproductive laborers in the home.

Looking back, I don't believe we totally understood the depth of the Miss America Protest or what we called "the appearance issue." We had talked about it in terms of comfort, fashion dictates, and how beauty competition divides women. But more importantly, we were targeting and challenging, however consciously or unconsciously, the *uniform* of women's inferior class status. After all, what really lies beneath this "appearance thing" is male prerogative and control. It's not only about sexual attractiveness versus comfort; it's about power. It's about constantly reminding both women and men that we are "the other," as Simone de Beauvoir phrased it. Granted, having to wear a suit and tie may be uncomfortable for men, but at least it identifies them with the class in power: men in suits. High heels, skirts, hose, and breast harnesses are not only physically inhibiting and torturous, they are insistent visible and tactile reminders of women's inferior class position vis-à-vis men. They are the uniform of the oppressed sex class in the West, not unlike the bound feet of Chinese women before the Communist revolution.

This is why what seemed like such a frivolous and petty issue to some has remained so entrenched in our culture and its sexual politics. As such it has been subject to the backlash and backsliding that has characterized the movement since the mid-1970s. As the Women's Liberation Movement lost its momentum and power after the liberal cooptation of the great radical upsurge of the late 1960s and early 1970s, pressure intensified to wear this uniform of the oppressed—high heels, Wonder-Bras, skirts, and all the rest of it—and women have lost much of their ability to resist, just as we have in many other areas of our lives.

As I write this in 1996, much of what we began to fight for nearly thirty years ago seems far out of reach. Today the Women's Liberation Movement—and the world-changing hope, truth, and energy it aroused and led—has been largely replaced by wheel-spinning individual forms of struggle, which can bring only token success to a few women, if that. It is crucial that women know and acknowledge that it was the power of women organized and working in groups in the Women's Liberation Movement that made our lives change for the better. It is only the persistence and stronger organization of both that movement and the groups that comprise it that can make change last and expand. It is also necessary to understand that the Women's Liberation Movement was pioneered by ordinary women (like me) with no special access to money or the halls of power. Those women came later when the ground had already been broken, and many even helped slow the movement to a saunter.

These are just a few of the many, many historical truths women need to grasp in order to gain the insight and courage to push on to women's liberation. Young women, especially, must take in these lessons so that instead of being intimidated by the activism of the 1960s, they will realize that they are basically like us and that, like us, they, too, can make change. If youth learns to build on the knowledge that lies in our history, they can go even further than we have. Who knows; together we may even be able to throw open the gate.

2. PAYING THE PIPER: DID I BLOW MY LIFE?

> *The older people of the Soviet Union . . . will often say to you, "Are you telling me that I lived my life in vain, that all of my sacrifices, all the hardships, everything that I accepted for this idea was in vain and that I blew my life?"*
>
> Guardian, 12/27/89

Like many active women's liberationists I have reached mid-life with little financial, social, or emotional security. Men, children, career, and sometimes even friends went by the wayside in the years of struggle. And like many people who have paid the piper, I have had my times of remorse (even of occasional bitterness, of which I am not proud) about the state in which I found myself. In the wake of the *Webster* decision in 1989 (in which the Supreme Court began to dismantle abortion rights granted in *Roe* v. *Wade)* and the many other rollbacks in women's liberation in the past decade, I often found myself asking, "Was it worth it?" As I wrote a feminist friend in August 1989:

> Life has been damn hard for most everyone I know—both in and out of "the Movement" (there's been so little movement, I feel funny even using that term) these past ten or so years. I have had some pretty bad bouts of depression and burnout, and even some times when I've had to focus on just getting through to keep from going down all the way. The worst was in the early '80s when the full impact of the "sacrifices" began to hit home—turning 39 with no man in sight and with little hope of having a child and the introspection that comes with that. Even having a man in my life some of those years didn't help a whole lot.
>
> A trip to Nicaragua in 1985 in support of the Sandinista Revolution was an enormous help as it focused my attention on something other than "self" and put my problems into a broader perspective.

No one completely escaped the "Me-ism" of the '80s; it wasn't just a Yuppie disease. I think it's in large part due to the isolation, self-imposed and forced on us by our culture (or lack of it). In Nicaragua people were warm and lively, full of hope and plans, hungry for knowledge and discussion. The arts were flourishing and feeding people's souls and most of it was free (having been purchased at a high price, however).

Though we were often physically uncomfortable there, coming back to the U.S. was an awful culture shock; I was in sort of a walking coma for several months. Here nobody wanted to discuss life except in a most superficial way. Books, movies, records, and live music were becoming unaffordable and lacking in quality. The energy and stimulation that I used to receive from them just wasn't there. People didn't even have the time or money to get together for dinner any more. There's a debilitating loneliness that results from such isolation and the worst thing is that it becomes comfortable after a while. It's easier to just stay to oneself than to make the effort to socialize in both the broadest and narrowest senses of that word.

For a time I thought it was just me or us Movement veterans suffering from the sacrifices we had made, but one day about a year ago my neighbor was telling me how lonely I must be, since it had been nearly two years since my mate and I had broken up. She then blurted out, "But it's even worse to be with someone and still be lonely." She's been married 25 years and had three kids.

Also after the *Webster* decision and other horrible setbacks, I was really feeling that it hadn't been worth it because they were going to take it all away anyway. All that sacrifice for nothing. I then had a serious consciousness-raising session with myself and asked if I would have wanted to live the past 20-plus years under the conditions for women of pre-1968. When I began to realize all the ways my life would have been circumscribed, I began to feel a real panic welling up. It wasn't the "sacrifices" that I had made that were bothering me so much as that we hadn't been able to go further—far enough to really solve the problems we had raised and are still facing—and we were sort of caught out on the proverbial limb. More and greater sacrifices were no doubt necessary, and even worse was the lack of a movement to give the hope and possibility of getting any more gains.

Even the women I know with good paying jobs, men, and/or children aren't much happier or having much more fun than I am. And having children is no guarantee of someone to take care of you in your old age, though it improves your chances, I suppose. There's got to be a better solution than being so dependent on one or two individuals anyway, be they children or friends. Life in the U.S.A. in the 1980s is the pits for nearly everyone but the wealthy, and I'm even a little sympathetic with those women.

Anyway, since this little talk with myself, which I'm sure could be greatly improved upon if it included the experience and observation of others, I've been feeling a lot less depressed and a little less burnt out.

I know the panic and fear that getting older engenders—especially without money and family. But in my dread, I try to remember it's not, at root, a problem of, or for, my comrades individually, or even of the Movement, but of this stinking, decaying capitalist system and its greedy grabbers bleeding and endangering us all with increasing intensity and in ways we never dreamed of, like the massive downsizing and making so many of the remaining jobs temporary and insecure, and often with longer hours. The capitalists have made our lives so difficult that people don't have the time or energy to do things right. That's one reason for the "shoddy" work of the U.S. work force that we hear so much about. I think we should call this decade "The Great Burnout."

I certainly haven't solved the immediate and future problems of relative poverty and time to do political work. What I miss most is the Movement with its forward thrust, community, sense of purpose, excitement of new discoveries and victories. I miss the Movement more than I miss a child, money or even a man. It's lacking all that's really the pits. And having a child or a man without the Movement to make things more equal is more work, more oppression, more exhaustion.

The above letter was written nearly a year ago. Sometimes I feel like I've come out of a long, dark tunnel. I'm still trying to understand those years and what brought me back out into the light. Some feminists say they are also feeling better than they have in years; others say not. One important thing that helped a lot was feeling other women's outrage in 1989 at both the *Webster* decision and the Nancy Klein case (where a so-called right-to-lifer legally intervened to stop an abortion that had been authorized by a husband hoping to aid the recovery of his badly injured and comatose wife). It wasn't just the usual complaining (which I hear and do a lot of), but outright, unapologetic, gut anger. When anger and indignation are routinely suppressed, despair and/or cynicism, both enemies of revolution, set in. Having my feelings affirmed in some kind of action by other women for the first time in years was not only good for my own mental health, but served as an inspiration to labor and struggle—and to sacrifice. Also seeing young women get concerned and active—at least about this one issue—gave me a sense of hope. Hopelessness had been a big part of the burnout.

Other things were happening, too. I went to a conference on SNCC (Student Nonviolent Coordinating Committee), which was also something of a reunion, held in Hartford, Connecticut, in April of 1988. Listening again to all those wonderful people who changed history (and my own life) was a shot of adrenaline. In March of 1989, Redstockings held an event marking the twentieth anniversary of their abortion speak-out in New York, which provided a brief chance to discuss the current situation with friends/veterans of the Women's Liberation Movement. Lavonne Lela sent me a copy of Sally Roesch Wagner's book, *A Time of Protest: Suffragists Challenge the Republic 1870–1887,* which was filled with stimulating and useful information about the nineteenth-century women's rights struggle. It was the first book on women's history I'd read in years that I just couldn't put down and that helped me sort out some of my own jumbled thoughts and feelings.

Then, too, I was just sick and tired of being so depressed and down all the time. When I spoke in several college classes about the early Women's Liberation Movement, I realized I needed to present something more than a despairing, beaten down, aging feminist waxing nostalgic for the "good old days." I wasn't even sure the positive feeling for the Women's Liberation Movement, which I still had, was coming through the gloom I was feeling. I needed to get myself back into some kind of fighting shape in order to make any ongoing, meaningful contribution.

And one day it dawned on me how much worse it would be as—ahem—"a spinster" in pre-1968. While there are times when I've missed not having a man in my life, I don't feel I have to constantly apologize for my life alone, as I would have if the Women's Liberation Movement had never happened. Though this is a couple-oriented society, many single women are no longer asking, "What's wrong with me?" In fact, now that my childbearing years are behind me, I'm rather looking forward to this new state.

But then there are other enormous problems looming, like how to survive alone—financially, emotionally, and physically—as an older woman, and how to deal with the male dismissal of both women's intellect and sexuality, which seems to increase with age.

The struggle for women's liberation is far from over. I don't want to go back and I don't believe most women really want to, no matter how tough things are right now. I know where I'm headed even though it's clear that the optimistic sixties slogan of "Liberation in Our Lifetime" is not to be. There are battles that can still be won in our lifetimes, even if the dreams of equal relationships and family lives and meaningful work that fueled our engines in the early Women's Liberation Movement are not to be realized by our generation. We may be *pushed* back, but we won't *go* back. We who remember what we came from know there's nothing there for us. As Matilda Joslyn Gage wrote in her final editorial in the *National Citizen and Ballot Box* in October 1881:

> To those who fancy we are near the end of the battle or that the reformer's path is strewn with roses, we may say them nay. The thick of the fight has just begun; the hottest part of the warfare is yet to come, and those who enter it must be willing to give up father, mother and comforts for its sake. Neither shall we who carry on the fight, reap the great reward. We are battling for the good of those who shall come after us; they, not ourselves, shall enter into the harvest.

> —Quoted by Sally Roesch Wagner in her introduction
> to the 1980 edition of *Woman, Church and State,*
> by Matilda Gage, 1893

There are a lot of people in the world these days being forced to decide which way to go—the former Soviet Union, Eastern Europe, and Nicaragua, for example. Retreating to capitalism as a means of achieving "democracy" and a "better standard of living" is no more the solution than moving back to women's status before 1968 is for us in our struggle for liberation. The real question is not so much whether we should go forward, but how best to do it.

POSTSCRIPT: 1996

As I reread the above, I worry that it sounds a little too depressing and pessimistic. True, I've paid the piper in many ways, as have many other women, other people, who have put struggling to change the world above their personal lives. Yes, it's tough living with the consequences. But not only am I grateful for the gains that the Movement has won, I can't bear to even think of having missed the experience of participating in the cutting edge of the Women's Liberation Movement. Without it, my life would have been less rich, less interesting. The heyday of the Movement was the best time of my life. Seldom since have I felt so alive and been so grounded about my place in the order of things. As my mind grew muscles, my spirit soared, and my heart found a happiness in the sisterhood of struggle that I yearn for and look for to this day. If I hadn't taken the risk of getting involved, I would not have the satisfaction of knowing that my life—blown as it may be by some standards—has counted for something, of feeling part of the great ongoing struggle to free women and humanity from the oppressions that keep us all from realizing our best dreams.

So did I blow my life? Hell, no! But I'll have to remember that the next time I come up short on the rent.

Catching the Fire

Rosalyn Fraad Baxandall

WERE THESE PROTO FEMINIST ACTS?

As a teenager, I was wild and out of touch with my feelings and vulnerabilities. I had learned bravado as a coping strategy while being bounced from relative to relative between the ages of three to eight while my mother was sick and my father, changing careers, went to medical school. Even then, though only eighteen months older, I was my younger sister's powerful caretaker. In taking care of Harriet, I took care of the fragile part of me, which no one saw but Harriet, who loved me. The oldest of three girls, I was cast in the "competent" role. Which meant having few needs myself or, rather, not letting them show.

Child and teen, I was not particularly "feminine" in its 1950s meaning, nor interested in stereotypical "girl" activities like shopping, makeup, and clothes. Adventurous, I hung out with the boys more than most girls did, mainly playing baseball and wrestling; I could even beat a few! Once I pinned Dennis Diamond, a very appealing class shrimp, down on the ground with an audience watching, sat on his stomach, held his arms, and asked him to kiss me. Although I was the victorious one, I remember needing to be kissed to prove that he found me appealing. I needed his male stamp of approval to feel liked as well as mighty. My craving for male approval led to a reputation for being what we called "fast." I felt that sexual admiration would chip away all my nonconforming edges. Sex made me, the tough gangly girl, appreciated, and also confirmed my "girlness."

My first sexual experience aside from playing doctor when I was five occurred when I was thirteen. Dennis and Robert, a huge burly boy, and I used to walk in the scary Bronx woods, climbing the rugged terrain looking for condoms. Once they challenged me to undress and show them my vagina, and they would show me their penises. Always the derring-do, I went first. After my turn, they refused and said if I told anyone I'd look like a pervert. I felt violated by the experience and quite ashamed, but when I told Susan Szekely and a few of my other girlfriends, I made it seem as if the boys were cowards and I Miss Intrepid. I actually half-convinced myself I was. So, early on, there were two, often seemingly contradictory, aspects to my "proto" feminism. I was used by the guys, but I transformed the experience to an advantage, to show my bravery and macha.

In fifth through seventh grade in my public school in the middle-class Bronx, I alone broke a barrier of conformity by dressing in men's clothes. I would dress in my dad's shirts and ties, grease my hair with Wildroot Cream Oil Charlie, and sometimes wear long tight skirts and brown loafers. My take now on this attire was that it reflected my body and personality type, bold, blond, rangy, tall, and skinny in a world where the ideal Annette Funicello type was short, pleasingly plump, and perky. Unconsciously I must have understood that I couldn't live up to the norm—neat, busty, dark, thick and curly hair—so I introduced a new standard rather than fail. I hoped this would make me noticed and interesting rather than a total fool. It worked. I wasn't among the most popular girls in the class, but I was solidly in the top ten.

But my popularity made me feel like a fraud. I hadn't had the guts to be an outsider, which I felt I truly was; my inside and outside didn't fit. In my formative years I'd lived with my religious Catholic relatives and was never considered as one of their own. My parents were communists in the time of McCarthy and totally unlike my friends' parents. My father was still in school—what an embarrassment! My mother, a lawyer, was taking time out to try being Susie Homemaker, unsuccessfully. She wore leotards around the house, didn't enjoy housework or her children, and was overly familiar with my male chums, sometimes telling dirty jokes.

In sixth grade I led a rebellion to admit the girls to shop class. Actually my motivation was mixed. On the one hand, I wanted to stir up trouble; on the other, I preferred to learn carpentry, rather than cook coddled eggs in a miniature kitchen. Shop class would mean more time with the boys, and prove that I could do anything as well as they could. I never thought about my refusal to take cooking and sewing as a step forward for women until Susan Szekely (now Edmiston), my best friend from grade school, wrote an article about our vanguard feminism for *Redbook* in May 1975. It is ironic that what in my memory was a failed revolt, showing my boy craziness, was to her a feminist rebellion with me the audacious leader and her the timid follower.

Home at Last

What I'd like to convey—what I think has been neglected in the books and articles about the women's liberation movement—is the joy we felt. We were, we believed, poised on the trembling edge of a transformation. All the walls and boundaries inside and outside us might be knocked down. There was a yeastiness in the air that made us cocky and strong. Sure, there were splits and backbiting among us, but there was also fun and great times. For me, the women's liberation movement was love at first sight. The minute I heard about it, in 1967, I joined and began attending meetings—study groups, consciousness-raising sessions, and guerrilla theater—three days a week. Feminism solved my life's puzzle: It showed me I wasn't a weirdo. I felt we activists had all sprung from Medusa's head and were truly sisters. Like romantic love, the movement also generated many illusions. My joining was, as they say these days, overdetermined. I come from a communist family of all girls, whose grandmother marched in suffrage parades, and whose conflicted mother, a lawyer and art historian, was then sacrificing her ambitions by staying home with her kids and hating it.

Did I have a choice? In high school *The Second Sex* was my Ann Landers. I read and reread every wilted page for advice. In the sixties in college, then in graduate school (1970–1972) and working, I'd been active in the civil rights and antiwar movements. Yet my activism in these movements flowed from obligation and outrage, not from a sense of my own struggle. I learned a lot, had fun, and shed some bourgeois skin, but didn't feel these movements were mine or represented me.

The Women's Liberation Movement

Oh, the ecstasy and the agony of New York Radical Women and Women's International Conspiracy from Hell (WITCH) in 1967 and 1968, the heady days, when the media followed our every action and women joined in droves, too many to organize or even contact! The early consciousness-raising sessions, meetings, and weekend retreats created a frantic energy, hope, and feelings of at last belonging and being at home somewhere. Suddenly I had new eyes to see with and a new way to look at the past and the future. Thought and action, mind and body meshed. Women were catching the fire and coming together to change the world. Changes started with everyday life and the relations between women and men. His inconsiderate ways of making love; his refusal to share housework; his arrogant assumption, reinforced by the society at large, that his work was most important—all those hidden injuries now had names: male chauvinism, class privilege.

I was mainly active in New York Radical Women (1967–1969), the first women's liberation group in New York City, and Redstockings (1969 to 1971). The early consciousness-raising groups were combative, not the live-and-let-live, I'm-OK-you're-OK, sisterly sweetness later called by the media and women's groups "CR" or "women's lib." We sat in a circle and each in her turn answered a question agreed on for that evening. Of course we often strayed. We talked as honestly as we knew how about sex, school, street hassles, our childhood, the men in our lives. Discussion was intense because we were speaking about subjects formerly whispered or entirely suppressed. Orgasms: do we fake them? what gives us pleasure? Housework: who does the dishes and laundry? Who vacuums? Who takes out the garbage? Some spoke animatedly for ten minutes, others whispered a few sentences. We would challenge one another, often too roughly, but this harshness actually helped us learn from each other. We interrupted each other when someone said something that didn't sound authentic, or was antiwoman, racist, or elitist. In this process, we learned from each other.

It was liberating to blame men and see how they benefited from our labor and love. We began to put our energy into understanding women, and therefore understood ourselves. We gave up being the perennial martyrs to the men in our lives. Yes, we were overly angry and our analysis was often one-dimensional. But we were finally letting out years of rage and learning where this rage came from. The subtleties of theory had plenty of time to get fine-tuned.

We expressed individual rage, but on behalf of a more communal political and economic radicalism than is imaginable now. The aim was to challenge the systems through which the classifications of "masculine" and "feminine" are constructed and maintained. We saw structures of race, class, and gender as interconnected, and we knew that social deformations had to be corrected through radical institutional transformation. In contrast to Gloria Steinem and company, who now see the self as the last frontier, we downplayed the role of the individual. We never dreamed sexism could be solved by changing one man or one woman. That's why we created a social movement and worked out our ideology collectively.

In our consciousness-raising groups, we talked about our abortions and the inadequacy of birth control, and from these discussions followed the first public speak-out to tell the world what it was like to have illegal abortions. Later we lobbied and marched to repeal all abortion laws and make abortion free, safe, and available on demand. In 1968 we New York Radical Women spoke out about how the Miss America contest made us feel inadequate and ugly. Our consciousness raising led to action, so we picketed Atlantic City, hung a women's liberation banner inside the hall where Miss America was crowned; one person got arrested. After our actions we evaluated what we had done and learned from our mistakes. We realized that our Freedom Trash Can, where we collectively threw our "instruments of torture"—bras, girdles, hair and eyelash curlers—had been antiwoman. In criticizing women who used beauty enhancers, we had failed to understand why women must waste time and money on daily makeovers. A new, prowoman line began to emerge from our sessions of criticism and self-criticism.

Redstocking was prowoman, which meant that we each tried to understand the sexual and political dynamics of everything women did: why women tried to please and manipulate men, and why they stayed in bad marriages and dressed in uncomfortable clothes. We saw that other feminists condemned women. For example, we understood that in order to keep some jobs, especially service and clerical work, women needed to wear makeup and give in to their bosses' outlandish demands. We understood why women with many children and brutish husbands preferred marriage to welfare. In retrospect, maybe taking the woman's side and accepting her reasons for being obsequious to men wasn't always helpful. Maybe such formulations excused women (like myself) who could have been pushed to change. But we were trying, for once, to err in women's direction.

Today I can't believe my own chutzpah. When I talked fearlessly at that abortion speak-out, it did not occur to me that I could lose my job, or be thought immoral or plain foolish. On the nationally syndicated David Susskind television show, the first women's liberation talk show featuring the new feminism, where I appeared with representatives of NOW, I criticized my husband and all men. What made me and most of us intrepid was that we weren't alone. We were part of a growing movement, and we felt we weren't only speaking for ourselves to improve our own lives but to improve the lives of women everywhere. Sisterhood was powerful; we believed our slogans, which in turn gave us more courage. The feedback was immediate. Our Miss America action and abortion speak-out were lead items in the national media. Every time the Susskind show was reshown, New York Radical Women and I would receive hundreds of letters from women all over the country, telling their stories and wanting to join.

Unfortunately New York Radical Women was a small-time operation, without funds, even without recognized leaders. Unlike the anti-war and civil rights movements, which raised funds so that cadre could be full-time organizers, we were all volunteers, in between and after jobs, so we couldn't take advantage of our growing organizational opportunities. Redstockings did at one point get an apartment to use as an office, but there was no staff, although a faction around Kathie Amatniek kept pressing for leadership, organization, and a developed program. We didn't read all the Susskind mail, much less answer it. Radical feminists had touched a nerve—women's rage at inequality—and women throughout the United States were ready to act. If we had only had computers, what we might have done! Where are those letters now? Though a small cache may remain, mostly we threw them out. We had no idea then of what a precious resource this was, the tales of the trials and troubles of hundreds of women from all over the country.

Men's traditional ways of organizing seemed inappropriate for us, but we never came up with a full-blown feminist alternative, one geared to our mode of integrating the personal and political. Both in New York Radical Women and Redstockings, we subscribed to a new form of organization, never articulated fully. It entailed no chairs and no hierarchy, innovations that came from the civil rights and antiwar movements. At the same time, every woman knew who had prestige and power and who didn't. Because power was unacknowledged, it was harder to expose abuses of power. Jo Freeman, an early Chicago feminist, dubbed this "The Tyranny of Structurelessness."

MARRIAGE, PERSONAL AND POLITICAL

I married Lee Baxandall six months after college and had a child in 1967 during these early years of the women's liberation movement. Even though it was a difficult and an untraditional one, I needed that marriage. It was the springboard for my militant feminist activities and the rock I clung to. The institution allowed me to take militant stands and still feel loved by the enemy. As radical feminists espousing what we called a prowoman line, we were clear that the enemy was not some amorphous blob that one couldn't identify; the enemy was the men with whom we lived and for whom we worked. We believed that it was men who had to change and that we could force them to do it. We actually had truth squads where we confronted one another's mates. Judy Thibeau's husband, John Gabree, worked at *Penthouse* magazine. About six of us stormed into his office and demanded he resign from the sexist rag. To our surprise, he did.

There were divisions among radical feminists on the question of marriage. Most of the women in New York Radical Women and Redstockings were single. Kathie Amatniek, the unanointed leader, was single and pro-marriage. She argued that marriage, in contrast with free love, gave women more leverage and protection. Amatniek, who later called herself Sarachild, was a Harvard graduate with a real ability to write, think, and provoke, which I found stimulating, but some found intimidating. Others in the group, like Shulamith Firestone, who wrote the first radical feminist book, *The Dialectic of Sex: The Case for a Feminist Revolution,* and Ellen Willis, who was a rock critic and wrote for the *Village Voice,* were antimarriage, repelled by the domination inherent in all patriarchal institutions. I understood that I gained social privileges from the society by being married. Marriage gave me legitimacy and adult status; it enabled me to be radical and provocative. Between 1968 and 1970, the media often chose me to represent the militant radical feminist view because I was a blond, sweet-looking, regular, everyday American gal with a husband and child. I talked tough but looked mainstream and gave audiences cogent, catchy concepts that reflected our group's thinking.

We did consciousness raising about marriage in Redstockings and discussed the pressure to marry. Some of us action freaks were in WITCH, a small guerrilla theater band made up of Yippie women and theater people. Armed with our critique of marriage, we decided to invade a commercial bridal fair at Madison Square Garden. Our flyer said, "Confront the Whoremakers." We gained access because Judith Duffet worked at *Bride Magazine* and got us tickets. Of course she was fired after what we did. We entered the Garden dressed as brides in chains with commodities dangling from our odd-looking gowns. We performed an unwedding ceremony in a sacred circle chanting:

> We are gathered together here in the spirit of our passion to affirm love and initiate our freedom from the unholy state of American patriarchal oppression.

> We promise to love, cherish, and groove on each other and on all living things. We promise to smash the alienated family unit. We promise not to obey. We promise this through highs and bummers, in recognition that riches and objects are totally available through socialism or theft (but also that possessing is irrelevant to love).

> We promise these things until choice do us part. In the name of our sisters and brothers everywhere, and in the name of the Revolution, we pronounce ourselves Free Human Beings.

There were about a dozen of us, and we were seen as such aliens that at first no one could quite look at us. As we sang antimarriage songs (now dubbed raps), we released white mice underfoot, because we imagined the brides resembled mindless mice. Crowds gathered. We hardly had time to begin our skit before the police arrived. We exited, police hot on our tail, brides-to-be and salesmen screeching, and white mice trampled. At that stage it seems we were not prowoman enough to identify with the brides. As for the mice, this was before the animal liberation movement.

The extremes of the bridal fair aside, we often disagreed about marriage. I was married but not strongly promarriage. My marriage was shaky because my husband was neither traditional nor reliable. I was caught in a bind because I believed Jean Paul Sartre's existentialist ideas of freedom and hated the idea that I was supposed to chain Lee by obligation. I was incapable of pushing my husband to be faithful or to support me emotionally or financially if he didn't freely so desire. My ambivalences and principles gave him permission to have affairs with whomever he wanted, which turned out to include women in the movement, our baby-sitter, and eventually my divorce lawyer. Probably Lee didn't need this permission, but the women's liberation movement was a welcome new source of women in his life. Naively I felt lucky that Lee encouraged my constant political activity, my going away for days at a time. He typed leaflets for the movement and appeared reasonable in comparison to other men who were jealous of our camaraderie and the time the movement required. I didn't realize my husband was taking out his hostilities in other ways, and if I did half-know about his affairs, I didn't really acknowledge them till later. I was so caught up in movement prairie fire that I wasn't ready to let anything, certainly not marital strife, quench the flames.

We both worked: he twenty or so hours a week and me forty to make about the same salary. I did gain from having two incomes and a man around to help occasionally with housework and child care. Always, though, I did the lion's share. It was the sixties and one didn't need much money to live well. We had simple demands. Lee was from a conservative family in Oshkosh, Wisconsin, and I introduced him to a more cosmopolitan life. He now makes his living and devotes his life to the movement for nude beaches or, as he prefers to say, "clothes optional, free beaches."

In 1969 I was on a radio show with Shulamith Firestone, Anne Koedt (who wrote "The Myth of the Vaginal Orgasm"), Ti-Grace Atkinson (who was part of the Feminists, a radical feminist group that believed in celibacy, because sex per se was a mental and physical drain), and Flo Kennedy (an older African American, lesbian lawyer who co-wrote an early book on abortion as a feminist right, and ran for president on the Feminist Party ticket in 1972). Kennedy was a feisty character who saw the media as the chief exploiter of women and advised women to "girlcott" certain products. They were all vociferously antimarriage, and although they didn't in fact attack me, at some point in the show I began to take their antimarriage invectives personally. I felt compromised by my own contradictions—the antimarriage married mother—and could hardly contain my tears. Unfortunately, I remember my feelings more than the actual dialogue except that Ti-Grace Atkinson likened marriage to cancer and Shulie decried pregnancy as barbaric. Stoically, I managed to carry on; I counted on my much practiced ability to repress my conflicts and sound militant and right-on no matter what else was happening. Later this distancing mechanism scared me.

DAY CARE

As one of the few New York Radical Women with a small child, and a full-time job, I joined with other mothers in 1967 to start Liberation

Nursery, in the Lower East Side, on Sixth Street between avenues C and D. This was the first feminist day-care center in New York City. We rented a dilapidated storefront for less than a hundred dollars a month and later demanded the city support us; eventually it did, and we hired and paid some of the mothers. Mothers, and an occasional dad, worked in the center on a rotating basis. My son's dad couldn't take working in the nursery because he had neither the inclination nor the know-how to cope with a dozen infants. I felt it was one of the hardest tasks I had to do, but I did it.

Most of the women working at the nursery were married. A few were single, and almost all of us became single after a few years. Some were hippies and some were on welfare. Many of the mothers—all white—had been actively involved in the civil rights movement. Many of them had sampled New York Radical Women, but were disquieted by the argumentative consciousness-raising sessions and grew impatient with talk. Unlike me, with resources, career expectations, and only one child, most of them had two young children and lived closer to the edge. They shared many women's liberation goals, but unlike the majority of the women in the first feminist groups, they had to make child care a priority. Also, some of them felt that children came first. Many mothers of young children live in an enclosed child-centered cocoon with little space in their lives for anything but necessity. Split people like me were more rare in the day-care movement, but there must have been others. I, too, was enveloped by mothering, but I also longed for another self, one separate from my son.

We established a fine day-care center, but it took time. Taking my turn working once a week in the center was strenuous and stressful. I had to plan activities for all twelve or so kids, and frankly, I was never gifted at arts and crafts, music or games. Luckily my working partner, Mimi Wolff, was a musician and exceedingly energetic. I preferred the politics of day care and hassling with the city over its stringent, out-of-date rules. For example, the city required centers to use only china dishes and of course we used paper. In the city's attempt to coopt me, I ended up on Mayor John Lindsay's Task Force on Day Care. We won some victories; some standards were lowered. But in hindsight, I realize that some of these victories may have been mistakes. Some of the rules—like hiring trained teachers and providing a certain amount of space per child—make sense, but at the time, we were so eager to expand women's access to cheap, convenient day care that we could only see the regulations as making community-controlled day care impossible for those in need. There are now probably all sorts of abuses in the casual storefront day-care centers. But the fact that we had made some changes catapulted us on to further actions. You could fight city hall and gain things the state didn't want to give.

In Liberation Nursery, there were splits about child rearing, mainly between those who believed in structure, routines, and cleaning up (including me), and those who believed in the permissive approach: what the child wants the child gets, and we'll deal with the mess later. Those who wanted a totally laissez-faire approach eventually started another center.

Like many mothers, we were insecure about our kids' behavior. This overidentification with one's child was heightened in our day-care center because our values were communal. We wanted the best for all the children, but actually, we were most involved with—and anxious about—our own. There were no experts, and we spent hours trying to figure out why Che bit and Tanya didn't talk. (In the 1980s, Che changed his name to John.) We expected nonsexist behavior, and we couldn't fathom why none of the children were as fascinated as we adults were by the anatomically correct dolls on which we spent great sums of money.

I myself felt more responsible for my child's hang-ups than I did for my own. I could always blame my problems on my parents—now Finney would blame me! Luckily, Phineas Baxandall, now 30, was easy, and in spite of his parents' mistakes, he adjusted and excelled. However, he was never deliriously happy in our communal day care. I've speculated about why. Maybe he was too young, or we were inexperienced in amusing and educating toddlers and infants. But he still has a few close friends from Liberation Nursery and a few years ago he was very disappointed to be out of the country when the nursery organized a reunion. In 1972 the Liberation Nursery received permanent city funding and moved into a large building. Started as a communal effort to respond to our child-care needs, it is still in operation, a lasting institution, now with a professional staff and a city subsidy

It's interesting to me that most books on the women's liberation movement neglect the early feminist day-care efforts. Is one reason the resistance of women like me to being stigmatized as mothers? I tried not to talk about my son in order to avoid typecasting. This must have been successful because friends in the movement were often surprised to learn I had a child. I never confronted my movement friends or tried to get them to take part in my child-care life. I enjoyed my separate universes and didn't want them linked. Perhaps I feared I might be forced to choose between them, and that choice would be painful.

No doubt as part of backlash, writers then and now associate the movement with lesbians, abortion, and political correctness, rather than admitting that the radical women's movement changed the lives of all women, of course including lesbians and women needing abortions. Even Ellen Willis wrote an article for *The Village Voice* twenty years later bemoaning the fact that our movement never addressed child care. But we did. The demand for child care was an essential part of the women's liberation program and early marches called for child care. Most radical feminists were not anti-child, they simply ignored children. (A few, especially Irene Peslikis, Anne Forer, and Kathie Sarachild were child-friendly, and Kathie encouraged me to write about my day-care activities in *Woman's World,* a Redstockings newspaper.)

In fact, women in the movement established many day-care centers. Other mothers started half a dozen in New York City, and dozens of others throughout the country. In order to get more space for day care, we occupied unused, dilapidated buildings, held teach-ins and cultural events to win community support, and repaired those buildings to make them fit for day care and women's centers. Day care was a demand of both the Columbia and Harvard University strikes of 1968. The center that Columbia was forced to provide still operates. Mothers organized to discuss funding, feminist curricula, and fighting the city bureaucracy. We had a coalition of centers and held conferences that included women from Boston and Connecticut. We published papers. Several of the mothers who worked in Liberation Nursery went on to careers in day care, but when my child graduated from day care, I felt that I had, too. But by then, we had made day care into a field, and a sense of urgency about it was in my bones. Though I was excited that I no longer needed to be so involved in Fin's schooling, yet I couldn't resist, and ended up the vice-president of the PTA (of course a man was always president).

My son may have suffered because I spent time at work and meetings and he was often with other parents and baby-sitters. I rationalized this by saying he was better off with a variety of parenting styles and that he seemed content. My own mother had spent my childhood years at home and resented it. I rejected that model. Phineas had wonderful hippie baby-sitters, people more mellow than I was, who became almost family members. They loved Phineas and enjoyed hanging out with us. I ended up becoming the legal guardian for one, Vicki, a runaway, who now has her own child. Vicki's friends substituted and hung out as well. My boundaries, never tight, kept expanding.

PAID WORK, DAY CARE CONTINUES

At the same time that I was working to build the day-care center, I was working full-time as a community organizer at Stanton Street Settlement on the Lower East Side and for Mobilization for Youth, the first poverty program, doing welfare rights ombudsman work. We acted as a buffer between the locals and their landlords, the welfare department, the Housing Authority, the police, and any bureaucrat or tradesmen they faced. I tried to bring women's liberation consciousness to the job. For example, at Mobilization for Youth we discovered that young females dropped out of the Job Corps in larger proportions than the males. In interviewing the female teens, I found that many of them had children and were staying home to care for them. Wherever I went women needed day care. I got permission to establish an informal drop-in childcare center for Job Corps members in an apartment in a public housing project, and briefly I helped staff the center. Because we were against red tape and asking too many questions, the center was so casual that one day there would be no children and another day too many. Several times mothers parked their babies there and they never picked them up again. These children ended up in institutions or emergency foster care. On occasion, I ended up bringing children home with me, unable to locate someone I hadn't gotten enough information from.

I also ran a group for teen girls in the Job Corps. The subject matter was open, but we talked mainly about sex; they had many questions, even though they acted knowing. I pushed abortion and birth control, but they weren't receptive. For them, getting pregnant was an important rite of passage. Of the ones who got pregnant, more than half dropped out, feeling, I suppose, that they had failed and wanting to avoid me. Some of these mothers touched something in me, and I became very close to them and their families. I remember scraping money together, telling them how to pretend they were married, and accompanying them to the Sanger Clinic for birth control. This was the only cheap, nonmedical way to obtain contraceptives at the time.

THINGS FALL APART

By 1971 the glory days were winding down. Many more women were joining Redstockings groups, but most had not come up through radical movements. Probably half of the women in the original New York Radical Women had not been in the new left either, but we were all radicals. Some of the early feminists were working class and didn't aspire to be bourgeois. They understood that only collective action, not individual change, would emancipate women. Perhaps I'm being romantic, but the founding mothers were a rebellious bunch. The new breed, often professionals, were timid and psychologically oriented. They thought consciousness raising was about self-help, not social change. They didn't think in collective terms, because having grown up with money, they could usually solve their problems without others. Instead of starting a child-care center, they could hire a babysitter; instead of counting on a friend to help them move, they would call in professionals. This new breed didn't understand that there were contradictions between their personal goals and our radical socialist ideals. It was hard to fight them because they didn't believe in battling and had more traditional feminine and bourgeois ways of smoothing over conflict.

The differences became clear to me when a feminist media group and some of us veterans tried to take over the *Ladies' Home Journal*—at least, that is what we thought we were doing. Our idea was to talk to the secretaries, try to get them to organize and confront their bosses about *Ladies' Home Journal's* lack of relevance to most women, including themselves. However, this demonstration was led by some of the new career types, who came armed with their vitae. They didn't want to change *Ladies' Home Journal* in a major way; instead, they wanted to write feminist pieces for the magazine. The eight pages of one issue that they won was an advance, and better than nothing. Susan Brownmiller, a leader of this takeover, recently informed me that they were surprised by their success and that they donated the $10,000 they got to the New York City Women's Center.

Ti-Grace Atkinson, Shulamith Firestone, and I saw that the career types were in the majority, and, while they were negotiating with the editors, we walked silently down the backstairs. We had assumed the action would be a real takeover, just like the time we took over *Rat*, the new left underground newspaper. We assumed that feminists would run the *Ladies' Home Journal* and change every aspect of the magazine. Our demand was for a new order, not for positions in the male hierarchy.

When I would recruit new members for Redstockings or give talks on the women's liberation movement, I began to feel I was on automatic pilot, that my words no longer had authenticity. This frightened me. I began feeling I needed to learn and study more about the history of feminism. Marion Davidson of New York Radical Women had once suggested that the group read history. When I began to do so, I realized there was much to learn—that in fact I knew nothing. I was also getting burnt out and needed quiet space to think and read. By 1970 going back to graduate school seemed the solution, so I became a graduate student at Columbia and started moderating my feminist activities, cutting back to one or two meetings a week. I found graduate school somewhat of a waste, except as a breather. I wanted to learn women's history and at that time no one else knew much, certainly not my male professors. So I was on my own. I did get help from a study group, the Atlantic Patchwork Quilt, which was studying working-class women's organizations. Sarah Eisenstein, Linda Gordon, Priscilla Long Irons, Ros Petchesky, Susan Reverby, and Meredith Tax were part of that endeavor and we learned from each other.

My marriage, which had been difficult, soon became unbearable. Sisterhood is powerful, but it also hurts sisters. My husband's affairs with my friends started eating away at me. Of course I confronted these so-called sisters and even made scenes. I threw the suitcases of one of them—Juliet Mitchell, a visiting English feminist—out the window. These sisters' explanation was always, "I thought you wouldn't mind, you seemed so liberated." Hmm . . . well, why didn't you ask me? I was bothered because I hated my jealous rages and believed in sexual freedom, but couldn't live with it. Although Lee didn't want the marriage to break up, he would neither stop nor see a marriage counselor. Because I feared I wouldn't be able to handle being a single mother, I stayed longer than I should have. But finally the situation felt intolerable and I figured I'd prefer being Lee's lover than his wife. Separating was painful, even more painful than I had imagined. My energy collapsed and finally I saw a psychiatrist. This helped somewhat; my sister, Harriet Fraad, a feminist psychotherapist, helped even more.

Lee moved and traveled widely. He was not a devoted dad. He saw Phineas twice a year for two weeks. Despite my fears beforehand, I found single parenting easier than hassling with Lee about other women and child care. Besides, I knew many single mothers, and together we worked out cooperative arrangements, having our children sleep over at each other's houses, so that we all had some free time.

In the past twenty years I have learned a lot from male lovers. Though sexism is a strong force, individual men are far weaker and more vulnerable than I had imagined growing up in a female household that venerated its one male. In the women's liberation movement we had an ideology that defined men as such threatening enemies that I was surprised at men's fragility. But oddly enough, at the same time that I saw men as all-powerful, I had illusions about the power of feminism; I expected it to change the world and certainly change men and women far more quickly than it has. I naively assumed continuous progress, things getting better, not worse.

I never imagined twenty years of conservative rule, nor the steady watering down of feminism by professionals, liberals, and self-help artists. Many of the women I had identified with, the real, gutsy feminists, were worn out, and nobody else came forward to open up space for radical change. Just as the moderate African-American groups needed Malcolm X for ideas and initiatives, the liberal feminists needed us radicals. We invented consciousness raising and women's self-help networks; we awakened consciousness about sexual harassment, pornography, and rape; we created strong ideas that grabbed headlines: "male chauvinism," "sexism," "sisterhood is powerful." We began the process of organizing secretaries and other blue-collar women workers; we demanded that men share housework and child care. We wrote germinal articles, new histories, critiques of sexist education and literature. I still feel furious that the moderates stole our ideas and slogans and then wrote articles and books that ignored our contributions. I knew something was wrong, but neither I nor my friends had the energy, organization, woman power, resources, or analysis to fight back. So, with the decline of radical feminism and the new left, a milder, less confrontational feminism came to the fore, eclipsing our more militant history. Without radicals to push from the edge, the moderate, well-funded "revolution from within" feminists compromised away many of the initiatives we had begun. In the culture as a whole, the tide was turning against us. Conservatives captured the helm. We even have had to fight for the right to abortion all over again. By 1973 the guts had been taken out of the women's liberation movement and it was no longer innovative or exciting for me.

All the same, feminism continues to be a large part of my life. I teach and live women's history. The story is ongoing . . .

I'd like to thank Harriet Fraad, Elizabeth Ewen, Linda Gordon, Wini Breines, Sheila Rowbotham, Nancy Krieger, Kathie Amatniek, Lucinda Cisler, James O'Connor, Michael Lipsky, Winston Mvusi, Bill Stott, Phineas Reed Baxandall, and especially Ann Snitow for their helpful and sometimes ignored suggestions.

Primary and Secondary Contradictions in Seattle: 1967–1969

Barbara Winslow

Many women have written about the "click"—that transformative moment when everything falls into place and one becomes a feminist. For me, there was no one click, but a series of personal and political events in 1967–1969, during the formative years of the women's liberation movement in Seattle, Washington. That movement transformed my life—sometimes I think it saved my life—and gave it direction.

In the student movement in which I had been active, we spoke of "contradictions." The primary contradiction was the class struggle, whose resolution, according to orthodox Marxists, was necessary before all other social problems could be solved. These social problems, called secondary contradictions, were racism, sexism, and the oppression of youth.

I was born in 1945 and raised in an affluent Westchester suburb north of New York City. I hated Scarsdale. In the sixth grade, I was sent to the school psychologist because I had actually said that I hated living in Scarsdale. I often took unpopular positions, and paid a social price for them. In a class debate over the death penalty, I was roundly booed for my opposition to capital punishment. I was the only kid in my class in 1952 to support Adlai Stevenson over Eisenhower.

My mother was a very contradictory role model. She was (and is) an extremely smart, capable woman. A graduate in political science and history from Wellesley College, she had hoped to work for the foreign service in the State Department and had taken the civil service exam. However, marriage to my father, an executive in the hosiery and women's apparel industry, changed her plans. Instead she became a tireless civic worker. She served on the state board of the League of Women Voters and played an important role in changing New York State's voter registration laws. She was a member of Scarsdale's Planning Commission, Ethics Committee, Parks and Recreation Committee, Committee for the County, the Village Club, Women's Club, the school PTA. For a while she was even acting mayor of Scarsdale. In 1956, the *New Yorker* profiled my mother in "They Darned Near Killed Luella," meaning, obviously, from overwork. In addition to her political and organizational skills, she was a terrific amateur golfer. Her lowest handicap (for those of you who understand golf) was at one point a 4. She won eleven straight club championships.

But I believe my mother was frustrated by her role as wife and mother. She gave up tennis and took up golf because she could beat my father at tennis. She ended up being able to defeat my father at golf as well. She really wanted a *professional* career in politics; I think she hoped to run for public office. But, as my mother told me many years later, my father wanted her home every night for dinner. So she gave up her political ambitions in order to maintain her marriage and family life. In the 1950s and 1960s there were few alternatives. Little if any support was given to women who chose a full-time professional political career over marriage and motherhood. My mother was, on the surface, the model of an emancipated woman within marriage. Recently she told me that she believed my role models were my grandfather, a professor of chemistry at Columbia University, and my father. Both men, she told me, believed strongly in women being independent. If that is true, it is something I do not remember. Instead, I believe my mother, with all the contradictions in her life, is my role model and major influence.

I was an alienated mess of contradictions at Scarsdale High School, both a cheerleader and a beatnik-wannabe who got involved in a small way in the Civil Rights Movement. I occasionally cut classes at school to go into New York City to participate in the picketing of Woolworth's Five and Dime, for the Woolworth chain refused to serve food to African Americans or to allow them to sit at the lunch counters. I also argued endlessly and bitterly with my parents about their lives, my life, and our politics. My grades were so terrible, and I was so unhappy that my parents decided to send me away to school. At first they attempted to convince me that I would be happy at some very preppy all-girls boarding school, but, after I put up a terrible fight, they found a small progressive private school in New Hope, Pennsylvania.

I loved Solebury. There I was able to live with myself and my very strange contradictions as a bleached blond cheerleader who at the same time protested the Bay of Pigs and the Cuban missile crisis. While at Solebury, I became committed to issues of peace and justice. I also learned about dope, sex, and rock 'n' roll. Antioch College was the college extension of Solebury. There I became a history major, had co-op jobs in Chicago and New York City, and spent a year and a half in England, working in London and studying at the University of Leeds. I married my college sweetheart in 1967 and followed him to the University of Washington in Seattle. He had been awarded a prestigious National Defense Education Award (NDEA) Fellowship to study Russian history. I was going to finish my B.A. at the university, which I did in 1968, and immediately began to work on my Ph.D. in U.S. history.

For my first year in Seattle, I was *Mrs.* Winslow, a devoted and loving wife. He was a prominent campus radical—handsome, charismatic, a great speaker and organizer, as well as the president of the University Committee to End the War in Vietnam. He was also an intimidating political opponent. I was content and comfortable to be in his shadow. My friends were his friends. I went with him everywhere, never even going to meetings or activities without him. One night at a party, friends told me that they were going to call me *Mrs.* Vietnam Committee because they didn't know my name. Ed Mormon, who was involved in the campus chapter of SDS, was so bothered by my passive role at meetings that he gave me a lecture. "You must speak up, you have a contribution to make." To which I replied, ever so sweetly, that anything I wanted to say my husband could and would say—only much better.

Political activity in Seattle centered mainly, but not exclusively, at the University of Washington. Beginning in 1966, a Trotskyist group called the Freedom Socialist Party held a series on Women in U.S. Society at the alternative Free University. The FSP had broken from orthodox Trotskyist positions on a number of questions, and it was the only old left group that considered "The Woman Question" (as it was called in the old left) of paramount importance.

In November 1967, two women, Judith Shapiro, a professor of economics, and Susan Stern, a graduate student in social work, attended the classes and invited me to a meeting that would discuss women's issues. I asked my husband if I could go. I believe it was the first political meeting I attended without him, and I was extremely uncomfortable. About twenty-five women showed up in the basement of Susan

Stern's home. Clara Fraser, one of the leaders of the FSP, Judith Shapiro, and Susan Stern did most of the talking. The women decided to form a women's liberation group, Seattle Radical Women. I didn't say one word at the meeting because I wanted to find out what my husband's opinion was before I got involved.

However, this was not the first time I had thought about or discussed the issue of women and feminism. I had read Betty Friedan's *The Feminine Mystique* when it first came out, and was excited because Friedan seemed to be writing about my mother's life. Also, I enjoyed provocation, and this book had elicited a furious reaction from a wide range of reviewers. In 1964, I embarked upon a research project for an experimental independent study sociology course at Antioch. Because I was interested in Friedan's arguments, I chose the topic "Women in American Society." What this meant in reality was that I read almost every book on "American Women" in the Antioch Library and wrote a lengthy and incoherent essay. The two books that stood out in my mind as hysterically hostile to women were Wylie's *A Generation of Vipers,* and Lundberg's and Farnham's *Modern Women: The Lost Sex.* In 1966 I also read Masters and Johnson's *Human Sexual Response,* hoping to learn new sexual techniques. Instead, I came across a set of provocative ideas about female sexuality. When I was a student in England, I took a number of history and sociology courses from Marxist professors, where, occasionally, the role of women in capitalist society was discussed. I wrote my soon-to-be husband, asking him what "The Woman Question" was all about. His answers were sympathetic to the then orthodox position taken by Marxists.

By the time of my marriage, I already had strong opinions on the subject of abortion. My parents had founded a Planned Parenthood clinic in my hometown. My father, who had always tried to discuss issues of sex and sexuality with his daughters, assured me that if necessary they would support me if I ever needed an abortion. Two of my closest high school friends had to get illegal abortions, and a woman I did not know at my college died from an illegal abortion. Then in 1966, when I was in Europe, I had to end a pregnancy. Getting an abortion in Europe was not as dangerous as it was for most women in the United States, but it was both painful and humiliating.

My aunt and uncle helped me get a semilegal abortion in Switzerland. In order for women to get an abortion, a psychiatrist had to recommend the procedure to a doctor. You had to convince the psychiatrist your life would be ruined and you would be driven insane if you had the baby. We concocted a crazy story that I was from one of the most prominent families in the United States, that my father was running for the U.S. Senate, and that I was engaged to some famous man. My future husband was not the father of this baby, and furthermore my mother was mentally unstable and might have a breakdown if she knew. I had to tell the psychiatrist this wild implausible story in French. He signed the form, and I got the abortion. Later, I found out that he didn't believe my story after all. He signed the form because he was convinced that my uncle got me pregnant. All along the doctor knew I had been lying, but he just wanted to make me jump through his particular hoops.

What I learned from that experience was that women with connections could always get abortions, but even middle-class women had to go through humiliating and painful rituals to exercise control over their bodies and choices. While my abortion was to be painful, I knew I wouldn't die and I was relieved. But nonetheless I was also furious that the only way a woman could get an abortion was to pretend to be crazy. I believed then, as I do now, that women should be able to get abortions without any explanation or justification.

In January 1968, when I was 23 years old, I noticed a lump on my breast. My husband and I went to a doctor, who immediately scheduled a biopsy. He explained that he would take a slice out of the lump and that, if it was malignant, he would immediately perform a radical mastectomy. I asked him why this had to be done so fast. Why couldn't I have some more time to think about it? The doctor replied that if I had a lot of time to think about this radical procedure, I might get scared, change my mind, and not agree to the operation. Given that I was raised not to challenge the authority of doctors, I thought his answer made sense. "Good," said the doctor and handed a medical form for my husband to sign. "Why does he get to sign the form?" I asked. I will never forget the doctor's words: "Because women are too emotionally and irrationally tied to their breasts," and if they are married it is better for the husband to sign the form. This was an outrage. But what could I do? Those were the rules, and there was no alternative. My husband signed the form that gave him control over my breasts. Fortunately, the biopsy showed there was no malignancy, except perhaps a sexist malignancy in the minds of the medical establishment.

At about the same time, I was applying to graduate school. I thought about applying for an NDEA, and why not? My grades had been as good as my husband's, and an NDEA grant was not only prestigious, but financially generous. The office secretary told me that the history department was not going to recommend any women that year. The policy was to ensure that men could get into graduate school and not be drafted. I was stunned, confused, and angry. How could I complain about such a policy? I was adamantly opposed to the war in Vietnam and the draft. However, while I was glad that the history department was helping men stay out of the army, excluding women was patently unfair. I wrestled with these contradictions and came to the conclusion that it was probably better for men not to be drafted than to protest the policy.

Looking back at the events that affected my deepest choices about health and education, I wonder now why I didn't fly into a rage, assault the doctor, tear up the history graduate office, and then single-handedly form a women's liberation brigade. When I tell these stories to younger women—to my current radiologist and gynecologist—they can't even believe a world like that once existed.

At the same time that I was discouraged from applying for an NDEA, the local SDS chapter sponsored a meeting to discuss "The Woman Question." I believe this was the first women's liberation meeting held at the University of Washington. Clara Fraser, the speaker, focused mainly on the ideas raised in *The Feminine Mystique*. I remember timidly asking Clara if Friedan concentrated too much on middle-class suburban women to the exclusion of the lives of working-class women (trying to show off what Marxism I had learned), and being soundly criticized for not understanding the contradictions of women under capitalism. Nevertheless, I wanted to learn more about and be involved in feminism.

Clara Fraser was a pivotal figure in the development of the women's liberation movement in Seattle. She was (until 1998) an active important community figure in Seattle. I was always in awe of her. Clara had been a long-time member of the Socialist Workers Party until she left and organized the Freedom Socialist Party. She had played a leading role during the 1948 Boeing strike in Seattle, a fact remarkable for someone who was both a Trotskyist and a woman. She also had roots in Seattle's African-American community. She was one of the few white revolutionaries in Seattle who had the guts to argue with the Black Panther Party when she thought they were wrong. She was, for instance, probably the only person who argued with the Panthers about their positions on women's liberation. She had a commanding, as well as sectarian, oratorical presence and her debating style reminded me in some ways of my husband's, politically both completely fearless and self-confident. In consequence, she was one of my early women's liberation role models.

In late April and May 1968, the UW Committee to End the War in Vietnam had planned a week of antiwar activities, including rallies, forums, and marches. We were heady with excitement about taking on the university and its repressive policies on free and loud speech. I was already on disciplinary probation for violating university rules regarding the use of loudspeakers. We were also thrilled about events taking place all over the country—the growth of the Black Power movement and the antiwar movement. We were ecstatic about the student revolt at Columbia University, and inspired when we read that Columbia women demanded equal political roles during the sit-ins.

During this week of protests, the University of Washington's Men's Commission, controlled largely by the fraternities, announced that Men's Day, a traditional event held at the university, would include a display of antique cars, a Phil Ochs concert, and an appearance by a Playboy bunny, Reagan Wilson. (For Women's Day, the sorority-controlled University Women's Commission brought the wife of the governor, who presided over a sorority tea.) We were convinced this was another fraternity plot to dissipate antiwar activity. Ironically, this event was being used by the Men's Commission to raise scholarship money for African-American students coming to the University of Washington. Susan Stern and another student activist, Barbara Arnold, pointed out the larger implications of the Playboy bunny's appearance. They called a Radical Women meeting to plan a women's liberation protest. The women decided that we would put paper bags on our heads, storm the stage, and chant satirical lines inspired by the *Book of Common Prayer*. Part of the chant went, "Reagan Wilson, you are an empty vessel." I thought the whole thing seemed stupid; worse, I believed that no one would understand our protest. I could not imagine myself walking on a stage with a paper bag over my head. I really was too afraid and too self-conscious. My husband also agreed. Or was it the other way around?

Despite my misgivings, I went to the protest to see what would happen and to offer what I thought would be silent support. I think the purpose of Wilson's appearance was to promote the magazine, as opposed to recruit women to pose. I took a seat along the aisle, and very soon seven Radical Women with paper bags on their heads stormed the stage, sat down in a circle, and began to chant. Unfortunately, no one understood what the women were chanting because the paper bags muffled their words. Then a group of fraternity and student government men grabbed the women, started punching them, and dragged them off the stage.

I was panic stricken. This was a terrible series of events. No one would ever know what these women had tried to do. Everyone in the audience would think that a bunch of women had just gone crazy. I decided I absolutely had to act. That's why, though I had never spoken before in public, all of a sudden I was on this stage with a Playboy bunny. In front of 450 people, I explained that this was a women's liberation demonstration. We were tired of being treated as sex objects; we wanted to be treated like human beings. No one comprehended the politics of what I was saying: people were screaming at me, telling me to get a husband (which I already had), get lost, or get laid; others yelled that if I was so tired of being considered a sex object, why did I wear miniskirts. I tried to explain that women were doing constructive things, like protesting the war. At this point Reagan Wilson interjected that she did all she could for the soldiers by sending them pictures of herself. I couldn't believe what I was hearing.

The meeting came to an abrupt halt. I found myself surrounded by angry and incredulous students, mainly women, who could never explain to my satisfaction why they had been interested in the first place in attending such an event. I was told I was being unladylike and unfeminine for protesting. I tried to point out that in the past women had had to struggle and protest, rally, and demonstrate just to get the vote. I talked about women in the abolition, civil rights, and black liberation struggles. Since I had just read George Dangerfield's *Strange Death of Liberal England,* I talked about how the Pankhurst women initiated mass nonviolent civil disobedience for the vote; that one day suffragettes broke every window in downtown London, that they went to jail en masse, went on hunger strikes, and endured forcible feedings. Some student body official ordered me to leave the stage. I was terrified, but I refused. I just kept on talking to the audience about what I thought women's liberation was all about.

By this time, word of the melee had spread to an antiwar rally that was taking place at the same time. SDS and antiwar sisters and brothers came running into the auditorium. Rick Sortun (who had been an All-American football player for the UW Huskies, and at that time was a second-string guard for the St. Louis Cardinals as well as a UW student) and Vic Svacek, a political science major, who was as big as Rick, tore down the aisle. Vic bellowed, "Who hit a woman?!" "No, no Vic," corrected Judith Shapiro, who also came running in, "not who hit a woman, *who hit a comrade!*"

I was then dragged off the stage. Only then did I realize what I had done. I rushed into the nearest women's bathroom and threw up. When I was finally reunited with my sisters, we were surrounded by hostile students. Barbara Arnold had been socked in the face and had a nasty black eye. Others had had their hair pulled or been scratched and bitten. Student government people told us we were going to face more disciplinary action. We were astounded; we had been punched, scratched, and kicked; we hadn't hurt anyone, and yet we were going to be disciplined. Susan Stern, who was also married to a prominent campus radical, and I were brought in front of the dean of students and introduced as Mrs. Robbie Stern and Mrs. Cal Winslow. At that moment I had had it. Indignantly, I stomped my foot in front of the dean and announced, "I am not Mrs. Anybody. I am Barbara Winslow."

The next day, our protest made the front page of three newspapers. The University of Washington *Daily* headline stated "Playmate Meets Women—Radical Ones," with a picture of me confronting the bunny, and my skirt was shorter than hers! The Seattle *Post-Intelligencer* headlined "Guys Gulp, Coeds Sulk at 42-24-36!" Only the *Helix*, Seattle's underground paper, carried a sympathetic article, written by George Arthur, an SDS member, who had been a supporter of women's liberation from the very beginning.

I wish I could say that from that moment on I became a truly independent woman, but it was the first time I had ever spoken up on my own. Yet because I made the front page of the University of Washington *Daily*, I became an early spokesperson for the women's movement. From then on, I felt as if I had something to say that I could say better than my husband.

Our demonstration had exhilarated us; we felt confident and strong. Even the men in the antiwar movement and SDS respected us, especially since some of us got threatened with disciplinary action and others got punched. After that, it seemed that almost everything pushed us into activity. Radical lawyers at the University of Washington Law School had invited Flo Kennedy to speak at the university. She met with us, and emphatically encouraged our activities. Over Memorial Day, we staged our second public protest. We wanted to show our sympathy with the women of Vietnam—not as victims, but as fighters against U.S. imperialism. Fewer than a dozen of us dressed in black pajamas, wore Vietnamese straw hats, carried plastic machine guns, and counter-marched in the Memorial Day parade that was held at the Seattle Center. Some members of our group handed out leaflets explaining our solidarity with the women of Vietnam and our opposition to the war. Looking back at that demonstration, I am amazed at our gutsy behavior. I can only imagine what would have happened, for example, during the Gulf War if a group of women, dressed as armed Iraqi fighters, demonstrated their solidarity with Iraqi women in the middle of a military parade. In so many ways, we acted without fear.

By the beginning of the summer, we set up study groups so that we could read and discuss women's issues, but there was hardly enough material available to read. Those of us who had access to the University of Washington library began to check out all books that dealt with women; articles, leaflets, journals about women's liberation were also beginning to circulate. We couldn't get enough of them. I was taking a graduate history course on the American frontier. I chose as my research topic: Why Western States Supported Women's Suffrage.

On July 4 of that year, Draft Resistance–Seattle held a combination picnic, rally, "be-in," and rock-fest—a day of music, food, games, and speeches. I was asked to give a speech about women's liberation, the first woman to speak about women's liberation at a large antiwar/antidraft rally in Seattle. I was expected (and I wanted) to tie in opposition to the draft, the war, and racism to a Marxist, class analysis of women's oppression, all in five minutes. I agonized over that speech, writing and rewriting. Unlike some women in other cities, I wasn't heckled or booed. In fact, I got applause, and lots of people came up and congratulated me. However, later both the content and delivery of my speech were criticized by Clara Fraser as well as by my husband. I am sure nothing I could have said would have satisfied every political faction and tendency attending the rally. The more orthodox Trotskyists of Radical Women were critical of any "line" other than their own. My husband concentrated his criticism on my delivery, a practice that continued throughout my marriage.

Seattle Radical Women and the Freedom Socialist Party also embarked upon a very ambitious six-week educational series on "The Woman Question in America." I was asked to speak about women and the American labor movement. In 1968, there wasn't a lot of scholarly information accessible about women and labor. I relied mainly on Eleanor Flexner, *Century of Struggle,* and Philip Foner's multivolume series *History of the Labor Movement in the United States.* Both authors excited me, for it was the first time that I had read about the lives and struggles of working-class women. I spent a lot of time preparing the talk and I know I presented new information to everyone at the meeting.

During both the planning and the classes themselves, political differences between the women in the FSP and the new left emerged. The FSP wanted Radical Women to be modeled on the lines of a Leninist vanguard formation complete with democratic centralism. In our minds this meant a replication of old left organizational forms, which we believed would only contribute to the continuation of hierarchical male-dominated structures. We of the new left wanted a decentralized organization. We believed in participatory democracy. The discussions and arguments were endless and confusing. Also, some of the more politically sophisticated women like Judith Shapiro explained to me that in reality, the Freedom Socialist Party wanted Seattle Radical Women to be their front group. She meant that while there would always be some nonaligned women in Seattle Radical Women, RW would always be organizationally and politically dominated by the FSP and would exist primarily as their recruiting conduit. By midsummer, fed up with the fighting, the overwhelming majority of us younger, new left women left Seattle Radical Women and founded a new group, called Women's Liberation–Seattle.

In Seattle, my political activities and personal evolution were all tied up with configurations of the old left and the new left. Much has been written—for example, by Sara Evans and Alice Echols—about how the male chauvinism of the Civil Rights, antiwar, draft resistance, and student movements gave birth to the women's liberation movement. However, the Seattle women's liberation movement developed in its formative years with the support of the larger radical movements, because in Seattle, the old left, that is the Communist, anarchist, and Trotskyist movements, had a tradition of interest in and some support of "the woman question." Women had been more visible as local (as opposed to national) activists, as well as in leadership positions in the old left than women were in the new. Many people from the old left expressed their shock at the contempt that men from the new left showed to female comrades. But further, in Seattle, SDS, the University Committee to End the War in Vietnam, and Draft Resistance–Seattle were founded by people who were either red diaper babies or had trade union backgrounds. Therefore they were tolerant of younger women fighting around women's issues. It was not until the breakup of SDS in 1969 that the Seattle new left exhibited its wretched excesses of male chauvinism.

Because of the support we received from other left organizations and individuals, Women's Liberation–Seattle began as a committee of the Peace and Freedom Party (PFP), a third party, radical electoral alternative to the Democratic Party. In fall 1968, after the University of Washington fall term began, Women's Liberation–Seattle was also a committee of SDS (WLS-PFP-SDS). The two main planks of the PFP were opposition to the war in Vietnam and support for the black liberation struggle. In a number of states in 1968, including California, New York, and Washington, the Peace and Freedom Party got on the ballot. Eldridge Cleaver, the minister of information for the Black Panther Party, was the national presidential candidate, and each state picked a local vice-presidential candidate.

We women wrote the party platform on women, and when we presented it to the convention, there was no dissent nor patronizing corrections. However, we never questioned the candidacy of Eldridge Cleaver nor the attitude of the Black Panther Party to women (Cleaver is alleged to have coined the phrase "pussy power" when asked about women's liberation). It never occurred to us to challenge our all-male presidential ticket. It especially never occurred to me, since our vice-presidential nominee was my husband. However, we did demand changes in past practices. We insisted that women chair all the meetings. We argued that women needed the experience, because in the past, only men had chaired meetings. We also established a rule that the chair had to call on a woman after a man spoke. In these ways, we hoped, we would end the tradition of women's silence.

By fall 1968, there were three women's liberation groups: Seattle Radical Women, Women's Liberation–Seattle (PFP/SDS), and the Majority Union. The Majority Union published Seattle's first women's liberation publication, a journal called *Lilith,* named after the myth of a prior creation of an upstart woman before Eve. The Majority Union had been founded by anarchist women. While relations between Majority Union and Women's Liberation–Seattle were friendly, and we jointly produced leaflets, the Majority Union opposed working in an electoral organization such as the Peace and Freedom Party. Seattle Radical Women, which by now was dominated by the Freedom Socialist Party, was hostile to the Women's Liberation–Seattle (PFP/SDS) and Majority Union. Radical Women was contemptuous of the new left and saw itself in competition with the two groups. Furthermore, after the majority of us left Seattle Radical Women to form a new group, the remaining few RW members were understandably bitter.

So aside from going to meetings and subcommittee meetings, and raising "the woman question" wherever we went, there did not seem to be any women's liberation actions for us, until one evening when Judith Shapiro brought in an announcement about a Fascinating Womanhood meeting. *Fascinating Womanhood,* a book written by Helen Andelin, who was connected to the Mormon Church, discussed ways in which women could be more exciting to their husbands by being totally servile and stupid as housewives, wives, and mothers. (It was the predecessor of Marabel Morgan's *The Total Woman.)* By demonstrating against this reactionary meeting, we could reach the press and a larger constituency. Excitedly, we sent out a press release to the women's editors of the two major papers and informed the other women's groups that we were going to infiltrate this meeting. We also decided that we would not talk to any male reporters or answer questions on whether or not we were married or had children. As far as we were concerned, all women's opinions were valid, and we did not need the title of "wife" or "mother" to give legitimacy to women's analyses.

From the moment the fifteen of us walked into the meetingplace, we knew we were going to have a good time getting into trouble. Some stayed outside and leafleted while others wearing dresses went into workshops, asking provocative questions such as Why get married?

Why be a housewife? Why not oppose the war? Before long some burly church elders began to physically escort us out. But not before we started yelling. All this fascinated Joan Geiger of the *Seattle Times,* whose article reflected her amusement and sympathy with us. The headline ran "Seattle Women Clash over the Right to Slavery and Freedom." Geiger wrote, "Inside women congregated together to learn (for a fee) to be childlike, submissive (but saucy) wives. Outside women handed out leaflets decrying any attempt to 'relegate women to a subordinate role.' " She went on to describe how we challenged FW to a debate on the parts of the textbook that disturbed us the most, 'revere your husband and honor his right to rule you and your children.' " Geiger also mentioned that the husbands of the protestors (including mine) were outside handing out leaflets. Geiger included the obligatory put-down of both sides at her conclusion, but enough in the article commented positively on women's liberation and spotlighted our group. Finally, Women's Liberation–Seattle had gotten off the ground. We had made news by doing something specifically for and about women.

Meanwhile, summer and fall events—the Democratic convention in Chicago, the Hubert Humphrey/Richard Nixon/George Wallace campaign, the continuation of the war, and the assassinations of King and Kennedy, the growth of the Black Panther Party, as well as the May/June events in France and other international events in Czechoslovakia and Mexico City—inspired hundreds of students to join the local SDS chapter when the fall university term began. The news about the first Miss America protests had also galvanized us. Women's Liberation existed across the nation. We had sisters everywhere.

One of our major activities was protesting all three major candidates. We leafleted Boeing workers for a week before George Wallace came to speak. We had been frightened by his large vote from blue-collar white workers. We staged a large anti-Nixon rally. But our most eventful protest was against Hubert Humphrey for his position supporting the war in Vietnam. Borrowing a red, white, and blue maternity dress, I disguised myself as a pregnant woman (inside my "womb" was a loudspeaker), and, along with a PFP contingent of 100 or so went into the balcony to engage in a Humphrey Heckle. Our heckling was so loud that we enraged the audience, who demanded that we be thrown out. When Humphrey walked onto the platform, I stood up, pulled the loudspeaker out from under my dress, and led the chanting of "Dump the Hump!"

The police came in and began ejecting people. The first person they grabbed was William Apple of the *New York Times*. Then the cops threw me on top of him. According to the article appearing in the next day's *Times,* when he asked if I had been hurt, I replied, "Of course not, I'm a liberated woman." That was how my parents learned about women's liberation. When they called me, they were more concerned that I had been hurt than by the political ideas I had been trying to convey. Furthermore, and understandably, they wanted me to graduate from college and not get arrested. Like many parents of that period, they supported their kids' beliefs but not all their actions around their beliefs.

Contrary to what later critics of the women's liberation movement have claimed, we were never hostile to children, parents, full-time housewives and mothers, or mothers who worked outside the home. One of the first issues we took on was free child care for all university staff, students, and faculty—and that was because so many of us did have young children. We focused on the University of Washington, not only because so many of us were students, UW staff, faculty, and faculty wives (yes, it was an official term), but also because the UW was the second largest employer in Seattle, second only to the Boeing Corporation. Our day-care committee developed into the organization that later created child-care facilities at the UW. We also planned to challenge the university's female exclusion policies, and the School of Dentistry's open refusal to accept any women students. We took on the Health Center, demanding that contraceptive information and devices be given to all students. By 1970, we had initiated, and later finally won a major lawsuit against the University of Washington citing massive sex discrimination at every level of the university. We transformed the UW Women's Commission from an institution that served only sorority women into a commission that developed meaningful programs for women. One of its most notable publications was *How to Have Intercourse Without Getting Screwed,* a comprehensive pamphlet regarding women's reproductive health. After 1970, the UW, like most institutions of higher learning, was forced to change its policies and institutional structures in an attempt to end gender discrimination.

We knew about the importance of consciousness-raising groups for developing women's political consciousness, theory, and practice. One of our first rap-group meetings discussed Masters and Johnson's *Human*

Sexual Response and Anne Koedt's "The Myth of the Vaginal Orgasm." This meeting was intensely emotional. One woman spoke about how she always felt she was sexually dysfunctional; another woman described faking orgasm; another confessed she preferred mutual masturbation to intercourse; one woman was excited because this information would improve her sex life. At the end of the meeting we were all crying, for we had realized one meaning of the slogan "the personal is political."

Yet for me, while I understood the importance of the slogan, I did not want the political to become too personal. In spite of the fact that I did not want to be "Mrs. Anybody," and that I was a dedicated women's liberation activist, I was afraid to take the radical essence of feminism into my personal life, and in particular, into my marriage. For this reason, I always felt I was a fraud in our rap groups. One particularly painful session dealt with "who drives the car." We spent the meeting talking about why men never allowed women to drive. Some of the women said they now insisted on doing 50 percent of all driving; others spoke of the need to learn auto mechanics so they wouldn't be dependent upon men. I admitted, to everyone's shock, that I could never challenge my husband on the issue of driving the car. The fight to be able to drive combined with his constant (and undeserved) criticism of my driving was not worth the principle of women's liberation—or so I thought. The same applied to housework. Our rap group read and applauded Pat Mainardi's "The Politics of Housework." We talked about why only women are housewives, why housework is drudgery, the political economy of housework, and how to get men to do housework. Yet I continued to do all the housework. Like driving the car, I thought it wasn't worth the fight. Besides, I rationalized, my husband was totally supportive of my women's liberation activities, why fight over something as unimportant (?) as housework? Looking back, I can see I was committed to staying in a marriage even though our interpersonal relations went against my feminism. But at the time, I believed my marriage enabled me to be a politically active feminist.

Living the traditional sexual division of labor worked well for my entire marriage despite the contradiction. I did the household work, and he mowed the lawn. We both worked as students and graduate student assistants. In our real world of political activity, he was a leading spokesperson against the war and racism; I did the women's liberation work. He never said my work was secondary to his; he never complained when I went to meetings; he never demanded that household chores come before my political activity. He encouraged me to speak publicly, yet often (heavily) edited my speeches and always criticized my delivery later.

I believed then that I could not have stepped forward in the way that I did without his support. He was my shield. My marriage protected me. I also loved him very much. I thought he was the most wonderful person in the world, and I assumed everyone else did as well. We were a very close, and at the same time, a very closed couple. We never had public disagreements on political issues, or, more accurately, I never disagreed with him publicly or privately on *anything*. Years later, a number of friends from Seattle told me that people saw us as a political monolith, a two-person permanent faction or clique. Looking back, I now realize how much power that gave him in our relationship and how it prevented me from being able successfully to challenge his clear domination of the most personal aspects of our marriage. I never saw our marriage as an equal partnership.

I also saw my role as taking care of him personally as well as politically. My first political organizing effort went to ensure that he was reelected chairman of the UW Committee to End the War in Vietnam running against the Socialist Workers Party (SWP) and their youth group, the Young Socialist Alliance (YSA), in spring 1968. Like a lioness protecting her young, but in this case it was my husband, I threw myself into the complex fight. I collared all our political and personal friends, explained the situation both politically and personally, and begged everyone to come to the meeting and vote for my husband and his slate. I had never before been so politically aggressive without my husband next to me. To everyone's shock, the meeting was both packed and stacked. My husband and his slate won the election. The opposition correctly denounced me for packing the meeting. In the end, my husband, and therefore I, decided to leave the UW antiwar committee to devote more time to SDS and PFP.

In 1991, I spoke with the woman who was the leader of the SWP/YSA at the time. We were no longer political adversaries but colleagues, and I was interviewing her for a book I am writing about the Seattle women's movement. We talked about that election campaign, and it was then that I realized that my first successful political organizing campaign had nothing to do with either women's liberation or feminism, but with saving my husband's leadership position in a group that he subsequently left.

In Women's Liberation–Seattle, I preferred the political discussions that enabled me to avoid dealing with the personal/political contradictions. We had endless discussions about exploitation and oppression. Are we slaves? serfs? workers? Are women an oppressed class? a caste? an oppressed sex? We engaged in the then-famous "Jackie" debate: "If all women are a class, does that mean that Jackie Onassis is oppressed under capitalism?" Our rap group decided that while Jackie might be oppressed as a woman, under capitalism, we wouldn't feel sorry for her, but would demand that she become a class traitor and give her millions to the movement. We debated whether or not women in the household produce use value or commodities. If labor is a commodity under capitalism, what do we call the unpaid labor of housewives? How can women's unpaid housework be accounted for in the Gross National Product? Are women exploited primarily as workers or consumers? Can we organize women as housewives?

Because of our geographical isolation, we were spared many of the divisive debates going on among women and women's groups in places like New York, Boston, Washington, or Chicago. We were not being divided along the lines of politicos and nonpoliticos, for all of us in Women's Liberation–Seattle identified in one way or another with the broad left.

We set up a speakers' bureau, whereupon over fifty organizations invited us to come and speak about women's liberation. I even spoke at the Women's Guild of the Seattle Symphony Orchestra. Unlike some other women's liberation groups, we did not discourage the development of spokeswomen. Our policy was to make each member a spokeswoman. We always sent two members to a speaking engagement, one more experienced than the other. That way, newer members would learn in a supportive, mentoring environment.

We had our first chance to educate the broader left about women's liberation when we read that the Student Mobilization Committee Against the War in Vietnam (the group that replaced the UW Committee to End the War in Vietnam) was sending women into dance halls. Their press release stated that the women were going to talk antiwar politics as they danced with the GIs. Immediately we called a protest meeting. Over three hundred people came to listen, argue, and debate the role and participation of women in the antidraft and antiwar movements. At first, the members of the Student Mobilization Committee accused us of being afraid to be feminine. "What's wrong with being pretty?" "What's wrong with GIs liking attractive women?" "If they'll listen to an attractive woman speak out against the war, what's wrong with that?" "We're not sleeping with them; we're just talking to soldiers about the war." We had to struggle with our arguments. After all, we too were totally opposed to the war and the draft. But we did not support the infamous slogan, "Girls say yes to boys who say no." Instead, many of us had gone down to the Shelter Half, the GI coffee shop in Tacoma, Washington, and talked politics with the soldiers.

In January 1969, the state Peace and Freedom Party brought Fannie Lou Hamer, the legendary civil rights activist and leader of the Mississippi Freedom Democratic Party, to speak in Seattle. At the UW, I was asked to speak on abortion rights on the same platform with Mrs. Hamer. I gave a short presentation about woman's liberation and a woman's right to abortion. Then Mrs. Hamer spoke. She praised my presentation and then told the audience that she was opposed to women having abortions, but she had never thought much about the subject. She told us she had been sent to a hospital and upon her release, she discovered she had been sterilized against her will and without her knowledge. The entire audience was stunned. Because of Fannie Lou Hamer, our abortion committee always recognized the issue of forced sterilization.

The Washington State Peace and Freedom Party put out three issues of a radical newspaper called *The Western Front*. I was the women's liberation editor. My first reportorial assignment was covering the January 1969 abortion hearings in Olympia, Washington, the state capital. In 1966, a group of liberal doctors, clergy, and social workers had begun studying the possibility of reforming Washington State's laws that outlawed abortion. They had worked very quietly behind the scenes because their hope had been to liberalize abortion laws without much public fuss. The hearings marked the beginning of the abortion reform campaign. Women's Liberation–Seattle set up an abortion rights committee, which played a significant role in the subsequent successful liberalization of the state's abortion laws.

The Peace and Freedom Party collapsed by March 1969. Its demise meant that Women's Liberation–Seattle was a committee solely of SDS. Our local SDS chapter had been supportive of women's liberation from the beginning. Most of us in SDS had also been in the PFP, and we had carried many of our organizational ideas about women into SDS. Women chaired meetings and were public speakers; women's issues and reports from the women's committee were always discussed by members; our SDS RAP (Research and Propaganda) groups were named after women: Harriet Tubman, Mother Jones, Elizabeth Gurley Flynn, Clara Zetkin, and Sojourner Truth.

Because of the supportive nature of our particular SDS chapter, we were constantly shocked at the male chauvinism of SDS national officers and travelers. Mike James, who was active in Chicago JOIN (Jobs Or Income Now), came to a meeting in Seattle in late fall to give a talk about organizing white workers. The meeting was packed. James was explaining in an affected SDS accent (their fantasy of a southern, white, male [stupid] worker) how to relate to white workers. At one point he said, "and then sometimes we all get together and ball some chick." Silence. There wasn't even a gasp in the room. Jill Severn, a member of Radical Women, stood up and in a clear voice wanted to know "what did that do to the chick's consciousness?" Again, silence. James did not know how to answer the question and began to backtrack. He finally admitted that they never really ever gangbanged women; they just said they did to appear tough. After that confession, the meeting erupted. The women surrounded Jill and congratulated her. We were thrilled at her timing and her presence of mind. We were also floored at James's remarks. We resented the fact that male SDS national leaders would breeze in and out of Seattle, cavalierly make passes at every SDS woman, yet at the same time show complete indifference to our women's committee. We couldn't stand this behavior, but we didn't do anything about it, either. In January 1969, we had a one-day teach-in on women's liberation; 250 people attended. We invited Bernadine Dohrn, then interorganizational secretary of SDS. Even though she was a woman, she was as appalling as any of the male SDS leaders. She mainly criticized the women's liberation movement for not being anti-imperialist. She picked fights with many Women's Liberation–Seattle members and spent most of her time with male SDSers. We were generally happy to see her leave.

What finally convinced us that there was something wrong with the politics of SDS toward women occurred during our participation with a group of women who were on strike for the first time against the Perfect Photo Company. One of the strikers was married to the president of the local AFSCME union at the University of Washington. He was an ex-member of the Communist Party and a supporter of SDS. We had worked with him and his union during the United Farm Workers' Strike. He asked members of Women's Liberation–Seattle and Radical Women if we would help his wife by coming down to the picket line. Since this was the women's first strike, and since they were very inexperienced about unionism, picketing, and demonstrating, he thought we could be of help. At 5:30 the next morning about thirty of us, including some men, showed up on the picket line. We carried signs that said Women's Liberation–Seattle. I had never been on a labor picket line before, and I was very excited. At last, this was a way to prove our commitment to supporting the struggles of women workers. It was also a way to make a real connection between their exploitation as workers and oppression as women under capitalism. We also thought, in all arrogance, this was the way to organize workers. Unfortunately for us, none of the strikers showed up that day. Our picket line prevented a number of scab cars from driving into the plant. Finally one car rammed into one of us. Furious, we surrounded the car, and started banging on it with our picket signs. My husband reached into the car, turned off the ignition, and threw the keys under the car. Immediately the police swept in and arrested fourteen of us. My husband was not arrested. I was thrown into a police car, taken to jail, and charged with profanity and resisting arrest. We spent several hours in jail, singing civil rights, union, and Wobbly songs, before we were released on our own recognizance.

That afternoon, there was an emergency SDS meeting to discuss what to do about our relationship to the strike. I could not believe my ears. All of a sudden it appeared that SDS had been transformed. The SDS campus leaders (mainly men) began talking about why we shouldn't support this strike. They reminded us that SDS was committed to fighting racism and imperialism, and that this strike had nothing to do with either. To me it was outrageous that a small group of middle-class white men were snottily critiquing the actions of a group of older working-class women who earned only minimum wage, who had been ignored by their union leadership, and who were on strike and fighting back for the first time in their lives. We were told that unless these women gave up their white skin privilege (!), SDS would not support their strike!

We refused to accept that directive. We tried to find ways to talk to the women and continue our strike support work. However, the union leaders had successfully convinced the striking women they wanted nothing to do with women's liberation and SDS. We were unwelcome on their picket lines and at the union meetings. After much soul-searching we realized our mistakes. Instead of storming onto their picket line and creating havoc, we should have met with the women, listened to them, followed their leadership and direction, and learned from them. Our future activities with women at the workplace looked very different from our behavior during the photofinishers' strike.

By now, a core group of us were arguing that Women's Liberation–Seattle should no longer be a committee of SDS but rather an independent, autonomous women's organization. We were not arguing that women should leave SDS. We wanted to stay in SDS, but we also wanted to focus on issues affecting women. The WLS-SDS was evenly divided over the issue of independence. The debate that took place in the committee and in our chapter was not particularly bitter or acrimonious but rather cold and detached. Judith Bissell and Karen Daenzer presented one proposal stating that the "role the women's liberation committee has actually played has practically speaking been phased out." The task now was for SDS as a whole to develop a program regarding women within "the over-all anti-imperialist context." Judith Shapiro, Lee Mayfield, and I replied that the work of ending women's oppression could never be phased out, and just as Blacks (the language of the time) had their own independent organizations to organize the struggle against racism, so should women have their own organizations to lead the struggle for women's liberation. We further pointed out that no one in SDS would dare argue that Blacks didn't need separate organizations; why should women's work always be relegated to a committee of some other group? The majority of SDS agreed to disband the women's liberation committee. It was in effect a contradictory victory for an autonomous women's liberation movement.

I was involved in all this frenetic political activity while a graduate student. My academic experiences also forged my feminist activism. How could a fellow student describe the nineteenth-century United States as a political democracy when all women and Black men in the South couldn't vote? "What does that have to do with anything?" he sneered. Our professor said nothing. Like most women graduate students in the sixties, I got little direction and mentoring from my graduate professors. By the time I took my oral and written Ph.D. exams in U.S. and British women's history in 1973, I knew more about women's history than they did.

Since I was an SDS and WLS member who had a history degree, I began to speak and write about women in history at meetings. In 1969, when SDS commemorated the fiftieth anniversary of the Seattle General Strike, I spoke about women in the Seattle labor movement and the role of Anna Louise Strong. I gave presentations on the history of International Women's Day, the history of the women's suffrage movement, and women in the labor movement. With a group of women, including Mary Rothschild, I worked to develop the first introductory course on women at the University of Washington. When I finished my M.A. thesis in the summer of 1969, I had decided that I wanted to develop my own Ph.D. program in women's history. I was going to England for a year to study with E. P. Thompson.

At the time I left for England, Women's Liberation–Seattle was flourishing. We were free from having to debate the factional issues ravaging SDS. While we were aware of and debated other issues raging within women's organizations in other cities, our geographical isolation postponed faction fights and splits. Our abortion rights subcommittee was involved in the campaign to liberalize Washington State's abortion laws, and played a significant role in the 1970 abortion rights victory. Our working-women's committee spawned the organization of clerical workers at the University of Washington. There was a Women's Liberation–Seattle chapter at Seattle Central Community College. We were able to publish our own newsletter, *And Ain't I a Woman.* A number of our members became founders of the first lesbian liberation organization, Seattle Gay Women's Alliance. Everything was possible.

In 1992, I began researching a book about the women's liberation movement in Seattle. I decided to write this book because much of the history of the women's liberation movement in high school and college texts as well as in more academic books does not correspond with my experience, and also because so little is known about the Seattle women's movement and its contributions to the struggle for women's liberation. I have in my room four boxes filled with original documents, press releases, minutes, leaflets, journals as well as my three-hundred-page FBI file. Recently, I went back to Seattle and interviewed former sisters and comrades. Many of my interviewees refreshed my memories of our struggles and helped me gain insights into my personal relationships.

What I realize is that I inverted the conventional Marxist paradigm by resolving my personal secondary contradictions first: I got a Ph.D., spoke in public about women's liberation, stayed politically active, wrote a book, became a history professor, played competitive tennis (on a 3.5 tennis team) while raising two daughters as a single mother. However, I was not able to resolve the primary contradiction; that is, I was never able to take the radical and liberating essence of feminism into my marriage. In fact, the breakup of my marriage, while personally devastating, enabled me to do what my earlier rap groups could never do— take my insights of the early years of the women's liberation movement, equality, mutual respect, challenge to traditional roles and hierarchies, and sexual freedom into all my personal relationships.

I get upset and am in disagreement with much of what is being written about the sixties in general and with the women's liberation movement in particular. I want our history to be written by people who were activists and partisans, who wish to convey the sense of liberation and transformation. Younger women are writing histories of our movement that some of us who were participants do not even recognize. Politicians, media pundits, and Camille Paglia–wannabees describe us as being racist, anti–working class, anti-Semitic, elitist, antisex, and hostile to mothers and children. Many of the writings of the sixties, like *The Sixties Without Apology,* are too defensive, too apologetic for me. The sixties was one of the greatest decades in U.S. history. As "ecstatic utopians" we struggled to create an egalitarian society, and liberating relationships, which challenged the hierarchies of class, race, gender, and sexualities.

In the Wilderness of One's Inner Self:
Living Feminism

Lourdes Benería

> *. . . not fulfilling our parents' expectations, often going against their expectations by exceeding them. It means being in alien territory and suspicious of the laws and walls. . . . It means being internal exiles.*
> **Gloria Anzaldúa, Making Face, Making Soul: Haciendo Caras**

> *The soul can shrivel from an excess of critical distance, and if I don't want to remain in arid internal exile . . . , I have to find a way to lose my alienation without losing my self.*
> **Eva Hoffman, Lost in Translation: A Life in a New Language**

One day in the fall of 1968, my graduate school friend Harriet Zellner came to class with a button that read "FEMINISM LIVES." We were Ph.D. students in economics at Columbia University, she a full-time student and I on maternity leave; she a native New Yorker and I a foreign student from Catalonia, Spain, still lost in translation from the warmth and protection of my European Latin culture to the great diversity, sophistication, richness, harshness, and alienation of New York City life. I looked at the button with curiosity, wondering what that message was about. I had not heard of the Columbia Women's Liberation group, but Harriet had attended some of their meetings and she seemed full of enthusiasm and passion about their plans and discussions. Rachel DuPlessis and Kate Millett were among the participants in the group and their discussions around sexual politics, Harriet said, were creating many waves on campus. What could "women's liberation" mean in general and to me in particular? Her proud smile when questioned about the button made me feel small; even though I did not know what it was all about, I would not have dared to show it off on my coat's collar. But I *was* intrigued.

INITIAL REACTIONS

My first reaction to the new wave of feminism was denial, even though I was unconsciously drawn to the conversations I had with Harriet and other friends involved in the women's movement. I had, after all, been carrying on my own individual struggle for years. Born in Boí, a village in the central Pyrenees mountains at a time when the Valley of Boí did not have a road, we had a five-hour horse ride to get to the nearest town with a bus that would allow us to travel to what seemed to us remote urban centers. My roots were in that picturesque valley of six small villages, centuries old, with homes close together as fortresses, built with thick, gray stone walls and blueish slate roofs, homes still shaped by the needs of a nineteenth-century subsistence economy in the process of disappearing. To me, that medieval cradle had been deeply patriarchal, protective, loving, and nurturing while also authoritarian and oppressive. The youngest of six, I had grown up practically as an only child; my much older brothers and sisters had left the household when I was still a child—except for my oldest brother, the *heir* in a deeply ingrained patriarchal system of primogeniture. I was sandwiched between the two generations born before and after the Spanish Civil War: a little girl surrounded by adults, with great pressures to obey and submit to authority, to follow traditions, norms, and social conventions. The influence of deeply ingrained Catholicism was all-encompassing, overwhelming, inescapably reaching all corners of one's existence and daily activities. It was buttressed by that dark and repressive period of Spanish history that followed the 1936–1940 Civil War. My childhood was nourished, or should I say malnourished, with the stiff and self-enclosed environment of Franco's dictatorship.

To be sure, there were other forces, other influences, like the beautiful twenty-minute walk across the valley done twice a day during my first years of primary school and, between the ages of nine and twelve, a one-hour walk across a mountain twice a week to attend school at a neighboring village. On these walks I felt the taste of freedom, the magnificence of life and nature, the power of the humble early spring violets unfolding through the melting winter snow, my curiosity awakened by the unknown valleys behind the horizon, the power of dreaming. And there was also the human factor: a strong sense of community, of belonging, of roots immersed in centuries-old history, the wisdom and strength of some adults in my extended family and village that turned life into a continuous lesson on human wisdom and intelligence, the inviting sophistication and urban culture of a few summer visitors, the interesting accounts of a great storyteller and deeply patriarchal uncle who nevertheless was proud of a girl's accomplishments, and the constant questioning of a child's mind in the face of life's contradictions and unknowns. In retrospect, an elementary school teacher about thirty-five years my elder, my cousin Maria, stands out as that wonderfully contradictory person, loving and controlling at the same time, who made me understand what I did and did not want to be like. Strong and independently minded in many ways, she taught me that women could read books and newspapers and discuss politics as much as men.

To many Americans and to urban people in particular, my long walks to school may seem like a lack of privilege, even poverty. This was not the case. Within the traditional and relatively egalitarian social structure of the Pyrenees, my family was quite well off. My ability to go to school away from my village, to follow a good teacher, was viewed as a privilege that few children could have. Within the local economy, my family could rely on plenty of domestic help even though, by the standards of a consumer society, we had very few of the consumer goods that an average working-class urban family now takes for granted. A radio was considered quite a luxury, and it was given a privileged location in the kitchen/dining room. Our house was large and with the standard accessories of traditional village life, but without the comforts of a modern home. We had a wonderful cellar to store barrels of table wine and olive oil, as well as home-produced delicacies such as hams, salamis, and cheeses, often representing the supply of a whole year, but the home decor was austere and not too comfortable by modern standards. We had plenty of wood to burn but no central heating. We had horses to take us to other towns and to transport tourists in the summer time. And we had sheep and other cattle for our own consumption and for business. Hence, my class background cannot neatly be defined in terms of modern society. The urban people I had met seemed to have a higher standard of living. They also seemed more sophisticated and savvy, and they spoke Catalan with what they (and we) thought was a "better" accent. Yet, deep inside, we met their rather common air of superiority with proud skepticism and often with oppositional contempt.

I was immersed in village life until I turned thirteen, at which time I was sent to (Catholic) boarding school for three years. A step away from rural life, it was my first stay in the provincial capital where I finished secondary schooling. It was an important phase in my formal education but also a source of internalized repression, particularly in matters of morality, sexuality, and social conventions of 1950s Spain. Protected and sheltered from the outside world, the nuns in charge of the school were eager to prepare us for bourgeois living, not quite our upbringing in most cases, and to teach us to serve God and patriarchal society.

Urban life arrived for me when I registered at the University of Barcelona in 1956. My father had died in 1954 and, in one of my last conversations with him, he had suggested that it was not necessary for me to have a university degree; what I needed was some basic skills to help with the family business. Although I didn't dare challenge him openly, that conversation reinforced my conviction that going to the university, following the steps of one of my sisters, was definitely what I wanted to do. Why I eventually decided to major in economics, not exactly what a *nice girl like me* was expected to do, was a source of constant inquiry on the part of family and friends. I finally developed a couple of quick, functional responses. I said that economics was a way of getting a variety of very practical jobs. For the more intellectually minded, I pointed out that I wanted to learn about the difference between capitalism and socialism. But I didn't have a good response for those concerned about economics not being a very "feminine" profession, or for being among only three women out of a class of seventy-five. Perhaps my feminism began unconsciously out of the pressure to answer these questions.

Barcelona and student life represented a more systematic opening to critical thinking, not so much through the exposure to inspiring teachers—there were very few in the tightly controlled francoist university—as through the multiple dimensions of city life. This period was a turning point in my political awakening. My identity as a Catalan had always been beyond doubt; I spoke Catalan as the primary language. But my traditional background had not encouraged me to see this identity in political terms. I had at times joined the chorus of those who protested against the imposition of Spanish in the schools or against the prohibition of registering Catalan names officially (they had to be translated), or protested not having Catalan newspapers or the symbols of

Catalan culture and identity displayed in public. But this was the first time that I understood, for example, the conflicts fought through the Spanish Civil War in profoundly political and historical terms, including nationalist and identity issues. From then on, my politics would be clearly defined as anti-Franco and antidictatorship.

I also began to question the role of the Catholic Church, not only as a reactionary force within Spanish politics but as a reactionary influence in my life. Religion was for me one of the most profound and difficult-to-confront sources of patriarchal power. Its presence can be typified by the gender divisions of a winter Saturday night in my household. There were the women, sitting around the fireplace, knitting, talking, or doing household chores. There were the men playing cards around a table: my father, the village priest, and other men representing the village symbols of male authority. The women were ready to serve them whenever they needed drinks or food. Card playing went hand in hand with conversations about community affairs, business, politics, religion, and life in general. As a child, I stood by the table, following the game with great interest and quietly listening to the multiple conversations. The priest, a venerable old man who had baptized everyone under thirty in the village, was the authority figure whose habits, virtues, vices, and weaknesses were well known to all. He would not have been as welcome in other homes as he was in mine, for not all families took religion equally seriously. Some, in fact, had distinguished themselves for their anti-clericalism and anarchism during the war, a source of tensions still ambiguously alive. As a child, I understood the religious aspects of these tensions better than the political ones, and my experience in boarding school did not do much to clarify these connections. It is in this sense that my university years helped me obtain a clearer view of the multilayered complexity of (apparently simple) village life.

If Barcelona began to open a new world for me, a stay in Paris during the summer of 1958 was a further turning point. I went as an exchange student to work at a bank at the heart of the city; I lived in the Cité Universitaire, which offered a totally new experience of autonomy and freedom. Paris was a sudden break from the closeness, protectiveness, and parochialism of Spanish life under the dictatorship. (Incidentally, even younger Spanish generations seem to have difficulties in comprehending the depth and scope of the limits and rigidities with which my generation grew up.) My decision to go to Paris was made without consulting my family; I had found the job through a student association and presented my family with a *fait accompli*. I had even managed to get my first passport by myself, a real accomplishment given the intricacies and bureaucracy of Franco's policed passport agencies.

I initially came to the United States with a Fulbright scholarship, as a graduate student. Although I did return to Spain after obtaining a master's degree, Marvin, the American man whom I eventually married in Spain, became the key reason for my returning to the United States and registering as a Ph.D. student at Columbia University. Both the marriage and the return had been difficult and excruciating decisions. I did not want to leave Barcelona; my identity as a Catalan, as a Spanish citizen, and as a political and social being in a Latin culture was bound up with deeply felt roots and strong attachment to place. I had found living in New York City for one year very interesting but had no desire to prolong my stay. I was aware of the opportunities that the move involved, of the possibilities to transcend boundaries. America was both attractive and scary.

But what then could Harriet's button mean to me? My own border-crossing struggle had been one without a name. I barely knew anything about feminism other than as an episode of the historical past. The catchy expression in 1968 was "women's liberation," which seemed pretty explicit and direct about meaning and purpose. At some very deep level, I understood immediately what feminism was about. "It's about women becoming themselves," I wrote in a rough first approximation in my diary, after having gone for a coffee with Harriet and another friend also involved with the Columbia group, "and about getting rid of conventionalisms and inhibitions that limit women's individual and collective growth."

To struggle for women's growth seemed frightening for many reasons that I did not want to recognize. First, I identified the movement as American and thus as rather alien to me. I often thought that feminist discourse was too individualistic, too concerned with the self, too anti-family and antimale. Further, I wrote in my diary, "I rather like 'feminine' traits, and I am not ready to give them up," assuming that being a feminist meant to become more "masculine." But gradually I became immersed in the questions raised by feminism, energized by issues highly relevant to me. "It's amusing," I wrote in another diary, "that these days

[September/69] I find myself involved in women's lib activities without having planned to do so or feeling fully part of it; unconsciously I realize that I am hearing voices that speak to me directly." That fall I wrote a short paper with the title "Scattered Thoughts on Women," which I used to clarify my ideas and to answer many of the questions often raised by male colleagues. At a meeting of the Union for Radical Political Economics that I attended, one of them had asked Harriet and me, with a condescending smile, what was it that women wanted! So I prepared a list of requests, with a first attempt at theorizing. Although I have not been able to locate a copy of the paper, my recollection is that it questioned women's concentration in domestic work, the gender division of labor in and outside of the family, and the process of socialization by which women saw many doors closed to them.

Yet despite my effort at clarifying these basic ideas, I was still uncomfortable describing myself as a "feminist" (whatever that might have meant to me then). It seemed to imply a greater identification with the cause than what I was prepared for. I had read the article "I Am Furious (Female)," which had been written, in the summer of 1969, "as an attempt to formulate perspectives for the Women's Caucus of the New University Conference."[1] It was an attempt to analyze the plight of women and justify why, in the authors' words, "[t]he ultimate goal of a radical women's movement must be revolution." That was a tall order, I thought. In retrospect, I see that the article was quite a sophisticated and erudite analysis of women's condition from a "radical" (in its 1960s meaning) perspective. But I felt intimidated by this radical message; I was not prepared for "the revolution," nor for the militancy it called for.

I became part of a consciousness-raising group at a time when that group had already functioned for almost two years (1969–71). The openness with which women spoke of their intimate lives in the group seemed very American to me. In a certain way, it intimidated me, but it was "liberating" to hear that other women were encountering similar problems with the world surrounding them: patriarchal schools and sexist colleagues, husbands, lovers; that they were angry, often unconsciously so, at

---

[1] The paper's title was reminiscent of a rather popular Swedish film, *I Am Curious (Yellow)*. It was the result of a collective effort and it was written by members of the Columbia and Harvard chapters of the New University Conference: Ellen Cantarow, Elizabeth Diggs, Muriel Dimen, Kate Ellis, Janet Marx, and Lillian Robinson.

gender asymmetries; that they felt guilty when they resented their unequal share of housework and child care; that I was not the only one who had to confront the consequences of years of sexual repression; that challenging male authority was difficult, painful, and threatening. The group dissolved when I was just beginning to enjoy it; symbolically enough, I had arrived when the rest of the women had become tired of it.

I then became a member of one of the several groups of women in New York City that tried to reconcile feminism with left politics. They were named Marxist-Feminist (M-F) to indicate their interest both in left and feminist politics, and represented a post-consciousness-raising effort to combine feminism with the goals of a study group. M-F I had been formed in the mid-seventies and included women who pioneered a great deal of earlier feminist writings. Mine was M-F II, created in 1976, a group with an oscillating number of twenty to twenty-five women that for me generated very important human, intellectual and political bonds. The group lasted until the early eighties, with new women joining while others left. The list of accomplished women from the group is long and diverse, among them Jessica Benjamin, Carol Cohn, Harriet Cohen, Muriel Dimen, Kate Ellis, Sherry Gorelick, and Rayna Rapp. In these groups, I was always part of some minority: as a non-American, as a Latin, the only one with roots in medieval times, the only one (or so it seemed to me) with such terrible fear of speaking in public. I made an enormous effort to fit in, to accommodate to what a few years later would be labeled the white middle-class women's movement. It was often difficult to connect my own experience to that of others since it seemed so remote to our shared New York City life. In many ways it was easier for me to relate my experience to my Spanish-speaking friends, but the membership of the M-F groups (the number grew to five) was mostly white, middle-class, from New York City and urban, with a large proportion of Jewish women. For the most part, I felt comfortable in the group, although at times also distant. In fact, it was not until many years later, when privileged middle-class feminism and the liberal coldness and elitism of the Ivy League became an issue for me, that I realized how, despite my many lived experiences with American feminism, I felt again the ambiguity of the outsider within, with my Latin roots surfacing strongly in that rich but difficult and lonely territory of the ever-changing borderlines. I realized then how much that accommodation had been accomplished by my naively brushing aside my own "difference."

GRADUATE SCHOOL
AND MOTHERHOOD

When I became pregnant during my first year in the Ph.D. program, I received a leave of absence from Columbia. Once my first son, Jordi, was born (in 1965), it seemed "natural" to have another baby; the notion of having a second child seemed an easy choice. Thus my second son, Marc, was born in 1968, the year that Martin Luther King, Jr. and Robert Kennedy were assassinated. I had grown up without questioning that, if I got married, I would be a mother. It was "natural," it seemed. In my village, child care was a shared family and community task. I was not familiar with the notion of a baby-sitter, let alone day care, until I arrived in New York City. Being paid for taking care of a baby? I had taken care of my nieces and nephews many times; the idea of it being a paid activity seemed strange. Having babies in the grand metropolis was clearly not what it was like in the Pyrenees, or even in a city like Barcelona where the role of the family was much stronger than in the United States. I had not been prepared for the limitations of the nuclear family; neither was I ready for the mental and physical stress created by uninterrupted child care and by motherhood responsibilities that never go away. I strongly felt the need to transcend domestic responsibilities. It was not surprising then that my desire to return to graduate school did not take long to surface. I decided to register again when my youngest son was ten months old. It was a difficult decision and I was aware of the obstacles involved, but I did not realize that it would be such an *enormous* struggle.

When I returned to Columbia in the fall of 1968, there was not a single day-care center in New York City's Upper West Side. The difficulties of dealing with child care soon made me a nervous wreck: unreliable baby-sitters, our precarious graduate-student finances, mother/child separation anxieties, and the difficulties of following tight schedules and finding time to read and do academic work all contributed to my decision to withdraw in the middle of the semester. Marvin and I soon became active members of the Columbia University Day Care Coalition. The group organized many sit-ins, demonstrations, petitions, and negotiations with the university administration and the City of New York; it eventually succeeded in getting a building from Columbia. Thus, a beautiful building at West 106th Street and Riverside became a day-care center, which we named the Children's Mansion. We saw it as a success that had been, to a great extent, nurtured by feminist politics and persistent work among the parents involved. My youngest son was among the first kids to register. The Children's Mansion was a truly multicultural institution, with children from different social and ethnic backgrounds. I was very grateful and proud of our accomplishment, which represented a crucial difference for my return to graduate school in the fall of 1970.

I was the only woman with children among the graduate students in economics. Among faculty and students, it seemed as if nobody cared about my special status and difficulties. But this time I was determined to finish my degree. Here feminism was very helpful. It gave me the impetus I needed in moments of doubt and it provided the emotional and intellectual support for my determination. The return to graduate school reinforced my feminism: I did not have a single woman teacher throughout graduate school. Male hegemony and privilege among faculty and students seemed overwhelming, a fact that women students now seem to forget. My household responsibilities often meant that I had to miss what for me were some of the most exciting activities: those taking place at the margin of required academic work, often organized by students around issues related to what we used to call "the movement," feminism included.

America, the civil rights movement, and the Vietnam War had radicalized me. I had not expected that "the land of affluence and freedom" could have the levels of poverty and urban squalor that I saw in New York City. Michael Harrington's *The Other America,* which summarized eloquently the problems affecting millions of people suffering from poverty amidst plenty, had a strong impact on me. The assassinations of Martin Luther King, Jr., and of Malcolm X were symbolic of the many events that made me think about the depths of racism; this was a time when I thought that U.S. racism had no parallel elsewhere (I have learned better since then, particularly with the current and growing xenophobia in Europe). The Vietnam War represented the international dimension (the favorite word at the time was "imperialism") of an economic and social system that generated unequal power relations and oppressive institutions for many. I did not know much about Marxism, but I began to think that it offered a paradigm conducive to addressing many of the questions about power, inequality, and exploitation in which I was increasingly interested. This was also the focus of the hyphenated M-F groups, even though the relative weights of the M and F were different for different people, with the F eventually tilting the balance in its favor.

Little in our graduate program responded to the radical questions of the time. On the contrary, the hegemony of orthodox thinking was alienating. I found no encouragement to concentrate on issues that interested me. But I persevered in my struggle with imposed canons and with teachers who seemed distant and arrogantly hegemonic. Fortunately, I was not alone and, in addition, there *were* immediate rewards to being a student: the tangible accomplishments of school work, even when small, the obstacles conquered, the acquisition of new skills, and (when graduate work was less absurd) the sheer joy of learning. But there were also many costs: "motherly" anxiety and guilt, stress, repressed anger at having to accommodate to what felt like an oppressive educational program. I was older than the average graduate student, and I often felt alienated from the world that surrounded me, with the exception of a few friends.

Having grown up in an extended family and with a strong sense of community, the limitations of the nuclear family and urban life in New York City seemed overwhelming. Hence the constant effort at reproducing the extended family: inviting friends to share meals and other activities, becoming members of baby-sitting pools, looking for collective living arrangements with some friends. Twice we looked at brownstones with the purpose of arranging collective living with other friends with children, but New York City brownstones, for all their charm, had not been built for collective living. Sharing housework and child care was a continuous struggle, which deepened my feminist questions: Why was it that women were assumed to be responsible for domestic work and child care? And why should we (women) have to be grateful when men merely "helped"? Why was it that, at the end, it was me who would have to wash the dirty pan left in the sink? I remember the first time that the difference between child *bearing* and child *caring* (that wonderful distinction in the English language) became so vivid to me. Yes, women carried babies in their wombs and we had breasts to nurse them, but there was nothing biological about the association of women with child rearing and domestic work. Biology was not destiny! The gender division of labor was a social construct! This may seem too obvious in the 1990s; in the 1960s and 1970s, we were discovering it, bit by bit.

Thus I was perfectly ready for the passionate discussions about domestic work that became prevalent in the early seventies, like the Domestic Labor Debate among M-F circles. Was domestic work "productive" or "unproductive"? What role did it play within the economic system? Did the wage earner—usually male—"exploit" the housewife—usually female? The intellectual discovery of the crucial role of house-work, not just within the family but within the larger society, was a moment whose excitement may be difficult to comprehend for the younger generation of feminists. The sense of breaking new ground, of gradually forging new intellectual tools, of mapping out how the personal *was* political were exhilarating and rewarding processes. But the frustrations of using the master's tools soon began to appear. "Who the hell cares whether domestic work is *productive* or *unproductive!*" said Harriet Cohen one day when our M-F group was discussing readings on the domestic labor debate. "All I want to know is why it is that women are stuck with it." I understood her anger and rebellion against andro-centric paradigms perfectly well. I have since mentioned her remarks innumerable times.

Despite the difficulties associated with child rearing, I enjoyed deeply every stage and every step of motherhood. Rereading my diaries, I am stunned at how often I wrote about the enormous joy I experi-enced from my sons. It's the multi-layered joy of seeing those little crea-tures grow and BECOME, with or without our help; the unfolding of life in all its dimensions; it's about feeling the most committed and unselfish love, and the most enduring human bonds. It always seemed as if each stage of motherhood was flying by much too fast to fully grasp its specific pleasures: hearing the first sounds and words, the first broken sentences, the exciting development of the power of language, the unex-pected and intelligent thoughts of wisdom from a child's mind, the voices traveling throughout each corner of the house, the adult-child playing, the intimacy of bedtime story reading, the discovery of humor and the first jokes, the beginning of logical conversation and under-standing, the sweetness of interdependence, even the closeness brought about by tensions and expressions of anger. These did not come in unproblematic ways. In my feminist groups, I soon discovered that my difficulties with setting clear-cut mother/child boundaries were also experienced by other women. Where was it that my sons began and I ended, and vice versa? Why was it that when dad and mom worked at their respective desks mom would never close the door? Thus I learned to work with constant interruptions. My background had prepared me well for such "skills." As with so many women, my well-being was tied to the satisfaction of demands by others. Despite my strong inner tensions, I had learned to give priority to the will of those who surrounded me. My own needs were often not allowed to surface to a conscious level, let alone to be expressed in a clear, direct, and explicit way.

Thus I remember having a negative reaction to Shulamith Firestone's book *The Dialectic of Sex*. Published in 1970, it received a great deal of attention for its call for, among other things, a "feminist revolution" that would free women "from the tyranny of their reproductive biology by every means available." The means included the use of technology to free women from pregnancy, a sort of feminist twist to Huxley's *Brave New World*, I thought. My reaction was quite spontaneous: I did not want be freed from the biological experience of child *bearing;* pregnancy had been a wonderfully rich experience and a lesson about the power and the marvels of our bodies. I would not have wanted to miss it. But why did biological reproduction have to be a source of oppression and gender inequality via child *caring?* Firestone's book also included a call for the elimination of the family, pure and simple! The kind of family she was describing had many features different from the one I grew up in and it was difficult for me to identify. But I did not dare to criticize the book in feminist circles; it was quite popular and I felt vulnerable at the borderline of my political difference, my different reaction, an impression that would return repeatedly. I still feel angry when I remember how it seemed as if I had to apologize for being a mother and having two children and a husband (and two sons on top of it! if at least they had been girls!!). Here feminism was not very helpful. Interestingly, in the late seventies, motherhood became not only acceptable among circles that had earlier rejected it but a matter of celebration and a source for rethinking women's identity. As Marylin Young, a brief M-F II member, put it once, some of us had a tendency to do the wrong things at the wrong time. Some of us had roots in societies in which being a mother was not even viewed as a choice, except when the alternative was marrying and serving God *Him*self!

One of my fears about marrying an American and living in the United States was to have children who would be ashamed of a mother from a different culture and with a foreign accent; the prospect of being their "other" filled me with anxiety. I had known sons and daughters of Spanish-speaking parents from Latin America who seemed embarrassed about their background. It was a painful realization. I was determined not to let my cultural heritage fade in the background. I spoke Catalan to my sons from the day they were born but, as they became social beings, English dominated at home and outside of it. Their Catalan (and Spanish) would probably not have survived had we not managed to visit the Pyrenees practically every summer. Thus, both of them grew up trilingual and with multicultural identities. As I write this essay, Jordi, a Ph.D. student at UCLA, is about to leave for the Bolivian Amazon to explore ideas for his dissertation. Marc, living in Madrid for the last three years, is working on a film in the Jordanian desert, a British production with an American director. My fears proved to be unfounded: they are proud of their multicultural roots and of their Pyrenees mother.

THE JOYS AND PAINS OF PERSONAL CHANGE

The early stages of feminism were for me an incredibly rich source of accelerated personal change and growth, an unprecedented challenge to understand myself and others, a source of openness and of self-assertion, a supportive force in the long and often painful trip that had been given the name of "liberation."

In the words of Ann Cornelisen, in her book *Women of the Shadows: The Wives and Mothers of Southern Italy,* I had been a "woman of silence." Its full meaning became clear to me at a meeting of my M-F II group in which I was to comment on the book, at Barnard College. Three of us were in charge of preparing for the group's discussion on "growing up in different forms of patriarchal families." We soon realized that the three of us had come from strongly religious and patriarchal families: Hedda Kaplan, from an orthodox Jewish family from New York City's Lower East Side; Hyla Sherer, from a Protestant pastor's family in Kentucky, and I from a Pyrenees traditional Catholic family. My chosen themes were "sex and class at my family's dining table" and "the sexual politics of a winter's Saturday night at home." I also passed around an album of selected family and village photographs that would help the group understand the setting.

I was happily surprised when I noticed the interest with which the account was received. I had often felt embarrassed by my rural background, not only in the United States but in Spain as well. In the United

States, when asked where I was from, I had often said Barcelona, and not necessarily to avoid explaining where my village was located; being from Barcelona automatically made me an urban person, presumably less of a target for negative assumptions about my mountain roots.

My experience was very different from that of the southern Italian women described by Cornelisen. But I did find, I said, some sentences with which I identified. When I began to read the quotes, my voice suddenly trembled and tears clouded my eyes: "They are women of tremendous strengths, these women in the shadows. . . ." The room, with perhaps twenty-five women sitting around a large seminar table, was in absolute silence and I could barely continue reading: "one of their strengths, and not the least, is their silence, *which outsiders have understood as submission*" (emphasis mine). When I dared to lift my eyes, I saw many faces looking, some of them teary also, as in communion with my past and present. It was a difficult but precious moment!

Twenty-eight hours later, my mind was still repeating, "they are women of tremendous strengths . . ." and "outsiders understand their silence as submission," while my tears continued flowing. There were my mother and my sisters in my mind, and so many other women of silence; they had much strength despite their submission. I had heard my father and mother repeat an old Spanish proverb, *"la mujer y la pera la que calla es buena"* (a woman and a pear are best when silent). My mother had lived up to it, and I had clearly heard the message from her. But the message had not killed the strength. In the United States, I had found that aggressiveness and verbal articulation were often equated with intelligence and worth. Students who spoke up in class had a head start over those of us who, fearful of and not used to speaking in public, remained silent and often ignored. I had grown up, as had many women in other cultures, with the opposite values. I had in fact learned to protect myself with silence, and I understood that it could be used as a sword, as "a strategic defense against the oppressor," as anthropologist Susan Gal has put it. It can also be a punishment of those who abuse authority over us. I do not, however, recommend the strategy; the withdrawal from communication that silence represents can be very painful. It can also create distance from those we love.

It took me years and a fierce willpower and determination to overcome "silence." How ironic that I chose a profession in which public speaking became increasingly an important part of my work. The facility with which my American classmates asked questions and made comments in class both fascinated and intimidated me. The words "outspoken" and "articulate" were not part of my upbringing, nor were they objectives for a girl to pursue. In my rural culture, it was important to be charming, to be liked, to be "feminine" and modest, to have a sense of duty, to be responsible and trustworthy. I had learned the message that outspokenness was not a virtue, at least not for women. My mother had another proverb for that: *"molt soroll i poques nous"* (Catalan) or *"mucho ruido y pocas nueces"* (Spanish), which she used to put down people who talked a lot without much substance. But she had no proverb praising the ability to talk eloquently and with depth, to express oneself, to voice one's needs, to communicate with others. Instead, women had to learn to understand and even to guess the needs of others so as to quickly try to meet them. This was what I have called "the antenna effect," typified by the dynamics at my parents' dinner table; the women learned to tune in and understand when we had to get up and get bread or water or wine or dessert. The men did not have to learn such skill; all they needed was to ask, with their presumed authority.

To be sure, there were also class dynamics at work at our dinner table. We often did not have to get up from the table because, at least until the early 1960s, my family had domestic help, a maid for household work and hired men to take care of sheep, cattle, and other family business. In the table's hierarchy, I sat next to those who worked for a wage, my parents at the other end and the rest of us sitting mostly according to age. I identified with the nonfamily members, not just because we sat and laughed together but because we shared the same authority figures. Yet when the conversation was about business, it was dominated by men across class lines. The women listened. It was not that they did not have strong opinions; they simply kept them to themselves. And yet, as in many rural societies, women did not necessarily feel under-valued; they were aware of the importance of their work for family and community well-being. Despite a clear-cut gender division of labor, women's skills were intertwined with those of men on a daily basis and in important tasks, within the family and the community. They did not seem to be isolated in the sense that an urban housewife often is, and loneliness was not an issue. On the contrary, the problem, at least for me, was lack of privacy and of a room of my own, despite a large home with plenty of bedrooms. (I remember vividly the many times I locked myself in the bathroom, reading a book; it was the only place where my privacy was respected.)

One result of silence for women was passivity. We learned to respond as dutiful daughters, and respond well rather than to speak up or take initiatives; we learned to follow rather than lead, to accept rather than ask difficult questions. Rebellion and critical thinking did not surface easily; it was kept within one's mind or for very special, rare moments of family intimacy. But it was there: hidden, subterranean, wrapped up with layers of guilt and a strong sense of duty. Patriarchy was deeply ingrained, and male authority was accompanied by warmth and protection. How difficult it would be to confront the loving patriarchs (fathers, brothers, uncles, father figures, boy friends, lovers and husbands)! Having grown up without siblings to struggle with (due to differences in age), I had not learned to fight with my peers, let alone with authority figures. Nor did I know how to express anger, particularly when the intensity of its accumulation was scary.

My cathartic experience in my M-F group was not only about overcoming silence. It was equally about revealing my origins, about not being embarrassed by them, about breaking the inner tension that results from feeling the pride and strong attachment to place and roots while internalizing urban biases and stereotypical presumptions of social worth and status. It was about discovering that having medieval and rural roots was not only acceptable but interesting to my friends. It was about being myself. The weight of urban biases in my consciousness had been deeper than I cared to understand. As symbolized by my tremendous effort at getting rid of my Pyrenees accent when speaking Catalan, I had spent a great deal of energy to ensure that I be accepted in the different circles I encountered. I did that quite successfully, mostly by accommodating and adjusting. The Barnard College experience represented a turning point. I was revealing, even crying out, parts of my life that I had not fully understood before. And the nakedness, although painful, was liberating! I am deeply grateful to the women in M-F II who listened and cried with me.

In this sense, the feminist groups I participated in were a great opportunity to confront issues of personal growth. Here feminism for me was crucial, a source of support, inspiration, and empowerment, a challenge. It was also a source of inner tensions, one of the areas in which I had to deal with the conflicts and ambiguities that Gloria

Anzaldúa calls "borderlands," or the shadowy areas between different cultures. Again, I made a great effort to adjust, to be part of a "women's movement" whose meaning I often had to "translate," with flashbacks from my background. A book I read in the summer of 1972 symbolized these ambiguities. The book was *Mujeres Españolas (Spanish Women)*, written by Salvador de Madariaga, a well-known historian and author who had spent many years in exile after the Spanish Civil War. His main thesis was that the "flavour" of Spanish life was based on women's special "predominance" in social life: "Our women have never had the need for 'liberation,' 'emancipation' or for other trifles[2] and utopias, and they have been indifferent to the agitation brought to them by bourgeois women from other countries." He then pointed out the large number of Spanish women that had distinguished themselves in the past for their "large spirit, intelligence and culture." The book provoked me to a degree not correlated to its worth, perhaps because it touched some difficult questions. Was I becoming too "Americanized" and removed from my own culture? Was feminism part of this process? I finally decided to write a critique of the book, emphasizing that the women in its chapters did not represent a feminist sense of emancipation. Reading Madariaga, whom I had met in London when I was twenty-one, was like a thermometer measuring how much I had changed. I had seen him as an accomplished intellectual and father figure to whom I listened attentively; now I was ready to confront him.

Madariaga was a writer and a historian, not an economist. One of my most difficult battles as a feminist has been that of dealing with my deeply ethnocentric profession. I often did not identify as an "economist"; it felt like a strange identity removed from myself. In graduate school, it seemed as if integrating feminism with economics was an impossible task; the way the questions were posed, the tendency of the profession to defend the status quo, its insensitivity to many of the issues that interested me, and the central role given to economic rationality and to "economic man" were stumbling blocks for my identification with the profession. I even considered transferring to another department. But I was still attracted to the depth that economics can give to understanding social issues. I resisted writing a dissertation on

---

[2] The beautifully cacophonous Spanish word is *zarandajas*.

women, as some of my fellow graduate students did, because I wanted to show that women could work on "male topics" as well. Hence I chose a topic dealing with education and economic development in Spain during the 1940–72 period. However, when gathering data on education, I found it broken down by sex, and I became increasingly more interested in showing the gender differences in education during the period. After all, it was all about the men and women of *my* generation. I did not include this topic in my dissertation, but I wrote a paper whose title tells a lot about the period and about my interests at the time: "Women's Participation in Paid Production Under Capitalism. Spain, 1940–72." It was my first paper given at a professional conference and my first published academic work. I felt passionate about it; I didn't about the dissertation. In retrospect, the paper was the first piece in what soon became the center of my work in academia and outside of it: women and work; gender and international development.

Looking back, I feel that I have been involved in a wonderful project, that of transforming knowledge and action through a feminist lens. I have enjoyed linking my work to that of many women across the globe and understanding the different economic, social, cultural, and political frameworks in which our lives have unfolded. To be sure, there have been failures and disappointments, and there is much left to do, but I am conscious of having been involved in one of the fundamental movements for social change of the late twentieth century.

I want to thank Dennis Gilbert, Sherry Gorelick, and Breny Mendoza for their comments. Many thanks also to Muriel Dimen, Kate Ellis, and Lillian Robinson for helping me remember.

Clenched Fist, Open Heart

Alice J. Wolfson

In 1969, as a young and passionate feminist living in Washington, D.C., I fearlessly stood up at a Senate hearing delving into the dangers of the birth control pill, crowded with lawmakers, spectators, and the press, raised my hand and demanded to be heard. I was ardent, I knew I was right, and I believed with all my being that the feminist "revolution" was just around the corner. Today, as a lawyer, I am often terrified to stand before a lone judge in a relatively empty courtroom. The contrast is not lost on me; I often ask myself what has changed in the intervening years.

The disruption of the Senate hearings on the birth control pill (the Nelson pill hearings), born out of a pure and burning anger over the lack of control women had over their bodies and their lives, has been described as "one of the most important feminist actions since the riots for the vote fifty years earlier."[1] To this day the picture taken of me and several of the other women involved appears in newspapers and magazines around the world. Although I had always believed that the issue of informed consent and the action, which resulted in the first patient package insert for a prescription medication, was significant, I had no idea at the time that those months of intense activity and organizing would result in the birth of the women's health movement. It is from this perspective that I have begun to trace the path that led me first to feminism as an ideology and eventually to the then nascent women's health movement.

Like so many other early feminists of the so-called "second wave" (the suffragists being the acknowledged first), my political roots lie first in the "ban the bomb" movement, the civil rights movement, and lastly, the antiwar movement. I have often thought that without the antiwar movement feminism would have taken much longer to reemerge as an important political force. Though women did not play a particularly

---

[1] Linda Grant, *Sexing the Millennium: A Political History of the Sexual Revolution*, NY: Grove Press, 1994.

significant leadership role in the first two movements, they were entirely peripheral in the antiwar movement, acting as the "good wives" for the "soldiers" whose battle was being waged. In those times such contradictions, dormant for so long, became increasingly palpable disparities between our growing political awareness as women and the stereotypical, traditional roles we were playing. The result of the inevitable collision was the new feminist movement.

I entered my first consciousness-raising group in 1968, in New York City. I wish I could remember more about the group or who all of the women were. I do, however, remember our tentative hesitation as we began to choose a reading list, deciding to explore the origin of women's oppression by reading Engels, Marx, and Wilhelm Reich. We had still not evolved to the point where women revolutionaries were considered significant early reading material. And I remember how the discussions, which started off scholarly, quickly became personal, and how the group developed its own early version of the "personal as political" politics that would later come to characterize the women's movement.

In 1969 I moved to Washington, D.C., because my husband, who was a doctor and whom I had met at an antiwar demonstration, had been drafted into the Public Health Service and was stationed there. Leaving New York, my friends, and my job was difficult for me, but being "political" and a "feminist" was its own subculture; within a short time I had found a small group of feminists who began meeting informally and started a group called D.C. Women's Liberation. As with so many women's groups in those days, abortion was a key issue. Abortion was still illegal. Women, all of us but most particularly poor women, were dying, and groups like Concerned Clergy were running underground railroads to provide safe abortions for thousands of women. But because D.C. was and is a black city, very early on it became clear that we could not address abortion in isolation from the issues of sterilization abuse and population control.

One of the early demonstrations I recall organizing was a picket line outside of D.C. General Hospital, the only publicly funded hospital in Washington, D.C. We were protesting the disproportionate numbers of black women who were being maimed and were dying from botched illegal abortions. The day we appeared outside the gates of the hospital happened to coincide with an interns' and residents' strike protesting the deplorable conditions in the hospital. It was immediately clear that if we wanted to be politically effective in a 76 percent black city, we could not see abortion as a single issue but were going to have to make the connections to other women's health issues. I attribute this growing awareness of the interconnection of issues of race and gender to my own emergence as a health feminist.

Out of these demonstrations came an organization known as the D.C. Women's Liberation/Welfare Rights Alliance. Together we worked on the issues of abortion, sterilization abuse, and numerous other health concerns affecting poor women and children in the city. There was one joint action that was particularly successful and typical of the daring acts we were all so willing to do. Because of the D.C. General demonstrations, the mayor had been forced to appoint a special task force on health whose purpose was to identify the major health problems in the city. The initial meeting was to be a fancy catered dinner in a downtown hotel. Our small group investigated and discovered the meeting's location and the cost of the meal that was to be served, and set about to disrupt the meeting. With ten dollars bail money stuffed in our boots (we expected to be arrested, a regular occurrence in those days), we burst through the doors just as the task force, numbering some fifty people, had seated themselves at the dinner table. Armed with paper sacks full of peanut butter and jelly sandwiches, we ousted the invited notables from their seats, substituted the peanut butter sandwiches for the appetizers, and "liberated" the microphones. By the end of the evening, D.C. Women's Liberation/Welfare Rights Alliance had placed several of its members on the task force.

It was in the context of these citywide health actions that I first heard about the Nelson pill hearings. Before I tell this part of my story, it is important to explain what it meant to be a young radical living in Washington, D.C., during those times. All of us lived fairly inexpensive marginal lives, living in communes, sharing resources, since none of us worked at full-time jobs. We had political meetings all day long. Whenever we heard about anything that was happening, we would just go up to Capitol Hill and check it out. The week of the pill hearings, the Women's Liberation Health Committee was having a meeting. Discussing whether or not to attend the pill hearings sparked personal conversation about our own experiences with the pill. All four or five of us had taken the pill at one time, but all had discontinued it because we had experienced unpleasant side effects. None of us, luckily, had become deathly ill. At that time, we didn't even know you could. We also didn't know that the pill had been recklessly marketed to 8.5 million women and that it was a common medical practice for a woman to be given a bag of pills and not examined again for a year. My own side effect had been hair loss. I had gone to several doctors about it, concerned that I could be going bald in my twenties. None of the doctors related the hair loss to the pill until I made the connection. The other women in the group had experienced similar problems. We were curious. We went to the Hill to get information. We left having started a social movement.

As I recall, on that first day we were all able to get seats together and we sat in a row and listened. As the testimony unfolded, we were appalled. Not a single woman was testifying, not a single pill user, not a single female researcher. All of the information that was coming out was frightening. "Estrogen is to cancer what fertilizer is to wheat," said one scientist. The "risk versus benefit" ratio favors the pill, said another. Risk to whom, benefit to whom, we wondered. But still we listened in silence. To this day I do not remember exactly what tipped us over— what comment became too much to bear. All I remember is the outrage mounting. At first we politely raised our hands, but of course we were ignored. I think they told us later that the Senate didn't take comments from the floor. And then we were on our feet raising our hands. Still they wouldn't recognize us. That's when we began to call out our questions. "Why wasn't the pill tested on more women before it was marketed?" "What happened to the women in the Puerto Rico study?" "Why weren't we told about the side effects so we could make informed choices?" "Who benefited and who was at risk?" "Why weren't any women testifying?" How dare the male-dominated medical establishment decide for women what they should and shouldn't know about their bodies?

When we started to speak aloud, the attention of the entire room turned on us. The press rotated its cameras and microphones from the august senators to the miniskirted women. So began a series of demonstrations, "which developed the first mass consciousness of women's control over their bodies."[2] Not knowing how to respond, the senators

---

[2] Linda Grant, "What Every Woman Knows," *The Guardian,* October 22, 1995.

quickly broke for lunch. That night a clenched-fisted women's symbol appeared on the national news and the question of informed consent for women became public around the country and the world. It was during that first disruption that Barbara Seaman, author of *The Doctor's Case Against the Pill,* an exposé of the dangers of the pill and the sexist nature of its marketing, asked us to meet with her. Together we began to strategize about ways to open the hearings to women's concerns. Barbara was an established writer and very much "straighter" than I was in those days, but we immediately struck up both a friendship and a working relationship. Barbara lived in New York and had many contacts with the medical establishment and the senators running the hearings. She would feed me information about some secret meeting or hearing, and our D.C. Women's Liberation group would immediately set up a demonstration. To call us activists would be an understatement. We believed fervently in our cause and we were ready to hit the streets or, as it were, the halls of Congress, at a moment's notice. And we had no fear! The more outrageous and original the action, the more we liked it and, of course, the more press attention was lavished on us.

Whereas our protest the first day at the hearings had been a spontaneous reaction, as soon as we realized the importance of the issue we quickly organized into a militant force devoted to disrupting the hearings, getting the information about the side effects of the pill out to women around the country, and forcing the Senate to demand that the Food and Drug Administration (FDA) commissioner approve a packet of information to be included with every package of pills so that women, not their "autocratic, patronizing, and paternalistic" doctors, would make the choice about whether or not to use this form of birth control.

We thought a lot about the tactics for impending demonstrations. Realizing that the senators would look foolish trying to oust the women who were taking the pill from hearings about the pill, we formed into attack brigades. Our costumes were designed to allow us to blend in as well as we could given our long hair and decidedly countercultural appearances. Out went our jeans and on came our dresses and suits, miniskirted though they were. Armed with the bail money in our boots, we came early and stationed ourselves at the end and in the middle of the rows in the hearing room. We each had two questions to ask in a carefully orchestrated order so that each time a guard attempted to evict one of us, another would rise at the other end of the room or in the middle of a particularly inaccessible row. Although there were only about thirty of us, we far outnumbered the guards, and our meticulous planning made it impossible for them to shut us up. On one day I remember the hearings being shut down, and Senator Robert Dole asking me to meet with him and begging me to let the hearings continue. "Only if you present our point of view," we told him. "Only if you have women testifying."

One day we handed out leaflets with an attached pill demanding: "Take this pill now. Think about it circulating through your system as you listen to the rest of these hearings. Caution: This Pill may cause:" and the leaflet went on to list the various side effects that the experts were reporting. Remember, for the 8.5 million women then taking the pill, this was the first indication of any potential health hazards. The leaflet then asked a series of questions, among them: Why are no women testifying? Why is the profitable relationship between doctors and drug companies whitewashed by the press and in these hearings? What kind of reparations will be made by the white male medical establishment to women who have been used as guinea pigs in this mass experiment? Why isn't there a male contraceptive? Why is it safer for a *man* to go to the moon than for a *woman* to take the pill? Thirty years later we still don't have answers.

At a certain point we realized that we were never going to get at the truth if we left it to the senators, the doctors, and the FDA. So we organized our own questionnaire and eventually our own alternative pill hearings. "Senator Gaylord Nelsen's hearings are being run by men and controlled by men. Women are considered fit only to be experimented upon. We may die if we take the pill, but we are not allowed either to tell of our experiences or to ask questions of the witnesses," we told the women who participated in our hearings. We sent hundreds of questionnaires documenting women's experiences on the pill to women's groups all over the country. The tabulated results were published by the government along with the rest of the testimony from the Senate hearings.

The pill hearings and the demonstrations that followed were like "on the job" training for health-care issues. We really hadn't known when we started how powerful both the drug industry and the population-control establishment were. At that time, world population control was considered a major problem for the United States. The leaders of the big five population-control organizations read like a *Who's Who* of the ruling class. These men considered population control to be so important that it was worth the risk of killing and sickening an unknown number of women to achieve. We actually didn't know when we started that the "benefit" that was being hailed by the scientists chosen by Nelsen was to the world population "problem." We didn't know that the risk to individual women wasn't important except, perhaps, if there were legal consequences. Before *Roe* v. *Wade,* our suggestion that the safest method of birth control was a barrier method augmented when necessary by legal abortion was considered a radical position. The issues, however, were always interconnected; part of the strategy to achieve informed consent for the pill was the struggle to legalize abortion.

The turning point in my consciousness came when Barbara Seaman told me about a "secret" FDA meeting that was being convened to evaluate English data allegedly linking the pill to heart disease and strokes. On April 1, 1970, armed with Barbara's information, three of us were able to push our way into the room where the doctors were meeting to discuss the data. When they threatened to call the police, throw us out, and have us arrested, we threatened to call the press and expose the fact that the FDA was arresting women who were simply trying to learn about the side effects of a drug that they had approved for marketing to healthy women without adequate testing. Apparently, in the face of the negative publicity, they decided that the better part of valor might be to let us stay.

What we heard was mind boggling. The data concerned the dangers of the pill, particularly its association with stroke and heart attacks, but doctors clearly did not want women to be informed. Nor did they want to warn women about what to look for, such as severe headache, double vision, etc., in order to avert a stroke. "Tell a woman to watch out for headaches, and she'll have one," said one of the healers charged with protecting our health. "I'll get too many calls; my wife will kill me," said another. (This particular concern resulted in the word "contact" your doctor being substituted for "call" in the warning. This was eventually approved.) Horrified at the thought of malpractice suits, all of the doctors agreed that they had to eliminate any suggestion from the warning that a woman's doctor should have discussed the side effects before she took the pill. In today's world, where product liability and medical malpractice lawsuits abound, it's probably hard to believe, but back then, the medical establishment felt invulnerable. They showed an intense lack of respect for all patients, and for women patients in particular.

Eventually we were promised that all packages of pills would be required to include an informational brochure. Before the wording could be finalized, a draft would have to appear in the *Federal Register* with a thirty-day period allowed for comments from the public, including the drug industry. We watched and waited, but when nothing appeared in the *Federal Register,* we held a sit-in at the office of Secretary of Health, Education, and Welfare (HEW) Robert Finch. We sat around, those of us with babies publicly nursing in the rather posh waiting room, and refused to move until he agreed to schedule a meeting with us. I remember several employees walking in, taking one look at us, and saying: "Oh lordy, the revolution has come to HEW!" A few days later, when Finch finally agreed to a meeting, I asked Barbara Seaman to join us. After the meeting, Finch agreed to a very watered-down warning as a package insert. The final pamphlet, published by the American Medical Association (AMA), had a sketch of me on it, or so everyone said. I represented the woman who needed to have the information to make an informed choice. I suppose they chose my image not just for the irony of it but because I had done so much media work related to the pill, appearing on David Susskind, Phil Donohue, and other nationally televised and radio talk shows. A picture of me disrupting the hearings appeared in such faraway places as *Der Spiegel,* a German newsmagazine. The demonstrations, with national and international attention, had succeeded. For the first time in pharmacological history, patients were given the right to know of the potential health-threatening side effects of a prescription drug.

As a result of the knowledge and experience I gained during the pill demonstrations, I evolved an analysis that viewed the health-care system as a microcosm of the entire political system. Remembering and applying my Marx and Engels from my early women's group, I saw that doctors were the ruling class and women were the proletariat, or maybe even "lumpen." While changing all of society appeared to be a monumental task, even in those days when we all felt so powerful, I passionately believed that it was possible to have an impact on women's lives by changing the power relationships in the health-care delivery system. From that point forward, I devoted all of my political energy to what has now become known as the women's health movement. In the early seventies this movement consisted of loose groupings around the country, some providing direct care, such as the Feminist Women's Health Centers, and others, like D.C. Women's Liberation, doing what we called "impact" work.

Population control was another hot issue. I recall one demonstration at an international population control meeting where my collective, Daughters of Lilith, attentively sat in the audience, looking somewhat normal, at least for us. At a prearranged signal, we all took off our coats to reveal witches' outfits, placed witches' hats on our heads, and jumped onto the stage, grabbed the microphones, and put on a bit of guerrilla theater. I don't remember the whole skit, but I do remember the recurring refrain: "You think you can cure all the world's ills by making poor women take your unhealthy pills." Each time we chanted it, we threw handfuls of pills at the members of the panel and the audience.

During this same period, 1970 through early 1971, Barbara Seaman and I did a lot of work together in an attempt to open up the FDA to consumer scrutiny. We were a two-woman brigade, demanding informed consent, showing up at every meeting having to do with women's health, and acting as if we belonged. Eventually, simply by refusing to move when they tried to oust us, and by having good relationships with certain members of the press, we succeeded not only in opening the previously secret meetings but also in seating consumers on the advisory committees themselves.

All the time I was doing this work, I was a part of D.C. Women's Liberation and on our governing board, which we called Magic Quilt. (We were determined not to mimic anything that appeared to smack of the male establishment.) D.C. Women's Liberation was a wonderful and diverse organization that remained a powerful political force on the left in the city until the gay/straight split in the women's movement that happened in Washington sometime in 1971. It seems incredible, looking back on it, that we could have allowed such a thing to happen. A small group of gay or gay-identified women successfully imposed an ideology identifying male children as the enemy and refused them access to the Women's Liberation office. These women, perhaps twelve or fifteen in number, eventually formed a collective called The Furies. Several of the women were from out of town. One was a powerful and magnetic force, who, under other circumstances might have been charming; but because of the deliberately destructive effect she had on the organization, I have always wondered if she was an agent. Although it is possible that some of the women who believed that male children were a barrier to feminism held this position not superficially but deeply, this belief seemed thoroughly irrational to me. It succeeded in destroying the women's movement in Washington, D.C. At the time, I was pregnant with my first child. Despite the fact that my theoretical background was still somewhat weak, I instinctively knew that these women were not going to make a revolution that I—or anyone—would want to be a part of, if the only way we could become a part of it was to give up our male children.

I remember the summer day that I sat, seven months pregnant, with two women from my collective, The Daughters of Lilith, women whom I had worked with and loved, and was told that I could still choose to be a part of the feminist revolution, to be a "woman-identified woman," and join The Furies, if I was prepared to give up the baby if it were a boy. I was appalled and deeply hurt, but several women with whom I had worked closely did, in fact, give up their boy children to their ex-husbands so that they could join the "revolution." Once, this same group of women broke into my home and wrote on the wall that they hoped their love could be strong enough so that the next time they came I would join them. It's hard to believe that such a small group could be so powerful but the out-of-town leaders had chosen well. They courted the strongest and most visible women and were able to close the doors of D.C. Women's Liberation in months, after years of our successful work.

During the time I was pregnant, I had been selected by a loosely knit coalition of American women's liberation groups to attend an international conference of women in Budapest. The reason for our attendance was to meet with Vietnamese women to begin planning an American women's liberation–Vietnamese women's conference to take place in Toronto and Vancouver, Canada. After months of planning, the conference took place sometime around my fifth month of pregnancy. I was on the planning committee and had already been in Toronto about a week when the conference began. I left in despair after the second day, saddened and mystified by an evolving ideology that allowed white American women to accuse North Vietnamese and Laotian women, some of whom had walked for a month to meet a plane to bring them to the conference, of being the cause of the war because of their "heterosexual" identity.

While I opted out of this part of the women's movement, I continued with my women's health work. Although there were ideological struggles here as well, somehow the concreteness of the work and the tangible results that we were sometimes able to obtain seemed to protect that part of the movement from the extremism that existed in other places. On September 1, 1971, I gave birth to my first son, Noah. My life and options as a feminist were forever changed by his birth.

After the breakup of the women's movement in Washington, D.C., I entered what I now refer to as my Marxist, Leninist, Maoist, or sectarian phase. It felt really important to me to figure out where we went wrong—how early feminist ideology that seemed so right to me could result in a movement that would identify male children as the enemy, bar male babies from the women's liberation offices and coffee houses, and actually debate when a male baby became the enemy. What started out as one study group of "straight" women, dropouts from the now-dominant movement, searching for answers, eventually ended up with about 200 people in study groups throughout the city. Everyone on the left in D.C. who was not in a black or gay group was studying Marxism-Leninism-Maoism and everyone was looking for guidance and unequivocal answers. I am embarrassed now to think of these times and the ideas I mercilessly propounded with the righteousness that only a true believer can summon. No matter how much I searched, however, I simply could not sign on to an ideology that idealized the family and had an authoritarian and judgmental view of homosexuality. Unlike a lot of the women who seemed able to leave their feminism behind, at least temporarily, and join male-dominated sectarian groups, I continued to work on women's health issues, particularly the pill, estrogen replacement therapy (which was now being linked to endometrial cancer), and informed consent.

In 1974, while pregnant with my second son, I began to have discussions with Barbara Seaman and Belita Cowan (another health feminist from Michigan) about the need for a national presence to create and put forth a woman's health agenda. The early meetings of the group that later became the National Women's Health Network were held in the basement of my home in Washington, D.C. In the fall of 1975, when my son Eric was an infant, we staged an inaugural demonstration in front of the FDA headquarters in Bethesda, Maryland. Holding placards with slogans such as "Feed your pills to the pigs at the FDA" and "Must we die for love?" women from all over the East Coast gathered to protest the lack of pre-market testing of the pill, the continuing deaths, the lack of adequate research into less harmful and invasive methods of birth control, the indiscriminate use of hormones, and a general lack of informed consent. The demonstrators shouted the National Women's Health Network into existence. Today it is the largest membership organization in the country devoted solely to women's health issues.

In 1977 I moved, with my family, from Washington, D.C., to San Francisco. My husband and I had decided that because the boys were so young, 2 and 5, and the move was traumatic for them, I wouldn't try to find work until we had all settled in. During those early days in San Francisco, I didn't have a car and would walk my son Eric in his stroller up and down 24th Street, the shopping street that defined my Noe Valley neighborhood. One day I noticed a sign reading "Coalition for the Medical Rights of Women." I wandered up steep stairs of a giant Victorian to find a wonderful group of committed feminists doing health work on a local level that was very similar to the work of the network. The two primary issues at the coalition when I first discovered it were unreliable Pap smear results including many false negatives, and DES (diethylstilbestrol), the drug given to pregnant women in the forties and fifties to prevent miscarriage, which, at that time, in the seventies, was known to cause vaginal cancer in some of the daughters and genital tract abnormalities in almost all of the daughters. As with so many other drugs marketed to women, DES was prescribed long after researchers and the drug companies knew that it did nothing whatsoever to prevent miscarriages. Shortly before finding the coalition, I had begun attending meetings to plan a demonstration protesting the passage of the Hyde Amendment, which only four years after the passage of *Roe* v. *Wade* cut off public funding for abortion. With the passage of the Hyde Amendment it was clear to me that, starting with the poorest and the weakest among us, abortion rights for all women were in jeopardy. Political groups that had organized around abortion as a single issue disbanded once abortion was legalized and the battle appeared over. The single-issue strategy had failed. It was apparent that the strategy we had developed in Washington, D.C.—a multi-issue reproductive-rights analysis, placing abortion into the whole spectrum of reproductive choice—was the only effective way to organize. With about six of the women who had participated in the planning of the Hyde demonstration, all of whom identified themselves as socialist feminists, I formed the Committee to Defend Reproductive Rights (CDRR) and immediately affiliated it as a project of the Noe Valley group, the Coalition for the Medical Rights of Women. At that time, reproductive rights was a new concept and there were struggles with the single-issue groups over dominance in the movement. It is interesting to see that now both NARAL and Planned Parenthood have adopted the reproductive-rights analysis that socialist-feminist groups like CDRR and CARASA (Committee for Abortion Rights and Against Sterilization Abuse) pioneered.

CDRR did extremely effective and innovative organizing work with a particular emphasis on winning back from the anti-abortionists the "hearts and minds" of the public through alternative media work. We pioneered the use of bus advertising and public access media, and published a hands-on "how to" book with precise instructions on use of the public access media by public interest groups. The book was very well received and was distributed nationwide. We also used a lot of the tactics that I had used as a part of D.C. Women's Liberation, and staged constant demonstrations, including street theater. CDRR was also the named plaintiff in a case brought by the American Civil Liberties Union, which has been successful in maintaining public funding for abortion in the state of California. I was the executive director of CDRR from the time I founded it in 1977 until I left to go to law school in 1986. During this time I was also on the board of directors of the National Women's Health Network and traveled throughout the United States to meet other women's health groups. The combination of my activities enabled me to bring a local perspective to the network and a national perspective to CDRR.

The entire time that I worked in the feminist and women's health movement, I was married and eventually was the mother of two sons. While I attended endless meetings and brought my kids to vast numbers of demonstrations, I was always extremely committed to my mothering and felt strongly that I would not sacrifice my kids to my politics. I had the gut feeling that it didn't matter how many minds I might change if I lost the hearts and minds of my own children. Perhaps this is why I stayed away from the more radical wing of the feminist movement. My D.C. experience left me wary of groups that were completely woman identified. I have never supported an analysis that excluded half the human race, two of whom were my own sons. Nevertheless, I have remained a committed feminist throughout. I have always felt that one of the oddest things about my life during the time my children were young was that I worked all day and often at night with women, at the same time that I lived with three men. The only other female presence in my house was the dog, whom I insisted had to be a girl. At times the contrast made me feel crazy, but I now think that the dichotomy kept me grounded. I know it always acted as a modulating influence on my feminist perspective.

In 1985, a year after my oldest son, Noah, was diagnosed with leukemia, I applied for and was accepted to law school. Why did I do this after all that time in the feminist movement? I'm not exactly sure, but I know that at least part of the reason was to become financially self-sufficient so that I could eventually have the option to leave my marriage, which had changed over the years and could not survive the weight of a sick and dying child. Why law school? Increasingly, it seemed as though the issues I was working on were being decided in the courts and not on the streets. As the sixties and seventies gave way to the eighties, the larger feminist movement, the movement that had seemed so revolutionary, the movement that wanted not a piece of the pie but a different pie, dissipated. Initially I believed that CDRR's socialist-feminist perspective would enable the abortion issue to act as a springboard for women to understand and become politicized to the larger issues. In the absence of a cohesive feminist movement there was, however, nowhere for the women to go, no larger revolutionary movement to feed into. CDRR became an end in itself, and eventually, I felt it was time for me to move on and to make some real money.

Of course, law school is hardly the feminist revolutionary capital of the world. But it was the place where I began to have a real understanding of what power was all about. It occurred to me that law school was the training ground for the future ruling class of the country. After all of my years in politics, I found this aspect of the experience very interesting. Midway into my second year of school, Noah, whose leukemia had been in remission, relapsed. Law school, the women's health movement, feminism were left behind. My life was completely focused on the final and losing battle for my son's life. On May 31, 1988, at the age of sixteen, Noah died. Nothing has shaped my life more, nothing has influenced me more, and nothing has been harder to bear than his death. CDRR, the network, my friends, the community I had spent a lifetime building were all wonderfully supportive. I remember once saying to someone, "If I live to be one hundred I will never be able to repay my friends for what they have given to me." She answered, "You already have. You gave your friends a chance to become heroes and most of them did." And they were.

Nor were my politics and political training left behind even in this struggle. When Noah was first diagnosed in 1984, the blood transfusion link to AIDS was just getting out. Our local blood bank refused to allow us to have donor-specific transfusions arranged for him, claiming that there was no danger; it was too cumbersome; and it was too expensive. One of my dear friends, a sister from the Washington, D.C., days who was also living in San Francisco, called and asked what she could do. "Take on the blood bank," I said. The mere threat of a group of mothers picketing in front of the blood bank for safe blood for a sick child caused them to cave in immediately.

After Noah died, I dropped out of everything except school, to which I had forced myself to return because I didn't know how else to let Eric, my younger son, know that he had to go on. Since he had to go back to school, so did I. Somehow we both did it. He's in college and I'm a lawyer. During that time I did not have the heart or the energy for politics, the women's movement, women's health, or anything but numb survival and my community of friends. Now, when I look at what I have accomplished in the years since Noah's death, I am amazed. When people ask me how I did it, I truly cannot give an answer. I just did.

Today I am saddened by the lack of a cohesive vision for social change. My activism was always been inspired by my belief that we would succeed, that we would make a revolution, that we would change the pie. I believed in it so strongly that before moving from New York to D.C., I recklessly ran up a large bill at Bloomingdale's. I was convinced that no one would make me pay my "Bloomie's" bill after the revolution. I think I was fearless because I was convinced I was right. Time has mellowed me. I no longer know what "right" is, I'm often frightened in court, and I finally paid off my Bloomingdale's bill.

Not too long ago I had a conversation with my mother about my son. "Would you have chosen to have Noah if you knew you were going to lose him?" she asked. "Yes," I answered, "every minute of his life was worth it." I feel the same way about my political work. While it saddens me to have failed at making the revolution I thought was a certainty, I am proud that I tried and I know I would do it again.

A Marriage Disagreement, or Marriage by Other Means

Alix Kates Shulman

Early in 1969, when my children were five and seven, I wrote "A Marriage Agreement," proposing that the tasks of child care and housework be divided equally between husband and wife. Like most women of my class and generation born in the United States before World War II, I had accepted, if sometimes grudgingly, traditional gender arrangements whereby the home belongs to women, the world to men. But during the previous year, when the electrifying ideas of women's liberation had lifted me out of my marriage into the world, I had become sensitized to the issue of traditional divisions of domestic labor by reading sister-Redstocking Pat Mainardi's satirical broadside "The Politics of Housework," then circulating in mimeograph (subsequently published in the 1970 collection *Notes from the Second Year*), which wittily detailed her mate's ploys for avoiding housework. That housework was up for political grabs, subject to maneuvering and negotiation, was only one of many previously unexamined premises of private life whose political bases were suddenly being exposed in the powerful light of feminist analysis. In a marriage complicated, unlike Mainardi's, by the presence of two impressionable children, I came to see domestic equity not only as simple justice but as one means of transforming society by reforming the rearing of the young.[1]

Before the Marriage Agreement, I had been writing for over a year, having begun on the morning I dropped off my youngest child at nursery school, freeing me for three hours a day. (Actually two and a half hours, after subtracting fifteen minutes to deliver her and fifteen minutes to collect her.) I wrote secretly at first, fitting my writing into the cracks between domestic duties, thinking it too self-centered and pretentious an

---

[1] In the following decade, this would be a major thrust of Dorothy Dinnerstein's *The Mermaid and the Minatour*, Harper & Row, 1976; Adrienne Rich's *Of Woman Born*, Norton, 1976; Nancy Chodorow's *The Reproduction of Mothering*, University of California Press, 1978, among other feminist analyses of the family.

activity for one who had, as the times required, dutifully renounced personal ambition in favor of family life, and I sent out my stories under a pseudonym so that not even my husband (to whom I'd made the mistake of showing my first effort only to hear him declare it "a shambles") would know I was doing it. My earliest writings—a children's book (with one human character, a boy), three chapters of a never-finished family novel, a long letter-to-the-editor of *The Village Voice,* and several short stories, including one about a baby-sitter, another about an abortion, and finally one called "Traps," about a woman leaving her husband—were written before I found the movement, but as it was only a few months later that I began attending meetings the two activities, writing and women's liberation, those twin threats to my marriage, are inextricably connected in my mind.

Like so many lives, mine began to change drastically as soon as I connected with the movement. Among the mostly childless women in both small groups I joined—Redstockings, which favored theory, and WITCH (Women's International Terrorist Conspiracy from Hell), which favored action—I was surprised to find myself suddenly valued for the very identity I had long felt ashamed of: for being a genuine full-time housewife-mother. Those spunky young women, mostly in their twenties, treated me like a treasured resource instead of the useless has-been I considered myself at thirty-five, and I began to shed my diffidence—first in the group, then in my writing, though I prudently continued to hide from my husband the subversive nature of both. Even the marginal literary subject matter, female and domestic, to which I'd felt confined by my limited experience began to seem increasingly tenable subjects for fiction, and under cover of my pseudonym I started to submit my work to the new feminist journals suddenly springing up.

All at once, instead of finding humiliating rejection letters in my secret post office box, I began to receive acceptances. Now there was an audience for "Traps," which appeared pseudonymously in the second issue (Winter 1970) of the feminist literary journal *Aphra* and eventually, in a slightly altered form, as the opening scene of my 1972 novel *Memoirs of an Ex-Prom Queen.* My first personal essay was a piece I volunteered to draft for my Redstockings group when someone pointed out that despite our extensive consciousness raising on the topic of sex we had no sex article to hand out. Around the same time, through a contact with the (male) editor of a young-adult book series on "Women of America," I began a biography of the (then) forgotten anarchist Emma Goldman,[2] whose works had all long since gone out of print. Based on my research I wrote essays on Goldman and on her sister anarchist Voltairine de Cleyre for the new *Women: A Journal of Liberation* (Spring and Fall issues, 1970), whose editors finally convinced me in the name of feminist courage to drop the pseudonym and sign my name.[3] Childless Goldman was impatient with women who remained in unhappy marriages, cavalierly asking (like certain Second Wave feminists, whose gibes I sometimes fielded) why they didn't simply leave their husbands; to which de Cleyre, despite having refused on principle to marry the father of her own child, responded hotly: "Why don't you run when your feet are chained together? Why don't you cry out when a gag is on your lips? Why don't you raise your hands above your head when they are pinned fast to your sides?"—a disagreement in which I took a more than scholarly interest.[4] So much interest, in fact, that by the time I came to write my Marriage Agreement I had done sufficient brooding on "the marriage question"—and had developed enough feminist confidence—to dare to revise my life in light of it.

My impetus for the Agreement, which I intended as a critique of the inequities of both conventional marriage and divorce, was based on my own recent bizarre experience with divorce lawyers. (The first working

---

[2] *To the Barricades,* T. Y. Crowell, 1970.

[3] Ardent feminist though I was, my consciousness changed slowly. Except for the story "Traps," published under my pseudonym, all my early writings were signed with my married name, Alix Shulman; not until 1972, just before publication of my first novel, did it occur to me to reclaim my maiden name, Kates, even though I had for several years been cheering the work of such self-named feminists as Kathie Sarachild, Betsy Warrior, and Laura X. Since by that time I had already published three children's books, two edited collections, and one biography all under the name Alix Shulman, I felt it would be imprudent to switch midstream to my maiden name, Kates, so I compromised by inserting it in the middle. But I've always regretted that I didn't drop my married name then. When I was finally divorced in 1985 I tried to shed Shulman in my private life—the name on my checkbook, for instance, is Alix Kates—but even then I wondered how my children must feel seeing me shed their name.

[4] When feminist friends occasionally directed the same question to me, asking, "When are you going to leave that husband?" I regularly quipped back, "Not until you're ready to help me take care of my kids."

title for the piece was actually "A Divorce Dilemma and a Marriage Agreement.") My ten-year-old (second) marriage had become increasingly shaky as my husband, the father of my children, preoccupied by a new business he'd opened in a neighboring state and a clandestine love affair he'd begun there, was spending so little time at home that I felt virtually abandoned. His betrayal particularly galled since in marrying him and starting a family I had myself renounced sexual adventure and quit my editorial job to accept as graciously as possible what I, as a 1950 graduate of white, middle-class Cleveland Heights High School, took to be my fate. Feeling the press of time (thirty was then generally considered the outside age for having a first child; when I met my second husband I was twenty-six), I had struck with my husband the traditional, if unspoken, romantic deal: I would be the devoted wife and mother, he would be the family man, the good provider.

(I remember the moment—back before we had children—when I was first stung by the profound injustice of the arrangement. I was standing at the sink washing the dinner dishes when, as he often did, my husband approached me from behind, untied my apron strings, slipped his arms around my waist, and began kissing the back of my neck to lure me away from the sink; when I shook him off, objecting that I needed to finish the dishes, he turned me around, looked me over with an expression of such disenchantment I can see it still, and said in a voice full of sorrow how dull, how matronly I looked in an apron, standing over a sinkful of dishes.)

Tied down by two small children, I had strenuously opposed his new business, knowing that it would take him away from us, but he had gone ahead with it anyway. In turn, when he'd opposed my testifying about my illegal abortions as risking his reputation, I'd defied his wishes. Now, humiliated and angry over his affair (with a woman more than twenty years his junior, whom he finally married many years later) and terrified that the children would be deprived of their father's physical, emotional, and financial support (the little money I earned by freelance editing scarcely paid for the baby-sitter I hired a few hours a week), I fought back with all the strength I'd developed in the movement, soon taking a young lover of my own. The same feminist understanding and confidence that enabled me to stand up to my husband despite my dependency turned my love affair into a grand passion, complete with the orgasms I (like so many other heterosexual middle-class women of my generation, as we were discovering through consciousness raising) had never experienced in fifteen years of marriage. Energized by my affair, bursting with sexual bravado, no wonder I volunteered to write the sex article for my Redstockings group. I titled the piece "Organs and Orgasms" and brazenly ended it with the admonition, "Think clitoris!"—one my husband, incensed by my admission that I'd long been faking orgasms, adamantly refused to heed.[5]

Gradually our marital battle escalated until at the end of each skirmish we were threatening one another with divorce grenades—now he would brandish the word, now I would, but in the end I was the bolder one. Or perhaps simply the more reckless. After all, what mere marriage could match the movement for excitement? Like other newly fledged feminists trying our wings, I was sometimes carried away by our own wishful rhetoric, soaring high into the clouds where feminism seemed invincible. Under the movement's spell we sometimes fancied raising our children together and growing old in joyful women's communities that would satisfy all our needs for companionship, sex, autonomy, power, family, free of oppressive—or merely dull—marriages. Imagining women's autonomy, we demanded free, round-the-clock, universal child care and explored all sorts of alternatives to traditional marriage: free love, serial monogomy, lesbian partnership, communal families, celibacy. Or we imagined ourselves as roving vigilante bands who through our indomitable solidarity would enforce our justice and wring compliance from men unable to live without us. For, contrary to media reports, women's liberation was not monolithically opposed to marriage. True, the group called The Feminists was against it, limiting to one third of their membership women who lived with men, and Boston's Cell 16 was associated with a policy of celibacy; but my group, Redstockings, while sometimes divided on the issue, was concerned less with overthrowing the institution than with overhauling it to better serve women's interests by somehow forcing men to be responsible mates and reliable fathers. Staying in the heterosexual arena to do close combat—planting, as it were, a subversive in every bed—

---

[5] *Evergreen Review,* June 1971; and *Woman in Sexist Society,* edited by Vivian Gornick and B. K. Moran, Basic Books, 1971. A decade later I wrote a second sex article contextualizing the first: "Sexual Bases of Radical Feminism," *Signs* (vol. 5, no. 4), Summer 1980.

was widely seen as a far more effective way to topple male supremacy than was any separatist path. Indeed, one triumph of the early movement was making men responsible for child care at large movement gatherings.

Nevertheless, many women did extricate themselves from intolerable relationships, and many others raised their standards of the tolerable. But with two children to care for and a hefty rent, I always returned to the nest before dark. Though our marriage was strained to the breaking point, I could not bear the thought of our children fatherless. Despite our love affairs neither my husband nor I really wanted divorce, with our children so young and our entire domestic establishment at stake—though I, emboldened by the power and thrill of the movement and at once bolstered and shaken by its critique of marriage, was more willing than he to pull the pin and lob the deadly weapon.

Just as my husband and I had once searched among obstetricians for one who would quietly agree not to breathe life into a seriously deformed newborn, so now, inspired by feminism, we searched among lawyers for one willing to draw up a radical separation agreement that would give us joint custody of our children. (*We?* Rather, *I* searched, dragging us off to one lawyer after another in hopes of devising the sort of innovative divorce that would somehow render my husband at once a dependable hands-on father and a civilized hands-off mate—as if divorce were simply marriage by other means.) In the late sixties, however, it was not yet legally feasible to obtain joint custody in the state of New York. Although the idea had been explored experimentally in California, elsewhere it was still widely considered harmful to children for subjecting them to the vicissitudes of their parents' disputes and leaving them without a clear-cut line of authority. The first lawyer we went to, a smug, square-jawed traditionalist, literally laughed us out of his office—to my husband's relief and my fury. When we consulted movement lawyers, both leftist and (that newly emerging breed) feminist, whom I expected to be sympathetic to my ideas, they echoed the straight lawyer, warning us that if we didn't have a standard adversarial divorce we would be guilty of "collusion" and the divorce might not hold up (divorce by agreement was invalid, though all this would be changed by New York's 1975 divorce-law reform); worse, if we insisted on joint custody, every time we had a disagreement or squabble the State would be free to step in and interfere, even, if it so chose, stripping us of custody of our children altogether.

"Which is not so farfetched, given your political activism," cautioned movement lawyer Carol Lefcourt. Acutely aware of the government's infiltration and subversion of the movement, I suddenly saw what folly it would be to invite Big Daddy into the heart of my family, no doubt to take the side of little daddy. Best not to marry at all, advised Lefcourt, but if married already, especially if there were children, safer not to be divorced.

Frustrated and fuming even as I laughed at these ludicrous legal conundrums so oddly confirming of the anarchist case for having as little as possible to do with the State, I followed the lawyers' advice. Yet I could hardly fold my wings and meekly surrender to the status quo. If the law could not accommodate us, then why not sidestep it and design our own joint custody? In lieu of divorce, the finality of which terrified both me and my husband anyway, I decided to draft a private agreement to suit our needs. Instead of the unstated, conventionally gendered patriarchal rules we had unconsciously lived by before, I would formulate principles we could embrace consciously.

My husband, a large-minded but deeply traditional man, obligingly acquiesced—whether to ward off divorce, or out of conviction, or simply to humor me, I'll never know. I do know that when I tried to involve him in thinking out our arrangement he took little interest. Perhaps he thought it trivial. Perhaps in the face of my relentless, to him fanatical, feminism he was merely practicing avoidance. Maybe he regarded the domestic concerns of such a document as outside his domain despite our struggles. Or maybe he was just too preoccupied to be bothered. In any case, he left it to me. But then, why not? What had he to lose? With no sanction for the arrangement but our goodwill, if ultimately it didn't work out and shove came to slam or bam came to bolt, we could always hire two tough lawyers to slug it out.

It was with feminist irony, idealism, audacity, and glee that I sat down to compose my Marriage Agreement. Utilizing the methods of inquiry and self-examination I'd been developing through consciousness raising, I wrote down every task and detail of child care and housework I could think of, no matter how small, in order to discover and expose exactly what was involved in those trivial pursuits. Trivial? I'd show them trivial—and rub their noses in it!—from brushing the children's hair, packing their lunches, phoning around for a baby-sitter, to cleaning, shopping, cooking, or stripping and remaking the beds. If these tasks were too insignificant to mention, then no father should mind doing them; and if some of them (like helping with homework) were as important as I thought, a father should treasure them. Having dropped out of Columbia's Ph.D. program in philosophy more than a dozen years before, it pleased me to apply my dormant analytical and critical skills to the minutiae of domestic management. The daughter of a lawyer, myself a lawyer manquée, I took special pleasure in the precision of the document.

The criticisms it later sparked centered mainly on the details, though I'd tried to make clear in my commentary that these would obviously vary from family to family, and that the schedule must be flexible, subject to frequent revision and renegotiation. As my good friend, Jungian analyst Barbara Koltuv, who followed with a marriage agreement of her own, told a reporter, "Part of the reason for thinking out a contract is to find out what your problems are; it forces you to take charge of your life. Once you have the contract, you don't have to refer back to it. The process is what's important."[6] But to me, the soul of the Agreement—even more important than the process—was its founding principles.

PART I. Principles.

1. We reject the notion that the work that brings in more money is more valuable. The ability to earn more money is a privilege which must not be compounded by enabling the larger earner to buy out of his/her duties and put the burden either on the partner who earns less or on another person hired from outside.[7]

This principle goes for the jugular of traditional marriage by challenging the basic rationalization of the division of labor in conventional nuclear families: money for services (which had been the unspoken basis

---

[6] Susan Edmiston, "How to Write Your Own Marriage Contract," *New York* magazine, December 20, 1971.

[7] This and the following excerpts are taken from the version published in *Redbook,* August 1971.

of mine). To name earning power *privilege* was to challenge the very basis of value and strip the arrangement of its cover of justice. With what delight I penned that second sentence! And if it was unjust for the "the larger earner to buy out of his/her duties and put the burden on the partner who earns less," then how comparably unjust must it be to put the burden on someone who earns still less. Let the man do his job, not buy out of it. Herein lay the utopian core of the document, its challenge to class society, plumbing purposes deeper than domestic guidelines. In the long wake of this first principle must eventually come equitable pay, universal child care, class and gender justice.

> 2. We believe that each partner has an equal right to his/her own time, work, values, choices. As long as all duties are performed, each of us may use his/her extra time any way he/she chooses. If he/she wants to use it making money, fine. If he/she wants to spend it with spouse, fine. If not, fine.

That last sentence was my code for sexual freedom, one of several messy subjects, including finances, that I wasn't prepared to see muddy up the document. If this principle freed my husband to spend as much time as he liked in Pennsylvania as long as he pulled his weight at home, it also established my right, for the first time since I'd found the movement, to attend meetings as many nights as I chose without having to feel either negligent or guilty. It also gave me the right to go into my room and close the door to write, even with the children still awake or dirty dishes in the sink, when my husband was on duty. Quite a contrast to the way I'd felt as recently as 1967 when, on the eve of committing civil disobedience at a military induction center in protest against the Vietnam War, I'd begged my husband's indulgence (and, if necessary, bail money), knowing that if I were arrested I wouldn't get home in time to make dinner or get the children ready for school the next morning. And when my husband had tried to move us all to rural Pennsylvania to be near his work, I had felt willful and selfish refusing to go, knowing that a wife was supposed to follow her husband's job. No longer.

> 3. As parents we believe we must share all responsibility for taking care of our children and home—not only the work but also the responsibility. At least during the first year of this agreement, *sharing responsibility* shall mean dividing the *jobs* and dividing the *time*.

In principle, jobs should be shared equally, 50-50, but deals may be made by mutual agreement. . . . The schedule may be flexible, but changes must be formally agreed upon. The terms of this agreement are rights and duties, not privileges and favors.

After these *Principles* followed *PART II: Job Breakdown and Schedule,* detailing chores and tasks involved with *(A) Children* (Mornings, Transportation, Helping, Nighttime, Baby-Sitters, Sick Care, Weekends) and *(B) Housework* (Cooking, Shopping, Cleaning, Laundry).

The Agreement certainly upended the original basis of our marriage—and my husband often complained that I was changing the rules on him, just as I, seeing the family man I'd married become a traveling man, accused him of changing the rules on me. Nevertheless, in good faith we both believed that reestablishing our relations on an egalitarian basis was bound to improve them, freeing us from guilt and recriminations. I would no longer complain about his absence from the dinner table and he would no longer complain about my housekeeping. As it turned out, my husband, with higher standards of housekeeping than mine, did more cleaning than I. (A would-be bohemian, in my first marriage I had refused to own either a vacuum or a broom.) On my side, working as I did at home, I did more child care than he. But we genuinely tried for 50-50, even if our compliance was somewhat erratic.

A few months after we began following the Agreement, we were rewarded when one of our children memorably said, "You know, I used to love Mommy more, but now I love you both the same."

That remark signaled to me that the time had come to write about and try to publish the Agreement. The first introduction I attempted told the divorce saga, complete with the ironies that had inspired me. But after a first draft I abandoned that strategy as tactless, introducing the document instead with a brief history of our domestic arrangements, pre-children and post-:

When my husband and I were first married, a decade ago, keeping house was less a burden than a game. We both worked full-time in New York City, so our small apartment stayed empty most of the day and taking care of it was very little trouble. Twice a month we'd spend Saturday cleaning and doing our laundry at the laundromat.

We shopped for food together after work, and though I usually did the cooking, my husband was happy to help. Since our meals were simple and casual there were few dishes to wash. . . . Our domestic life was beautifully uncomplicated.

When our son was born, our domestic life suddenly became *quite* complicated; and two years later, when our daughter was born, it became impossible. We automatically accepted the traditional sex roles that society assigns. . . .

The article then goes on to describe the great changes and strains that overtook our marriage once I left my job to stay home with the children.

Entitled, simply, "A Marriage Agreement," the piece first appeared in the second issue of the new feminist journal *Up from Under,* in August 1970. Over the next several years it was reprinted, with slight modifications, in such disparate magazines and books as *Redbook, New York* magazine, *Women's Liberation: Blueprint for the Future,* the premiere issue of *Ms., Life* magazine, and eventually—indeed, to this day—in many sociological, feminist, and legal textbooks and anthologies, including the standard casebook on contract law compiled by Harvard Law School's late Lon Fuller.[8]

Like other feminist proposals, mine was initially greeted with wildly divergent responses: it was called liberating or stultifying, reasonable or cracked, lucid or legalistic, principled or petty. Despite the upheavals of the sixties, the idea of shared child care and housework was then still widely considered unnatural and fatal to the male ego. And not only by traditionalists: in those days radical men, too, often felt justified in dismissing feminism as politically lame because of its concern for such distracting questions as who does the dishes. Even certain feminists, while agreeing with the principles of the Agreement, objected to its "legalistic" tone and purported rigidities. By the time of its apotheosis in a six-page spread in a 1972 *Life* magazine cover story, the Marriage Agreement was the subject of much debate in the popular press, where it was sometimes celebrated but more often derided by such antifeminist critics as Nor-

---

[8] *Up from Under,* August–September 1970; *Redbook,* August 1971; *New York* magazine, December 20, 1971; *Women's Liberation: Blueprint for the Future,* ed. by Sookie Stambler, Ace Books, 1971; *Ms.* magazine, Spring 1972; *Life* magazine, April 28, 1972; Fuller and Eisenberg, *Basic Contract Law,* West Publishing Co., 1972.

man Mailer, Russell Baker, Joan Didion (in a front-page article in the *New York Times Book Review*), and (a little later) the infamous S. I. Hayakawa, who as president of San Francisco State College had summoned state troopers to suppress the 1968 student strike.[9]

Even editors willing to publish it tried to subvert it. After it appeared in *Redbook* (under the editors' title "A Challenge to Every Marriage" and their cautious hedge that they found it "provocative"), more than two thousand letters poured in, one of the largest responses in *Redbook*'s history. I was heartened to find that though some readers were hostile, far more were supportive, and all but a few took the proposal seriously— hardly surprising, given *Redbook*'s predominantly housewife readership. But when I published my analysis of the two thousand–plus letters in *Redbook* a year later (September 1972), I was appalled to find the editors going beyond a mere disclaimer in their headnotes to misrepresent my entire analysis. I had avoided using percentages in my article because so many of the most thoughtful letters were too complex to categorize readily, but no such scruples restrained the editors, who reported their own percentages of letters *for/against/undecided* (36/53/11) as if they were mine, and edited my key paragraph to make it appear I agreed with them.[10] I immediately protested such high-handed treatment and reluctantly gave my own, very different summary figures (60/30/10) in a long letter, which was printed on the Letters page over an editorial apology.

Still, controversy was exactly what I wanted. I remember the mounting excitement with which I read Mailer's notorious attack on

---

[9] Norman Mailer, *The Prisoner of Sex,* Little, Brown & Co, 1971; Russell Baker, "Ms., Kiddismo and Law," *New York Times,* December 28, 1971; Joan Didion, "The Women's Movement," *New York Times Book Review,* July 30, 1972; S. I. Hayakawa, *Through the Communication Barrier,* Harper & Row, 1978.

[10] The altered paragraph was the one in which I summarized my conclusions about the letters. Here is what *Redbook* printed:

". . . most readers—many more than I ever imagined—generally agreed with our ideal of equality between husband and wife. (I *think* most readers agreed, whether their tone was angry or sympathetic.) They seemed to feel that the traditional sex roles might not be appropriate for everyone, or even for most people, and that a more equitable arrangement might have to be worked out between couples. The majority of readers, however, questioned our means for achieving equality through a formal written agreement."

Here is what I wrote in my manuscript:

feminism, first serialized in *Harper's*—the same excitement with which I had once relished philosophical debate, the subtleties of law, sexual adventure but had traded for family life. As I came to his concluding section that opened by quoting in full the *Principles* of my Marriage Agreement I exulted over having hit the mark. "No, he would not be married to such a woman," wrote Mailer of himself in the third person. "If he were obliged to have a roommate, he would pick a man. The question [with which he began his inquiry, Who finally would do the dishes?] had been answered. He could love a woman and she might even sprain her back before a hundred sinks of dishes in a month, but he would not be happy to help her if his work should suffer, no, not unless her work was as valuable as his own."[11] Oh, exquisite triumph! The first principle of my Agreement, that a woman's work was by definition as valuable as a man's—indeed, that the comparison was henceforth impermissible, not least because absent the opportunity that must follow domestic equality no one could know what women might do—this Mailer could not swallow.

Perhaps it was the Agreement's very reasonableness that made it seem so threatening, transgressive, outrageous to men like Mailer. In fact, that tantalizing combination of reasonable and outrageous that colors so much early Second Wave feminist writing may account for the wide range of reader response. For though I certainly meant my proposal in earnest, I also relished the ironic face in which I presented it: a sardonic lift of eyebrow as I laid out the principles, a curl of the lip as I listed the tasks in excruciating detail, a wicked chortle as I mocked man's self-importance as a mere ruse for getting out of the dishes. The Agreement became another of those sly inside jokes, so common in

---

"... many more readers than I ever imagined agreed generally with our ideal of equality between husband and wife. I think *most* readers did, whether their tone was angry or sympathetic. Most of them questioned our means for achieving equality via a formal written agreement; many found our lifestyle untypical and our goal perhaps Utopian. Nevertheless, there seemed to be widespread agreement that the traditional sex roles might not be appropriate for everyone, or even for most people, and that a fair arrangement might have to be worked out instead of taken for granted."

Thus, *Redbook*'s version implies that the majority of letters were *against* the experiment, whereas I found the majority *in favor of it*.
[11] *The Prisoner of Sex*, p. 165 (Signet ed.).

those days, that knowing women crowed over together but that many men just didn't get—or perhaps, being its butt, got only too well.[12]

Though in his footnote to my article Mailer had carelessly cited *Off Our Backs* instead of *Up from Under* and had misspelled my last name with an *Sch,* at least he got the title right. Not so many another, who persistently referred to the Agreement as a Contract. Perhaps the mistake was set in motion by the inclusion of the Agreement (under its own name) in a sidebar in Susan Edmiston's provocative essay, "How to Write Your Own Marriage Contract," published in the premier issue of *Ms.;* but when the error took on a life of its own despite my repeated objections, I could hardly avoid concluding there were political motives at work. *Agreement* sounds amicable and voluntary, whereas *contract* sounds adversarial and legal. Our arrangement, which we had established in part precisely to escape the law, had no legal status or intention; we simply wanted to divide up the duties for our own education and convenience, to improve things at home. Yet how easy to undermine our simple idea by substituting one word for another. Does this sound far-fetched? Consider: though I granted permission to Hayakawa to quote from my article only on condition that he use the word *agreement* instead of *contract* and even saw corrected galleys that met my condition before I sent in my written permission, in the finished book there was *contract* back in place in every instance where it had been changed to *agreement* in the galleys. Consider: though I got *Life*'s firm promise to use my title before I granted permission or signed a release, *Life* got around the restriction by using a huge one-word title "CONTRACT" on one page opposite a sentence describing it on the facing page, in letters a fraction the size, as "A 50-50 Marriage Agreement." In the table of contents *Life* used the title "Living by Contract," and on the cover,

---

[12] Several years later I met Mailer at a book party for a children's anthology to which we had each contributed a story and introduced myself as the author of the Marriage Agreement.

NM: That was a dumb idea.

AKS: Only if you didn't get it.

NM: You mean it was supposed to be ironic? I missed that.

AKS (throwing Mailer's own familiar slur back at him): That's because you antifeminists have no sense of humor.

NM (pausing to scratch his head, as he fails again to get it): Hmm. That's what I always say about you feminists.

beneath a small photo of my husband and me—one of four pictured examples of "Marriage Experiments" that included "Unmarried Parents in a Boston Suburb," a "Collective Family in a Big House in Berkeley," and a "Frontier Partnership in Idaho"—appeared the caption "Work-sharing Contract in New York," with no mention of *agreement* at all. Perhaps a mainstream journal like *Life* must inevitably try to tame and depoliticize everything between its covers: in the galleys of the article, the reporter, Patricia Coffin, had me spending my free time at art galleries instead of at political rallies. When I objected to this falsification it was corrected, but the offending *contract* remained.

Still, under whatever title, that *Life* coverage did help to get people thinking about alternatives to conventional marriage, including the controversial idea of domestic equality—so well, in fact, that when the magazine decided to do a follow-up of the major stories of the year for their late-December wrap-up issue, their April 28 report on "The Marriage Experiments" was among those selected. Good for the movement—but for one hitch: when Pat Coffin called to set up another interview, I had to tell her that my husband was on the West Coast and couldn't be reached.

What I didn't tell her was that, his business having recently folded, he had followed his young lover, then a student at Berkeley, to California. We had separated only months after the Agreement appeared in *Life*. Much had happened to us in those brief months, including the nearly simultaneous publication of my first novel and collapse of my husband's business—events that together loosened our ties; but *Life* readers, ignorant of our private history, not knowing that our Marriage Agreement was three years old could easily presume a causal connection between the Agreement and our precipitous separation. Thinking of the fun Mailer and the others could have with the news of our breakup if they got wind of it, I dreaded an exposé—particularly when Pat Coffin suggested that perhaps she could interview each of us separately. I managed to put her off by fudging my husband's address, but I was terrified she would somehow discover his whereabouts.

When *Life* unexpectedly announced to the world that it would be folding before the end of the year, I was jubilant. Indeed, so powerfully did I feel the swelling force of the movement that I wondered if perhaps it wasn't my personal feminist genie that had delivered *Life* its death blow to save face for me and the movement. (Just as, following the signing of a book contract some months earlier, I'd suspected my genie of exterminating the editor who had laid a hand suggestively on my knee, and would again some months later suspect her of conveniently delivering back to me my compromising love letters only hours before my lover's fatal heart attack. Oh, the power of the movement!)

I realize this confession may be construed in some quarters to feed the notion that feminism destroys marriages—a charge akin to the one that feminism destroys fetuses. In that feminism offers women the possibility of autonomy, giving them permission to leave a bad marriage or terminate an unwanted pregnancy, both accusations are partially true. Before feminism, divorce, like abortion, was often regarded as scandalous; until the 1970s, in many states the only ground for divorce was (criminal) adultery, the only ground for abortion threat to the mother's life, while now, thanks in part to feminism, divorce and abortion are widely accepted as basic rights. But that's only part of the story. As I once pointed out to a man who accused me of having caused his wife to run off with the baby after reading one of my novels, *he* may have had something to do with it, too. True, a few women, torn by ambivalence and carried away by the movement's rhetoric that seemed at times to condemn all marriages (and families) as oppressive, committed acts they later regretted—ending relationships, postponing pregnancies, leaving children—only to change their minds after it was too late. But many others acted without regret and some like me struggled in the name of feminism to improve family life by making it more equitable, flexible, and thus viable. As I wrote for a "Symposium on Marriage" in the feminist literary journal *Aphra* (Fall 1973—several years before New York reformed its divorce law): "Children will continue to be born and reared. Adults may fairly be expected to make sacrifices for them. Marriage insures that women will not be the only ones to make those sacrifices." My feminist intent was neither to bring down nor to shore up marriage but to improve women's lot within and without it.

Now, many years after my second divorce, looking back across a quarter century of social change to try to recover the feelings that led to my Marriage Agreement, I wonder if writing it was an act of political imagination, personal conciliation, or feminist revenge. I do remember the elation with which I wrote it; and I also remember that later, as I read letter after wistful letter from *Redbook* readers applauding the Agreement and envying me my "understanding husband" or begging for the secret of how I managed to get him to go along with it, I sensed an uncomfortable disparity between my power and theirs. It was not only that I had class and other privileges many of them didn't share, like rewarding remunerative work and no more toddlers at home. At that point, unlike most of them isolated in their disappointing marriages, I, fueled by feminist insight, anger, and pride, felt the power of a burgeoning movement backing me. The unspoken sanction for my Agreement, the secret force behind it (and a reason, perhaps, to call it a contract after all?) was my bottom-line willingness to divorce him if he wouldn't agree. I puzzled over the effect on the movement of admitting this straight-out: would it help or hurt the cause?—help it by revealing the necessity of struggle, goodwill notwithstanding, or hurt it by exposing the all-but-prohibitive stakes? And later, as it became increasingly clear that our Agreement did not really "work" despite our best intentions—that, since my husband's work took him so often out of town, I continued to do most of the parenting (and gladly, too, knowing how much calmer and freer we each felt during our long stretches apart), and for the same reason, by default as it were, he let the housework slide, and eventually our marriage, like so many, foundered—I wondered which was better for the movement, particularly in face of the conservative attacks: to hide these failings or confess them?

But why, I wonder now, should the "failure" of my marriage, or any marriage, have seemed to me so potentially embarrassing for the movement—any more than the cancer death of food-reformer Adele Davis should have so scandalized the health-food movement? As if a person, or a marriage, should be immortal, or as if our marital breakdown must be laid at the door of our singular Agreement rather than of our accumulating disagreements. When dozens of feminist activists, myself included, had staged a sit-in on March 18, 1970, at the editorial offices of that bulwark of traditional gender roles, the *Ladies Home Journal,* to demand a platform in its pages for feminist ideas, one of the reasons we selected that magazine was to challenge its famous monthly column, "Can This Marriage Be Saved?" (which Redstocking Ellen Willis proposed retitling, "Can This Marriage"). Yet, despite that action, two years later I evidently still thought it my duty to shield *Life*'s audience from the truth about my own marriage, as if the point were to save it.

The truth? Like every ideal, our Marriage Agreement fell far short of the standard it proposed; indeed, it failed. Worse, its failure was as emblematic as it was personal: in the absence of economic equality and/or a strong movement, decades after women's liberation launched the battle over housework married men in the United States still do precious little domestic labor—only 10 percent more than they did two decades earlier, according to one survey. *The Second Shift* (Viking, 1989), Arlie Hochschild's important study of divisions of domestic chores among married, predominantly middle-class working couples in families with young children, reports that what the women's movement began is now a "stalled revolution": only 18 percent of the husbands in the study did half the housework, 21 percent did a moderate amount, and 61 percent still did little or none, though their wives held down outside jobs. And even among couples who share more equitably in the work at home, "women do two-thirds of the *daily* jobs, like cooking and cleaning up—jobs that fix them into a rigid routine" while men do less frequent tasks like fixing appliances or changing the oil in the family car. *Families on the Faultline* (HarperCollins, 1994), Lillian B. Rubin's examination of working-class families, shows that many working-class men who would not even pay lip service to gender equality two decades ago are now "quite sensitive to the needs and wishes of their wives"; yet because they fail to translate this sensitivity into action, the housework question is now often "a wrenching source of conflict."[13] In fact, according to Hochschild, "the most important injury" to women in unequal marriages is not the unfair leisure gap between the sexes, not women's exhaustion from the double day, but rather that they "carry into their marriage the distasteful and unwieldy burden of resenting their husbands."

---

[13] Rubin notes that housework more than child care is at issue in these families, "for despite the enormous ferment in family life over these last decades, the cultural definition of the good parent has changed little. Parenting . . . remains woman's work. It's mother who's still held accountable for [the children's] moral development, their emotional stability, and their worldly success or failure. Father need only make a living for them to satisfy his part of the bargain. Any unanticipated ripple in the children's development is quite simply mom's failure." [80] The exception is in black families: "Black men are the most likely to be real participants in the daily life of the family and are more intimately involved in raising their children than any of the others. . . . Compared to their white, Asian, or Latino counterparts, the black families look like models of egalitarianism. Nearly three-quarters of the men in the African-American families in this study do a substantial amount of the cooking, cleaning, and child care, sometimes even more than their wives." [92]

Conflict, discontent, resentment: a bitter legacy. And with consciousness changing so much faster than practice, and far more on the part of women than of men, discontent and resentment must be at record highs. Hard on the children (like our own, who unfortunately were spared none of the hardships of growing up in an embattled household, for after that first separation my husband and I got back together and remained married until the children were grown); hard on everyone involved. Still, an improvement over the cavalier dismissal of housework as "trivial," and better by far than the unconscious, prefeminist alternatives, which, in any case, have become increasingly untenable now that most women, regardless of class, race, or age of children, hold down outside jobs.

Yes, our Marriage Agreement failed, and our marriage after it. But the unbearable status quo, to challenge which I had written the Agreement in the first place, also collapsed—fell in a whirling freefall that, like so many utopian fictions and experiments, landed us somewhere we never imagined. Once the feminist challenge pushed open the door on traditional marriage and took a good look inside, it could not be the same again. Even though the goal of domestic equality between cohabiting parents is honored—like the marriage vows themselves—mainly in the breach, at least it is now a commonplace, no longer an outrage. Despite the gloomy news on actual housework done, the *ideal* of egalitarian marriage has steadily grown (espoused by 48 percent of the wives in Hochschild's study if only by 20 percent of the husbands), that of traditional gender roles within marriage has steadily shrunk (down to 12 percent of the wives and 18 percent of the husbands), and the rest (40 percent of the wives and 62 percent of the husbands) are somewhere "in transition."

Parenting is still profoundly gendered, and the nuclear family is still the setting vastly preferred for child rearing, but in fact fewer and fewer children grow up in a traditional household or even one where both biological parents reside. Instead, to accommodate paternal flight or enact eternal hope, there has been an irrepressible proliferation of new *de facto* forms of family life—from jumbled, blended, divorce-extended families to single-parent, lesbian, or gay domestic partnerships, and even the occasional innovative experiment. In a May 14, 1994, column in the *New York Times* Peter Steinfels proposed a "thought experiment" doing away with legal marriage altogether: "The state would have nothing to do with it. The whole business would be strictly a private agreement. . . . The only thing that would be essential is that the couple—or the triad or the quintet—agree freely. . . . The number, the sex, the hierarchy or permanence of spouses in any household would be no more a matter of legal requirement—or ultimately, of social concern—than the number or size of the rooms."[14]

Such proliferation ensures that even in the face of punishing institutional biases that restrict nontraditional families' rights, traditional hierarchical marriage will not again be monolithically entrenched. But it does nothing to correct or even address the gendered division of labor that permeates our society. It is this domestic inequality, not the form or legitimacy of marriage, that continues to worry me. Not that I don't have a cheer for every imaginative or brave attempt. But the inevitable slippage between intentions and their outcomes, particularly in the absence of strong organized feminist movement, keeps me asking cautiously of each, Who will benefit, who will lose, and who will wind up with the housework?

---

[14] "Beliefs" column by Peter Steinfels, *New York Times,* May 14, 1994, p. 28, col. 1.

On Becoming a Feminist/Lawyer

Nadine Taub

Of course, I forget how I became a feminist. I feel like my awakening, like most lawyers', was late. For example, I remember a lunch in Newark with a later well-known lefty lawyer, probably in the spring of 1969, when, as a fairly new law graduate, I was beginning my work in a community law office. He asked me what I thought of what he called "women's lib" complaints. Well, I didn't know.

I think my becoming a feminist was probably a combination of being ready, blundering into a historical moment, happening to see important things to work on, and then being shaped and directed by that work. Some relevant facts: I was born in 1943 and grew up in a small midwestern college town, the middle child of a hard-working, academic father and an equally hard-working, in-the-home mother. They were people who said that it was important to have something to do. I ultimately became a lawyer and, since 1973, have been in charge of the Women's Rights Litigation Clinic at Rutgers Law School.

Growing up, I simply could not do what was expected of a young woman. I was elected president of the student council in the tiny university high school I attended, but I couldn't get asked to the big school prom. I was supposed to do better socially when I got to Swarthmore College but didn't. Nor was there much to my social relationships in law school. Indeed, it wasn't until I was on my way to becoming my own person that I could hook up with a fine, also own person—to whom I've now been married over 20 years.

I think this inability to meet role expectations ultimately proved very useful. Unable to fall, early and easily, into the trap of being a wife and mother, I had to do something. Though I had no experience of political struggles, I'd been brought up with some sense that racial discrimination was wrong. In college, I'd picketed and marched and even been arrested (to my parents' pleasure) as part of early civil rights demonstrations. In the year after college, I spent a little time in tenants' rights groups, but I never took a leadership role and was, in fact, often put off by the in-group in charge.

Yet, as always, I saw myself as doing something and applied to law school. But, Yale, like all law schools then, was definitely an institution built around male norms. Yes, there was a small women's restroom on the second floor, but it wasn't very convenient, and it had a rest space like the ones required by the U.S. protective labor legislation. Yale thus joined in the law's message that women are special, that we have female problems and need to retire, and above all that a woman's real role is as wife and mother.

At Yale, you made your mark by getting on the law journal, being chosen for a popular seminar, having access to professors, and by making top grades. Because I didn't make it by these standards, I didn't know that I could criticize them. It didn't occur to me that I might play the lawyer role in our extracurricular mock trial, but I was naturally happy to serve as a witness—a prostitute. Nor did it occur to me to talk to the handful of other women in my class of almost two hundred, and certainly not to the "law wives."

My gender socialization did help me, though, post–law school. Many of the men set off to make money, but as an unmarried woman it was socially acceptable for me to consider taking lower-paying public interest work. As everyone said back then, I would never have to support anyone besides myself. In addition, my belief that I must do something probably had its gendered side. For whatever combination of reasons, I thought it was important to help people. In this doing-for-others, I stretched and grew.

I got a job in a just-getting-started legal services office in the Bronx. It was 1968, and there wasn't yet much talk out loud about my being that novel creature, a young woman lawyer. Nor was I particularly aware of being a woman. Certainly, I was totally unaware of my relations with the primarily Black female support staff and was just worried that clients and others would take me for a secretary. I remember with pleasure the tenant, the one with the brown paper bag holding the twelve mice she'd caught in her apartment, just exclaiming when she saw she had a girl for a lawyer, "Isn't that the damnedest thing!"

Only in retrospect did I notice that every time I, a white woman, had to work late, so did one of the office's other five lawyers, all male. I'm pretty sure when one of them had to stay, he did it by himself. I still don't know what I think about this, even in light of so many subsequent years of discussion about gender issues. It was a storefront office in a poor, predominantly Black neighborhood. I'm guessing the Black boss made a judgment about potential risks—to the program as well as to me. I was treated differently, seen—no doubt realistically—as more vulnerable. But weren't those boy lawyers at risk, too? Yes, but not really to the same extent. There was no question of my staying late to keep *them* safe, but would I have been any help if I had stayed? I guess I would like to have been part of a conversation about this difference, and about what to do.

From the legal services storefront in the Bronx, I went in April 1969 to a Newark storefront established by the state American Civil Liberties Union following the 1967 riots. I was "boss" with a secretary and one other equally inexperienced lawyer in the office. "Inexperienced" was my predominant evaluation of myself—when I thought about it—but I didn't that much. I felt like I was representing "the community" and the community was moving.

I think this was my first real sense of movement involvement. I represented rent strikers; I lawyered for folks fighting for affirmative action (politically as well as legally); I defended demonstrators; I sued the cops; and I helped some individuals. I liked and respected the people I represented; I cared about what they were fighting for and felt we were fighting together. We (I) won sometimes; though, with hindsight, I know it helped that the years of these early cases were 1969 to 1972, a time when the courts were responding to politicized demands for justice from the civil rights and legal services communities. Because I was engaged in doing something for somebody else, I functioned well—working long and hard and seemingly effectively—without the paralysis I felt in situations where I myself was up for judgment. It didn't occur to me to get mad when a judge couldn't help saying I was as good as a real lawyer.

In 1968, just after I graduated from Yale, the climate at law schools started to change. Men who went to graduate school were no longer exempt from the draft, and a visible number of women found places in law schools. Rutgers Law School in Newark was one of the first to admit significant numbers of women. With their new numbers, their energy and motivation, and because of the times, this cluster of women at Rutgers, all white and mostly middle class, showed a kind of group awareness unthinkable only a few years before. They formed consciousness-raising groups, got women's courses added to the law school curriculum, and started the *Women's Rights Law Reporter*.

But consciousness raising requires risk-taking, a willingness to be vulnerable. And such risk-taking is far more likely when people know and already trust one another to some extent, when they are enough alike to hope to be understood. Since it's more likely that you will overcome detachment and caution with women a lot like you, how can we get the benefits of speaking personally and, at the same time, understand that women have very different experiences from each other?

For whatever reasons, consciousness raising was never my way into feminism. For me, back in the late sixties and early seventies, the things that happened in the world, and the things I did were more important than my few efforts at group talking. I had become an activist in that Newark storefront, and much of my feminist consciousness came from that experience. While still there, I had begun to work on the women's challenge to the New Jersey criminal abortion statute.

It was Nancy Stearns who brought me into this work. A veteran of SNCC working at the Center for Constitutional Rights in New York, she was attempting to get courts to see that abortion laws denied women their fundamental right to liberty. I vaguely knew that her New York case included depositions in a Greenwich Village church, a "speakout" to get across what illegal abortion was actually like for women, and to make women feel they could talk about it and be part of efforts to challenge the law in court.

A similar case was starting in New Jersey and since I was one of the few eligible women lawyers in town, Nancy Stearns asked me to share her load. At first I didn't understand what was at stake or what it was all about. I was a single woman who had never been pregnant and had never been in a circle of women who needed to get abortions—or so I thought. Later I learned from a college friend how another college acquaintance had nearly died from an illegal abortion, and when the school found out, it had almost kept her from graduating. And I finally grasped my mother's old, veiled allusions to needing and getting an abortion when, as a Depression newlywed, she simply could not afford a child. But I didn't yet know how an unwanted pregnancy left you almost alone and worried out of your mind, driving you underground to risk your health and future well-being, or constraining your life with a however loved, terribly needy child.

I opened the file under the label "Health." However, as I did my assigned task of assembling the arguments of the long list of women who were mounting the legal and political challenge, I began to get it: women were trapped by unwanted pregnancy and man-made laws denied them the most basic autonomy. My job was to fit together all the pieces Nancy and others were writing to make the brief smooth and convincing. Of course, typically, I ended up reading all the relevant cases and putting into my own words how the consequences of compelling pregnancy by legally denying the abortion option (loss of job, loss of education, continuing guilt for a child adopted away, etc.) deprived women of the right to liberty the Constitution supposedly guarantees to everyone. When we won the first round of the case two-plus years later, I placed the closed file under the heading "Women."

As an announced feminist, I kept learning by doing. In the fall of 1973, I began teaching a Women's Rights Litigation Clinic at Rutgers Law School–Newark that many of the same women students who had worked on the abortion case had persuaded the school to initiate. One of the clinic's early projects was to convince the federal courts that for a woman to be subjected to her boss's sexual demands violated fair employment laws. It was that work with the clinic students, that process of explaining to each other and to the court the impact of the usual power differential, of being perceived inevitably as a sexual object, that made me able to understand just what sexual harassment is all about, and, along with others, begin to bring it into the realm of law.

Another among the cases I took on at the clinic involved a suit on behalf of a woman who was locked up by the Newark police as a "material witness" when she complained of being raped. The irony was that the man she charged skipped bail. Several years into the case, however, he was caught and tried. My client, a Black woman in Newark, was painted not only as a willing partner, but also a prostitute. This was like the cases I had brought earlier against the police in various North Jersey communities, complaining of their racially motivated conduct. But because what happened was a thing that happens to women, this case was much more personally painful. I was learning this was my fight; when I worked on women's issues, I was going beyond service to others. When the criminal trial resulted in the man's acquittal, I really didn't want my husband to touch me.

We found we were examining our experiences as women as much as the law, and we found students and faculty could work together as colleagues. For example, in doing that work on the early sexual harassment case, it was by talking to one another that we were able to explain to ourselves and to the court why sexual harassment violates laws against sex discrimination.

It was hard to learn to teach, to get students to do their best, to distinguish between what I knew and they knew, and to know when to take over. It was hard to balance the needs of the real cases and real clients—that were so important to us all—against the needs of the students to learn by doing. Being unsure of my role compounded these problems. Perhaps because I was new to teaching and because we were able to work together, it was hard to shift from identifying with the students, who got me hired and gave me rides, to seeing myself as one of the faculty—a faculty that in those days often focused on my inadequate credentials and the political (and therefore not worthy) nature of my work.

I was in a political women's lawyer group where I was quiet about these problems, unable to ask for support. But as more and more in our women's crowd went into legal teaching, I saw them finding each other to talk about what they were facing, and I saw them working together to make a mark on the established organizations and institutions. Now that I'm no longer knocking myself, I can recognize once again that change takes numbers.

Well, I made it through tenure (which seems to me something to forget, like the bar exam), but I doubt that there is real acceptance of what I believe in. Probably what mattered was some grants, some newspaper and TV coverage of clinic victories, some publications. It is my guess it mattered more to people at Rutgers that the Rockefeller and Ford foundations gave me a lot than that I put together a wonderful group of activists and theorists who produced two books on reproductive laws for the 1990s. I'm afraid I also got indoctrinated, infused, and infected with their ways of measuring achievement. Now I too worry about how much I publish and where (their "where") I get invited and who (their "who") has heard of me. I really don't think the others from my women lawyers crowd are free of this, and it's only harder when we deny it. Sometimes, I'm glad that it turns out that I can only do what I believe in; often I just obsess about the grades academia gives to grown-ups.

Of course, this is related to a bigger worry. Feminism as a discipline is so acceptable in academia now. Give us a job and benefits, and we produce incomprehensible words and footnotes and "fight" with each other. Of course I see that we couldn't stay the way we were at the beginning, either in terms of jobs or struggles. And I do think we are trying to figure out ways to carry on, to progress. But it's awfully hard to stay true to the vision.

Reflecting on my teaching experiences has complicated my understanding of the possibilities for escaping the confines of hierarchy and gender roles. As time goes by, I really do know more about the relevant law and other matters about getting what we hope for done than the students working with me. When they read precedent-setting cases about sex discrimination, they see that some of them were mine. Plus my hair is getting gray. It is harder and harder to see and be seen as an equal. A traditional teacher model, often more natural and more successful for a male, seems the inevitable alternative. Still, though, I have been recharged recently by hearing some wonderful ideas I had never thought of from clinic students. I ask myself if being respectful to students is enough. How can I manage authority without being authoritarian?

Many good things have happened since "my awakening." I have seen changes in the law that helped change women's lives. I have had the pleasure of making some of those changes myself. I helped women get the same government benefits men get. I've helped make procreative choice real—for those who need medicaid to pay for abortion, for those who need protection against coerced sterilization, for those who seek the care of midwives, and for those who stand to be robbed of choice by hazardous workplace conditions. I have also helped to establish legal remedies for sexual harassment at work and at school. I've been involved in more struggles, and have seen other victories, but that's enough for now.

Perhaps most important, these gains have often come about through a special feminist way of working together. But as I age, see others age, and see feminism absorbed by the establishment, I worry about how we will retain and sustain these new ways of working. Despite our generation's increasing age and fatigue, we must all always remember we have found ways to combat sexism and must continue to use them.

"For the People Hear Us Singing, 'Bread and Roses! Bread and Roses!' "

Meredith Tax

I grew up in the fifties, a time when nothing could be talked about, at least in my family. My immigrant grandparents had come to the United States to save us from pogroms and starvation; my parents had worked their way through the Depression and World War II and made it into the suburbs so that we could go to good (i.e., white) schools. We should be grateful, keep our heads down, and not ask questions. Of course my poor mother, whose family were the only Jews in a small Wisconsin town, had no idea how to teach me to be a middle-class suburban girl. I was a misfit, shy and angry, with my nose forever buried in a book—often some classic feminist text I read over and over, like *Hedda Gabler, Saint Joan,* or *Little Women,* for I was a premature feminist. I had no language for it, just knew the life offered girls was boring and unfair. Sometimes I thought of myself as a suffragette. In sixth grade I passed around a petition saying we should elect a girl as class president for a change. I told my family that when I grew up, I wouldn't get married; instead I would go to New York, be an actress, and have lots of boyfriends.

Who would marry me? my family replied.

I chose a college, Brandeis, that I sensed would be more tolerant of weirdness than people in the 'burbs. But it was not fundamentally different in its vision of women. In 1964, I went to graduate school in London, where I did research for three years on marriage and comedy in the period following the English Restoration. But war and revolution were on the front page every day—the civil war in Nigeria, the Six-Day War, the war in Vietnam. And the war at home—in 1967, there were race riots in 127 U.S. cities—Detroit, Newark, Atlanta, Boston, Chicago, New York among them—as blacks signaled their frustration with a society that just would not change. Martin Luther King said the United States was the greatest purveyor of violence in the world. One hundred and fifty thousand people marched on Washington to end the war. I started to meet guys who had burned their draft cards. What about me? In 1967, I went home to the United States for a visit and reality crashed in on me. I returned to London and had a nervous breakdown, unable to sleep for weeks, feeling I couldn't hold back any longer yet terrified to move forward, knowing my temperament was such that, once I committed myself to politics, it would be the end of "my brilliant career." I had formed myself in opposition to the suburban world I came from, but as an artsy bohemian, not a political radical. These self-definitions became obsolete overnight.

So I joined the Stop It Committee, a draft resistance group of anti-war Americans in London. At first I just went to meetings and asked questions. But Linda Gordon was a member, and she soon suggested I run for the steering committee. Interesting idea. Before long I went cold turkey on my thesis and was doing politics full-time. In 1968, I decided to return to the United States—that was where the war had to be stopped. As I remember it, on the plane back, Linda handed me a magazine.

It was the first issue of *No More Fun and Games,* published by Cell 16, a Boston women's liberation group. I remember catching my breath: Women had their own group? Then, as I read, I began to smile, for I recognized the voice: angry, raw, full of pain combined with a kind of bitter triumph at seeing the situation for what it was. It sounded just like my own voice. It was the voice of the women's liberation movement being born.

Nine months later Cell 16 called the first women's liberation conference in Boston, on May 11, 1969, at Emmanuel College, where Roxanne Dunbar taught. Trude Bennett and I began to plan a workshop on women and psychology. By psychology, we didn't mean Freud. We meant the way it felt to be a woman.

Our workshop left me reeling. I had never heard such talk—about the most intimate things. I was not one to open up to strangers, but rethinking my own history as I prepared for the conference, I had begun to construct a mythology of my own life, starting with what I called my "political breakdown" in London the year before. The night after the conference, I wrote down my memory of this breakdown—the tone may sound overheated, but 1969 was a time of overnight epiphanies and my self-dramatization was low-key, compared to many.

[A year ago] I had no connections. . . . There were so few people . . . I felt relaxed with, able to be off guard with, to *touch*. I was
surrounded by a glass wall the rest of the time, sometimes in panic,
often in resignation. The pain of this isolation was never as intense
as in college, when I felt as if I were choking, when I could see my
own breath on the window of my solitude. I didn't panic very often
but it was always a possibility. My inability to function was the
index of the fact that the world had finally succeeded in communicating to me what it was like. . . . The thought of Vietnam and of
life in the ghetto became absolutely intolerable, yet I could think of
nothing else. . . . Merely to exist with such perception was pain. . . .
I had no choice but to fight the causes of that pain, or to spend the
rest of my life fighting a rearguard action against my realization of
it—which would be to go mad.

People at the conference responded strongly to what I said. I got a
little scared at the intensity of feeling flowing back and forth and the
revelations I had made to people I didn't know and might never see
again. What was my responsibility to these women? What was theirs
to me? Unnerved, I wrote in my diary that night, "I am so effective
sometimes it terrifies me. I feel I must use this ability to change lives systematically in all directions, and when I can't see the way at once, I want
to cry."

To give expressive leadership is exhilarating, draining, and terrifying. It is not just self-expression; it is letting the spirit speak through
you. At certain historical moments when change is possible, collective
energy fills the air like static electricity, shooting out sparks. Some people can channel it; they know how to express what a group feels and
point it the way it wants to go. Like dowsing rods or Geiger counters,
they absorb and feed back feeling, indicating energy and direction.
Often this gift is a burden. Sometimes it feels like hubris, sometimes
prophecy.

After the Boston conference at Emmanuel College, I became
obsessed with questions of organization and strategy. If women's liberation was serious, and it felt more serious than anything else in the world,
we needed a plan. You can't make a revolution without a plan. I couldn't
figure one out by myself. I didn't know enough. I needed a group.
NOW was out of the question; they weren't revolutionaries. Cell 16 was

a cadre group; they said they didn't want new members. A couple of project groups seemed to be growing out of the conference, but those weren't enough to do the job. We needed an organization with a program. My head exploding with ideas, I wrote in my journal, May 24, 1969:

> [Small] groups would be given strength and purpose by relating to a program of analysis and demands. . . . A program gives people a way of relating to the movement, a reason for joining it, and something to "join"—to enter an experiment with. Instead of saying to people, "Some women are doing this and some that," you can say, "Women's liberation wants this and that, and is working to get it this year by doing this and that."

I thought, what if a small group of women worked on strategy over the summer? And what if each simultaneously started another small group to spread the discussion? Surely we could get together a program for women's liberation by September. Then we would form an organization! In my inexperience and grandiosity, I had no idea I was asking people to do the political equivalent of inventing the atom bomb in the kitchen. So I typed up a proposal and took it to Linda. She was appalled: how could one little group set itself up as strategic leaders for the whole women's movement? It was so elitist!

But she cautiously agreed that it wouldn't hurt to try to pull things together a little. We might as well call a meeting to discuss it. A handful of us met at her house the next week, and then again four days later, this time preparing by reading a *New Left Review* article by Juliet Mitchell giving a structural analysis of the oppression of women. My journal entry conveys the feeling of these early discussions—all our ideas were so fluid, we were so intense yet easily shaken, that one comment could suddenly tip a whole political decision:

> The talk [at the meeting tonight] was much less uptight and hostile than last time. But people are still pretty resistant to organizational ideas. This mostly takes the form of skipping from subject to subject and never arguing through anything. . . . Linda [thought of a way] . . . to solve the dual problem—organization and theory—how to work out analysis and program in a nonelitest way. [She said] we should call an open meeting of some sort and

people would divide into groups to write papers analyzing different aspects of the [oppression of women]. . . . It was on the verge of being adopted when Jean Tepperman said that it made her feel very sad because what she felt she really needed—a political collective that would talk about all kinds of things—wouldn't happen. . . . [So I said why didn't] each of us . . . invite the people—two or three—whom we considered were where we were politically—anticapitalist, etc . . . [to a meeting] to set up a bunch of political collectives like our own, which would discuss strategy and organization with a view to formulating a program. This was accepted with great relief.

Our initiating group, soon to be called Collective No. 1, ended up with eleven members: Fran Ansley, Trude Bennett, Michelle Clark, Linda Gordon, Marya Levinson, Grey Osterud, Sara Syer, Jean Tepperman, Judy Ullman, Wendy Towner, and me. The larger group we called together first met on Friday night, July 24, 1969, and began to meet regularly each Friday in the living room of Hester Butterfield's mother's house near the Radcliffe Yard. By September it had coalesced into a citywide organization called Bread and Roses. Our name came from a women's labor song from the Lawrence, Massachusetts, strike of 1912—"Hearts starve as well as bodies, Give us bread but give us roses!"—for we were conscious radicals, trying to learn from the past, trying to figure out ways to unite our antiwar, antiracist politics with women's liberation in order to bring about permanent social transformation.

But to embody these desires in a strategy and program—that was harder. We didn't know how to do that. The best we could do was draw up lists of demands as long as your arm, covering everything from abortion rights to jobs to sex. These lists were meant to bring us somehow from the present to the revolution—we had no idea how. We spoke of revolution the way old-time anarchists used to talk about *Der Tag*—that great day when everyone would suddenly wake up, pour out into the streets, and declare a general strike. Only our revolution would be more complete than those of the past, because women would have equal power.

By this time I had begun to write. I had always wanted to be a writer but had held back, not only because I had nothing to say, but because there was no one I wanted to say it to. Now I had both a subject and an audience, gifts from history.

A young woman is walking down a city street. She is excruciatingly aware of her appearance and of the reaction to it (imagined or real) of every person she meets. She walks through a group of construction workers who are eating lunch in a line along the pavement. Her stomach tightens with terror and revulsion; her face becomes contorted into a grimace of self-control and fake unawareness; her walk and carriage become stiff and dehumanized. No matter what they say to her, it will be unbearable. No woman can have an autonomous self unaffected by such encounters.

This became a four-part essay, called *Woman and Her Mind: The Story of Daily Life.* A section was published by the New York Radical Feminists in *Notes from the Second Year,* edited by Anne Koedt and Shulamith Firestone. *Notes* wouldn't print my whole essay because they felt the second half was too socialist; Roberta Salper, a New York socialist feminist, would only print the second half because the first was too radical feminist. (I thought New Yorkers were impossible. We weren't sectarian in Boston.) The excerpt in *Notes* was picked up by the Liberation News Service, a movement version of the Associated Press that sent packets once a week to hundreds of underground papers. Then the whole essay was published as a pamphlet by the New England Free Press, a Boston cooperative that produced and distributed movement literature. Appearing in the spring of 1970, *Woman and Her Mind* became one of the founding documents of the women's liberation movement as it exploded into existence. By the time the New England Free Press folded in the eighties, its editors estimated they had sold 150,000 copies of my essay by mail, at prices ranging from thirty-five to fifty cents.

People told me my work had changed their lives. Without such assurances, I might not have been able to give myself permission to keep doing something as pleasurable as writing, for finding a strategy for women's liberation was a heavy burden. I began to search history for prototypes, digging into the archives in the Schlesinger library to find the connections between class, race, gender, and revolutionary strategy. I found wonderful stories but, drowning in detail, could make no sense of them. Nobody else seemed to have a better grasp than I did. Most did not even seem bothered by our lack of a long-term plan; they were willing to live from day to day. But I couldn't stand the anxiety.

Looking back, I ask myself, why? Why didn't I just go on with my writing? I had a book contract by this time, and was doing research that fascinated me on the history of women and working-class organization. Other people in the movement managed to go on with their lives, go back to school, develop careers. Why did I have such ants in my pants? I think the stakes were higher for me because I never knew who I was until the women's movement. Without it, I had no community, no place I felt at home. I loved the women's movement so much, I couldn't bear the thought of its failing to achieve its highest aims. Though I had little sense of the risks involved, I was trying to be practical: women's liberation required a revolution so I would just have to find out how to bring one about.

Ultimately, the desire for a strategy that had made me push to form Bread and Roses propelled me out of it, in search of answers to my questions: How do you make a revolution that works for women instead of selling them out after the seizure of power? How do you build the kind of movement that will unite women across class and racial lines and not be twisted to serve elite interests? How can you tell when small reforms may add up to revolution and when they are just reforms? By 1971, these questions were driving me crazy. Inevitably, I began to read the only writers who addressed such issues: Marx, Engels, Lenin, Mao Tsetung. They didn't say much about women but they knew a lot about revolution.

In addition, as my own answers ceased to satisfy me, I began to pay more attention to those of my husband, a red diaper baby who had learned Marxism at an age when most boys were being bar mitzvahed. He had dropped out of college to work for a union but by this time he was drifting, working in a factory on his own, without being connected to any union or organization. He desperately needed a political context for his work, but neither of us—especially me—thought much of the Marxists we had met. The Communist Party people were so lame they seemed to be in a time warp and I simply could not suspend my disbelief in the Soviet Union as an example of liberation. The people in Progressive Labor were just rich kids from Harvard pretending to be workers. But in 1971, we began to meet people who had lived in China, people who knew about the Cultural Revolution firsthand. They said

China really was different from other revolutions. It was an exciting thought, worth pursuing.

In 1972, we left Boston to do factory work in a midwestern industrial city. In 1973, we joined the October League (OL), a Marxist-Leninist "pre-party formation" led by people who'd been heavily involved in Students for a Democratic Society (SDS). During my time in the OL, I worked on an assembly line in a TV factory, then in an electronics factory, and finally as a nurse's aide in a small private hospital. Until then, I had led an almost completely segregated life, not by choice, but because I grew up in a segregated city, went to college before affirmative action programs, and became politically active only after the early unity of the civil rights movement had become racially polarized. Because I had no experience with anyone but white people, I did not have enough political grasp to understand how to fight the *de facto* segregation of the antiwar movement and women's movement. In my years in the OL, I began to learn—not from theory but from the experience of being white in places where the work force was almost entirely made up of African-American and Hispanic women. Since that time, most of my political work has been on a multiracial basis. Being in all-white political meetings or social gatherings no longer feels natural to me; I see them as the product of political choices, however unconscious.

Learning how to live in a multiracial world was important to me personally. Since race is at the heart of the way every contradiction comes up in the United States, it also affected my ability to think strategically. In other ways, my OL experience was mainly negative. Even before I joined, I'd had trouble with their line and practice in relation to women, but there were so many things I needed to learn that I decided to reserve judgment and keep my mouth shut. But, in fact, I could no more keep my mouth shut than fly, and the OL leadership had a nose for error. I asked too many questions and I asked them in the wrong tone of voice, disagreed about too many things and challenged leadership too often. Inevitably, I was expelled. This meant I was attacked and ostracized by everyone I had worked with, including my husband—he had to choose and it was easier to replace a woman than a whole political context.

So in August 1975 I became a single mother. I had no money and only dubious survival skills, was alienated from my family (who disapproved of the course I had taken) and was working at the time as a nurse's aide, earning so little I was eligible for food stamps. I barely survived. Finally, I decided I had to return to the Northeast, where at least I had friends who would talk to me. In 1976, my father died and my mother gave me his car, which I was able to sell for a thousand dollars. With this nest egg, I moved to New York, where, with difficulty—my résumé was truly bizarre—I got a job as a secretary. I badly needed a support group, and friends from Bread and Roses now in New York— Sarah Eisenstein and Ginger Goldner—pulled together a women's group that helped me reconnect with the broader women's movement.

By 1977, the movement was in weird shape. A huge gap seemed to have developed between people doing practical work, who had little idea of how their work connected to anyone else's, and people doing theory, whose ideas were increasingly academic and cut off from practical consequence. Then Representative Henry Hyde started his campaign to cut off Medicaid funding for abortion and, to my surprise, I knew what must be done. Apparently I *had* learned how to think about strategy differently; I seemed to be doing it. The feminist movement's biggest problem was its whiteness and middle-classness. There were minority and working-class feminists, but they had little connection with what they saw as the feminist movement. Consequently, the movement's strategy on abortion—and everything else—must be directed toward building a path to a multiracial feminist movement. That meant white feminists would have to think about abortion differently in 1977 than they had in 1969—they couldn't just dramatize themselves, or treat it as an aspect of sexual freedom, or stake everything on a change in the law, or isolate abortion as a single issue, or make it part of a general health-care program. They would have to find a strategic link with an issue that concerned Third World feminists.

CESA (the Committee to End Sterilization Abuse), founded several years before by a Puerto Rican doctor, Dr. Helen Rodriguez-Trias, had already begun to work on the issue of sterilization abuse, a considerable problem for both African-American and Latina women. Members of CESA, particularly Karen Stamm and Ros Petchesky, became part of the process that led to the formation of CARASA, the Committee for Abortion Rights and Against Sterilization Abuse. Together we began to develop an analysis of reproductive rights that has now become so strong that few people care to remember how different the prevailing ideas were just fifteen years ago. Ros Petchesky has been particularly important in developing this analysis, and linking U.S. women activists with others in the Third World—an alliance that had stunning impact on world policy at UN conferences in Cairo and Beijing.

My work took me in a different direction. I was immersed in CARASA for three years. During much of this period I was working full-time as a legal secretary or editorial assistant. I was also the mother of a six-year-old daughter, Corey, born in 1974. Though I still wanted to write, I was too exhausted. And though I gave a tremendous amount of time to CARASA, I was practically the only woman with a young child and could not seem to get people to respond appropriately to my being a single working mother. After a while I got sick of sacrificing all my time with my daughter to meetings and phone calls, with no help from anyone with child care.

I had been trying to finish my history book, *The Rising of the Women,* for years, but had had no time. And the political climate was clearly changing. The mass movement was not going to keep expanding indefinitely, around reproductive rights or any other issue; we were entering a more conservative period, when we would have to defend what we had won and would make few new gains. Rather than continuing to spin my wheels doing activist work, I decided it was time for me to act like an intellectual and develop my ideas, pending the time when it became possible to build a mass movement again.

In 1979, I got laid off from an editorial job and was able to collect unemployment. This enabled me to finish my history book, *The Rising of the Women,* which was published by Monthly Review Press in 1980. Then I got a substantial advance on a proposal for a historical novel, *Rivington Street,* published in 1982 by William Morrow. Around the same time, I also wrote *Families* (Little, Brown, 1981), a children's picture book that showed a spectrum of different family structures, from single parenthood to the extended family to gay and childless couples, as if all were normal, rather than presenting the traditional family as normal and the rest as peculiar. I also married a second time, developed asthma, and had another child, my son Elijah.

Then, in 1986, I attended a Congress of International PEN, the writers' organization. Norman Mailer, then president of PEN American Center, presided. I could not help noticing that all the speakers seemed to be men, mostly white and rather advanced in years. Someone counted—only 16 out of the 117 panelists were women. Had we gone back to the 1950s? A number of women complained to Grace Paley, who was on the PEN board; she raised her hand and announced that some people were unhappy about the small number of women on the program and had decided to hold a meeting at lunchtime the next day to discuss it. I chaired the meeting. Two hundred people came. We drew up a protest resolution, elected spokeswomen, and said we would occupy the hall unless they got time to present it at the plenary. We went on to form a women's committee in PEN American Center. Three years later, I began to try to organize a women's committee in International PEN; it was accepted in 1991, at a PEN Congress in Vienna. Finding through hard experience that this work needed an independent organizational base in order to work with the necessary freedom, Grace, I, and a number of others have recently formed a new human rights organization, Women's WORLD, which stands for the Women's World Organization for Rights, Literature, and Development. We have just published a pamphlet manifesto called *The Power of the Word: Culture, Censorship, and Voice.* Thus, for the last ten years, most of my political work has been concentrated on questions of women's voice and gender-based censorship, and much of it has been international.

I love this work and think it is critically important, but my writing has not done equally well. In all the years since 1986, I have published only one book commercially, my second novel, *Union Square.* All my books went out of print, except for *The Rising of the Women,* which is hardly distributed. *Families* stayed in print for fourteen years, then, in 1994, became the target of a censorship campaign led by the Christian Coalition in Fairfax Country, Virginia, who felt it "glorified divorce" and objected to the inclusion of a lesbian couple. When their campaign affected sales, rather than fight to defend the book, Little, Brown put it out of print. I am happy to say that the Feminist Press decided to reprint it, showing again women's need for an independent organizational base, especially in hard times. And these are hard times for American writers; the publishing industry, increasingly conglomeratized and interested only in the bottom line, does not keep old books in print, particularly radical ones, and does not welcome new oppositional voices.

To work so hard to strengthen women's voices in the rest of the world and find it impossible to make my own heard in my own country makes me very unhappy. I feel like one of the last surviving members of a nearly extinct species—the committed left-wing feminist. And yet I know my species is not extinct, though we have been pronounced so again and again by the media, who never wanted to recognize our existence for more than ten minutes in the first place. Publishers have been telling me "there's no market for feminist books anymore" since 1977, when McGraw-Hill dropped *The Rising of the Women,* a history of relations between labor, socialist, and suffrage women before World War I, because they had decided the feminist movement was dead. After many years of work on censorship issues, I have concluded that censorship in the United States wears the face of the sales rep, the marketing manager, the spin doctor, all those who service the corporate monoculture that now controls publishing and is being imposed upon the rest of the world. As we say in *The Power of the Word:*

> The media have made possible a new form of cultural domination, the global monoculture, which has become a threat to cultural diversity and specificity the world over. . . . A parallel development has taken place in the publishing industries of Europe and North America, where production is increasingly concentrated in the hands of a few transnational conglomerates . . . a film company, an oil company, a newspaper company, etc. These conglomerates make few concessions to individual editorial taste; their interest is the bottom line and they see writing as just another product, like soft drinks or sneakers. . . . The growing world domination of the North American commercial monoculture . . . is an extremely unhealthy development, the equivalent in culture to the hegemony of commercially bred seeds and the practice of monoculture in farming. Both drive out diversity. Both impoverish the soil they feed on. Both produce sterile seeds, without a living relationship to their environment.

I still believe in the power of the word to transform reality and I know how to think about strategy better than I did in 1971. I know the word is central to women's movements, which are based so much on individual changes in consciousness, set in motion by other women's testimony and lives. I am frustrated by my inability to get my own words into the hands of those who I think need them. Of course this feels like my own problem, like failure, but is also a social problem affecting anyone who questions traditional ideas about gender, class, and race in conservative times.

Inevitably, conservatives will try to block, ridicule, and marginalize our writing, and to obliterate even the memory of our questions. Women writers have to organize to keep one another going, and to ensure that our words and questions survive.

How? That's the problem I'm working on now.

We Called Ourselves Sisters

Priscilla Long

1969. **Cambridge, Mass.** We—my husband and I—lived in a prison-green, aluminum-sided apartment building, a slum that came with a kid upstairs who set fires in the basement. Exhaust fumes from Brookline Street seeped into the bedroom, rain leaked into the bedroom closet. The backyard grew weeds and trash. Indoors I tended a solitary gardenia whose blossom filled the house with fragrance. At twenty-eight, Peter had just emerged from prison, where he'd spent two and a half years for refusing the draft. He was a graduate student in political science at Boston University. I had just quit an editorial job at a publishing house. I knit sweaters, made candles, read books. I marched in antiwar demonstrations. And, that first year of our marriage, I joined the women's movement.

After six months of unemployment, I took a job dishing up coleslaw at a fish restaurant. The context of my career change from editor to kitchen worker was neither marriage nor the women's movement but my ambition to be a writer. I'd kept a journal since the age of sixteen, for some years writing copious entries including much dreadful poetry. By 1969—I was twenty-six—I had published my first article and had edited a collection of essays. But my first decade of writing had proceeded without guidance or encouragement, and things gradually deteriorated. The writing dwindled. I quit my editorial job because I couldn't accept the failure of my writing. I didn't know how to work at writing, but I left room for it by refusing to excel at any other profession, especially not one so densely populated with failed writers.

Downward mobility cohered with the anti-establishment ethos of the times. Like many political activists I lived on the margins of society

Special thanks go to Bethany Reid, Esther Altshul Helfgott, Raelene Gold, and Margaret Crastnopol for their insightful support. I am grateful to Barrie Thorne, Connie Field, Dotty LeMieux, and Lise Vogel for generously sharing their notes and memories. The essay was immeasurably improved by friends who perceptively commented on drafts: MariJo Buhle, Joan Amatucci, Scott Driscoll, Jerry Richard, Peter Irons, Karen Franklin, Saul Slapikoff, Louis Kampf, and Ellen Cantarow.

by choice. These margins, in the strong economy of the sixties, could provide a rather commodious way of life. Earlier in the decade I and my comrades of the counterculture had furnished our apartments from the excellent choice of chairs and sofas provided on "big trash night." Regular trash night supplied kitchen utensils, bolts of cloth, Oxford shirts in perfect condition except for a missing button or two. Youth was not the only difference between then and now: in 1969 you could live on a minimum-wage job.

I lived and breathed the politics of the time. The women's movement of the late sixties was for me inextricable from my first arrest in 1963 at a sit-in to integrate Baltimore's Gwynn Oak Amusement Park. It was inextricable from the four days we spent in a Baltimore County jail eating White Tower hamburgers for breakfast, lunch, and dinner. It was inextricable from Vietnam, from the burgeoning news of body counts, body bags, bombs. It was inextricable from the campaigns against the war, the marches against the war, the chants—*Hell no, we won't go*—against the war.

1969. Cambridge, Mass. We held our first meeting at my apartment while Peter went to a movie. We were a dozen women in our twenties, all active in the antiwar movement. In one way or another we each looked askance at capitalism, favoring some form of socialism or anarchism or pacifism. We had read *The Autobiography of Malcolm X*, James Baldwin, Simone de Beauvoir, at least a smattering of Marx. Probably half of us had been arrested for civil disobedience either in the civil rights or the antiwar movement, and we took our arrests as a matter of pride.

Five of us were married, five single. Two of us, Ruth,[1] who had a Ph.D. in English literature, and Marcia, worked as full-time mothers raising small children. Both Adrienne, a clergywoman, and Clarissa staffed the offices of local draft resistance organizations. Libby worked as a secretary and Jackie worked for *The Old Mole*, a radical newspaper. Anna and Carrie studied sociology as graduate students at Brandeis. Nina worked at the New England Free Press, the collectively operated printshop whose pamphlet series included the first edition of *Our Bod-*

---

[1] To protect confidentiality, I have changed the names of the members of my women's collective. All other names in the essay are unchanged.

ies, Ourselves. I was soon to begin the kitchen job. We were white, from a mixture of class backgrounds. We were two Jews, one Mormon, the rest, including the clergywoman, more or less lapsed Protestants or Catholics, all rather secular in outlook.

We called ourselves a women's collective and we met weekly for a year and a half. Our initial focus was to share the stories of our lives for what they could tell us about society. Above all, we believed that the personal was political, that, to give an obvious example, a woman or person of color who feels inferior has internalized the sexism and racism of society.

Our association was intense and complex, but in many cases we did not become friends. Our self-revelations unfolded apart from intimacy in the ordinary sense of the term. Many friendships did develop in the women's movement, of course. But it was just as likely that the woman across the room revealing her most private feelings and experiences would become, not a friend, but an intimate sort of stranger.

In general, and not only in the women's movement, the year 1969 was an intense time of "letting it all hang out." There was more music, more dancing, more nakedness, more shouting, more sex, and much more talk. The study group—people getting together to read Marx or Marcuse or E. P. Thompson—became a common social form. It was a year of war and escalations to war, of massive antiwar demonstrations, of the Beatles, the Rolling Stones, the Grateful Dead. It was a year of teach-ins, be-ins, love-ins, of strobe lights, happenings, pot, acid. The craze for California hung thick in the cultural air, and so did fear, the anxious fear of the draft.

The year 1969 saw all the trends and tendencies of the decade in full swing: the back-to-the-country movement, the craft movement, the turn to soybeans and whole grains, the rise of food co-ops, the burgeoning of beads and Afros. It was a sexualized decade, a decade in which the ideal became to experience everything. Twenty years later it has become a feeding trough for right-wing quippers, but they miss the point, the values, the complexity, the hundred subgroups, the way a summation or an epithet might (or might not) capture or caricature one or two groups but miss ninety-eight others. The politicos alone—from the Black Panthers to Women Strike for Peace—could be divided thirty or forty ways according to activities, strategies, approaches.

That was one side of the sixties. The other side most people have forgotten. In 1969 I had never seen a woman bus driver. I had never been treated by a woman doctor or dentist, never taken my cat to a woman veterinarian, never heard a woman speak at a rally. On television all the newscasters were men. As an Antioch College student earlier in the decade, I'd taken some forty courses of which one, French, was taught by a woman professor.

Discrimination against women was open and rampant, and I had experienced it directly. In 1965 the *New York Times* barred women from its Antioch co-op job running copy, so I took the one at *Newsweek*. *Newsweek* hired women to run copy, but denied them access to the training program provided for aspiring male writers. Alas, I was an aspiring female writer. I did not respond with indignation, only with a deepening sense of inferiority. Then, that spring, a month after my twenty-second birthday, I was beaten up and raped by a violent stranger. My sense of self had been shrinking. At this point it disintegrated.

In the sixties I knew, successful women were successful at pleasing men. People saw female professionals, particularly if unmarried, as failures in the womanhood department. I remember hearing sneering noises about bluestockings even at the radical place Antioch College was. I remember groups of men ranking the passing women according to degree of femininity. Reading my own journal of my nineteenth year (1961), I find that I myself believed the most important task confronting a woman was to make herself beautiful.

As college graduation approached, I vacillated insanely between the twin poles of love and work. Love won. Not the thing itself but the hope for it, the idea of it. It corroded my ambition as a writer, corroded any possibility of a career as a historian (I had majored in history). I decided not to go on to graduate school after college because, I reasoned, I wanted to get married.

In 1965, after keeping a journal for seven years, I concluded that I had nothing to say. I gave up writing in my journal, not resuming until 1969. Thus I became invisible even to myself. I didn't know what I do now, that everyone has something to say, that you write to find out what it is. I didn't see how the culture was erasing me, or how I was joining it to silence myself.

The women's movement did not come a minute too soon. At our first collective meeting, in the spring of 1969, I said something about the importance of "loving relationships." There was a discussion about kittens (not on the agenda). Thinking about the position of women in society was new to us: that spring we floundered from topic to topic. (It is startling to remember that the first issue of *Ms.* was three years away.) The theme of sex roles percolated constantly in our conversations. (Peter and I began negotiating over who would cook, who would wash dishes.) Some of us began taking an interest in automobile mechanics, in light sockets and plumbing fixtures. Others in Boston began working on reproductive rights and on violence against women (a subject upon which I was too traumatized to speak). Slowly, women began entering trades like printing and construction, and professions like medicine and law.

We all believed in day care, that society shared responsibility for children. I myself initiated a free Wednesday afternoon playgroup for three- and four-year-olds, starting with kids in the neighborhood. I loved the kids and I loved being good with kids. But I also see my little playgroup in a darker light. I was always willing to provide a social service, to take up an organizational task. I never said no, I never put myself first. I was reliable, responsible, cheerful, always willing to help. Rather than pursuing creative goals or career goals, I invariably put the community before myself.

Even after I began seriously to work at writing, including daily practice, studying grammar books, taking a night course in writing the sentence, another in writing the paragraph, others in poetry, in fiction, and so on, I persisted in putting the community first, in helping others to edit their work instead of writing, in leafleting or stuffing envelopes or making phone calls instead of writing. What I got back from political activism over the years was community, the love of friends and comrades, respect, admiration, appreciation, recognition. Besides, in social activism I, an atheist, was living out the strong sense of morality I'd gotten from my deeply religious family background. In contrast, writing was a pleasure, done for myself, selfish. It was a long time before I could put it first.

Our women's collective helped to start the Boston women's organization, Bread and Roses, and we became the outreach committee. We spoke to classes and meetings. We gave little talks with facts and charts showing how women were paid 60 percent of the wages of men. We argued that the prevailing images of women as emotional, sexual, and illogical and of men as rational, nonsexual, and logical served discrimination. All of this was news to everyone. We presented our talk to a Harvard class on the family and it was like throwing a lit match into dry straw: the students ranted and raged at each other for the rest of the semester.

I also continued doing my part to stop the war. I was arrested at a demonstration at Boston University to block Marine recruiting there. At the trial we defendants watched policeman after policeman lie under oath about what had occurred. Our case was dismissed after the judge viewed an amateur film that showed the police beating us up rather than the other way around. We enacted this drama and its legal aftermath with an almost euphoric sense of camaraderie among ourselves, men and women. But in general the antiwar movement was shaken to the core by the emergence of feminist consciousness in its ranks. One particular organizational meeting found the men sitting on one side of the room and the women on the other. We carried out the agenda at the top of our lungs. (The issues were condescending attitudes on the part of the male leaders, male chauvinism, and the question of who would lead and who would do the shit-work.)

In the women's movement I discovered women artists, women writers, women political figures. But, ironically enough, it was Peter who asked one day in 1970, "Why don't you write a biography of Mother Jones?" Fascinated by this white-haired, charismatic organizer of coal miners, I began the research, remembering my love of libraries, the silence, the musty smell of old books. The voices of the past became as real to me as anything in the present. I noted in minute detail everything from evolving technology to labor struggles, gathered in my compulsive net every glimpse of the women of the coalfields. I floundered in the material for years before I began to grasp it. Eventually I wrote not a biography, but a history of coal mining.

In 1970 various Bread and Roses women formed a women's history group, and I added these meetings to those of my women's collective. In the history group each of us was researching or writing some aspect of women's history or feminist criticism. Our discussions and discoveries in making visible the past experience of women became pleasurable, at times thrilling. It was exhilarating to learn of women like Sojourner Truth, who delivered her great speech "Ain't I a Woman?" to the first women's rights convention in 1848; women like the anarchist Emma Goldman; the suffragists Elizabeth Cady Stanton and Susan B. Anthony.

We had not grown up with these names; they were new to us and provided new models on which to shape our own lives.

Eventually the young scholars in our group—Lise Vogel, Ellen DuBois, MariJo Buhle, Linda Gordon, Maureen Greenwald, Sharon Strom, Lillian Robinson, Meredith Tax, Linda Hunt, among others—would publish their now well-known books. We took pleasure in our community of women, basked in a new sense of self-worth, carried out our newfound work with a prideful sense of its historical significance. In some ways I enjoyed more genuine friendship in the history group than in my original women's collective. Still, for all the worthwhile work we did together, we did not inevitably form bonds of "sisterhood," as we myopically believed. There were no guarantees against competitive hostility, against confidences betrayed. Indeed, our very concept of sisterhood was rather idealized, as if among real sisters competition does not exist along with love and attachment.

In 1971, I began teaching women's history in a university extension program. For two semesters I took sixty hours each week to research lectures on subjects like sexuality in the nineteenth century; women in the labor movement; a history of household technology. The hundreds of books we now have on such subjects had yet to be written: preparing the lectures and delivering them to my warmly appreciative class (all women, mostly older than myself) stands as one of the thrilling intellectual experiences of my life.

In my historical research, as in my life, I was drawn to working-class life. My father, the dairyman on a 350-acre farm, had worked himself to the bone for his dream of a farm of his own, a goal he never achieved. My sisters and brother and I had grown up driving tractors, feeding calves, and milking cows, but we ended up enamored of cities. Perhaps because our parents believed strongly in education and read to us constantly throughout childhood, we took pride in our intellectual interests. As we grew older we increasingly wanted out of farm life. My mother got us out, but that left my father empty-handed.

Years later, without fully realizing it, I was still carrying his values and his wounds, and it was no simple matter to set them aside to pursue a professional career, whether intellectual or creative. In this attachment to the world of my childhood, and to my father, I was living out one of the dynamics of American working-class history: the cultural and psychological complications of upward mobility. Money represents opportunity but lack of money is not the only problem. In a submerged way that I couldn't have explained, I sensed that upward mobility would amount to betrayal of my father.

This conflict hovered somewhere near the center of my life, but because it had not emerged into full consciousness, I could not articulate it in my women's collective. For other reasons as well, our self-revelations could be less than totally revealing. We looked for common experiences, and ignoring anything that could divide us, we did not explore experiences relating to class.

I had strong intellectual interests, but I hadn't been raised to pursue professional goals. My mother began a Ph.D. at age thirty-one, but out of economic insecurity persistently urged me to attend secretarial school. By the time I turned thirty in 1973 I tended to view professionals, including a few good friends, as privileged beings whose experiences were about as similar to mine as hang gliding is to shoveling coal.

By the early seventies the economy was beginning its decline from the affluent sixties, when rent was cheap and jobs were abundant. The activist community, possibly the only place in society where people of all classes mixed as equals, began to show cracks, as some people undertook or continued training for professional endeavors and others began to slip into less well-paid paths, paths their class backgrounds had perhaps inadvertently prepared them for. There was the hidden reality, the taboo subject, that some political activists had resources (trust funds, inheritances, or just affluent parents ready to help with the down payment on a house) while others did not.

In progressive circles, admiration for working-class life was strong. Activists from such backgrounds felt pride in their connections to working-class experience, whereas those from middle-class backgrounds often felt an anxious sort of guilt. The two groups coexisted without communication. In a kind of shadow theater, many middle-class activists began or continued preparations to advance in professional careers or in other ways to secure their financial futures.

During periods of political activism, like the thirties or the sixties, working people tend to be honored, respected, given their due. During periods of reaction, like the eighties, they are disparaged. In one way, my own pride in my connections to working-class life was not misplaced. It was this sense of pride, writ large, that gave us the turn to a more comprehensive history of working-class communities and struggles, not to mention women's studies, black studies, and so on. It was this sense of pride that fueled my study of coal mining, year after year.

Yet I along with many activists from working-class backgrounds—especially but not only women—had no concept of working in my own self-interest. I may have been a sturdy, cheerful, intelligent person, but my self-confidence in arenas that required striving for achievement in competition with others was nonexistent. I dreaded competition in part because I'd lost the competition for my parents' affection and, during my black-sheep years, could do nothing right in their eyes. At the same time, I was very good at, say, hawking newspapers on the street. The problem with my dream of being a writer was that my writing had yet to emerge from utter mediocrity. Minimum-wage jobs—telephone clerk, cleaning woman, artist's model, filling orders for Rounder Records—these brought in enough money to live, as today they would not. They required little thought and no risk of failure.

Numerous activists—mostly but not only men, mostly but not only the offspring of professional fathers if not mothers—understood what I did not: that a person could work for herself in ways that didn't oppose, that might even serve, the interests of the community. They pursued their careers while also contributing to the work of social change. I see now that in periods of political activism the possibility exists for discussion and learning between these two groups. No one should be hired for a low-paid staff position in a movement office without a discussion about their plans, savings, aspirations, opportunities, resources. A related discussion ought to be an ongoing part of activist culture: how to contribute to social change and also take care of oneself; how to develop abilities that will serve the community but also satisfy personal aspirations and ambitions.

In my women's collective in 1969 or 1970, we began systematically presenting our autobiographies. Certain vivid moments in our stories remain in mind. One woman, who was pregnant, a friend we thought we knew well, revealed that this would be her second child, that as a teenager she'd given up her first for adoption. Another woman, Anna, a single graduate student in her late twenties, showed us her family album of photographs. I had a complex moment of revelation: that a single person could surround herself with silverware and photo albums; could, in a word, make a home for herself. Marcia, the mother of a little boy, spoke mainly of her mediocre marriage, which, however, was held together by the couple's passionate sex life consisting entirely of anal intercourse. When she realized that she alone among us enjoyed this pleasure, her story ground to a halt and after a moment of shocked surprise, she exclaimed, "You don't know what you're missing!"

My own autobiography embarrassed me acutely. I spoke of the farm; of rust stains on our clothes from the water pipes; of canning and freezing and plowing; of how cold the farmhouse was our first winter in Maryland. I spoke of my parents' angry quarrel, which had continued throughout my childhood. From our farm background my twin sister and I attended, with the aid of large scholarships, Moravian Seminary for Girls, where we were popular and highly regarded despite certain discrepancies between ourselves and others. (We washed our hair with dish detergent, they with shampoo.)

Now it is easy to mention all these matters, but as I told my story to my women's collective it did not seem to add up to a woman's experience. It didn't add up to anything that I could grasp, and at one point during my presentation I disintegrated into hysterical giggling. None of us knew what to make of my experiences feeding the pig, or my puzzlement, in boarding school, over the method by which people determined precisely on which day they were dirty enough to take a bath. (The system of bathing every day, dirty or not, came to me as a revelation.) In my case, what we did *not* share was simply greater than what we *did* share. The most perceptive comment on my autobiography was, "What are we to make of this Ma and Pa Kettle story?" It was a great relief when several months later Meredith Tax, a key Bread and Roses organizer, called together a subgroup of women from working-class backgrounds to talk about *that* experience.

In my women's collective, we ruminated at length on the subject of monogamy. Was monogamy oppressive to women, a relic of the time when a married woman was her husband's property? Was free love, love given or withheld without regard to convention or legality, more liberating to women? On this topic our level of abstraction zoomed up to the stratosphere. We began, I think, not with our own lives but with Frederick Engels' *The Family, Private Property, and the State*. Also, we were great admirers and probably romanticizers of Emma Goldman, the turn-of-the-century anarchist and believer in free love. We did not have Alice Wexler's biography to inform us that Goldman's love affairs were fraught with pain. We did not understand the importance of self-esteem and how it affects a person's relationships, monogamous or not. This discussion was no doubt a stepping stone to the idea that a woman's body belongs to herself alone, but I myself don't remember actually coming to that thought at the time. It probably also marked the beginning of a cultural shift that widened the room for women outside of marriage.

What were our real relations with men? I am speaking here of heterosexual women. Certainly, it was a time of fairly extensive sleeping around, a time when couples who remained monogamous were not proclaiming the fact from the rooftops.

To what extent did we who were heterosexual continue to focus our need for love and recognition exclusively on our relationships with husbands and lovers while repudiating the world as a source of the same? I am thinking of a friend who received a major prize from her university and calmly declined to attend the ceremony to receive it. And I was honored, in response to an essay I'd written on Mother Jones, by a simple but heartfelt letter of support from a leading scholar in my field. I was pleased but did not bother to answer. Another friend, a visual artist, hid her work out of sight for years. Here was the world, offering support, love, praise, honor, recognition. Here were we, turning it down. Did we then crave such recognition all the more from the men around us?

In the midst of the elaborate discussion on monogamy taking place in my women's collective, my husband and I became nonmonogamous. He became involved with another woman, and I became involved with first one man, then another, then another. On my side, this arrangement did not work out according to my fantasies. At the time, my clandestine longing was to be married to two husbands, one of them Peter. Since then I have wondered whether my relative lack of jealousy was connected to low expectations for myself. I've wondered whether the situation recapitulated my childhood, in which I was one of several closely spaced children who got virtually no individual attention.

Peter and I were fiercely attached to one another, but at the same time our relationship left a lot to be desired. He had emerged from prison angry, the legacy of more than two years of daily humiliation, including the sexual harassment of the strip check. He was ambitious, brilliant, and frustrated because years behind on his career. We had our tender moments, but all too often he took out his rage on me, never physically, but in a barrage of hostile, derogatory commentary. To complicate matters, I did not understand his drive to succeed, and did nothing to support his ambitions. He in turn felt annoyed at my downwardly mobile tendency. Both shame and my intense loyalty to Peter precluded my ever mentioning our difficulties in my women's collective.

I found myself stumbling into the saddest period of my life, a time of brief love affairs and low-paid work. Still, I continued to work on writing and on researching the coal industry. I continued, but in a state of hopelessness, compulsively taking notes on a vast subject that seemed to grow more vast by the day.

At the age of thirty I took a job as a cleaning lady. I was employed by Maid for a Day, a company that drove you to the house to be cleaned and picked you up six hours and twelve dollars later. My first house stands as my first experience of real suburbia. I was let off at a prim ranch house with a flagstone walk curving to the front door. The woman of the house greeted me pleasantly and gave me instructions before going out.

I began to clean a spotlessly clean house. The toilet was pristine, without ring. The bathtub gleamed like an advertisement. I was supposed to dust, but there was no dust. I vacuumed the carpets without pleasure, no gritty clicking sounds in the hose. I fell into a state of anxiety, for I had no idea how to clean an immaculate house for six hours. Perhaps she would return to watch me going through these sham motions. My sense of values was offended. I had been brought up to work hard, I had always worked hard. I saw I was being hired not to clean but to enhance some other woman's status. Moreover, the house was aesthetically repulsive, decorated in beige timidity and bland convention. It contained nothing beautiful, nothing interesting, not a single book. It was none of my business to have these thoughts as I dusted the gleaming furniture, but I did have them. I felt, not empathy for this woman's apparently vacuous existence, not sisterhood, but pure, scandalized hostility.

Within the women's movement, sisterhood was in better but not perfect condition. By 1971, rifts had developed between lesbians and heterosexuals, between radical feminists and socialist feminists, which, generally speaking, we in Bread and Roses were. Moreover, women from varying cultural backgrounds such as Jewish feminists and black feminists began to feel the need to explore their own experiences as distinct from those of other women. The movement had begun with the notion of the common oppression of women; without renouncing that framework, increasingly we began to recognize the diversity of women's experiences. I did not understand (as I do now) that diversity does not preclude empathy, that empathy is quite possible across vastly different backgrounds.

In 1971 our original woman's collective fell apart in the following bizarre manner. First, two of our members became lovers. One of them, Charlotte, was married, the mother of an infant; the other, Libby, was single. Next Libby began sleeping with Charlotte's husband. (Or perhaps this happened in a different order.) For a few weeks both women extolled the benefits of triangular domestic arrangements. After which Libby formed a monogamous relationship with Charlotte's husband, leaving Charlotte to a life of single motherhood. Charlotte remained a lesbian.

At the same time, political differences were pulling apart our umbrella women's organization, Bread and Roses. A split developed between women who felt that sex inequality constituted the main contradiction in society as against those who felt that it was class inequality. Obviously I was on the class side. Neither position excluded the other entirely but the different emphases resulted in different strategies: the center could not hold. Both Bread and Roses and my women's collective fell apart, but of course feminism was here to stay.

My history group continued meeting for another couple of years. It typified the women's movement in Boston, which now tended to re-form around specific projects: organizing secretaries; a women's center; the *Our Bodies/Ourselves* project; a study group on mother-daughter relations that included sociologists Barrie Thorne and Nancy Chodorow; a shelter for battered women, and so on.

As my women's collective was breaking up in 1971, Peter and I began living separately, which we continued to do for five years. His career began percolating quite nicely and at the same time he struggled to become the generous and sweet man he is. We ended up married for 20 years. I cannot here relate the saga of Peter and me except to say that, now divorced, we remain close friends.

I learned the printing trade and became (in late 1973) a co-founder of Red Sun Press, a collectively run printshop that did commercial printing while contributing to community and social-change efforts including, of course, feminist efforts. I continued working on my research and writing, getting up at five each morning to write before I left for work.

The women's movement was full of contradictions, as we used to say, old ways conflicting with the new both within ourselves and among ourselves. It could not have been otherwise. As it turned out, sisterhood was not as powerful as we liked to think. Even so, our accomplishments were utterly transforming. Who can imagine, at this point, the virtual exclusion of women and people of color from the medical, legal, and academic professions, or from the printing trade or the plumbing trade? Who can imagine a return to an era when violence against women was unquestioned? Certainly, we have a long way to go, especially to achieve structural social and economic changes that offer the possibility of a decent life for all women. But our work—along with that of others—is everywhere evident. And contrary to the stereotype of sixties activists selling out to Wall Street, each of us—my source here is the grapevine—continues to do one thing or another to further the cause of equality for women.

A Fem's Feminist History

Joan Nestle

The Lesbian Herstory Archives was born on a shore washed by two oceans—the old sea of Greenwich Village bar nights and working-class butch-fem communities and the younger sea of fierce lesbian feminism. In 1973, when a group of us from the newly founded Gay Academic Union formed a consciousness-raising group, these two bodies of experience were well represented. Julia Penelope and I from the old days, Deborah Edel and Pamela Oline from the new.

Sitting in that group, I already felt like a seasoned veteran of lesbian feminism even though it had been only two years since my entry into the gay activist movement via the old Firehouse on Wooster Street and its resident tenant, the Gay Activist Alliance. We, the lesbians in GAA, had already formed the Lesbian Liberation Committee, which would eventually turn into Lesbian Feminist Liberation, the oldest lesbian feminist group in the country. I had already been part of a Marxist-feminist study group, the only lesbian present, and for a brief time, a feminist artists group. Groups formed quickly in the early seventies, allowing for a cohesive theoretical and political community.

That cohesiveness, however, that forward-looking, solidified code of behavior and perception demanded from old-time lesbians like myself a certain kind of amnesia. Having emerged in 1958 into the public lesbian bar community as a young fem woman, I had behind me a decade of lesbian living and loving that formed a complex sense of self—criminal, erotic, independent, exiled. I knew what I liked in bed and I pursued the butch women who welcomed my desire. I played with dildos and loved penetration. I was queer and a fem, and a fem was not the same as a woman.

I quickly learned in the early lesbian feminist groups that this past of mine was not a valued contribution, that, in fact, it embodied the enemy, but I was offered something in return, a cultural exchange—feminism for fem, woman for queer. Suddenly the stigma of deviancy was lifted, and the pain of being a freak—the legacy of the medical world of the fifties—went into hiding. Another history took its place—the legacy of patriarchy, the cross-cultural, eternal oppression of women. This 1970s anger and solidarity of response, the shared communal moments in darkened theaters and women's centers, the growing acceptance of our own abilities and our anger at men—gay and straight, who seemed not to understand that a new paradigm was being born—all made possible the birth of the Lesbian Herstory Archives, a feminist undertaking by lesbians who wanted to control their own stories. These stories reflect the layering of consciousness that is lived history; my own story is an example of this.

One summer night in 1971, lesbian feminism walked into my fem life in a very concrete way. It was the weekend, and I was sitting at a round table in Kookie's, a bar for lesbians that had been holding sway on 14th Street on the outskirts of New York's Greenwich Village for a few years. Larger and flashier than my old hangout, the Sea Colony on Abingdon Square, this gathering place boasted of red patterned wallpaper, low hanging chandeliers of cheap tinkling glass, and a large dance floor. Kookie herself strode around the floor, blond hair teased high, keeping track of how fast we emptied our glasses. One night she had stopped at my table and shoved her pinky into my glass to suggest I needed another drink. Kookie was a businesswoman, and we were her trade.

But this was the beginning of the seventies, not the late fifties when I had entered public gay life by finding the world of lesbian bars strung out along the narrow streets of Greenwich Village. Dark and dangerous, haunted by the police, these bars were places that we carved into homes, homes where we found touch and friends and learned about how to be a queer in the late McCarthy period of this country. Butch and fem women in their forties and fifties carried their worldly ways to us here. The bar was a delta, gathering the richness of lesbian experience on its smoky shores. Here we met women who proved in their stances and in their stories that social isolation could be borne, that familial rejection could be outlived, that the state with its sexual policing laws could be outwitted. Here we also learned the terror of bar raids and the limits of an outlaw geography.

As the fifties shifted into the sixties, the police that I had grown accustomed to confronting in the Village bars became the state troopers of Baltimore and Alabama; the mounted troops of Washington, D.C., became the carefully dressed undercover FBI agents snapping our photographs at every demonstration. Active in the civil rights, antiwar, antinuclear armament movements, I had become experienced in confronting the more decorous face of the armed forces of the state. I was just beginning to see the connections between these liberation struggles and my own fem life; I had even begun to believe that "freaks" such as us deserved to live our lives without constant terror of disclosure or attack.

But that night in Kookie's I was sitting at my table, putting my desire before my social knowledge, just wanting to be with the community I had known for over ten years. Hunched over my drink, making desultory conversation while my skin picked up every movement around me, I suddenly heard the sounds of a demonstration, a sound I knew so well but never thought to hear in this world, the lesbian bar. I looked up to see a group of young women, dressed in jeans and flannel shirts waving flyers in Kookie's face while she shoved them toward the door. I watched as from a distance; how could this be happening in my outlaw world? These were women, not police; what was the nature of their invasion?

This is how feminism entered my world, forcing me to bring together what I had learned from the two previous decades: that desire, even policed desire, could create worlds, and that political communities could change worlds.

I found out later that the young women were members of the Gay Liberation Front, and the leaflets were about the meetings that were going on regularly at a retired firehouse on Wooster Street. Up to this point, the Women's Liberation Movement had seemed irrelevant to me. I had been working since I was thirteen, living on my own since I was eighteen, and trying to come to terms with a mother, the only parent I had ever known, who had worked every day of her adult life and who had too many lovers to keep track of. I was a queer, a fem, a self-taught socialist who flourished in the streets many other women were afraid of—the Women's Liberation Movement as represented by Betty Friedan or Gloria Steinem and even at times by Kate Millett was a world away. How could I join forces with this middle-class, highly educated, self-confident group of women without betraying the women I had known in the bars—the long-haired prostitute; the struggling hairdresser; the passing woman; the hard-working, hard-living butches who became all courtly gestures when in pursuit of a woman, and finally, without betraying myself, a yearning independent fem woman?

But I had learned from other social movements to recognize that special moment when change opens a door, when one's home has grown too narrow and one's needs too big, when a revised social vision offers the deepest political gift, a healing to wounds that have sunk so far below the surface they feel like breath. I had to follow the trail of those leaflets, just as I had to follow the short-haired butchy woman I had met in Pam Pam's in 1958 to the door of the Sea Colony. I had to find the cobblestone street in front of the firehouse, I had to meet the women who said, "The personal is political." Something was dawning in me, another way to understand the experiences of my young life. My personal life, the way I loved, had made me the target of hatred and had engendered deep shame in me, and yet I also had been strengthened beyond my years by that same love. I understood in my bones that the choices we made or thought we made were complex meeting grounds of class and, in my case, desire. On the way out of the bar, I picked up a fallen leaflet and tucked it into my pocket.

The next month found me at the weekly meeting of the Gay Activist Alliance, a militant gay civil rights group that had started to have public meetings in 1970 in the aftermath of the Stonewall Rebellion in 1969 and was known for its chaotic meetings and for its direct street actions, or zaps as we called them. That night I stood pressed against the stone wall of the jammed first floor of the firehouse. All the wooden chairs were taken, mostly by white young men in tie-dyed T-shirts and long ponytails. Some of them I would come to know—Arnie Kantrowitz, Marc Rubin, Jim Owles, Morty Manfred, Arthur Bell. Our attention that night was focused on the raised platform that served as a stage and the heated discussion that was taking place. I saw Nath Rockhill, a solid smart woman, that night, and Ginny Vida, a stalwart organizer and zap participant. A few other women were scattered around the room, looking very different from the women I had known in the bars; they were dressed for action not allure: flannel shirts, jeans, and work boots.

Later that night I heard the first discontented murmurings of the women who called themselves lesbian feminists: "We need our own space." While we participated in the weekly mass meetings and in the spontaneous protest marches, we also met in a small group to plan women-only events. We did this sitting in a circle, a geometric form I was going to become very familiar with as feminist consciousness-raising groups became more and more a part of my life. In many similar meetings around the country, lesbians were exploring the possibilities of separatism, first as a necessary step to winning autonomous physical spaces and then, influenced by the decolonizing ideas of Black nationalism, as an expression of a theoretical stance of self-inheritance.

One evening at such a meeting, I had to face the consequences of walking through the door I had chosen. Two older women with gray hair worn in the butch DA style had ventured into the meeting. They pulled up two of the wooden folding chairs resting against the wall and joined the group, sitting in its outer ring. I turned toward them, feeling the wind of the bars at my back, torn between them and the new friends I had made. As the meeting progressed, I left to go downstairs to use the bathroom and stood in line behind two of the younger women from the group.

"Did you see those two gray-haired women who just walked in?" one said to her companion. "Why do they have to look like men? I hope they don't come back."

Those women never did, and I did not speak up for them in 1971 because I wanted so desperately to be part of the new world of lesbian feminism, and I hadn't yet learned from feminism how to honor its principles by valuing my own stigmatized life and those who shared it with me. What I was learning, however, was that our rallying cry, "the personal is political," was a double-edged sword, promising both liberation and punishment.

In our monthly meetings, I met women like Ginny Apuzzo and Jeanne O'Leary, none of whom shared my bar-days history. I was amazed at their ambitions, their unfettered claims to positions of power, even the small world of power that the Firehouse represented. In those days, I often felt like an immigrant trying to become a citizen of a new country. The stigma of sexual deviancy as I had known it was so heavy that I had never thought about the stigma of being a woman. Only once, ten years before, did I remember their coming together in a way so clear I could not avoid seeing the connection.

In 1962, I was a senior at Queens College, an English major who had to take the dreaded written comprehensive exam to graduate. I stayed home from the bars that weekend, took amphetamines and prepared for the challenge. During the exam, I became the sexually deviant rebel who loved literature. I wrote for myself, and every answer was a letter of gratitude to the authors for what they had given me, for the worlds of lyrical beauty and psychological complexity that my own life had been too bleak and too hectic to embody. When I was finally told the news, by a woman professor, that I had passed with distinction, the only one to do so, she said in glowing praise, "Because of how the essay was written, we all thought the author was a man—you write like a man." Even in my exhausted state, I knew that my victory had been tainted. These words echoed in my head. If she only knew I was queer, I thought. Maybe when I was smart, I was not a woman.

As I read over the words I have written so far, I understand so much more about why I needed feminism, perhaps more than many. As a working-class young woman, I just assumed things to be my destiny—like subordination, like marginal survival. And the world I moved in—before the seventies—had reflected that back to me, even the world of political activism of which I was a part. Until I started to meet with other women, without men present, I had never been able to be more than a silent and respectful observer. This is why I was so awed by the directness of the young women I was meeting in those early days of lesbian feminism.

I decided early on to join the ranks of the newly emerging lesbian feminist movement in New York as it evolved from these Firehouse days, not because of its leaders but because of the moments of community it created. First we formed the Lesbian Liberation Committee, still meeting under the auspices of GAA. Our first goal was to increase the presence of women at the Firehouse. We asked the men for one day when the second floor would be a women-only space. This was the first expression of separatism in the New York community, and it was fueled both by a practical organizing sense and a growing theoretical understanding that negotiating around male power, even gay male power, wasted too much lesbian feminist energy, and that our agendas for social action were not always the same.

Thus were launched the famous Sunday afternoon gatherings. More lesbians than I had ever seen in one place—the bars were small—gathered outside the huge open doors on Wooster Street waiting for the two o'clock program. Transforming the bare stony space into a cabaret, we would arrive early enough to cover the tables with checkered tablecloths, putting a candle on each table and making sure the reedy sound system on the small raised platform that passed for a stage was ready. Then we each took up our allotted tasks to make sure the afternoon

went smoothly. Several times I worked in the kitchen, cleaning and filling the huge coffee and tea urns. What I saw through the partition of
the kitchen wall was a new world being born. Women in their movement uniforms of flannel shirts, pants, work boots—laughing, talking,
clapping as performers like Kay Gardner or Alix Dobkin sat on that little stage giving their all. Sometimes there were panels, newly created
experts from our own ranks, discussing sexuality or separatism or their
mothers. My own mother made her way to the Firehouse on one afternoon, to sit with other parents, some of whom cried as their lesbian
feminist daughters proudly claimed their right to love women. While I
felt none of the sexual tension in that room that I had thrived on in the
bars, I did feel a rationality of self and purpose, a political cohesiveness,
an openness that cleared my head and heart. After twenty years, I still
can feel the sun shining on that street, hear the shouts of greetings, see
my new comrades in their bib overalls, breasts hanging free, the Firehouse doors wide open waiting for us to enter.

From these Sunday afternoons came the strength and determination to break away from GAA completely and form an autonomous lesbian organization: Lesbian Feminist Liberation, a group that still exists,
hosting thousands of lesbians at its yearly Gay Pride Dance. Here in this
separate space, lesbians lived out the tenets of "The Woman-Identified
Woman," the Radicalesbian position paper that became the anthem of
the seventies. "What is a lesbian? A lesbian is the rage of all women con-
densed to the point of explosion," read its opening blast. Back in 1958,
my driving need had been desire; the public lesbian feminist stance of
the early 1970s demanded both less and more of me.

Still, an understanding started to form in me, a nebulous cloud of
possible connections between sexuality, class, feminism, and my fem self.
So, I became part of the first wave of lesbian feminist consciousness-
raising groups. The groups were numbered, the first having the stars—
women like Kate Millett, Alma Routsong, Jill Johnston—and then came
the troops, working their way down the ranks. Once a week, my group,
number 5, met in one of our homes to discuss a personal topic that had a
politic embedded in it. Friendships, sex, mothers, coming out, work—
every week we went around our circle speaking as women about our lesbian lives. For the next five years, I learned to learn with other women in
a variety of CR groups: a Marxist-feminist group, a Gay Academic Union
lesbian CR group—out of which the Lesbian Herstory Archives would be

born. These groups were emotional and dramatic, sometimes funny, sometimes overwhelming. I learned new ways of seeing my woman's life, new understandings of gender oppression, a new language, but I also learned the boundaries beyond which the politic could not go. So—as I said to begin with—we could talk about sex, but not about penetration, not about dildos, not about butch-femme, not about desire. We could talk about our work, but not about class as it expressed itself in the groups, most of which were dominated by middle-class women.

These silences were made to be broken, however, by the insights of feminism itself. While I was learning to value women for perhaps the first time in my life, I was also chafing at the new code of decorum. More and more I resented the severing of my old fem lesbian life from the consideration and respect of the new era. I realized that my experience as a sexual deviant had given me insights into certain issues like pornography, prostitution, and gender questioning that while not the prevailing ones in the lesbian feminist seventies and eighties were too important to be buried.

In the 1950s, lesbian sexual desire had been my politic. Nothing else could have armored a young working-class woman against the loss of such certitudes as marriage and motherhood. Now as I moved through my job, as I walked my streets, as I tried to jettison my self-hatreds, feminism—the feminist understanding of how a "woman" is constructed in our society—became an indispensable ally to me. My challenge then became to bring desire, fem desire, and the clear sight of feminist analysis into the same room.

The way I chose to do this was through the use of history, my own and my community's. In 1966, I had started teaching in the SEEK Program at Queens College. In order to be the best teacher I could, I started to read books on colonization, the cultural experience of my students whether they were African-American or Puerto Rican—the two communities of young people whose street rebellions had brought the program into existence. (Ironically, the bar in which I had perfected my fem ways, and in which I had met the forces of the state, was called the Sea Colony.)

One evening, after a long day of teaching, in our lesbian feminist group, Julia Penelope [Stanley] and I began reminiscing about the lesbian past, a subject we would come to look at in very different ways; we had known each other in the "old days," the bar, butch-fem days, and we had a sense of the fragility of lesbian culture, how easily each generation's markings had been swept away. "You know," I remember her saying, "just because we have our own presses now [Daughters, Diana] doesn't mean that patriarchy will allow us to exist."

At about the same time, in 1974, I read a book by Albert Memmi, *The Colonizer and the Colonized,* which contained the sentence, "The colonized are condemned to lose their memory." This sentence kept coming back to me as we drafted the early principles of the archives collective. Memmi's concept and my whole life became part of a resistant personalized fem feminism that was expressed in my work with the Lesbian Herstory Archives, that lived in the apartment I shared with my lover, Deborah Edel. Deborah, who had come out into lesbian feminism, and I had become lovers in 1975, and though our "married" relationship ended eleven years later, our commitment to the archives never has. I realize now that our relationship was a living bridge between the two worlds of resistance—queer fem street survival and lesbian feminist tenacity.

The archives, in its material sense, had a very humble beginning: ten milk crates containing the combined personal donations of the women in the CR group and some international lesbian journals were emptied onto wooden shelves in a small room in our Upper West Side apartment. For twenty years, the collection grew and grew, taking over more and more of the apartment, giving a home to cherished stories of lesbian life told in a myriad of ways, to the thousands of women who came to use the collection's resources, and to myself as well. I, too, had found a home, a home for all the different personal and political parts of my life, for my woman self and for my lesbian self—which were not always the same thing and certainly did not always share the same history—but both had been reshaped by the dignity of feminism.

Feminism as it lived in Deborah gave me the gift of revisiting the red-lit backroom and the young fem girl who had walked late-night city streets to find her lovers. She held me while I made my way back into the pain of being called a freak. She worked tirelessly to sustain the symbol of my historical and psychological unification—the archives. Feminism as it lived in my chosen friends inspired me to enter a public debate about the complexity of lesbian desire. Feminism, because it was a source of ideas about the body, about socially constructed selves, about the shifting outlines of class, race, sex, and gender, became my queer theory twenty years before the 1990s academic version.

When I gave tours of the ever-expanding collection to the hundreds of visitors who came by every year, I could piece together a lesbian history I could live with, one where a Lavender Menace T-shirt worn by a woman protesting NOW's intolerance of lesbians in 1971 shared a shelf with the pasties of a lesbian stripper from the fifties; where a pair of hobnailed boots and a hard hat bearing a lambda, the insignia of the gay rights movement, the gifts of a lesbian woman who had worked in the Buffalo steel mills in the late sixties and early seventies, lived in the same room as photographs of Eleanor Roosevelt and her lesbian friends from the 1930s. I would pull out photographs of butch and fem women from decades past and show them to young women still exploring their sexuality. Without denying the present-day lesbian feminist movement, I could honor the differences of the past and make living connections to the present. Finally, I had found a way to bring my own meaning to the words that had enticed me, "the personal is political."

In the 1980s, I began to write about the old days. Strengthened by ten years of lesbian feminist involvement and my work with the archives, I let the memories of my freak time, of my street time, of my taxi driver and whore time, of bouffant hairdos and the fish time, of DAs and pinky rings, of vice squad raids and bathroom lines, of hips raised on pillow days, of "let's see what kind of a man you are" days, of my sun-coming-up-in-the-morning-as-we-emptied-into-the-street days come flooding through. The archives gave honor to my memories; it brought together old friends who had been waiting in the shadows of the new sun.

In 1981, my article entitled "Butch-Fem Relationships: Sexual Courage in the 50s" was published, after some debate, in the sexuality issue of *Heresies,* a journal exploring feminist culture.

The *Heresies* essay marked the beginning of my integrated feminist and lesbian public self. While I knew that butch-fem sexuality had been held in scorn for most of the early lesbian feminist years, I also knew that we needed to look at and understand our near-history. We needed to understand both the pleasures and the struggles of our sexual selves. We had spent a decade fighting on so many fronts—the reproductive rights struggle, the ERA battle, the anti–violence against women campaigns, the anti-imperialism movement, the never-ending effort to pass a gay civil rights bill in this city—that we had not had the time to look at a specific lesbian desire that had been a community's organizing principle before we had a movement. Knowing the courage it still took to be an open lesbian woman in the early 1980s, I naively thought this reclaiming of a past audacity would be an exhilarating moment of connection.

In 1982, at the Barnard Sexuality Conference (The Scholar and the Feminist IX: Toward a Politics of Sexuality), I learned that I had miscalculated the emotions with which the lesbian near-past would be greeted. The morning of the conference was bright with the coming of spring, but I approached the campus with trepidation. A swirl of phone calls the night before had alerted me to the storm of protest that had gathered over the conference, resulting in the pulling out of circulation of the conference's program, a wonderfully inventive booklet giving previews of the panels and bibliographic guides. Members of New York's Women Against Pornography had been infuriated at the scope of the discussion, at its inclusion of butch-fem and S/M "sexual perverts," as we had been labeled in one of the late-night telephone calls to the college. That morning I had to pass a picket line of women wearing black T-shirts proclaiming their position on pornography and handing out leaflets condemning the conference's inclusion of butch-fem and S/M sexuality. I had not known what a battle I was going to face, but ten years of feminism and twenty years of queerdom had given me the wisdoms I needed to pursue the vision of an inclusive women's history, a history calling on the lesbian body to speak its complex desires.

The Barnard conference in fact opened a whole terrain of unexplored sexualities that would become important in the discussions of the 1990s. But the Barnard conference also made the necessity of remembering our complex sexualities and our pasts clearly pertinent. For the repression of that conference brochure indicated how fragile and vulnerable were documents, artifacts, and analyses exploring sexuality. Once again, I was convinced of the importance of the archives project.

Now in 1996, the Lesbian Herstory Archives lives in its own home in the Park Slope section of Brooklyn, in a three-story limestone building bought by the contributions of all the different kinds of lesbians there are and others, too, gay men and straight mothers and fathers who want their children to be remembered. Twenty-two lesbian women coordinate its activities and often, when I am there, I have to be introduced to the new projects that they are working on. Some wear leather, some wear skirts, some wear jeans, all are younger than me and all call themselves feminists as well as many other things. Deborah and I sit at the meetings, she fifty-one, a feminist butch woman, and I fifty-six, a fem feminist, the co-founders of a lesbian cultural and research foundation that is entering its twenty-seventh self-possessed year, watching again the wonder of a lesbian and feminist dedication to re-imagine the world.

Days of Celebration and Resistance:
The Chicago Women's Liberation Rock Band, 1970–1973

Naomi Weisstein

In Chicago, one cold and sunny day in March of 1970, I decided to organize a feminist rock band. I was lying on the sofa listening to the radio—a rare bit of free time in those early hectic days of the women's movement. Perhaps a meeting had been canceled. First, Mick Jagger crowed that his once feisty girlfriend was now "under my thumb." Then Janis Joplin moaned with thrilled resignation that love was like "a ball and chain." Then the Band, a self-consciously left-wing group, sang:

Jemima surrender.
I'm gonna give it to you.

I somersaulted off the sofa, leapt up into the air, and came down howling at the radio: "Every fourteen-year-old girl in this city listens to rock! Rock is the insurgent culture of the era! How criminal to make the subjugation and suffering of women so sexy! We'll . . . we'll organize our own rock band!"

My epiphany was influenced by the fact that my closest friend, Virginia Blaisdell, had started playing in a feminist rock band in New Haven. Judy Miller, a fellow political activist in New Haven, decided that she wanted to play drums. She bought herself the glitziest, snazziest, light-blinking-on-and-off drum set she could find, and parked it on Virginia's doorstep. "Teach me how to play these things, and we'll start a rock band," she said.

But until that bright cold day in March I didn't think we could pull off a feminist rock band in Mayor Daley's brutally repressive Chicago.

Chicago was not a city you wanted to venture out in after dark, even to hear your favorite rock group. White Chicago was a scared, silent, violent balkanized city. It seethed with ethnic tensions. Rape was epidemic. Vivian Rothstein, co-founder of the Chicago Women's Liberation Union, told me that most women she knew in Chicago had been raped by a stranger, an unusual and chilling observation, since most rapists know their victims. Except for a couple of streets on the north fringes of Old Town, there were no "free spaces" like San Francisco's North Beach or New York's Greenwich Village, where a seriously dissenting culture might start to develop. One couldn't hold as much as a poetry reading without the Red Squad showing up.

But that day I said to myself, "Fuck it." If I were able to find musicians in a city where no family would teach their daughter "devil" instruments like drums and electric guitar, then I would form a rock band. If the police broke it up but didn't kill us, then it would just be good publicity. Why not?

Of course there was more to my desire to organize a rock band than this small epiphany on a cold sunny afternoon in Chicago. I wanted to form a rock band because I was dissatisfied with the state of feminist consciousness in the Chicago women's movement and, in particular, in the Chicago Women's Liberation Union (CWLU), the magnificent citywide umbrella organization that we had created, which nonetheless often placed its version of socialism ahead of feminism. For instance, a returnee from one of the Venceremos Brigades that went to Cuba to harvest sugar had described at a CWLU meeting how she preferred to cut cane with the Cuban men because the Cuban women were so "politically undeveloped." When I queried her preference, another CWLU'er whipped out her little red book and started quoting Mao Tse-tung. Some women at the meeting sighed with relief to see the problem so easily resolved. Watching this scenario unfold, I thought I was hallucinating. Where was the feminism?

The idea of direct cultural intervention in order to change consciousness was held in low esteem by most of the CWLU leadership at that time. This was due to another assumption we had inherited from the New Left, that if we changed the structures that maintain our oppression (such as if we won equal pay for equal work) consciousness would follow. I had started to disagree. Structural change is absolutely necessary if we are to overthrow our oppression, but it is not sufficient;

we also need to change our consciousness. Structure is the tip of the patriarchal iceberg. Submission gets inside our heads, and we're only going to get it out if we create alternatives to the dominant and dominating culture. We had to go through the culture, both mainstream and Left, with a fine-tooth comb, confronting everything from why we thought that a working-class revolution—indeed any revolution— was more important than a feminist revolution, all the way to why we believed, along with the mainstream culture, that male domination and a little bit of cruelty would always turn us on. We all identified with the counterculture; rock was considered "our music": dangerous, sexy, and our harbinger of the social changes to come. No matter that rock assaulted women more savagely than anything in popular culture before it; many of us lived cocooned in rock's sound, oblivious to, or even worse, delighting in, the message.

"What about rock?" I said to myself, boiling over with my new idea. Rock, with its drive, power, and energy, its insistent erotic rhythms, its big bright major triads, its take-no-prisoners chord progressions, was surely the kind of transforming medium that could introduce ecstatic feminism into our culture, and thus help us to change our consciousness.

The task would be to change the politics while retaining the impact. In subsequent weeks, while I looked around for musicians for the band, many people told me, some with huge sneers, that it couldn't be done. Rock was its own thing, they said, and you couldn't mess with it. "Art and politics don't mix," they said. I dismissed this. Rock was the preeminent theater of sexual politics; in this sense, rock was already deeply political. Moreover, as a red diaper baby, and the daughter of a musician mother, I had grown up on political art—not simply agit-prop, or socialist realism, but frontier creation. I loved Bertold Brecht and Kurt Weill's *Threepenny Opera* and Lenny Bruce's morally outraged prefeminist, anti-authoritarian and brilliant stand-up comedy. Coming from such a background, I thought that if you could pull off *both* the art and the politics, political art could be wonderful—liberating in itself. It was a thrill to contemplate trying to make feminist rock.

And so I organized the Chicago Women's Liberation Rock Band. My goals were much too ambitious—a common problem at the time—but the band turned out to be remarkably successful in achieving many of the goals. For starters, we actually got an effective group together. After the first shake-down months (at our debut performance in Grant Park in August of 1970, we had thirteen singers all bellowing happily to their individual muses), we grew into a distinctive troupe of hip, even talented, if inexperienced musicians. High school dropout Sherry Jenkins was our resident rock genius with her wonderful gravelly whiskey voice and lyrical lead guitar. There was no rhythm that our hippie rhythm guitarist Pat Solo, then Miller, couldn't master. She was also wildly comical. Bass guitarist Susan Abod was steeped in rock, if just starting out on the fret board. Both her bass line and her song lines were lyrical and inventive. Sanya Montalvo and Susanne Prescott provided a double drumming rhythm.[1] As for myself, I had seven years of classical training on the piano plus an additional two years of jazz piano. But my more important function as a performer in the band was to provide and direct theater and comedy, two areas in which I had some talent and experience.

Learning how to play a rock beat was our biggest problem, since most of us had gained our musical experience in classical or folk music. In addition, few of us had experience with ensemble playing. But we practiced, and we performed and we listened to each other's favorite groups.

We were explicitly, self-consciously political about our performances, while avoiding leaden sloganeering. To combat the fascism of the typical rock performance where the performers disdain audiences and the sound is turned up beyond human endurance, we were interactive with our audiences, rapping with them and asking them which songs they liked while keeping the sound level at a reasonable roar. We were playful, theatrical, and comical,[2] always attentive to performance. We sang "Poppa don't lay that shit on me," to the tune of the old-time dirty song, "Keep on Truckin', Mama," in carnival fashion, with slide whistles and whoops of derision, the audience laughing and singing along:

> *Poppa don't lay that shit on me,*
> *It just don't compensate.*

---

[1] Kathy Rowley and Stephanie Hirsh also performed with us for a while.
[2] For a discussion of humor and women, see Naomi Weisstein, "Why We Aren't Laughing Any More," *Ms.*, Nov. 1973: 49–51, 88–90.

Poppa don't lay that shit on me,
I can't accommodate.
You bring me down,
It makes you cool.
You think I like it?
You're a goddamn fool.
Poppa don't lay that shit on me . . .

(Virginia and I wrote this song during a visit I made to New Haven in late June of 1970.)

"Don't Fuck Around with Love" offered a parodic voice-over above a sentimental fifties doo-wop chorus: "Love is wonderful / Love is peace / Love moves the mountains / Love cuts the grease." "Secretary" described a typical pissed-off working day: ("Get up, downtown / don't you wish you could get out of this? / no trust / big bust / doesn't all those mumbles ever bother you?") At all times we wanted our politics to be artful, to be revolutionary poetry.

We were an image of feminist solidarity, resistance, and power, and audiences loved us. Just the fact that we were all women standing up on the stage playing our heavy-duty instruments into our heavy-duty amplifiers was enough to turn many women on. We also received a wildly enthusiastic response from a range of different groups, including the crowd at the Second Annual Third World Transvestite Ball, and the fourteen-year-old black girls at a summer camp for inner-city children. At Cornell University, where we played with the New Haven Women's Liberation Rock Band, women stripped to the waist and danced together in undulating circles. Outside the room, angry fraternity boys were threatening to attack: "Put your clothes back on," sang Jennifer Abod (Susie's sister) without shaving a beat, "We're in a hostile situation." The women kept dancing. "No we won't," they sang back. "We're free. We are . . . FREE." At the inner-city camp, the girls made us play Amy Kesselman's "VD Blues" six times before they would let us pack our bags and go home:

I went to the preacher, said preacher can you help me please?
. . . He looked at me and said, girl, get on your knees.
I went to the doctor and said doctor can you help me please?
. . . He looked at me cross-eyed and said,
You've got A SOCIAL DISEASE!

Everywhere we went, we would be mobbed at the end of a performance, with the audience hugging the band and other members of the audience. And the band hugging the audience. And all of our faces wet with tears of joy.

"Secretary" and "Mountain Moving Day" were our strongest songs, and sometimes, when we were really on, they utterly transformed our performance. A gig we played at the University of Pittsburgh in April of 1971 is etched in my memory. The room was large and bright, and we were on stage and at our instruments before the mixed female and male audience showed up. (This was a rule with us. In accord with our subversive resolve to be audience-friendly—unheard of with male rockers—we tried always to be on time for a performance.) When the room was filled, Sanya did a cracking drum intro and Susie sang Kathy Rowley's adaptation of "I don't need no doctor cause I know what's ailing me." Then I went to the mike, and assuming the leering voice of your average low-life male sexist, I said, "A women's liberation rock band. Farrrr . . . Out! Farrrrr . . . fucking out. Hey, I'd like to see you chicks in your gold lamé short shorts and feathers on your tits." I went on to imitate Mick Jagger singing "Under My Thumb": "There is a squirrelly dog, who once had her way . . ." Then I asked the audience: "And do you know what he says then? he says, 'It's alright.' " Pause. "Well, it's not all right, Mick Jagger, and IT'S NEVER GOING TO BE ALL RIGHT AGAIN. [CHEERS FROM THE AUDIENCE] *IT'S NEVER GOING TO BE ALL RIGHT AGAIN!*"

The audience didn't stop screaming for five minutes.

Susie and Pat's adaptation of my setting and additional verse for Japanese feminist Yosano Akiko's "Mountain Moving Day" was our final song. I played a soft sixteen-bar piano intro in Dorian mode (like "Greensleeves"), and Susie joined with a descending sixteenth-note bass and sang:

The mountain moving day is coming
I say so yet others doubt it.
Only a while the mountain sleeps.
In the past, all mountains moved in fire.
Yet you may not believe it.
O man, this alone believe

Pat and Sherry's true harmonies amplified the last line:

> *All sleeping women now awake and move,*
> *All sleeping women now awake and move.*

Susanne, who formerly played in a marching band, then did a haunting martial snare-drum roll, as if to call legions of women to battle.

> *Can you hear the river?*
> *I can see the canyons as they stretch out for miles*
> *But if you listen you can hear it below*
> *Grinding stones into sand.*
> *Yet you may not hear it*
> *O man, this alone hear*
> *The waters now will tear the canyons down,*
> *The waters now will tear the canyons down.*

Again, folks in the audience began to scream and sing with us. Usually Sherry and I would play a fugal coda to bring the excitement down at that point. But it was no use. This audience shouted and wept and rushed up on the stage and hugged our instruments and hugged us, and surely, we felt, we had produced a new world that would never go away, that would never fail us.

Driving back to Chicago, we had a flat tire and pulled off into a rest stop surrounded by tall trees. It had rained in the morning, and huge blurry clouds were racing northwards. The trees, probably wild cherry, were just beginning to sprout little lavender buds, tiny bird tracks across the hurrying sky. We became silent and stood against the car. It was April of 1971, and we were getting good, and we were making history.

Every weekend, we crisscrossed the Chicago area, flew or drove to Colorado Springs, Bloomington, Madison, Pittsburgh, Lewisburg, Toronto, Ithaca, Indianapolis, Buffalo, Boston. (I flew as "Susan Young" at youth fare.) Audiences invited us back, and by the second visit knew half our lyrics. A cult began to form. We flew east to Boston to make a record for Rounder Records (1972),[3] which became an underground

---

[3] *Mountain Moving Day: The Chicago and New Haven Women's Liberation Rock Bands and a caste of millions.*

classic for many feminists. This is when that congeries of styles and songs called Women's Music began.

The band lasted three years and broke up in an agony of hatred and hidden agendas. This fact is not unusual; it even happened to the Beatles. But the way our band broke up reflected all the conflicts that were devastating the radical women's movement at that time. The band was a microcosm of what was happening all over the country: we were losing our women's movement and there was no one to tell us how to stop the dissolution.

There were many reasons for the band's failure. As the radical movements of the preceding decade receded, conflicts that once seemed easy to resolve, such as those of lesbians versus straights, now seemed almost insurmountable. We began arguing too much and rehearsing too little. But there were two conflicts in particular that finished us. These conflicts lay at the millenarian heart of the prefigurative[4] politics of the women's liberation movement.

The movement's utopianism included the ideas that (1) any woman should be able to do anything as well as any other woman; and (2) there should be no leaders. We soon learned these ideas were untenable, but we persisted in hoping that if we were good enough feminists, we could abolish inequality of skills and function without leaders. The contradictions between what we knew to be true, versus what we pretended was true, destroyed us.

In our band, the first conflict expressed itself as a tension between expertise on the one hand and, on the other, enthusiasm-in-place-of-expertise (or "militant amateurism"). Our early women's movement said that any woman could do anything, if given the right social context and sufficient social support. (I said something like this myself in the early

---

[4] Wini Breines used this phrase speaking about the early New Left to indicate utopian political actors who tried to incorporate their ultimate vision within their contemporary politics. See Wini Breines, *The Great Refusal: Community and Organization in the New Left, 1962–1968*, New York: Praeger, 1982, e.g., p. 6: "The crux of prefigurative politics imposed substantial tasks, the central one being to create and sustain within the live practice of the movement, relationships and political forms that 'prefigured,' and embodied the desired society."

days.[5]) I think this principle worked at the beginning, when our rock band was the first of its kind. Women appreciated our rough edges, our ragged style, which conveyed the message that the audience itself could do things formerly considered taboo for women. But we owed it to our audience to grow smarter with them, to become the best musicians we could. Some members of the band were willing to take up this challenge, but others were not. Feeling that the band needed a sharper beat, one day I suggested to one of our drummers that she take some lessons. She replied somewhat contemptuously, "I'm good enough for *this* band." The telling thing about this exchange was that nobody followed up. The myth about equality in skills was so strong that not one of us had the temerity to say, "You're *not* good enough for this band. Get better, or quit."

The second, and related, conflict that did us in involved the question of leadership. This question was to rend the women's movement from coast to coast. Committed, as I have said, to what turned out to be a myth of equal skills, the movement applied the same kind of thinking to leadership, declaring that there should be none. For instance, as my reputation as a public speaker increased and my speaking invitations multiplied, the CWLU decided that I should refuse further invitations, lest I emerge as a "heavy." I willingly went along with this. (Instead, I organized intensive speaker training sessions, where I taught inexperienced women the skills that I had picked up.) But no matter how self-abnegating leaders were, it was not enough. Utopianism morphed into cannibalism, and the movement ate its leaders: in city after city, they went down.[6]

Here is how the leadership conflict played out in the band. We built the group painstakingly, and through much interpersonal struggle, as an egalitarian collective. Thus, for instance, every member wrote songs, and these were accepted by everyone in the band with few questions

---

[5] See Margaret Strobel, "Consciousness and Action: Historical Agency in the Chicago Women's Liberation Union," in Judy Gardiner, ed., *Provoking Agents*, Urbana: University of Illinois Press, 1995. Also see Naomi Weisstein, "Psychology Constructs the Female; or The Fantasy Life of the Male Psychologist," *Feminism & Psychology*, vol. III, no. 2 (1993), 195–210. See other articles in this issue of *Feminism & Psychology* commemorating the twenty-fifth anniversary of the original publication of "Psychology Constructs the Female."
[6] See Alice Echols, *Daring to Be Bad: Radical Feminism in America: 1967–1975*, Minneapolis: University of Minnesota Press, 1989.

asked, although friendly adaptations and amendments were usually received enthusiastically. But, in spite of our laid-back social style and our values of structurelessness and leaderlessness, I was clearly the theatrical director, theoretician, and spiritual healer of wounds. If only by dint of a chronological advantage and a frenzied drive—and totally committed, as I was, to a deeply utopian egalitarianism—I was nevertheless "mother" to the band, its *de facto* leader. When the women's movement started trashing its leaders, the band turned on me for all the roles I had played. Its solidarity split open, and I came under attack.[7] After I and Virginia Blaisdell published a piece in *Ms.* on the band's strengths and triumphs,[8] I was attacked by the band for egotism: "Why did you sign your name to the article?" some members asked. Interestingly, nobody questioned the importance of the article, just that I should take credit for it.

The band needed my experience and skills, but they did not want to admit this. A gig we played at Bucknell University in 1972 made this clear to me. The audience was ferociously hostile, riled by an earlier speaker and angered by the fact that only half the band showed up. (In pre-performance confusion, they had taken the wrong plane.) Huge fraternity boys were screaming and baring their canines in the middle of the floor like turf-threatened gorillas. At one point, Sherry put an empty coke bottle on my piano and grabbed a microphone stand because she thought they were going to rush the stage. I offered to calm the audience with some stand-up comedy. Concerned about my leadership role, the band refused to let me do this. Instead, another band member, inexperienced in such situations, haltingly read my lines, further enraging the crowd. At this point I—gulp—improvised a new monologue, producing (eventually) giggles, then guffaws. The band was furious at me for my success in reversing the audience's mood.

---

[7] Catharine R. Stimpson describes a similar dynamic in women's studies today: "Feeling vulnerable, faculty, staff, and students then make too many demands on women's studies programs. They are to provide an impossible model of egalitarianism and cooperation, a haven of principle, a nurturing sanctuary. If a program or a 'leader' lapses for a moment, complaints flow as if the two were the unforgivably never-good-enough mother. And nothing, nothing is ever the fault of the complainant. I am woman, hear me suffer, hear me protest, hear my innocence." Stimpson, "Women's Studies and Its Discontents," *Dissent*, Winter 1996, 71.

[8] Naomi Weisstein and Virginia Blaisdell, "No More Balls and Chains," *Ms.*, 1972: 25–27.

To paraphrase Tolstoy, unhappy disputes all have their unique quirks and kinks; it is beyond the scope of this paper to dwell on ours. I should point out, however, that by talking about "the band," I don't mean to imply a monolithic consensus about trashing me. As these dynamics go, one person started the attack. As it turned out, when I left the band, she attacked the leader who took my place. In varying degrees, the rest of the band was reluctant to join the confrontation she had set up, but their silence gave the trashing the appearance of unanimity. Their inability to stand up for me stemmed from the ideology and culture that had so recently infected the women's movement. Band members were just plain scared to oppose the new dogmatism. They didn't want to appear politically stupid. After all, hadn't the CWLU decreed that I should stay silent? Maybe, reasoned some of the band members, I shouldn't be performing at all.

How much the band actually relied on me was to be sadly revealed when I left Chicago.[9] When I had been gone three months, I read in the CWLU newsletter that the band had dissolved. The group described its death as a Higher Form of Life: "women's music lives and grows." But the reality was that the band had died—women's music doesn't necessarily live and grow. Though from the seventies to the nineties, many wonderful kinds of women's music did,[10] it was rarely the kind played by the CWLRB: bust-out bad-ass visionary political poetry. The band dissolved because we were not honest about the skills we needed to develop and because trashing had replaced compromise and generosity as the dominant political modus operandi of the radical women's movement.

Recently, I heard the audio portion of a video tape of a CWLRB performance that took place shortly after I left Chicago. It is labeled "last concert," and I hear Susie on the tape announcing this to the audience. My husband, Jesse, who has seen the tape, tells me that it is fragmentary, black and white. It makes me nostalgic, bringing back both the conflicts

---

[9] For this part of my feminist struggles in science, see Naomi Weisstein, " 'How Can a Little Girl Like You Teach a Great Big Class of Men?' The Chairman Said, and Other Adventures of a Woman in Science," in Ruddick and Daniels, eds., *Working It Out: Twenty-Three Women Writers, Artists and Scholars Talk About Their Lives and Work*, New York: Pantheon, 1977.

[10] See Lucy O'Brien, *She Bop: The Definitive History of Women in Rock, Pop and Soul*, NY: Penguin, 1995, and ed. Barbara O'Dair, *Trouble Girls: The Rolling Stone Book of Women in Rock*, NY: Random House, 1997.

and the euphoria of the period. For the rest of my life, I'll always be obsessed with the conflict between the band's ecstatic side and its amateurish side. Through the poor tape, we nonetheless see Susie (a natural performer) working like mad to keep a lively tempo for "Poppa." Sherry's deadpan voice shouts out, "Keep on truckin, everybody . . . there's plenty of space back there to truck." And Pat Miller Solo's slide whistles and banjo-rhythmed guitar makes an old-time honky-tonk festival out of the song. The audience is delirious, cheering like crazy.

Why is the audience cheering so hard? Many of the other songs are done quite poorly, revealing—at least to someone familiar with the band's previous performances—the extent to which the band has disintegrated. The demoralization that the band members are feeling as the drummer loses the beat and the singers can't stay in tune is palpable.

And yet, in the grainy shadows of that last tape, the audience is ecstatic, because beyond the CWLRB's flaws, beyond the disintegration of the last performance, the band still conveys celebration and resistance. Its performance deliberately sets up a prefigurative politics of strong, defiant women, absolute democracy, the players and the audience together in a beloved community. Through the intensity of the medium, through our bad-ass revolutionary poetry, the band shouts the news: we can have a new world, a just and generous world, a world without female suffering or degradation. It is an irony that the utopianism that had destroyed us was the same ingredient that made our performance so powerful.

After the death of the CWLRB, I played with the more durable New Haven Women's Liberation Rock Band, whose dominant forces were Virginia Blaisdell and Jennifer Abod. (Blaisdell was a professional musician who could play trumpet, French horn, drums, piano, and even electric bass, and directed the beginner musicians into a tight ensemble sound. Jennifer Abod—Susan's sister—had the family's stunning dramatic presence, and a deep blue voice she could have taken to Hollywood.) Later, when I became professor of psychology at SUNY, Buffalo, I sat in with a South Buffalo lesbian band. But it was never the same. I mourned my band, and the radical women's movement that fell apart in that same period; for years, I mourned it. The Women's Liberation Rock Band was, in feminist Chelsea Dreher's words, "Like a lover who abruptly walked out on you and never did tell you why."

—*For Susie, Sherry and Pat: time sharpens the intensity.*

The Art of Getting to Equal

Nancy Spero

In September 1972, A.I.R. (Artists in Residence), the first all-women's cooperative art gallery in the nation, and a direct result of Women's Liberation Movement energy, opened in New York City at 97 Wooster Street. Nancy Spero was one of its six founding members. Though it has moved and changed, A.I.R. still exists.

What follows is a collage-scroll, like Spero's own work. It was sequenced by Rachel Blau DuPlessis and Ann Snitow, primarily from interviews and conversations between Spero and Amy Schlegel (the AS of the text, 1994–96), with fragments from interviews of Spero with Jeanne Siegel (1984, 1985). The questions interviewers put to Nancy Spero below sometimes project a feminist scenario onto her life which she recasts. An interviewer asks the artist about early repression or disaffection with early works, projecting a move from silence to speech. Spero says, no. An interviewer pushes for the image of Spero's husband, Leon Golub, as a competitor, or as the big male artist, the arbiter. Spero says, no. An interviewer wonders if three children weren't a dangerous interruption for a woman artist. Interruption and difficulty, Spero concedes, but not the danger, no.

Behind these denials one glimpses yet another feminist scenario. Spero wanted both her ties and her freedom; she experienced the strain; she twisted and turned and contrived to collage all these ill-fitting things together—forming her style. The power and exuberance necessary to keep it all going was prodigious. An encounter with this energy in Spero is one way back into the cultural atmosphere of feminism in the early days of the U.S. Women's Liberation Movement. Many of Spero's works include fragments of texts so insulting to women that women viewers often feel a frisson of horror or rage that fits perfectly with the careening images of passion or destruction she sets circling through rooms or waving in banners.

> *Marduk caught Tiamat in his net, and drove the winds which he had with him into her body. And whilst her belly was thus distended he thrust his spear into her, and stabbed her to the heart, and cut through her bowels, and crushed her skull with his club. On her body he took his stand, and with his knife he split it like a flat fish into two halves, and of one of these he made a covering for the heavens.*
> From Torture of Women, a quotation from Sumer, 5000 B.C.E.

In the late sixties and early seventies, feminists tried to change the rules about what women could hope for. An ideal of sacrifice gave way to a dream of having more, and Spero rode on the back of that change, hanging on to marriage, children, work, and politics. Like everyone, she cut her own deal with rebellion. She had her kids (and responds irritably to the interviewer: "Why not?"), had her partner-husband, had her work—even if for several decades she was on the traditional double shift and hardly anyone was looking.

Gradually, she took up more and more space. Leaving the grand gesture of oils, she used paper—but the paper started to scroll out in all directions; her female figures started to put on a thousand faces—from mythic to mundane. By the 1970s, Spero was having her own grand shows—entirely on her own terms—figures dancing along walls, riding up onto ceilings, anarchic, mismatched, borrowed, cobbled together. Feminism had given her the viewers she deserved, and she met them with delight.

Spero is among the women artists driven by the feminist wish to represent women in motion, not fixed in a male gaze or adored in repose. She has devoted herself to feminism—its ideas, its struggles—and is one of those who has shaped its aesthetics, its early institutions.

NANCY SPERO: Leon [Golub] and I [married in 1951] are always battling the art world. Our primary concerns were our sons and our art. The preoccupation with our art must have been difficult for them.

AMY SCHLEGEL: With your work and three children, was there ever a time in the 1950s and early 1960s when you weren't totally tired? You must have been exhausted for a good twenty years.

NS: Thirty years.

AS: Raising the kids and painting at night . . .

NS: Night work, largely a consequence of my inner clock, became my essential work time when the children were young. I still work at night. I had the freedom of the uninterrupted night. I remember that fatigue when the first two were infants—they are very close in age. I kept telling myself, "I'm an artist," forcing myself to work late every night in the studio. I couldn't let up. I was proving to myself and to the world and . . .

AS: To Leon?

NS: To Leon, sure, but primarily to myself, that I was an artist.

AS: You and Leon appear to have led relatively traditional lives in certain respects, despite the unpredictability of existence as professional artists.

NS: Yes and no. Our partnership has been a strong base, unacknowledged publicly until recently, a constant art dialogue which has been crucial and consuming for both of us. I've always had my studio where we've lived. Our homes have been mostly work spaces—from our first, a garage in an alley in Chicago, to our present-day loft in downtown New York. The kitchen table is the only social area! When our sons were younger and still in school, the fact that we were both artists and lived this way—without the convention of furnishing a home—was a source of embarrassment for them. It's probably a source of pride for them now.

AS: Did you ever think twice about the drawbacks of having had children so soon after getting married?

NS: I didn't reflect on it. Why shouldn't artists have kids?

AS: The family came first . . . It was expected . . .

NS: I was an artist and a mother, why not? But then the feminists came in the early 1970s and said, "Forget it! We're gonna go out there and 'do our own thing.' " I joined in but also I was already doing my own thing. I hadn't talked much about my children in the fifties because, at the time, to me domestic issues were taken for granted. Then, in the new women's groups in the late sixties and early seventies, I didn't talk much or at all about my children, because I was so intent on the public issues of investigating the art world and how I could best invade it. I didn't mind the women's movement's silence about motherhood, because I had always separated my art ambitions from family life.

AS: Can you recall your very first feminist "intervention"?

NS: Actually, it was a prefeminist action. In the summer of 1967 two dancers, Sarah Petlin and Marian Hunter, invited me to join in crashing a stag party for our mutual friend, the art critic Max Kozloff. A great idea! Sarah and Marian had heard that a stripper might be hired to jump through a cardboard cake and that porn movies would be shown. This so irritated us that we had to retaliate—disrupt the party. We bought some disposable aluminum pie plates, chocolate pudding, canned whipped cream, and other gooey food substances, and slapped together some "pies." When we burst in, the lights were out and the men were watching "blue movies"—hardly recognizable as pornographic now, they were so naive and blurred (innocent days!). We threw our pies aimlessly, making a huge mess. Sarah plopped a tray of pies over the head of the eminent Harold Rosenberg!

AS: It's a great story to hear now, in retrospect, but I'm sure they didn't think it was funny at the time!

NS: This was our reaction to what we considered the stupid male bonding of the stag party—men visually consuming the female body in the porno films. A few days afterwards, I encountered the painter Paul Jenkins in Central Park as I was riding my youngest son home from school on my bike. Jenkins shook his finger at me and said, "You ruined my new suede suit." I felt a sort of regret, but I was pleased, too.

My artwork of that period reflects anger—anger at my lack of a voice, the lack of a dialogue in the art world, and anger at the U.S. intervention in Vietnam. The *War Series* (1966–69) was done in response to the Vietnam War. I wanted to represent the convergence of state violence with male sexual aggression. To emphasize this, I exaggerated phallic-shaped anthropomorphic depictions of bombs with wild heads, vomiting poison onto the victims below, and helicopters consuming and shitting their victims' remains. I envisaged these works as manifestos, a kind of exorcism of war and total destruction—of not wanting my sons or anyone else's to fight and die in this dirty war, any war. Male bombs (the trunks of the bombs became torsos) with huge penises are a jab at male power; yet I painted female bombs as well, to represent the contradictory roles of women, stereotyped as nurturing and caring, yet forced to be complicit in such aggressions. Women in powerful positions can be as brutal as men in wielding power.

I abandoned oil painting in 1966 as both a personal and a political act.

JEANNE SIEGEL: In thinking about your move away from painting to collage, accompanied by your new unconventional format, I am tempted to conclude that it was a response to macho painting—so-called heroic painting dominated by male artists. Were you conscious of that at the time?

NS to JS: I was reacting to the self-importance of oil painting, its value as a commodity; I wanted to undermine this notion. It was important that I discard what I felt was an "establishment" product and critique not only the art world by implication, but the politics of war.

NS to AS: Abandoning oil painting and switching to paper was a definitive kind of self-realization. Even though I had railed against self-importance, I wanted to expand—I just wanted more space. The confining spaces of small work needed to be augmented—a longer gesture. I had subversive ideas about space in the *War Series* and the *Artaud Paintings*. I wanted to get out in the world and occupy "my" space; it was to become an extended layer of space, primarily horizontal, but also vertical, which could continue virtually indefinitely in extended linear formats.

In 1968–70 when I went to the meetings of the activist group the Art Workers Coalition (AWC), it was primarily male artists who led theoretical discussions and actions, ignoring issues of sexism in their grasp of leadership. As important as the AWC's discussions and actions were, I couldn't enter with enthusiasm in their male-oriented goals.

[AMY SCHLEGEL EXPLAINS: The AWC designated itself "the conscience of the art world." Its initial demands to museums were that they should expand their audience and include more living artists in their temporary exhibitions and permanent collections. Next, AWC took the position that museums that did not publicly take a stand against the Vietnam War were complicitous with the war effort, which it saw as linked with racism and oppression. Sexism was added to this list by the art critic Lucy Lippard, one of the most vocal female AWC activists, but in no way was sexism a central focus of the group.]

NS: I didn't go frequently to Art Workers Coalition meetings at Museum [an alternative, ad hoc exhibition space on Broadway, active from about 1968 to 1971], partly out of irritation at the demanding male attitudes and also because my youngest son, Paul, was only seven in 1968 and I was painting at night—as I still do. I contributed work to anti-Vietnam protests like the L.A. Peace Tower (1965) and the two *Collage of Indignation* exhibitions in New York City (1967 and 1970, at Loeb Student Center, NYU, and the Huntington Hartford Museum). But it wasn't until the formation in 1969 of WAR (Women Artists in Revolution), a splinter group of the AWC, that I became seriously active.

As a political action and discussion group, WAR provided a meeting ground for all sorts of women artists who were angry and wanted action. We were confronting the facts of our status as women artists, and we became increasingly impatient at the exclusion of women artists from galleries, national and international exhibitions, coverage in art magazines and newspaper reviews, and studio faculty positions at colleges, universities, and art schools.

Eight of us went to John Hightower at the Museum of Modern Art demanding parity. Then, early in 1970, a group of other women artists interested in challenging the status quo planned to picket the Whitney Museum, so I started participating in the Ad Hoc [Committee of Women Artists] as I wanted to join the picket. I wrote an article about this action, "The Whitney and Women: The Embattled Museum." Here are the opening paragraphs, written in 1970 and published in January 1971 in *The Art Gallery.*

Papa's little bed pal. Lump of love.   —James Joyce

The latest act in the New York art scenario might be called "The 'Second Sex' Versus the Whitney Museum."

Last spring, Women Artists in Revolution (WAR), a group of politically oriented women artists, met with the curators of the Whitney Museum to protest the museum's discrimination against women artists and to demand a women's exhibition. The Whitney currently is offering in response a "theme" show: "Women Artists—Works Selected from the Permanent Collection." How naive and how dense to assume that this exhibition would have any relevance to the problems of women artists! This exhibition is simply a cop-out.

Recently, a group of activists including the critic Lucy Lippard and artists Poppy Johnson, Brenda Miller, and Faith Ringgold has demanded the admission of fifty percent female artists in the Whitney Annual. They have bedeviled and harassed the Whitney: bits of paper carrying their demands, uncooked white eggs, hard-boiled black eggs, Tampax, etc., have been scattered about the museum, while visitors have been given impromptu indoctrination courses. Most recently, unknown parties have distributed fake Whitney Museum press releases stating that the Annual would include fifty percent women artists.

Is the dissatisfaction of women artists with the Whitney Museum justified? A few simple statistics indicate that it is. In the 1969 painting Annual, 143 artists were represented, of whom exactly eight were "lumps of love." The total over the last five-year period, 1965–69, has been 729 artists, of whom a mere sixty are "papa's little bed pals." These facts are conclusive evidence of the past disparagement of women artists. This year there will be a total of 100 works in the Whitney Annual, of which exactly twenty-two will represent the "second sex." A sorry response. . . .

We picketed the Whitney, standing outside in the cold with placards, speaking to passersby, interviewing visitors inside, explaining the disparity of female to male artists in the exhibition. Four percent women! In the following Whitney Biannuals the percentages went up to 20 to 25 percent, and remain that way.

All these exchanges made me realize how women artists are excluded from public discourse. Earlier I had felt excluded, and had thought this was due to the nature of my work. After all, my work wasn't mainstream; I was addressing issues that were really anathema to the New York scene, political issues, women's issues, that were absolutely *verboten*. And my work wasn't formal. It wasn't minimal. It was tending toward what could be defined as expressionist. So I thought I was forever swiveling on the edge of the art world because of who I was. My politics may have been part of it—but then I was beginning to see that ultimately I had been excluded by gender discrimination. It didn't matter who I was. The other women on the picket did work that in no way resembled mine. What joined us under a kind of political umbrella was the exclusion of women artists.

[Spero's next group involvement was with A.I.R.]

AS: Do you think that A.I.R. was a radical feminist experiment?

NS: It wasn't a radical feminist group, but we were aware of our unique status as a nonprofit, conceptually and politically alternative, all-women's art gallery. A.I.R. was an exciting, powerful coming together of previously unaffiliated women artists—challenging the art game from new perspectives. A.I.R. became momentarily chic in the early 1970s. The gallery had a sensational opening in September of 1972 and got a lot of media and art world attention, which lasted for about two years. But the male art world is sophisticated in the way it occasionally patronizes new interests and shunts others aside. After that burst of attention, I was forced to acknowledge that despite A.I.R.'s success, any women's group is stigmatized by the fact of its being an all-women's enterprise; a women's group can become a ghetto.

AS: How did the group form? What was the process?

NS: Barbara Zucker and Susan Williams had the initial idea. Then they called a meeting with Dotty Attie, Mary Grigoriadis, Maude Boltz, and myself. We decided it was a great idea to form an all-women's gallery. The six of us invited fourteen other women artists from a huge slide registry of women artists compiled by the Ad Hoc Committee of Women Artists. The twenty of us met in 1972 and showed each other our work.

Many in the group didn't want the term feminist applied to their work, while other women artists would not even consider joining A.I.R. because of feminism's seemingly negative connotation.

AS: So the connotations of feminism in the art world circa 1972 clearly were not positive.

NS: It was mixed. The term generated a lot of controversy then as it does today. I am proud to be categorized as a feminist artist. For me, feminism holds the promise of a rethinking of conventional models, a questioning of the status quo, an addressing of inequities. In A.I.R., we were twenty disparate individuals. Our work was often lumped together and categorized as "feminine" because we were women artists. When is a group of male artists characterized as "masculine" artists? In fact, our art reflected the range of work going on in the entire art community. We were different personalities, all ambitious, often argumentative, and all facing near insurmountable barriers in the art world—so the goals of sisterhood weren't easy.

AS: Can you discuss gender in relation to race and class in the A.I.R. collective during the 1970s?

NS: While I was aware of the problems of racial representation and ethnicity, I'm afraid as a group we didn't explore issues of race and class often enough, because our primary concern was our individual role as artists. But Howardena Pindell, the only black artist in A.I.R., was vocal in her efforts to get the work of artists of color recognized and was effective in making us and other artists keenly aware of issues of race. Ana Mendieta, Cuban born, was also involved with issues of women artists of color; she curated a show in 1980 at A.I.R. ("Dialectics of Isolation: An Exhibition of Third World Women Artists of the United States"). She was particularly concerned with the status of Latin American artists in New York City.

There was other agitation and action by artists of color in the early seventies. Faith Ringgold, among others, was angry—angry as a black woman in a white society that oppressed her, and angry that she was marginalized as well for being a woman artist. Faith Ringgold's was a powerful and compelling voice.

AS: You were one of the few at A.I.R. who spoke out against a desire to integrate with the mainstream. In Irene Sosa's 1993 video documentary about your work and life, *Woman as Protagonist,* there is an excerpt from a film by Hermine Freed containing a poignant moment from the early days: a small group of A.I.R. members are sitting on the floor in a circle and one member says, "I think in about a year from now everything will be okay; we'll be able to show with men again," and you disagree and say, "No, no, absolutely not; that's not possible; I'm adamant about keeping separate for quite a long time; anything less would compromise the radicalness of our position." I think to some extent you still feel that way about women's oppositional stance vis-à-vis the mainstream.

NS: It has to be both ways. Separatism is a necessary phenomenon and essential in certain circumstances, as it was for me in the 1970s. Women artists still have to infiltrate museums and galleries to gain presence and have a role in shaping how the visual arts affect the way we look at our contemporary world.

AS: What exactly did you find liberating about the Ad Hoc Committee of Women and A.I.R.?

NS: Participating with a diverse group of women artists with a common goal—free of male control!

What Feminism Means to Me

Vivian Gornick

I'd been sent out by the *Village Voice* to investigate "these women's libbers." It was November 1970. "What's that?" I said to my editor. A week later I was a convert.

In the first three days I met Ti-Grace Atkinson, Kate Millett, Shulamith Firestone; in the next three, Phyllis Chesler, Ellen Willis, Alix Kates Shulman. They were all talking at once, and I heard every word each of them spoke. Or, rather, it was that I heard them all saying the same thing because I came away from that week branded by a single thought. It was this: the idea that men by nature take their brains seriously, and women by nature do not, is a belief not a reality; it serves the culture; and from it our entire lives follow. Simple, really. And surely this had already been said. How was it I seemed never to have heard it before? And why was I hearing it now?

It remains one of life's great mysteries—in politics as well as in love—readiness: that moment when the elements are sufficiently fused to galvanize inner change. If you are one who responds to the moment you can never really explain it, you can only describe what it felt like.

I had always known that life was not appetite and acquisition. In my earnest, angry, good-girl way I pursued "meaning." It was important to do work that mattered (that is, work of the mind or spirit), and to love a man who'd be an appropriate partner. These, I knew, were twin requirements: interwoven: one without the other unimaginable. Yet I grew into a compulsive talker who could not bear solitude long enough to study: I did not learn to command steady thought. I read novels, daydreamed an important life, mooned over boys. Although I moralized endlessly about seriousness, it seemed I could pursue the man, not the work. This, however—and here we have something crucial—I didn't know. I did not know I could do love but I couldn't do work. I was always thinking, When things are right I will work. I never thought, How come although things are not right I can still obsess over this boy or that?

In my mid-twenties I fell in love with and married an artist. I was all set. I had a desk to sit at, a partner to encourage me, a sufficiency of time and money. *Now* I would work. Wrong again. Ten years later I was wandering around New York, a divorced "girl" of thirty-five with an aggressive style who had written a couple of articles. Beneath the bluster the confusion was deep, the aimlessness profound. How did I get here? my head throbbed each day, and how do I get out? Questions for which I had no answers until I heard the "women's libbers." It seemed to me then that I saw things clearly. I was old enough, bored enough, exhausted and pained enough. The lifelong inability to take myself seriously as a worker: *this* was the central dilemma of a woman's existence.

Like Arthur Koestler getting Marxism for the first time, it was as though light and music were bursting across the top of my skull. The exhilaration I felt once I had the analysis! I woke up with it, danced through the day with it, fell asleep smiling with it. I became impervious: the slings and arrows of daily fortune could not make a dent in me. If I held onto what feminism had made me see I'd soon have myself. Once I had myself I'd have: everything. Life felt good then. I had insight, and I had company. I stood in the middle of my own experience, turning and turning. In every direction I saw a roomful of women, also turning and turning.

That is a moment of joy, when a sufficiently large number of people are galvanized by a social explanation of how their lives have taken shape, and are gathered together in the same place at the same time, speaking the same language, making the same analysis, meeting again and again in New York restaurants, lecture halls, and apartments for the pleasure of elaborating the insight and repeating the analysis. It is the joy of revolutionary politics, and it was ours. To be a feminist in the early seventies— bliss was it in that dawn to be alive. Not an I-love-you in the world could touch it. There was no other place to be, except with each other. We lived then, all of us, inside the loose embrace of feminism. I thought I would spend the rest of my life there.

What went hand in hand with the exhilaration was the quickly formed conviction that work was now something I could not do without. Loving a man, I vowed, would not again be primary. Perhaps, in fact, the two were incompatible. Love-as-I-had-always-known-it was something I might now have to do without. I approached this thought: blithely. As though it would be the easiest thing in the world to accommodate to. After all, I'd always been an uneasy belligerent, one of those women forever complaining that men were afraid of "women like me."

I was no good at flirting, it was a relief to be done with it. If love between equals was impossible—and it looked as though it probably was—who needed it? I pressed myself against my newly hardened heart. The thrill and excitement of feminist reality made me glad to give up sentimentality, take pleasure in tough-mindedness. The only important thing, I told myself, was work. I must teach myself to work. If I worked, I'd have what I needed. I'd be a person in the world. What would it matter then that I was giving up "love"?

As it turned out: it mattered. More than I had ever dreamed it would. Yes, I could no longer live with men on the old terms. Yes, I could settle for nothing less than grown-up affection. Yes, if that meant doing without I was prepared to do without. But the idea of love, if not the reality, was impossible to give up. As the years went on, I saw that romantic love was injected like dye into the nervous system of my emotions, laced through the entire fabric of longing, fantasy, and sentiment. It haunted the psyche, was an ache in the bones; so deeply embedded in the makeup of the spirit it hurt the eyes to look directly into its influence. It would be a cause of pain and conflict for the rest of my life. I love my hardened heart—I have loved it all these years—but the loss of romantic love can still tear at it.

It was always there, threatening, this split in me about love, yet I never spoke of it. I never spoke because I didn't need to speak. I didn't need to speak because it was bearable. It was bearable because I had made an important discovery. The discovery was my secret ingredient, the thing that made my cake rise each morning. It was this: As long as I had a roomful of feminists to come home to I had built-in company for life. I'd never be alone again. The feminists were my sword and my shield: my solace, my comfort, my excitement. If I had the feminists I'd have community, I could live without romantic love. And I was right: I could.

Then the unthinkable happened. Slowly, around 1980, feminist solidarity began to unravel. As the world had failed to change sufficiently to reflect our efforts, that which had separated all women before began to reassert itself now in us. The sense of connection began to erode. More and more, we seemed to have less and less to say to one another. Personalities began to jar, conversations to bore, ideas to repeat themselves. Meetings became tiresome, parties less inviting.

At first, the change in atmosphere among us was only a glimmering suspicion (so solid had feminist comradeship seemed!), but slowly it became an unhappy conviction, and then an undeniable reality. One day I woke up to realize the excitement, the longing, the expectation of community was: over. Like romantic love, the discrepancy between desire and actuality was too large to overcome.

I fell into a painful depression. Existential loneliness ate at my heart: my beautifully hardened heart. A fear of lifelong solitude took hold of me.

Work, I said to myself. Work hard.

But I can't work hard, I answered myself. I've barely learned how to work steadily, I can't work hard at all.

Try, I replied. And try again. It's all you've got.

The first flash of feminist insight returned to me. Years before, feminism had made me see the value of work; now it was making me see it all over again with new eyes. A second conversion began to take place: the one in which knowledge deepens. I understood that I would have to face alone the very thing my politics had been preparing me for all along. I saw what visionary feminists had seen for two hundred years: that power over one's own life comes only through the steady command of one's own thought.

A sentiment easy enough to declare, the task of a lifetime to achieve.

I sat down at the desk, as though for the first time, to teach myself to stay with my thoughts: to order them, extend them, make them serve me. I failed.

Next day I sat down again. Again, I failed.

Three days later I crawled back to the desk and again I came away defeated. But the day after that the fog cleared out of my head: I solved a simple writing problem, one that had seemed intractable, and a stone rolled off my chest. I breathed easier. The air smelled sweet, the coffee strong, the day inviting.

The rhetoric of religious fervor began to evaporate in me, replaced by the reassuring pain of daily effort. I could not keep repeating "work is everything" like a mantra when clearly it *wasn't* everything. But sitting down to it every day became an act of enlightenment. Chekhov's words stared back at me: "Others made me a slave but I must squeeze the slave out of myself, drop by drop." I had tacked them up over the desk sometime in the early seventies, and my eyes had been glazing across them for more than ten years. Now, I read them again: really read them. It wasn't "work" that would save me, it was the miserable daily effort.

The daily effort became a kind of connection for me. The sense of connection was strengthening. Strength began to make me feel independent. Independence allowed me to think. When I thought, I was less alone. I had myself for company. I had myself, period. I felt the power of renewed wisdom. From the Greeks to Chekhov to Elizabeth Cady Stanton: everyone who had ever cared to investigate the nature of human loneliness had seen that only one's own working mind breaks the solitude of the self.

A hard truth to look directly into. Too hard. And that is why we yearn for love, and for community. Both laudable things to want in a life—but not to yearn for. The yearning is a killer. The yearning makes one sentimental. Sentimentality makes one romanticize. The beauty of feminism, for me, was that it had made me prize hard truth over romance. It was the hard truth I was still after.

Everything I have just written: I have lost sight of times without number. Anxiety, boredom, depression: they overwhelm, they blot me out, I "forget." Slavery of the soul is a kind of amnesia: you cannot hold onto what you know; if you don't hold onto what you know you can't take in your own experience; if you don't take in experience there is no change. Without change the connection within oneself dies. As that is unbearable, life is an endlessness of "remembering" what I already know.

So where does that leave me? In perpetual struggle.

I have endured the loss of three salvation romances—the idea of love, the idea of community, the idea of work. With each loss I have found myself turning back to those first revelatory moments in November 1970. Early feminism remains, for me, the vital flash of clarifying insight. It redeems me from self-pity, bestows on me the incomparable gift of wanting to see things as they are.

I still struggle with love: I struggle to love both my hard heart, and another human being at the same time—and with work: the daily effort remains excruciating. But when I make the effort I am resisting the romance. When I resist the romance—look steadily at as much hard truth as I can take in—I have more of myself, and feminism lives in me.

Sisterhood in Black and White

Barbara Omolade

I have walked a narrow path up a steep mountain with white women and their feminism on one side and my people, Black, nationalist, and contradictorily, very American on the other side. Because of tortured racial histories and troublesome gender confusion, it has been difficult for me to organize and advocate for both Black people and women while also addressing the social realities of Blackness and femaleness. Aware of being both Black and female, I have often slipped and slid up and down the sides of that narrow path.

The term "feminism" has never adequately described the thinking of those diverse groupings of women whose only commonality is the socially constructed colorlessness of their skin originally called "white" by marauding European sailors and mad scientists. I have known too many different kinds of white women friends, school chums, and comrades to be deceived by false generalities about their "race" or gender. The concept of "feminism" as some sort of all-inclusive theme of unique sisterhood seems a false stretch for embracing the diversity of white and other women.

In this same way, "Blackness" seems too thin a term for describing people too profound or complex to be limited by the word "race" or the color "Black." The fervor of our shrill and rhetorical calls for nationalism cannot match our historical location or significance because we, African Americans, are a unique people occupying a powerful and pivotal place in the American nation.

Since the mid 1970s I have, with difficult insistence, dwelt among, and not merely visited, both the Black-people and the white-feminist sides. Sometimes I have felt like an envoy and ambassador shuttling between two alien nations. Sometimes as avenging warrior, I have defended each one's causes to the other. At other times I have sought refuge in one side, after being disgruntled and fed up with the failures and weaknesses of the other. After nearly twenty years, living in two political cultures—one feminist, and the other nationalist—has become as fluid and natural to me as speaking two languages. While rustling through old papers, trying to create order out of the last two decades of notes, diaries, speeches, and other writings, I have discovered my chaotic chronicles of those early tentative steps in these two political cultures. This essay describes my work in "white feminist organizations" and organizing within Black Brooklyn's myriad of political and social groups from 1976 to 1982.

By the late 1970s white "girls," who only a few years before were awed by Blackness, usually in the form of Afroed, militant, male gladiators, became fired up with their own words and womanhood. These white women grew closer together, bonding ostensibly around their femaleness, but ultimately also around their whiteness.

During this same time, many Black men and women like me were moving closer toward Africa. When I wrapped my head in African cloth and wore African clothes, I became embraced by and joined similarly clothed others. Their embrace seemed to eradicate all the uncertainty and confusion surrounding the experiences of my racially integrated schooling and hippie lifestyle in the white world and my childhood memories of family and community. Certain that I had discovered my true home in Africa, I repudiated all that was white.

In the seventies, I became an African woman and lived nestled with my children and my husband in a community of other newly discovered Africans. I floated above his male privilege and our mutual poverty, convinced that the specialness of being African would take care of everything. Although he was not involved in my daily activities, my husband was essential and significant in my life.

Each day I was surrounded by Black women who regarded each other as African sisters and who believed being married and mothers were privileges. We also discovered our own special talents and skills in these female relationships. We worked together on food co-ops, craft shows, and catering; we shared information about nutrition and child care. Like most women in the world our women's consciousness was raised by our common work of child rearing and household chores. The very activities and roles criticized and condemned by feminists empowered us.

We African women recognized and supported our husbands' attempts to become patriarchs and heads of their families. The sexist aspects of these attempts were peripheral, or at least they were offset by the powerful sisterhood our African-ness unleashed. We women looked to each other for dependable and consistent support.

Even Black feminists have written African-American nationalist women like me out of their feminist discourses because they view us as simplistic and deluded baby makers for even more deluded Black men. The fact is I became a nationalist for the same reasons Black men did—to restore *their* manhood as well as *my* womanhood, while reclaiming *our* self-determination as a people with a history and culture beyond bondage and before America. Even before I got married or became a mother or a nationalist, I was searching for that lost and underdeveloped but essential part of my self. Being African enabled me to live without the shame or regret of being a woman of African descent. My search ended when I became supported, empowered, and loved by other Black women and Black men in an African-based community. My last name, "Omolade," is a lasting homage to my connections to that "African" home in the United States.

However, I was challenged and stretched to go beyond my African nationalism and family life. First the unique "socialism" of China diverted my attention from exclusively focusing on Africa. After viewing Shirley MacLaine's film of her multiracial women's delegation to the People's Republic, I longed to travel to China. I realized loyalty to Africa need not mean isolation from other people and groups. In fact, the Chinese had supported African countries and groups of visiting African-American nationalists. (I eventually traveled to China in 1978 under the auspices of a national racially mixed organization.)

In 1973, while I was nursing my third child, my nationalism was further transformed by reading Gerda Lerner's *Black Women in White America*. Living an "African" lifestyle enabled me to avoid the difficult past history of Africans within the United States. I had spent many years studying precolonial African history and culture and shaping my daily life around African art, cooking, and religion. Although I had studied history and American studies in college, I knew little about the history of African or African-American women or that women like me were historical beings.

After reading Gerda Lerner's book, I was suddenly burning with questions about how women survived the transition from African woman to slave mother. I yearned to know how my female foremothers lived and survived slavery and segregation. Like many other Black people, I had mentally run away from recognizing our past of colonialism and enslavement and had embraced a more glorious historical period in the history of Africa. In this sense, my intimate and personal questions about how Black women in the past took care of their children linked the past with my own daily life. I knew this past began in Africa, but living as an idealized African was no longer enough. I embarked upon a historical and scholarly quest to understand what had happened to my people, especially women.

The need to answer these questions led me to pursue a master's degree at Goddard College's off-campus independent study program. In this way, I reasoned, I could remain within my community, take care of my children, but also study about African and slave mothering. Rather than focus on the academy and professoriate, my goal was to become a public historian like John Henrik Clarke and Alex Haley. I didn't need a degree to do this kind of public history, but I hoped the Goddard Program could give me structure and resources.

In 1973, my nationalism was further challenged by my extended family's attempt to move to a more African-like setting in rural Jamaica. Once there, we, or at least I, confronted the limits of Black postcolonial cultural nationalist dreams of a return to a pristine pre-European Eden. The generous but poor people in the hills of Jamaica often drank only sugar water and made stews from roots. They worked sporadically as migrant laborers or hotel staff. They dreamed of coming to America. We, however, believed we could live in Jamaican splendor and comfort without being caught in the obvious contradictions of class. Our African dream depended upon our ability to exploit "the natives" and join the bourgeoisie. But we had neither the color, wealth, nor connections to join the exiled American bourgeoisie. Nor did we want to become part of the Jamaican peasantry and live even more poorly than we had in the United States. After only a few weeks, I returned to the United States grateful to live at the center of the capitalist West where at least I could achieve a decent working- or middle-class life for myself and my children.

Yet another blow to my African dream state came from my father, who had achieved that decent working-class life for his family. Along with other rebels with or without causes in my generation, I had rejected my father's mundane and straitlaced life to pursue the adventurous and elusive dreams of Africa and other idealized places. He saw failure in my marriage and in my dreams. He actually cried when he saw my living arrangements and begged me to let him take care of me and the children. In 1975, with Jamaica and his death still haunting me, I broke away from my marriage and extended family, hoping to provide a decent education and home for my children, then ages 3, 5, and 6, by working at whatever job I could find.

WHITE "SISTERS": A NATIONALIST WOMAN IN THE HEART OF WHITE FEMINISM

My first post–African commune job was as co-coordinator of a battered women's shelter established in 1976 by the YWCA and National Congress of Neighborhood Women (NCNW). Ironically, I had been one of those Black women who believed that women deserved to be hit by their husbands. Only a few years before, I counseled my sister-in-law to stay with her husband after he hit her, convinced that what I then saw as her verbal aggression must have been the reason for the abuse.

My knowledge of feminism and the women's movement had been gleaned from mainstream media and rabid antiwhite nationalism. But I hid my ignorance, naiveté, and political incorrectness from my new feminist employers. I kept code switching during the hiring process by remembering past friendships with white women. I got the job, grateful for a paycheck even from the "enemy."

My plan was to work for "them" for a while and go back to an African lifestyle by opening a school for Black children or starting a crafts business. I believed my job at the shelter was going to be helping some self-righteous, pampered white women who sniffled every time their man yelled or cursed. So I never thought my new-found employment would clash, conflict, or complicate my nationalist allegiances. I fortunately have a demeanor that exudes confidence and self-assurance, but though my face was calm, inside my eyes were widened, and my jaw dropped, when I saw that the first women in the shelter were Black working-class women with their sons.

The battered women in the shelter were Black like me. They were or had been married to Black men. They worked and had children. During the first weeks I heard their stories of blood, broken bones, police calls, and flight. Most had endured years of physical abuse and had tried to leave many times. Until the battered women's movement and shelters, women like them had no place to escape violence and abuse.

I first learned about feminism and the women's movement through daily counseling battered women and developing a shelter for them. In fact, my shelter experience introduced me to the violence against women within Black families and communities. There was nothing at all being done within nationalist organizations or cultural nationalist communities to help Black battered women. I also hadn't found any Black women's organization or group working on domestic violence. Yet many Black women called the shelter for help.

At home at night I was called by cultural nationalist women who were being beaten by the same brothers who had written poetry about African queens and who were active in Black political work. I never had time to slip into the illusion that spouse abuse was the practice of unpolitical Black men, drug addicts, or just plain mean men. Ironically, my work in the "white" woman's battered women's shelter revealed aspects about my own "African" community that had been hidden or that I had idealized.

The monies for the shelter came from a "pork barrel grant" of monies obtained by state legislators Karen Burstein and Carol Bellamy for a sprawling board of thirty women mainly from the YWCA and NCNW. My job was described as co-coordinator of the internal shelter activities. But when I was hired, there was no shelter, so the job really involved working with the other five staff members to create a shelter and its program.

From March to July, we established a pilot project at the Brooklyn YWCA that included a nine-bed shelter, hotline, counseling, and community-education project. From July to August, three staff members including myself moved the program from the Y to its permanent location, a former maternity hospital in Brooklyn. The shelter opened in September 1976, and within three weeks was functioning at capacity with a total of thirty-nine women and children. We were among the first such shelters to include both battered women and their children. We sheltered 145 residents: 52 women and 93 children in 10 months and we served at least 500 women on the hotline. We had established the only battered women's shelter in Brooklyn and the largest shelter for battered women in the country.

The work was eclectic and daunting. We worked with the police to shore up orders of protection and to bring women to the shelter. We advocated with the welfare department for emergency grants. We established a child-care program and worked with contractors to provide washing and kitchen facilities for shelter residents. We recruited and organized volunteers to assist residents and to staff the hotline. We offered room and board to a woman in exchange for evening and weekend coverage. However, as a core staff member, I could be contacted at any time, so the shelter became central to my life.

Our staff was supposed to be a model feminist collectivity for it was assumed that women in the shelter would discover healing, security, and sisterhood from the staff as well as each other. Female volunteers were expected to add to this model of women working together. Shelter planners, however, underestimated the differences and difficulties of a newly constituted staff trying to work when there was no common bond or frame of reference among us except our commitment to creating a battered women's shelter. The staff included only one paid counselor, but no maintenance, kitchen, or secretarial staff. Although we should have equally shared these tasks, not every staff member wanted to do this daily and unglamorous work.

One staff person worked exclusively with other battered women's groups in the city rather than mobilize local community support from churches and organizations. Some staff were hired on a part-time basis in order to raise money and to do research. The work of admitting women, meeting and training volunteers, working with contractors to set up the physical arrangements, and creating the shelter's program increasingly fell to me and two others who were white and lesbian.

Without any clear lines of authority, power, and direction, each staff woman set her own agendas, timetables, and goals. There was both a power vacuum and the absence of a cohesive staff with coordinated roles and responsibilities. In short, the collective model was not working.

In a report to the board, I criticized the peer-counseling model of the shelter. "The model failed in any comprehensive and consistent way to adequately deal with the basic problems, with helping the women cope with economic and ethnic discrimination. Without serious consideration of this discrimination, poor women seeking economic security will fall back into dependent, potentially violent relationships."

Although I had no more authority than other staff members, I attempted to coordinate the staff's work. I was increasingly asked by board members to represent the shelter at press conferences and fund-raising meetings. Six months after I was hired, I had become an articulate, accomplished, and knowledgeable leader in the shelter.

However, board members hovered over me and the staff, sometimes butting in and bullying, and sometimes supporting us. Their lack of experience in creating an ethnically mixed shelter for abused women and their need to micromanage every decision soon clashed with the staff's increasing knowledge about the shelter's needs and operation. Shelter planners optimistically thought women would leave the shelter after six weeks, resettle in apartments, and join supportive women's groups. Since they were not involved in the daily work of the shelter, few board members realized the trauma of dependence and fear suffered by the women. Many were too emotionally paralyzed to quickly move on. Others were beaten down by poverty and discrimination. Black and Latina residents faced housing discrimination and had to spend many more frustrating months in the shelter than white residents. Moreover, language and culture played a key role in keeping Latinas in the same neighborhoods as their batterers. Passivity, poverty, and desire pulled many residents back to their batterers as soon as they were physically and emotionally patched up. There were few miraculous leaps from battered woman to self-sufficient feminist among our residents.

Furthermore, many board members, volunteers, and staff were unfamiliar and often unwilling to examine the issues and tensions in the shelter that contradicted their feminist visions of sisterhood. Staff who worked closest with women in the shelter had learned to see and hear beneath feminist rhetoric into the real lives of the residents.

Still heady from attempts at creating a "soft revolution" using their white woman's power, board members attempted to rule the shelter more like autocrats and new conquerors than as sisters. Board members envisioned grand publicity campaigns, idealized battered women victims, and minimized references to other "issues" such as poverty and racism. I define that shelter period as a frontier zone—not only was I new to feminism, but feminists were just beginning to translate their consciousness raising into organizations and institutions.

In spite of the desire to establish a feminist institution beneficial to battered women, a rather straightforward power struggle developed between the board (management) and the staff (labor) with racial, class, and homophobic undertones. The board's vision of making everything collective collided with the recognition by myself and the two most active staff members that the board needed to relinquish its authority to an executive director who could manage and supervise the shelter's staff and program.

The shelter board was composed of about thirty professional and politically sophisticated and well-educated white women, while the two or three Black women board representatives were less privileged. There were no women of color on the board who matched the experiences and class of the white board members. When issues of power and policy were involved, the white board members ignored the contribution of the Black women. In one of my recommendations to the board, I demanded it be expanded to include women of color who "have the skills, verbal and organizational, that can deal with the board on an equal level and have equal input and impact on its issues."

Because of these demands and positions, I began to pose an "uppity" challenge to white feminist racial politics and the board's authority. At one meeting I said,

> the shelter grew out of the interest of mainly white middle-class professional feminists and is an attempt to establish a feminist shelter for battered women most of whom are not only Black and Hispanic but non-feminists and racially oppressed.

But before I could consolidate my own power base, gather enough resources for the shelter's second year, and systematize the shelter's program, it was all over: the board fired the entire staff.

Fortunately a supportive board member helped me find another job. In January 1977, a month after being fired from the frontier work of the shelter, I found myself at the center of second-wave feminism, working for the Women's Action Alliance, a national woman's organization in a mid-Manhattan office building several floors down from *Ms.* magazine.

The Women's Action Alliance had been formed in 1971 as a clearinghouse on women's issues and program. It housed a library of periodicals about women's issues and organizations, including the *Women's Agenda* magazine and the National Women's Agenda, an association of national women's organizations. In addition, the alliance established the Non-Sexist Child Development Project (NSCDP), which produced materials, workshops, and presentations for interested educators and parents. I was hired to assist the director of the NSCDP. My work included travel to conferences and schools to showcase the project's philosophy and products. But most of all, I enjoyed the chance to learn about the activities and politics of the women's movement that swirled around the Alliance's activities.

I soon became involved in Alliance office politics when a Puerto Rican member of the clerical staff was "summarily" dismissed for taking work home during office renovations. Both program and clerical staff protested her firing to the executive director, pointing out the disparity between the clerical and program staff. Not surprisingly, there was also a need for clear and written personnel policies. As a result of the protest, I was appointed to serve on a staff and board Personnel Advisory Committee to develop those policies.

A few months later I was given the enviable assignment to coordinate the Women's History Project, which included organizing a three-week institute in women's history at Sarah Lawrence College, and a culminating program at the Smithsonian Institution. Historians Gerda Lerner, the institute's director, Amy Swerdlow, and Alice Kessler Harris organized the curriculum of the institute. Later institute alumnae pressured politicians to establish March as Women's History Month.

Although the institute was successful and I was gaining recognition as a leader within the Alliance and among women's organizations, six months later I resigned from the Alliance, charging the organization and the new executive director with racism. I stated that

> racism at the Alliance is pervasive, subtle, and devious, permeating policy directions, program implementations, and interpersonal relationships. It makes effective work from Black women a minor miracle. It means every aspect of the work is a battle ground for inclusion. . . . The same old-girl network permeates every program area: white, middle-class women who have limited family or cultural obligations. The hiring practices of the last six months . . . have been the same kind of woman—white. There is little reason to think this will change, especially since I am the only Black woman on staff.

Although I was the only Black woman on the staff when I left the Alliance in 1980, it hadn't always been so. Before me there had been several other Black women at the Alliance. One of them had also challenged the Alliance's unfair treatment of women of color. When Black women staff members were together, we laughed at the hypocrisy and cried at the insults of being Black and female in a white feminist organization.

However, it seemed the longer I worked in the white women's movement, the more I learned about Black women and our own movement.

While at the Alliance I became friends with Susan McHenry, the first Black woman editor at *Ms.* magazine. In 1978, she edited a major article about Black feminism and about Michele Wallace's book *Black Macho and the Myth of the Superwoman.* In her role as journalist, Susan seemed to know about everything and everyone in the women's movement. Around the time of the Wallace profile, Susan McHenry organized a short-lived women's group with Michele Wallace and a few other Black women. We studied Michele's book and classic feminist writings, which introduced me to feminist literature as well as made me see the value of documenting my own experiences and viewpoints.

Working at the Alliance also enabled me to travel to conferences and workshops where I met and learned from other feminists. On one such assignment, in 1979, I attended a Black woman's history conference organized by Darlene Clark Hine at Purdue University. There I met Betty Thomas of the National Council of Negro Women and many other Black women who were feminists scholars studying Black women. I heard Kalamu ya Salaam, a Black male journalist from New Orleans, discuss his workshops and book, *Why Black Men Should Stop Raping Black Women.*

After that conference I felt more comfortable openly describing myself as a feminist because I knew that "feminism" was not solely a "white woman's thing." There were many Black women feminists and Black male supporters of feminism. My connections with other Black feminists and supportive Black men helped me to overcome my doubts about working in the "white women's movement." I stopped hesitating and pursued writing and public speaking in feminist circles.

In 1979, the organizers of the Barnard College Scholar and Feminist Conference asked me to fill in for Michele Wallace and lead a workshop on Black women and feminism. My presentation at that workshop was expanded into an essay, "Black Women and Feminism," which appeared in *The Future of Difference,* a volume of the conference proceedings. For the next several years I participated in many Barnard Scholar and Feminist Conference planning committees, challenging the limited role of women of color in their work.

In spite of our knowledge and work as feminists, Black women continued to be marginalized within the movement. Susan McHenry, Audre Lorde, and I protested and organized against the exclusion of Black women from conferences such as the Second Sex Commemorative Conference on Feminist Theory held in 1979 at NYU. I believe Susan made an unannounced presentation during one of the plenary sessions. In the meantime a few of us faced down the angry conference organizer, who tried to limit our participation to the one or two workshops that in her words "were designated for us." The last paragraph of Susan's letter to the conference said it all, "There can be no conference on feminist theory without the inclusion of women of color on every level so in that sense I feel that the Second Sex Conference has already tragically failed."

Black women like Susan and me were integral parts of second-wave feminism but our roles were always being contained, discouraged, and limited by white women who in spite of their so-called "feminist politics" replicated existing power relationships, which minimized and subordinated us because of our race. Nevertheless, by the late 1970s there were enough of "us" to create a "Black sisterhood" unintended by the "white" women's movement.

We Black women continued to hack away at and expose white female racism at conferences and organizations that purported to be feminist. In many ways, we were still part of an old civil rights mode that protested against the exclusion of Black people from anything that was white only. But we were not only protesting, but shaping and creating our own kind of feminist politics.

We were also attracting the attention of many white women seeking a more relevant and connected sisterhood. The fear of Black women's power and abilities and denial about the significance of race caused many white women scholars to place French feminism at the center of their politics and intellectual work. The 1979 Barnard Scholar and Feminist and the Second Sex conferences celebrated and highlighted Simone de Beauvoir and other French feminists, but marginalized Black women's participation. However, many white women participants at the Barnard conference found it difficult to understand the intricacies and relevance of French feminist arguments and cried with delight and connection at Audre Lorde's brief and powerful message about language. In spite of racist opposition by white women, Black women were moving from the margins to the center of second-wave feminism.

By outstripping and challenging the exclusive focus of second-wave feminism on gender and sexism, Black women insisted that an understanding of race and gender exploitation was essential, not subordinate, to feminism. Moreover, since most of the world's women are women of color living in communities and countries devastated by colonialism and underdevelopment, Black feminist views and politics in the United States were more relevant to women's organizing and politics in the rest of the world than the second-wave feminism of white women.

BLACK SISTERS: WOMANISM IN THE HEART OF NATIONALISM

My family and community experiences were more similar to women's experiences around the world than to those of many of the white and Black feminists I worked with in the women's movement. At that time, I was a Black single mother living in the Black community and raising three school-aged children. My community was beset with problems of poor schools, economic devastation, and police brutality. After my work in the women's movement, I returned to a community and family demanding my attention and support.

I worked and associated with white women during the day, knowing they lived in neighborhoods and apartment buildings that would never rent apartments to women like me. Many of the feminists I met were married or in relationships with financially successful professionals and intellectuals. I met only one or two women who had sole or primary responsibility for rearing children especially within a working-class community. After all the speeches about women's changed roles made by many of my feminist colleagues, most lived lives of class and racial privilege. In contrast, every week I found myself pushing a shopping cart full of groceries and laundry in a poor Black neighborhood.

I faced the contradiction of being applauded by many white women for being outspoken and articulate while my children, especially my daughters, were often punished by white female teachers for expressing themselves. Once my youngest daughter was unfairly punished by a teacher for being too outspoken, yet this same teacher admired a recent speech I had made. She didn't see the irony in applauding me for the very practice for which she punished my daughter. As a Black parent I had to put aside my intellectualism and feminism and defend my children and household against the racism of white teachers, principals, and landlords whether they were male or female. I also knew that taking care of my family included participation in Black community efforts and nationalist politics. I pushed myself to participate in demonstrations and meetings sponsored by progressive Black organizations.

During the late 1970s the largest Black organization in Central Brooklyn was the Black United Front (BUF), a mass organization that held large protest marches against police brutality and encouraged liberation struggles around the world, especially those fighting apartheid in South Africa. It was organized into international, housing, veterans, culture, education, health, and women's committees, which sponsored many events and weekly community forums.

Work in BUF offered me an opportunity to use the skills, insights, and information I had learned in the Alliance to build *our* organization and "nation." My feminist experiences, in turn, sensitized me to the value of working with Black women and to exposing the male chauvinism and sexism in BUF. Once I was treated rudely when I criticized the male moderator of a BUF-sponsored Black Women's Forum for misusing the discussion period and not allowing me and others to ask questions. The moderator asked, Who did I think I was to criticize him? In my protest letter to him, I answered, "As a Black woman at a forum on the Black woman, I felt that my question and other questions were more important than your tirade . . . I am a Black woman with a right to speak in an open forum without being insulted and berated by anyone."

Interestingly, a representative from BUF responded to my letter, I am sure at the urging of Black women in the organization's leadership, by inviting me to write a column for their journal, *Black News*. For the next several years, from 1977 to 1981, I wrote many articles on subjects such as spouse abuse, women in South Africa, slavery, and ancient Africa. My articles gave me an opportunity to make the political connections between feminism and nationalism. Unknown to Alliance staff, I wrote most of the articles at work.

BUF's positive response to my written protest also encouraged me to join its Women's Committee, which was the largest, most financially solvent, and best organized of all BUF's committees. In April 1979, five months after writing my protest letter, I spoke at one of the BUF weekly forums about relations between Black males and females.

Through my efforts, the Ms. Foundation funded the Women's Committee's participation in a March on Washington to protest the attacks on affirmative action. Our committee chair reported that ". . . the Black Women's Committee showed strong organization, perhaps the best of all participating groups. The chants 'Send Bakke Back!' 'The People United Will Never Be Defeated' were most effective; education on the buses was good . . . there was no criticism to be made of our efforts."

Although I enjoyed cross-fertilizing feminism and nationalism, my family life was suffering as the work in both areas intensified. While working with the BUF Women's Committee, I was also coordinating the Women's History Institute for the Alliance. When the BUF Women's Committee chair asked me to organize an education campaign, I had to decline, saying,

> After the meeting I went home at 9:30, my children had not eaten, they were asleep, my son had been crying because he thought something had happened to me. I did not pay attention to the time during the meeting, because I was involved and committed. The next day, he had an asthma attack which meant searching for child care and leaving the girls alone after school. I blamed myself for going through with the meeting knowing I couldn't because of my family responsibilities. . . . I have to continually balance priorities and concerns in the best way I know how. Sometimes I am just too tired to come to meetings, other times I want to spend time with my children and friends. I can't keep up with what you want me to do.

I continued to participate but only in special projects of the Women's Committee and occasionally I spoke at forums or moderated workshops. My work with BUF was especially meaningful because of Safiya Bandele. When I met her at the Sisterhood of Black Single Mothers, she was one of its most active members, an officer in BUF, and a counselor at Medgar Evers College. Safiya was an example for me of Black female leadership because of her integrity and compassion especially for the "sisters." During the late seventies it seemed that Safiya could become even more powerful, especially because the Women's Committee was so strong.

In 1980, Safiya became an officer in the Black United Front when it expanded into a national organization. However, women's issues and antisexism efforts remained absent from the overall enterprise. At the founding 1980 convention, the Women's Committee became bogged down and divided over the issue of declaring polygamy a form of male chauvinism. I wrote in an unpublished article describing the struggle,

The passing of the motion condemning polygamy, domestic violence and rape as forms of male chauvinism in the Women's Committee and the national assembly degenerated frequently into a "them" and "us" shouting match with the "leftists" on the one side, and "cultural nationalists" on the other. The polygamy issue also tended to obscure the question of participation in the *political leadership* of the NBUF by women in general and Black "feminist" and/or "leftist" women in particular.

This "polygamy" debate at the national BUF founding convention was actually about the effectiveness of the ideology and practices of cultural nationalism. In spite of the intent to replicate African communities and families, most polygamous marriages formed by cultural nationalists had disintegrated. Paradoxically, many of those women most supportive of polygamy at the conference were those who had already experienced and personally rejected it in their personal lives. Hence, the polygamy debate at the conference was a showdown between the Black left and Black cultural nationalist male leadership in which they and their respective women used the issue of polygamy to dominate and overwhelm the agenda of the Women's Committee. The use of women's committees and issues as pawns for male power plays occurred in many Black nationalist organizations throughout the country.

I find in my notes from 1980 the following comments:

What might be missing from these opinions as each group and person tries to come to terms with the issues of male chauvinism and polygamy is that Black women were yelling and screaming around an issue they felt strongly, real strongly about, in spite of their respective male supporters. So no Black men in the context of the convention could have done what they used to do during the seventies—SHUT THE BLACK WOMEN UP. For in spite of the lack of an articulate theory or development of a concrete plan of action by Black women nationally, Black women in bits and pieces have begun to see their issues and themselves as important in critical new ways. Black women were in so many ways taking themselves seriously—reacting for or against polygamy, defending/debating, speaking to the general body. Their feelings had emerged in a volcano of energy about themselves. It is (can be) a continuation of Black women's struggle for self-definition within male-dominated Black organizations and social relationships.

For years Safiya and I attended many meetings of Black women that would begin with expressions of concern about the oppression of Black men and youth. However reluctant they were to make any public statements or stands opposing the "brothers," these women soon shared personal experiences of male chauvinism and sexism in their family and political lives. Safiya and I were not sidetracked by the initial "solidarity talk" because we knew these same sisters would at some point share their rapes, beatings, and difficulties at the hand of many of the same Black men they publicly supported. In spite of the loyalty of Black nationalist women toward their men and organizations, demands for leadership roles and better treatment for women soon spread.

Some organizations attempted to address the issues structurally by assigning male and female leadership to local chapters, promoting individual Black women and supporting women's initiatives and committees. However, these organizations failed seriously to programmatically address the destructive impact of male chauvinism in Black political work and its impact on personal relations. The rage and disaffection of Black women was ignored. Consequently, many Black progressive and nationalist organizations and groups fell apart over the "woman question."

Although I remained optimistic about the power of Black women activists, they did not fight for self-definition in male-dominated organizations. Scarred by sexism and male power, many Black women permanently abandoned Black radical politics. Others became active in electoral, community, and social efforts where they often faced other forms of male chauvinism. Some developed their own businesses, private schools, and community programs. A few became active in the women's movement and worked with white women and other women of color. Finally a few women like Loretta Ross and Nkenge Toure managed to use their nationalist experiences in BUF and other organizations to develop new forms of Black feminist political work such as the Washington, D.C., Rape Crisis Center.

Although I was a member of the Sisterhood of Black Single Mothers (the Sisterhood), I only began to see its significance as a Black feminist organization after Safiya and I became more involved with Black women in nationalist political groups. Founded by Daphne Busby in the early 1970s, the Sisterhood was one of the first post–civil rights era organizations in the country exclusively committed to Black women. By focusing on support for single-mother families, the Sisterhood challenged patriarchal, middle-class, and even cultural nationalist assumptions of women's roles and the family by affirming their completeness and strengths. The Sisterhood sought to debunk the myths and distortions about Black single mothers and their families.

Because it was an autonomous organization run by and for Black women in their communities, the Sisterhood did not have to measure its programs according to abstract ideological principles. The Sisterhood had no need to apologize for anomalies in either nationalist or feminist customs and practices. Under Daphne's leadership, the Sisterhood creatively and powerfully reflected the complicated intertwining of race and gender, family and women's power. Therefore, the Sisterhood's programs were eclectic, expansive, and inclusive in their support for Black single mothers and their families.

A 1977 newsletter describes the breadth of the Sisterhood's work. Rereading it, I find that during a six-month period, Safiya and Daphne represented the organization on radio programs and at the National Association of Black Social Workers, the Urban Corps Conference, the Women for Racial and Economic Equality (WREE) Conference in Chicago, and the National Conference of Panamanians. Safiya spoke to students at a School for Pregnant Students, at Our Lady of Charity Church. Articles about the Sisterhood appeared in magazines. The Sisterhood held meetings and picnics for the membership. Safiya also presented a tribute to her grandfather in the newsletter.

Daphne was as much at ease discussing the Sisterhood in white feminist settings as she was speaking in the Black community. I was surprised when Daphne asked me to accompany her to a session of the International Women's Tribunal: Crimes Against Women held at Columbia University. The session featured a number of feminist issues such as critiques of patriarchal family, support for lesbians, as well as information about violence against women, subjects unmentioned in Black organizations.

With unparalleled boldness, Daphne also fostered work with supportive Black men, many of whom were single fathers. The Sisterhood once held a conference with all male moderators. One of the workshops was moderated by a Black man and a white woman representative from Women Against Pornography, who showed their anti-pornography slide show.

The conference was one of several Sisterhood efforts to create environments that promoted friendship between Black women and men. Unlike many white women's organizations, which attempted to distance themselves from men, and unlike Black nationalist organizations with their contentious male-female struggles, the Sisterhood attempted to strengthen social relationships between Black women and Black men.

Daphne believed that Black single mothers deserved opportunities for social activities with and without their children. Although some feminists and womanists might view these efforts as nothing more than heterosexism, nevertheless, the Sisterhood met the needs and wishes of many of its membership for fun and recreation.

Inspired by the Sisterhood, Daphne Busby, and Safiya Bandele, I embarked on creating opportunities and situations for Black female self-determination independent of either Black male or white female organizations and politics. During 1981, I called together a few Black women to plan an organized response to the large number of murdered and missing Black children in Atlanta. The response became a Mother's Day March for Action: Protect and Defend Our Children, sponsored by our Coalition of Concerned Black Women. The march of mainly women and children was one of the few led and organized solely by Black women.

SISTERHOOD AND PEOPLEHOOD: THE PATHS MERGE

The march brought me to a juncture where the paths of nationalism and feminism merged. Only a few years before they had seemed inevitably separate, but now, I became aware of their commonalities. The marginal yet supportive place of Black women was integral to the way these groups framed their politics. Black women's secondary status was based upon narrow and rigid constructions of ideological categories where feminism meant white female power and nationalism meant Black male power.

White women's claims of sisterhood were conveniently put aside as they climbed over and through Black and other women for coveted positions, resources, and status. Feminism has been undermined by white women's unexamined and outrageous acts of racism. White women activists frequently bypassed and ignored the experiences, expertise, and institutions of Black people, while attempting to get Black women to work for them without allowing them any role in defining the policies and directions of the women's movement. In addition, most white feminists have failed to address the role played by their own privileged nationalism and white power in subverting the stability of Black communities and families. Second-wave feminist claims that sexism was more significant than racism, and feminism more progressive than nationalism were nothing but unabashed claims by white women vying with Black male nationalists and white male leftists for control of Black female loyalty and labor for their cause, as well as for hegemony over the social-protest movement.

Although there were many active Black feminists within nationalist organizations, Black women's dominant political consciousness and identity has been almost exclusively shaped by Black resistance to racism. However, in the same ways that race undermines white women's attempts at creating a viable feminist movement, blindness to the significance of gender has blunted the effectiveness of Black politics. By closing off a serious examination of gender, Black nationalists have become unable to explore internal divisions and dilemmas that prevent the internal development of an effective political agenda which could benefit *all* Black people. I am frankly afraid when I hear some Black nationalist woman's adamant and unexamined put-down of feminism, because I and others have learned about the closeted, silent space of the personal lives of many Black women who have been victimized and humiliated by the sexism of Black men. The avoidance of a gender analysis has allowed Black women to mask their actual experiences with Black men. And no matter how they try to comfort, understand, rationalize, or explain Black male violence against Black women, it can't legitimately be viewed as anything but a stumbling block to Black unity. In fact, much of the divisiveness within the Black community and movement can be directly traced to the unbridled and unexamined expression of Black male chauvinism. And what political framework can we use to explain this raw use of male power and brutality, except feminism?

While working in the midst of these white women who were often racist and narrow, I learned to see myself and all women differently. I will never again be so quick to dismiss and to disconnect other women's joy and pain from my own life and experiences. I no longer view white women as an enemy, nor feminism as a threat to my loyalty and consciousness as an African American.

White feminists effectively prodded women to expose their personal experiences to a political examination and praxis until now, even those who detest feminism have accepted many feminist views on women and work, violence against women, and women's broader role in society. White feminist campaigns to expose the silenced and ignored issues of rape, incest, and domestic violence benefited all women. Although early Black feminists of this period, such as Angela Davis, Frances Beal, and Toni Cade Bambara, provided analysis and debate, many second-wave feminists created identifiable and concrete projects and programs around women's experiences with reproduction and sexual violence. The way white feminists framed these issues has benefited all women, exposing us to and teaching us about issues we have either silenced or ignored.

The feminism I identify with was awakened and shaped by my experiences in the white women's movement, but it did not stop there. In fact, like many Black women, my notions and practice have challenged and outstripped the narrow, but often effective, focus of that movement. Feminism led me to more objectively examine gender within the Black community and its movements. It taught me to connect my personal relationships with Black men to my work in Black political organizations. I learned to view Black men more realistically, with greater sympathy for the personal struggles hidden by their sexism and bravado. My Black nationalist brothers' powerful analysis of white racism and Black nationalism has taught me how to use their framework to resist and protest against oppression. Their politics showed me *how* to use feminism as a tool for examining sexism within the Black community.

My experiences have produced a bifurcated angle of vision about feminism and nationalism. Although what I learned and experienced within both feminist and nationalist organizations merged within me, this does not imply that race and gender should be collapsed into each other, for they represent separate social constructs with differing histories. I have simply concluded that there is no effective Black agenda without the inclusion of women's issues and one of those issues is invariably male chauvinism. There is no effective feminist movement without the inclusion of Black women's leadership and perspectives and without opposing white racism and elitism.

I didn't realize it then, but the work of Black women threatened the intentions of both nationalist and feminist organizations. If racial and gender categories were made porous and flexible enough to include us, then the power structure of those organizations would be challenged. Black women have a strong work ethic of effectively completing agendas and programs with limited resources and usually offer valuable insights about the needs and experiences of working and poor people. Our plain talk about real issues and universal—or category-transcending—concerns about compassion, equality, and justice reinforce our speaking on behalf of the unrepresented and unprivileged groups. I am not suggesting that every Black woman actually performs in these ways, but that we embody and represent these elements to feminist and nationalist power structures.

I have also noticed similarities between Black and white women who counseled other women at the Woman's Survival Space and the Sisterhood of Black Single Mothers. Though both groups can be considered as pioneering "feminist" models, much of their work was, in fact, a continuation of women's traditional efforts to offer support to other women. In an ahistorical perspective typical of that time, the women who developed the shelter and the Sisterhood believed themselves to be unique. They failed to connect with Black and white female social workers and nurses who have also worked with populations of needy women. In the absence of these connections, many wheels of building successful ways to care for women were reinvented, and many opportunities to radicalize and expand the work of professional women caretakers were left unexamined.

Both the Sisterhood and the shelter used resources from the state, foundations, and churches to empower and heal women. But much of the time of women workers in these groups was spent competing for grants, writing reports for funders, and meeting state and other regulations. Caught between meeting the demands of their funding sources and the needs of their constituency, these groups found it difficult to consistently and actively connect the personal problems facing Black and poor women with structural solutions such as adequate housing, decent jobs, and better medical care. Instead, the work of both the Sisterhood and the shelter rested upon the notion that personal experiences of sisterhood could heal troubled women. Often these women were emotionally patched up just enough to enable them to function, but not enough to challenge the fundamental forms of political and economic inequality that oppressed them.

Yet organizations such as the Alliance and BUF that purported to address racial and gender inequality more structurally had failed to do so. In spite of the rhetoric of inclusion and challenge implied in the multiple issues of the Alliance's work as a national information clearing-house for women's issues, and in spite of BUF's attempts to develop a national mass-based political organization, both were more interested in enabling a small group of white women and Black men to attain orga-nizational power over information, decision-making, and resources. The Alliance, using the methods of corporate lobbyists, and BUF, using the protest tradition of labor union and political parties, demanded redress and resources from the state in the name of women and Black people. However, their methods were derived from the same white men whom they viewed and spoke of as privileged adversaries. In fact, the grassroots, community-based elements of nationalist and feminist orga-nizing were downplayed in favor of enabling the leaders of these groups to become recognized "players" in the national political arena.

Many of us who worked with prominent and promising feminist and nationalist organizations during the 1970s and 1980s believed we were creating changes in the relationships of women and Black people to state power. We assumed ourselves the advanced guard of the next wave of the civil rights, Black power, and women's movements, but we were, in many ways, the last of the 1960s-style radicals.

Nationalist and feminist politics and their representative groups and organizations no longer dominate or even participate in the public discourse. However, identity politics remains an important means for racial, ethnic, and gender groups to define their own particular strengths and issues. But this form of political organizing has limited value because few groups are able to remove their ideological blinders long enough to define an effective agenda based on concrete rather than rhetorical and opportunistically constructed group needs. The failed legacy of feminist and nationalist identity politics goes beyond their exclusion of Black women, but rests in their inability to realize that women, racial, and ethnic groups all live under a common political and economic system that ultimately controls the organization of race and gender.

Greater participation by Black women might have helped these groups understand that feminism and nationalism are not mutually exclusive and contentious categories, but malleable frames of reference for political organizing among working- and middle-class people. How-ever, both nationalist and feminist organizations framed their issues and causes in ways more germane to the urban privileged intellectuals that they were than to the people whom they claimed to represent. Identity politics often disregards the fact that most people—including Black people and women—live and frame their lives around family, work, and religion, more than abstract ideologies.

Yet the organizations I worked with gave only minimal attention to these issues. Only the Sisterhood of Black Single Mothers and the shelter focused primarily on women's experiences within the family, while BUF and the Alliance downplayed that side of daily life. In many groups, I often felt I had to silence and suspend the importance of my family obligations and experiences. While the Alliance focused more on women's work than the other groups, none made any attempts to connect with labor unions or workplace issues. In fact, paid employment was treated as an afterthought of political organizing, something one did in between meetings and conferences. As for religion, one of the organizations was even housed in a church, but no group seriously addressed the question of religion, faith, or a relationship with God, which was so central to people's daily lives as well as to past and contemporary social movements.

Feminist and nationalist politics have been eclipsed by conservative social movements that have rendered our protest mode obsolete, ended our financial support, and wearied our best efforts to make the national and personal efforts of organizing meaningful. From the vantage point of the merged politics that I experienced and from my own personal journey, I can see how necessary the combined strengths of the shelter, the Sisterhood, the Alliance, and BUF were for mounting viable campaigns that could effectively address issues of morality and ethics as well as justice and equality. However, a much needed critique of past work is necessary for feminists and nationalists to more effectively address the changed social context. Feminism still offers a challenge to the blinders that distort and obfuscate the truth about gender, sexism, and women's lives, while the protests of African Americans demonstrate to all how to expose and fight against racism.

I am convinced that both nationalists and feminists have used too much precious time and effort bashing conservatism as if all its elements and positions are to be condemned. At first I joined in the almost knee-jerk antagonism toward everything conservative, but more recently, I have found myself agreeing with their privileging of family and moral values. I, however, continue to believe that struggles against racism and sexism are dimensions of a larger effort toward improving family and that nationalist and feminist voices remain vital for examining the differences and inequalities among us while we create a common democratic community.

For although we remain walled in by the social constructions and constrictions of race and gender as well as by our class positions and the cultural and ethnic heritage of our families and communities, those walls are more porous than we usually recognize. In contemporary society, the ideas and actions of one political culture must necessarily have an impact upon those in other political cultures. Not only can we study and view the "other" across these porous boundaries, but in many situations, such as my own, we can walk through and embrace the other's culture as our own.

Black Women's Activities Personal Diary (1977–1982)

The following are events culled from my personal records and papers that show that Black women were organizing events and conferences focusing on themselves and their issues during the years when historical accounts of second-wave feminism had them marginalized.

The list ends in 1982, at the stage when Black women were beginning to critique the women's movement and increasing their role in furthering feminist (and womanist) theories and practices.

1977　　　　Workshop Participant
　　　　　　Intrafamily Violence: The Battering Wife Emerges
　　　　　　Annual Conference of New York State Association of
　　　　　　Human Service
　　　　　　SUNY–Brockport, New York

1978　　　　*Welfare Mothers Workshop*
　　　　　　Women's Center, Brooklyn College
　　　　　　The Ida B. Wells Lecture Series—monthly lectures
　　　　　　October–December, sponsored by Division of Special
　　　　　　Programs (Andree McLaughlin, chairperson), and Division of Student Services (Robert Johnson, dean of students), Medgar Evers College, Brooklyn, New York

　　　　　　December 29
　　　　　　Letter to Job after attending the BUF Black Women's
　　　　　　Forum

1978–1981

　　　　　　Ahidana's Black Woman's Conference evolved into *The Black Woman's Group Retreat;* guest leader was Patricia Rosezelle; organized by Tayari ya Salaam

1979　　　　January
　　　　　　Black Women: Who We Are, What We Are, Where We Are

sponsored by the Coalition of 100 Black Women at
Marymount Manhattan College, reported in *Amsterdam
News* on 2/3/79 by Annette Samuels, who emphasizes
the difference between this conference and one sponsored by the National Black Feminist Organization in
1973—male participation (25% of the panelists including Dr. Roscoe Browne, president of Bronx Community
College) and white and Hispanic [sic] women were part
of the conference.

March 1–3
Kansas Black Women's Conference sponsored by the
Kansas Black Women's Conference Committee (an ad
hoc group of women from several Kansas communities
organized, funded by the Kansas Committee for the
Humanities); "Choice or Chance . . . The Life Cycle of
the Black Woman"; Nikki Giovanni, keynote speaker

March 30–31
Participant
Conference, *The Black Woman: Her Past, Present, and
Future,"* Africana Studies and Research Center; first
time I heard a Black woman, Bettye Thomas, call herself
a feminist; heard Kalamu ya Salaam speak about rape
and Black men (sent by the Women's Action Alliance
as part of the Women History Institute preparation);
Patricia Hill Collins conducted a workshop.
Purdue University
Organized by Darlene Clark Hine

Speaker "Black Woman, Black Man"
Black United Front
Women's Committee

Slide Show/Discussion
"Women in China"
Women's Center, Brooklyn College

May 5
We Black Men Must Stop Raping Black Women
Presentation by Kalamu ya Salaam, editor of the *Black Collegian* magazine, "Women Hold Up Half the Sky," Chicago, Illinois

May 12
Featured Speaker
Black and Blue—A Daylong Workshop on Battered Women
Sponsored by Women Hold Up Half the Sky, Chicago, Illinois
Organized by Patricia Rosezelle, a professional workshop leader and community activist, active in the civil rights movement and anti-draft movement

Black United Front—Women's Committee
Minutes of Meetings: 3/7, 3/13, 3/20, 3/27, 4/10, 5/1, 5/22, 6/18
Letter to Brenda Andrews on October 10, 1979, about my work with the Women's Committee

September 20
Black Women's Symposium on the Socialization of Black Women, sponsored by the National Advisory Council for Women's Educational Programs and Texas Southern University
Houston, Texas
Participants: Sarah Lightfoot, etc.
To explore the impact of socialization on the development and achievements of Black Women; identify those characteristics associated with success in education, business, politics, and develop recommendations for strengthening the socialization process through better educational experience.

October 26
Paper *Black Women and Education*

Association for the Study of Afro American Life and History Conference

November 12, 13
Black Women: An Historical Perspective
First National Scholarly Research Conference on Black Women, sponsored by the National Council of Black Women, Inc. Gerda Lerner, Sharon Harley, went with Susan McHenry, editor at *Ms.* magazine; a wonderful oral history presentation by Sue Bailey, co-founder of the National Archives for Negro Women in 1939 and the first editor of *AfraAmerican Women's Journal* (republished), who sent a letter she was ailing; Ruth Sykes, staff at NCNW for over 25 years, and Jeanetta Welch Brown, the first secretary of NCNW, added to Sue Baily Thurman's report.
Washington, D.C.

1980   Workshop
Women's Center, College of New Rochelle

Seminar on Polygamy
Women's Committee
Black United Front

Workshop
Creative Arts Team
New York University

Speaker
Histories and Experiences of Black Women
Black Women's Week
Florida State University, Tallahassee, Florida

July
My response to articles on feminist leadership by Gloria Steinem and Charlotte Bunch: "The Leadership Crisis: Are Women the Answer?"

Fall meetings to plan the *Black Women and the Law Conference* (1981), organized by Lauren Anderson, associate director of National Conference of Black Lawyers

September 5
Minority Women: Problems and Strategies sponsored by the Mid-Atlantic Regional Convention of the Women's Studies Association University of Maryland (didn't attend)

November
Bernice Reagon at Barnard College, the Women's Center Reid Lectureship includes a public lecture, a luncheon, and an informal workshop co-sponsored by the Barnard Organization of Black Women

1981   March–July
Black Women: Why Feminism?
The Yulanda Ward Memorial Project: Black Women and Feminism co-sponsored by Black Women's Organizing Collective, D.C. Feminist Alliance and Feminist Law Collective
Yulanda Ward, a Howard University student from Houston, Texas, a housing organizer, who was murdered in D.C. She developed a proposal for a project entitled Black Women and Feminism (the project is a result of the proposal); Gwen Braxton, participant

Reported in *Amsterdam News* on October 31, 1981, that the The Coalition of 100 Black Women held a meeting composed of 40 Black women "educators, legislators, social psychologists, lawyers, etc., from fifteen geographic areas . . . to structure themselves for action." The article says that the coalition has "taken the lead in establishing an advocacy forum on behalf of Black women across the nation."

Speaker
Women Under Apartheid
Dikes Against Racism Everywhere, New York

March
Organizer Coalition of Concerned Black Women
Mother's Day March for Action: Protect and Defend
Our Children May 10, 1981; Letter to members on
May 21, 1981, trying to keep on organizing

*Black Working Women: Directions Toward a Humanistic
Context for Social Scientific Research*
A Working Conference sponsored by the Center for the
Study, Education, and Advancement of Women at the
University of California. "The purpose of the four-day
research conference is to convene a small interdisciplinary group of women who have completed significant research on black working women. The conference
will provide an opportunity to review the social sciences
and humanities literature and to exchange informed
perspectives on the research conference topic." Participants included Barbara Christian, Harriet McAddoo,
Aileen Hernandez, Julianne Malveaux.
Berkeley, California

July
"Black Woman's Summit" recalling 1895, First National
Black Woman's Summit. Newspaper article reports that
over 500 women preregistered to attend the Summit at
Howard University. Called by Congresswoman Shirley
Chisholm and Mrs. Mona Humphries Bailey of Seattle,
national president of the Delta Sigma Theta Sorority,
Inc. Keynote speech by Addie Wyatt, international vice-
president of the United Food and Commercial Workers
International Union AFL-CIO.

Ongoing support of Black Women in South Africa
See "Black Women Under Apartheid in Azania," in
Black News; and "Women in Southern Africa" by Safiya
Bandele (December 1981) and *SASAA—Sisters Against
South African Apartheid*—founded by Karen S. Daugh-
try of House of the Lord Church (wife of Herbert

Daughtry, co-founder of Black United Front); goal was "to form a coalition that would directly support the struggle of women and children in South Africa, who have been fighting against the racist, oppressive government in their country."

1982   Speaker
            Black Family Under Siege
            Mapinduzi Organization

            Speaker
            Women, Nuclear Disarmament and U.S. War Drive

            Speaker
            Afrikan Street Carnival, Brooklyn, N.Y.

            Women's Place in Politics
            Voter Education Program
            Church of the Master, Harlem, New York

            The Politics of Reproduction and Abortion
            Women's Section
            Black United Front

            Black Solidarity Day
            Black United Front

            August
            Black Convention 1982: A Call to Convene the Black Population of NYC "The time has come for Black New York to meet in convention for the purpose of defining our goals and fashioning a program of action to develop plans and strategies and most essential to reaffirm our commitment to struggle against racism at home and abroad."

The Buried *Yes*

Minnie Bruce Pratt

CHAPEL HILL, NORTH CAROLINA, 1973 WOMEN'S DANCE

She is not the first woman I've ever danced with. In high school I had a friend, a girl who sometimes held my hand in darkness; once or twice she whirled me around our music practice room. And at the senior prom the girls outnumbered the boys, so I went with my best friend, LaJuana, but we didn't actually dance. But this lanky studious woman is the first grown-up woman, a married woman like me, experiencing sisterhood at my first women's dance at Elizabeth's house that she shares with Linda. Not yet the collective house at Laurel Avenue in Carrboro, or the one on Green Street in Durham, but a graduate student's shared duplex where the women who consider themselves part of Women's Liberation have come tonight. Now I belong too, because I've written one review, on a book about androgyny, for the local *Feminist Newsletter*. Now she and I dance one dance, no spark with her except the thrill of asking for that dance by choice, not by default. No conversation, although I wonder about her work, a history graduate student who teaches storefront classes on women because the university won't let her do it for credit. Later her book on the roots of our new movement of women in the black civil rights movement gives me a context for my political theory. But tonight she is just a partner for one song at a dance I've come to almost to spite my husband, who worries when I do women-only things. I'm fighting with some of the women in the English department also, because I want to close the Women's Caucus social events to men. Joy says, "John will feel funny," and I say, "No offense to John, but women often go places without their husbands." I don't know how to articulate what I can see, an enticing vista, what it might be like to talk among ourselves without always having to answer the men, or reassure them. What kind of new plots might we come up with, what kind of endings invent at a potluck of just us? Dancing with

Sara (who doesn't seem especially interested in me) I glance around the room, and see, pressed into a corner on the margins of the dance floor, half-lying under a coffee table, two women making out. One, in a boy's cap, nuzzles the other's neck. I am repulsed and attracted. I'm watching something taboo, pornographic, a peep show. But my body tingles as if I've raised a foot or hand bent too long in one position and the nerves have come suddenly alive. When I get home my husband asks me nothing. On Sunday afternoon I walk through the garden to meet our new neighbors. He's an ex-truckdriver minister who was thrown out of seminary for political reasons; he's marched in Washington. He's a poet and handsome, like my husband. Standing next to him, I get as hot as if kneeling, hands in dirt, in the garden, a heat that lasts until he asks me to do him a favor, type up his notes for his evening sermon. I spend the rest of the afternoon saving seeds in the garden, morning glories, scarlet climbers, cockscomb, and princess feather. I bend over withered vines, and crush desiccated herbs in my hands, basil, dill, thyme. I lift up my fingers to smell the pungent oils.

Fayetteville, North Carolina, 1976–1977 Equal Rights

One afternoon, when I am the speaker at a branch library, out near the mall, I debate a local representative of the Eagle Forum, Phyllis Schlafley's right-wing women's auxiliary. She and I wrangle over constitutional interpretations until she throws out a line like a whip: equal rights for women will make homosexual marriages legal, and also men and women will have to use unisex toilets. I pause, stunned, and look at the ten people in the audience, who look back at me for a response to this statement that accuses: Either you like women too much, you're a lesbian, what you want is legal sanction for perverted sex. Or you don't like women at all, you want to be a man, what you really want is his filthy penis. At some point her accusations merge, and I become a perverted lesbian who wants a penis like a man, and filthy sex with other women. Her words uncoil through the room like lines of electric wire nailed to a fence. I muddle through my answer. Nothing in our meetings about legislative reform and the Equal Rights Amendment has prepared me to defend a connection between women's rights, same sex love, and a flexible gender expression for men and women. I say of course we are for women, divorce law reform, equal pay. I say of course there won't be gay marriages or shared bathrooms. I try to say that lesbians are women too. I make a boundary around womanhood a few feet larger than hers. Just beyond it my woman lover and I lie together, in a king-size bed in a motel room. We're on our way to Philadelphia, to a National Organization for Women conference, a long drive up and shared expenses with another woman member. My lover puts her fingers on my mouth to shush me because of the other sleeper there, she twists her fingers between my thighs, into my pubic hair. What kind of a woman can I be in public, outside this hidden room? The electric wire marking off space allowed for woman, for man. To touch the boundary is danger.

After the meeting, I go with some of the audience to a restaurant. We have cherries jubilee and coffee, a white woman stockbroker complains about quotas, a white housewife says that smiling at her husband feels like slavery, two women make jokes about queers. Two African-American women who work for the county say, "You'll have to change your language if you want us to participate." Later, a NOW member reprimands me: it's unnecessary to push lesbians on the audience. A year before she had been upset when she learned I was a lesbian; she was offended that I had not trusted her enough to tell her. She'd said abruptly, "Being afraid to tell me is your problem, not mine." I have had an ongoing argument with her about organizational support for an African-American woman suing the county for discrimination; she doesn't want to endanger grants for our program funding. Jerk back from crossing the boundary.

After another library meeting, consciousness raising on rape, seven of us go to AJ's for beer. MC raped by a friend, Sue and Deb by their fathers. We get loud, noisy, annoying. Three white men in suits walk past us. One stops, puts his hand on Regina's shoulder: "Solving the world's problems?" Regina says, "I don't know about that, but take your hand off my shoulder." I say, "We don't know you; we don't want to talk to you." Put barbed wire up between me and the intrusive hand that fondles, that rips, that pats and then slaps. Wrap my body in barbed wire when I go out in public, unwind it at night to be with my lover, both of us drinking to numb the pain that tracks across our arms, our breasts, our thighs. When we fight, sometimes she mocks me, "You are so queer." I wonder what kind of woman I would be past these boundaries. Maybe someone naked in a silk robe. The contours of my body shift as fluid as the fabric, skin flexible as silk. How much of a man would I be, how much of a woman? Who would I lie naked with, slipping off the robe of my skin?

An Activist Love Story

Paula Allen and Eve Ensler

WHERE WE STARTED

Eve

Inspired by Simone de Beauvoir, Janis Joplin, Grace Slick, Adrienne Rich, the Deadly Nightshade, Toni Morrison, Robin Morgan, Sylvia Plath, my feminist English literature professor Joan Peters, drugs, my general anger and distrust of men (based on a violent and incesting father), an incredible attraction to women both sexual and emotional, a deep hunger for a mother and an ongoing obsession to liberate her from an oppressive marriage, inappropriate sexual involvement with a series of older male professors, I became a feminist. Initially my efforts were devoted to organizing a feminist organization at Middlebury College between 1973 and 1975. Here was a university that supposedly advocated the equality of the sexes, with hardly any female professors, no women's studies courses, a very jock-minded, fraternity-based, sexist environment. Organizing women here was difficult, but eventually paid off. We created WAC (Women's Action Coalition), a strong group of over 50 women who brought feminist speakers, films, and poets to the campus. We ran a feminist radio show once a week and produced a feminist literary magazine. We infiltrated classrooms with feminist books and speakers. We ran consciousness-raising groups. We fell in love with each other and we fought hard to win a sex discrimination case for a feminist professor.

All of this was amazing training. In these early days I discovered how impossible it was to be a good leader. I had no boundaries. I was desperate to control women, to drag them into my way of thinking. I did not, for example, understand the difference between facilitation and fascism. I was a depressed alcoholic, covering my emptiness and low self-esteem with this driven rage and hatred of men that fueled and infected my work.

In 1975 I graduated from college and bottomed out. I got lost in the streets and bars of San Francisco and New York City. I found myself reenacting my childhood, engaging in abusive, dangerous situations with violent men while I was in blackouts. I was wildly promiscuous, acting out my self-hatred, participating in self-humiliating situations night after night. The alcohol and early abuse of my childhood had split me. On one hand I was a militant feminist, on the other I was waitressing in Mafia bars wearing tuxedo tops with black fishnet stockings and high heels. I was a mess of contradictions. I could not live what I believed.

In the years that followed, I eventually got help. I got sober and began to look inside, to unweave this mess of contradictions, heal this split. When I returned to political organizing, I returned with a new consciousness. I worked in a grassroots peace group in New York City in my neighborhood, CANDU (Chelsea Against Nuclear Destruction United), and this time the issues of leadership, process, empowerment were as important as nuclear disarmament itself. We did hundreds of local-based actions. I was transformed by this group and the humble day-to-day work: leafleting, mailings, speaking, marching, and civil disobedience.

Paula

I wish I could name the exact moment when feminism burst within me. In a sense, there was such a moment, but it was the result of thousands of other moments that came before. I grew up in Detroit, polite, predictable, heterosexual, obedient—a real pleasure to be around. I had a perfect symmetrical pixie haircut and wore a funny little orange sundress. But I had another self which I kept more private, developing her within the confines of my room and mind. I was really growing up angry, questioning, demanding, highly sexual, a Lesbian. In this other persona I created myself as a female superhero—masked, tightly clad in black clothes, big breasted, fearless—scaling walls.

By the time I left Detroit and arrived at Boston College, I decided the best way to celebrate my freedom was through sex and acid. I did both often and even managed excellent grades, but toward the end of the first year, I realized I had enrolled myself in an institution just like that of my high school: conservative, segregated, and boring. True freedom came—I quit, became a waitress and bought a camera. My Pentax camera became my love. I had found a means of expressing that self which I, for so long, had hidden. Making pictures allowed me visibility. I began with pictures of shadows, then shadows with people, then people without shadows, then packed my camera and moved to New York City.

I wandered through neighborhoods developing photo projects and presented my growing portfolio to stock agencies and magazines, using the feedback (rejections) as my education. It was in 1980 at my job, printing in a color darkroom, that I first experienced feminist feelings and desires without yet knowing the word. National Public Radio was on and announcing the upcoming Women's Pentagon Action. Thousands of women would be gathering in Washington to defy the Pentagon, the workplace of imperial power. Women would be encircling the building to protest the arms race. I found the idea of the action completely thrilling. I had to be there.

I phoned *Newsweek*, asked for the assignment editor, and told him he had to send me (he had no idea what the WPA was or who I was). I persuaded him that it would be a big mistake not to have an assigned photographer present. He offered me the assignment and five hundred dollars.

For the first time in my life I witnessed the bravery of women in activist struggle. I documented women in red, screaming and enraged, beating drums; women in mourning creating a graveyard on the Pentagon lawn, commemorating women victims of patriarchy and war; women encircling the Pentagon singing songs as the windows filled with workers' faces; women in defiance blocking the entrances, weaving themselves together with yarn. It was here that I experienced a dual revelation. Photography could be a means of activism in that I could make women's actions and histories visible. I also realized that these women I was photographing were not merely documentary subjects—they were me. Not only did I share their fear of nuclear war, feel angry at prevailing militarism, and long for a women's community, but I was discovering a bravery and a sense of outrageousness in myself I hadn't known I possessed.

FALLING IN LOVE

Six years later, in 1986, we met at the Cornelia Street Cafe in New York City. Paula was jet-lagged, emotional, just off the plane from Greenham Common Women's Peace camp in England via southern Lebanon. Eve was exhausted and terrified as her new play, *The Depot* (a play about a middle-aged woman's liberation through her experience in a women's peace camp), was just about to be performed for the first time. In this heightened state, a state that was to last really for the next nine years (and still continues), we bonded, fell in activist love, found the commonality of the issues we pursued in our work (photography and writing), and discovered our mutual passion for anarchy and civil disobedience.

Greenham Common

Paula

In August 1981, a Welsh housewife led a group of 50 women, children, and men to Greenham Common United States Air Force / Royal Air Force base. They marched 125 miles in protest of NATO's decision to site 96 American cruise missiles there by December 1983. A total of 464 land-based cruise missiles would be deployed in Europe, each missile with the capacity to destroy 15 cities the size of Hiroshima. The development of more and more "sophisticated" weapons and guidance systems by the United States and the USSR suggested the possibility that a limited nuclear war could be fought and won in Europe.

Nine days after the marchers had arrived at Greenham Common, four women chained themselves to the fence at the main gate and requested a televised debate on the subject of cruise missiles with the Ministry of Defense. Their request was denied. Some of the marchers, now joined by other supporters, made a decision to stay and set up a peace camp.

Six months later it was decided to make Greenham a women's only peace camp. Making it a women's only space challenged the hierarchies characteristic of a patriarchal society. It encouraged women to take part in disarmament, develop confidence, and voice opinions in an environment where each woman's perspectives and feelings were equally valued. Men, however, were welcome to visit and encouraged to continue their support of the camp off-site.

Women began to arrive from not only England, but all over the world. Having been forbidden by the authorities to live in campers or erect permanent structures, the women built "benders"; domelike environments created by hanging plastic sheets over tree branches. Wood pallets became mattresses. Straw insulated the ground, and candles provided light and heat. Eventually other camps were established along the nine-mile perimeter fence at all the entrances to the base.

Every day women decorated the fence with photographs of loved ones and words such as PEACE, WE SAY NO, CRUISE OUT, and by weaving spider webs, snakes, and dragons. On one side of the grim metal-link fence were hundreds of soldiers preparing for the arrival of cruise missiles, and on the other, challenging fear and destruction, were the women reclaiming the base with brilliant colored threads of hope and trust.

The women's camp—a remarkable manifestation of women's courage, vision, and determination—became a vital emotional force within the peace movement. We were women from every conceivable background united in our opposition to cruise missiles and our firm belief in nonviolent direct action as a means of change.

It was at Greenham that I not only developed my skills as a documentary photographer, but I discovered my powerful activist self. I began to participate in actions, blockading entrances and roadways. I used bolt cutters to dismantle the fence and was dragged off by police. I learned to build fires in the pouring rain and cook a meal for fifty. I developed a sense of humor and theater. I paid attention and had opinions that were heard. I was now an out Lesbian in love with another Greenham woman. I was in awe of all the women who arrived at the camp, feeling love and respect for these women with whom I developed community, created home, took risks, and envisioned change.

All actions—there were hundreds—were organized and carried out by women. We were daring and took risks; we were uninhibited, playful, and constantly surprised and pleased by what we could accomplish together.

Thirty thousand women held hands and encircled the base. Five thousand blockaded the entrance and roadways. Two thousand removed large sections of the perimeter fence. Forty-four, using ladders, climbed the fence, formed a circle on top of one of the missile silos, and danced. Twenty women occupied the sentry box at the main entrance, sang songs, and answered the phone. On Nagasaki Day women entered the base and gave the commander an origami crane as a symbol of peace. On Christmas, women climbed the fence dressed as Santa Clauses with sacks of presents for the soldiers. On a warm spring day, women dressed in teddy bear suits climbed the fence and picnicked on the runway.

My last time at Greenham was in 1987. I had made thousands of photographs and had developed a reputation as a "peace photographer" not only by the women of Greenham, but also by the British press, who regularly published my work. As an activist I was firmly rooted in my desire to work in women-only groups, to work creatively and nonviolently and to take action, without my camera, when I felt the necessity.

FROM THE PLAY "THE DEPOT" BY EVE EASLER

I did an action, old nursey, careful, believe in the law me, did an action. I cut through the fence with nine other women and drew peace signs on the guard's little house. And I almost got arrested. [to guard] Where were you? You're supposed to be on morning duty. You got a nice buddy there. He actually punched me in the face. See. I was laughing. I don't know why. I felt so excited. Like I was a kid. Like I was doing exactly what I wanted for the very first time. He told me to stop spray painting his little house. I didn't. I just kept laughing. This made him angry, I guess. The next thing I know he punches me.

The thing I didn't know was that both Matthew [her husband] and Sandrah [her daughter] arrived during the action and they were watching the whole thing. Oh my God, Matthew was in shock. He couldn't believe it—the military of the United States, punching his own wife. He went slightly crazy, started screaming at the guard, started to come right on through with us. The other women had to restrain him. I think your buddy may have helped win him over to the cause. He's a slightly violent version—but I think he's with us. Sandrah was terrific. At first she was very withdrawn. She stayed back away from me. Then after awhile she came over and she told me that kids at school had called me all kinds of names—the same names I used to call the women here—lesbian, commie, loonie. It had upset her a lot. But then she saw the action. She was so proud. She kept saying she couldn't believe it was me. She told me she missed me so much, that her daddy was kind of nuts without me and that when it rained she imagined me washing away forever. Then she cried and I cried. We have always cried well together. I must admit that for that one moment I wanted to go home and crawl up in bed with Sandrah and take a long nap. Fortunately she didn't ask me to come home. As a matter of fact, she said she might come and stay next weekend. What can I tell you. It feels good. All of it. Good. Right. Here. Now.

Eve

I wrote *The Depot* because I was moved and obsessed with women's peace camps. I believed they were defining a space for the possible transformation of political and emotional reality. It was clear that radical new thinking and actions occurred there. Women had found a way to collect themselves into their power and originality in protesting and refusing a male-driven system.

I was a playwright. Peace camps were intensely theatrical. The camp site itself was like a set. Everything occurred there, eating, talking, sleeping, arguing, peeing, chanting, singing, weeping. It was an emotional set as well. Women got real there, defenses got stripped away through a variety of forces. Sitting in a concentrated way with the thought of nuclear destruction (for example) for three days, like a global meditation. Your life was there, literally on the ground. You experienced your fears, you dreamed them and talked about them. Defenses got stripped away by exhaustion too, by dirt, by sweat, by having to live inside a group of highly opinionated and emotional women.

I was interested in the process of transformation I'd seen occur to myself and women who spent time in peace camps, how the bonding of women, the safety of a "woman only" space had given freedom to voices and opinions and selves. This transformation process was what theater was about—a character beginning one way and through the process of the journey becoming someone else.

Joanne Woodward was really responsible for my writing *The Depot.* She was very active in the nuclear disarmament movement. She wanted to find a way other than giving speeches to get to people. The material had to be funny. We had to reach people without their knowing it— moving them, entertaining them. This was a difficult thing for me, not hitting people over the head. I simply didn't trust people to hear the message unless I clobbered them with it.

We worked for several months on the script, me writing, integrating my experience of peace camps with interviews I had done with women from Greenham Common and Seneca. When we had a first draft, Joanne decided she wanted to direct it. We contacted Shirley Knight and she wanted to perform it. The three of us worked for months, shaping the text, finding the lead character of Barbara. We wanted the story to be about an ordinary woman who comes to an extraordinary place through her time at a peace camp. Our process together was remarkable. It was truly one of the great times of my life. Three women, all of us feminists, all different generations. Joanne and Shirley were the great women of the theater. They taught me about economy and humor and passion and subtlety. We rehearsed for hours in churches, in high school auditoriums. We ate brown rice cakes and we stopped apologizing for having an agenda. We were openly using theater to radicalize people, to move them, upset them, stir them out of their apathy and fear. We traveled for two years all over North America going from the Kennedy Center, where we performed for Congress, to the Nevada test site, where we performed at a mass demonstration.

COMMITMENT

In our separate ways, we (Paula and Eve) had both been developing as activists and artists, attempting to find ways to integrate these two aspects in our own lives. We were both concerned with women empowering themselves, documenting their voices and visions. We were each involved in unraveling violence. Paula was photographing wars and conflict as a journalist in Lebanon, Northern Ireland, Poland, and Chile. Eve was writing plays about characters who had suffered violence in families, in homeless shelters, in war. We both focused on the women who defied authority, refused domination, and continued in spite of the violence, whether it was a loving mother in Belfast or a homeless woman who stirred rebellion in the shelter.

With several other women, Paula and Eve founded Anonymous Women for Peace in 1987 as a way of immediately responding to current issues. The group only existed when a woman in the group felt a need to call for an action around a specific cause. There were no flyers, mailing list, high organizational structure. It was more like a guerrilla group. The tenets of the group were simple—the action had to be outrageous, funny, and immediate. The group lasted for almost four years. In that time we were able to initiate both small events and mobilize mass actions.

We initially organized peace camps, which became the center out of which all our other actions grew. We organized and participated in six women's peace camps in New York City. Three of these camps were in Madison Square Park and three were in Battery Park.

Peace Camps

At 9:15 p.m. the women lit candles and we walked through the park to the water. Ships moved on engines of light, like capsized hotels, like huge electrified sugar cubes. At the sea-wall the women made another circle of their flames. And then they told each other why they were there and where they'd come from and what they hoped for. This wasn't a media event, a photo opportunity, an attempt to levitate the Pentagon, guerrilla theater. Nor was it, as in China's Cultural Revolution, a struggle meeting or a Speaking Bitterness. It was more a gathering of fugitives reaching out from what they knew in their separate solitudes to make a community of conscience, to ease into their witness and signifying.

John Leonard, Newsday, 1988

Bagels, rats, plastic, banners, paint melting in the rain, consensus, police, tents, more plastic, Stacey, romance, more police, flashlights, menstruation, no sleep, dirty fingernails, no nukes in the harbor, stop the violations against women, homeless women, singing by the river, candlelight vigils, square dancing, no men as protectors, we need men as protectors, women protecting women, only women, origami cranes, honk for peace, office workers, flyers, rat patrol, Tom Orr's lasagna, Ann on a bench at 3 A.M., Laura's "wet ones," Tina's port a jane, nurse Jennie with her emergency box, love in the dirt.

For six years we camped in the parks in May or June, each camp focusing on the most pressing concerns. We camped in solidarity with the women of Greenham Common. We camped to protest a planned nuclear navy port in New York Harbor. We camped to say no more rape and to reclaim our bodies, our earth, our rights, our history, our power.

We came from different organizations and orientations. Some of us came from Mobilization for Survival, from CANDU, from Women's Pentagon Action; some came from Greenham, from War Resisters League. Some pulled up in taxis in the middle of the night.

We were straight women and gay women. There were longtime activists and the newly curious and the totally pissed off, the intellectually superior, anarchists, socialists, democrats, women on motorcycles, women in office jobs, artists, married women, women politically opposed to marriage, women whose hair was perfect after sleeping in the dirt all night and women who smelled strong, women who read *Vogue* magazine and women who read Lesbian porn.

The peace camp was an anomaly in New York City. First of all it transformed the dark, dangerous park into a safe, cozy place decorated and determined by women. By being a public space, by being connected to issues, by being a women's camp, women became politicized.

We were inspired by the notion of stopping life as usual, of putting our bodies on the literal ground to say no more war, no more desecration, no more nukes, no more rape, no more violence. The stakes were this high. Our willingness to be there inspired the surrounding community. It made them less cynical, more hopeful. They came to spend afternoons with us. They bought food. They handed out our flyers. They got angry.

The camps became a gathering place for women to share ideas, and desires, to vent rage, to express sorrow, and to dream. It seems we lived in peace camps for a long time.

ACTIONS

The peace camps created bonds, made women safe enough to continue with their activism and to take bigger risks. Ironically, the camps had created a home for us—an emotional, spiritual, political place we could return to in ourselves and with each other. Really, the peace camps motivated the continuing years of more expansive, outrageous, and challenging actions.

NEVADA TEST SITE

Twenty Anonymous Women raise the money through a 1989 letter-writing campaign to fly to Nevada, to sleep in the desert, to stop the testing of nuclear weapons. Unfortunately, we only know city camping: rats, loud truck noises, taxi horns, hungry passersby. We know nothing about scorpions, snakes, cold desert nights, radiation dust, camping equipment, fires, erecting tents, making food—survival.

We invade the test site with hundreds of other protesters. As we are handcuffed and arrested by armed state troopers with mirrored sunglasses we perform the can-can for a crowd of cheering thousands. We are held in outdoor cages in the desert for hours without water with hundreds of other protesters from across the country. Then, still in handcuffs, we are crowded in buses and transported for three hours to an unknown destination in the middle of the night.

Women have claustrophobia attacks. Women sing. Women weep at the nature of violence and the obvious desecration of the earth and disregard for our lives. A convoy of support vehicles follows. They wait for us and are there cheering when we're released. Later that night, the hard desert ground actually feels comforting after being locked up in those buses. The earth feels safe and expansive and welcoming. It's the lesson we've come to learn.

Weaving in D'Amato's Elevator

In 1991 we stand on the street corner for an entire day and give passersby quarters to call Senator Alfonse D'Amato's office and register a protest against his support of the war in El Salvador. We tie his phone line up for eight hours. We take Polaroids of passersby posing with a life-size photograph of Senator D'Amato.

A week later seven women weave themselves with yarn into the elevator of Senator D'Amato's building. We tape the hundreds of Polaroids on the elevator wall. We then "occupy" the elevator, riding it up and down in search of the "Peace Floor." The superintendent of the building discovers us and shuts the elevator down, locking us in the dark. We are now woven together, unable to move in a closed dark place. Claustrophobia builds. We decide to moan for the dying women and children of El Salvador. We are very loud because we overcompensate for our terror. Our moaning carries through the entire building, bringing out hundreds of worried and confused onlookers.

They open the elevator door so we will stop moaning, but we don't. The police arrive and the press. It is now an event. A female police officer, very unhappy to see us, throws us against walls and brutalizes us, ripping through our weaving with a huge butcher knife. Bruised and roughed up, we are carried through a now huge crowd to a police car where we are arrested and taken to the station.

Stickering

Every Christmas between 1988 and 1991, a group of Anonymous Women make hundreds of antiwar toy stickers: "These toys are dangerous to your children's mental and emotional health." We choose a huge Toys 'R Us, usually in New Jersey, and invade it with our stickers. We work in pairs and we work quickly, stickering as many war toys as possible—guns, nuclear weapons, bombs, etc. Building our courage as we go, we even sticker toys that are already in people's carts.

One Christmas, two of us get busted and have to rip off hundreds of labels, but this is successful, because the packages of the toys look damaged when the stickers are ripped off and the store has a hard time selling them.

RED ACTION

Twenty Anonymous Women, dressed in red, invade Mariel Hemingway's restaurant on the Upper East Side to protest her participation in the TV miniseries, "Amerika," a program designed to rejuvenate terror of communism. Having made reservations, we occupy a few tables and then take off our coats, revealing our shocking red outfits. We place red napkins on tables, red carnations in the table vases, red dye in the water glasses.

We don't make it beyond red drinks: cranberry juice, Shirley Temples, Virgin Marys. Angry management and reluctant waiters attempt to usher us discreetly out the door. There is nothing discreet about us. Some of us have already joined other diners, engaging in conversation about the miniseries. Others leaflet the restaurant. The police arrive. We are moved outside and permitted to stay as long as we keep moving, so we sing "America the Beautiful" in front of the restaurant windows. We can-can (as usual) and snake dance in our red.

BRUNCH AT THE PLAZA

Anonymous Women invite Donald and Ivana Trump to join New York's homeless for brunch at the Plaza in the middle of February. We request that the Trumps donate 1.3 percent of their net worth for housing for the homeless. The nature of the action is to dramatize the incredible discrepancy between rich and poor. The Trumps never RSVP, but two thousand homeless people arrive by foot, on school buses, by subway, and in vans for brunch.

There are long tables covered with white tablecloths and flowers set up outside the Plaza. There are waiters in tuxedos and balloons and banners. There are performances by homeless women and art events. There is so much food—turkeys, chicken, salads, chili, and cakes, donated by hundreds of individuals and fifty restaurants. One man, moved by the event, sends a sterling silver tray filled with finger sandwiches from the Plaza.

WHAT IS ACTIVIST LOVE?

Eve and Paula

Being an activist means being aware of what's happening around you as well as being in touch with your feelings about it—your rage, your sadness, your excitement, your curiosity, your feeling of helplessness, and your refusal to surrender. Being an activist means owning your desire. The history of women has been a history of the denial of desire.

We fell in love with each other's refusal to be silenced, buried, undone, or contained. We fell in love with each other waking up at 5 a.m. in a soggy plastic tent, our sleeping bags intertwined. We fell in love rubbing each other's feet for hours on trains to and from demonstrations in Washington. We fell in love as we were thrown into paddy wagons and it was dark, but we could feel each other's warm, sweaty skin as we sat, pressed together. We have continued our love affair in other countries and other contexts. We volunteered in a women's homeless shelter for eight years. Paula photographed. Eve interviewed women and wrote a play. We made a book together. We went to Berlin and witnessed the wall coming down—the turquoise, purple, and golden paint being chipped away. We had nightmares in a hotel room in Berlin where Eve remembered being an incest survivor because the wall was coming down. Political events often mirror the unconscious. Activism becomes the ignition, driving the internal and external worlds to a point of intersection and then, openness. When you stand up in solidarity with another woman, that moment becomes an act of love. We found each other through action. We claimed our desire.

To Hell and Back:
On the Road with Black Feminism in the 1960s & 1970s

Michele Wallace

It gets harder and harder to say why and how I became a black feminist twenty-six years ago when I was only eighteen. Over the years, I feel as though I have passed through at least three or four different lives; I've been old, over the hill, in despair, and even nearly dead more than once. I have also been reduced to infancy and total helplessness more times than I care to remember. The girl I was at the chronological age of eighteen is only a vague memory to me, someone I once knew and understood a long time ago.

More to the point perhaps, I had no inkling at eighteen that I would still be explaining twenty-six years later why or how I, as a black woman, became a feminist. The necessity of doing so is all the more aggravating as I have come to realize in the past decade that my feminist ethics and my racial pride are no more than the tip of the iceberg so far as my identity goes.

Some unimaginative types, most persistently in the provinces, continue to believe that a black woman must be brainwashed by white culture in order to voluntarily call herself a feminist. In fact, it has never been easier for me to be a black feminist than it is right now. Perhaps because I haven't been anything else for so many years, I find it difficult to imagine how women who are not feminists stand themselves. Essentially, I've given up on most other kinds of speculative political thought or activism anyway, so why not go completely futuristic and visionary? You might say that my preferred political perspective has taken on an almost science fiction–type improbability.

Granted I have to admit that part of the security and satisfaction of my present life is inextricably linked to my ten-year-old relationship with the so-called "enemy"—hubby bear Gene, the love of my life and my soulmate. I am also cognizant of the fact that many Americans, maybe particularly black Americans, are laboring under the misapprehension that feminism precludes marriage and/or a satisfactory relationship with a male.

But the problem of loneliness and isolation, which is perhaps global, or at least postmodern, hasn't much to do with feminism, or even with its opposition. The odds are very much against any of us finding and/or remaining with the "right" person (if you still believe in such a thing) for all sorts of substantial socioeconomic and cultural reasons. Start with the fact that looking probably doesn't help, and that nothing in our upbringing, in our culture, or our history (aside from the popular notion of romantic love, always unrequited) teaches us to value our own time enough to want to find the "one" that we're living to mate with, the other half of our solitude. Is it luck or acculturation that renders some of us blissfully settled with what feels like just the right complement, and others of us consigned to roam, or to settle for a restless autonomy? (I don't believe that shit about a Zen-like isolation, such as Zora Neale gave Janey at the end of *Their Eyes Were Watching God.*)

My observation is that those who really need somebody, find somebody. Those who don't, wander, enriching the world all the more as they go, as a result. Apart from everything else that has to do with our complex individual psychological development, as social critic Barbara Ehrenreich has said, the social structure of patriarchy in whatever form you choose—from the U.S. Senate to the church—has become increasingly unstable. This means that the economic and political function of the nuclear family is deteriorating beneath our feet. So what are we who are so suddenly orphaned turning into? Nobody quite knows. Basically, you're on your own when it comes to the conceptualization of a mate, or whether or not you even bother.

As it happens, I am a feminist. I have mated, although I haven't had any children. All of this has to do with shifts in the patriarchy, which is to say if the patriarchy (and along with it old-fashioned capitalism) weren't on shifting ground, a woman like me probably would have had children. But, as it happens, I find myself frankly relieved that I haven't dared. Between the needs of my sister's three, the demands of my vocation as cultural critic, and my pleasure at being a perpetual child to my husband's parent and vice versa, there has never been any space. Sometimes I think of the four children I might have had, or of the four abortions, and the fact that they were for three of the brightest, most interesting men I've known. The children would have been fascinating if they had survived their unwilling parents. Which was a risk I still stand unwilling to take. Given that there are so many other unwanted children—visibly grown and otherwise—in need of recognition, courting, and nurturance, I prefer the living to the dead.

For the umpteenth time, I find myself reflecting on the myriad factors that led me down the curious path of my feminist persuasion, never satisfied with the answer, wanting to tell a story about it that will finally satisfy everybody, including me. I would have to say I have been inclined to revolutionary politics and radical gestures of one kind or another at least since the seventh grade, perhaps in rebellion against elementary school at the exceedingly dull and pedantic Our Savior Lutheran School in the rural Bronx.

To give you some idea of the extent of the brainwashing in this parochial institution, my typically colored family regarded my sister and me with horror as we plastered our bedroom walls with pro-Nixon stickers during the presidential campaign of 1960, which (no thanks to us) Kennedy finally won. When we started bringing home jokes about Jews and Catholics, my mother thought it high time that we move on. Indeed the pivotal occasion was a run-in with the racism of my sixth grade teacher about which I subsequently wrote a short story (my first, a prizewinner and published three times) in my sophomore year at college.

After Our Savior, our next stop was the ultra-progressive, ultra-rad and boho New Lincoln School, no longer in existence but then located in a lovely old building on 110th Street on the mutual borders of black Harlem, Spanish Harlem, and the Upper East Side. My fellow students ranged from the son of Susan Sontag (David Rieff) and the daughter of Harry Belafonte (Shari Belafonte) to the sons and daughters of the likes of Robert Rauschenberg, Maureen O'Sullivan, and Zero Mostel.

Other luminaries-to-be were Tisa Farrow (sister of Mia), Robin Bartlett and Deborah Offner (actresses), Stanley Nelson (the filmmaker), Jill Nelson (the writer), Adrian Piper (the artist), Billy Boulware (the TV director), Suzanne DePasse (film and TV producer), Thelma Golden (a mere baby), and so on and so forth.

This isn't just a list of the rich and famous but rather is meant to give some idea of how abruptly New Lincoln managed to change my vision of things to come. It was like going from a warm bath to an ice-cold shower. Suddenly I was no longer in Dick-and-Jane land but in something like real time. It may have been the fashion among a certain tier of the well-off and famous to toy with a radical milieu in education, but this game didn't cohere with my mother's ambitions for me. She was more serious. Thanks to the rise of unionization among both teachers (my mother and my aunt) and General Motors assembly-line workers (my stepfather), financially I regarded us as comfortable, but no matter how much I fantasized, we still weren't rich.

As it so happened, just as we were making the momentous change to New Lincoln, everything else in the world was changing as well, which continued to lend my experience at New Lincoln a certain gravity.

The first year I was at New Lincoln, in the seventh grade, John F. Kennedy was killed in the streets of Dallas. I can remember trying to explain to my best friend of the moment, the daughter of a soap opera star, why I was unable to cry about it—after all, what was he to me? In the same school year, under my most beloved teacher Helen Myers, we studied Eastern cultures, from the food (which we prepared in cooking classes) and religions to the history and literature; for my project, I led my class in a day of Buddhist observance.

During the year I was in the eighth grade, just as I was getting to know him, Malcolm X was shot down like a dog in the Audubon Ballroom. This event positively rocked Harlem, the community I lived in, and my youngish parents with it. No one uptown was ever quite the same. Meanwhile, I was directing my fellow students in a production of *The Diary of Anne Frank,* a book I adored, along with the memoirs of Helen Keller, and every other book I could find about the growing up of sad little girls. Once I had lost my religious faith among all those irreligious leftist Jews at New Lincoln, I never regained it.

Going to New Lincoln was the first of many radicalizing transformations, interior and exterior. Among my classmates were red diaper babies and the children of those who had been blacklisted by McCarthy, sometimes overlapping with the rich and/or famous. What may have been happening was that the taint of McCarthy was finally washing away in the blood of the sixties. Our assemblies featured peace activist folk singers, speakers from SNCC and the Civil Rights Movement. We listened to the music of Leadbelly and John Cage and we sang the songs of Pete Seeger in our classes.

The first anti–Vietnam War demonstration I attended was a class outing in the eighth grade. But the major proof I now have that New Lincoln was exceptional is that it no longer exists in these evil times. It simply vanished, like cheap housing.

Meanwhile, as a full-time resident of Harlem, I was going to the Apollo with my neighborhood friends every Saturday afternoon. We watched show after show, as long as they let us, of the Drifters, the Supremes, Jerry Butler, Jackie Wilson, the Temptations, the Marvelettes, Curtis Mayfield and the Impressions, Smokey Robinson and the Miracles, Marvin Gaye, Gladys Knight and the Pips.

Schoolmate Jill Nelson and I started a singing group with two other girls at New Lincoln modeled after the Marvelettes and we actually dared to perform at the eighth-grade dance our version of "Please Mr. Postman"—a humbling experience.

So it should come as no surprise that at the fragile age of thirteen, and in the midst of a local and international world that seemed convulsed with revolution and upheaval, that I decided that life would no longer be possible without first meeting Smokey Robinson. I was very much a doer and at least this was something I could do. So it was just the most natural thing in the world for me to call the Apollo Theatre while he was featured there and ask to speak to his manager. I told him that I was a reporter for the school newspaper (my school had none), and that I wanted an interview with Smokey.

Having actually gotten an appointment for the next day, somehow arranging to miss school and with my most grown-up makeup on, my sister, my best friend, and I trotted over to the stage door of the Apollo our hearts in our mouths, and were ushered in to meet not only Smokey Robinson and all the Miracles but also all of the various Temptations, and Wilson Pickett as well. At the time I didn't even know who Wilson Pickett was. That day I had a preview of something I wasn't quite ready to know yet about the second-class world of black celebrity: the fact that they were so accessible, in comparison to what my white classmates went through to get a peek at the Beatles or other white stars, and that backstage at the Apollo was so unbelievably shabby, killed whatever romantic notion I had previously had of their tier of showbiz.

So at fourteen, as we were entering the "Soul" period in popular music, I was already disillusioned about the magical powers of rhythm n' blues. The fan in me was dead. With somewhat more serious political intentions, I took myself alone down to the SNCC office to volunteer to go South on the bus rides. The lessons of the six o'clock news, bringing bulletins from the front in Mississippi and Vietnam, had not been wasted on me. I was genuinely surprised when the workers at the office suggested that I was too young. I have no idea what made me think they needed me but I was hopelessly in love with Stokely Carmichael.

Then at fifteen, I was sent off to Paris for the summer with my beloved grandmother, Momma Jones, a Harlem fashion designer who called herself Madame Posey, who was most intent on gaining admittance to the showings of the couture collections. My mother, Faith Ringgold, the artist, was approaching her mature development as an artist and needed time to paint. It was the summer of 1967, and the revels to come in 1968 were already very much in the air on the Left Bank. At French lessons at the Alliance Française on the Boulevard de Raspail, my sister and I rubbed shoulders with an international student clientele, enabling us to escape periodically the protective gaze of Momma Jones.

On those escapades, I was intent on pretending to be older. I have no idea how successful I was, but I remember much of this period as a time when I had no clear boundaries: I had convinced myself that I looked at least nineteen or twenty to the young Africans, Caribbeans, Italians, and Greeks gathered there. Smoking French cigarettes and drinking espresso helped bolster my courage. I have no idea if I fooled anyone. It seemed as though wherever we traveled, the newsstands were always screaming the latest scandal of the Civil Rights Movement in the South. Between that and Vietnam, it didn't feel like such a great time to be American.

After the summer of 1968, when I assistant-taught dance at the School of Music and Art, I flopped all over the place during my senior year in high school. I was an extremely indifferent student, my one claim to fame that I managed an incredibly high score on the SATs after two prior attempts. Boyfriends were already commandeering a good portion of my attention.

Having decided somewhat haphazardly to audition for Juilliard, I sabotaged myself by quitting my preparatory work at Arthur Mitchell's new dance school in Harlem in the middle of a class with the Master Karl Shook because, I told myself, ballet was simply too apolitical. I ended up with Barbara Ann Teer's New Age National Black Theatre for a spell, a cathartic experience for me because of its philosophy that middle-class Negroes were brainwashed and in need of debriefing. It held out the promise of a transformative blackness. Working there was a ritual healing; it was a place where you could discard all your inhibitions, of which I had a ton. I was so incredibly self-conscious, it is hard to imagine now. Meanwhile I was getting a lot of attention, mainly because of the way I looked. I had had exzema in my early adolescence and been as homely as a flea, but I had been cured by a fancy Fifth Avenue dermatologist and now I was beautiful, or so everybody said.

At New Lincoln, since I was seriously getting into my militant and fed-up-with-whitey phase, I started a black student organization that never could find much to protest in a private school that was already 25 percent black. I finally hit on boosting Puerto Rican enrollment as a demand.

By graduation, I can only suppose (since I was in a semiconscious state) the curriculum was in such disarray from keeping pace with the reverberations of JFK's assassination, the Columbia riots, SNCC, the Peace Movement, the sexual revolution, and the marijuana craze, all of which seemed to come to a head that year, that we hardly managed to produce a yearbook. Classmates Chris Rauschenberg and Tim Lutz took a lot of crazy, lopsided photographs.

During graduation, I was actually in another zone. I remember that I had begun to wear my hair in an uncombed style, something like the early stages of what we now know as dreadlocks. At the ceremony, Momma Jones complained that the parents looked as bad as the kids. In particular, she pointed out to Faith the tangled hair and blue jeans of Robert Rauschenberg, who was sitting with John Cage just in front of them. "No wonder we can't get Michele to comb her hair." Some of the kids had on jeans. Some were barefoot. Some showed clear signs of the fact that they were smoking marijuana with their parents on a nightly basis. The music had been written by students, and was sublimely dissonant and jarring, after Cage.

For me, it was not a sobering moment but the reverse. I had no desire to go to college so far as I knew but wanted to graduate immediately to autonomy and revolution. My guidance counselor, Verne Oliver, had taken the precaution of applying to Howard University (my choice) and the City College of New York on my behalf. I guess Faith was busting out all over in her development as an artist and hadn't the time, energy, or fortitude to devote to my situation after having spent so much money on private schools and camps.

Becoming a black feminist in the seventies had not only to do with the times but it also had everything to do with being the daughter of the ambitious, fiercely militant, and driven black artist, Faith Ringgold. My family was made up of women who were either superwomen of one kind or another, or women who just couldn't cope on almost any level. From an early age you were expected to declare which one you would be, although I didn't learn this until much later.

In retrospect, I imagine that I was driving my mother, who had never wanted children to begin with, crazy. She seemed to have little idea how bad things could get. Remember, this was the sixties, which had followed the fifties, forties, and thirties, the latter humbling decade the one in which my mother was born. After so much money on private school, etcetera, how much could go wrong?

When Faith sent my sister and me to Mexico for the summer, I can fully understand why she was relieved to finally have us out of her hair for a short time, although in her place, I would not have allowed my girls out of my sight, but then that may also be why I have never had children. I could never stomach the odds.

As for me then, I was seventeen and simply mad for revolution; my sixteen-year-old sister, Barbara, who was nearly fluent in Spanish and French and quick as grease, wasn't much better. Mexico City, which had been the scene of student revolution the summer before, turned out to be precisely the right place to continue my research. Given my sister's facility in Spanish, it didn't take us long to join a commune in the countryside outside of the city. When I told Faith that I had no desire to return to the United States but wished to spend the rest of my life in Mexico, I was ordered home not only by her but also by the U.S. government. To make a long story short, I ended up in a facility for juvenile delinquents on 16th Street.

Up until this time, I was no feminist. Rather my thesis had been that I and my generation were reinventing youth, danger, sex, love, blackness, and fun. But there had always been just beneath the surface a persistent counter-melody, which was becoming a full-scale antithesis, what I might also call my mother's line, a deep suspicion that I was reinventing nothing, but rather making a fool of myself in precisely the manner that untold generations of young women before me had done. The synthesis of the two lines—my mother's cautionary tales and my own joie de vivre—merged into our joint vision of black feminism, the ground upon which my mother and I could mutually agree long enough for me to grow up.

Of course, I am saying this in retrospect. We didn't just wake up one morning as a black feminist mother-daughter team. The radical feminist protest at the Miss America Pageant had happened in 1968 and had gotten a lot of attention in the press in New York. Although the press coverage was designed to turn people off, it did just the opposite for me. I remember that being my initial moment of interest because I had always deeply resented the institution of the Miss America Pageant and had already figured out that life was possible for a woman without a bra.

In the fall of 1969, after my adventure in Mexico, and my debriefing in the Sisters of the Good Shepherd Home for Girls on 16th Street, I went off to Howard University, a place designed to acquaint you with the shortcomings of black female status if ever there was one. Between the fraternities and the Black Power antics, misogyny ran amok on a daily basis down there.

In the spring of 1970, I returned to New York and night school at CCNY. In my absence, New York had become a seething hotbed of all kinds of feminist activity. Faith and I were very shortly radicalized within the frenetic and inclusive goings-on of the downtown art scene.

A major organizing principle during these times, despite the reluctance of present historians to admit it, was the overarching unity of everybody on the left—feminist, black, hippies, druggies, socialists, and Marxists—in opposition to the war in Vietnam. If you are too young to remember it, then try to imagine what it might have been like if the pro-Nicaraguan movement or the anti-Apartheid Movement in regard to South Africa had been a thousand times bigger, then maybe you'll be close. Remember also that an astonishing array of major leaders, from MLK, Medgar Evers, and Malcolm X to both JFK and Robert Kennedy, had been taken out, more or less, right in front of our eyes. What with a paranoid and closeted J. Edgar Hoover lurking about and watching us all, no one who had any claims to a position of progressive leadership had any idea when their number might also be up. Baldwin's melancholy refrain during this period was, "Martin, Malcolm, Medgar, and me."

My recollection has always been that Faith and I came to feminism at the same time, although I now suspect that I was following her lead in the way that an offspring can sometimes follow a parental lead without necessarily being aware of it, especially since I was an inveterate Momma's girl right through my early twenties. Through those early years of the seventies, I frequently accompanied and assisted my mother in her various radical forays into the antiwar, anti-imperialist art movement of the times. With Faith's assistance and support, I founded an organization called Women Students and Artists for Black Art Liberation (WSABAL) as an activist and polemical unit to advocate the kinds of positions in the art world that are now identified with the Guerrilla Girls.

Particular high points were when we participated in raucous art actions at the Museum of Modern Art and the Whitney, when we occupied the offices of Thomas Hoving at the Metropolitan, and when I wrote the words for the poster for the Judson Memorial Flag Show (participants ranged from Carl Andre to Kate Millett), which was ultimately closed by the attorney general's office, whereupon Faith as well as Jean Toche and John Hendricks (now Yoko Ono's personal curator) of the Guerrilla Art Action Group were arrested and became the Judson Three. Somewhat reluctantly, and with only half my attention, I sometimes collaborated with Faith when she used texts as she did in her "Political Landscapes" series.

In the meanwhile, I also managed to move slowly but steadily toward completion of a bachelor's in English at CCNY, studying creative writing under such notorious enemies of feminist indoctrination as the late Donald Barthelme, Earl Rovit, John Hawkes, Mark Mirsky, and Hugh Seidman. At various events around town, I met Audre Lorde, Toni Morrison, Alice Walker, June Jordan, Nikki Giovanni, Sonia Sanchez, Clayton Riley, who all seemed to me stunningly attractive, articulate, and bigger than life. They used to say what I now realize were perfectly outrageous, revolutionary things and they were photogenic. Clayton had been my sister's teacher; I encountered Walker, who seemed shy and retiring, at meetings of black feminists. Even then, to fledgling black women writers, Morrison was a queen. I, myself, wrote and published relatively often, and got the chance once or twice to read my black feminist poetry in the company of such feminist luminaries as Audre.

Among the many thoughtful editors of my writing during this period were Kathie Sarachild at *Women's World,* for whom I wrote my first black feminist essay, "Black Women and White Women," in 1971; Robin Morgan, who was associated with *Rat;* and Theresa Schwartz, editor of *The New York Element,* for whom I covered the Panther Convention in D.C. in 1974, at which Huey Newton and Jane Fonda made a notorious pair.

My best feminist buddy and mentor then was Pat Mainardi, now professor of art history at CUNY and Brooklyn College, with whom I spent the summers in a country house in a one-horse town called Craftsbury, Vermont. Together she and I, artists Irene Peslikis and Marjorie Kramer started an ill-fated left-wing publication called *Women and Art.*

I can remember distinctly Shulamith Firestone, the minimal artist Robert Morris, then director of the Museum of Modern Art, Robin Morgan, and various New York Panthers visiting our apartment in Harlem. Sometimes I had the sense that we were making history. I certainly thought we were on the verge of a revolution.

In the summer of 1973, Faith and I went to Europe—she to Germany, to Documenta, and I to meet a friend in Madrid, where I spent a sybaritic week of dancing all night and sleeping all day. The only touristy thing I did was visit the Prado and that I did every day like clockwork, in order to inhale the dusky magic of their Zurbarán paintings. I felt invigorated by the Prado and by Franco's totalitarian Spain. It was so quiet, so safe, and so cheap, unlike the world I'd come from. I made up for the lack of political stimulation by having a passionate affair with a military stranger whom I met in a discotheque. Perhaps a foreshadowing of my future husband, he too was from South Carolina.

Nevertheless, as I grew older, I became more and more aware that I was often operating under the shadow of a heavy funk. I was depressed a lot.

Sometimes I look back on the mid-seventies and feel as though I spent more time taking cold showers to break through my numbness than anything else. When I finally graduated from CCNY in 1974, it seemed something like a liberation of sorts. I considered myself a veteran feminist by this time. For reasons that now escape me, I was wearing psuedo-African apparel, geles, long dresses, sandals, no makeup, and so forth. The assumption that was usually made about me was that I was a Muslim, which won me some respect on the street, more than you might get in a miniskirt. Yet here I was, this very opinionated black feminist, who had real problems with the Black Muslim agenda.

The general idea of the long dresses was to cover as much of my body as possible and thereby impede the course of the various sexual propositions from strangers, which followed me everywhere I went. Apparently, it seemed worth being mistaken for a Muslim woman. Meanwhile, I was also occasionally agoraphobic, bulimic, and often had a nightmare of inadvertently strolling the streets in the nude.

By the fall of 1974, new friend Margo Jefferson (then a writer at *Newsweek*) had helped me get a job as a book review researcher at *Newsweek,* which furnished me with entry to all sorts of magic New York worlds, from the Newport Jazz Festival to the Public Theater to a variety of literary shenanigans and shindigs. I worked on both the Erica Jong and the Toni Morrison cover stories. I first met Ishmael Reed on the telephone. From my spartan office in the Newsweek building on Madison Avenue, in the illuminating company of fellow researcher Robert Miner, and under the mentorship of senior editor Jack Kroll, I was able to call anywhere in the world provided I knew the number.

Michael Wolff, a white friend (we were introduced by a mutual black male friend who was gay), worked in a job of similar prestige at the *New York Times,* and we made a habit of chainsmoking, drinking scotch, and crashing high-profile New York literary parties together. I kept hoping that I would one day meet Norman Mailer, whose antifeminist rants I secretly found hugely entertaining.

It was around this time, I believe, that I became one of the founders of the National Black Feminist Organization along with Faith and a whole bunch of the usual suspects. I was still urgently passionate about a variety of feminist causes in the abstract. Occasionally, I was asked to write sexy short pieces for *Ms.* I received all sorts of moral support from Margo and Marie Brown (then editor at Doubleday), who never stinted on expense account lunches. As usual, chum since high school Jill Nelson and I continued our protracted commiserations over the fate of black feminism. In particular, I remember Jill, whom I had known since seventh grade in New Lincoln, as somebody who I thought really understood me. Neither of us had yet turned out the way our parents had expected.

Together with the poet Pat Jones, Faith, Margo, and I organized the Sojourner Truth Festival of the Arts in 1976 at the Women's Interarts

Center, at which Ntozake Shange performed something from *For Colored Girls*. This also turned out to be the scene of a major public confrontation between my mother and me, one that resulted in a lot of tears on my part and in my getting my own apartment. About a year later a new group called the Sisterhood began meeting at Alice Walker's house in Brooklyn to talk about what, if anything, black women writers should do or say about feminism. Also, a little later, around 1978, a black feminist study group, which included Susan McHenry and Barbara Omolade, began to meet to discuss black feminist texts and to ponder what our role should be in the movement.

In 1974, I met Ross Wetzsteon at a party at Mark Mirsky's house. If I wanted to write for the *Village Voice,* Ross told me, he would be glad to introduce me there. He took me to a vivacious and saucy Karen Durbin. As feminists, we immediately bonded. I ended up working with her on my first two *Voice* essays—one about being a black feminist called "Anger in Isolation: A Search for Sisterhood," in which I talked about the difficulty of black feminist movement in that we black women had neither the will nor the means to risk standing together against black men on any issue. The other article explored my experience of growing up a black American princess in the Harlem of the fifties and sixties. Both essays were struggling to articulate the peculiarly paralyzing specialness of being one of the few members of an educated, black middle-class elite. We were the talented tenth that Du Bois imagined but never really got to see.

It was with the articles in the *Voice* that I first became a public black feminist in New York. Perhaps my greatest hit had been my back-cover profile of Frankie Crocker, then and still the program director and head DJ at WBLS-FM. It was my luck that James Brown just happened by the studio the day I was visiting. Of course, in my article, I gave them both black feminist hell, as was my style in those days. So much so that when Ntozake first met me when I interviewed her, she said that she was glad that the *Voice* had chosen me because I was just the person to put an end to all the ridiculous voyeuristic speculation in the mainstream media regarding her various suicide attempts.

Of course, it didn't turn out that way, but that's another story. But I can remember being hungry for the kind of fame she had then. Everybody knew, I thought, that the possibility of radical politics was over. But at least you could be famous and then tell them all to fuck themselves.

The writing for the *Voice* in the mid-seventies got me my editor, Joyce Johnson, who took me with her to Dial Press, which also published most of Baldwin's books. Margo introduced me to Maxine Groffsky, who would become my literary agent. In 1975, Maxine helped me draft a proposal for a book on black women and Joyce got me a modest advance ($12,500), whereupon I immediately quit my job at *Newsweek* and once again moved away from home uptown with Mom to a mouse-ridden apartment on Greene Street.

In a matter of a few months I had whipped up the essential core of what I thought would be a single chapter on black men. But then Joyce argued that it should be the centerpiece of the book and that I needed only another large section on black women. We then began together the laborious process over a period of two years of editing what was called "Black Macho" and constructing the much more difficult to write section of the book that would be called "The Myth of the Superwoman."

Meanwhile, since my money was low, my guardian angel Margo recommended me to her friend Helen Epstein for a job teaching journalism at NYU. At twenty-four, I was suddenly a university professor (actually my rank was lecturer) in a school that had almost no black faculty. It was a common occurrence once I moved into the NYU housing in Washington Square Village to be frantically queried by middle-aged white women in mink coats whether or not I had any free days for housework. I was always so stunned, I can't recall what I would say. I wasn't used to living around white folks.

It was not unusual for my editorial sessions with Joyce to result in tears: mine. Frankly, most of her qualms were over my head as a writer. I had the distinct impression that she might have been perfectly comfortable drawing out our revision process for another year or even two, but I put my foot down. I needed a book as soon as possible. Talk about waiting to exhale.

What helped me conceptualize both my book and my life, as much as anything else during this time, was a book that Helen was working on about children of concentration camp survivors. Helen focused her first book on the riddle of her relationship to her own parents, who had survived the Holocaust. She set out to discover what made such people so inscrutable and difficult, and how it affected their children. In the process, she was also learning a great deal about who she really was; in particular (or so I imagine now) how to wake up from the pain that survivors and their descendants sometimes find so crippling. For the first time, I began to realize, through my discussions with Helen, and through therapy, that I too might be considered the adult child of the walking wounded, and that this fact, as well as my feminism and my blackness, had much to do with who I was.

As *Black Macho and the Myth of the Superwoman* approached the galley stage, old friend Robin Morgan submitted my text for review to Gloria Steinem and Alice Walker. Needless to say, they liked it a lot (which isn't to say they wouldn't later change their minds) and, through a process of elimination and the ministrations of a new black female editor who would become another best friend (Susan McHenry), I ended up with a double excerpt and a picture of me on the cover of *Ms.*

Then the whirlwind began over the way I looked and dressed for TV appearances, the way I spoke, what I did and didn't say. *Ms.* asked me to take my braids out so they wouldn't interfere with the cover lines. *The Today Show* insisted that I be interviewed with someone who could debate my inflammatory positions.

Afterwards, all I can remember hearing from the publicity people at *Ms.* and Dial was that I was wearing the wrong colors, the wrong accessories, and I didn't smile enough. I am sure I was probably as animated as a piece of wood on camera, so these complaints were merely their best attempts to get through to me. I don't think anybody ever realized how paralyzed with fear I usually was in any kind of public appearance. While Dial Press wondered whether I should be described as a black feminist in their press materials, *Ms.* wondered whether I was up to snuff as a black feminist spokesperson (I was not).

Meanwhile, although I had dedicated the book to her, my relationship with Faith had reached an all-time low. Not nearly as famous then as she is now, she didn't feel as though I had given her sufficient credit for my miraculous feminist rebirth.

I had started therapy with an Adlerian the year I graduated from college. We had put all our eggs in one basket. The theory was that professional success was supposed to cure whatever was ailing me psychologically. Au contraire, I was more a mess than ever. I was drinking and smoking heavily, even doing the occasional illicit drug, and hating myself on a daily basis for not being pretty or smart enough. My boyfriends then are now too excruciating to remember.

Then the sniper attacks started rolling in. But what could I expect after not having given any thought at all to allowing Dial to feature the most inflammatory paragraph in the book on the jacket cover. "I am saying . . . there is a profound distrust, if not hatred," my inner child proclaimed in black type against a white background, "between black men and black women that has been nursed along largely by white racism but also by an almost deliberate ignorance on the part of blacks about the sexual politics of their experience in this country."

In *Black Macho and the Myth of the Superwoman* I had indiscreetly blurted out that sexism and misogyny were near epidemic in the black community and that black feminism had the cure. I went from obscurity to celebrity to notoriety overnight. Quite suddenly, I was a frequent guest on *The Today Show, Phil Donahue,* and "the six o'clock news" from Newark to Pomona; I was reviewed, attacked, and debated in *Essence, The Nation, The New York Times, The Washington Post,* and *The Black Scholar,* by my own people more than anyone else, and my photograph was everywhere. At twenty-six I had written the book from hell and my life would change forever.

When I did readings and talks, black folks came at me with book in hand quoting chapter and verse. Meanwhile I was completely at a loss to explain how the book had actually come about. In a way, I still am. I think now that *Black Macho and the Myth of the Superwoman* was one of those manuscripts that was never supposed to see print, which, indeed, wouldn't see print in today's more competitive and specialized marketplace.

The result of an unhappy alliance between a perfectionist unfeminist aesthete and a young, nihilistic, black, feminist, militant half-crazed and sexually frustrated maniac, the text could only hope to crash and burn, which it promptly did after first driving a lot of people crazy, including me.

Nevertheless, it documents a crucial stage in my development, and perhaps in yours, in learning the lesson that human perfectibility is not a possibility, that men are people too, and that there aren't any answers in life yet. While I don't think of *Black Macho* as the Holy Grail, I am not dismissive of the book. Indeed, I believe it to be one of those immortal texts destined to be misread and misunderstood in its own time, but to survive whatever onslaughts are hurled at it. Somewhere in the future it will find its home. Or perhaps it will just help make the future. Just because I gave it birth doesn't mean I understand it.

Moreover, *Black Macho* belongs with other celebrated documents of the heady times of the sixties and seventies, most of them not exactly gospel: from Cleaver's *Soul on Ice,* George Jackson's *Notes from Soledad,* Baraka's *Home* and *Dutchman,* and Angela Davis's *Autobiography* to Toni Cade Bambara's *The Black Woman,* Robin Morgan's *Sisterhood Is Powerful,* Ti-Grace Atkinson's *Amazon Odyssey,* and Jane Alpert's "Mother Right."

In the process, I learned a lot of things, many of them impossible for me to verbalize. But one thing I can say is that no matter how you slice it, humanity still has a lot of fixing to do. Although I am hardly dead yet, I am no longer young; nor do I any longer feel as though the burden of change is on my shoulders, or my generation's shoulder's, alone. I am prepared to stand aside, to watch others try and, blissfully, to watch the crowd go by. Nevertheless, I continue to believe that feminism, in all its myriad and contentious incarnations, will always be part of, although not the only, prescription, until somebody comes up with a cure.

Skirting

Yvonne Rainer

It must have been sometime in 1985 that I bragged to a friend, "I'm no longer afraid of men." I hadn't trucked sexually with "them" for at least four years—I was fifty years old—and it would be another five years before I would venture into intimacy with a woman, although I had already begun to call myself a "political lesbian." The question continues to vex me as to why I spent so many years fooling around with what now seem to have been preordained doomed heterosexual partnerships. The answers are as numerous as the day is long. (1) I didn't possess foresight and couldn't make use of a constantly unraveling hindsight. (2) The prospect of "working at" the relationships with the help of a succession of professionals always held out the possibility of imminent "success." (3) Until the late eighties I was more attuned to heterosexual feminism than to the gay rights movement and therefore was not given, or could not give myself, permission to tune in to another level of desire. (4) Compulsory heterosexuality.

But it hadn't always been that way. My first "liberation" came at age eighteen when I moved out of my parents' house across the bay to Berkeley. While I was browsing in a bookstore the most beautiful woman I had ever seen struck up a conversation with me. Tim was twenty-five, a graduate student in psychology at UC Berkeley, and "bisexual." She took me to her house, told me her life story, talked about her conquests. I fell in love. Tim was worldly-wise, wore Navajo jewelry, had studied modern dance, could discuss anything and everything, had an I.Q. of 165 (so she said), and long flowing black hair (I had chopped off my hair bowl-fashion shortly after falling in with some socialist Zionists from Hashomer Hatzair in my third year in high school). Although we slept in the same bed, she refused to make love to me, her reason being that she didn't want the responsibility. I confided to her that the woman in my sexual fantasies looked like Marilyn Monroe or Jayne Mansfield. She said that a woman like that would probably want someone more butch than me. It was 1953.

The foregoing anecdote can be situated in its proper historical context when I confess that shortly thereafter I got myself picked up by an ex-G.I. in a North Beach bar, thereby unwittingly launching a life of compul*sive* heterosexuality. This may sound like a harsh judgment, a view through the spiky gauze of aging, a change in sexual preference, and breast cancer (I had a mastectomy over a year ago). Yet it cannot be said often enough that for a young woman in 1953 everything in the culture militated toward pleasing men. I suspect that my bisexual mentor was no exception. Tim's bisexuality may have served as a refuge when she became too uncomfortable in the lesbian underground. As for me, the heterosexual assumptions of the dominant culture, coupled with a lion's share of traumatic (so what else is new?) deprivations in early childhood, guaranteed a scenario wherein a docile Goody Two-Shoes compulsively (and impulsively) falls into bed with every Big or Little Daddy that comes along. Insofar as the fifties sanctified virginity as a way of preparing women for lifelong monogamous bedlock, my scenario was not as unexpected as you might think.

My parents were totally unfit to raise children in a reasonable way (in fact, farmed me and my older brother out to various foster homes until the ages of seven and eleven, but that's another story). In the 1920s, as anarchists and vegetarians, opposed with equal fervor to the evils of the State and carnivorism, they had been social rebels, but by the time I was an adolescent in the late forties, their latent puritanism surfaced to mesh with the sexual conservatism of the era. It was only a matter of time before I would transform the terms of their former radicalism, acting out in the bedroom a rebellion against both social prohibitions and parents while seeking through compliance with the sexual expectations of men the love I had been denied as a child. (A shrink I consulted in the late fifties said I was the most compliant person he had ever met. And of course far be it from him to steer me in the direction of a differently gendered sexual partner!)

So it transpired that I conveniently "forgot" the implications of my lesbian desires. Libidinal amnesia was subsequently compounded by prolonged exposure to psychotherapeutic revelations of my mother's insufficiencies, with the—happily, temporary—consequence of a deepening distrust of women. The return of a women's movement in the early seventies coincided, in my case, with the disintegration of an emotional house of cards. Busy with "my brilliant career" of dancer and choreographer, I had hardly taken notice of the gathering tumult of feminist voices. A white, unconsciously ambitious artist, oblivious to art-world sexism and racism, ensconced in the profession of dancing (a socially acceptable female pursuit), protected from the reality of my ambitions by skulking in the shadows of male artists, I started reading *Sisterhood Is Powerful* in 1971 as a seven-year relationship blew up in my face, necessitating a long haul—aided and abetted, and in some respects impeded, by feminist essays—out of the ashes of an almost successful suicide attempt. Shulamith Firestone and Valerie Solanas figured prominently in my enraged demise and recovery.

I had never thought of myself as belonging to an inferior class, especially as I began to achieve recognition in my field. Hadn't I gotten a Guggenheim before he did? Wasn't he always encouraging me and taking pride in my success? Hadn't he said that he hated "false modesty" when I tried to claim I wasn't ambitious?

Excerpts from Firestone's analysis of romantic love in *The Dialectic of Sex* still read with a burning clarity:

> Thus "falling in love" is no more than the process of alteration of male vision—idealization, mystification, glorification—that renders void the woman's class inferiority.

> However, the woman knows that this idealization, which she works so hard to produce, is a lie, and that it is only a matter of time before he "sees through her." Her life is a hell, vacillating between an all-consuming need for male love and approval to raise her from her class subjection, to persistent feelings of inauthenticity when she does achieve his love. Thus her whole identity hangs in the balance of her love life. She is allowed to love herself only if a man finds her worthy of love.

Yes, it was the light from *his* eyes as I described the making of "Trio A"—the dance that was to become my signature piece—that first illuminated my achievement. This may have taken place in Monte's, or maybe the San Remo, in the Village, over double vodka martinis in the winter of 1965. I watched his expression change from polite attention to intense appreciation, even wonderment, as I described the details of creation. I was saved.

> In a male-run society that defines women as an inferior and parasitical class, a woman who does not achieve male approval in some form is doomed. To legitimate her existence, a woman must be

more than woman, she must continually search for an out from her inferior definition.

I extracted what I needed to fuel my woman-scorned fury. The corruption of love by power inequities in the "sex class system" produces the proverbial song and dance:

> . . . while men may love, they usually "fall in love"—with their own projected image. . . . It is dangerous to feel sorry for one's oppressor—women are especially prone to this failing—but I am tempted to do it in this case. Being unable to love is hell. . . . As soon as the man feels any pressure from the other partner to commit himself, he panics. . . . He may rush out and screw ten other women to prove that the first woman has no hold over him. . . . for him to feel safely the kind of total response he first felt for his mother, which was rejected, he must degrade this woman so as to distinguish her from the mother.

Hot stuff! But Firestone's recasting of Freud and Marx and Solanas's apocalyptic vision did more than fuel my outrage. Their—and a welter of other feminist—writings gave me permission to begin examining my experience as a woman, as an intelligible and intelligent participant in culture and society rather than the overdetermined outcome of a lousy childhood that had previously dominated my self-perception. I began to come of age reading this stuff. Change, of course, comes with greater difficulty than the reading of a couple of books. The struggle to throw off the status of unknowing collaborator in victimization—at both ends of the domination scale—is uneven and ongoing. But after 1971 my work began to reflect with ever more confidence the details of daily life and implications of "being a woman" in western culture.

By the mid-seventies women in the New York art world were flirting and dancing with each other at parties. It was as though the women's movement had heaved a cornucopia of same-sex sexual fantasies into the face of heterosexual propriety. While real-life lesbians were battling for recognition at NOW conferences, we ladies of illusion were riding a backlash of resentment at our real and imagined oppressors, indicting our failed straight love affairs in displays of wanton—if not libidinous—abandon. Maybe some of us ended up in bed. Not me. I was all show and no go.

"The movement" had penetrated, but I still wasn't calling myself a feminist. It was hard to shake off those received notions of feminists as upper-class women from the twenties and thirties who wore plus fours and rode horses, like Vita Sackville-West or Nancy Cook and Marion Dickerman, the gals with whom Eleanor Roosevelt hung out. (Clearly, a tacit homophobia was operating here. Marilyn and Jayne's departure from the center stage of my fantasy life had occurred with some consequence; it had opened the door to a very specific mistrust.) Furthermore, I thought to be a feminist you had to be politically active, and I wasn't, at least not in that arena. It wasn't until 1975, when Mimi Schapiro convinced me that feminism is as much a state of mind as a matter of activist alliances, that I dared to use the term self-referentially.

At that point I had made two feature films, *Lives of Performers* and *Film About a Woman Who . . .* , both of which dealt in an elliptical fashion with aspects of my own real-life melodramas. With one foot in a quasi-minimalist verité and the other in soap opera, I was struggling toward some hybrid form that I hoped would encapsulate and redound with everything from catharsis to pathos to irony to bathos, give or take the baby and the bathwater. My subject matter for the most part was heterosexual romance and conflict from a woman's point of view, and the form issued from the broadest definition of narrative: There was no beginning, middle, or closure, no climax, no denouement, no character development, no plot. But there was lots of language that dealt with the trials and tribulations of a she, a she who was here to stay and would have her say.

Some people have called those early films "pre-political" or "pre-feminist." In any case, *Film About a Woman Who . . .* became a focal point for more than one brouhaha among feminist film theorists over issues of positive versus negative imaging of women, avant-garde versus Hollywood, strategies of distanciation versus traditional conventions of "suture," elitism versus populism, documentary versus fiction, and so forth. The debates go on, but in more muted fashion with regard to feminism, as theoretical center stage has been preempted by postcolonial and queer theory, both of which concerns, I should add, were woeful omissions in straight white middle-class feminist discourse in the 1970s and early 1980s. Another reason the feminist film wars have somewhat subsided is that as the sheer volume of women's output in film and video began to accrete, it became apparent there are almost as many styles, strategies, and tactical choices manifest in women's work as there are women producers. Progressive feminism does not reside exclusively in any one mode of representation.

But fifteen and twenty years ago the debates over formal procedures were heated, and in several instances a bit nasty. If my films have become more "accessible" in the sense of availability, it is because I found a distributor who pegged my work as marketable and acted accordingly. As for accessibility in the sense of intelligibility, I still believe in the necessity of certain kinds of narrative "distanciation," a belief that may lack the polemical fervor that characterized my espousals of ten years ago, but which nevertheless continues to inflect many of my decisions. The goals remain the same: to jar the spectator out of comfortable identification (or repulsion) into critical detachment, to complicate and compound the spectator's relation to the immediate scene with additional information, analysis, or emotional affect, and to give comic relief.

I could now write about relationships with "my last men" and the ten-year gathering of courage and need that propelled me toward a particular woman, and not only to "women." I would have to give credit to the examples of younger lesbian and gay friends, their courage and determination and high spirits. I would have to describe getting caught up in Gay Pride marches, getting tired of loneliness, and, most important, inviting Jayne and Marilyn back into my living room from the back porch to which they had been banished for so many years.

I've always looked at women's bodies. Everyone knows that women ogle each others' bodies. We used to be told that we look in order to compare, to see what attracts men. It was a competitive gaze, we were told. Uh-uh. We look because we like them, because women's bodies please us, and it pleases us to look.

Toward the end of the Stonewall 25 march, my lover Martha and I sit down on a railing in Central Park near three women in their late fifties and early sixties. I shall call them Constance, Doris, and Alice. (Not being a journalist, I neglect to ask their names.) They are carrying signs that identify them as NOW activists from Vermont and New Hampshire. We chat about this and that. Finally I muster my nerve and say, "Could I ask you ladies some nosy questions? I'm a filmmaker doing research on aging and sexuality . . . Did you come out late in life or have you been out for a long time?" Alice instantly retorts, "What makes you think we're out?" I gulp. Does she mean they're not out or that they're not lesbians? I say, "Well, you're *here!*" Alice explains that they're here to support gay and lesbian rights as twenty-year activists in NOW. Doris and Martha exclaim in one voice, "It wasn't always that way!" Alice is quick to add that they're all "just good friends." "But you never know," Constance interjects. "Life is full of surprises."

"Ain't I a Feminist?": Re-forming the Circle

Shirley Geok-lin Lim

In 1969, at the age of twenty-four, drawn by two prestigious fellowships, I entered the graduate program at Brandeis University. In doing so, I left not only my country and community; I also left behind someone with whom I was desperately in love and who would not forgive my rejection of his proposal. I was determined to be a writer and a scholar, a destiny that I believed could not be achieved in the traditional, patriarchal, racially divided culture of my homeland, Malaysia. Except for the funding from the fellowships, I was completely penniless, even as, ironically, my impoverished father in Malaysia, with five children still living at home, was counting on my stipends to help the family.

My entry into the United States repeats a familiar feminist narrative: a young woman forsaking marriage, society, and security for the uncertain struggles of a professional and creative career. Indeed, in a reference letter he wrote for my admission to the University of Malaya in 1963, the Malacca High School headmaster, Colonel Christopher Wade, a British graduate of Sandhurst Military Academy who had mustered out of the Queen's Army to help administer my part of the British Empire, predicted that I would become one of the first feminists in the new nation, this at a time when I and other young Malayan women were wholly unfamiliar with that word. It is true that in my teens I had loved reading *Little Women* and *Jane Eyre*, two women's books that miraculously had slipped into the male-dominated library collections of British colonial education. Little wonder also that years later in the United States, I so deeply identified with the heroines in Anzia Yezierska's *Bread Givers* and Miles Franklin's novel, *My Brilliant Career.*

The feminism that Colonel Wade prophesied, however, had its source not only in images and ideas common to yearning Western girl-women full of desires, designs, and hurts. My tomboy attributes were specifically formed in rebellion against the cultural values and female models of a multicultural, colonial, Asian-based society. Writing for a volume that focuses on "second-wave U.S. feminism" therefore poses a particular tension for me: my feminism spans and embraces a more transnational territory than "the United States." This rupture, between "Asian" and "American," explains why I began to publicly identify myself as a feminist only in 1987, over twenty-five years after Colonel Wade's prescient proclamation of my pubescent "feminism."

When I arrived in Boston in August 1969, I landed in the midst of a feminist revolution. Welcomed, upbraided, parodied, reviled, and end-lessly reinterpreted, the feminist movement was and is a central social revolution of the twentieth century. Its struggles have been more effec-tive in achieving social change in the United States than other civil rights struggles for class, race, and sexual equality, and this success is evident everywhere: in the justice system and department stores, on the television evening news, in the divorce courts, in schools and colleges, and in the home. So pervasive and deep were the changes that in some sense every woman in the United States during the period between 1968 and 1988 could be said to have been "inside the movement." Like every woman, I benefited. I could wear jeans and go braless with-out facing social opprobrium; use contraceptives and pursue a career without the interruption of unwanted pregnancies; travel to confer-ences without fearing harassment. I gained abilities and felt joys that most women, until the second half of the twentieth century, never knew—in a body whose reproductive organs I could control, and with the confidence to decide what I wanted for myself. The movement has made possible for ordinary women like me a freedom that very few women historically have been privileged to enjoy—freedoms unknown to the empresses of China or Marie Antoinette, and especially to my grandmothers, mother, and aunts, poor Asian women precariously sit-uated between feudal and colonial societies and an emerging, modern-izing nation-state.

But much as I have benefited, and profound as I find the insight that private life is political life, the ideological articulation of U.S. Feminism with a capital "F" contains a narrative that is not mine at all. The historian Sara Evans argues that " 'new left' politics nourished the seeds of a new feminism" and vividly traces the course of the women's liberation movement through "early meetings," "tentative conversations," "a bountiful dinner," to explain the emergence of a "new collective consciousness" that manifested itself in mass transformations—"Young women's instinctive sharing of their personal experiences soon became a political instrument called 'consciousness-raising.' " The capital "F" in Evans's narrative of American Feminism, to my mind, also denotes the social capital that these movement Feminists possessed, a social capital that most third-world immigrant women simply did not have in the sixties and many still do not enjoy today. By social capital I mean the old-girls network, the same-o same-o circles, telephone trees, college connections, neighborhood kaffeeklatsches, Sullivanian West Side parties, and church organizations. Evans notes, "Anyone could form a group anywhere: an SDS women's caucus, a secretarial pool, a friendship circle, a college dorm, a coffee Klatsch": these small groups, formed almost instinctively, provided a "free space" marked by intimacy and support where women "could share with mutual trust the intimate details of their lives."

One problem with "safe spaces," however, is who gets defined as outside these spaces—one whose identity can easily be discovered through her absence. The condition that makes possible the intimacy and mutuality so celebrated as a core value in Evans's history is exclusivity. The very smallness of the consciousness-raising groups, which allowed trust to flourish, meant that large numbers of other "nonmutual" women were not admitted. In the women's liberation groups covered in Evans's account, women of color, immigrant women, blue-collar women whose class and familial positions did not permit them the time to participate, women who did not easily share the cultural values that enabled them to openly discuss "the intimate details of their lives," women with different political consciousnesses, were absent. To say that early consciousness-raising groups "formed almost instinctively" is to reveal that the members of these groups were unaware that what they saw as universal ideas and cultural experiences were thoroughly alien to masses of other women. Class and race norms, not instinct, fused the unity Evans describes as a movement strength.

In this historical construction of Feminism, I was clearly no Feminist. Living in Cambridge, Massachusetts, I heard my Anglo-Euro-

American (AEA)[1] college acquaintances plan for baby-sitters and car rides to their women's groups; but even as a graduate student in a prestigious university, I was never invited to attend one of the many consciousness-raising groups that Evans's history made out to be so democratically accessible. Of course I felt the exclusion—it signified then that I did not belong. But more profoundly, it deepened the intellectual, psychological isolation that any woman struggling for a life different from the one traditionally laid out by her community already endures.

In the sixties and seventies, "the personal is the political" operated within an unproblematized and uninterrogated ideal of "the personal," which paradoxically reproduced at a local level those social and political exclusions and power-subordinations that AEA Feminists had so acutely suffered in male-dominant organizations. At least for heterosexual women of color, who could and did share their lives with men, intimacy with the (male) other was possible; the personal existed as a space for relationship and struggle. But these same women remained unrelated and thus deeply alienated from AEA Feminists, whose definitions of the "personal" and the "intimate" afforded women of color little space.

This exclusion is repeated even today, in those subtle dynamics of discrimination to which Feminists are ever sensitive in patriarchal society but to which they appear oblivious in their sororal circles. These dynamics encompass seemingly trivial relations as well as significant intellectual disagreements. As in: AEA Feminist academics greeting each other affectionately and doing lunch, while ignoring a minority woman colleague on the sideline. As in: AEA Feminists producing what gets labeled all-embracing "theory" while criticizing the work of minority women colleagues as unreflective "identity politics," more stuck inside a limited "I." (Once again, AEA Feminists claim the universal ground, failing to recognize the limits or particularities of their own stories; once

---

[1] In this paper I use the term "Anglo-Euro-American" or "AEA" instead of "white" to signify the political difference between women who are privileged by their identities within a mainstream Anglo-European-American civilization and those who by skin color, minority identity, language, and religion are discriminated against in this mainstream American national model. I discussed the tension between hegemonic AEA feminism and minority feminism in greater detail in my 1993 essay, "Asian American Feminism and Anglo-American Hegemony: Living in the Funny House."

again, they place minority women on the side with their work reduced to special cases that may or may not augment thinking at the capital "F" center.)

In each of these examples of discrimination, the minority woman has to understand the AEA Feminists' actions not as expressions of private individuals ("Who I choose to have lunch with is my own affair"), or of the operation of universal criteria (abstract theory is superior to personal narrative). She must also resist the little voice that says, "Of course AEA feminists have the right to choose their own company, and who can blame them for wanting to hang out with their own kind? Of course my lifestory is inconsequential next to Freudian, Lacanian, or Derridean theory." That is, the minority woman has to analyze the personal at work in her experiences within ideological vectors, and understand her marginalization not as deserved but as politically produced. She has to resist the hegemonic power that trivializes her critique as the politics of resentment.

The minority feminist has to claim/write her feminism in the same way that European and white American women, such as Simone de Beauvoir, Betty Friedan, or Gloria Steinem, did: she must be ever vigilant in her relationship to AEA Feminists, prepared whenever necessary to call AEA Feminists into question in the same way that AEA Feminists have called into question patriarchal power operating under the guise of democratic association. For example, AEA Feminists have challenged all-male professional clubs that excuse their sexism by invoking the right to free association; they have questioned male appeals to objective and hierarchically situated knowledges.

Given the exclusivity inherent in AEA Feminists' "instinctive," "intimate" groups as they raised and are raising their consciousness, it is little wonder that many women of color have resisted the appellation "feminist" to describe themselves. At the 1994 Melbourne Sixth International Feminist Bookfair, for example, a West Indian and an African writer, caricaturing Western feminism, argued that they were not feminists: they were not middle-class women who blamed men for all the ills in the world; they actually liked men; and they saw racism and colonialism as greater evils than gender discrimination. Madhu Kishwar, the founder and editor of the leading Indian women's publication *Manushi*, published a seminal essay titled, "Why I Do Not Call Myself a Feminist," in which she "openly challenged being labeled feminist." She based her resistance to the "label" on the fear of alienating "large sections of potential readers," as "it would inevitably evoke associations with the women's movement in the West, which was known in India mostly through simplistic stereotypes." Her journal, she argued, was "concerned not just with women's equality, as the term 'feminist' would imply, but with the protection of the human rights of all disadvantaged or discriminated groups." Similarly, in the United States, many women intellectuals of color have carefully disarticulated their political agendas from those of "Feminists."

The minute I change that Western capital "F" to a small one, the picture changes. For such reluctant feminists as myself, the small "f" signals the shared and common identity of women's gender as a social category marking women as a group below the class of men. Women's issues have become visible globally as the twentieth century draws to an end. In a wide range of public and private issues, including questions of reproductive rights, quality of life, economic empowerment, education access, political representation, and marriage laws, a host of societies have been undergoing a process of transformation, in response to modernizing pressures and especially in response to changed material conditions, such as overpopulation, urbanization, and industrialization. Arguably, the movement for women's liberation today is everywhere where there are women. Whether directly or indirectly, women everywhere today are inside a social process that is feminist in formation.

Feminism is a woman's thing. To be a feminist is to be a woman in her full implication with contrary desires and conflicting cultural expectations. In the changes taking place from traditional national economies to a late-capitalist global structure, from rural to urban, from agricultural to industrial, from isolated to technologically open, women have moved from traditional cultures into a (post)modern era and so from feminine roles into the feminist position of contradiction, complexity, and conflict. The social, economic, and cultural concerns of third world and minority women on the path of transformation—between the discontentments and given certitudes of traditionally structured societies and the distortions and irresistible promises of modernization—are inevitably feminist in cast.

Just as the former slave Sojourner Truth asked to be added to the category "woman" with her famous question, "An't I a woman?" now third world and minority women should be asking, "Ain't I a feminist?"

In short, non-AEA women should not give up the analytical usefulness of the idea(l) of feminism any more than they should give up the useful common ground of the category "women" simply because AEA Feminists have excluded them from their Feminist stories. There is a potent and liberatory power in affirming our relations to each other as women, relations that can only be formed through collective discourse, when we share our different histories as nonwhite feminists with each other. My argument is that third world and minority women need to acknowledge a position that recognizes the global commonality of women's struggles for civil rights, that recognizes that other women are linked *as women* in our political, material, social, psychological, and spiritual struggles.

For me the fundamental marker of a shared feminist identity is the possession of the female body—the vagina which has been consecrated as sacred and vilified as profane, the womb which has anointed woman with supreme power and degraded her with abject vulnerability, the breasts which have been worshipped as a natural force and mutilated as an artificial appendage. Because feminism is a noumenal phenomenon in which woman's body and mind are simultaneously engaged in producing understanding and knowledge, only women can be feminists. Only women can understand the critique of the vaginal orgasm through their bodies as well as through their minds. Only women can grasp the tension between maternal longing and professional ambition in its ambient contradictory force. Women's concerns with their body image have often been trivialized by men and by some feminists as expressions of personal vanity and social frivolity. But women's subjectivity cannot be understood without a deconstruction of the phenomenology of the female body.

Until I was twelve I did not see my body as separate from my self. For much of my childhood, we were so poor that the only mirror we children shared was a small, stained eighteen-by-twelve-inch glass, which hung too high on the wall for me to see more than my face chin-up. The absence of a long glass in which I could preen or worry over hair or waist or legs or other body shape meant that I grew into adolescence with hardly any sense of my body image. Moreover, with seven brothers and no sisters, mother-abandoned, and with only a remote stepmother who did not speak to me, I entered puberty without a clue as to the mysteries of a woman's body—menstruation and child bearing, for instance.

In feminist cautionary tales of women's dangerous jealousy, women are warned against obsessive dependency on their mirror images. Using the voice of the mirror to form their self-esteem, women must inevitably arrive at the impossibility of their beauty myth, and end in murderous pathology. However, with no mirror and no older or younger female to relate to, from eight to twelve, I lived directly in a world of senses and ideas, steeped in physical sensation and books, an external life like that of my brothers, and one that contrasted sharply with the traditional socialization of women in Malaysian culture.

While I sometimes felt shame at my wrinkled, worn-out frocks, I chiefly delighted in the strength, flexibility, and mobility of my physical body. I felt this delight most keenly when I began ballet classes, in love with the motion and lightness of bodies lifting off in jetés and spinning against earthly gravity in dizzying pirouettes. Going through our ballet exercises at the barre in the unmirrored convent school hall, I saw my body only in my mind's eye, not as an idealized type but as a series of movements.

Imagine my shock at the end of that year, at the photograph of myself in my short practice tunic, head in three-quarter profile, trunk lifted high and arms outstretched in a point posture. The photographer had posed me in a classic stance, his camera freezing an already stationary image, for the annual ballet class individual portrait. I saw a strange body, tense, with muscular calves and a strained face—surely not me!—and nothing like that mental image of floating tulle and spirit that I had imagined of my body in dance. Of course now, after years of conscious feminist resistance, I can see the beauty of that strong lean young body, the female body of determined muscle and force so much like photographs of the sprightly Isadora Duncan or the short Anna Pavlova that I was to study later. But back then I recoiled at the gap between material physicality and idealized shape. The hurt of that image of myself, so much a body and so little a spirit, remained with me for years.

This first detested photograph was followed by so many more. Over the years, even with group portraits, I would pore over the particular image of my body, foreign in every way, the strange half-smile, the body forever in some kind of uneasy pose, my critical eye noting the disjuncture between what the camera saw, what the world sees, and what I knew was inside that image, something fierce and hard not captured by the image. Yet, while like most women I suffered from the way my body could not be what I wanted it to be, I never let go of the belief that "I" was something other than that deficient body—something by far nicer, more radiant, more emphatic. And gradually, I have become more reconciled to this physical body, can even see in later photographs a woman as attractive as any other.

The implicit drift of this brief digression may appear to many politically sensitive readers as narcissistic. "Narcissism" is a term raised to implicate women's concerns with their body image, sexuality, and social relations as less than socially ethical. The accusation of narcissism is usually made only when it is woman gazing at her reflection, while male self-reflexivity has traditionally been privileged as appealing to universal humanistic concerns. Western male autobiographies and fictions, from William Wordsworth's *The Prelude* to J. D. Salinger's adolescent anti-hero in *Catcher in the Rye* and Saul Bellow's, John Cheever's, and John Updike's intellectuals, middle-class suburban husbands and philanderers, have historically placed the male character at their center without arousing disgust over their narcissism. The empowered male reader speaking through reviews and within a tradition of male writing resonates to concentrated masculine constructions and rewards them with prizes, while he finds women's self-reflexive narratives wearisome for their reflections of women's subjectivity. The impatience of radical social feminists with women's personal, self-reflective narratives, criticized for their "bourgeois," "liberal" elements, echoes the impatience of these male readers.

But such rigorous rejection of self-narratives in which social identity is explored and interrogated through the historical categories of color and race needs to be carefully examined; there is a counterpossibility: the necessity to continue the writing of such discourses of identity. When a "subaltern" arrives at a self-conscious position that permits self-voicing, that kind of agency is not to be easily or prematurely left behind. The self-reflective gaze can be posited as a necessary step out of narcissism, and into social reflexivity and empowerment, for how can a "woman" begin to act if the importance of gender is not confronted? Carolyn Kizer calls women "narcissists by necessity," for they must struggle to insert their voices and self-reflexive consciousnesses, which remain unrepresented or underrepresented in many national canons, whether in Western, Asian, or African nations.

In the 1970s the sharp debates over open admissions at the City University of New York were expressed as issues over merit, academic excellence, accountability, privilege, and so forth. As a green-card-holder from Asia, I was outside every interest group represented in the contentious discussions. For four years I taught in CUNY, first at Queens College, then at Hostos Community College. Although I experienced these years as a free-for-all, even then I was aware of enormous social forces that worked to the advantage of individuals of certain groups and to the disadvantage of others.

There is no doubt that the United States, and particularly an American city like New York, is hard on every individual. Blond white women lost their innocence in New York; Jewish guys with newly minted Ph.D.s in history from Harvard took low-paying clerical jobs in nonprofit organizations because they could not find positions in a university. Walking along Bleecker Street or uptown along Broadway any day in New York one could always see unhappy, lonely, depressed, poor white Americans. Failure and desperation are human conditions that resist racialization. You don't have to be a person of color to fail; whiteness does not automatically endow social success.

But in America, as in Malaysia, I was aware of the layered nature of the individual, an agent composed of a distinctive temperament, skills, and talents, but also embedded in a social sphere and dynamic that offered resources that she could call upon—family ties, college connections, professional networks, community relations. In Malaysia, for all my sense of alienation and outsidership, I had been surrounded by these social resources, which, as I rebelled, I often experienced as constraints. But in New York the social resources I had taken for granted or resisted at home were suddenly other people's. I had to start, as it were, tabula rasa, in building those dynamics and networks that are intrinsic to individual achievement, though in New York, composed of fresh immigrants, both American and foreign, pouring through its five boroughs daily, it is eminently possible to construct new contingent communities.

Teaching in the city's higher education system, I was aware that opportunities and constraints operated simultaneously. A young immigrant woman speaking English with a Malaysian accent, my "exoticism" and "exceptionalism" made me an attractive and safe professional, but insofar as I could not be placed as representative of any of the interest groups contending for power within CUNY, these same qualities also marked me as "unserious," minor, and marginal. An intellectual in the traditional sense needed a constituency, an author an audience—and insofar as I identified myself as a Malaysian, I could not speak as an intellectual or a writer in New York.

Of course this negative role was self-inflicted. I could, as some Asian Americans did, identify with New York's Chinatown community. In the seventies, *Bridge* was publishing out of Chinatown, and by the eighties Jack Tchen had come up from Princeton and set up the China-town Historical Project. The geographical space of Chinatown played a big role in my psychic life. Once a week, taking the IRT from Brooklyn, and then the D train, I would get off at Canal Street and wander down through Mott, Elizabeth, and Broadway. The tiny crowded grocery shops reminded me of Malacca, my hometown. They smelled of peeling onion skins, dried fish, salted napa cabbage, the nitric of pork sausages, a brown kitchen ambience of soya sauce, sesame oil, and pungent five spices, which soothed my homesickness, smells which I took back with me in the form of leaky packages of Cantonese roast pork and roast duck to my home above Prospect Park, a neighborhood in which I was always the only Asian American shopping at the local supermarket. Each journey through the narrow car-clogged pedestrian-thronged side-walks of Chinatown was a small moment of imagined return to an orig-inal, more vivid society—a phantasmal connection that helped me stay "in touch," but in touch through a simulacra of homeland that was as commodified as a Disneyland attraction.

Yet what's to critique about such possibilities? For centuries relo-cated groups have constructed loyal replicas of their original spaces in unlikely places—Roman garrisons on the swamps along the Thames, mosques and minarets in the river valleys of Castille, Catholic cathe-drals on Macao by the mighty Chinese hinterland, Spanish forts and haciendas in the steamy island of Luzon. Where European imperial forces have dropped phantasmagorias of colonial administrative archi-tecture in Africa or Asia, these Government Houses and Capital Centers have been interpreted as material evidence of political change. But shelves stocked with dried squid and persimmons, fresh bokchoy, and quivering tofu squares, restaurants crowded with citizens feasting on alien dim sum and Szechuan eggplant also provide persistent evidence of cultural transformation in the West, not as dramatically manifested as Western military conquest of Asian territories, but perhaps as legitimately material.

If the only space in all of New York that I could find to allay an exile's nostalgia was in Chinatown, I was unapologetic for it. But at the same time that I was overcome weekly by the desire for a Chinatown fix, it was impossible for me to identify with Chinatown. A compulsory ghetto shaped by white America's anti-Asian prejudices, by housing discrimination, redlining, and other insidious acts of racism, Chinatown was not a neighborhood I wished to live in: it was a distorted, grossly misshapen materialization of Asian-American society. It was a fetishization of Asia, disassembled into, displayed, and sold as edible, exotic parts to the thousands of Manhattan, Long Island, and out-of-state tourists who thronged the curio and grocery shops and restaurants, and who viewed the inhabitants not as Americans but as freak-foreigners. Each time I shopped in Chinatown I felt the impulse to avert my eyes from the waiters, the sellers of jadeite grapes and celedon vases. I imagined their hopeless humiliation, imagined how they must be subjected daily to the gaze of a stream of English-speaking white tourists, a gaze that casts them as un-Americans, different, strange, Chinese. As an English-speaking Chinese American, I projected on to them my fantasy of white stereotyping of the Chinese. Imagining their rage and shame, I felt also my own rage and shame at their complicity in the construction of this phantasmagoric ghetto, their manipulation of these exotics of identity.

I have never overcome my status as an outsider to Chinatown, and the guilt that tags along for what appears to be the inability to form the simplest of ethnic community identifications. Yet despite the ideological stance taken by many Ethnic Studies academics and Asian-American activists—that Asian Americans must look to their ethnic communities for their source of identity formation—I believe many Asian Americans—who find themselves in a variety of locations in U.S. culture—are conflicted about naming an ethnic enclave as the necessary site of political consciousness and organization. As we critique white supremacists who locate their discourses of rights in a race-bounded identity, so too we must resist the dangerous binary of fixed, ideologically raced loyalties against a centric Other, recognizing that Asian-American political and social agendas are not chauvinistically restricted to ethnic enclave or even ethnic community but must be enacted across a national spectrum. To paraphrase a famous saying of Hillel, "If we are not for us, who will be? If we are only for ourselves, what are we? If not now, when?"

The question "What are we?" is the central American question that draws together all Americans, Native, Euro-American, Jew, Black, Latino, and Asian, and that remains unasked as long as we continue to construct "we" as separate individuals or as separately segregated group identities. In either case, the "we" is sharply limited. "We" are each separate individuals; or "we" are members of a community that can now usually only be constructed along narrowly defined ethnic collectives—the Asian-American community, the Black community, the Native American community, the Chicano community. Ironically, the vaunted autonomy of the individual as supreme subject is reproduced in U.S. race discourse by the insistence that race is a full individual identity. It is as if racialized communities fear that without the regulated boundaries policed by ethnic separatists, the repressive AEA value of assimilation will triumph and differences valued by other communities will melt and disappear. In the 1970s and 1980s, resisting stereotyping as the essentialized, racialized Chinese, I was left with no group identity, the identity of the assimilated "white" American being as alien to me. It was chiefly through the rich resources I found in the theory and practice of feminism that I was able to transform this liminal habitation into a "home."

Throughout the 1970s and 1980s I was prey to self-doubt and self-division. My intellectual "I" interrogated and undermined my writing "I" with intense, deleterious asides. I was teaching long wearying hours in a community college and raising a child in outer suburbia with little sense of community for support. Audience, reception, even language choice and genre choice were concerns I grappled with alone.

I had written poems, essays, and short fiction from a very early age in Malaysia. The itch for fame may appear ludicrous in a young colonized female subject, a brown unkempt and hungry child in the tropics, but desire for self-immortality through letters does not fall into gendered or classed lines. Situated in the crisis of English education in the

United States in the early 1970s, I was still able to imagine a role for myself in the geographical, national territory of my birthplace. A Malaysian poet in exile, I wrote my first book of poetry while I was teaching in the South Bronx, negotiating among Black, Puerto Rican, Jewish, and Anglo-Saxon identities. *Crossing the Peninsula* received immediate attention in the British Commonwealth countries, winning the 1980 Commonwealth Poetry Prize, but not in the United States, a neglect which I took as a confirmation of my resident alien identity. Above my college desk I scrawled, "Only disconnect," reversing E. M. Forster's liberal dictum as an ironic reminder of my alienation.

I began to get at the gut of this alienation by dealing with a highly problematic relationship with a woman. E. was a colleague whom I had known distantly for about three years when she began to initiate a closer friendship. At that time, pregnant at the late age of thirty-four, I was grateful for her attention, her advice on motherhood (she was the mother of two), her confidences on office politics, and her generosity in sharing clothes and toys. At about the same time, frazzled by the addi-tional stresses of child care and increasingly unhappy about the tensions between my professional and creative work and the community college position I had taken in order to be with my husband, I began therapy with a woman social worker. If I had focused chiefly on sexual relations with men in my early womanhood, entering my midlife, I was begin-ning to find areas of connection and emotional satisfaction in these two different relationships with women.

Abruptly, however, E. withdrew her affection. One morning she walked past me in the corridor without a sign of recognition. When I pursued her, demanding to know why she had changed, she denied any knowledge of her behavior, even as she continued to ignore me, and to treat me coldly. Frustrated, tears streaming, I would drive home from the college, wondering what I had done to anger her. I discussed my wounded feelings interminably with my husband, who could not understand my hurt, my sudden insecurities. "Sometimes people change and just go different ways," he suggested.

Finally, when it became clear that E. had grown implacably hostile to me, I had to ask myself why I was so needy and what I could do to overcome the emptiness left by the loss of the relationship; I sharply missed the warm conversations, the Saturday visits with the children playing together, the laughter as we shopped for clothes. Growing up with many brothers and no mother or sister, I had made a mystique out of female friendship; E. was not the first woman I had loved who had then turned to reject me. My loneliness for female companionship, my urgent desire to hang out with women were—as I was feeling them then—inappropriate displacements of my childhood desires for a mother and for sisters. Friendship between women was, is, a precarious adventure when it is not normalized within familial, kinship, and social units, or stabilized by communal traditions like college ties or church membership. The intensely intimate one-to-one friendships that I had sought rose from and fed a childhood legacy of neurosis.

Examining my need for women's friendships and my experience of inappropriate neediness, I decided I would be better off seeking the support of more formal groups of women than the emotional dependencies that resulted from singular pairings. Still depressed by the break with E., I called five women colleagues teaching in different colleges in the New York–Westchester region and asked if they were interested in forming a writing group. These women became my major feminist community from 1983 until I left for California in 1990. Members included dramatists, poets, and scholars, senior professors and recent Ph.D.s, Jews, Irish and Anglo-Americans, South Asians, and Asian Americans, divorced, single, long-married and newly married women, mothers and women without children, women over sixty and women in their twenties. We did not identify ourselves as feminists, but we guarded our gender identity. These monthly meetings were crucial interventions in the academic careers of many of us. Through the millennia, women have fallen into silence, defeated by isolation. I owe a great deal of my resilience against despair and my mental toughness to these women whose affections and imaginations buoyed me when other conditions would have sunk my efforts. Such a semi-organized women's community was my response to the failed sisterhood I experienced with E., recognizing that for me paired "sisterhood" is fraught with unbearable emotional neediness and jealousies and that a community of women offers necessarily more flexibility and wisdom than can be found in these pairings.

At the same time, I remain conscious of the contradictions inherent in a "feminist" practice that remains only at the level of individual politics and ad hoc solutions. A central problem facing feminists is how to form collectives that widen to include divergent communities rather than constrict to confirm an ideology. I look for such communities through acts of the imagination and through my teaching. Thus, since my naturalization in 1980, I have struggled with the question of America with a different valence, a struggle I treat more fully in my memoir, *Among the White Moon Faces*. I now accept a binational and transnational space as the field of my cultural work, that is, I write, speak, and teach as an American and also as a Malaysian-Singaporean Chinese. The histories of these societies speak in the tremors of my voice, in my values, perceptions, resistances, and yearnings.

This acceptance has brought me to a different recognition of America. Until very recently, hearing my voice on a radio interview I felt a distinct frisson of alienation—the shock of disconnection between my internalized chronometer of American voice and speech and the accented voice that is mine and other Asians. Now, on hearing an Asian-accented English, including my own voice reading Wallace Stevens's, Gwendolyn Brooks's, or my poems, I take confidence in an expanded notion of the American voice: that the broad nasal tones of the Vietnamese American running for office in California or my own clipped, British-trained, Chinese-inflected, Malay-stressed dancing over vowels and consonants are as much American English as the Brooklyn, New York, midwestern, Southern and Western drawls that continue to defeat the television anchor's influence. That musicality, different from other American speech, no longer worries me like a hidden deformity: for better or for worse, it has also become part of the broad-running waters of American English, mixing further with other accents while keeping its peculiar tang.

The plural vision of the United States that makes such disalienation possible was legitimated by the civil rights struggles of African Americans, feminists, and American left-wing activists, a historical coalition of race, gender, and class concerns that has transformed American society to make it more genuinely democratic and just. Knowing this history, even though it is partial, the minority feminist must seek to overcome her disadvantage of belatedness to claim her place in that coalition. The circle has to be re-formed to achieve a more inclusive America. Unlike the women in my writing group, I am much more willing to assert my feminist identity, perhaps because, as a new American, I am more aware of the political necessity for coalition, and have found, through the historical struggle of all women for life, liberty and the pursuit of happiness, my place in the circle of humanity.

WORKS CITED

Anderson, Benedict. *Imagined Communities.* London: Verso, 1983.

Evans, Sara. *Personal Politics: The Roots of Women's Liberation in the Civil Rights Movement & the New Left.* New York: Vintage, 1980.

Kishwar, Madhu. "Why I Do Not Call Myself a Feminist." *Manushi,* No. 61, 1991: 2–8.

Kizer, Carolyn. "A Muse of Water," *No More Masks: An Anthology of Poems by Women,* ed. Florence Howe and Ellen Bass. New York: Anchor Books: 170.

Lim, Shirley Geok-lin. "Asian American Feminism and Anglo-American Hegemony: Living in the Funny House." *Tulsa Studies in Women's Literature,* 12:2, Fall 1993: 279–287.

———. *Among the White Moon Faces.* New York: Feminist Press, 1996.

Some Responses

The net of The Feminist Memoir Project *was cast to capture a brilliant period of feminist activism we editors saw receding from popular memory at an alarming, accelerating pace—with political consequences we worried about but could not predict. The memoirs we asked our authors to write reminded us of the early feminist culture we desired to record, but, as we said in our introduction, we do not see that past as a sealed-off episode; we seek not nostalgia but continuing engagement with the questions modern feminism has so vividly posed.*

So, at the end of our project, we have tried to give the wheel of memory one more turn. We wanted still more second thoughts, controversies, feelings, and counterinterpretations to create on the page something of the dynamism that makes feminism so alive. We have added another round of voices by asking a number of feminists to read the entire collection of essays and to respond. Some were women we'd invited to write before but who hadn't gotten around to it, and some were women who weren't born when this wave of feminism began.

One of our original writers, hearing of this process, asked, "What right have they to comment on my memories?" What right, indeed. As Ann Janette Rosga and Meg Satterthwaite put it: "From what stance can one comment critically on memoir?" For example, the willingness to tell the stories of race is rare enough to be valuable in itself; knowing these stories tells us, as Barbara Smith observes, why different feminists have such different memories, why we never were simply one movement. Each one sets her own boundaries on her material and claims her own epistemic privilege, that is, her right to interpret herself. This right to invent new understandings of women's experiences was one thing feminists claimed and often established. But the story never ends there. The integrity of each voice we have included has not prevented us from want-

ing conversation and response. Hence we asked our responders to write as they chose—adding memories, talking back, thinking through. Although these pieces come at the end, they are not the last word. Let there be no last word.

RBD and AS

Notes from the Aftermath

AnnJanette Rosga and Meg Satterthwaite

From what stance can one comment critically on memoir? Our position as political-intellectual daughters of the feminist movement—heirs to all that is good, bad, and undecidable in this legacy—seems at once overdetermined and difficult to name. The pieces in this volume seem to us to represent much of the full spectrum of our inheritance. There is much here we've found inspiring; even more, humbling. And a fair amount that makes us cringe, as perhaps only true daughters can—those who are both indubitably *of* this heritage and yet/still outside of it. For each of us, a defining feature of our entry into feminism was that it occurred *ex post facto*. We weren't there. We studied feminism-as-critiqued. The "third wave"—marked chiefly by a decentering of the unmarked (hence, white and middle-class) Woman—was well underway by the time we reached college in 1986, as was the conservative "backlash." Many of the contributors here are in conversation with this panoply of critics. Much of the prose exudes varying degrees of longing to correct the record, but the critiques themselves are here too: perhaps this is feminism's most enduring strength and its bane, a relentless self-criticality. For us, this volume offers us an account of our debts; it complicates that "straw woman," the seventies feminist, and it challenges us to find an adequate measure of our own places in this history.

Meg

I became a feminist at the same moment I became a lesbian. No, I was not born a lesbian, or a feminist. I was born in 1969, a petite little girl who grew up trying to please, trying to erase the impact of her footprints on the world, and even, as a seven-year-old Southern Baptist, trying to save my mother's sinning soul. *She* had found feminism after I was born, in a quest to regain a self crushed under years of wife-and-mothering. She divorced my father; lived with a man who was ten years her junior; smoked things she was not supposed to smoke; did primal scream therapy in the basement. She became a massage therapist and a dental hygienist, a secretary and a whole string of pink-collar things.

Her low wages made us eligible for the subsidized breakfast and lunch program at school, despite my father's skyrocketing income and our extended family's solid middle-class status.

I became a feminist far later than I should have. My mother gave my sister and me *Free to Be You and Me* and told us we could be anything we wanted to be. She taught us about sex and babies and periods so early that I got in trouble in first grade for giving the other kids in my class too much information on the playground.

Knowing I was supposed to be equal, I blamed it on myself when I didn't do as well as the boys. I will never forget my teacher stopping the whole class in second grade to point out how *good* I was when I did my classwork while the class bully punched my arm repeatedly and called me names. "She just ignores it," the teacher said. "See how good Margaret is." And I was good, for eight more years at least. Then, at sixteen, I became a punk rocker. A political punk rocker. I had realized that the world was "fucked up" and I saw in "the scene" a way to erase a little of the bad I did every moment of my existence by being a white American, by buying clothes made by children in sweatshops, by treading on the earth my ancestors stole and then covered with asphalt, by breathing.

I became a part of an anarchist collective in D.C. and welcomed the male-dominated world of Straight Edge, a small community that, following the lead of the band Minor Threat, determined it was not a good idea to "drink, smoke, or fuck." I welcomed that. Fucking was definitely something I was not interested in doing. Instead, we poured our energy into organizing sparsely attended benefits for homeless shelters (always featuring all-male bands), did guerrilla theater to protest U.S. involvement in Central America (the guys always played the CIA agents and *contras,* we young women were *campesinos* and community organizers, gunned down by their fake guns), and planned brief, illegal moments of sabotage (I will leave these undescribed). It felt like home.

That was where I met my first boyfriend. Both relieved the other was also into Straight Edge, we entered a nonpenetration agreement. After a year or so of dating, this became unacceptable to him and my entry into the adultish world of compulsory heterosexuality had begun. Despite my anarchist pretensions, deep down I was afraid of not being "normal." I had secretly read *Rubyfruit Jungle* and recognized my desires; I hoped it was a phase and decided to work hard at ensuring I matured beyond it. In those days I was reading underground 'zines and anarchist philosophers; the scene was deeply pre–Riot Grrrls and feminists were nowhere on my radar screen, partly because I considered them bourgeois sellouts. I was ready for the Revolution, and I was sure I would never make it to my thirtieth birthday. A nuclear bomb would have dropped, or I would have killed myself, or the Revolution would have begun.

Then, in college, I started to see the larger world. I recognized that in my despair I was not taking responsibility; in my grandiose view that I could reject whole-hog all that I was and stood for as a white, middle-class American, I was not finding an enduring place from which to do the work I would need to do my whole life. I was burning out. And assigned to read Virginia Woolf and Toni Morrison and Simone de Beauvoir, I was finding a way, miraculously, to say no to my boyfriend. I don't know how that happened, because for six months I had told myself that I "owed" him what he "needed," and legs spread, I would turn my head and try to hide the tears each time he fucked me. Partly it was talking to other women, realizing this was not the standard thing. This was not even the revolutionary thing. This was, I finally came to see, possibly even an abusive thing. Two years later, I was on fire from reading Adrienne Rich and Audre Lorde and Catharine MacKinnon and I was in love with my best friend.

Feminism, for me first a deep communion with words and books and the texture of the page communicated eloquently by teachers I both revered and idealized, became my life's breath. A three-month period stands out in my memory; I could barely sleep at night I was so hungry for feminist words. I spent hours in the library and in my room at night, reading and rereading, copying down words and writing in my journal. I felt I was on a quest for an answer, but I wasn't sure what the question was. I waited with candles burning for a revelation. When it came, it shattered my relationship with my best friend. I never told her I was in love with her; I never told her I was a lesbian; I never held her after the final fight we had, nasty, cruel, and fraught with subterranean truths. I walked away when I got the note in my mailbox: "please return my photos." I never did. She returned each and every image of me: every snapshot, every card I wrote her, every letter. Erased me from her life. The books that had brought me to the revelation—the words of feminists—were there to comfort me when the pain hit:

they helped me analyze what had happened, showed me how to understand what it meant to come out, to grasp onto the hope of finding a place in the world where my voice could be useful. For me, feminism replaced the Revolution.

Anjie

I was born in 1966. My father served in the army for a couple of years after that. I was into my twenties before I realized that I had no idea if he'd been to Vietnam, before I had an inkling of what that might mean: "that" being both whether he went, and why I never knew. All I can remember is the pictures he showed me of himself in fatigues with his buddies, all dog-tags a-dangle, drinking beer, looking happier than I ever remember seeing him in life. All that was left of the military in him was a well-exercised tendency to terrorize. He kept his reign over us in shape, like his pecs and abs.

I must have been about nine years old when my baby-sitter explained to me that feminists burned their bras. Since this was also the first time I gave any thought to the *notion* of a bra, I was especially confounded by the image. In the telescope of my memory, it wasn't much longer before my mom was dancing around in the living room to an eight-track recording of Helen Reddy's "I Am Woman, Hear Me Roar!"

Because I came of age in the postmodern era, I can have an almost aesthetic appreciation for what might otherwise be only painful: the fractured and clashing narratives my mother and I tell each other about the role of feminism in our lives. I am convinced that, among other powerful forces of history, feminism saved my life. It gave my mother the potency to flee my father's violence, and to fight in court for the right to take her children with her. It gave me a context within which to understand, in retrospect, how we ended up moving from a house with extra pork chops in the freezer to living in a trailer park on fried tortillas. It explained to me where our car really went when it disappeared one morning and my mother said it'd been borrowed by aliens from a UFO. (Granted, this was a good deal later than when the information would have been most useful, but after-the-fact comprehension ought not to be disparaged.)

My mother, on the other hand, having surpassed her love of Helen Reddy, now believes feminism was the harbinger of the downfall of both civilization and her life as a woman. She's an ardent and active member of the Patriot Party who blames the U.S. government for the Oklahoma City bombing, and she has spent years developing a dangerously hostile relationship with the IRS. Feminism, to her, is an insidious tool of the devil, responsible for what she now sees as her long-ago failure to accept her proper spousal role and, ultimately, for the "confused" state of her lesbian daughter. She believes, with a force of conviction that easily rivals my contrary own, that feminism destroyed her life.

Today I am a new teacher at a small midwestern liberal arts college; though I don't teach Women's Studies proper, feminism suffuses what and how I teach. I've had several dozen conversations in the past two years with other faculty or faculty-to-be about whether or not it makes sense to "teach women's studies," about how one might do so now. Now that the category "woman" has been so thoroughly problematized, now that the making of categories itself is widely understood to be one of Power's central mechanisms.

I was ushered into intellectual adulthood by feminist teachers, and I think of myself as someone who would never—could never—lose sight of the profound distance covered by feminist activism. I was never one of those students who couldn't imagine, or who consistently "forgot," that women didn't always teach college, that they (these foremothers of my generation) endured a suffocating breadth and diversity of sex-based constraints. And still, this passage from Priscilla Long's essay, "[I]n 1969 I had never seen a woman bus driver. I had never been treated by a woman doctor or dentist, never taken my cat to a woman veterinarian, never heard a woman speak at a rally," takes my breath away. Before I went to college, I had a series of jobs—this was in the mid-eighties—in which my direct supervisors were *always* women; often, the highest authority in the workplace was a woman. I went to college from 1986 to 1990, during which time I believe I had a total of *three* male professors. During both college and graduate school, my mentors and advisers were among the leading feminist scholars in this country. If I can help it, and I almost always can, I only go to women doctors (though I'm less picky about my veterinarians and bus drivers), and it's never occurred to me at rallies to wonder where the women speakers are because they're everywhere.

I cannot say the same about women of color, at least not to the same degree. And therein lies a tale. . . .

In any case, I'm certainly never at risk of forgetting the fact that this life of mine is a historical accomplishment of astonishing proportions. At the same time, I'm also aware that a substantive gap between my understandings of feminism, my views on the utilities and dangers of the category "woman," and those presented by many of the writers here is inevitable. The very success of the movement these writers initiated *makes possible* my questioning of its precondition: the aphrodisiac of global sisterhood.

We are the postrevolutionary feminists, in the post-easy-labels period of U.S. history. From this vantage point, two key features in these memoirs cannot help but discomfit us: the prevalence of a language of discrete identity categories, and the suggestion of a widely presumed model of social change, articulated in various ways by the authors' memories of their belief that the Revolution was just around the corner.

On the question of identity, perhaps we are doomed, for to para-phrase Stuart Hall, as soon as you shut the door behind identity, it's crawling back in through a window. Even as they are asserting their early and constant attention to the issues of race, class, and colonial power, these authors, with few exceptions, describe clashes and coali-tions that took place between unified representatives of coherent group identities. And this, no doubt, is a problem of history-telling—for if events were narrated in such terms at the time, how is one to re-narrate them now without keeping alive the reality-making force of those very terms? If one crucial task of memoir is to render a sense of the moment as it was lived, these pieces are compellingly vivid reenactments of a par-ticular—and lingering—kind of identity politics.

Nonetheless, the seeds of what would eventually develop into what some consider the pitiless fracturing of identity categories, and what others celebrate as the long-overdue death of the phallogocentric sub-ject, are evident in many of these memoirs. Elizabeth Martinez's "pine-willow" foreshadows articulations of identity as nonessentialist but still rooted in location. Barbara Epstein's early criticism of purism in the New Left and women's movements suggests the limits of rigid identity boundaries, as does Barbara Omolade's "bifurcated angle of vision about feminism and nationalism." Lourdes Benería's careful evaluation of women's silences and family roles cross-culturally is suggestive of what has become the first step in feminist scholarship: recognition and appreciation of contextual factors in defining identities. Minnie Bruce Pratt's essay reminds us that at least some of early feminism was at pains to interrogate the boundaries of that most rigid identity distinction: sex itself ("perhaps there is a third space that is *lesbian,* not *woman,* not *man*"). And finally, Shirley Geok-lin Lim's piece clearly incorporates recent critiques of "identity" when she writes, "as long as we continue to construct 'we' as separate individuals or as separately segregated group identities . . . the vaunted autonomy of the individual as supreme subject is reproduced [as it is, for instance] in U.S. race discourse by the insistence that race is a full individual identity."

On the question of Revolution, or models of social change, our reading of these texts is again profoundly shaped by our location. We have come of age in a time that saw the fall of the Berlin Wall and the failure of statist communism; the public despair over America's "decline" as a self-assured and openly neocolonialist power; and the simultaneous shift in focus from the state to the multinational corporation as the locus of struggle over cultural, political, and economic power. In this space, the Revolution seems like a dream not only impossible in its logistical and tactical details, but also stark and frightening in its inevitable results. Instead of working with a sense of certainty and urgent zeal toward a clear goal, we find ourselves taking steps that lead only to the next uncertain juncture.

Perhaps we, as young Anglo-American feminists, are the inheritors of the grief that came from these authors' lost center: postmodern children of our modernist mothers. They searched for the center that would not hold; we start from the spinning debris that resulted when that search imploded. We begin from that loss, keepers of a pain that both is and isn't ours, and we work to find hope in the awareness of always-already partial visions. Seeing through our eyes can never be anything but incomplete. There is no place to stand for a whole view; no fulcrum from which to rock the world.

And, as we learned from many "third wave" feminists, this can be a place of hope. This *must* be a place of strength and creativity. For in coming to voice, in becoming feminists, we discovered that our selves, our white, highly educated, pink-collar, lesbian, activist selves with U.S. passports, credit cards, and loan debt, would always necessarily be both oppressor and oppressed; hegemonic and counter-hegemonic; both/and; never either/or.

Shirley Geok-lin Lim describes the challenge this way: "A central problem facing feminists is how to form collectives that widen to include divergent communities rather than constrict to confirm an ideology." The voices collected here are ambivalent about such a project, some still smarting from the sting of a lost (some claim stolen) vision, power, and the promise of momentous change. But many voices resonate deeply: the chapters by Michele Wallace and Vivian Gornick, for instance, convey a sense of humility about the limits of conscious human control over the directions, forms, and pace of social change, without constructing that humility as a source of despair.

The feminist lesson for which we are most grateful is one that teaches us not to require a tight, clear sense of preplanned direction. Rather we seek the triumph that comes after working long, hard hours to find a moment of consensus in coalition, a moment of understanding in the presence of difference, a breath collectively taken because of—rather than in spite of—divergent views considered respectfully.

"Feisty Characters" and "Other People's Causes": Memories of White Racism and U.S. Feminism

Barbara Smith

In November 1973, I attended the first Eastern Regional Conference of the National Black Feminist Organization (NBFO) in New York City. It is from that event that I mark my involvement in the second wave of the women's movement. Although I had been the only Black participant in a consciousness-raising group, had read *Sexual Politics* and an early newsprint edition of *Our Bodies, Ourselves,* and was a charter subscriber to *Ms.,* I did not become actively involved in feminist organizing until the NBFO conference. Despite my growing awareness of gender oppression as both a social reality and in my own life, I could not imagine joining a white women's organization.

Finding NBFO and other Black feminists gave me the context and support I needed to claim feminism for myself. It was like coming home. The NBFO chapter we started in Boston in early 1974 eventually became the Combahee River Collective. About a year and a half after the NBFO conference I came out as a lesbian and was finally able to acknowledge my long-hidden desire for other women. My meeting other Black lesbian feminists made me believe that it was possible to be out, to have a community, and to survive. I am sure that the reason I have been able to maintain decades of commitment to the struggle for women's freedom is that I came to feminism in a specifically Black feminist milieu.

The Feminist Memoir Project offers countless reminders of how fortunate I was not to have entered feminism through a white door. What strikes me hardest about many, although not all, of these accounts is how unwelcoming and even dangerous the early years of the women's movement were for women of color. Many of these memoirs, written in the late 1990s, also reveal how little some feminists' consciousness about race has evolved.

The perniciousness of racism in the women's movement is not a new revelation. What this collection helps clarify are the specific attitudes and assumptions that contributed to its segregation from the very beginning. Although *The Feminist Memoir Project* offers many insights about a remarkably exciting and little documented period and also reveals that the movement marginalized other groups besides women of color, what it most signally provides for me is a history, in participants' own words, of how racism was initially institutionalized within feminism.

Women of color contributors to this volume address the paradoxes and contradictions of the movement from various perspectives. Shirley Geok-lin Lim explains why the "safe spaces" of the first consciousness-raising groups were not really open because of unexamined "class and race norms" that excluded "women of color, immigrant women, [and] blue-collar women." Barbara Omolade observes that "white women grew closer bonding ostensibly around their femaleness, but ultimately also around their whiteness."

A number of contributors describe their groups' rationales for white bonding. White women's desire to organize against their own oppression and the hostility they often encountered from white men in the left fueled a competitive mentality. Dana Densmore states:

> Suddenly the progressive causes we had always worked for were revealed as having been other people's causes. Was it possible we could finally be turning to the most radical cause of all?

Not only did this mentality result in antileft political stances, but in withdrawal from antiracist politics, which were reductively viewed as male. The equation of women with whiteness and race with maleness, persists to this day and as always ignores the multiple oppressions and multi-issued political agendas of women of color.

Some writers give the impression that racial divisions were necessary and inevitable if white women were to be successful in building a feminist movement. Jo Freeman writes:

> Race and class were constant concerns. Even though there were no minority or working-class women in our group, there was an unspoken assumption that 'their' approval was necessary for our legitimation. But there was no way to obtain their approval. Our contacts with minority women were few, despite our roots in the Civil Rights

Movement and community organizing projects. . . . A couple of black women came to our early meetings but didn't come back. We accepted the fact that blacks wanted to keep their distance from whites and assumed this applied to other minority women as well.

"Our contacts with minority women were few!" Indeed what is ironic to me is that white women can remain so clueless about race despite some involvement in the Civil Rights movement. Some contributors express great hostility toward those white women who were concerned about Black women's opinions of how white women were generally defining women's issues. Some describe relationships with Black women in the movement in extremely tokenizing and condescending language. For example, both Dana Densmore and Rosalyn Baxandall describe two different Black women as "feisty characters."

Appallingly, Black activists' demands for autonomous organizations in order to determine Black political agendas during this period are cited as a legitimate excuse for not altering the all-white composition of early women's organizations. White women's comfort level with de facto segregation, which they had experienced since childhood, and their lack of significant connections to women of color in their daily lives, were much more likely causes.

Elizabeth (Betita) Martinez offers a vivid description of the white solipsism and isolation that ultimately forced her to leave New York Radical Women:

"It was almost entirely white but that did not bother me at first. . . . Then came the night that Martin Luther King was assassinated, April 4, 1968. The streets of New York and the nation, the hearts of people everywhere, were filled with rage. But at our women's meeting, nobody mentioned King's death, no one said we should talk about it before our usual business (some who might have done so were absent). . . . It was a night to realize that if the struggle against sexism did not see itself as profoundly entwined with the fight against racism, I was gone." Martinez did not abandon feminism, but eventually worked with other Chicanas to challenge sexism within the Chicano movement.

Another telling perception is the number of contributors who contend that the best days of the movement were over by the mid or even early 1970s. Often their declaring the end of the movement coincided with their decision to leave it. Anselma Dell'Olio writes of 1975: "Most depressing of all, the movement felt brain-dead." Rosalyn Baxandall remarks: "Many of the women I had identified with, the real, gutsy feminists, were worn out, and nobody else came forward to open up space for radical change. . . . By 1973 the guts had been taken out of the women's liberation movement and it was no longer innovative or exciting for me." In fact the 1970s saw the growth of feminists of color organizing (often led by lesbians) all over the country. This organizing perhaps reached its peak in the early 1980s. This was also the period when those issues that had divided many of the movement's constituencies—such as racism, anti-Semitism, ableism, ageism, and classism—were put out on the table. The most progressive sectors of the movement responded to the challenge to transform their analysis and practice in order to build a stronger movement that encompassed a variety of feminisms.

A few white contributors evidence that their politics have been affected by the feminism of women of color, but most write as if our organizing never occurred. One indication that some early feminists still operate in a racial time warp is their shocking use of the term "Negro" when describing past events, although they do not use "girls" or "chicks" when referring to women during the same bygone era.

In 1997 there is still a feminist movement in the United States. Its most vital elements are grassroots activists who are committed to linking diverse communities and struggles. This is the part of the movement that never got major media attention, nor does it get to speak out in mainstream contexts about feminist issues. The women's movement is still portrayed as a white, bourgeois, heterosexual monolith that organizes well-orchestrated campaigns against a *film* about Larry Flynt, but maintains complete silence about New York police officers' *actual* attempt to lynch Haitian immigrant Abner Louima by eviscerating him with a bathroom plunger.

Meredith Tax writes:

Because I had no experience with anyone but white people, I did not have enough political grasp to understand how to fight the de facto segregation of the antiwar movement and women's movement. . . . I began to learn—not from theory but from the experience of being white in places where the work force was almost entirely made up of African Americans and Hispanic women. Since that time, most of my political work has been on a multiracial basis. Being in all-white political meetings or social gatherings no longer feels natural to me; I see them as the product of political choices, however unconscious.

Learning how to live in a multiracial world was important to me personally. Since race is at the heart of the way every contradiction comes up in the United States, it also affected my ability to think strategically.

I wish there had been more words like these in *The Feminist Memoir Project*. Ironically, Tax recounts how difficult it is for her, as a "committed left-wing feminist," to get her writing published.

The battle to build a women's movement that addresses the life circumstances and priorities of all women continues. Unfortunately, what many of these memoirs reveal is why this effort has been so difficult. When I described this book to a friend and comrade, Naomi Jaffe, who was active in New York City feminist groups in the late 1960s, she reminded me of what Black feminist Flo Kennedy said about the debate in 1971 about whether feminists should support Black and Puerto Rican prisoners' rebellion at Attica. Kennedy's statement brilliantly sums up the kind of feminism in which I believe, the kind of movement that can change the world. She asserts:

"We do not support Attica. We are Attica. We are Attica or we are nothing."

My Memoir Problem

Ellen Willis

For me, this book arrived at an ironic moment. Just as the larger public was getting into the memoir form in a big way, I, ever the crank, was finding it increasingly problematic. Over the years I had had many occasions to defend the importance of personal writing for accumulating knowledge and dispelling myths about women's lives—and to roll my eyes at socially conservative critics, usually though not always male, who denounced such writing as the self-indulgent, narcissistic publicizing of private matters that were shameful or trivial or both. (That this vein of polemic is by no means exhausted is evident from the collective freak-out that recently passed for criticism of Kathryn Harrison's memoir of her affair with her father.) For that matter, some of my own writing had been the object of these charges. Yet it seemed to me that as women's writing about their experience became more acceptable, both in the mass media and in the academy, it had also become more formulaic, a repository of packaged epiphanies. Periodically, new and revitalizing voices would emerge, speaking of lives and cultures previously excluded from the conversation; over time they too seemed, on the whole, to travel a familiar route from fresh to canned.

It's not that I never find individual memoirs that interest or even compel me. But I rarely have the impulse to read a memoir, and—more to the point in this context—I no longer look to memoirs as a likely source of radical insight. On the other hand, the stories *The Feminist Memoir Project* promised were not simply about the connection between personal and political, but about the connection of individuals with a political movement, with political history. Surely that would make a difference?

Reading the manuscript of *The Feminist Memoir Project,* I was riveted, by turns delighted and amused, irritated and appalled, confirmed and challenged, at times deeply pained, almost always overwhelmed with recognition. How could it be otherwise? I know many of these women personally, know of most of the others, lived through my own complicated version of the history we collectively made and individually perceived and now remember in our distinctive and sometimes incompatible ways.

There's nothing canned about these essays: despite the presence of several of the movement's literary heavyweights among its contributors, the book has the unprocessed flavor of early feminist writing. If the essays can be said to have a common thread, beyond the movement itself, it's defiance of the relentless decoupling of feminism from radical politics. The writers make clear that it was feminist activism—not only feminist ideas—that changed their lives. Implicitly they also argue that it was the ideas and actions of radicals that transformed the culture. A different kind of memoir, to be sure. And yet the difference didn't resolve my anxieties about the form, but rather gave them a particularly disconcerting spin.

As I read essay after essay (virtually all of them in one sitting), I began to feel an oppressive sense of isolation. Who were my fellow readers supposed to be? I was having trouble imagining anyone but charter members of second-wave feminism and other sixties social movements, or historians of those movements, reacting to most of the pieces with anything but uncomprehending puzzlement. The writers' animating assumptions—that huge numbers of young people had serious aspirations to transform society and their own personal lives and relationships; that the ideas and vocabulary of radical left and feminist politics were as much a part of the public conversation as, say, the right's anti-government rhetoric is today; that people made life-changing decisions based on those ideas; that economic survival was unproblematic enough so they could afford to make such decisions—are so alien to contemporary thinking as to create a formidable communication gap. And the writers' language keeps falling back on the tropes of an earlier era, for the simple reason that in this period there exists no legitimate public language in which to describe utopian vision or systemic opposition. The conceit of the memoir—especially the memoir with a political theme or intent—is that the details of an individual's life can illuminate the social world in which that person moved. But in this case it's more likely that the opposite is true, that only a detailed rendering of the social world of early feminism—the kind of account a historian or novelist might provide—could make these individuals' lives intelligible to readers who have grown up on what feels like another planet.

Eventually, of course, there will be a new wave of social and sexual rebellion to provide the missing context for these pieces of intimate history; the true audience for this book may be the next generation of utopians. In the present, however, the book represents the flip side of my memoir problem: the gap between the radical sensibility of these memoirs and the depoliticized reader mirrors the gap between the denatured feminism of so many contemporary memoirs and the radical ideas and passions that inspired the explosion of women's personal writing in the first place. In an age of political exhaustion, intellectual stasis, and attenuated hope, I can't help suspecting that memoirs are less likely to give me what I need than social and cultural criticism. The women's liberation movement championed experience as the fount of ideas; yet this book is nothing if not striking evidence that ideas are also the fount of experience. Paradoxically, the writers' vivid evocations of lives shaped by activism inspired by the power of ideas make me hunger for, well, theory. Perhaps it's time to concentrate on cultivating the visions that will impel us to reinterpret our experience and forge the new politics from which new stories will come.

Sisters in Struggle:
A Belated Response

Beverly Guy-Sheftall

My mother, Ernestine Varnado Guy, was probably the first feminist I ever knew. She left my father when I was in the eighth grade, moved back with her parents, never remarried, and raised her three daughters to be independent, self-reliant, and resourceful. When I was in the ninth grade, she petitioned the Memphis public schools to waive their home economics requirement for all female students and demanded that I be allowed to take typing, which was reserved for juniors and seniors. This act of "feminist" defiance on her part sent several clear messages to me early on—that learning to be a homemaker was relatively unimportant; that the skills of a typist would be more useful to me as a serious, college-bound student; and that one could resist authority. Whenever I reflect upon my journey to feminism, I always invoke the memory of my mother, who died too soon at age 62 of breast cancer, before I got a chance to say to her how much she had influenced her first, sometimes contrary, daughter.

In one of our last conversations during her final hospital stay after I had shown her my recently published book on Spelman College (the second book I'd co-edited), she told me how proud she was of my accomplishments and what a good daughter I'd been though, I reminded myself, I had not followed the conventional route of motherhood and was soon to be divorced. "She prefers to produce books," my mother thought out loud. I was pleased, I thought to myself, that she had forgiven me and given me permission, in her own subtle way, to continue my intellectual passions.

When I was approached about becoming a contributor to *The Feminist Memoir Project,* I thought again of my mother and agreed because I was also frustrated by the erasure of Black women in popular and scholarly histories, television documentaries, and magazine articles about the "second-wave" women's movement. I was tired of seeing mainly white women's faces and hearing white women's voices in retrospectives about the women's liberation movement of the sixties and seventies. I was also annoyed at having to explain to Black folks, even academics, for most of my young adult life why I identified as a feminist. During the late seventies, as the women's movement grew in momentum and as the Civil Rights Movement receded, it seemed, into the background, some Black women scholars left Black Studies or tried to infuse gender there—often a difficult enterprise. A few of us associated ourselves with Women's Studies and advocated loudly for paradigm shifts that would more adequately address race/class/ethnicity issues and eradicate frameworks that were constructed from the notion that "woman" is a monolithic category. Others tried to maintain a foot in both camps so that Black feminist perspectives would permeate both disciplines, one of which had been historically insensitive to gender and homophobia, and the other one of which had been insensitive to race and class, and too bound up in Western epistemologies and cultural contexts.

It was especially difficult to be a Black woman committed as intensely to the eradication of racism and sexism and heterosexism during this early period. We were sometimes perceived within the African-American community to be disloyal to the race, anti-male, white-oriented, and lesbian, this last perhaps seen as the worst of these evils. It was hard to convince many in the community that Black women, and some Black men, had been thinking and writing "feminist" since the early 1900s and that their perspectives came from their analyses of their own realities rather than from an embrace of white feminism; my book *Words of Fire: An Anthology of African American Feminist Thought* (New Press, 1995) was my own response to these misconceptions and erasures.

Even among Black women, the constituency we cared most about, we Black feminists were heavily criticized. As has been the case with the more recent Clarence Thomas, Mike Tyson, and O. J. Simpson cases, I recalled the endless and painful arguments I've had with my sisters, including some of my closest friends over the years, about the need for a feminist analysis of these complicated situations and the problem of defending Black men at all costs.

In order to better understand what other Black feminists faced inside and outside our communities, I recalled having read Michele Wallace's 1975 *Village Voice* essay, "Anger in Isolation: A Black Feminist's Search for Sisterhood" (published before her controversial, much-maligned *Black Macho and the Myth of the Superwoman),* which was one of the earliest narratives by an African-American woman to trace the development of her feminist consciousness. I remembered the joy I experienced after reading some years ago three more lengthy memoirs— Shirley Chisholm's *Unbossed and Unbought,* in which she named sexism rather than racism as her biggest hurdle; *Color Me Flo,* Flo Kennedy's radical Black feminist manifesto; and Pauli Murray's *Song in a Weary Throat,* a compelling portrait (published in 1987 posthumously) of one of the most important figures in the Black women's liberation movement and "second-wave" feminism. These cross-generational autobiographical narratives and many other texts, especially Toni Cade's ground-breaking anthology *The Black Woman* (1970); bell hooks's first book, *Ain't I a Woman: Black Women and Feminism* (1981); Barbara Smith's *Home Girls: A Black Feminist Anthology* (1983); and Paula Giddings's *When and Where I Enter* (1984), helped me to claim feminism unapologetically despite the hostility I sometimes experienced at work and at conferences.

I can still remember exactly how I felt as an eager graduate student in the eighties after stumbling in the Emory University Library upon Anna Julia Cooper's pioneering *A Voice from the South by a Black Woman of the South* (1892),[1] a largely ignored text that I and other Black scholars would later appropriately label the first published monograph of African-American feminist thought. I was literally awestruck when I read Cooper's insightful and original pronouncement, which she wrote in 1892 long before there was any mention of Black feminism: "The colored woman of to-day occupies, one may say, a unique position in this country. . . . She is confronted by both a woman question and a race problem, and is as yet an unknown or an unacknowledged factor in both."

Perhaps, most importantly, I recalled my earliest involvement with the women's movement, many details of which are vague and difficult to reconstruct with certainty. It was 1968 and I was a graduate student at Atlanta University pursuing an M.A. in English. I don't remember how I came to be involved, or what in particular drew me to those Sunday afternoon gatherings at Sandra Flowers's small apartment in a working-

---

[1] Anna Julia Cooper's *A Voice from the South* (Aldine Publishers, 1892) has been reprinted by Oxford University Press (1988) in the Schomburg Library of Nineteenth-Century Black Women Writers series, edited by Henry Louis Gates, Jr.

class neighborhood near the campus, which I came to realize much later were consciousness-raising sessions; I don't even remember the circumstances under which I met Sandy, who else attended, exactly what we talked about, or how long I went. What I was able to recall was that I was a regular participant, along with at least ten to twelve other young Black women, in what we now know was a major strategy of "second-wave" feminism—women gathering informally, usually in living rooms, sharing their individual experiences of being female.

In preparation for the writing of my own memoir for this collection, which I never completed, I spent a great deal of time going through old folders so that I could trace the evolution of my involvement with feminism. The most startling discovery of all in my file cabinets were faded mimeographed documents entitled "Statement of National Black Feminist Organization," "Standard Questions You Might Be Asked—Suggested Answers That Might Work," "Points Taken from the Platform of The National Black Feminist Organization," and "N.B.F.O. Suggested Reading List." The documents (no bylines) must have been generated soon after 1973, the year the National Black Feminist Organization was founded, which was long after our CR group in Atlanta had disbanded.

I reread the powerful opening paragraph of the "Statement," on the left of which was an image of the now-familiar female symbol but with a twist—in the center was a clenched fist, reminiscent of the Black Power Movement:

> The distorted male-dominated media image of the Women's Liberation Movement has clouded the vital and revolutionary importance of the Movement to Third World women, especially Black women. The Movement has been characterized as the exclusive property of so called "white middle class" women and [the] only Black women seen involved in this Movement have been seen as "selling out," "dividing the race," and an assortment of nonsensical epithets. Black Feminists resent these charges and are therefore establishing THE NATIONAL BLACK FEMINIST ORGANIZATION, in order to address ourselves to the particular and specific needs of the larger, but almost cast-aside half of the Black race in Amerikka [sic], the Black Woman. . . . We will encourage the Black community to stop falling into the trap of the white male Left, utilizing women only in terms of domestic or

servile needs. We will remind the Black Liberation Movement that there can't be liberation for half a race. We must together, as a people, work to eliminate racism from without the Black community which is trying to destroy us as an entire people, but we must remember that sexism is destroying and crippling us from within.

Finding these cherished documents made me bemoan the absence still of a comprehensive history of the contemporary Black women's liberation movement and reminded me that standard histories of the women's movement, which I continue to read nevertheless, are still somewhat useless in this regard, even the most recent ones. In any event, subsequent histories need to be tested against this criterion—how they incorporate and analyze the involvement of Black and other women of color in various kinds of feminist organizations and in feminist movements more broadly defined.

Because I also felt it was important for future generations of Black women and men to know something about the personal struggles of their sisters who self-identified as feminists during a critical juncture in both African-American and women's history, I decided to join this project. I thought my story would be distinctive in some ways because unlike many Black feminists of my generation (with whom I had developed close personal ties), I had lived and developed politically primarily within southern Black urban communities.

In addition, helping to edit *Sage: A Scholarly Journal on Black Women* (1983–1995), the first Black feminist publication focused on women of African descent locally and globally, made me aware of the limitations of conventional feminist theory, which has historically decentered or made invisible the activist, intellectual, and cultural work of a particular group of women who have been central to the development, nevertheless, of feminist thought and praxis. In many ways *Sage* emerged in 1983 because of the failure of both Black Studies and Women's Studies to adequately address the experiences and thinking of Black women around the world. Our editorial practice was affected in many ways, therefore, by the erasures and gaps in Black Studies and Women's Studies scholarship. *Sage,* we believe, has been critical to the development of Black Women's Studies and has helped in the reconceptualization of Women's Studies as a more inclusive field of study; we also believe it has helped to promote greater gender sensitivity in the field of Black Studies.

What will probably not be surprising, given what I've shared about why I was interested in the project in the first place, is my disappointment at the small number of narratives by African-American women, who were, of course, critical in the development of the contemporary women's movement. It may have been the case that others, like myself, were unable to meet the deadline for submission. I read the introduction and was not surprised by the predictable picture of "second-wave" feminists being mostly white, though there is the clear acknowledgment that the Civil Rights Movement was the major stimulant. I longed for references to Black women who were important in the early days of the women's movement—Flo Kennedy, Pauli Murray, Aileen Hernandez, Margaret Sloan, Frances Beal, Brenda Eichelberger, Audre Lorde, Loretta Ross, Alice Walker, to name a few. I was pleased about references to critiques by women of color about white feminism and its insensitivity to difference. I was happy to learn more of the extraordinary history of a movement that had a profound impact upon my own personal and professional growth, but was disappointed by the conflicts, collisions, schisms, and errors that editors of this anthology were intent upon *not* sweeping under the rug. I recognized the importance of this side of the story, and welcomed the candor of the painful admissions of many of the contributors. It was important, as well, to see that the movement still lives, despite its flaws, and to be reminded that significant changes have occurred in the life of the nation since the sixties because of civil rights and feminist struggle.

I read with particular enthusiasm what three very different African-American women (whom I know) remembered about their involvement in civil rights, Black nationalism, and the women's movement. I'm not convinced that the interview following Barbara Emerson's narrative was necessary, though it is possible that the editors were frustrated when they discovered that this "daughter" of "the movement" had not written about the women's movement at all. Though Barbara indicates that she didn't really see gender issues as a youngster while she was immersed in the Civil Rights Movement, I wondered if she had revisited as an adult that period with respect to its lessons about gender. What Barbara does reveal in the interview is her ambivalence about white feminism as a young civil rights worker in the South; she also asserts that her feminist consciousness came later—mainly as a result of a failed marriage and the experience of being a single parent. What Barbara's narrative underscores for me is the connection to feminism that comes with lived experience. "Certain things were possible because this movement had started to change the way that people think . . . I became a feminist indirectly, and I suspect that that's the route that most women took."

Michele Wallace's story and feminist politics are more familiar; she is the daughter of the well-known feminist/artist Faith Ringgold, and joined her mother in the development of the feminist art movement. What links Barbara and Michele, despite their very different backgrounds and histories, is the militant politics of their father and mother, respectively, which helped to shape their own political perspectives and activism. They were both courageous young women, as well, with an early commitment to social change. However, Michele paid a dear price within the Black community when her writing catapulted her into the public arena as an angry Black feminist bent on maligning the Civil Rights Movement and demonizing Black men. With the publication of *Black Macho*, made worse by its appearance in excerpt form in *Ms.* with her on the cover, Michele was demonized by Black men and women alike for having, in her own words, "indiscreetly blurted out that sexism and misogyny were near-epidemic in the Black community and that Black feminism had the cure. . . . At 26 I had written the book from hell and my life would change forever." Michele's essay here helps to explain the personal/political context in which this important and perpetually controversial Black feminist text emerges.

Like Michele, one of the founders of the National Black Feminist Organization, Barbara Omolade is an important figure in the history of contemporary Black women's activism; she and Michele were also both involved in a Black feminist study group in New York in the late seventies. Her self-identification as a nationalist, her location within Black working-class communities as a struggling single mother, her early involvement with white feminist organizations in which she experienced blatant racism and classism, and her pioneering work in the battered women's movement enable her to see "second-wave" feminism in particular ways that I would argue are critical for the readers of this volume.

Without these narratives, it is more difficult to understand the battles Black feminists were compelled to fight on two fronts during the sixties and seventies. They struggled with white feminists around issues of race and class and within their own communities around issues of gender and their involvement with feminism.

These very different autobiographical reflections are finally about resistance and the sheer determination and courage of a diverse group of women committed to helping change the world, which always begins with personal struggle and transformation. We will not understand the contemporary women's movement within the United States without knowing more about the women who helped to get it going, sometimes with tremendous personal sacrifice. They were transformed by the work and, in turn, changed the world in which we now live. We need more stories, more remembrances, more calls for action, more analysis, especially from those among us whose voices have not been heard or else have been forgotten. *The Feminist Memoir Project* points us in the right direction and inspired me to work further and tell my own story.

How Many Lives Are Here . . .

Kate Millett

How many lives are here, since for every woman who tells her story in feminism in this ground-breaking collection, there are a thousand others, ten thousand others. For these "representative lives" are only one sampling of a great historical wave. It came at us full tide and from all sides and swept our lives into action, sudden meaning, a transforming vitality, a consuming energy that is still unspent.

History broke over a generation of women who were changed utterly and in the process changed their own times, a change still going on around the world, change still hardly reckoned yet, a chain reaction that will set still others in motion. And it begins with such small steps: a pamphlet, an evening between friends, a challenge at a meeting, then a demonstration, then a network of consciousness-raising groups. It begins with an atmosphere arising out of the great example of the struggle for black civil rights and with the passage of a civil rights law that, virtually by accident, empowered women as well, and thus opened a path. It also began because of a disastrous and unpopular war and resistance to that war by a left whose male chauvinism became insupportable. Yet another path opened. And there was always the example of our foremothers once we could see our way back to them and see ourselves as another wave of the longest revolution. Women came together from different political directions and backgrounds, formal and informal groupings, in neighborhoods or places of study. They explored and agreed, disputed and disagreed, analyzed and synthesized, proclaimed and pronounced and denounced and roughed out a style and an agenda of goals we are still hotly pursuing.

Women's Liberation became an explosion. The women in this collection were on the front line of this movement and felt its first energy, that explosive moment. Feminism became enormous and took on issue after issue: wages led to law and then to health; sexual self-definition led to abortion and then to lesbian rights; the image of women led to advertising and textbooks or toys and war. As you read, you can see a historical phenomenon like this begin with afternoons among "a gang of four" friends positing an autonomous left feminism in Naomi Weisstein's Chicago apartment, which would lead to the Chicago Women's Liberation Union, which sprouted a school and women's studies, a speakers bureau and child care and even a rock band whose triumphs and failures seem a metaphor for the times.

"Every day someone else became a lesbian," Amy Kesselman muses, remembering this time of discovery and change. Out of whirls of activity and experiment came genuine service and solid achievement. The stories here are stories of risk taking: Anselma Dell'Olio's vital immigrant past and her brave forays into feminist theater, Barbara Epstein's thoughtful ambivalence in the face of communism. There was fun in the Lavender Menace "zap," impudence and daring and humor. There was daring in the Chicago "Jane" project that performed eleven thousand abortions before legalization. There is pain in Roxanne Dunbar's stories of rape, even in a rapist's conviction in court: suspended sentence and a two hundred dollar fine. There is another pain in Weisstein's and in Jo Freeman's and other accounts of "trashing," doctrinaire attacks on women by other women, and there is a fine courage in Dell'Olio's denunciation of it as "Divisiveness and Self-Destruction."

There is movement building here, the nervy excitement of meetings and organizations, the march of groups in cities: Bread and Roses, Radical Women, WITCH, Redstockings, the Sisterhood of Black Single Mothers and the Woman's Survival Space, women's peace camps, the Herstory Archives. A woman's law movement came into being, a woman's health movement. The romance of politics was always an inner struggle, as Vivian Gornick reminds us, a battle with the self for discipline and strength, or for class or racial or ethnic identity, as Priscilla Long and Meredith Tax, Barbara Omolade, Michele Wallace, Lourdes Benería, and Shirley Geok-lin Lim demonstrate. Or for autonomy within marriage or recognition for relationship, as Alix Kates Shulman and Joan Nestle work it out from different poles of origin. The turmoil of the very self in transformation while it tries to transform the culture around it. It has not changed enough, nor have we. The divisions of class and race beset us still. This being America, the role of black feminism must become pivotal, crucial, the linchpin securing the wheel itself, if U.S. feminism would be liberatory to feminism worldwide. And though we come together across class, class divides us still. As it was meant to do, and means to do still in an increasingly ruthless capitalism, the so-called "global economy" presenting itself as iron necessity. The stakes get bigger, tougher.

"What I'd like to convey"—Rosalyn Baxandall fills in the essential—"what I think has been neglected in the books and articles about the women's liberation movement—is the joy we felt. We were, we believed, poised on the trembling edge of a transformation. . . . There was a yeast-iness in the air that made us cocky and strong. Sure there were splits and backbiting among us, but there was also fun and great times. For me the women's liberation movement was love at first sight."

Really, after all, this is a love story: love for ideas that had come alive in political action and possibility, love for a vision of freedom and for the camaraderie that brought that liberation into being. We called it sis-terhood. It was euphoric and over the top, excessive and insufficient all at once. There were terrible shortcomings in how this movement faced differences in race and class, which are slowly being redeemed. There were downs and depressions, times when support fell through and community failed: Jo Freeman and Carol Hanisch give powerful and moving testimony here. There is an emptiness afterwards and a slightly elegiac tone at the end of a great many of these pieces.

The social transformation that has come about since, the gradual unfolding and extension of feminism into every corner of our lives and into so many societies worldwide, had its kernel as well as its parallel in accounts like these, lives like these. And it goes on. The "click" of recog-nition and resolve will continue among other women now, younger, or distant, or yet to come.

CHRONOLOGY

Rachel Blau DuPlessis and Ann Snitow

This partial, highly selective, but suggestive chronology illustrates the premise for this book: the interpenetration of local, particular, and personal decisions and events with large, historical, macro-events. Small-scale, individual, precise, micro-changes experienced by our participants are here presented in conjunction with the large-scale, general historical shifts and incidents of these years. Our contributors' names signal their participation or connection with the event. The combinations of small and large in this chronology illustrate how the political and personal coincide, collide, and mesh.

February 1, 1960 African-American students (organized by CORE—Congress for Racial Equality) stage a sit-in at Woolworth's in Greensboro, North Carolina, protesting refusal of service in a public accommodation. Also in 1960: high school students join in pacifist protest of air-raid drills in New York City (Epstein); Committee for a Sane Nuclear Policy (SANE) organizes a meeting on peace and the end of the Cold War. The contraceptive pill is introduced.

1961 Berlin Wall is constructed. President's Commission on the Status of Women is formed; Eleanor Roosevelt is chair. August 1961 Student Non-Violent Coordinating Committee (SNCC) Campaign to register Black voters in Mississippi. Also in 1961: first national convention of Student SANE (Epstein).

June 1962 Founding of SDS (Students for a Democratic Society) with the Port Huron Statement. October 1962 Cuban missile crisis.

1963 Betty Friedan's *The Feminine Mystique* is a best-seller. Gloria Steinem's exposé "I Was a Playboy Bunny." Suicide of Sylvia Plath.

Assassination of distinguished Civil Rights organizer Medgar Evers, Mississippi; April-May 1963, Birmingham Civil Rights nonviolent demonstrations. Martin Luther King, Jr., writes "Letter from a Birmingham Jail."

July 1963 Barbara W. Emerson, about to enter her final two years of high school, goes to Georgia to join the Civil Rights Movement, in which her father, Hosea Williams, is a key leader. In 1963 contributor Priscilla Long is arrested in a sit-in to integrate an amusement park. August 28, 1963: the March on Washington sponsored by the Civil Rights Movement; Rev. King's "I Have a Dream . . ." speech. September 15, 1963: 16th Street Baptist Church in Birmingham, Alabama, is bombed; four Black girls are killed.

November 22, 1963 Assassination of President John F. Kennedy.

1964 Freedom Summer in Mississippi. Congress passes Civil Rights legislation, prohibiting discrimination in public accommodations and employment, signed into law July 1964. It includes Title VII, barring sex discrimination in employment. In August 1964, the Economic Opportunity Act (the "War on Poverty") is passed. Also in August, the result of the Tonkin Gulf incident gives war powers to the president.

Early demonstrations against the war in Vietnam (Wallace). Fall 1964, Berkeley Free Speech Movement.

January 1965 Lyndon Johnson and Hubert Humphrey are inaugurated. In February, there is a voter registration drive, Selma, Alabama; the effort results in racist attacks, beatings, deaths. February–March, there is significant escalation of the war in Vietnam. March 1965, Civil Rights March from Selma to Montgomery, Alabama, is protected by Alabama National Guard. February 21, 1965, Malcolm X assassinated in New York City. March 1965, Significant sit-ins against the U.S. war in Vietnam begin in Chicago, Michigan. Teach-ins about the war in Vietnam in Berkeley (Dunbar). In May, a National Teach-In against the war in Vietnam is attended by 100,000 on 100 campuses. Marches against the war in a number of places, including Los Angeles, San Francisco, New York, and on April 1, antiwar march on Washington, D.C. "Flower Power" phrase coined by Allen Ginsberg.

In 1965 Mary King and Casey Hayden write a position paper on the status of women in SNCC, "Sex and Caste: A Kind of Memo" (circulated widely, then published in April 1966 in *Liberation)*. Women of this generation begin experiencing job discrimination. On June 7, 1965, in *Griswold* v. *Connecticut,* the Supreme Court invalidates the birth control law that had banned use of or circulation of information about birth control.

Summer 1965 SCOPE (Summer Committee Organization and Political Education Project) in the Civil Rights Movement; a number of future feminists work in it (Emerson, Freeman). It concentrates on voter registration. In June 1965, there are five days of Civil Rights protest in Chicago; in August 1965, six days of rebellion in the Watts ghetto, Los Angeles, California, leaving 34 dead, 4,000 arrested.

1965 Beatles film *HELP!* whose insouciance had a large impact, as Martinez points out.

1965 Congress passes the Voting Rights Act, eliminating literacy tests and poll taxes, and mandating federal supervision of voting.

1966 In November 1966 Juliet Mitchell's "Women: The Longest Revolution" is published in *New Left Review,* an important British journal of analysis. In 1966 opposition to the war in Vietnam grows; SDS is one of central antiwar youth organizations (Epstein). Chicago has radical antiwar activity (Kesselman). There are demonstrations in San Francisco, Boston, Philadelphia, and an antiwar Stop It committee in London, England; Meredith Tax is present. Draft calls at 50,000 a month, with the end of automatic student deferments. In 1966–69 Nancy Spero is making art work—called the *War Series*—concerning the Vietnam War and the "convergence of state violence with male sexual aggression."

1966 James Meredith's March against Fear, Mississippi. "Black Power" is enunciated as a concept. There are tensions around issues of sexuality and the treatment of women in the Civil Rights Movement; Blacks to organize autonomously. In 1966 SNCC votes to expel all white staff members (Emerson, Freeman, Martinez).

October 1966 NOW (National Organization for Women) founded (Dell'Olio). Betty Friedan serves as its first president, 1966–70.

1967 NOW holds first national conference, featuring a "Bill of Rights for Women." In 1967 *New Left Notes* (SDS) prints women's statement about "male chauvinism" in the organization, setting it in a disparaging context. In 1967, Shulamith Firestone and Jo Freeman make a feminist critique of SDS after an in-fight in SDS.

After the National Conference for New Politics in Chicago, September 1967, the West Side Group (a women's group) is formed in protest about the treatment of women radicals—see Kesselman's essay.

In 1967 Women's Liberation movements begin their rhizomic and effervescent growth. In spring 1967, Berkeley women's consciousness-raising groups formed. There is women's liberation activity in Chicago, in Seattle (Winslow, Freeman, Kesselman). Early debates will take the form of politicos (radical women) versus feminists (women radicals; "feminist" was not a term then used), although these were differently inflected in different cities. Summer 1967: In a "prefeminist action" women artists (including Nancy Spero) in

New York City crash a stag party for male art critics (who were also their colleagues and friends) and disrupt the party with a custard pie event. New York City feminists protest and desegregate Help Wanted ads in *New York Times*. 1967, New York Radical Women is founded (Baxandall, Martinez). 1967 Feminists and young radical mothers open a feminist day-care center: Liberation Nursery in New York City. The anarchist/feminist protest SCUM Manifesto published by Valerie Solanas.

In 1967, contributor Vivian Rothstein attends a peace conference between antiwar Americans and Vietnamese from both North and South. By August 1967, 15,000 Americans have been killed in Vietnam, troop levels exceed 475,000, and bombing tonnage exceeds that of World War II.

In April 1967, Martin Luther King, Jr., calls on African Americans and others to boycott the Vietnam War. June 1967, Mexican Americans occupy the courthouse in Tierra Amarilla (see Martinez); Chicanos in New Mexico seize lands formerly Mexican. In 1967, there are Black riots and uprisings in more than 100 cities in the United States, including Newark, Detroit, Atlanta, Boston, Chicago, New York, Louisville, Cincinnati (see Taub and Tax). The Kerner Commission is appointed to investigate causes and propose remedies. In July 1967, a Black Power conference is held in Newark, New Jersey.

In August 1967, Thurgood Marshall is appointed the first Black justice on the Supreme Court. Also August 1967, The first Black riots in Washington, D.C., as well as in Milwaukee, New Haven, Providence. Rev. King calls for organized mass disobedience.

January 1968 Dana Densmore hears the words "Women's Liberation" for the first time from her mother, Donna Allen, founder of Women Strike for Peace. In 1968, Joreen [Jo Freeman] publishes *Voice of the Women's Liberation Movement,* the first national newsletter of the movement, emanating from Chicago (see Densmore and Freeman). In 1968, Shirley Chisholm is the first African-American woman to be elected to the U.S. House of Representatives.

Tet Offensive begins January 30; March 1968, the My Lai massacre in Vietnam (not generally known until two years later) (discussed by Dunbar).

February 29, 1968 The Kerner Commission report released: "Our nation is moving toward two societies, one black, one white—separate and unequal."

April 4, 1968 Assassination of Rev. Martin Luther King, Jr. (spoken of by Emerson and Martinez). Rioting occurs in 100 cities; 21,000 federal and 34,000 state troops are mobilized.

1968 Prague Spring and May '68 in France; international student and left protest movements. In 1968, there are spring demonstrations and strikes on many university campuses, including Columbia and Harvard, around issues of racism, antiwar protest, and the complicity of university research in the war effort. Antiwar protest at University of Washington (see Winslow). San Francisco State president Hayakawa uses state troopers to suppress student strike (mentioned by Shulman).

June 1968 SDS convention: women hissed and thrown out for demanding that women's liberation become a plank of the national platform.

1968 Confrontation between a *Playboy* Bunny named Reagan Wilson and Barbara Winslow, University of Washington, Seattle. In 1968, a Grinnell College "nude-in" protesting *Playboy* recruitment on campus (see Freeman). In 1968 struggles for day care became an issue within and immediately after the Columbia Strike, and the Columbia University Day Care Coalition is organized, winning a center called "The Children's Mansion" by 1970 (see Benería).

June 6, 1968 Assassination of presidential candidate Robert Kennedy.

1968 Massacre of protesting students in Mexico City.

July 1968 at the Free School of the Boston Draft Resistance Group, Dana Densmore and Roxanne Dunbar meet and form a group for women's revolution. On July 4, 1968, the formation of the Female Liberation Front for Human Liberation in Boston. On July 4, 1968, Barbara Winslow gives a talk on women's liberation to a demonstration and rally of Draft-Resistance-Seattle. In 1968, Seattle Radical Women and the Freedom Socialist Party sponsor a mini-course on "The Woman Question in America." In 1968, Beverly Guy-Sheftall attends a CR group in Atlanta along with about twelve other Black women.

August 1968 In Sandy Springs, Maryland, a meeting of New Left women from SDS and the Civil Rights Movement to discuss women's liberation (discussed in Densmore, Dunbar, Freeman). In New York City, Boston activist Dunbar meets feminists in Redstockings and NOW activists Ti-Grace Atkinson and Flo Kennedy, and visits Valerie Solanas in prison. Boston women publish the first theoretical journal of the women's movement, *No More Fun & Games: a Journal of Female Liberation* (Dunbar, Densmore, Tax).

August 1968 Police riot at the Democratic National Convention, Chicago; arrest of seven male antiwar activists and Bobby Seale of the Black Panther Party: they are called "The Chicago 8."

September 7, 1968 Women's Liberation stages the Miss America Pageant Protest, Atlantic City (see Carol Hanisch and Ros Baxandall). Also in September 1968, with the slogan "The Drag Queen Is Everywoman," Boston women use a film about a female impersonator to organize for female liberation (Dunbar). In fall 1968, Women's Liberation–Seattle activists invade a meeting of "Fascinating Womanhood," an early antifeminist and fundamentalist organization (Winslow). A "Feminism Lives" button on another Columbia University student inspires contributor Benería in fall 1968. In late 1968 Boston feminists picket the Playboy Club (Densmore, Dunbar). WITCH is founded on Hallowe'en 1968. Pat Mainardi writes "The Politics of Housework."

September 1968 Roxanne Dunbar, Betty Friedan, and Rona Jaffe (novelist) appear on live TV to debate and discuss the women's movement. Also in 1968, contributors Kate Millett, Rosalyn Fraad Baxandall, Anselma Dell'Olio, along with Jacqui Ceballos appear on *The David Susskind Show* as "Four Angry Women."

November 1968 Lake Villa, Illinois: the first national gathering of about 200 women's liberation activists from about thirty cities in the United States and some from Canada. In attendance from this book: Kesselman, Densmore, Freeman; also discussed in Dunbar. In 1968–69, feminist consciousness-raising groups abound (mentioned in Benería and Wolfson). December SDS resolution supporting women's liberation begins a debate among feminists about working in "mixed" organizations or in all-women political organizing.

January 1969 Richard Nixon inaugurated. September 1969, the Chicago 8 Conspiracy Trial opens to political streetfighting ("Days of Rage").

In 1969, Robin Morgan and Kenneth Pitchford create the women's liberation symbol—a raised fist inside the glyph for "female" for the second Miss America demonstration. "Bread & Roses," by Kathy McAfee and Myrna Wood (June 1969); "Toward a Female Liberation Movement," by Beverly Jones and Judith Brown, widely circulated, as was a Marlene Dixon article "Why Women's Liberation?"

1969 There is increasing pressure on abortion laws. Concerned Clergy is active in running underground railroad (see Wolfson); several groups—in Seattle, in Washington, D.C., in New York City—begin speaking out against forced sterilization of poor women (Wolfson; Winslow). Abortion increasingly linked to women's health issues, as Wolfson points out. In March 1969, there are women's counter-hearings, testimony about illegal abortions, conducted by Redstockings, and others (see Hanisch). In 1969, "Jane" (an abortion referral service) is begun by Heather Booth in Chicago (Kesselman).

April 1969 U.S. Supreme Court strikes down laws controlling the reading/viewing of "obscene" material.

Early 1969 "A Marriage Agreement" by Alix Kates Shulman written; published and reprinted in journals and books through the early 1970s. 1969, first edition of *Our Bodies, Ourselves* from Boston Women's Health Collective. Lucinda Cisler's legendary bibliography of works about women circulates by mail-order. Naomi Weisstein's important critical analysis " 'Kinder, Kuche, Kirche' as Scientific Law: Psychology Constructs the Female," written 1968, begins to circulate widely.

1969 New York: Congress to Unite Women. Cell 16 performs a then-scandalous hair cutting (Densmore).

1969 WAR (Women Artists in Revolution) splits off from Art Workers Coalition (AWC), an activist group of artists on the issue of sexism in the art world (Spero). In 1969, New Feminist Cabaret Theater does traveling gigs in colleges and universities across the United States (Dell'Olio).

1969 Berkeley strike for a Department of Ethnic Studies.

1969 D.C. Women's Liberation/Welfare Rights Alliance demonstrates at the lethargic but well-connected task force on health problems in D.C. In 1969, U.S. Senate hearings on the birth control pill (the Nelson Hearings) disrupted and interrupted by feminist activists from Washington, D.C., to protest the exclusion of testimony about its negative and dangerous side-effects (Wolfson).

May 1969 Discussions of feminism in the *New York Times,* including a review of the New Feminist Repertory Theater (Dell'Olio). In May 1969, Cell 16 in Boston holds a women's liberation conference. Tax attends, along with Dunbar; Tax and Trude Bennett lead a workshop on women and psychology. Summer 1969, Women's Caucus of the New University Conference position paper "I am curious (female)" (Benería).

June 28, 1969 Stonewall Rebellion: police raid New York City gay bar; gays, lesbians, and men in drag fight back; five days of riots mark the symbolic beginning of gay militancy.

July 1969 "Redstockings Manifesto" published. A group of Boston women found a collective called Bread and Roses to unify antiwar, antiracist, left politics with women's liberation (see Tax). New York Radicalesbians form. In 1969, Chicago women found the Chicago Women's Liberation Union (CWLU), a separate left women's organization (Kesselman; Weisstein).

CWLU ends in 1977. Male authoritarianism in the antiwar movement drives many women into the women's movement (Epstein). Marge Piercy's feminist analysis of the left movement, "The Grand Coolie Damn," is written. At the same time, in 1969, Jo Freeman identifies a number of strains and fissures within feminism—reform versus radical, and the strong tensions about celebrity and press attention—but continues a kind of missionary work for the movement at the same time that she feels frozen in it by "trashing" (Freeman; Dell'Olio).

July 20, 1969 Apollo XI space missions—first manned landing on moon. In August 1969, Woodstock music festival.

1969 Feminist pressure within the professions and professional associations begins to be manifest. Women's Caucuses, for instance, form in the American Political Science Association.

1969 Ad Hoc feminist coalition in New York City stages a sit-in and demonstration at the *Ladies Home Journal* to demand that it reflect some modicum of feminist, or increased female, consciousness (Baxandall). The *Journal* publishes a special supplement in August 1970. In spring 1969, Nadine Taub is asked by a male lawyer about "women's lib" complaints (Taub). New York feminist groups invade a Bridal Fair at Madison Square Garden (Baxandall).

November 1969 Second Moratorium against the war in Washington, D.C.; tear gas used on demonstrators.

1970 The legal voting age changes to 18 (from 21).

1970 Significant publishing of feminist work: *Notes from the Second Year. Sexual Politics,* by Kate Millett. Shulamith Firestone, *The Dialectic of Sex: The Case for a Feminist Revolution. The Black Woman: An Anthology,* ed. by Toni Cade [Bambara] includes "Double Jeopardy"—Frances Beal's influential analysis of racism and sexism as interlocking systems of oppression. *Sisterhood is Powerful: An Anthology of Writings from the Women's Liberation Movement,* ed. Robin Morgan, a mass-market compilation of a number of the pamphlets, position papers, analyses, and testimony from the women's movement, collects much influential work, including Redstockings manifesto, WITCH documents, lesbian and Black women's analyses. Leslie Tanner, *Voices from Women's Liberation,* with an emphasis on left position papers and feminist analysis.

February 1970 The widening of the war to Laos. In February, the Chicago radicals are found not guilty of conspiracy to incite to riot.

March 1970 Chicago Women's Liberation Rock Band formed (Weisstein). The Feminist Press is founded by Florence Howe. New York City groups picket museums of modern and contemporary art, protesting the exclusion of women artists and artists of color from both historical and contemporary shows (Spero). In 1970 Jo Freeman travels in Europe (Holland, Norway, Sweden), engaging with incipient and active feminist groups in a variety of places.

During 1970, Dolle Mina is founded in the Netherlands; Mouvement de la Libération des Femmes organizes in France; and the first Women's Liberation Conference is held in England.

1970 Women's liberation activists at the University of Washington initiate a lawsuit charging massive sex discrimination in the university; they later win (Winslow). Study groups in feminist history and theory begin forming in many places. An example is the Great Atlantic Patchwork Quilt with contributors Priscilla Long, Meredith Tax, and Rosalyn Baxandall as members. Feminist newspapers begin publishing in a number of cities, including Berkeley, Washington, Iowa City. Some of the periodicals of the women's liberation movement include *Off Our Backs* (Washington); *It Ain't Me Babe* (Berkeley); *Up from Under* (New York); *No More Fun and Games* (Boston area); *Aphra* (New York); *Lilith* (Seattle); *Lavender Vision* (Cambridge); *Southern Journal of Female Liberation* (New Orleans); *Women: A Journal of Liberation* (Baltimore).

July Abortion laws liberalized in New York, Hawaii, and Alaska. Work on liberalizing abortion laws in New Jersey, through the Center for Constitutional Rights (Taub).

Discrimination against Women hearings held in June and July 1970 before the House Committee on Education and Labor.

The Second Congress to Unite Women; Rita Mae Brown sparks the Lavender Menace protest to assert lesbian rights as part of women's movement. 1970, Berkeley-Oakland Women's Union challenges the right of women members to belong to organizations that include men (Epstein). In 1970, Gay Activist Alliance and the Lesbian Liberation Committee are founded, in New York City (Nestle). "The Woman-Identified Woman," an influential position paper from the Radicalesbians, is written in 1970. During 1970–71 many Lesbian feminist consciousness-raising groups are formed.

April 1, 1970 Three feminist protesters enter a secret Food and Drug Administration meeting evaluating data allegedly linking the birth control pill and increased risk of heart attack and stroke (Wolfson). Later in the year the Washington, D.C., feminists hold a sit-in at HEW Secretary Robert Finch's office to pursue their demand that an informational brochure be placed in each packet of pills to alert consumers. Alice Wolfson and Barbara Seaman are a "two-woman brigade" monitoring all FDA meetings on women's health issues. The FDA warns physicians about the pill. In April 1970, the first Earth Day, organized by the ecology movement.

April 1970 *Newsweek* profiles "new feminists," including Jo Freeman. Spring 1970, Meredith Tax's pamphlet "Woman and Her Mind: The Story of Daily Life" is published, eventually selling 150,000 copies, and also often reprinted. Spring 1970, Michele Wallace, just graduated from high school and returned from Mexico and a year at Howard University, is back in New York, a "seething hotbed of feminist activity" and antiwar activity. Ideological disputes about the nature and conduct of the movement itself riddle the women's movement; resentment of "stars"; "tyranny of structurelessness"—in Jo Freeman's phrase (Kesselman, Dell'Olio, Baxandall, Weisstein, Freeman).

April 1970 U.S. troops in Cambodia. May 4, 1970, Four unarmed students protesting the invasion of Cambodia by the U.S. are murdered at Kent State University by the National Guard. At Jackson State University, two students murdered in protests. Students strike at more than 350 campuses nationwide.

August 26, 1970 The first march commemorating women's suffrage; Women's Strike for Equality. In August 1970 U.S. House passes the Equal Rights Amendment; Senate holds hearings about the Equal Rights Amendment.

November 1970 Journalist Vivian Gornick sent on an assignment to "investigate 'these women's libbers' "; a week later she "was a convert."

1971 "The Furies," a separatist Washington, D.C., feminist group, instigates severe criticism of other feminist groups (such as the Daughters of Lilith and D.C. Women's Liberation) on the subject of working with males, or consorting with any males, including boy children (Wolfson). Rifts develop in the women's movement over politics and identity (Long). In 1971, the romance of the Chinese Revolution affects many radicals, including feminists (Tax).

1971 Priscilla Long teaches women's history at a university extension program; first courses in women's history and literature begin in many places. Vivian Gornick and Barbara Moran publish *Woman in Sexist Society: Studies in Power and Powerlessness,* with theoretical and scholarly analyses with an interdisciplinary thrust from a number of fields, including sociology, psychology, art history, literary criticism, history, cultural analysis. 1971, *Notes from the Third Year,* ed. Anne Koedt and Shulamith Firestone; Adrienne Rich's "When We Dead Awaken: Writing as Revision"; and Tillie Olsen's "One Out of Twelve" galvanize and inspire feminist cultural analysis. In

1971, WEAL (Women's Equity Action League) sues 350 universities for sex discrimination, including the state systems of New York, New Jersey, Florida, California.

1971 Chicago Women's Liberation Rock Band plays gigs at many places, including Colorado Springs, Bloomington, Madison, Pittsburgh, Toronto, Ithaca, Buffalo, Boston (Weisstein). In 1971–72 Michele Wallace and her mother, Faith Ringgold, found Women Students and Artists for Black Art Liberation, participating in art actions of protest at a variety of major museums in New York City, and Wallace writes her first Black feminist essay, "Black Women and White Women," for *Women's World*.

March 1971 Lieutenant Calley is convicted of premeditated murder for his role in the My Lai massacre of civilians in Vietnam. In spring 1971, 800 Vietnam veterans throw their medals back at the U.S. Capitol in protest against the war; other expressions of resistance inside the military grow in number. May 1971 there are major antiwar demonstrations in Washington. June 1971, Pentagon Papers published, classified material about U.S. involvement in Vietnam.

1971 National Women's Political Caucus founded by Bella Abzug, Shirley Chisholm, Betty Friedan, and Gloria Steinem, among others, to try to influence the electoral process. The founding of Women's Action Alliance, a clearing house on women's issues and programs, includes Non-Sexist Child Development Project (Omolade). New York Radical Feminists hold a Speak-out Against Rape.

September 1971 Attica prison revolt, New York.

1972 Flo Kennedy runs for president of the U.S. on the Feminist Party ticket; Shirley Chisholm declares for the nomination for president as a Democrat, while George McGovern actually runs on Democratic ticket. Air war in Vietnam escalates; land troops are withdrawn somewhat.

March 1972 The Supreme Court rules unconstitutional former bans on sale or prescription of contraceptives to single persons.

1972 The founding of A.I.R.—Artists in Residence—the first all-women artists cooperative gallery in New York City. Opening show in September 1972 is a great success (Spero). In 1972, 12 percent of law students are women, up from 3.6 percent in 1961. Chicago and New Haven Women's Liberation Rock Bands cut a record ("Mountain Moving Day") for Rounder Records; the phenomenon of "women's music" can be dated from this moment (Weisstein).

October 1972 Watergate revelations about domestic espionage and sabotage carried out by Republican infrastructure; Nixon is reelected in November, but a significant constitutional crisis grows.

1972 A number of feminists enter a sectarian Marxist-Leninist-Maoist phase (Wolfson).

Title IX of the 1972 education bill prohibits sex discrimination in educational programs receiving federal assistance. There are many repercussions, including on women's sports.

In 1972, the first rape crisis centers and the first battered women's shelters open.

1972 *Feminist Studies* is founded; *Ms.* magazine begins publishing in July. Phyllis Chesler, *Women and Madness.*

January 22, 1973 Supreme Court decision *Roe* v. *Wade* allows for first-trimester abortions on the principle of privacy and strikes down restrictions on places that can provide abortions in *Doe* v. *Bolton.* April 1973, Abortion clinics open in Chicago (Booth in Kesselman).

Gender segregation in want ads struck down by U.S. Supreme Court. In 1973, there are victories for suits on job discrimination in such venues as AT&T, Civil Service Commission, U.S. Coast Guard. Women office workers begin to unionize.

1973 National Black Feminist Organization is formed; contributor Wallace is one of the founders (Omolade, Wallace). November 1973, Barbara Smith attends the first Eastern Regional Conference of NBFO. 1973, Barbara Omolade finds her black "nationalism further transformed" by reading Gerda Lerner's *Black Women in White America,* and by the attempt of her extended family to live in Jamaica. In 1973 Daphne Busby founds the Sisterhood of Black Single Mothers.

In 1973 Homosexuality is struck off the list of mental disorders by the American Psychiatric Association. Sisterhood and desire at a women's dance in North Carolina; Minne Bruce Pratt attends. In 1973, the Gay Academic Union founded (Nestle).

In 1973, Women are almost 45 percent of the U.S. workforce.

1973 Nancy Spero has her first solo show at A.I.R. Gallery; the Codex Artaud is shown. In fall 1973, Nadine Taub is the founder of the Women's Rights Litigation Clinic, Rutgers University Law School. In 1973 Women's Action Coalition at Middlebury College is founded (Ensler/Allen).

By 1973 58,000 American soldiers are dead in Vietnam; Nixon withdraws all land troops.

1974 Many suits about sex bias; many gender barriers fall, including mandatory maternity leaves for teachers (which had pushed them out of jobs); Little League open to girls; Merchant Marine Academy admits women; sex bias in housing is declared illegal. The Equal Opportunity Act forbids discrimination on the basis of sex or marital status.

1974 Foundation of CESA (Committee to End Sterilization Abuse) by Dr. Helen Rodriguez-Trias (Tax). In 1974, Coalition of Labor Union Women is founded; 58 unions are represented. The Combahee River Collective of Black Women begins meeting in Boston in 1974; they present "A Black Feminist Statement" in 1977.

August 9, 1974 President Nixon resigns due to complicity in Watergate conspiracy. In September, President Ford pardons Nixon, also announces amnesty for Vietnam draft evaders and deserters.

1974 Eleven women are ordained as Episcopal priests, in defiance of church law. Adrienne Rich wins the National Book Award for *Diving into the Wreck;* she accepts it with the two other women nominees, Audre Lorde and Alice Walker: "We symbolically join here in refusing the terms of patriarchal competition. . . ." In France, Luce Irigaray's *Speculum de l'autre femme* is published.

April 29, 1975 Fall of Saigon; end of the war in Vietnam.

1975 *Signs* is founded, a scholarly journal devoted to scholarly research on women and on gender. In 1975 Lesbian Herstory Archives founded to collect and reflect the complexity and diversity of the lesbian past in the U.S., by Joan Nestle and Deborah Edel. *Ms.* magazine publishes a somewhat sanitized version of Dell'Olio's essay "Divisiveness and Self-Destruction in the Woman's Movement," originally delivered in 1970. Gayle Rubin publishes her important theoretical analysis "The Traffic in Women: Notes on the Political Economy of Sex." Feminist scholarship begins and flourishes in many fields. In France Hélène Cixous publishes "Le rire de la Médusa."

In 1975, the U.N. International Women's Year Conference, Mexico City, begins the "U.N. Decade for Women"—1975–85. In the U.S., a "typical" family (working father, housewife, two children) is only 7 percent of the population.

Mid-1970s Several study groups begin trying to reconcile feminism and left politics (named Marxist-Feminist, or M-F groups) (Benería). One of their central pieces of intellectual work is the "domestic labor debate," about defining the economic value of unpaid domestic labor in the home. Mid-1970s, Some people think that "the action-oriented, visionary women's liberation movement . . . dissipates" (Kesselman). Mid-1970s, Nancy Spero does work investigating the "victimage" of women political prisoners.

1975 Barbara Emerson dates her sense of her own struggles as a Black woman as feminist struggles. 1975, The Great Southeast Lesbian Conference, including Lesbian Mother Workshop; Pratt attends.

1976 After much discussion about the need for a national agenda for women's health, the National Women's Health Network is formed; still functioning (Wolfson). In 1976, M-F (Marxist-Feminist) II study group forms; Lourdes Benería a member; the group lasts until the early 1980s. 1976, Sojourner Truth Festival of the Arts, Women's Interart Center, New York (Wallace).

The period is filled with "firsts" for women, including first woman to conduct the Metropolitan Opera, first Rhodes scholarships to women, first woman governor elected (Ella Grasso, Connecticut, 1974); women in NASA training; female sports reporters access to locker rooms (1978).

1976 National Alliance of Black Feminists is founded. Adrienne Rich, *Of Woman Born.* Dorothy Dinnerstein, *The Mermaid and the Minotaur.*

September 1976 YWCA and National Congress of Neighborhood Women (NCNW) establish a battered women's shelter, which also housed their children; Barbara Omolade is co-coordinator. 1976, First AIDS victims in New York. 1976–1977 Minnie Bruce Pratt debates a local representative of the Eagle Forum in Fayetteville, North Carolina. In the mid-1970s Eve Ensler works in a grassroots peace group in New York City (CANDU—Chelsea Against Nuclear Destruction United).

January 1977 Jimmy Carter inaugurated.

1977 Committee to Defend Reproductive Rights (CDRR) founded in San Francisco after pressure on *Roe* vs. *Wade* from the Hyde amendment, prohibiting abortions funded by Medicaid (Wolfson). After the Hyde amendment restricts access to abortion, feminists influenced by CESA (Committee to End Sterilization Abuse) form CARASA (Committee for Abortion Rights and Against Sterilization Abuse), with a full analysis of reproductive rights, not a single-issue focus (Tax).

1977 Barbara Omolade works at Women's Action Alliance as an assistant to the director of the Non-Sexist Child Development Project.

November 1977 First National Women's Conference in Houston; passes significant resolutions formulating and codifying a feminist agenda as it developed over the past decade—including issues of Battered Women, Business, Child Abuse, Credit, Disabled Women, Education, Elective and Appointive Office, Employment, Equal Rights Amendment, Health, Homemakers, Human Rights and International Conventions on Women, Insurance, International Women's Decade, Minority Women, Older Women, Offenders, Rape, Rural Women, Sexual Preference, Statistics, Women, Welfare, and Poverty.

1978 Publication of influential feminist scholarship and theory by Nancy Chodorow, *The Reproduction of Mothering;* Audre Lorde, "The Erotic as Power"; Adrienne Rich; Mary Daly, *Gyn/Ecology;* Barbara Ehrenreich and Deirdre English.

October 1978 Senate votes to extend the deadline for the ratification of the Equal Rights Amendment until 1982.

1978 A women's group of Black women includes Michele Wallace, Barbara Omolade, and *Ms.* editor Susan McHenry. In 1978, Michele Wallace's book *Black Macho and the Myth of the Superwoman* excerpted in *Ms.;* Wallace is on the cover and becomes somewhat notorious for the book. In 1977–81 Omolade writes a column for *Black News,* the journal of the Brooklyn Black United Front (BUF), a mass organization that expands into a national organization in 1980.

August 1978 The first Take Back the Night March in Boston; in November, there is a Take Back the Night March in San Francisco.

1979 Conference on Black women's history at Purdue University (Omolade). January 1979, Coalition of 100 Black Women sponsor a conference at Marymount Manhattan College: "Black Women: Who We Are, What We Are, Where We Are." *Conditions* publishes "the Black Women's issue" in Autumn 1979. Black women hold conferences and symposia in Chicago, New York, Houston. *Sturdy Black Bridges,* ed. Roseann Bell, Bettye Parker, and Beverly Guy-Sheftall is published.

March 1979 Three Mile Island, Pennsylvania—a major nuclear power plant accident.

1979 Barnard College Scholar and Feminist Conference; Omolade leads a workshop on Black Women and Feminism, and subsequently participates in many planning committees. Editors Snitow and DuPlessis also attend; DuPlessis gives a seminar that becomes her essay "For the Etruscans."

1979 Second Sex Commemorative Conference, New York University. Women of color, including Susan McHenry, Barbara Omolade, and Audre Lorde, protest the limited participation of women of color in the conference.

November 1979 The National Council on Black Women sponsors First National Scholarly Research Conference on Black Women (Omolade).

1979 The Moral Majority is founded by Rev. Jerry Falwell, opposing abortion, the ERA, and rights for homosexuals.

1980 Women's Pentagon Action; Paula Allen photographs it, and becomes a feminist (Allen/Ensler).

November 1980 Ronald Reagan elected; the term "gender gap" is proposed to analyze certain voting patterns. Iran hostages released after 444 days of captivity, minutes after Reagan is inaugurated.

1980 Eruption of Mt. St. Helen's. Murder of John Lennon.

1981 *Families* by Meredith Tax published, a children's book that shows a spectrum of different family structures. In 1994 it becomes the target of a censorship campaign led by the Christian Coalition. bell hooks's first book, *Ain't I a Woman: Black Women and Feminism.*

1981 The AIDS virus is identified.

May 1981 Mother's Day March for Action: Protect and Defend Our Children, a protest march about the murdered and missing children in Atlanta, sponsored by Coalition of Concerned Black Women. July 1981, Black Woman's Summit, Howard University. Billye Avery founds National Black Women's Health Project.

August 1981 Greenham Common protest begins in England, to resist the future siting of cruise missiles there. A peace camp begins, soon to be a worldwide focus of protest, with other demonstrations and camps at Seneca Falls, New York State, and in Nevada at the nuclear test site (Allen/Ensler).

September 1981 Sandra Day O'Connor becomes the first female justice on the U.S. Supreme Court. A domestic violence bill is defeated in the Senate, due to conservative campaigns against it.

1982 On June 30, the ERA is defeated, falling three short of the thirty-eight states needed for ratification.

The Barnard College annual Scholar and Feminist Conference takes up the issue of sexualities (or the sex wars, as they become known); sexual debates are rife within the feminist community (Nestle). 1982, Gayle Rubin writes "Thinking Sex: Notes for a Radical Theory of the Politics of Sexuality."

All the Women Are White, All the Blacks Are Men, But Some of Us Are Brave: Black Women's Studies, ed. Gloria Hull, Patricia Bell Scott, and Barbara Smith (containing, among other essays, Barbara Smith's "Toward a Black Feminist Criticism") is published by the Feminist Press.

1983 First U.S. woman to go into space (Sally Ride). Beverly Guy-Sheftall is a founding co-editor of *SAGE: A Scholarly Journal on Black Women.*

1983–1990 Shirley Geok-Lin Lim forms a women's reading group.

1984 Bombings and arson attacks against abortion and family planning clinics. Economic Equity Act helps women collect pensions and enforces child support.

1986 The U.S. Supreme Court finds that sexual harassment is a form of job discrimination. Women's Committee of PEN American Center founded; Women's Committee in International PEN founded in 1991 (Tax). Major pro-choice demonstration in Washington, D.C. Luz Alvarez Martinez founds National Latina Health Organization.

April 26, 1986 Chernobyl nuclear power accident.

1987 Anonymous Women for Peace founded by Paula Allen, Eve Ensler, and others; they organize six women's peace camps in New York City in Madison Square Park and Battery Park in summers from 1987 to 1992. Contributor Shirley Geok-Lin Lim identifies as a feminist, having spent almost twenty years "inside the feminist revolution, but not in the women's liberation movement."

1988–1991 New York women place antiwar stickers on war toys in mega-toy stores during the holiday season.

1989 George Bush inaugurated; Iran-Contra trial. Twenty Anonymous Women camp at the Nevada nuclear test site (Allen/Ensler). 1989, *Webster* v. *Reproductive Health Services* gives states the right to limit women's right to legal abortion. Fall of communism in eastern Europe; Berlin Wall falls.

June 4, 1989 Massacre of 2,000 prodemocracy protesters, Tiananmen Square, Beijing, China.

1991 The Gulf War. Clarence Thomas is confirmed as Supreme Court justice despite allegations of sexual harassment by Professor Anita Hill.

Notes on Contributors

Paula Allen is a social documentary photographer. During the past twenty years she has documented nonviolent revolutions such as the European nuclear disarmament movement, focusing on Greenham Common Women's Peace Camp, and Solidarity in Poland, and she has photographed in the war zones of Northern Ireland and Lebanon. Her work has been published in numerous magazines: *Newsweek,* the *New York Times Magazine,* the *London Independent, Ms., Paris Match, Art in America,* among others. Her primary focus has been on long-term projects, combining pictures and text, that record women's histories. Two such projects are "Angelina/Foxy," an ongoing photo essay (begun in 1985) of a homeless woman, mother of four sons, who fell in love with a pimp and became a prostitute, and "The Women of Calama," a five-year project, now in its concluding stages, documenting women in the far north of Chile who have been digging in the desert for twenty years for the bodies of their relatives disappeared after the 1973 coup. In 1991 Allen received a New York Foundation for the Arts Fellowship for her photographs of Irish Traveller girls living in Belfast, Northern Ireland. Allen's present work is an ongoing project documenting lesbians in a variety of countries, including Cuba, the United States, Ireland, and Poland.

Rosalyn Baxandall is chair of American studies at the State University of New York at Old Westbury. She is the author of *Words on Fire, The Life and Writing of Elizabeth Gurley Flynn,* Rutgers University Press, 1987; the co-editor of *America's Working Women: An Anthology of Women's Work, 1920–1970,* Random House 1976 (a new edition, three-fourths of which is new, was published in March 1995 by W.W. Norton and Co.); co-author of *Picture Windows; How the Suburbs Happened,* published 1997 by Basic Books, and co-editor of the forthcoming *The Encyclopedia of the Women's Liberation Movement, 1964–1976;* as well as the author of numerous articles and book reviews, on day care, working women, sexuality, reproductive rights, and race and gender in suburbia, 1945–1990. She is a member of the speakers bureau Speak Out and speaks frequently on campuses and in demonstrations.

She was on the board of Virago Press and New Feminist Library, and a consultant on the Multicultural Diversification for New York State and National Endowment for the Humanities films. For more than 25 years she has been a feminist activist. As one of the foremothers of the women's liberation movement in the late 1960s, she helped found several day-care centers and was on the Mayor's Task Force on Day Care. She was active with New York Radical Women, Redstockings, WITCH (Women's International Terrorist Conspiracy from Hell), CARASA (Coalition for Abortion Rights and Against Sterilization Abuse), and is now active with the Lower East Side Collective.

Lourdes Benería is professor of city and regional planning and women's studies and director of the Latin American Studies Program at Cornell University. An economist, she has also taught at Rutgers University, the New School for Social Research, the Autonomous University of Barcelona, the Complutense University of Madrid, Spain, and at other institutions. Her work on gender and development began with a job, in 1977–1979, as coordinator of the Programme on Rural Women, part of the World's Employment Programme at the International Labor Office, in Geneva, Switzerland. She is the author of *The Crossroads of Class and Gender* (with Martha Roldan) and editor of *Women and Development: The Sexual Division of Labor in Rural Societies,* of *Women and the Economy* (with Catharine R. Stimpson), and of *Unequal Burden: Economic Crises, Persistent Poverty and Women's Work* (with Shelley Feldman). She has also published numerous articles in journals and edited volumes on topics related to gender and international issues. Beyond academic work, she has been involved in feminist and political groups working on a variety of issues ranging from access to day care to anti–Vietnam War activities, political economy, peace movement, and solidarity work with women's organizations in Latin America.

Heather Booth has been organizing for social change since 1960, when she joined the demonstrations against Woolworth's, which was discriminating against Blacks sitting at their lunch counter in the South. She was active in the Civil Rights Movement, going to Mississippi for the Freedom Summer Project in 1964 with the Student Non-Violent Coordinating Committee (SNCC). In 1965, she began work with the emerging women's movement, setting up the first campus women's organization at her college at the University of Chicago and setting up consciousness-raising and action groups around the city. In that year she also started Jane, the abortion consultation service, and later (after her first child was born) the Action Committee for Decent Childcare. In 1973, with a back-pay award she won from a clerical union organizing effort, she founded the Midwest Academy, which has become one of the nation's leading training centers for organizers. She was a founder, co-director, and the president of Citizen Action, the nation's largest grassroots progressive consumer organization that had over three million dues-paying members, working on such issues as health care, campaign finance reform, and toxic waste. In 1990, she directed the Mobilization for Women's Lives, which brought out a million people around the country and in Washington, D.C., to demonstrate for women's right to choice. She has regularly been involved in elections related to these kinds of concerns. In 1992, she was field director for Carol Moseley Braun's successful Senate race. She is currently the field director for the Democratic National Committee. She has been married for 30 years to Paul Booth, whom she first met in a student sit-in, and who is now the director of organizing and the assistant to the president of the American Federation of State, County, and Municipal Employees. They have two sons, Gene and Dan.

Anselma Dell'Olio was born in California. She lives, translates, and writes in Rome and Milan.

Dana Densmore, women's movement theoretician. Active in female liberation movement in Boston, 1968–1974. Member of group Cell 16. Founding editor, prolific contributor, and later publisher of radical feminist journal *No More Fun & Games,* 1968–1973. Active with MIT women's group. Led many study groups and workshops. Numerous articles reprinted in anthologies; numerous write-ups and mentions in national magazines; numerous appearances on radio and television shows dealing with women's liberation issues. Co-founder of women's martial art Ja Shin Do in 1974, with schools in Boston and Washington, D.C. Researcher and editor for Women's Institute for Freedom of the Press, Washington, D.C., 1974–1976. Founded and directed Artemis Institute, a school for self-empowerment for women, 1977–1987. Faculty, St. John's College, teaching Great Books, 1987–1994. Master's degree, history of science, 1993. Currently independent scholar and co-director, Green Lion Press.

Roxanne Dunbar is a historian and professor in Ethnic Studies and Women's Studies at California State University, Hayward, where she has taught since 1974. In 1968, with other women in Boston/Cambridge, she founded the radical women's liberation group, Female Liberation—Cell 16, and its journal, *No More Fun and Games: A Journal of Female Liberation*. In addition to her theoretical essays on women's liberation, she has published numerous scholarly books and articles in the field of Native American Studies. In 1997, she published a memoir, *Red Dirt* (Vergo), about growing up in rural Oklahoma. *Red Dirt* was selected as one of the hundred best books of 1997 by the *Los Angeles Times*.

Rachel Blau DuPlessis (Temple University) has contributed to the formation of feminist criticism with the essays in *The Pink Guitar: Writing as Feminist Practice* (1990), the studies of poetry and the novel in *Writing Beyond the Ending: Narrative Strategies of Twentieth-Century Women Writers* (1985), and the analysis of the vocation of a woman writer in *H.D.: The Career of that Struggle* (1986). For almost fifteen years she was a member of the editorial collective of *Feminist Studies*. She is the author of *Drafts 15-XXX, The Fold* (1997), continuing the long poem begun in *Tabula Rosa* (1987) and *Drafts 3-14* (1991). She is the editor of *The Selected Letters of George Oppen* (1990), the co-editor, with Susan Friedman, of *Signets: Reading H.D.* (1990), and, as well, the co-editor of this volume.

Barbara Williams Emerson is a veteran activist and educator, having started as an organizer with the Chatham County Crusade for Voters at age 15. Her early involvement with the Southern Christian Leadership Conference, alongside her father, Hosea Williams, took her to movements in Selma and across the South, D.C.'s Resurrection City, Chicago, and eventually to New York City, where she has lived and worked for the past thirty years. During those years she worked with CORE in Harlem, organized the anniversary march of the "1987 Forsythe County March Against Fear and Intimidation," managed her father's bid for Congress, and returned home to Georgia for numerous holidays to participate in "Feed the Hungry." In 1989 she authored *Mississippi Freedom Summer Journal*, a chronicle of the 25th anniversary reunion that she organized for former volunteers in the voter registration project during which civil rights workers James Chaney, Andrew Goodman, and Michael Schwerner were murdered.

   Dr. Emerson currently serves as the Vice President for Program Development at the New School for Social Research and senior lecturer at the Robert Milano Graduate School of Management and Urban Policy. Emerson earned a B.A. in sociology from New York University. Her master's and doctorate degrees were awarded by Columbia University in community organization and planning, and administration, planning and policy analysis respectively.

Her academic career includes positions at Queens College of the City University of New York as a SEEK counselor, sociology faculty member, co-ordinator of the Presidential Advisory Council on Multiculturalism, and dean for Special Programs. She has published, lectured, and consulted nationally and internationally on higher education, women's issues, diversity, multiculturalism, student achievement, and her work in the Civil Rights Movement. She is the proud mother of Weusi Hosea Emerson, an educator who teaches the fifth grade at the Jackie Robinson School.

Eve Ensler's plays include *Floating Rhoda and the Glue Man* (published in *The Best Plays of 1993*), the acclaimed *Extraordinary Measures, The Depot* (directed by Joanne Woodward), *Scooncat, Loud in My Head, Lemonade, Ladies, Reef and Particle,* and *Cinderella Cendrillion* (directed by Anne Bogart). Her play *The Vagina Monologues* won a 1997 Obie Award and was nominated for a Drama Desk Award. Eve's new play, *Necessary Targets,* commissioned by the Joseph Papp Public Theater, was given a performance on Broadway starring Meryl Streep, Angelica Huston, and Cherry Jones, to benefit Bosnian women refugees. Eve has been an activist for over twenty years. She has been a founding member of groups such as CANDU (a grassroots peace group in Chelsea, New York, advocating for Nuclear Disarmament), Anonymous Women for Peace, and Women Helping Women. She has worked with homeless women for over ten years as an advocate, volunteer, and friend. Recently, she has focused her energies on supporting Bosnian women refugees, and stopping sexual violence toward women everywhere. She is a member of the Writer's Guild of America and the Dramatist Guild, and she teaches in the Dramatic Writing Program at NYU.

Barbara Epstein teaches in the History of Consciousness department at the University of California, Santa Cruz. For many years, she was a member of the editorial board of *Socialist Review.* She is now in the editorial collective of *Socialist Register.* Her book *Political Protest and Cultural Revolution* was published by University of California Press in 1991. Since then she has written a number of articles criticizing postmodernism. She is working on a book on why the left is in such bad shape in the United States.

Jo Freeman is a guerrilla scholar and unaffiliated agitator. She is the author of *The Politics of Women's Liberation* (winner of a 1975 American Political Science Association prize as the Best Scholarly Work on Women and Politics) and the editor of *Social Movements of the Sixties and Seventies* (1983) and five editions of *Women: A Feminist Perspective.* She has a Ph.D. in political science from the University of Chicago (1973) and a J.D. from New York University School of Law (1982). Her articles on feminism, social movements, law, public policy, sex-role socialization, organizational theory, education, federal election law, and political parties have been published in *The Nation, Ms., Valparaiso Law Review, Trans-Action, School Review, Liberal Education, American Journal of Sociology, Intellect, Political Science Quarterly, Acta Sociologica, Prospects, Signs, Pace Law Review, The Journal of Law and Inequality, off our backs,* and numerous anthologies. She currently practices law, politics, editing, writing, and a few other things in Brooklyn, N.Y.

Vivian Gornick lives in New York City, where she writes, thinks, talks, struggles, became a feminist, and has written six books: *In Search of Ali Mahmoud: An American Woman in Egypt; The Romance of American Communism; Women in Science; Fierce Attachments; Approaching Eye Level; The End of the Novel of Love.* In 1970, with B. K. Moran, she edited one of the first anthologies of feminist thought, *Woman in Sexist Society.* Her early feminist essays were collected in 1978 in *Essays in Feminism.*

Dr. Beverly Guy-Sheftall is founding director of the Women's Research and Resource Center and the Anna Julia Cooper Professor of Women's Studies at Spelman College. She has published a number of texts within feminist studies, including her dissertation, *Daughters of Sorrow: Attitudes Toward Black Women, 1880–1920* (Carlson Publishing Company, 1991), and most recently, *Words of Fire: An Anthology of African American Feminist Thought* (New Press, 1995). She is completing an anthology, *Traps: African American Men on Gender & Sexuality,* with Prof. Rudolph Byrd. She has been involved with the national women's studies movement since its inception and provided the leadership for the establishment of the first women's studies major at a historically Black college. Beyond the academy, she has been involved in a number of advocacy or activist organizations or collectives—the National Black Women's Health Project, the Black Family Project, African American Women in Defense of Ourselves, the National Council for Research on Women, and the Coalition of 100 Black Women. She also serves on numerous national advisory boards dealing with race and gender issues. She continues to be active in the international women's movement and teaches courses about global feminisms, the experiences of women of African descent, and comparative women's studies.

Carol Hanisch got her political consciousness raised in the Black-led Mississippi Civil Rights Movement in the 1960s. She was an original member of New York Radical Women in 1968 and active in Gainesville Women's Liberation in Florida from 1969 to 1973. Her 1969 paper "The Personal Is Political" explained and brought that concept into public usage along with "The Pro-Woman Line." An editor of the Redstockings book *Feminist Revolution,* she later founded the journal *Meeting Ground.* Her column "Frankly Feminist" enlivened the *Hudson Valley Woman* from 1991 to 1995. For the 75th anniversary of women's winning the vote, she created a dramatic reading, *Promise & Betrayal: Voices from the Struggle for Woman's Emancipation,* which she performs with TruthTeller Productions. Carol has also done working-class, anti-apartheid, anti-imperialist, and environmental organizing. She labors as a freelance graphic artist and editor in upstate New York, and continues to write, speak, and organize for women's liberation whenever possible. She can be reached at P.O. Box 1270, Port Ewen, New York 12466.

Amy Kesselman grew up in New York City and graduated from the City College of New York in January 1967. From 1967 to 1970 she was active in the New Left and the emerging women's liberation movement in Chicago, where she taught a course in Women's Role in Society at a local high school. In 1970 she moved to San Francisco, where, funded by the New University Conference, she organized women's studies conferences on the West Coast. After moving to Portland, Oregon, she went back to school to get a master's degree in history at Portland State University, where she was involved in the development of the Portland State University Women's Studies Program. She taught women's studies at Mount Hood Community College until 1977, when she entered a doctoral program in history at Cornell University. She is associate professor of women's studies at the State University of New York at New Paltz; the author of *Fleeting Opportunities: Women Shipyard Workers in Portland and Vancouver During World War II and Reconversion* (SUNY Press, 1990); and one of the editors of *Women: Images and Realities, a Multicultural Anthology* (Mayfield, 1995), an introductory women's studies textbook. She is currently working on a study of the women's liberation movement in New Haven, Connecticut, 1967–1975.

Shirley Geok-lin Lim was born in the British colony of Malaya, attended the University of Malaya during the tumultuous postindependent period, and received a Ph.D. in English and American literature from Brandeis University in 1973. An academic feminist who writes often of the differences and commonalities between Western and non-Western feminist practices, she is also an émigré/immigrant; her recent memoir, *Among the White Moon Faces: An Asian-American Memoir of Homelands* (Feminist Press, 1996), narrates a British colonial childhood, a postcolonial female *Bildung,* and struggles in forming an American identity. It received an American Book Award in 1997. Her first book of poems, *Crossing the Peninsula* (Heinemann), received the 1980 Commonwealth Poetry Prize. She has published another three books of poetry, two short story collections, and two critical studies of Southeast Asian Anglophone literature, and has edited a number of volumes of Asian-American writing and criticism. Her co-edited anthology, *The Forbidden Stitch,* won the Before Columbus American Book Award in 1990. Currently professor of English and Women's Studies at the University of California at Santa Barbara, she has published articles on Asian-American and third world women's writing, and serves on the editorial board of *Feminist Studies.*

A writer who lives in Seattle, Priscilla Long is currently at work on a book about creativity and women artists. She is a poet who performs her work with the Seattle Five Plus One. She is author of *Where the Sun Never Shines: A History of America's Bloody Coal Industry* (Paragon House, 1989), and has published scholarly essays on the labor organizer Mother Jones, on the women of the coalfields, and on the history of violence in the coalfields. She is also a regular reviewer for *The Women's Review of Books.* Her fiction and poetry appear in *The Southern Review, North Dakota Quarterly, The Seattle Review, Southern Humanities Review,* and elsewhere. She lived in Boston for fifteen years and was active in the Boston women's liberation organization Bread and Roses. She was a founding member of Boston's Red Sun Press, and worked as a printer at Red Sun for ten years. She also participated in the Lebanon Emergency Committee, a Boston group working for peace and justice in the Middle East. In 1984 she moved to San Diego, where she completed her history of coal mining and participated in CISPES (Committee in Solidarity with the People of El Salvador). In 1988 she moved to Seattle and earned an MFA in fiction from the University of Washington. Besides doing her own writing, she works as a freelance editor and writing coach. She is currently the treasurer of the Seattle local of the National Writers' Union.

Elizabeth ("Betita") Martinez is a Chicana activist, writer, and teacher. Her political work began over thirty years ago while she was living in New York. She worked full-time with SNCC, a major Black civil rights organization, in Mississippi and as coordinator of its New York office, as well as with the Black Panther Party. After moving to New Mexico in 1968, she began the Chicano movement newspaper *El Grito del Norte* and edited it for five years. Later she co-founded and coordinated the Chicano Communications Center, an educational and activist organization in Albuquerque.

Out of her movement experience came dozens of magazine articles over the years in *The Nation, The Village Voice, In These Times,* and other publications. She has published six books on social movements, including *Letters from Mississippi, The Youngest Revolution: A Personal Report on Cuba, Viva La Raza* (co-authored with Enriqueta Vasquez, and winner of the Jane Adams Children's Book Award), *The Art of Rini Templeton: Where There Is Life and Struggle* (bilingual), and *Guatemala: Tyranny on Trial* (as co-editor). Her best-known book is *500 Years of Chicano History,* a bilingual pictorial history widely used by schools, youth groups, and community organizations. It became the basis for her 1995 educational video *Viva La Causa!* shown at major film festivals.

She was previously a researcher on colonialism at the United Nations for five years, an editor at Simon & Schuster, and Books & Arts editor of *The Nation,* in New York. She writes regularly on Latino issues for *Z* magazine and other publications, and Op Ed pieces on Latino issues for the Progressive Media Project, based in Madison, Wisconsin. Her travels include Latin America, Europe, the former USSR, Eastern Europe, and Asia.

Living in the San Francisco Bay Area since 1976, she has worked on various Latino community struggles. She ran for governor of California in 1982 on the Peace and Freedom Party ticket, the first Chicana on the ballot for that office. Currently she works with several youth groups and the Women of Color Resource Center, and teaches ethnic and women's studies at California State University, Hayward. She also lectures across the country, at over one hundred universities and colleges in the last five years alone. During 1998 she will continue working with others to establish a national institute to strengthen relations between different peoples of color, in order to combat today's divisions and backward political trends.

Awards received since 1992: the Chicana Foundation for "Outstanding Latina Achievement"; the National Association for Chicano Studies for service to the community; the Bank of America and KQED as a "Local Hero"; MEChA for Lifetime Achievement; Center for the Arts, Yerba Buena Gardens, for "Outstanding Achievement"; California State Senator Richard Polanco, a proclamation of recognition; Alumni Resources for "Achievement, Vision, Excellence."

She has one daughter, Tessa Martinez, an actress.

Kate Millett was associated with Downtown Radical Women in New York, helped found Columbia Women's Liberation, and attended meetings of Redstockings, the Feminists, and New York Radical Lesbians. She also served as chair of New York NOW's Education Committee from 1967 to 1970, which published a critique of women's colleges called "Token Learning." In 1970 she published her doctoral thesis, *Sexual Politics*. Her other publications include *The Prostitution Papers, Flying, Sita, The Basement, Going to Iran, The Loony Bin Trip, The Politics of Cruelty,* and *A.D.*

Born in the Bronx, New York, in 1940, Joan Nestle is co-founder of the Lesbian Herstory Archives (1973), author of *A Restricted Country* (Firebrand, 1988; Pandora, 1996), and editor of *The Persistent Desire: A Femme-Butch Reader* (Alyson, 1992). With Naomi Holoch, she has edited three volumes of *Women on Women: Anthologies of Lesbian Short Fiction* (Plume, 1990, 1993, 1996), and with John Preston she edited *Sister/Brother: Lesbians and Gay Men Talk about Their Lives Together* (HarperSanFrancisco, 1994). In 1999, Vintage will publish an international collection of lesbian fiction, *Worlds Unspoken,* also co-edited with Naomi Holoch. A new collection of her writings, *A Fragile Union,* will be published by Cleis Press in 1999. In 1995, she retired from twenty-nine years of teaching writing in the SEEK Program at Queens College, CUNY. In 1997, after being diagnosed with colon cancer, she joined her latest CR group, sponsored by CancerCare. Once again she sits in a room of women fighting for their lives.

Dr. Barbara Omolade is currently on the faculty of the sociology department of City College, Center for Worker Education, an evening college program founded in 1981. She is a founding staff member of the center that meets the needs of working adults, mainly women of color. Her early years at the center were spent organizing within the university and her local community; however, she is now focusing on working with students to make the connections between work, school, and family life. "One day I realized that the same women I was trying to reach, and the same issues I was attempting to address, existed within the center."

Most important is her faith and commitment to her church: "Becoming a born-again Christian did not resolve all personal dilemmas and contradictions, rather it provided a guided spiritual community for living my life as a complete human being: body, soul, and spirit."

Barbara Omolade is the author of *The Rising Song of African-American Women* (Routledge, 1995) and is writing a book on African-American Teen Mothers.

Born in 1946 in Selma, Alabama, Minnie Bruce Pratt received her academic education at the University of Alabama in Tuscaloosa, and at the University of North Carolina at Chapel Hill; and her actual education through grassroots organizing with women in the army base town of Fayetteville, North Carolina, and through teaching at historically Black universities. For five years she was a member of the editorial collective of *Feminary: A Feminist Journal for the South, Emphasizing Lesbian Visions.* Together with Elly Bulkin and Barbara Smith, she co-authored *Yours in Struggle: Three Feminist Perspectives on Anti-Semitism and Racism.* She has published three books of poetry, *The Sound of One Fork, We Say We Love Each Other,* and *Crime Against Nature,* on Pratt's relationship to her two sons as a lesbian mother. The latter was chosen as the 1989 Lamont Poetry Selection by the Academy of American Poets, given the American Library Association Gay and Lesbian Book Award for Literature, and nominated for a Pulitzer Prize in Poetry. Her book of autobiographical and political essays, *Rebellion: Essays 1980–1991,* was a finalist in non-fiction for the Lambda Literary Awards, and her 1995 volume of stories about gender boundary crossing, *S/HE,* was one of the five finalists for that year's American Library Association Gay, Lesbian, and Bisexual Book Award. Pratt is working on a fourth volume of poems, *Walking Back Up Depot Street.* Pratt makes her home with novelist and historian Leslie Feinberg in Jersey City, New Jersey. She teaches women's studies, lesbian/gay studies, and creative writing as a member of the Graduate Faculty of The Union Institute.

Yvonne Rainer was born in San Francisco in 1934. She trained as a modern dancer in New York from 1957 and began to choreograph her own work in 1960. She was one of the founders of the Judson Dance Theater in 1962, the beginning of a movement that proved to be a vital force in modern dance in the following decades. "The Mind Is a Muscle" is her best-known choreographic work. During the Vietnam War she adapted parts of her choreography to deal either directly (as in public interventions) or indirectly (within the work itself), with antiwar and anti-censorship protest.

Since 1972 Rainer has completed seven feature-length films, beginning with *Lives of Performers* and more recently *Privilege* (1990) and *MURDER and murder* (1996). Noteworthy for a wry humor and emotional candor brought to bear on the everyday intersections of private and public life, Rainer's films deal with a number of issues, such as melodrama, menopause, racism, political violence, sexual identity, and notions of disease. Her films have been shown at major international film festivals.

In the mid-eighties Rainer participated in a number of abortion rights demonstrations with a group called No More Nice Girls. They wore chains and pregnant bellies and carried banners that read "No More Forced Labor."

AnnJanette Rosga is an assistant professor of sociology and anthropology at Knox College in Illinois. She holds a Ph.D. from the History of Consciousness program at the University of California, Santa Cruz. She has worked with several activist organizations on the issue of bias-related violence, and has written on the topics of police-community interactions and the social construction of hate crime.

Vivian Rothstein grew up in Los Angeles and attended the University of California at Berkeley, where she became active in mass civil rights campaigns and the Free Speech Movement. She joined the Mississippi Freedom Summer Project, 1965, and subsequently quit school to become a community organizer with JOIN Community Union, an SDS-sponsored project in Chicago. In 1967 she participated in a peace delegation to North Vietnam, where she met women active in the Vietnamese Women's Union, which became a model for the Chicago Women's Liberation Union, organized the following year.

Vivian continued to work on community advocacy issues through the 1970s and 1980s and for the past ten years has been executive director of a Southern California nonprofit that runs a network of shelters and emergency services for battered women, homeless adults, and homeless families. In 1992 she returned to Vietnam as part of a women's delegation sponsored by the Vietnamese Women's Union, during which she presented a portfolio of U.S. antiwar posters to the women's museum, where they are now on display.

Vivian writes on social issues and is working on a memoir of her experiences as an activist.

Meg Satterthwaite co-founded and chaired Amnesty International's network for lesbian and gay human rights from 1990 to 1996. She obtained her master's degree in literature and cultural studies from the University of California, Santa Cruz, in 1995. She served as an investigator for the National Truth and Justice Commission in Haiti, and is now studying law at New York University School of Law. She is active in a number of different feminist, antiracist, and human rights organizations.

In 1953, at twenty, Alix Kates Shulman rushed to New York City's Greenwich Village, which she imagined a better place to spend the fifties than Ohio. In the sixties she became a political activist, feminist, and writer. An early member of Redstockings, her activism has ranged widely, from helping plan the first national demonstration of women's liberation, the 1968 Miss America Pageant protest in Atlantic City, to teaching at the 1975 Sagaris Feminist Institute, to founding a Hawaii branch of the abortion rights guerrilla action group No More Nice Girls in 1991–1992. Besides numerous essays and short stories, she is the author of eleven books, including two books on the anarchist-feminist Emma Goldman, and four novels: *Memoirs of an Ex-Prom Queen* (1972, 1997), called by the *Oxford Companion to Women's Writing* "the first important novel to emerge from the women's liberation movement"; *Burning Questions* (1978), about the rise of that movement; *On the Stroll* (1981), about a shopping bag lady and a teen runaway; and *In Every Woman's Life . . .* (1987), a feminist comedy of ideas. Her 1995 memoir *Drinking the Rain,* about her solitary low-tech life on an island off the Maine coast, was a finalist for the *Los Angeles Times* Book Prize and won a *Body Mind Spirit* Award of Excellence. Hailed by the *New York Times* as "the voice that has for three decades provided a lyrical narrative of the changing position of women in American society," her work has been translated into ten languages. She has taught writing and literature at New York University, Yale, the universities of Southern Maine, Colorado, Arizona, and Hawaii, and has been Visiting Writer at the American Academy in Rome and Bellagio. The recipient of grants from the National Endowment for the Arts, the Lila Wallace/Reader's Digest Foundation, and the Rockefeller Foundation, she has just completed a family memoir, *A Good Enough Daughter* (1999).

Barbara Smith is the editor of *Home Girls: A Black Feminist Anthology* and co-editor of *The Reader's Companion to U.S. Women's History.* Her collected essays, *The Truth That Never Hurts,* will be published by Rutgers University Press in 1998. She is currently researching a book on the history of African-American lesbians and gays.

Ann Snitow has been a feminist activist since 1969, when she was a founding member of New York Radical Feminists. Her Ph.D. from the University of London is in literature and her first book, *Ford Madox Ford and the Voice of Uncertainty*—written in another life—was about the early mo ern novel in England. With Christine Stansell and Sharon Thompson, she edited *Powers of Desire: The Politics of Sexuality,* a central text in feminist debates about sexuality and its history. She has written germinal articles, among them "Mass Market Romance: Pornography for Women Is Different," "A Gender Diary: Basic Divisions in Feminism," and "Feminism and Motherhood." She writes for *The Nation, Ms., The Village Voice Literary Supplement, Dissent, The Women's Review of Books,* and *Feminist Studies,* among others, on a variety of subjects from the fiction of Angela Carter to the changes in Poland's abortion law—some pieces to be collected in her forthcoming book, *A Gender Diary.* A founder of the Feminist Anti-Censorship Task Force, of the action group No More Nice Girls, and of the Network of East-West Women, her most recent writing and political work is about the changing situation of women in East Central Europe and the former Soviet Union, where doing feminist organizing is a whole new story.

In the late sixties and early seventies Nancy Spero joined with other women artists in investigating the lesser status of women in the art world. These discussion/action groups were instrumental in raising awareness and formulating strategies. These were angry groups, often militant. This activism was increasingly correlated to the activism of her art. It was as if Spero were born from the head or vagina of Athena against the male progeny of Zeus! In addition to marching against the Vietnam War, Spero was active in WAR (Women Artists in Revolution) 1969–1970, the Ad Hoc Committee of Women Artists, 1970–1972, and subsequently co-founded A.I.R. Gallery with nineteen others, the first all-women's cooperative gallery in New York City.

She showed in the many burgeoning all-women exhibitions and every two years at the A.I.R. Gallery, notably "Torture of Women" (1974–1976), a linear sweep running 20 inches high and 125 feet long, and "Notes in Time" (1976–1979), an exaltation 20 inches by 225 feet. These were revelatory and exciting times, and Spero articulated her position as a female underground artist who gestured angrily at the perimeters of male territory. Her art infiltrated and became present in commercial galleries as well as museums, and other places, and by 1987 she had a major retrospective exhibition at the Institute for Contemporary Art in London, which traveled to Edinburgh and Northern Ireland. Another retrospective in the United States and commenced at the Everson Museum in Syracuse and culminated at Museum of Contemporary Art in New York City. More recently d a major retrospective exhibition with her partner, Leon Golub, at the American Center in Paris, and in the summer of 1996 they received the third Hiroshima Art Prize and had a joint retrospective exhibition and individual installations at the Hiroshima City Museum of Contemporary Art. Since 1988 the artist has done more than 20 site-specific installations: Frankfurt, Madrid, Chicago, Vienna, Paris, among other places and has been in innumerable international exhibitions. In summer 1997 Spero exhibited fifteen Vietnam "war paintings" at Documenta X in Kassel, Germany, and subsequently at the IKON Gallery in Birmingham, England, Galerie Montenay in Paris, and Crown Gallery in Brussels. Spero and Golub will exhibit jointly at Wayne State University in Detroit, Jacobo Borges Museum in Caracas, and Galerie Pro Arte in Hallein, Austria.

N adine Taub is a professor of law at Rutgers Law School in Newark, New Jersey, where she also directs the Women's Rights Litigation Clinic. She is a 1964 graduate of Swarthmore College and a 1968 graduate of Yale Law School. She has co-authored an undergraduate text, *The Law of Sex Discrimination,* 2d. ed., 1994, and a law school casebook, *Sex Discrimination and the Law: History, Theory and Practice,* 2d. ed., 1996. She also co-edited *Reproductive Laws for the 1990s,* 1989. Among the cases handled by her clinic are *Tomkins* versus *P.S.T.&G,* one of the first decisions recognizing the right to sue for sexual harassment on the job; the appeal of *Alexander* versus *Yale,* the first effort to hold a university responsible for sexual harassment suffered by students; and *Right to Choose* versus *Byrne,* the 1982 decision requiring New Jersey to pay for Medicaid abortions.

M eredith Tax: I went through the Wisconsin public school system, attended Brandeis University, and did graduate work at the University of London. In 1967, I became involved in the antiwar movement and, once it began, in the women's movement. My political passions made it difficult to negotiate a successful academic career and, between 1969 and 1979, I worked at a variety of jobs, including academic piecework; factory, hospital, and secretarial labor; and freelance writing, while defining myself primarily in terms of my political work, especially in the women's movement. In 1979, I began to be able to live on my writing, and since then have published many essays and four books; as a result, my movement work has been increasingly focused on issues of voice and censorship. With Grace Paley, I founded a Women's Committee in PEN American Center in 1986, then started a similar committee in International PEN in 1991. In 1994, I became president of

Women's WORLD, an independent nonprofit that treats women's freedom of expression as an international human rights issue, and sees gender-based censorship as a social mechanism essential to the subordination of women and maintained by institutions ranging from the family and schools to governments and police, and including free-market forces like publishers and reviewers. Women's WORLD attempts to fight this censorship worldwide through public education and agitation, defense of targeted women, and the encouragement of feminist institutions like women's presses and an international e-mail censorship hotline. I have been married and divorced twice, and am the proud mother of Corey Tax and Elijah Tax-Berman.

Michele Wallace: After one year on sabbatical and one year as Laurie New Jersey Chair of Women's Studies at Douglass College, this fall I will be returning to my permanent position as associate professor of English at the City College of New York and at the CUNY Graduate Center. During my two-year leave, I have done a fair amount of professional writing (for supplemental income), and have also been making steady progress toward the completion of the Ph.D. in Cinema Studies at New York University, occasionally interrupted by my attempts to assist my sister in parenting her three girls, two of whom are now adolescents. In the next year or so, there won't be much time for anything else with this program, and the balance of the writing of the dissertation, still pending, but at the age of forty-five, I am profoundly gratified to have job security doing something I rather like (teaching) in a place that generally (although not always) appreciates my feminist politics, and to have the support of a loving, feminist husband.

I have to admit (perhaps I shouldn't) I haven't got much faith in the efficacy of feminist activism given our present historical moment. Primarily I am concerned about the quality of life, from day to day, for myself, as well as others (in particular for my Mom and Dad, my husband, my sister, my nieces, and my numerous extended family on my husband's side) rather than life's ultimate meaning or purpose—a concept in which I no longer have any faith whatsoever, I'm afraid. More than anything, these days, I love to study the lives, and the myriad representations of the lives, of ordinary people, which is one of the ways I envision my dissertation topic, *A Genealogy of Race in ... can Cinema, 1889–1919*. My fondest hope is that it will also become ...d that all of you will read it.

...author of *Black Macho and the Myth of the Superwoman* and *Invis-* ...and the organizer of *Black Popular Culture,* I confess I have grown weary of sonorous statements, and long to recover the details I might have once overlooked in pursuit of the big picture.

K nown as a pioneer in what is now called cognitive neuroscience, Naomi Weisstein is professor of cognitive psychology at the State University of New York at Buffalo. She was on a Guggenheim Fellowship in New York City in 1980 and arranging to do a feminist comedy show with producer-playwright Eve Merriam when she fell ill with a devastating case of chronic fatigue and immune dysfunction syndrome, which has persisted to this day. Nevertheless, she still manages to do some of her scientific research, which aims to show the presence of active intelligent mind—of agency—in the most elementary neural circuitry of the visual system.

A lifelong feminist whose militance was sharpened by her experiences in male-dominated science after Wellesley and Harvard, Weisstein was a leader in the early feminist movement in Chicago: a founding member of the West Side Group (the first independent radical women's group, 1967); the Chicago Women's Liberation Union (1969); and the Chicago Women's Liberation Rock Band (1970). She also helped found American Women in Psychology (now a Division of the American Psychological Association), the Women's Caucus of the Psychonomic Society (1972), and Women in Eye Research (a caucus in the Association for Research in Vision and Ophthalmology, 1980). Her feminist essays have appeared in many publications and anthologies throughout the world. Her article "Psychology Constructs the Female; or, The Fantasy Life of the Male Psychologist (with Some Attention to the Fantasies of His Friends, the Male Biologist and the Male Anthropologist)" has been reprinted some forty times since its original publication in 1968, most recently in a twenty-fifth anniversary celebration/retrospective in the British journal *Feminism and Psychology,* where Weisstein urges feminists to stop rejecting science and to use it instead to figure out how to mount a resistance to the patriarchy.

E llen Willis is a journalist and a professor in the department of journalism at New York University, where she directs a graduate concentration in cultural reporting and criticism. She is the author of two books, *Beginning To See the Light: Sex, Hope, and Rock & Roll* and *No More Nice Girls: Countercultural Essays,* collecting her articles in *The Village Voice, Rolling Stone, The New Yorker,* and other publications. She has been involved in feminism since 1968, when she joined New York Radical Women. In 1969, she and Shulamith Firestone founded Redstockings. She has also been a founding member of the pro-sex abortion rights group No More Nice Girls, the Feminist Anti-Censorship Taskforce, and the Network of East-West Women. She was a member of the planning committee for the notorious 1982 conference at Barnard, "Toward a Politics of Sexuality," which brought to public attention the argument between pro-sex feminists and the anti-pornography movement.

Barbara Winslow was a founding member of both Seattle Radical Women in 1967 and Women's Liberation–Seattle in 1968. She participated in the women's liberation movement in England. In 1970, with Sheila Rowbotham (and others) she helped organize the first demonstration against the Miss World Beauty Pageant as well as the first women's liberation conference at Ruskin College. She attended the founding conference of the Coalition of Labor Union Women (where she first met Ros Baxandall at a radical teachers' caucus meeting) and was active in women's labor activities in Ohio in the 1970s. She helped organize and served on the National Steering Committee of the Reproductive Rights National Network. She was a member of the Cleveland Pro-Choice Action Committee, 1979–1984, as well as the Brooklyn Pro-Choice Network, 1984 to the present. She has taught women's history since 1971, beginning first at Seattle Community College, then Cuyahoga Community College, Cleveland, Ohio, and then throughout the City University of New York, CUNY. From 1991 to 1994 she was the executive director of the Coordinating Committee of Women in the Historical Profession/Conference Group on Women's History (now Coordinating Council of Women Historians), and is now on the executive board of the Berkshire Conference of Women Historians. She was an assistant professor of history at Medgar Evers College/City University of New York, and is now a visiting associate professor in the women's studies program at Brooklyn College. She has written *Sylvia Pankhurst: Sexual Politics and Political Activism* (St. Martins, 1996), and is currently writing a history of the women's liberation movement in Seattle, Washington. She lives in Brooklyn, New York, with her two daughters, and is politically active serving on the board of directors of the North Star Fund, a foundation that funds radical social change. A   ennis player, she is a member of the Brooklyn Raqueteers, which has   New York City championships. At this writing, her eldest daughter   air of her high school women's group, which is called Cell 16, and   daughter interned with the National Labor Committee, work-   Disney's sweatshops in Haiti. (Carry it on!)

Alice Wolfson is a veteran political activist who first became interested in health in the 1960s when she was on a Fulbright scholarship in England. Soon afterwards, Wolfson became involved in the antiwar/draft movement and eventually joined one of the first women's consciousness-raising groups in New York City. Early on, Wolfson recognized that women's health issues, especially population control and abortion, were vital to the women's movement agenda. She argued that the medical system provided a microcosm for understanding women's relationships with their bodies, and that until women gained some control over their bodies themselves, feminist changes would be impossible.

As a member of D.C. Women's Liberation, Wolfson was involved in the struggle to legalize abortion and moved from there to help form a national movement dedicated to providing women with informed consent regarding the birth control pill. That movement, which she led, was responsible for the first patient packet insert in prescription medication in the United States. From there, Wolfson went on to be one of the five founding members of the National Women's Health Network, on which she served as both a member of the board of directors and of the executive committee for many years.

After moving to San Francisco in 1977, Wolfson founded the Committee to Defend Reproductive Rights, in response to the cutoff of federal funding for abortions. Known as CDRR, the organization had national impact when it pioneered the use of bus advertising to bring the issue of abortion out into the open.

Today, Alice Wolfson has taken her years of experience as an activist into the legal profession. As an attorney, she continues her fight for women to have fair and equal access to insurance coverage. She has worked actively to obtain proper reimbursement for women who have suffered from faulty breast implants, and she is currently concerned with the issue of insurance discrimination based on genetic testing for breast cancer.

Wolfson's education includes Barnard College, Stanford University, and a year in England as a Fulbright scholar. In 1970, she was chosen to represent the American Women's Liberation Movement at a world conference of women held in Budapest. She has written and lectured extensively on women's health and consumer rights, including informed consent, reproductive rights, insurance coverage, and patients' rights.

About the Cover

Rally, Liberty Island, August 26, 1978, the day in 1920 when women's suffrage was ratified, and the day in 1970 when modern feminism stepped out in its first mass march down New York's Fifth Avenue to commemorate the earlier struggle. Seated front is 90 year old Isolde Dubic, a suffragist. The banner is the text of the Equal Rights Amendment to the Constitution which, despite the extension it received from Congress later in 1978, died unratified in 1982.